Contract Law

Contract Law

Rules, Cases, and Problems

Professor Seth C. Oranburg

ASSOCIATE PROFESSOR
UNIVERSITY OF NEW HAMPSHIRE
FRANKLIN PIERCE SCHOOL OF LAW

DIRECTOR
PROGRAM ON ORGANIZATIONS, BUSINESS, AND MARKETS
CLASSICAL LIBERAL INSTITUTE AT NYU LAW

JURIS DOCTOR
UNIVERSITY OF CHICAGO LAW SCHOOL

CAROLINA ACADEMIC PRESS
Durham, North Carolina

See catalog.loc.gov for complete Library of Congress
Cataloging-in-Publication Data

 ISBN: 978-1-5310-2077-4
eISBN: 978-1-5310-2639-4

Carolina Academic Press
700 Kent Street
Durham, NC 27701
(919) 489-7486
www.cap-press.com

Printed in the United States of America

To Talia, my partner in the greatest contract of life, marriage.

Contents

MODULE II | MUTUAL ASSENT

MODULE III | CONSIDERATION AND ALTERNATIVES TO CONSIDERATION

MODULE IV | DEFENSES

MODULE V | INTERPRETATION

MODULE VI | PERFORMANCE AND BREACH

═══════════════════════════

MODULE VII │ REMEDIES

═══════════════════════════

Table of Cases

Acknowledgments

Special thanks to the American Law Institute and the National Conference of Commissioners on State Laws for the general use of the Restatement of the Law (Second) of Contracts and the Uniform Commercial Code:

Restatement of the Law Second Contracts, copyright © 1981 by the American Law Institute. Reprinted with permission. All rights reserved.

Uniform Commercial Code (UCC), Article 1 copyright © 2001, Article 2 copyright © 2011 by The American Law Institute and the National Conference of Commissioners of Uniform State Laws. Reproduced by permission of the Permanent Editorial Board for the UCC. All rights reserved.

Thanks to my teaching assistants — Eva C.H. Scheiwe, Jacquelyn Pariseau, Amber Pavucsko, Hannah Schaffer, Nathanial "Nate" Ingerick, Alexandra "Lexi" Jones, Natheena Tyler, and CharLee Rosini — who helped refine this book while using it to foster great classroom experiences over several years. You kept me in touch with students' needs; I am grateful for your helpful feedback and suggestions. I thank all the students who offered constructive criticism, and I especially thank Abraham Webber and Jonathan Agustin for providing detailed comments.

Thanks to fellow teachers who contributed to this manuscript, especially Lisa Bernstein, Brian Bix, Wilson Huhn, Wes Oliver, Georgy Kuney, and Ashley London. Thanks also to the four anonymous reviewers. I have taken your comments to heart and trust that you will find your positive influence in this text.

I am grateful for consideration, advice, and time from many members of the Carolina Academic Press community; in particular, I thank my instructional designer Krystal Norton, my editor Carol McGeehan, and my publisher Scott Sipe for going above and beyond in supporting the production of this work.

Special thanks to the Institute for Humane Studies and the Classical Liberal Institute for financial assistance and research support. I could not have afforded to produce this work on time without you. I hope this book helps us achieve our mutual goal of connecting a community of scholars in pursuit of the good society. Thank you.

Any errors or omissions are probably mine, but I will blame autocorrect.

Online Materials

Additional content for *Contract Law: Rules, Cases, and Problems* is available on Carolina Academic Press's *Core Knowledge for Lawyers* (CKL) website.

Core Knowledge for Lawyers is an online teaching and testing platform that hosts practice questions and additional content for both instructors and students.

To learn more, please visit:
coreknowledgeforlawyers.com

Instructors may request complimentary access through the "Faculty & Instructors" link.

Contract Law

Introduction

Welcome to Contract Law! In this course, we study whether and how people can create obligations that courts will enforce. Studying contract law is an essential part of the first-year law-school curriculum because this subject teaches you how law defines and supports voluntary relationships between people. Through this course, you will learn:

- the process of contract formation by mutual assent,
- the consideration doctrine,
- defenses to contract formation,
- interpretation of written and oral agreements,
- the doctrines of performance and breach,
- the calculation of money damages, and
- the application of special remedies.

In addition to this doctrinal knowledge, contract law also provides an ideal background to learn legal analysis, such as:

- using treatises to understand common law doctrine,
- reading cases, statutes and codes,
- citing and explaining rules from statutes and cases,
- interpreting written language in context,
- distinguishing relevant from irrelevant facts,
- breaking down rules into simpler elements,
- combining rules into more complex statements,
- analogizing and distinguishing facts with case law,
- formulating arguments using the "IRAC" paradigm,
- evaluating relative strength of parties' arguments, and
- predicting how courts will resolve legal disputes.

Participating in this course can build your affective skills, too:

- engaging with groups of colleagues and faculty,
- critiquing others' written work,
- receiving criticism on your writing and analysis,
- sharing your opinions while listening to colleagues, and
- justifying your positions with logic and reason.

You will also develop an appreciation for how judges balance obedience to equal justice under the rule of law with safeguards for fairness and equity.

To succeed in this endeavor, you will need to be motivated, responsible, ethical, open-minded, and perseverant. This course provides an opportunity to cultivate these qualities.

You will find the course materials are organized into modules and chapters to help you understand how the pieces fit together into the big picture of contract law.

Modules represent large domains and categories of legal concepts. For example, our first module, mutual assent, deals with a variety of rules, cases, and principles that all relate to the process of formation of contracts.

Chapters represent more specific components of legal knowledge. For example, the module on mutual assent is split into three chapters — the offer, duration of the offer, and acceptance of the offer — to help you understand the phases of the contract formation process.

Within chapters, you will find specific rules of law, cases which demonstrate those rules, and practice problems that test your understanding of those rules. The rules come primarily from two sources, which will be explained in our first module: the Restatement (Second) of Contract ("**R2d**") and the Uniform Commercial Code ("**UCC**"). Some rules or modifications to rules also come from cases that you will read.

For example, the chapter on offers features rules defining "offer" (R2d § 24), distinguishing offer from preliminary negotiations (R2d § 26), and establishing requirements for offers such as reasonable certainty of their terms (R2d § 33). The chapter on bargains includes a case discussing whether an advertisement can be an offer (*Lefkowitz*) and a case about whether an offer is binding even when one party claims it was just a joke (*Leonard*).

Your first job is to read the rules and cases carefully. You may have to look up terms that are unfamiliar to you in a legal dictionary such as Black's Law Dictionary. You should refer frequently to the comments in the R2d and to commentary provided by your professor in writing, via video, and in class for help identifying and resolving tricky and counter-intuitive legal rules and principles. By actively reading and listening, you should remember and understand the rules of law.

The second step is to apply those rules to new scenarios. Cases show you how experienced lawyers and judges applied rules to the facts of those cases. Then it is your turn to work out hypothetical problems involving contractual scenarios that will be presented to you in a process known as application.

As the course progresses, you will have to assimilate multiple rules and relate them to one another. In other words, you will need to analyze complex sets of rules such that you can organize, classify, interpret, generalize, and combine them. This ability to inventory and utilize increasingly large sets of rules that apply to a common problem is vital for lawyering in the real world, since legal problems are rarely so simple as to be resolvable by a single rule or precept.

When you read cases, you will observe parties' arguments and judges' evaluations of them. But you will soon need to create legal arguments of your own based on your analysis of rules and your evaluation of facts. As you progress through this course, you will increasingly be asked to discriminate between relevant and irrelevant information, to decide what information benefits or hinders a given party's legal objective, and to draft intelligible legal arguments on both sides of a case. Ultimately, you will be able to synthesize an entire situation involving a conflict about a contract and resolve which party should prevail in a court of law.

To help you matriculate from novice to competence and proficiency in contract law doctrine, each topic proceeds via the same four steps. First, the course presents high-level concepts in a straightforward, conversational tone that tries to avoid legal jargon and to include illustrations and examples so that you gain a basic understanding of the ideas. Second, the course presents the rules of law as drawn verbatim from contemporary sources, so you become familiar with the legal lexicon and authorities. Third, the course presents cases that illustrate the legal concepts in complex, real-world situations accompanied by lawyers' arguments and judges' opinions. This helps you to see how the rules are applied and to analyze the purpose of the rules. Fourth, the course proposes practice problems so that you can test your understanding and practice your ability to formulate your own legal arguments and to evaluate the relative strength and weakness of cases.

As you engage with this course, try to keep in mind the notion that contract law enforces voluntary bargains because parties anticipated that exchange would make themselves better off, and their self-motivated transaction thereby increases social welfare. In order words, contract law is a way to facilitate the transfer of property to the person who values it most. This also explains why courts do not enforce certain contracts, such as a contract to assassinate someone, because while the bargain may increase the welfare of the party who ordered the hit (and the financial welfare of the hitman), those private benefits are outweighed by the public harm from murder.

This course teaches Contract Law cases from a discovery approach; that is, it illustrates how the law is necessary to solve real disputes in the real world. As you read cases in this book, try to conceptualize the legal issue as a problem that the law must to solve, and the rules as methods of solving such problems. That will help you learn how to apply legal rules to solve real-world problems. The goal is for you to emerge from this course of study not only knowing the rules of contract law, but also possessing new skills in resolving the complexity of civil disputes.

I wish you the best of luck in this course of study!

/s/ Seth C. Oranburg

What Is Contract Law?

Our study of contract law study naturally begins by discussing the nature, purpose, history, and evolution of contract law.

Contracts law regards whether and how people can create obligations that courts will enforce. Note that people must create their own obligations under contract law. In other words, contract law is voluntary: if you do not want to be liable under contract law, then you can choose not to form a contract.

This makes contract law different from other legal subjects. Criminal law, for instance, applies to you regardless of whether you agree with it or not. Consider the debate over assisted suicide, where terminally ill people like Theresa Hobbins asked doctors like Jack Kevorkian to end their lives. In that case, the Michigan Supreme Court ruled that the State of Michigan could impose criminal penalties for assisted suicide, regardless of whether both parties wanted to engage in that action voluntarily and willingly.

Criminal law, constitutional law, administrative law, tax law, and procedural law are all part of our "public law," which governs the relationship between persons and governments. Public law is not voluntary, at least not on an individual basis. You cannot decide that you are allowed to commit burglary or avoid paying taxes. You can only vote for lawmakers who you hope will change the public laws with which you disagree.

On the other hand, "private law" governs the relationship between persons. Private law is, for the most part, voluntary; that is, people decide whether to be bound by private law by choosing to engage in certain actions or transactions. Private law subjects include tort law, property law, family law, and contract law. In private law systems, the law provides a framework and regulations for structuring activity and resolving disputes. The goal of such systems is promoting individual autonomy.

Origins of Contract Law

The law of contracts is ancient. According to Professor Charles Auerbach, the oldest collection of contract law sources that are still used today was assembled by Rabbi Hillel in 200 B.C.E. The Jewish law of contract was derived from the five books of Moses (Genesis, Exodus, Leviticus, Numbers, and Deuteronomy) and Jewish oral tradition. Orthodox Jewish courts still apply these laws and principles today — although

Figure A. Moses and Aaron with the Ten Commandments.
Painting by Aron de Chavez (circa 1675). Public domain work.

the Divine principles underlying Jewish law are sometimes quite different from the philosophical justifications for law that are accepted by modern nations.

The Roman Law of Contracts is no longer employed today, but, according to Professor Alan Watson, it forms the basis for the enforcement of private agreements in most of the Western world. The earliest embodiment of Roman Law of Contracts was probably found in the Twelve Tables, a set of laws inscribed on twelve bronze tables that were created around 451 B.C.E. Those tables have apparently been destroyed, but their legacy survived. Some countries, such as South Africa, still base their legal system on the Roman *jus commune* (common law).

England, on the other hand, did not adopt Roman law wholesale. Roman law was introduced to England, along with French language and other Continental traditions, by the Norman Conquest of 1066. But England, at that time, was not a legal *tabula rasa* (blank slate). Rather, commercial disputes were resolved in various local courts. This varied legal tradition, mixed with Franco-Roman influence, was first canonized by King Henry II, who pronounced a unified national common law in 1154. After the English *Magna Carta* (great charter) was instituted in 1215 to provide for basic civil liberties and restrict the power of the monarchy, the English Court of Common Pleas was established to adjudicate actions between people (as opposed to actions which concerned the state or the monarch).

The English Court of Common Pleas heard contract disputes for hundreds of years, until it was finally merged with the English King's Bench, the Court of Chan-

Figure B. Roman civilians examining the Twelve Tables.
Unknown author. Public domain work.

cery and the Exchequer by the Supreme Court Judicature Act of 1873 — more than one hundred years after the American Revolution.

The American legal system is heavily influenced by its English predecessor. Prior to the Revolution, the British Government claimed to have the sole power to create courts in the American colonies. Courts in the American colonies generally borrowed from English law. You will even find citations to the King's Bench and other English courts in some early American case law. But even in this early period, when the Colonies were still under English rule, the American courts began to develop their own precedent and approach. As judges interpreted — and sometimes created — law to fit the needs of American commerce, a uniquely American Common Law of Contracts began to develop.

Law and Equity

Equity has a specific legal meaning which is somewhat different from the sociological usage of the term. The sociologic usage of the term has come to provide a counterpoint to equality (where equality means giving the same advantages to all people so that all people have the same inputs, whereas equity means giving more

Figure C. King John signing the Magna Carta reluctantly.
Painting by Arthur C Michael (1945). Public domain work.

advantages to less advantaged people so that all people achieve the same outputs). However, this is not what it means in law. Equity in law refers to a body of principles constituting what is fair and right and a particular set of remedies.

Equity in law originated in England in the Courts of Chancery. While the Courts of Common Pleas heard claims regarding the illegal breach of contracts and other private-law claims, the Courts of Chancery were a separate court system, which entertained cases where there was no legal claim but where some wrong needed to be redressed by some remedy. (Meanwhile, the King's Bench mainly focused on what we would now call criminal actions and other public law causes of action.)

Unlike courts of law, which were run by judges, courts of equity were originally preceded over by Chancellors who were trained as priests, bishops, or other

Figure D. The Court of Common Pleas at work. Unknown author. Public domain work.

Figure E. The Court of Chancery during the reign of George I.
Painting by Benjamin Ferrers (1732). Public domain work.

theologians. These Chancellors were known as "keepers of the king's conscience." They did not concern themselves with legal precedent or formal rules; rather, Chancellors would render decisions based on practical concerns and moral justifications.

In 1529, Sir Thomas More (venerated in the Catholic church as Saint Thomas More) ascended to the position of Lord High Chancellor of England under King Henry VIII. More was a lawyer, social philosopher, and author of the political sat-

Figure F. Portrait of Saint Thomas More (1523). Public domain work.

ire titled "Utopia." More reformed the Chancery by requiring a lawyer's signature to make any Chancery decision binding. This eventually resulted in Chancellors becoming lawyers themselves.

Most of the American colonies initially maintained the English division between courts of common law and courts of equity, but that distinction has been all but abolished today. As mentioned above, England merged its courts into a single system toward the end of the 19th century. Today, only a few American states have separate chancery courts. The most notable among them is Delaware, which specializes in handling corporate disputes and fiduciary litigation issues.

Today, almost all U.S. state courts can hear and enforce both matters of law and equity. The distinction between law and equity has thus been blurred. However, some differences remain. For example, equitable claims tend to require some element of justice, whereas a legal claimant may prevail merely by meeting the standards required by law. Many equitable remedies can also be limited as justice requires.

Moreover, equitable claims and remedies remain exceptional and extraordinary; that is, courts will prefer to find a legal remedy and will only resort to an equitable remedy to the extent that justice requires them to do so. R2d does little to distinguish legal and equitable claims and remedies; however, this book views that indistinction as an error. Most courts still regard equitable remedies as exceptional, so they will not be granted when a legal remedy is available. Students are encouraged to analyze legal claims and remedies first, only to explore equitable claims as remedies as a last resort, and to present arguments why justice requires the extraordinary imposition of an equitable remedy.

The Restatement of Contracts

America began as a British colony that imported British law, including the law of contracts. After the American Revolution and the formation of the United States of America, American law began drifting apart from English law. In the early days of the United States, states had a great deal more power relative to the federal government than they do today. State courts heard most contract claims, and contract law developed as a matter of state law. State law may vary, as one state is not bound to follow another state's precedent. Thus, Contract Law developed differently throughout the states.

This variety in the Law of Contracts between states creates some challenges for interstate commerce. Whether having different state laws and giving parties the right to choose among them is good or bad for commerce and society, the subject of much debate in commercial law. Theory aside, in Contract Law, there have been efforts to generalize and normalize the law among the states, and several prominent examples of these efforts are widely successful.

The leading effort to define (or create) a common law that is truly common throughout America has been conducted by the American Law Institute (ALI), an organization that was founded in 1923 to clarify, modernize, and otherwise improve the law. According to the ALI's website, "The ALI drafts, discusses, revises, and publishes Restatements of the Law, Model Codes, and Principles of Law that are enormously influential in the courts and legislatures, as well as in legal scholarship and education."

The ALI influences contract law through drafting Restatements. A "Restatement" is a legal treatise that purports to inform judges and lawyers of the common law. Some have criticized such Restatements for shaping and creating, instead of merely reporting the law. Despite such criticism, the ALI Restatements have been hugely successful. They are frequently cited by American courts as statements of "black letter law," which are propounded to be statements of legal rules that are no longer subject to reasonable dispute.

The First Restatement of Contracts was principally drafted by Samuel Wendell Williston, a professor at Harvard Law School. Williston espoused an "objective" view of contracts; that is, contracts are interpreted through the lens of a reasonable third person. For example, if, in the opinion of a reasonable third person who witnessed the contracting process, the elements of a contract were present, then a contract was formed — regardless of what the parties thought or what other circumstances might have informed their decisions and actions. In other words, if something looks like a contract, then it legally is a contract. Williston's objective approach to contracts reflected his preference for "legal formalism," an approach to law where the judge need only consider the facts in light of the law to evaluate a case — and where politics, morality and other normative issues are deemed irrelevant to judging.

The First Restatement of Contracts consisted mainly of black letter law. There was little commentary, and the notes were relatively short. This shortcoming made it difficult for courts to understand the reasoning for the ALI's pronouncement of rules.

Moreover, the First Restatement of Contracts reflected a way of thinking about the law that went out of favor. As American courts shifted away from legal formalism by the mid twentieth century, a new Restatement of the law of contract increasingly became necessary.

The Second Restatement of Contracts ("R2d") was drafted and promulgated in 1979 as part of a movement known as "legal realism." This movement is based on the idea that law cannot be understood in a vacuum; rather, law is a product of humanity and society. Practically, this approach means that courts must look for the parties' actual intentions when entering into a contract, even if the plain meaning of what they say or write would reasonably be interpreted by a third party to mean something else. R2d was principally drafted by Arthur Linton Corbin, a professor at Yale Law School who is sometimes credited with creating the modern law school model.

Despite the R2d foundations in legal realism, it increasingly feels like a creation of an earlier age. For example, the Restatement was created when virtually no one owned their own computer. Now we walk around with computers in our pockets on which we can purchase goods and offer services. The R2d does not account for the Internet of Things, smart contract, Web3, blockchain, or the multiverse, because these things did not exist when it was written. As the R2d shows its increasing incompatibility with a digital age, a new Restatement may prove to be necessary sometime soon.

But the law changes slowly, and, at present, the R2d is still considered to be the best authority on what is the common law of contracts in America. We will rely heavily on the R2d to learn contract law principles. Just keep in mind that the law of contracts will change during your lifetime of practice in the law. As a common law doctrine, contract law can change as judges create new precedent by deciding new changes. By practicing contract law, you can be part of that change.

The Uniform Commercial Code

In addition to Restatements, which are effectively very persuasive treatises on what the black letter common law is, the American Law Institute also produces "Model Codes," which are designed to be used as a basis for designing state law statutes. In our legal system, most contract law disputes are adjudicated as a matter of state law, so each state is free to make its own law without being bound by precedent from another state. This system allows for experimentation between states and optimizing laws for local populations, but discrepancies between state law can result in confusion and expense for interstate commerce.

The ALI developed the Uniform Commercial Code ("UCC") in 1952 to harmonize commercial law among all the states. The UCC extends well beyond contract law. In fact, the UCC is so extensive that each of its articles is the subject of an entire law school course. This course does not discuss the entire UCC because that would require several courses of study. Rather, this book only references Article 2 of the UCC, which deals with contracts for the sale of goods.

Scope of the Uniform Commercial Code.*

UCC Article	Title	Contents
1	General Provisions	Definitions, rules of interpretation
2	Sales	Sales of goods
2A	Leases	Leases of goods
3	Negotiable Instruments	Promissory notes and drafts (commercial paper)
4	Bank Deposits and Collections	Banks and banking, check collection process
4A	Funds Transfers	Transfers of money between banks
5	Letters of Credit	Transactions involving letters of credit
6	Bulk Transfers and Bulk Sales	Auctions and liquidations of assets
7	Warehouse Receipts, Bills of Lading and Other Documents of Title	Storage and bailment of goods
8	Investment Securities	Securities and financial assets
9	Secured Transactions	Transactions secured by security interests

Unlike the R2d, which is a treatise that is therefore only a persuasive authority, the UCC becomes a binding authority when enacted by state legislatures as a statute. All 50 state legislatures have adopted some form of the UCC and, in doing so, have rejected prior judicial doctrines that are contrary to that statute. In other words, courts must obey the UCC, while the R2d is technically a non-binding statement of what binding law should be.

But the UCC does not apply to all contracts. Rather, Article 2 of the UCC only applies to sales of goods. Contracts for services and sales of real estate and intellectual property are not governed by the UCC:

> Unless the context otherwise requires, this Article applies to transactions in goods. UCC § 2-102.

The UCC only deals with contracts for the sale of goods. Good are things that are moveable and identifiable at the time of sale, such as a ton of bricks or a barrel of monkeys. The UCC does not govern contracts for services, such as a promise to babysit; nor does it govern the sales of houses or land, which are not moveable:

---

* The American Law Institute and Uniform Law Commission proposed adding an Article 12 on Controllable Electronic Records to the UCC. If enacted by states, UCC Article 12 will provide a national framework for transactions involving digital assets such as cryptocurrencies.

The UCC was principally drafted by Karl Nickerson Llewellyn, who was Corbin's protégé and a Legal Realist. The adoption of the UCC, therefore, is seen as a triumph of Corbin's Legal Realism over Williston's Legal Formalism.

Why Does Contract Law Exist?

Contract law is private law, meaning, contract law involves the relationship amid persons. This contrasts with public law, which involves the relationship between individuals and the state. As the Roman lawyer in the third century Domitius Ulpianus explained, "*privatum, quod ad singulorum utilitatem*," meaning, private law is for the benefit of the individual.

How does contract law benefit individuals? Contract law provides a framework for enforcement of promises and agreements. Essentially, the state will enforce certain promises and agreement so that individuals can plan mutual affairs with more reliability on one another than can otherwise be achieved. Contracting thus has an essentially economic function. The purpose of contract law is to allow people to make the world better off through their private decisions to make themselves better off through trade.

Economics assumes that when a person makes a voluntary trade, that person does so in order to make themselves better off. For example, if you go to the record store (do those still exist?) and purchase a record for $10, economics assumes that you rationally did that because you prefer having the record more than having $10. Meanwhile, the record store only sold you that album because it valued having $10 more than having the album. After the trade, you and the record store are presumptively both better off, because you both now have something you value more than what you had before.

> *UCC § 2-105. "Goods" means all things (including specially manufactured goods) which are movable at the time of identification to the contract for sale.*

When one or more person in society becomes better off without making anyone worse off, that represents an overall improvement to social welfare. You are a part of society, and society is now better off because of the trade you made with the record store.

This prior example is of a spot trade, in which contracts did not necessarily come into play. But the value of contracts becomes obvious when you consider trades that cannot happen at the same time. To understand this concept, imagine that you have an apple orchid in Washington State. Every Fall your apple trees produce about two thousand apples. But you can only eat about one hundred of these apples, and you sell about nine hundred of them at your local farmer's market. The other thousand apples go to waste — and you are quite frankly sick of apples by November. Then you hear about an orange farmer in Southern California who has an annual surplus or

Figure H. Karl Llewellyn. *Source*: ACME Newspictures (1934). Public domain work.

oranges and call her. You offer to ship her one thousand apples when they mature in September if she agrees to ship you one thousand oranges when they mature in November.

Without contract law, you could not rely on a stranger's promise to ship oranges to you, so you might not be willing to ship apples to her first or even to enter into and count on this bargain at all. But, thanks to contract law, you have some assurances that the strange orange farmer will either ship your oranges when the times comes or will have to pay you the value of those oranges, so you can ship the apples in confidence that you will be made better off by doing so. Either way, you are better off than having a thousand apples rotting on the ground around you. Contract law allows you to rely on a stranger's promise to buy these apples when they are ripe, and that encourages you to create the orchard in the first place.

Subjective Meeting of the Minds versus Objective Mutual Assent

Before we get to the cases, let's consider what two of contract law's leading luminaries thought about the subjective and objective theories of contract formation and interpretation. While this oversimplification does not fully do them justice, we can better understand theories of contract interpretation by juxtaposing these two scholars as if they represent two reasonable ends of the subjective-objective spectrum.

Samuel Williston: Legal Objectivism

Samuel Williston was born on September 24, 1861, to a wealthy family in Cambridge, Massachusetts. The United States was embroiled in Civil War. Just four days prior, Lexington, Missouri was captured by Confederate forces. As the war raged on, Williston's family prospects declined. This setback, Williston later recalled "served as a spur to endeavor."

Williston went on to graduate Harvard College in 1882. He taught for three years and then went to Harvard Law School, from whence he received his juris doctor in 1888. While in school, he edited the Harvard Law Review and won a prize for his essay titled *History of the Law of Business Corporations Before 1800*. Over his 102 year lifetime, Williston published at least 36 articles in the Harvard Law Review alone.

Williston's greatest contribution to the law of contract was probably his treatise, The Law of Contracts, which he first published in 1920. In that treatise, he presented his objective approach as the third sentence in his module on general rules for the interpretation or construction of contracts:

> *The interpretation of a contract is the process of determining from the expressions of the parties what external acts must happen or be performed in order to conform to what the law considers their will.*

Note that Williston focuses on expression. His objective approach essentially holds that courts of law are obligated to construe contracts in terms of expressed intentions and not seek evidence on actual intentions where the expressed intentions are clear. Therefore, the court's role in interpreting contracts is relatively narrow:

> *Interpretation is properly the process of applying the ordinary legal standard to the words or symbols used in order to determine their meaning or sense.*

Williston's application of "ordinary" meaning to contractual words puts the burden on parties so say what they mean and mean what they say. This is a somewhat utilitarian philosophy based on various efficiencies. Courts are more efficient where

Figure I. Professor Williston. Public domain work.

they can resolve cases as a matter of law, without a jury and, preferably, without much need to hear evidence. Business transaction are more efficient where the outcome of written contracts is more certain and therefore less likely to go to court; and there is less risk of legal expense when the scope of a court's review is narrower.

But this rationale of attaching legal meaning to contracts stops making sense when the contractual parties should not be assumed to have legal knowledge. If parties are reasonably unaware of how to use words according to their legal meaning, then applying the legal meaning does not necessarily approximate the parties' intentions. For this reason, Williston applies different standards of interpretation to different classes of contracts.

> *In one division must be put not only formal contracts such as sealed instruments and negotiable paper, but also contracts where the parties have agreed on a writing or other fixed system as a memorial or integration of their agreement.*
>
> *In a second division must be put all other contracts. This class will include not only all oral contracts, but also any informal contracts of which there may perhaps be written memoranda.*

Williston's division of contracts into two classes, formal and informal, may have come from his experience growing up in the 1880s. After the Civil War and the Reconstruction, American society entered a period of industrialization that included the development of railways, steamboats, telegraphs, and telephones. These transportation and communication technologies enabled national business markets to exist across state lines. Perhaps there was some reasonable expectation that a meat packer in Chicago and a cattle rancher in Colorado, for example, would transact using standard forms and terms.

But people still continue to make simple and casual promises to each other. Simple contract parties might not be expected to use words by some standard legal meaning. For this reason, Williston held that informal agreements should be interpreted a bit more personally — although they still must be based on expressions:

> *In the second class [informal contracts], the standard of interpretation [is] the sense in which the party who used the words in question should reasonably have apprehended that the other part would understand them.*

This is still an objective approach in that is considers what was actually said and not what was privately thought, but it softens this approach by accepting the possibility that two people might have both attached the same meaning to an express term, and that the parties' meaning is different from the ordinary legal meaning. Williston goes on to illustrate this point:

> *Not only may A and B agree that holding up a hand means an agreement to buy or to sell a hundred shares of a particular stock, but it seems that they may agree that in the code which they are using, though it is a code peculiar to themselves, horse shall mean cow, or that buy shall mean sell. To be sure, clear proof will be needed in order to convince a tribunal that such was the agreement of the parties.*

Now how often do parties say horse to mean cow? I suppose that if one party can show the other had a cow named Horse, that sort of evidence should be admissible even before a strong objectivist judge in construing a contract for the "Sale of Horse."

Williston continued to champion the objective approach to contract interpretation throughout his lifetime. When he was 88 years old, Williston published a strong denunciation of the UCC Article 2:

> *All the contradictions of existing law and all the implications in the provisions of the Article. Some of these provisions are not only iconoclastic but open to criticisms that I regard so fundamental as to preclude the desirability of enacting that part at least of the proposed Code.*

Law of Sales in the Proposed Uniform Commercial Code Harvard Law Review, 63 Harv. L. Rev. 561 (1950). This indictment of the UCC was indicative of his over his strong objectivist philosophy, at least with regard to the law of sales, as the UCC generally takes a more subjective approach than R2d.

Does Williston's division of contracts into two classes, formal and informal, still make sense today?

Arthur Linton Corbin: Realist and Subjectivist

Arthur Linton Corbin was born on October 17, 1874, to a farming family in Cripple Creek, Colorado. His father served throughout the Civil War in the 12th Kansas Regiment. His mother was a schoolteacher. Corbin graduated from the University of Kansas in 1894, taught high school for about two years before matriculating to Yale Law School, from whence he earned his juris doctor in 1899. He became a full professor at Yale in 1909 and spent his entire career there, retiring in 1943. Some say that there he invented or at least popularized the casebook method which you are experiencing today.

Corbin also founded the American Law Institute and was the first reporter of the Restatement (Second) of Contracts. Meanwhile, he also compiled a treatise, CORBIN ON CONTRACTS, which was first published in 1952. Thus, 32 years and a World War separate the inception of these grand treatises. In discussing his approach to contract interpretation, Corbin paid homage to his predecessor Williston by acknowledging that both sides of this debate have merit.

> It is arguable whether the parties are bound according to their real will, or according to their will as manifested, in cases where differences are apparent between what was really intended and what was actually declared. It is easy to understand that this argument reflects the long-standing dispute between the subjective and objective approach to contract.

Despite his acknowledgement that objectivism had its place, Corbin generally pushed the Restatement away from rules and towards standards, giving the courts broader scope in reviewing contract cases and determining what promises were made thereunder.

Corbin is associated with a school of thought known as legal realism, which sought to expose and limit the role of politics in judicial decision making. The development of this school in the 1920s and 1930s makes sense when you think about what was occurring at that time. To give just one example, in 1937, via the Judicial Procedures Reform Bill, President Franklin Delano Roosevelt threatened to "pack" the Supreme Court with new appointees of his political persuasion if the Court struck down his "new deal" laws as unconstitutional.

> Ferment is abroad in the law. The sphere of interest widens; men become interested again in the life that swirls around things legal. Before rules, were facts; in the beginning was not a Word, but a Doing. Behind decisions stand judges; judges are men; as men they have human backgrounds. Beyond rules, again, life effects: beyond decisions stand people whom rules and decisions directly or indirectly touch.

Zipporah Wiseman, *The Limits of Vision: Karl Llewellyn and the Merchant Rules*, 100 Harv. L. Rev. 465 (1986–1987). Since judges are people—and since all people bring their own subjective perspective to interpretation due to their backgrounds and philosophies—they cannot be expected to determine the true meaning of words.

Figure J. Professor Corbin with his treatise. Copyright Yale Law Journal.
Reprinted with permission.

Rather, their job is to understand the meaning that the parties intended in order to effectuate the reasonable expectations of the parties to a contract.

This focus on the human aspect of law may have led legal realists like Corbin to the opinion that intentions are central to the creation of legal relationships. This notion that a contract is a meeting of the minds involving mutual consent accords well with Corbin's world view. Accordingly, he did not shy away from interpreting contracts even where partied' express intentions were indecipherable.

Karl Llewellyn, a student of Corbin who was also a legal realist and the principal drafter of the UCC, argued that scholars should consider the human and political aspect of law in poetic words that present the essence of this philosophy:

> *Where neither custom nor agreement determines the allocation of risk, the court must exercise its equity powers and pray for the wisdom of Solomon.*

3 Corbin on Contracts § 1333. Corbin's view is fairly expressed through R2d, to which he contributed a great deal as its first reporter, even though R2d was published in 1981, 14 years after his death. Since then, R2d has been lauded by progressive and derided by conservatives as an effort by Corbin and others to change the law to what they think it should be instead of restating the law as it was.

As you will see, not all courts have adopted the R2d's subjective approach.

Reflection

Contract law has evolved over thousands of years of human civilization. For millennia, courts have enforced private agreements so that people would be more willing to trade with strangers. The legacy of Roman law was passed to England through the Norman Invasion, where it mixed with local customs and then evolved along its own lines. The American colonies inherited the English system, then made it their own as the passage of time and the distance between the continents allowed the systems to drift apart.

Over its long history, contract law has really not changed its purpose. It was and is a system of voluntary liability that promotes individual autonomy in economic matters. The dual notions of freedom to contract (meaning, the right to make binding agreements) and freedom from contract (meaning, the right not to be bound without one's volition) have generally persisted throughout the ages.

That said, the details and nuances of contract law have changed and continue to change as culture, society, and technology evolve. Moreover, since contract cases are usually heard as a matter of state law and not federal law, the common law has not developed identically across America. The level of details and the degree of differences makes studying contract law challenging. This course attempts to make it easier to begin learning contract law by identifying what is truly common about American common law of contracts and teaching the principles that apply generally.

Module I

Contract Foundations

We begin our study of contract law doctrine by defining what is a contract. Contrary to popular belief, a contract need not be a written document (although some types of contracts must be properly evidenced by a signed memorandum). Rather, the most basic definition of a contract is: a set of promises that courts will enforce. This definition, in turn, requires us to define what is a promise. By unpacking the foundational definition in this way, we not only learn the deeper meaning of contract law, but also learn how to do the work of contract practice.

Contract practice is primarily about avoiding litigation through careful drafting. By thoughtfully unpacking and describing terms in a manner that clarifies and memorializes two parties' mutual understanding, the contract lawyer adds great value to transactions that thus become more certain and less subject to dispute. You will begin to develop those skills in this first module, where you are called upon to parse and explain the technical rules found in R2d and UCC. These skills are applicable to the interpretation of other treatises and statutes, such that the work you do here translates into higher capacity to do legal work in other domains.

But things do not always go as planned. Even careful drafting cannot eliminate every risk. Moreover, not all agreements are carefully drafted and some are not written down at all. There are many reasons for contractual disputes to arise, and then once again, the contract lawyer adds value by predicting how a court would evaluate the disputed agreement and advising clients on whether and how to negotiate, sue, or settle. This book will specifically teach you how to do that work by recognizing whether courts will enforce specific promises, how the court would interpret those promises, and what remedies a court will award for broken promises. That learning begins with unpacking and understanding the set of rules defining what a contract is and who can form a contract.

Chapter 1

What Is a Contract?

Contract law invokes its own use of language. Certain terms that are used in everyday parlance take on a special meaning in contract law. For example, in Webster's Dictionary, the word "bargain" is defined as "something acquired by or as if by negotiation." But, under contract law, bargaining is not synonymous with or even necessarily related to negotiating. Therefore, is it critical to look up the legal and contractual meaning of key terms and not to rely on intuition or common knowledge.

Rules

A. Contract

The first definition we encounter in this course is, fittingly, Section 1 of the Restatement (Second) of Contracts ("R2d"), which defines "Contract."

> *A contract is a promise or a set of promises for the breach of which the law gives a remedy, or the performance of which the law in some way recognizes as a duty.* R2d §1.

A "contract" is simply a legally binding promise or set of promises. Although lay persons may use the term contract to mean a writing that sets forth an agreement, note that a writing is not required by this definition. Contracts can be written or oral. Only a few specific types of contracts need to be evidenced by a writing, as you will learn when studying about the statute of frauds.

Note that there are several words in the definition of contract which have a precise legal meaning: contract, promise, breach, remedy, performance, and duty are all specific legal words whose meaning may be different from the lay meaning. To understand the meaning of the term "contract," we thus have to learn the meaning of the other terms used to define contract.

Let us look to the Restatement for more clarity on what these terms mean in a legal sense.

B. Promise

A contract is a promise or set of promises. In particular, contracts-at-law require a set of promises, while contracts-at-equity and formal contracts require just one promise. But, in any case, all contracts require promises. What, then, is promise?

Promise is defined in Section 2 of the R2d:

A promise is a manifestation of intention to act or refrain from acting in a specified way, so made as to justify a promisee in understanding that a commitment has been made. R2d § 2(1).

Once again, note there are special legal words here that require additional unpacking. In particular, the term "manifestation of intention" is probably not a term you use in everyday speech, and it certainly has a special meaning here. How can we learn the special legal meaning of such words and phrases? Let us turn to Black's Law Dictionary to look up the legal meaning of words like "manifestation."

Manifestation. A clear sign or indication that a particular situation or feeling exists; that which exhibits, displays, or reveals.

What can we learn from this definition? A manifestation is an external expression — as distinguished from a secret thought or an undisclosed intention. Therefore, contract law must be concerned with outward acts and clear signs, and not with hidden secrets.

Another vital source necessary to understand the meaning of special legal terms is found in the Restatement itself. After each rule, you will find a series of comments that help to explain the rule. It is often necessary to read these comments, so you do not make a mistake by attributing a common or lay meaning to a special legal term or concept.

Manifestation of intention. Many contract disputes arise because different people attach different meanings to the same words and conduct. The phrase "manifestation of intention" adopts an external or objective standard for interpreting conduct; it means the external expression of intention as distinguished from undisclosed intention. R2d § 2 cmt. b.

A "promise" is a manifestation of commitment to do or not to do something. The concept of manifestation, meaning an outward sign or expression and not a privately held thought or belief, is central to contract law. Although a person may harbor some secret intention, contract law will judge that person's obligations only by what clear signs or indications that person exhibits, displays or reveals.

Not all promises result in contractual obligations. As you will soon learn, parties can make gratuitous or illusory promises that are not binding as a matter of law. Promises may be morally binding, such that breaking that promise is viewed as a sin or causes feeling of guilt or blame, but contract courts are not arbiters of morality. Promises may be socially binding, in that failing to keep them harms one's reputation or standing in a community, but that is not a matter for courts to evaluate when posed with a contract dispute. Contract courts enforce only legally binding promises — and the first half of this course is dedicated to answer the question of whether a particular promise is legally binding.

For example, Grandpa promises to give Grandson $100 on Grandson's next birthday, and Grandson promises to accept the gift. This is an agreement, but it is not a contract. As you will soon learn, absent specific facts (such as Grandson's detrimental reliance on Grandpa's promise), this agreement lacks consideration, so it will be unenforceable as a matter of law.

The suffix "-or" is added to a verb to create a noun that refers to the person that does an action. The suffix "-ee" is added to a verb to create a noun that refers to the person who is affected by the action. The verb "promise," therefore, is made into the nouns "promisor" and "promisee" to refer to the parties relevant to this transaction.

The person manifesting the intention is the promisor. R2d § 2(2).

A "promisor" is the subject of the promise; that is, a promisor is the person who makes the promise. If that promise is legally binding, it may be considered an obligation, and the person who made that promise may be termed an "obligor."

Promisee. The person to whom the manifestation is addressed is the promisee. R2d § 2(3).

A "promisee" is the object of the promise; that is, a promisee is the person to whom a promise is made. A person to whom a legally binding promise, or obligation, is made is called an "obligee."

Beneficiary. Where performance will benefit a person other than the promisee, that person is a beneficiary. R2d § 2(4).

A "beneficiary" is a person who benefits from a promise, but who is not a promisor or promisee. Such a person may also be referred to as a third-party beneficiary. Such third-party beneficiaries may have certain rights to sue the promisor or even, in certain cases, the promisee.

What have we learned from these terms? We have learned that contracts are only formed when parties make external, outward, objectively understandable statements or clear and unequivocal actions that demonstrate a commitment to do or not to do something. In other words, contracts are formed by promises. The person who makes a promise is called the promisor. The person who receives the promise is called the promisee. And a third party who benefits from the promise but is not the promisee is called a beneficiary.

C. Agreements and Bargains

The common meaning of the term "agreement" simply means a harmony of opinion. In other words, the common usage of the term does not require any objective manifestation. Under the common usage, you might "agree" with a person who lives in Australia that the sky is blue despite never having met her. But this is not what is meant by agreement under contract law.

Under contract law, an agreement is active, not passive: agreement requires a manifestation by two or more persons whose words and actions objectively demonstrate their accord.

An agreement is a manifestation of mutual assent on the part of two or more persons. A bargain is an agreement to exchange promises or to exchange a promise for a performance or to exchange performances. R2d § 3.

Look at the structure of this provision. Did you notice that "agreement" and "bargain" are both defined differently? That means that an agreement is distinguished from a bargain; in other words, the terms agreement and bargain must mean two different things. In particular, the definition of agreement does not mention the word promise at all, whereas a bargain is defined as an exchange of promises. This is a distinction that makes a difference.

Under contract law, an "agreement" is an express mutual understanding between two or more parties, but it does not necessarily create a legally binding obligation. For example, if you call your friend in Australia and discuss your shared belief that the sky is blue, or that today is Tuesday, that is an agreement, but this is not a contract. It is not even a bargain. Indeed, it is not even a promise!

A "bargain" is a subset of agreements in which both parties agree to do something in exchange. Not all bargains are contracts; that is, not all bargains are enforceable as a matter of law. Even if parties agree to exchange something of value, that does not necessarily make their agreement into a contract. For example, if a minor agrees to purchase a diamond ring from a pawn broker in exchange for $10,000, the minor may be allowed to "void" the obligation. Since the minor's promise to purchase the ring is not enforceable by the pawn broker, this is not a contract. Or, if a hit man agrees to assassinate a targeted person for $100,000, this is clearly a bargained-for exchange, but courts will not enforce obligations to commit crimes, so the bargain is not a valid contract. Yet these are still bargains, because they involve an exchange of promises.

Note that the legal definition of "bargain" makes no mention of negotiating or haggling. The term "bargain" sometimes confuses students who associate bargaining with haggling or some other process of negotiation, but this is not what the legal term requires. Parties to a contract do not necessarily haggle or negotiate. Perhaps the symmetrical concept of "mutuality of obligation" conveys the concept of bargained-for exchange more naturally.

For example, if you go to the Apple store, purchase a new MacBook, you may choose to pay $200 for the AppleCare extended warranty, but you will not find any opportunity to "bargain" with Apple regarding the price or terms of that transaction. It is a take-it-or-leave-it offer. Nevertheless, you have in the technical legal sense made a bargained-for exchange, namely, your $200 for Apple's extended warranty coverage.

D. Contracts-at-Law and Contracts-at-Equity

Recall that a "contract" is a legally binding promise or set of promises. This logically means that contracts are a special type of bargain that involves legally enforceable promises, while a bargain is a special type of agreement that involves a manifestation of mutual assent; therefore, a contract is a legally enforceable manifestation of mutual assent.

Unfortunately, even the law is not always this precise. The term "contract" is sometimes used to include legally enforceable promises that are not based on a bargain. To be more precise, we can further distinguish between legal contracts, which are based on bargains, and equitable contracts, which are not.

A "contract-at-law" is an agreement between two or more parties to a bargain that creates legally binding (enforceable) mutual obligations between them. Contracts-at-law are formed of mutual promises, each voluntarily given in exchange for the other, which together create a mutuality of obligation that binds the contractual parties to one another. A contract-at-law must have the elements of offer, acceptance, and consideration.

A "contract-at-equity" is a legally enforceable promise that is not based on a bargain, but which still requires a promise. Contracts-at-equity may lack the element of bargained-for exchange (technically known as "consideration"), yet they are still enforceable for other reasons of fairness and justice, also known as equity. While contracts-at-equity do not need to have all the elements of offer, acceptance, and consideration as contracts-at-law do, contracts-at-equity must at least include a promise which would be unjust not to enforce.

In any case, contracts require promises. Remember that contract law is voluntary. Unlike death or taxes, which are mandatory regardless of one's intentions or actions, a person must manifest some intention in order to be legally bound under contract law to perform some action. This means:

Contracts are promises that courts enforce.

E. Reflections on Contracts, Promises, Agreements, and Bargains

Thankfully, the American Law Institute has made the work of understanding contract much easier that codifying it. The R2d, while not a perfect representation of the myriad approaches among all the states, is a reasonable approximation of the common law that is well organized and relatively easy to read. Meanwhile, the UCC has been adopted in virtually all U.S. jurisdictions, thus harmonizing the law of sales throughout the country.

This course will teach you the common law of contracts as found in the R2d while pointing out where the UCC differs meaningfully from the common law. Your first task in applying this knowledge will be to determine whether the UCC applies so that you will apply the appropriate body of law.

Cases

Reading Steinberg v. Chicago Medical School. The *Steinberg* case discusses the legal meaning of the term contract. The background of the case may be familiar to many students: a prospective student was rejected from a prestigious medical school. Having paid an application fee, the student-plaintiff argued that the medical school had formed a contract with him and others in a similar position. Under the terms of this contract, the prospective student argued, the medical school had promised to evaluate the admissions fairly and without bias. The prospective student then argued that the school broke its promise by evaluating the applications based on the ability of the applicant and his family to make large donations to the school. The issue before the court is whether the application constituted a contract, which turns on what is the meaning of a "contract" in a legal sense.

Although contracts are usually formed through a more obvious sequence of offer and acceptance, the definition of contract is flexible enough to contemplate many other situations. Even though there was no written document that said CONTRACT in all caps at the top, it is still possible that a legally binding agreement was formed through this application process. Read *Steinberg* to see how courts will evaluate such claims and how they will define a contract and its key elements in the process.

Steinberg v. Chicago Medical School

69 Ill. 2d 320 (1977)

DOOLEY, Justice

Robert Steinberg received a catalog, applied for admission to defendant, Chicago Medical School, for the academic year 1974–75, and paid a $15 fee. He was rejected. Steinberg filed a class action against the school claiming it had failed to evaluate his application and those of other applicants according to the academic criteria in the school's bulletin. According to the complaint [which is the initial document or "pleading" that starts a civil action in a court of law], defendant used nonacademic criteria, primarily the ability of the applicant or his family to pledge or make payment of large sums of money to the school.

The 1974–75 bulletin distributed to prospective students contained this statement of standards by which applicants were to be evaluated:

Students are selected on the basis of scholarship, character, and motivation without regard to race, creed, or sex. The student's potential for the study and practice of medicine will be evaluated on the basis of academic achievement, Medical College Admission Test results, personal appraisals by a pre-professional advisory committee or individual instructors, and the personal interview, if requested by the Committee on Admissions.

Count I of the complaint alleged breach of contract; count II was predicated on the Consumer Fraud and Deceptive Business Practices Act and the Uniform Deceptive Trade Practices Act; count III charged fraud; and count IV alleged unjust enrichment.

This was sought to be brought as a class action. [A class action is a lawsuit where a single person or small group of people represents the interests of a larger group who are similarly situated.] Accordingly, there were the customary allegations common to such an action.

The trial court dismissed the complaint for failure to state a cause of action. [Dismissing the complaint entirely means that the plaintiff will not be able to prove the merits of any of its claims or "counts."]

The appellate court reversed as to count I, the contract action, and permitted it to be maintained as a limited class action. It affirmed the circuit court's dismissal of the remaining counts II, III, and IV. [Accordingly, the trial court will need to decide the contract claim on its merits.]

The real questions on this appeal are: Can the facts support a charge of breach of contract? Is an action predicated on fraud maintainable? Is this a proper class-action situation? [This edited version of the case will only include portions that are relevant to the breach of contract claim.]

On motion to dismiss we accept as true all well-pleaded facts. [This is a civil procedure concept that essentially means the court will take the facts that the plaintiff alleges in the complaint as true and will then evaluate whether those facts add up to a claim that, if true, would merit legal relief, a "remedy."]

Count I alleges Steinberg and members of the class to which he belongs applied to defendant and paid the $15 fee, and that defendant, through its brochure, described the criteria to be employed in evaluating applications, but failed to appraise the applications on the stated criteria. On the contrary, defendant evaluated such applications according to monetary contributions made on behalf of those seeking admission.

> *A contract, by ancient definition, is an agreement between competent parties, upon a consideration sufficient in law, to do or not to do a particular thing.*

> *An offer, an acceptance and consideration are basic ingredients of a contract.*

Steinberg alleges that he and others similarly situated received a brochure describing the criteria that defendant would employ in evaluating applications. He urges that such constituted an invitation for an offer to apply, that the filing of the applications constituted an offer to have their credentials appraised under the terms described by defendant, and that defendant's voluntary reception of the application and fee constituted an acceptance, the final act necessary for the creation of a binding contract.

This situation is similar to that wherein a merchant advertises goods for sale at a fixed price. While the advertisement itself is not an offer to contract, it constitutes an invitation to deal on the terms described in the advertisement. Although in some cases the advertisement itself may be an offer (*see Lefkowitz v. Great Minneapolis Surplus Store, Inc.*), usually it constitutes only an invitation to deal on the advertised terms. Only when the merchant takes the money is there an acceptance of the offer to purchase.

Here the description in the brochure containing the terms under which an application will be appraised constituted an invitation for an offer. The tender of the application, as well as the payment of the fee pursuant to the terms of the brochure, was an offer to apply. Acceptance of the application and fee constituted acceptance of an offer to apply under the criteria defendant had established.

Consideration is a basic element for the existence of a contract. Any act or promise which is of benefit to one party or disadvantage to the other is a sufficient consideration to support a contract. [This is an older definition of consideration that still appears in some court decisions. More modern courts will define consideration as a bargained-for exchange or mutuality of obligation. *See* R2d § 71.]

The application fee was sufficient consideration to support the agreement between the applicant and the school.

Defendant contends that a further requisite for contract formation is a meeting of the minds. But a subjective understanding is not requisite. It suffices that the conduct of the contracting parties indicates an agreement to the terms of the alleged contract.

Williston, in his work on contracts, states: "In the formation of contracts it was long ago settled that secret intent was immaterial, only overt acts being considered in the determination of such mutual assent as that branch of the law requires. During the first half of the nineteenth century there were many expressions which seemed to indicate the contrary. Chief of these was the familiar cliche, still reechoing in judicial dicta, that a contract requires the 'meeting of the minds' of the parties."

Here it would appear from the complaint that the conduct of the parties amounted to an agreement that the application would be evaluated according to the criteria described by defendant in its literature.

Defendant urges [the case of] *People ex rel. Tinkoff v. Northwestern University* controls. There the plaintiff alleged that since he met the stated requirement for admission, it was the obligation of the university to accept him. Plaintiff was first rejected because he was 14 years of age. He then filed a mandamus action [which requests a court to compel performance of a particular act; here, apparently the plaintiff was hoping the court would compel Northwestern University to admit him], and subsequently the university denied his admission, apparently because of the court action. That decision turned on the fact that Northwestern University, a private educational institution, had reserved in its charter the right to reject any applicant for any reason it saw fit.

Here, of course, defendant had no such provision in its charter or in the brochure in question. But, more important, Steinberg does not seek to compel the school to admit him. The substance of his action is that under the circumstances it was defendant's duty to appraise his application and those of the others on the terms defendant represented.

A medical school is an institution so important to life in society that its conduct cannot be justified by merely stating that one who does not wish to deal with it on its own terms may simply refrain from dealing with it at all.

As the appellate court noted in a recent case in which this defendant was a party:

> *A contract between a private institution and a student confers duties upon both parties which cannot be arbitrarily disregarded and may be judicially enforced.*

Here our scope of review is exceedingly narrow. Does the complaint set forth facts which could mean that defendant contracted, under the circumstances, to appraise applicants and their applications according to the criteria it described? This is the sole inquiry on this motion to dismiss. We believe the allegations suffice and affirm the appellate court in holding count I stated a cause of action.

[Discussions regarding the tort claim of fraud and the class action issues omitted.]

The appellate court was correct in affirming the dismissal of counts II [consumer fraud and deceptive practices] and IV [unjust enrichment] of plaintiff's complaint and in reversing the dismissal of count I [breach of contract] of the complaint. It erred in affirming the dismissal of count III [fraud] and abbreviating the class represented by plaintiff.

The judgment of the appellate court is affirmed in part and reversed in part, and the judgment of the circuit court of Cook County is affirmed in part and reversed in part. The cause is remanded to the circuit court with directions to proceed in a manner not inconsistent with this opinion.

Appellate court affirmed in part and reversed in part; circuit court affirmed in part and reversed in part; cause remanded.

Reflection

The *Steinberg* case discussed what a contract is and how it can be created. It also previews concepts that will be discussed more thoroughly throughout this course. *Steinberg* defines a contract as "an agreement between competent parties, upon a consideration sufficient in law, to do or not to do a particular thing." With this definition, the court pointed to its most important parts, or basic ingredients: offer, acceptance, and consideration.

According to R2d §3, an agreement is "a manifestation of mutual assent on the part of two or more persons." The *Steinberg* defendant incorrectly defined this manifestation of mutual assent as a "meeting of the minds." As *Steinberg* points out, there does not need to be a true meeting of the minds because the agreement is not based on a person's secret inward intent but on their outward actions.

As you will learn through this course, a student or lawyer who wishes to comprehensively analyze whether parties formed a valid contract should make the following inquires: (1) what promise(s) were made? (2) are the parties capable of making legally binding promises? (3) were the promises framed as a reasonably clear and definite offer? (4) was that offer accepted before it was terminated? (5) were the promises given mutually, where one thing shall be done in exchange for another; and if not, is there some equitable reason why a promise should be enforceable anyway? (6) did any promise require a signed writing; and, if so, was there either a sufficient writing to evidence the agreement or some equitable reason why the promise should be enforced anyway? (7) are there any "defenses" that one or both parties might assert that absolves contractual liability?

If one determines that a contract was thus formed, the next question is what exactly does that require the parties to do or not to do. Then a court will inquire whether the parties actually did those things, and if not, what remedies should be provided to an aggrieved party.

As you might already be able to see, this entire inquiry turns on what promises were made. Therefore, an appropriate place to begin the study of contract law is by understanding the promise itself. Understanding what a promise is and being able to recognize both valid and invalid contractual promises is an essential skill for all lawyers who encounter contracts.

Discussion

1. What is a meeting of the minds? When does a meeting of the minds occur?

2. Why might it be easy or difficult for a court of law to determine whether a subjective meeting of the minds occurred?

3. Why did the *Steinberg* court determine that this specific application constituted a contract? What does this demonstrate about the legal definition of what is a contract generally?

4. Did Chicago Medical School make any promises to its applicants? Did the applicants make any promises to Chicago Medical School is exchange? When answering this question, make sure to cite the R2d's definition of "promise" and use that definition to perform analysis of whether any prospective manifestations constituted a promise.

> **Reading Pappas v. Bever.** Contracts usually take the form of a mutual set of promises "to do or not do a particular thing." But what does the law recognize as promises? The next case, *Pappas*, addresses the issue of what constitutes a promise, which is a question at the heart of contract law.

Pappas v. Bever

219 N.W.2d 720 (Iowa 1974)

McCORMICK, Justice.

Plaintiff William Pappas, receiver for Charles City College, appeals trial court's judgment denying enforcement of a fundraising pledge against defendant Sondra Bever, executor of the estate of Philip Bissonnette, Jr. No evidence was offered bearing on the meaning of the pledge instrument. The court held the instrument alone was insufficient to show the pledge was obligatory. We affirm.

In relevant part the executed form read as follows:

> I/we intend to subscribe to the College Founder's Fund the sum of Five Thousand — no/100 Dollars.
>
> I intend to pay ( ) Monthly ( ) Quarterly ( ) Semi-Annually (X) Annually
>
> over 60/36 months beginning 1967.
>
> Name Philip Bissonette
>
> Address 301 — 2nd Ave.

The form was printed except for the blanks designating the amount of the pledge, terms of payment, signature and address of the pledgor. Bissonnette paid $1,000 on the pledge in 1967 and $1,000 in 1968. The college closed in May 1968, and he made no further payments prior to his death May 15, 1969.

The same fund-raising project and pledge form were involved in *Pappas v. Hauser*, 197 N.W.2d 607 (Iowa 1972). There the court held extrinsic evidence could be considered in determining whether the parties intended the pledge to be obligatory or not. Such evidence showed the background of the fund-raising drive, preparation of the form and circumstances surrounding its execution, including statements attributed to the college's fund-raiser to the effect the pledge was only a statement of intention and not binding. Based upon this record the court held the pledge to be nonobligatory. Three members of the court concurred, specially on the ground they would hold the pledge form as illuminated by evidence of background and surrounding circumstances were nonobligatory without resort to the fundraiser's statements. There was no disagreement with the principle that extrinsic evidence is admissible, which throws light on the situation of the parties, antecedent negotiations, the attending circumstances and the objects they were striving to attain.

In the present case the pledge form stands alone, there being no evidence other than the instrument which purports to cast light on its meaning. Thus, we reach the problem not decided in the Hauser case, whether the pledge form standing alone is obligatory or not.

Without extrinsic evidence [extrinsic evidence is evidence that comes from facts and circumstances surrounding the contract and not from the written contract itself] bearing upon the intention of the participants, we must attempt to ascertain the meaning and legal effect of the pledge form by giving the language used in the instrument its common and ordinary meaning. No useful purpose would be served by repetition of the authorities treating the meaning of the word "intend" in various contexts. They are collected in *Pappas v. Hauser*. These authorities demonstrate that when words expressing an intention to do something in the future stand alone, they are not a promise and hence do not create an obligation. A mere expression of intention is not a promise.

The distinction between a statement of intention and a promise is explained in 1 Corbin on Contracts § 15 at 35 (1963):

> *A statement of intention is the mere expression of a state of mind, put in such a form as neither to invite nor to justify action in reliance by another person. A promise is also the expression of a state of mind but put in such a form as to invite reliance by another person.*

The language of the pledge form in this case, standing alone, shows nothing more than a statement of intention. There is no evidence the pledge was intended to be obligatory.

Even if the language were viewed as uncertain, the conclusion is the same. In this case, we are dealing with language printed on the pledge form by the fund-raiser, and doubtful language in a written instrument is construed against the party who selected it.

Plaintiff contends the fact two payments were made proves the pledge was obligatory. This is a bootstrap argument. The mere fact a person carries out in part what he said he intended to do does not convert his statement of intention into a promise.

It was plaintiff's burden to prove the pledge was intended to be obligatory. We agree with trial court he failed to do so.

Affirmed.

Reflection

By studying *Pappas*, we learn that a statement of intention, such as a pledge form, is simply a "mere expression of a state of mind," and therefore nonobligatory. When words expressing an intention to do something in the future stand alone, they are not a promise.

A promise is "a manifestation of commitment to do or not to do something." Promises require manifestations, which are outward signs or expressions that are not privately held thoughts or beliefs. A mere expression of an intention is not a promise.

Without the admission of extrinsic evidence in this case, it is impossible to determine the parties' intentions. Barring any outside evidence, by filling out the pledge form, Philip Bissonnette Jr. only made a mere expression of intention to donate to Charles City College. Bissonnette made no further manifestation of a commitment to donate to Charles City College. Therefore, the pledge was nonobligatory.

Discussion

1. What is the difference between a "promise" and a "mere statement of intention"? How should courts distinguish between the two?

2. What legal consequences result from defining a manifestation as a mere statement of intention and not a promise?

3. Why did the *Pappas* court determine the specific manifestation in this case was not a promise but rather a mere statement of intention? What does this teach about the general legal meaning of the term promise? Cite and use the R2d definition of "promise" in conducting this analysis.

Problems

Problem 1.1. Contract, Agreement, or Bargain?

For each of the following hypothetical situations, identify whether the parties have made a promise, a contract, an agreement, a bargain, or a mere statement of opinion, and explain your reasons why you have correctly identified the situation.

i. Sarah Seller orally offers to sell Greenacre to Carlton for $100,000, and Carlton orally accepts the offer.

ii. Bob the Builder is constructing a home for Harry Homemaker. Bob says to Harry, "I warrant that this house will never burn down."

iii. Harry Homemaker is bragging about his new house to his neighbor, Nancy. Harry says to Nancy, "This house will never burn down."

iv. Ernst Employer says to Wanda Worker, "I will employ you for a year at a salary of $5,000 if I go into business."

v. Stephen Stargazer remarks to his friend Tom, "That constellation over there is called the Big Dipper." Tom replies, "Yes, that's right."

Problem 1.2. The Monster and the Beast

The Beastie Boys, a hip-hop group, asked Zach Scaccia, a DJ known as "Z-Trip," to create a remix of their songs (the "Megamix") for fans to download for free to promote the Beastie Boys' then-upcoming album. Z-Trip was later contracted to work as a DJ for energy-drink manufacturer, Monster Energy Co.'s ("Monster") after-party for their annual snowboarding competition called "Ruckus in the Rockies." Nelson Phillips, responsible for planning Ruckus in the Rockies, spoke to Z-Trip for about 30 seconds and asked him if there was any music he could use for a web-edit of the event. Z-Trip replied that there was, and he could download it for free on his website. Later at breakfast, the two discussed the video, and that Phillips would not publish the video without Z-Trip's approval. Phillips believed he had permission to use the Megamix for their promotional video because it was "available for free download on his website . . . it's there for use. For free."

A few days later, Phillips e-mailed Z-Trip, with a link to the video, asking him whether he approved and once he did, he would post it on Monster's YouTube channel. Z-Trip replied with "Dope!" and asked him to also post a link where people could download it for free. Phillips emailed Z-Trip again, telling him the video was posted and Z-Trip again replied with "Dope!" The Beastie Boys sued Monster for copyright infringement for using the remix of their songs in their promotional video.

Monster brought a third-party complaint (a civil procedure concept where a non-party is brought into the case and can be held liable for plaintiff's claims) for breach of contract and fraud against Z-Trip. Monster argued that Z-Trip misrepresented himself as having the authority to license (permit the use of) the copyrighted material in the Megamix to third parties such as Monster. Monster further argued that Z-Trip breached (failed to perform) his obligations to Monster because Z-Trip promised to convey the right to use the Megamix, but Z-Trip did not have authority to convey such use.

Did Z-Trip promise Monster that Monster could use the Megamix for free in their promotional video?

See Beastie Boys v. Monster Energy Co., 983 F. Supp. 2d 338 (S.D.N.Y. 2013).

Problem 1.3. Harassment in Hawaii

Leland Gonsalves worked as a service department manager at a Nissan car dealership in Hawaii. One of the employees under his supervision, Neldine Torres, complained to Gonsalves's supervisor, Wayne Suehisa, that Gonsalves sexually harassed her on several occasions. Suehisa approached Gonsalves about Torres's complaint. Gonsalves denied them all.

Suehisa replied to Gonsalves, "You will get a thorough and fair investigation. You do not need to get a lawyer because this is only an internal investigation. Do not worry about losing your job; I am not planning on terminating you." The next day Suehisa circulated an inter-office memorandum detailing Torres's claims and Gonsalves's denial, in which Suehisa wrote "Torres will maintain her position, as well as Gonsalves."

Two weeks later, while the independent investigation was ongoing, Gonsalves emailed Suehisa complaining that Torres was creating a hostile work environment for him, that she was insubordinate, and that her job performance was poor. Suehisa ignored the email. A few days after that, the independent investigator determined that Gonsalves was the one creating a hostile work environment and concluded that Gonsalves should be disciplined for his unacceptable behavior.

Suehisa was disappointed by the report because Gonsalves was an otherwise effective manager. He thought about it seriously for three days, then, given the company's zero-tolerance policy for harassment, Suehisa decided to fire Gonsalves. In the termination letter, Suehisa wrote that the termination was based on evidence that Gonsalves had sexually harassed Torres.

Gonsalves was furious. He applied to forty to fifty other jobs but was rejected from each one. Gonsalves then sued Nissan corporation on the theory that Nissan's authorized agent, Suehisa, promised not to fire him, then broke that promise.

Did Suehisa promise Gonsalves that he would retain his job regardless of the findings of the investigation?

Did Suehisa promise Gonsalves that he would conduct a thorough and fair investigation of Torres's allegation?

See Gonsalves v. Nissan Motor Corp. in Hawaii, 100 Haw. 149 (2002).

Problem 1.4. Lifelong Employment

William Greene began working for Grant Building, Inc. in 1959. Greene allegedly agreed to work at a pay rate below union scale in exchange for a promise that Grant would employ him "for life."

In 1975, Oliver Realty, Inc. took over management of Grant Building. The president of Oliver Realty assured all former Grant employees that their existing employment contracts would be honored.

Greene explained the terms of his agreement to his new supervisor. The supervisor told Greene that he would look into the matter but never got back to Greene.

In 1983, Greene was fired from Oliver Realty. Greene brought an action for breach of contract against Oliver Realty.

Was a valid bargain formed between William Greene and Grant Building, Inc.?

Was a valid bargain formed between William Greene and Oliver Realty, Inc.?

See Greene v. Oliver Realty, Inc., 363 Pa. Super. 534 (Pa. Sup. Ct. 1987), app. denied.

Chapter 2

Capacity and Incapacity

Contract liability only results from intentional words or actions. This distinguishes contracts from torts, which can be intentional (like intentional infliction of emotional distress) or accidental (like negligence). Since contract liability must arise from intentional conduct, a preliminary question to ask is whether a party had the capacity to form legally enforceable intentions in the first place.

> *No one can be bound by contract who has not legal capacity to incur at least voidable contractual duties.* R2d § 12(1).

This general rule requiring capacity to contract is followed by several specific instances of incapacity.

> *A natural person who manifests assent to a transaction has full legal capacity to incur contractual duties thereby unless he is (a) under guardianship, (b) an infant, (c) mentally ill or defective, or (d) intoxicated.* R2d § 12(2).

The result of this rule is that contracts formed with people who are under guardianship, infants, mentally ill, or intoxicated may be voided or cancelled by the party who lacked capacity at the time of contracting. Once an incapacitated party regains its capacity, that party may reaffirm its obligations such that they can no longer be voided.

Once again, we need to be careful to learn the special legal meaning of terms used in contract law. You may have some ideas about what "infant" means, for example, but if you do not look up the precise legal meaning of this term, then you run the serious risk of getting the law wrong.

Rules

A. Guardianship

A "guardian" is someone who has the legal authority to care for another's person or property. A person who is under a guardian's care or protection is called a "ward." Also termed a conservator, a guardian may be appointed because of a ward's infancy, incapacity, or disability. A person under guardianship cannot contract.

> *A person has no capacity to incur contractual duties if his property is under guardianship by reason of an adjudication of mental illness or defect.* R2d § 13.

Guardianship is a legal state of affairs, where the state, through legal process, determines someone is incompetent to make decisions about their own person or property. This is a serious deprivation of freedom and civil liberties that is not taken lightly. A guardianship is almost always an involuntary procedure imposed by the state onto a person who thus becomes the state's ward. While a person is under such guardianship, that person lacks the legal power to make binding contracts.

B. Infancy

The second category of incapacity, "infants," counterintuitively, does not mean a little baby. Rather, an infant is a person who, in the eyes of the law, has not yet reached the full age of maturity. A more common term for such a person is a "minor." Under the common law of contracts, the terms infant and minor are synonyms.

Generally, an infant has the right to disaffirm or avoid contracts made while he or she is a minor. After reaching the age of majority, the former infant must promptly elect to disaffirm his or her obligation or agree to be bound by it.

> Unless a statute provides otherwise, a natural person has the capacity to incur only voidable contractual duties until the beginning of the day before the person's eighteenth birthday. R2d § 14.

But a major exception to this right of disaffirmance is that the infant is liable for any "necessaries" he or she buys. The problem with this exception is defining "necessaries." For example, if a minor rents an apartment while he could alternatively live at home, is that rental a necessary? If an infant orders a crate of ramen noodle soup while she could go to a soup kitchen, is that soup a necessary?

For example, if a car dealership leases a basic Toyota Corolla to an infant who lives in a rural area and needs a car to go to work in order to afford basic living expenses, the infant's power to void the contract are limited because the contract regards a necessary.

Corbin's treatise gives some guidance as to what constitutes "necessaries" such that infants who contract for them have a binding obligation:

> Things may be of a useful character, but the quality or quantity supplied may take them out of the character of necessaries. Elementary textbooks might be a necessary to a student of law, but not a rare edition of 'Littleton's Tenures,' or eight or ten copies of 'Stephen's Commentaries.' Necessaries also vary according to the station in life of the infant or his peculiar circumstances at the time. The quality of clothing suitable to an Eton boy would be unnecessary for a telegraph clerk; the medical attendance and diet required by an invalid would be unnecessary to one in ordinary health. It does not follow therefore that because a thing is of a useful class, a judge is bound to allow a jury to say whether or not it is a necessary.

Once you get past the archaic language, the point of the above passage is clear: what is necessary depends on the circumstances but should always be distinguished from luxuries.

C. Mental Illness

Mental illness results in incapacity to contract if the mental illness specifically impacts a person's ability to understand a particular transaction.

> *A person incurs only voidable contractual duties by entering into a transaction if by reason of mental illness or defect he is unable to understand in a reasonable manner the nature and consequences of the transaction.* R2d § 15(1)(a).

Additionally, mental illness results in incapacity where the illness impacts a person's ability to act reasonably in relation to a transaction and where the other party should detect this inability.

> *A person incurs only voidable contractual duties by entering into a transaction if by reason of mental illness or defect he is unable to act in a reasonable manner in relation to the transaction and the other party has reason to know of his condition.* R2d § 15(1)(b).

In the contract law context, "capacity" means the ability to perform a role, specifically, the ability to perform the role of giving or accepting binding promises. Contractual promises are binding only where intentionally given, so a person who does not have the capacity to manifest his or her intentions does not, by definition, have the ability to make binding promises.

But determining whether someone is so incapacitated as to render purported contractual decisions invalid is a rather complex matter. First, our scientific understanding of mental states and mental disease is still in relatively formative stages. Second, courts who review disputes months or even years after promises were allegedly made face additional problems in assessing alleged incompetency at the time of contract formation. For these reasons, there is a fair amount of debate about what standard for capacity should govern contract law.

Two examples illustrate how the general concept of mental incapacity requires more specific analysis regarding the nature of the transaction and the nature of the mental illness.

First, imagine that Debora suffers from depression, a mood disorder that causes a persistent feeling of sadness and loss of interest. A psychiatrist diagnosed her conditions and prescribed her medication for it, but Debora still suffers from what you might call "the blues." One day, Debora purchases a non-refundable airplane ticket to Cabo San Lucas because she thinks the vacation will help her feel happier. Later, she becomes anxious about the cost of the trip and decides to avoid the contract. In this case, Debora has full capacity to understand the nature of the transaction of buying plane tickets, so will be bound to the contractual terms.

On the other hand, Scully suffers from schizophrenia, a mental disorder in which people interpret reality abnormally. Schizophrenia may result in some combination of hallucinations, delusions, and extremely disordered thinking and behavior. During an episode of delusions, Scully become convinced that the Soviet Red Army is going to invade his hometown of Des Moines, Iowa, and he is the only person who can stop the attack and save his country. Scully places an order for a M4 Sherman Tank, a military weapon from World War II, under the mistaken impression that he will pilot it in the forthcoming battle. Scully did not understand that the tank he ordered was a replica that cannot fire artillery. Under these extreme circumstances, Scully can likely show he lacked capacity to make the contract to purchase the tank.

Unlike guardianship, which is a clear legal state, determining whether a person has a lack of capacity for reasons of mental illness is much more difficult. It may require testimony from medical experts about the nature of the illness.

D. Intoxication

The term "intoxication" may also differ legally from common or lay conceptions of the term. One may be too intoxicated to drive, for example, but still well within his capacities to contract. The legal standard for incapacity at contract law is that one must be so drunk or intoxicated from drugs that he does not know what he is doing. Moreover, the other party must have reason to know of the intoxication.

> *A person incurs only voidable contractual duties by entering into a transaction if the other party has reason to know that by reason of intoxication (a) he is unable to understand in a reasonable manner the nature and consequences of the transaction, or (b) he is unable to act in a reasonable manner in relation to the transaction.* R2d § 16.

For example, Aaron and Betsy have been communicating for weeks about the purchase and sale of a boat. One day, the parties conclude their oral conversation with Aaron presenting a clear offer to sell his boat and Betsy saying, "I'll think about it and get back to you as soon as possible." That night, Betsy drinks to the point of blacking out. While totally drunk, Betsy texts the seller with the simple message, "I accept your offer." Unless Aaron has some reason to know that Betsy was totally drunk—which would not be apparent from the text message—the contract is binding.

If, on the other hand, Betsy first texted, "Just took ten shots of vodka!" and then texted she wishes to accept Aaron's offer, then Aaron might reasonably know that Betsy was not competent to accept his offer at that time.

2 • CAPACITY AND INCAPACITY

E. Reflections on Capacity and Incapacity

Contractual liability is voluntary, and willingness to be bound by a contract is evidenced by a manifestation of intention to be bound by its terms. Therefore, the ability of parties to form and manifest intention is essential to the contract formation process. The law presumes that infants and people under guardianship lack this capacity to form an intention to be bound because of an inability to understand what that means. This presumption extends to the mentally ill and, to a lesser extent, to the intoxicated.

In the next module, you will learn what a manifestation of mutual assent looks like. But you should keep in mind that even when something objectively looks like mutual assent to an outside observer, it is possible that subjectively one or both parties did not actually understand the bargain or consent to it. This is just one of many examples of the tension between objective manifestation and subjective intentions that runs throughout contract law.

Cases

Reading Webster St. Partnership, Ltd. v. Sheridan. Contract law protects certain people from contractual liability as a matter of public policy. One such protection applies to minors and children, which are referred to in contract law as "infants."

"Infant" has a special meaning in contract law that differs from the plain meaning of the term. Most people use the term infant to mean a baby who is less than about a year old. Contract law, however, defines "infant" to mean someone who has not yet reached the age of majority, which is 18 years old in most states.

The question in the following case is not whether one party is an infant. This is usually a very simply factual inquiry with a binary result (infant or major). The tricky question, however, is whether such infant contracted for a "necessary" such that the contract is not voidable by the infant.

Before exploring what constitutes a necessary under the common law, think about why this rule exists. Put yourself in the position of someone who has received an offer to contract from an infant. You know this infant incurs only voidable obligations. Might that make you less likely to accept the infant's offer to contract? It should, because you will not have certainty that the infant will perform his obligations, and you will have no recourse for breach. While this rule protects infants from making bad deals, it also discourages people from making deals with infants at all, even ones that benefit the infant. For example, it is very hard for an infant to lease a car because the car dealers know that the infant could void the contract at any time.

This rule intended to benefit infants thus has the unintended consequence of creating a hardship for them. The way around that hardship is to make contracts for necessaries binding. If an emancipated minor is homeless, then renting an apartment would be considered a contract for a necessary in that case. Since that apartment is necessary, the contract will be binding on the minor, despite the capacity rule for infants generally. This should encourage landlords to rent apartments to minors who otherwise have nowhere else to live. But does it work?

Webster St. Partnership, Ltd. v. Sheridan

220 Neb. 9 (1985)

KRIVOSHA, Chief Justice.

Webster Street Partnership, Ltd. ("Webster Street"), appeals from an order of the district court for Douglas County, Nebraska, which modified an earlier judgment entered by the municipal court of the city of Omaha, Douglas County, Nebraska. The municipal court entered judgment in favor of Webster Street and against the appellees, Matthew Sheridan and Pat Wilwerding, in the amount of $630.94.

On appeal, the district court found that Webster Street was entitled to a judgment in the amount of $146.75, and that Sheridan and Wilwerding were entitled to a credit in the amount of $150. The district court therefore entered judgment in favor of Sheridan and Wilwerding and against Webster Street in the amount of $3.25. It is from this $3.25 judgment that appeal is taken to this court.

Webster Street is a partnership owning real estate in Omaha, Nebraska. On September 18, 1982, Webster Street, through one of its agents, Norman Sargent, entered into a written lease with Sheridan and Wilwerding for a second-floor apartment at 3007 Webster Street. The lease provided that Sheridan and Wilwerding would pay to Webster Street, by way of monthly rental, the sum of $250 due on the first day of each month until August 15, 1983. The lease also required a security deposit in the amount of $150 and a payment of $20 per month for utilities during the months of December, January, February, and March. Liquidated damages in the amount of $5 per day for each day the rent was late were also provided for by the lease.

The evidence conclusively establishes that at the time the lease was executed both tenants were minors and, further, that Webster Street knew. At the time the lease was entered, Sheridan was 18 and did not become 19 until November 5, 1982. Wilwerding was 17 at the time the lease was executed and never gained his majority during any time relevant to this case.

The tenants paid the $150 security deposit, $100 rent for the remaining portion of September 1982, and $250 rent for October 1982. They did not pay the rent for the month of November 1982, and on November 5, Sargent advised Wilwerding that unless the rent was paid immediately, both boys would be required to vacate the premises. The tenants both testified that, being unable to pay the rent, they moved from the premises on November 12. In fact, a dispute exists as to when the two tenants relinquished possession of the premises, but in view of our decision, that dispute is not of any relevance.

In a letter dated January 7, 1983, Webster Street's attorney made written demand upon the tenants for damages in the amount of $630.94. On January 12, 1983, the tenants' attorney denied any liability, refused to pay any portion of the amount demanded, stated that neither tenant was of legal age at the time the lease was executed, and demanded return of the $150 security deposit.

Webster Street thereafter commenced suit against the tenants and sought judgment in the amount of $630.94, which was calculated as follows:

Rent due Nov.	$250.00
Rent due Dec.	$250.00
Dec. utility allowance	$20.00
Garage rental	$40.00
Clean up and repair broken window, degrease kitchen stove, shampoo carpet, etc.	$46.79
Advertising fee	$24.15
Re-rental fee	$150.00
Less security deposit	($150.00)
TOTAL	$630.94

To this petition the tenants filed an answer alleging that they were minors at the time they signed the lease, that the lease was therefore voidable, and that the rental property did not constitute a necessary for which they were otherwise liable. Sheridan then cross-petitioned for the return of the security deposit, and Wilwerding filed a cross-petition seeking the return of all moneys paid to Webster Street.

Following trial, the municipal court of the city of Omaha found in favor of Webster Street and against both tenants in the amount of $630.94. The tenants appealed to the district court for Douglas County. The district court found that the tenants had vacated the premises on November 12, 1982, and therefore were only liable for the 12 days in which they actually occupied the apartment and did not pay rent. The district court also permitted Webster Street to recover $46.79 for cleanup and repairs. The tenants, however, were given credit for their $150 security deposit, resulting in an order that Webster Street was indebted to the tenants in the amount of $3.25. Webster Street then perfected an appeal to this court assigning but one error in terms which provide little assistance to the court in considering the appeal. The assignment of error, in pertinent part, reads as follows: "The District Court . . . abused [its] discretion and committed errors of law in improperly modifying the judgment of the Municipal Court. . . ." It appears, in fact, to be Webster Street's position that the district court erred in failing to find that Sheridan had ratified the lease within a reasonable time after obtaining majority, and was therefore responsible for the lease, and that the minors had become emancipated and were therefore liable, even though Wilwerding had not reached majority.

Webster Street is simply wrong in both matters. As a general rule, an infant does not have the capacity to bind himself absolutely by contract. The right of the infant to avoid his contract is one conferred by law for his protection against his own improvidence and the designs of others. The policy of the law is to discourage adults from contracting with an infant; they cannot complain if, as a consequence of violating that rule, they are unable to enforce their contracts. "The result seems hardly just to the [adult], but persons dealing with infants do so at their peril. The law is plain as to their disability to contract, and safety lies in refusing to transact business with them."

However, the privilege of infancy will not enable an infant to escape liability in all cases and under all circumstances. For example, it is well established that an infant is liable for the value of necessaries furnished him. An infant's liability for necessaries is based not upon his actual contract to pay for them but upon a contract implied by law, or, in other words, a quasi-contract. Just what are necessaries, however, has no exact definition. The term is flexible and varies according to the facts of each individual case. A number of factors must be considered before a court can conclude whether a particular product or service is a necessary. As stated in *Schoenung v. Gallet*:

> "The term 'necessaries,' as used in the law relating to the liability of infants therefor, is a relative term, somewhat flexible, except when applied to such things as are obviously requisite for the maintenance of existence, and depends on the social position and situation in life of the infant, as well as upon his own fortune and that of his parents. The particular infant must have an actual need for the articles furnished; not for mere ornament or pleasure. The articles must be useful and suitable, but they are not necessaries merely because useful or beneficial. Concerning the general character of the things furnished, to be necessaries the articles must supply the infant's personal needs, either those of his body or those of his mind. However, the term 'necessaries' is not confined to merely such things as are required for a bare subsistence. There is no positive rule by means of which it may be determined what are or what are not necessaries, for what may be considered necessary for one infant may not be necessaries for another

infant whose state is different as to rank, social position, fortune, health, or other circumstances, the question being one to be determined from the particular facts and circumstances of each case."

In *Ballinger v. Craig*, the defendants were husband and wife and were 19 years of age at the time they purchased a trailer. [In this jurisdiction at this time, people the age of 19 had not reached majority and were therefore considered infants]. Both were employed. However, prior to the purchase of the trailer, the defendants were living with the parents of the husband. The Court of Appeals for the State of Ohio held that under the facts presented, the trailer was not a necessary. The court stated:

> "To enable an infant to contract for articles as necessaries, he must have been in actual need of them, and obliged to procure them for himself. They are not necessaries as to him, however necessary they may be in their nature, if he was already supplied with sufficient articles of the kind, or if he had a parent or guardian who was able and willing to supply them. The burden of proof is on the plaintiff to show that the infant was destitute of the articles and had no way of procuring them except by his own contract."

Under Ohio law, the marriage of the parties did not result in their obtaining majority. In 42 Am.Jur.2d Infants § 67 at 68–69 (1969), the author notes: "Thus, articles are not necessaries for an infant if he has a parent or guardian who is able and willing to supply them, and an infant residing with and being supported by his parent according to his station in life is not absolutely liable for things which under other circumstances would be considered necessaries." The undisputed testimony is that both tenants were living away from home, apparently with the understanding that they could return home at any time. Sheridan testified:

Q. During the time that you were living at 3007 Webster, did you at any time, feel free to go home or anything like that?

A. Well, I had a feeling I could, but I just wanted to see if I could make it on my own.

Q. Had you been driven from your home?

A. No.

Q. You didn't have to go?

A. No.

Q. You went freely?

A. Yes.

Q. Then, after you moved out and went to 3007 for a week or so, you were again to return home, is that correct?

A. Yes, sir.

It would therefore appear that in the present case neither Sheridan nor Wilwerding was in need of shelter but, rather, had chosen to voluntarily leave home, with the understanding that they could return whenever they desired. One may at first blush believe that such a rule is unfair. Yet, on further consideration, the wisdom of the rule is apparent. If, indeed, landlords may not contract with minors, except at their peril, they may refuse to do so. In that event, minors who voluntarily leave home but who are free to return will be compelled to return to their parents' home — a result which is desirable. We therefore find that both the municipal court and the district court erred in finding that the apartment, under the facts in this case, was a necessary. Having concluded that the apartment was not a necessary, the question of whether Sheridan and Wilwerding were emancipated is of no significance. The effect of emancipation is only relevant with regard to necessaries. If the minors were not emancipated, then their parents would be liable for necessaries provided to the minors. As we recently noted in *Accent Service Co., Inc. v. Ebsen*:

> "In general, even in the absence of statute, parents are under a legal as well as a moral obligation to support, maintain, and care for their children, the basis of such a duty resting not only upon the fact of the parent-child relationship, but also upon the interest of the state as parents patriae of children and of the community at large in preventing them from becoming a public burden. However, various voluntary acts of a child, such as marriage or enlistment in military service, have been held to terminate the parent's obligation of support, the issue generally being considered by the courts in terms of whether an emancipation of the child has been effectuated. In those cases, involving the issue of whether a parent is obligated to support an unmarried minor child who has voluntarily left home without the consent of the parent, the courts, in actions to compel support from the parent, have uniformly held that such conduct on the part of the child terminated the support obligation."

If, on the other hand, it was determined that the minors were emancipated and the apartment was a necessary, then the minors would be liable. But where, as here, we determine that the apartment was not a necessary, then neither the parents nor the infants are liable, and the question of emancipation is of no moment. Because the rental of the apartment was not a necessary, the minors had the right to avoid the contract, either during their minority or within a reasonable time after reaching their majority. Disaffirmance by an infant completely puts an end to the contract's existence, both as to him and as to the adult with whom he contracted. Because the parties then stand as if no contract had ever existed, the infant can recover payments made to the adult, and the adult is entitled to the return of whatever was received by the infant.

The record shows that Pat Wilwerding clearly disaffirmed the contract during his minority. Moreover, the record supports the view that when the agent for Webster Street ordered the minors out for failure to pay rent and they vacated the premises, Sheridan likewise disaffirmed the contract. The record indicates that Sheridan reached majority on November 5. To suggest that a lapse of 7 days was not disaffirmance within a reasonable time would be foolish. Once disaffirmed, the contract became void; therefore, no contract existed between the parties, and the minors were entitled to recover all of the moneys which they paid and to be relieved of any further obligation under the contract. The judgment of the district court for Douglas County, Nebraska, is therefore reversed and the cause remanded with directions to vacate the judgment in favor of Webster Street and to enter a judgment in favor of Matthew Sheridan and Pat Wilwerding in the amount of $500, representing September rent in the amount of $100, October rent in the amount of $250, and the security deposit in the amount of $150.

REVERSED AND REMANDED WITH DIRECTIONS.

Reflection

Webster established that an infant generally does not have the capacity to contract. In order to protect infants, adults are discouraged from contracting with them. If an adult enters a contract with an infant, the contract may consequently be unenforceable.

However, the privilege of infancy is not applicable under all circumstances. Infants are liable for the value of necessaries. There is no strict definition for necessaries. What is defined as a necessary varies from case to case. In general, "necessaries" refers mainly to things that are useful and required for existence. However, many factors can influence whether something is deemed a necessary. What may be deemed a necessary for one party may not be deemed a necessary for another party. Generally, items are not deemed necessaries for an infant if their parent/guardian is able to supply them. Specifically looking at *Webster*, the apartment they leased was not a necessity because they were able to return to housing provided to them by their parents.

Another important note from *Webster* is that Sheridan was still able to claim infancy even though he reached majority while contracting. Since Sheridan vacated the property only 7 days after he reached maturity, he was still able to use his infancy as a defense against contractual liability.

Discussion

1. Who is an "infant" as defined in contract law? Why should the law protect infants?

2. Can you foresee any problems that might result from a legal effort to protect infants?

3. What are "necessaries"? Why is there an exception to the protection for infants from contractual liability with regard to necessaries?

4. What is a quasi-contract? Why did courts create the legal concept of a quasi-contract?

––––––––––

Reading Estate of McGovern v. Commonwealth State Employees' Retirement Bd. In the contract law context, "capacity" means the ability to perform a role, specifically, the ability to perform the role of giving or accepting binding promises. Contractual promises are binding only where intentionally given, so a person who does not have the capacity to manifest his or her intentions does not, by definition, can make binding promises.

But determining whether someone is so incapacitated as to render purported contractual decisions invalid is a rather complex matter. First, our scientific understanding of mental states and mental disease is still in relatively formative stages. Second, courts who review disputes months or even years after promises were allegedly made face additional problems in assessing alleged incompetency at the time of contract formation.

For these reasons, there is a fair amount of debate about what standard for capacity should govern contract law. The following case, *Estate of McGovern*, is an excellent discussion of the reasoning for and against the Restatement's approach to this thorny problem. Not only does *McGovern* present relatively straightforward and memorable facts, it also goes into significant depth as to what legal standard should be applied to such facts and why. As you will see, most of the Supreme Court of Pennsylvania refuses to accept the Restatement's approach to this issue. But then a well-reasoned dissent in this case supports the Restatement approach and goes into considerable detail as to how that approach shall work and why it will produce more equitable results.

After reading this case, you should not only have a better understanding of different legal standards about mental capacity to contract, but you should also have some arguments that will help you decide for yourself which legal standard is best.

Estate of McGovern v. Commonwealth State Employees' Retirement Bd.

512 Pa. 377 (1986)

FLAHERTY, Justice.

On January 9, 1981, Francis J. McGovern retired after thirty years of service with the Delaware Joint Toll Bridge Commission. In December of 1980, just prior to his retirement, Mr. McGovern executed and filed a retirement application in which he selected two of several options for payout under the retirement plan offered by his employer. Under the options selected by Mr. McGovern, he would receive a lump sum payment of $27,105, a joint survivor annuity paying him $750 monthly for life, and if he predeceased his wife, she would receive a survivor's annuity of $375 monthly for life.

Mrs. McGovern, who had been ill with Hodgkins disease since 1979, died of cancer on January 23, 1981. Five days later, on January 28, 1981, Mr. McGovern died. The Board determined that Mr. McGovern's estate was due the lump sum of $27,105.00 plus $499.92, a portion of the first month's annuity payment. Had Mr. McGovern chosen a living survivor annuitant, or no beneficiary at all, the sum of $151,311.45 would have been available to the living beneficiary or his estate.

Michael J. McGovern, Mr. McGovern's son, requested that the Board review the amount payable to the estate, on the grounds that his father was not mentally competent when he executed the retirement papers.

According to testimony of Michael McGovern, his sister, and friends of the elder Mr. McGovern, Mr. McGovern suffered during the last year of his life from alcoholism and apparent distress at the state of his wife's health. Although Mrs. McGovern was told in March of 1980 that she was terminally ill, Mr. McGovern, refused to acknowledge that his wife was going to die. Occasionally, Mr. McGovern would admit that his wife was seriously ill, but Mr. McGovern's friends testified that he was so sensitive to any conversation concerning his wife's health that they would never mention it unless he introduced the subject. When Mrs. McGovern was hospitalized for almost two months during the last year of her life, Mr. McGovern visited her only once, for five minutes, and would sometimes insist that his wife was malingering, or that she had a bleeding ulcer. Additionally, although Mr. McGovern had an alcohol problem for many years, when his wife's illness became apparent, he drank more heavily, even to the point of missing work and being too drunk to keep appointments. Finally, there was some evidence that Mr. McGovern was not always attuned to reality in other ways: after he retired, he would, on occasion, dress in his uniform and demand to be taken to work, and after his wife died, Mr. McGovern refused to eat and was heard having conversations with his dead father.

The Board advised the junior Mr. McGovern that his father's retirement documents were binding and could not be changed. On November 25, 1981, an administrative hearing was conducted at which Mr. McGovern contended that on December 17, 1980, the day his father completed his retirement application forms, his father did not have the requisite mental capacity to execute a retirement application. After hearing testimony from Mr. McGovern's friends and family, including a letter from the family doctor, and evidence from the retirement official who dealt with Mr. McGovern, a hearing examiner rejected this claim.

The Board affirmed the hearing officer, based on its conclusion that Mr. McGovern did, in fact, possess the requisite mental capacity on the day in question and that he understood the nature of the transaction.

Commonwealth Court reversed the Board, holding that it capriciously disregarded the evidence of Mr. McGovern's incapacity. We granted *allocatur* [Latin for "it is allowed," *allocatur* is used to denote permission to appeal to the Supreme Court of Pennsylvania] to examine whether Commonwealth Court applied the appropriate standard of review of the Board's findings of fact and whether that court's statement of the law of capacity to enter into a legally binding contract was correct.

[Discussion of the standard of review omitted.]

Since there is no allegation in this case that any party's constitutional rights have been violated or that the proceedings were irregular, the question on review is whether the agency's adjudication is supported by findings of fact which are, in turn, supported by substantial evidence.

The Board determined, in essence, that Mr. McGovern was mentally competent to execute his retirement papers and that he understood the nature of the transaction.

In support of this adjudication, the Board found that although Mr. McGovern had an alcohol problem and was distressed about his wife's illness with cancer, Mr. McGovern, some two months before his retirement, executed a will which even his son believed to be competently executed; he conducted his job over the years in a controlled and responsible fashion; he sometimes admitted and sometimes denied the seriousness of his wife's illness; he appeared coherent and responsive to the retirement official on December 17, 1980 during the meeting at which he selected his retirement options; and after the meeting of December 17, he sent a check to the retirement fund, as discussed at that meeting, to purchase his military buy-back retirement time.

Whether these facts support a conclusion that Mr. McGovern was legally competent to execute his retirement papers on the day in question will depend on the legal definition of competence.

It is well established that the State Employee's Retirement System creates a contract between the Commonwealth and its employees. When a member retires and elects a retirement option, he enters into a contract with the Board. If the benefit contract is freely entered into with an understanding of its terms, the contract cannot be set aside.

Here the contract is challenged on the grounds that Mr. McGovern lacked the mental capacity to enter into an agreement. Under Pennsylvania law, it is presumed that an adult is competent to enter into an agreement, and a signed document gives rise to "the presumption that it accurately expresses the state of mind of the signing party." To rebut this presumption, the challenger must present evidence of mental incompetency which is "'clear, precise and convincing.'"

This Court has held that where mental capacity to execute an instrument is at issue, "the real question is the condition of the person at the very time he executed the instrument or made the gift in question." . . . "We further held that a person's mental capacity is best determined by his spoken words and his conduct, and that the testimony of persons who observed such conduct on the date in question outranks testimony as to observations made prior to and subsequent to that date." "Mere mental weakness, if it does not amount to inability to comprehend the contract, and is unaccompanied by evidence of imposition or undue influence," is insufficient to set aside a contract.

Finally, a presumption of mental incapacity does not arise merely because of an unreasonable or unnatural disposition of property.

Contrary to these principles concerning the Pennsylvania law of competence, Commonwealth Court in this case adopted a new standard of competence based on the Restatement of Contracts, 2d. Section 15 of the Restatement, relied on by the court below, states:

> A person incurs only voidable contractual duties by entering into a transaction if by reason of mental illness or defect (a) he is unable to understand in a reasonable manner the nature and consequences of the transaction, or (b) he is unable to act in a reasonable manner in relation to the transaction and the other party has reason to know of his condition. R2d § 15(1).
>
> Where the contract is made on fair terms and the other party is without knowledge of the mental illness or defect, the power of avoidance under Subsection (1) terminates to the extent that the contract has been so performed in whole or in part or the circumstances have so changed that avoidance would be unjust. In such a case a court may grant relief as justice requires. R2d § 15(2).

This Court has never adopted Section 15 of the Restatement, which requires a post-hoc determination of reasonableness, and we decline to do so now. In fact, because the provisions of Section 15 establish new tests for incompetence which conflict with those previously established by this Court, Commonwealth Court exceeded its authority in purporting to adopt Section 15 of the Restatement.

Accepting, as we do, that the common law of incompetence as it has been articulated in our prior cases is the law that controls this case, even if it were conceded that Mr. McGovern may have been incompetent to execute any legal document at certain intervals of time within months of his wife's death, substantial evidence also supports the conclusion that on December 17, 1980, he was lucid and understood the terms of the retirement contract. This evidence, which consists of testimony of the retirement official who met with Mr. McGovern on December 17, is significant because it concerns Mr. McGovern's state of mind on the date in question. Moreover, in support of the official's observations, immediately after the December 17th meeting, Mr. McGovern mailed a check to the retirement fund to purchase his military buy-back time, which was discussed at that meeting. Such an act is consistent with the Board's determination that Mr. McGovern acted with deliberation and understanding on December 17, 1980.

It is our conclusion, therefore, that Commonwealth Court was in error in reversing the Board's determination, which properly applied the law of incompetency and which was supported by substantial evidence.

Ironically, the junior Mr. McGovern's explanation of what his father did in this case may be very close to the truth:

Q. Let me ask you the critical question. Why did he [the elder Mr. McGovern] designate a joint survivor of benefits on that application after all the counseling and the dialogue that you had with him regarding the pension? Can you attribute anything for that choice?

A. [The junior Mr. McGovern]. I think my father had . . . arrived at a frame of reference in his mind that was — permitted him to function, and I think that this frame of reference was totally out of touch with the reality of his real-life situation. I think he had convinced himself that my mother was going to outlive all of us and that he was just — he just refused to accept, I think he just refused to accept the truth that my mother was dying and that he decided that this illusion that he created for himself that he was going to live and that my mother was going to live and was not sick at all was the truth and that she was going to live for twenty years or whatever.

They were going to have a golden retirement together and that he decided to name her at the last minute to ensure that he was right; that we were all wrong and that he was right, that she was going to live forever. . . .

The real thrust of Mr. McGovern's claim in this case is that his father's designation of his mother as a secondary beneficiary was unreasonable and unwise. From some points of view, that may be true, but no one can say that belief that another will overcome a terrible disease and live is lunatic; no one can successfully assert that such a belief, even against the medical evidence, renders one incompetent. Such a belief may be, from some points of view, thoughtless, against scientific probabilities, irrational, and when combined with what amounts to a testamentary disposition of property in favor of the ill person as opposed to another who seems to be healthy, it may even be said to be selfish and heedless of the needs of others. But whatever may be said about it, it cannot, without more, be said to prove incompetence. Thus, the claim that is made here in the name of incompetence is in reality a challenge to the wisdom, the desirability, the thoughtfulness and the rationality of the disposition. But such a challenge may not succeed, for neither courts nor disappointed heirs may alter the disposition of the property of a deceased person merely on the grounds that that person acted in a way that the challenger believes to be irrational.

Order of Commonwealth Court is reversed, and the determination of the Pennsylvania State Employee's Retirement Board is reinstated.

LARSEN, Justice, dissenting.

I dissent. In view of the obvious diminished mental capacity of the decedent Francis J. McGovern, I would hold that the contract created by decedent's election of option 3 and the designation of his then terminally ill wife as his sole beneficiary is voidable. The evidence introduced at the hearing before the State Employees' Retirement Board (Board) is clear and persuasive. It shows that the decedent was laboring in a defective mental state when he signed his job termination and retirement papers on December 17, 1980. The decedent's flawed mental condition rendered him unable to act reasonably and deal with his retirement options in a reasonable fashion.

Contrary to the evidence, the Board found that the decedent "did not lack the requisites or mental capacity to execute his retirement application on December 17, 1980, and did understand the nature of the transaction." The Commonwealth Court reversed the Board, relying upon Section 15 of the Restatement of Contracts Second

The comment to Section 15 of the Restatement is particularly apropos.

Comment:

a. Rationale. A contract made by a person who is mentally incompetent requires the reconciliation of two conflicting policies: the protection of justifiable expectations and of the security of transactions, and the protection of persons unable to protect themselves against imposition. Each policy has sometimes prevailed to a greater extent than is stated in this Section. At one extreme, it has been said that a lunatic has no capacity to contract because he has no mind; this view has given way to a better understanding of mental phenomena and to the doctrine that contractual obligation depends on manifestation of assent rather than on mental assent. See [R2d] §§ 2, 19. At the other extreme, it has been asserted that mental incompetency has no effect on a contract unless other grounds of avoidance are present, such as fraud, undue influence, or gross inadequacy of consideration; it is now widely believed that such a rule gives inadequate protection to the incompetent and his family, particularly where the contract is entirely executory.

b. The standard of competency. It is now recognized that there is a wide variety of types and degrees of mental incompetency. Among them are congenital deficiencies in intelligence, the mental deterioration of old age, the effects of brain damage caused by accident or organic disease, and mental illnesses evidenced by such symptoms as delusions, hallucinations, delirium, confusion and depression. Where no guardian has been appointed, there is full contractual capacity in any case unless the mental illness or defect has affected the particular transaction: a person may be able to understand almost nothing, or only simple or routine transactions, or he may be incompetent only with respect to a particular type of transaction. Even though understanding is complete, he may lack the ability to control his acts in the way that the normal individual can and does control them; in such cases the inability makes the contract voidable only if the other party has reason to know of his condition. Where a person has some understanding of a particular transaction which is affected by mental illness or defect, the controlling consideration is whether the transaction in its result is one which a reasonably competent person might have made.

Illustration:

1. A school teacher, is a member of a retirement plan and has elected a lower monthly benefit in order to provide a benefit to her husband if she dies first. At age 60 she suffers a "nervous breakdown," takes a leave of absence, and is treated for cerebral arteriosclerosis. When the leave expires, she applies for retirement, revokes her previous election, and elects a larger annuity with no death benefit. In view of her reduced life expectancy, the change is foolhardy, and there are no other circumstances to explain the change. She fully understands the plan, but by reason of mental illness is unable to make a decision based on the prospect of her dying before her husband. The officers of the plan have reason to know of her condition. Two months after the changed election she dies. The change of election is voidable.

c. Proof of incompetency. Where there has been no previous adjudication of incompetency, the burden of proof is on the party asserting incompetency. Proof of irrational or unintelligent behavior is essential; almost any conduct of the person may be relevant, as may lay and expert opinions and prior and subsequent adjudications of incompetency. Age, bodily infirmity or disease, use of alcohol or drugs, and illiteracy may bolster other evidence of incompetency. Other facts have significance when there is mental illness or defect but some understanding: absence of independent advice, confidential or fiduciary relationship, undue influence, fraud, or secrecy; in such cases the critical fact often is departure from the normal pattern of similar transactions, and particularly inadequacy of consideration.

The above comment and illustration are specifically germane to the instant case. The final months of the decedent's life were pathetic. They depict an existence dominated by "delusion, hallucination, delirium, confusion and depression." During that time of progressive deterioration, the decedent's acts and decisions were influenced by his corrupted view of reality. His conduct often was based upon false perceptions. Such perceptions apparently prompted his selection of pension option 3.1.

The decedent may have understood the pension plan as presented to him by the pension officer but, the evidence establishes that he was unable to make a rational decision based upon the very real prospect of his wife dying before him. The decedent's wife and sole beneficiary, Loretta M. McGovern, was first diagnosed in October of 1979 as suffering from Hodgkin's disease. In March of 1980 she was informed that the disease was in its late stages. Upon being apprised of these medical findings, the decedent became despondent, his "drinking" habits worsened and he, at times, refused to accept the fact that his wife was terminally ill with cancer.

The majority expresses the view that a person who believes, contrary to scientific probability, that another will overcome a usually terminal disease and live is not rendered incompetent by holding such a belief. The majority goes on to say that this is true even if we consider that such a belief is irrational. These, however, are not the circumstances presented in the instant case. Here the decedent did not express a belief that his wife would overcome a terrible disease. Rather, the decedent, at times, flatly denied that Mrs. McGovern was ill, accusing her of malingering. At other times he seemed to acknowledge her illness. This kind of irrational conduct when considered in conjunction with the decedent's other aberrant behavior demonstrates a lack of mental capacity sufficient to render the decedent's pension option election voidable.

Additionally, the pension officer, James Kendig, who accepted decedent's application had reason to know of decedent's condition. Starting in early 1978, pension officer Kendig had many discussions with the decedent. Those discussions included face to face meetings and numerous telephone conversations. It was established that Mr. Kendig had reason to know of decedent's alcohol problem. Further, at the time of his application, the decedent failed to give Mr. Kendig comprehensible answers to questions concerning the health of Mrs. McGovern. Considering all of the evidence there was sufficient and clear proof of irrational behavior and debilitating alcohol abuse on the part of the decedent to render voidable his choice of pension option 3.

I would adopt the principles set forth in the Restatement of the Law of Contract Second, §15, apply those principles to this case, and affirm the Commonwealth Court.

I dissent.

Reflection

Estate of McGovern reflects the view that mental incapacity to comprehend a contract is based on the words and conduct of the person at the time the contract was entered. In other words, observations made on the date of entering the contract are more important than those made prior to or after entering the contract. R2d §15(b) reflects an alternative view and is one which *Estate of McGovern* declines to follow.

As you might have noticed, there is no perfect way to measure a person's mental incapacity. *Estate of McGovern* and R2d §15(b) conflict in two distinct ways on how to determine a person's capacity to contract. First, they disagree on what observations can be used. *Estate of McGovern* found that McGovern Sr. was able to comprehend the contract at the moment of application despite a history of believing his wife could overcome a terminal illness. The dissent, relying on R2d §15(b), believed that his history of delusions, hallucinations, delirium, confusion and depression corrupted his view of reality. Thus, these observations, which were before, during, and after entering the contract, could be used as proof that he was incompetent.

The second distinction is whether there is a reasonably competent person standard, and that the other person had reason to know. The majority in *Estate of McGovern* found that even if the decision of the deceased was unreasonable, irrational, and unwise, it does not automatically render him incompetent. There needs to be more to prove incompetence. On the other hand, the dissent argued that it wasn't that the deceased believed his wife could overcome a terminal illness but that, at moments, he believed she wasn't ill at all. Moreover, the pension officer had reason to know of McGovern Sr.'s condition and failed to give comprehensible answers on the health of his wife. Therefore, the deceased's corrupted view of reality, including denying his wife's illness, rendered him incompetent because he was not acting reasonably in the transaction.

Discussion

1. How does the rule applied in the *Estate of McGovern* opinion differ from the rule articulated by R2d? Which rule do you think is better, and why?

2. What are the advantages to a rule granting the defense of incapacity for the reason of mental incompetency in a wider range of case? How problematic would such a broad rule be for individuals or society?

3. Do you agree with the majority opinion or the dissent in this case? Explain your reasoning.

Problems

Problem 2.1. The Infant and the Lemon

Dobson entered an oral contract with Rosini Motor Company ("Rosini") for the purchase of a used automobile. At the time of contracting, Dobson was an infant. The two agreed that Dobson would pay $2,500 for the vehicle, and Rosini would bear liability for any expenses incurred by reason of repairs needed to put the vehicle in "proper working condition."

Dobson paid the purchase price. Two months later, Dobson was required to pay Apichell Motors, an automobile repair company, $350 for repairs. Another two months passed, and Dobson was forced to pay $450 to Apichell for even more repairs. The car continued to be mechanically defective.

Four months after the contract was entered, Dobson notified Rosini that he was disaffirming the contract and provided Rosini with the precise location of the vehicle. "Disaffirmance" is "the act by which a person who has entered into a voidable contract, as, for example, an infant, disagrees to such contract and declares he will not abide by it."

Dobson brings a claim against Rosini to recover the purchase price of the car and the amount he was required to spend on repairs.

Will Dobson be able to recover for the purchase price of the car, the amount he was required to spend on repairs, or both?

See Dobson v. Rosini, 20 Pa. D. & C.2d 537 (1959).

Problem 2.2. Bipolar Disorder & Contractual Capacity

Stanley Fingerhut was the sole general partner in a private and successful investment company. He wanted to buy a golf club and obtained an appraisal of Bel Aire Golf & Country Club that valued the club to be worth $21 million. Several months later, Fingerhut and his attorney drove to Bel Aire to meet the sellers (defendants) of the golf club to purchase it. Negotiations took place, and the price of $23.6 million was agreed upon. Fingerhut signed a binder (an informal agreement that states the buyer is interested) that was written by his own lawyer and gave the sellers a check for $200,000 as a down payment. The parties met again three days later, and, after six hours of negotiations, a contract was made. The next day, the contract was executed by all the parties, and Fingerhut paid a further down payment of $1.5 million. The rest of the price for the property was to be paid at closing (or potentially sooner).

In less than a month, Fingerhut, through his attorney, sent a letter to the seller. The letter stated "We were apprised for the first time that Mr. Fingerhut suffers from a manic-depressive psychosis, also known as bipolar disorder, a condition for which he has received medical treatment for the past years. We were advised, and competent medical authority will substantiate, that Mr. Fingerhut prior to the first meeting, and until recently, was in the manic stage of his illness and wholly incompetent and totally incapable of managing his own affairs during that time." The lawyer also requested that the binder and contract be rescinded and the $1.7 million to be returned to Fingerhut. The seller denied his request. Fingerhut filed a complaint asking for the contract to be rescinded and declared null and void and a return of the $1.7 million from seller.

Applying the standard set out in R2d § 15(b), should the court allow Fingerhut to rescind the contract?

See *Fingerhut v. Kralyn Enterprises, Inc.*, 337 N.Y.S.2d 394 (N.Y. Sup. Ct. 1971), *aff'd*, 335 N.Y.S.2d 926 (N.Y. App. Div. 1972).

Problem 2.3. The Italian Gambler

Mario LaBarbera is an Italian citizen and business owner who serves as a consultant for the pharmaceutical industry. He claims to suffer from gambling addiction, a condition he has been treated for in Italy. LaBarbera does not speak any English.

LaBarbera decided to visit Las Vegas and stay at the Wynn Hotel in late March through early April of 2008 after being recruited by Alex Pariente, an Italian-speaking employee and VIP host of the Wynn. While staying at the Wynn, LaBarbera gambled and lost $1,000,000 of his own money. The Wynn then extended $1,000,000 worth of gaming credit in the form of casino markers to LaBarbera. When LaBarbera checked out of the Wynn, Pariente brought LaBarbera the signed casino marker and asked LaBarbera to wire $1,000,000 to cover the debt. LaBarbera refused, claiming that he has no recollection of taking that debt, and claiming that the signature on the agreement was not his. The $1,000,000 marker was left unpaid. The Wynn then filed a breach of contract action to collect $1,000,000 in unpaid casino markers from LaBarbera.

At trial, LaBarbera claims he has no recollection of the debt, and that even if he did take that debt, he was intoxicated at the time and therefore should be allowed to void the agreement. LaBarbera claimed that Wynn employees continually brought drinks he did not order, that he was especially intoxicated while gambling, and that on one occasion, he became intoxicated to the point where he became physically ill and vomited.

The Wynn claims that LaBarbera never complained or brought attention to his intoxication while he executed multiple gaming markers over several days. The Wynn cites to cases showing the extremely high burden required to prove a voluntary intoxication defense and claims that LaBarbera's argument fails because he cannot identify any specific facts about how much or how long he drank.

Should the court allow LaBarbera to void the alleged agreement to borrow $1,000,000 from the Wynn?

See LaBarbera v. Wynn Las Vegas, LLC, 134 Nev. 393 (2018).

Module II

Mutual Assent

Contractual liability is voluntary. A person is obligated to perform contractual duties only when he, she, or it has outwardly manifested an intention to be bound by contractual terms. Moreover, as you will learn later in the module on Consideration, for a contract to be enforceable as a matter of law, it must not create only one obligation but rather a contract must create two or more obligations which are given in exchange for each other. This set of mutual obligations is known as a bargain. "Mutual assent" is where two or more parties outwardly display their intentions to be bound by the terms of a particular bargain.

This module will teach you how to recognize a legal bargain and to evaluate what exchange that bargain contemplates. You will accomplish this by learning three topics which represent the three phases of mutual assent: offer, duration of the offer, and acceptance.

Chapter 3

Bargains

Generally, contract formation requires parties to agree to a bargain. A bargain usually involves an exchange of promises. Therefore, the usual contract involves two parties who promise to give something or do something for the other in return for something in exchange.

For example, John offers to sell his Honda Civic to Henry for $10,000 on Friday, and Henry agrees to purchase the car. In this typical contract, the parties have exchanged promises: Johnson promises to deliver the car to Henry, and Henry promises to deliver the cash to John. This is a typical contract, formed by an exchange of promises, which is a type of bargain.

Rules

A. Contracts-at-Law

Recall the definition of bargain: "A bargain is an agreement to exchange promises or to exchange a promise for a performance or to exchange performances." R2d § 3. The typical contract requires a bargain:

> *Except as stated in Subsection (2), the formation of a contract requires a bargain in which there is a manifestation of mutual assent to the exchange and a consideration.* R2d § 17(1).

Such typical contracts may be called contracts-at-law or informal contracts when necessary to distinguish them from the atypical types. The term "contract" generally refers to contracts-at-law or informal contracts. The vast majority of contracts are such informal contracts, also known as contracts-at-law, and so we can use the term "contract" when we mean this typical form. For the most part, we will focus our study these typical, informal contracts-at-law.

However, you should note that there are two exceptions this rule. There are special cases where contracts do not require bargains. We will briefly discuss those special cases, known as formal contracts and contracts-at-equity before returning to the typical case of contracts-at-law.

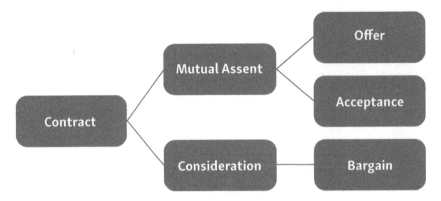

Figure 3.1. Components of an "informal" contract-at-law.

B. Formal Contracts

Before studying this typical contract formation process, briefly note that there are a few special types of contracts that do not follow the typical rules. Recall that Subsection 1 of R2d § 17 said that the formation of a contract requires a bargain *except* as stated in Subsection 2. Now let's look at that Subsection 2.

> *Whether or not there is a bargain a contract may be formed under special rules applicable to formal contracts or under the rules stated in §§ 82–94 [regarding contracts without consideration].* R2d § 17(2).

Thus, there are two exceptions to the rule that contracts require a bargain. The first exception regards "formal contracts," which are subject to special rules and do not necessarily require a bargain. The five types of formal contract are:

(a) *contracts under seal, a historical artifact involving the imprint of a signet ring into wax affixed to the document, which is not recognized in most modern jurisdictions;*

(b) *recognizances, such as bail bonds;*

(c) *negotiable instruments, such as certificates of deposit, promissory notes, bearer bonds, certificates of shares of stock, and other investment securities;*

(d) *negotiable documents, such as warehouse receipts, bills of landing, and other documents of title; and*

(e) *letters of credit, which is a promise to honor demands for payment.*

Contracts under seal, recognizances, negotiable instruments, negotiable documents, and letters of credit are made enforceable through special processes involving special rules. We will not be studying the special rules for such formal contracts because those rules will be covered in subject matter specific courses dealing with those particular kinds of agreements. Instead, we will be talking about ordinary contracts, not formal contracts, so that the rules we learn apply to the vast majority of contracts. You should simply be aware that there are such things as formal contracts, such as letters of credit, which may not require consideration due to peculiarities in historic common law of merchants or state statutes.

C. Contracts-at-Equity

Recall the general rule that the formation of a contract requires a bargain and that there are two exceptions to this rule. The first exception is formal contracts. The second exception regards promises made under the rules stated in R2d §§ 82-94. What are these rules?

R2d §§ 82-94 comprises the section titled "Contracts without Consideration." We have not yet learned the Consideration doctrine, which is the subject of its own entire module. But the short version is that consideration is a bargained-for exchange. R2d § 71. Thus, we see that R2d §§ 82-94 simply refers to contracts that do not require a bargain.

What is the basis for enforcing promises that are not part of bargains? In the absence of bargain, courts enforce promises because principles of fairness and justice require them to do so. There are some promises which, while not contracts-at-law, should be kept. For example, in a famous case, a brother invited his widowed sister to move onto his land. She moved without giving him anything in exchange for his generous gift. This is not a bargain, because there is no exchange, and so it is not a contract-at-law because contracts-at-law require a bargain. The brother then attempted to evict the widow, who would thus become homeless and destitute, along with her children. In that case, the court enforced the brother's promise as a matter of equity, or fairness, even though the legal elements of contract formation were not met.

We will deal with the enforcement of promises that do not include bargains when we learn the Consideration doctrine. The two main cases where contracts are formed without bargains are called "promissory estoppel," also known as a promise made for a benefit previously received, and "equitable estoppel," which is sometimes called a promise reasonably including action or forbearance. We will study these two doctrines as equitable exceptions to the consideration doctrine.

Now that you are aware of the exceptions, let us continue with understanding the majority rule: in general, contracts require a bargain. In fact, we will use the term "contract" to be synonymous with "informal contract" or "contract-at-law."

With those exceptions set aside for now, we shall proceed with our study on the typical formation of contracts through a bargain.

D. Manifestation of Mutual Assent

Contracts require parties to manifest their mutual assent to a bargain. It is not enough that two parties intend to be bound by a set of promises. Both parties must actually manifest their intentions for a contract to be formed.

A manifestation is a clear sign or indication that a particular situation or feeling exists; or the act of appearing or becoming clear. By sign or indication, the law means some outward sign, such as a statement or observable action. Privately held beliefs do not impact contract formation if they remain unknown to the contracting counterparty.

> *Manifestation of mutual assent to an exchange requires that each party either make a promise or begin or render a performance.* R2d § 18.

A manifestation is an outward exhibition or a clear sign of a situation or feeling. For example, a smile is a manifestation of happiness. But what if someone smiles when they are truly feeling unhappy? Then the sign does not reflect the truth. People are surely capable of manifesting false signs and signals. What happens when someone falsely manifests an offer?

To put this another way, what happens when the offeror's objective manifestation does not match his subjective feelings? Objective refers to externally verifiable phenomena, whereas subjective refers to an individual's secret thoughts or hidden feelings.

The general rule is that courts apply an objective theory of contract interpretation. Even though contracts are sometimes referred to as a meeting of the minds, modern courts generally do not actually require parties to subjectively agree in their minds. Courts only require that the parties manifest assent, giving the semblance of agreement.

The objective theory of contract interpretation means that mutual assent is evaluated objectively or apparently. Whether or not a manifestation is an offer depends on whether a reasonable person would understand the words or conduct to constitute an offer. It is not necessary for the offeror to actually desire the bargain he presents.

The term "meeting of the minds," which implies a subjective agreement as well as an objective one, is thus a dead letter in most modern courts. A fake smile has the same impact as a real one, so long as the observer cannot reasonably tell the difference.

The R2d makes this clear in Section 18, comment c, regarding a sham or jest: "If one party is deceived and has no reason to know of the joke the law takes the joker at his word." Contracts are a serious matter, and one should not make offers lightly.

In the case of *Lucy v. Zehmer*, one party claimed that the contract he wrote and the negotiations leading up to its formation were just a joke. If one of the parties takes the joke seriously, or if one party is deceived and has no reason to know of the joke, the law takes the joker at his word. Even if the deceived party should have reasonably known that the contract was a joke, there may be a claim for fraud or unjust enrichment by virtue of the promise made.

Contract law also recognizes that actions can speak louder than words.

> *The manifestation of assent may be made wholly or partly by written or spoken words or by other acts or by failure to act.* R2d § 19(1).

A meeting of the minds is both unnecessary and insufficient to contract. It is not enough that two parties intend to be bound by a set of promises for a contract to be formed. Both parties must actually manifest their intentions. Privately held beliefs do not impact contract formation if they remain unknown to the contracting counterparty.

E. Misunderstanding: Failure of Mutual Assent

As you will learn in the later chapters on defenses to contract formation, a "mistake" is a belief that is not in accord with the facts, meaning, an erroneous perception. A "misrepresentation" is an assertion that is not in accord with the facts, including an erroneous statement. A misrepresentation by one party may induce a mistake in the other. In both cases of mistake and misrepresentation, there is some distinction between beliefs and facts. This distinction may make a contract avoidable, even though it does not fundamentally undermine the notion that both parties objectively assented to a particular deal.

A "misunderstanding," on the other hand, is a more fundamental problem to contract formation. A misunderstanding occurs where both parties have a true belief, but that belief it not shared. There is a limit to the adage that contracts do not require parties to mean the same thing (subjectively) but to say the same thing (objectively) that occurs where there is no objective way to determine what they both said. The most famous example of this involves the Two Ships Peerless, a case where two parties agreed to ship cotton on a ship named Peerless, but, ironically, it turned out that there were two such ships. The court had no reasonable means of determining which of the two ships was objectively meant by the parties' mutual manifestations, and so there was no mutual assent.

In other words, a misunderstanding occurs where parties have different beliefs about some material fact. There is no mutual assent, and therefore no contract, where parties have a misunderstanding.

> *There is no manifestation of mutual assent to an exchange if the parties attach materially different meanings to their manifestations and neither party knows or has reason to know the meaning attached by the other.* R2d § 20(1)(a).

This definition raises the question of when one party has reason to know of the meaning attached by the other. According to R2d § 19 cmt. b., "A person has reason to know a fact . . . if he has information from which a person of ordinary intelligence would infer that the fact in question does or will exist." R2d also expressly attributes greater responsibility to a person of higher intelligence, although it does not attribute lesser responsibility to a person of lower intelligence. The R2d's various standards of responsibility on the basis of levels of intelligence appear outdated. See, e.g., Henry D. Schlinger, *The Myth of Intelligence*, 53 Psych. Rec. 15–32 (2003). It may be difficult or impossible for a judge to determine whether a party has superior or inferior intelligence vis-à-vis an ordinary person, especially where modern psychology has not determined how many types of intelligence humans have, nor how to measure it objectively.

F. Reflections on Mutual Assent

The unifying principle of contract law is voluntary agreement. Parties choose whether or not to make promises. Then contract law may require them to keep those promises. Contract law will not bind parties to promises they did not make.

Before you jump to the conclusion that this is unfair, recognize that other areas of common law—such as property, torts, and restitution—and many forms of statutory law will hold people responsible for non-promissory actions. For example, if a doctor treats a patient who is unconscious, she might be entitled to payment under the law of restitution and unjust enrichment. A landowner who recklessly disregards a known hazard on his property may be liable for injuries to visitors under the law of property. A celebrity who profits by promoting a baseless investment opportunity may be liable under the securities law. Contract law does not operate in a vacuum, although law school may initially give students that impression.

Thus, contract law focuses on parties' willingness to enter into a transaction. In general, contract law requires both parties to express this willingness under specific conditions. The remainder of this module covers those conditions, which are analytically separated into three phases: offer, duration of the offer, and acceptance of the offer.

Cases

Reading Lucy v. Zehmer. The *Lucy* case has become a law school favorite, perhaps because its colorful characters and vivid details make it easy to remember. But while the facts are fun, it's equally important to extract the holdings and reasoning, which tell us how contract law will be interpreted more generally.

The central lesson in this case comes from the fact that one party claims to have been "just bluffing" when he bargained and agreed to sell his farm. In technical terms, the seller has a subjective and privately held belief that the bargaining was just a joke. Unfortunately for the seller, however, the joke was not obvious to the buyer and to a third-party observer.

As you read this case, think about why contract law focuses on objective and outward manifestations that signify assent to be bound by contracts, instead of focusing or including what parties privately thought or secretly believed at the time of contract formation. What might be the reasoning for the requirement of an objective manifestation of intent to be bound by

contractual terms? How might commerce and the economy function differently if the law enforced private opinions and secret beliefs instead of focusing
on what parties objectively say and do?

Lucy v. Zehmer

196 Va. 493 (1954)

BUCHANAN, J., delivered the opinion of the court.

This suit was instituted by W.O. Lucy and J.C. Lucy, complainants, against A.H.
Zehmer and Ida S. Zehmer, his wife, defendants, to have specific performance of
a contract by which it was alleged the Zehmers had sold to W.O. Lucy a tract of
land owned by A.H. Zehmer in Dinwiddie County containing 471.6 acres, more or
less, known as the Ferguson farm, for $50,000. J.C. Lucy, the other complainant, is
a brother of W.O. Lucy, to whom W.O. Lucy transferred a half interest in his alleged
purchase.

The instrument sought to be enforced was written by A.H. Zehmer on December 20, 1952, in these words: "We hereby agree to sell to W.O. Lucy the Ferguson
Farm complete for $50,000.00, title satisfactory to buyer," and signed by the defen-
dants, A.H. Zehmer and Ida S. Zehmer.

The answer of A.H. Zehmer admitted that at the time mentioned W.O. Lucy
offered him $50,000 cash for the farm, but that he, Zehmer, considered that the offer
was made in jest; that so thinking, and both he and Lucy having had several drinks,
he wrote out "the memorandum" quoted above and induced his wife to sign it; that he
did not deliver the memorandum to Lucy, but that Lucy picked it up, read it, put it in
his pocket, attempted to offer Zehmer $5 to bind the bargain, which Zehmer refused
to accept, and realizing for the first time that Lucy was serious, Zehmer assured him
that he had no intention of selling the farm and that the whole matter was a joke.
Lucy left the premises insisting that he had purchased the farm.

Depositions were taken and the decree appealed from was entered holding that
the complainants had failed to establish their right to specific performance and dismissing their bill. The assignment of error is to this action of the court.

W.O. Lucy, a lumberman and farmer, thus testified in substance: He had known
Zehmer for fifteen or twenty years and had been familiar with the Ferguson farm for
ten years. Seven or eight years ago he had offered Zehmer $20,000 for the farm which
Zehmer had accepted, but the agreement was verbal and Zehmer backed out.

On the night of December 20, 1952, around eight o'clock, he took an employee to
McKenney, where Zehmer lived and operated a restaurant, filling station and motor
court. While there he decided to see Zehmer and again try to buy the Ferguson farm.
He entered the restaurant and talked to Mrs. Zehmer until Zehmer came in. He asked
Zehmer if he had sold the Ferguson farm. Zehmer replied that he had not. Lucy said,

"I bet you wouldn't take $50,000.00 for that place." Zehmer replied, "Yes, I would too; you wouldn't give fifty." Lucy said he would and told Zehmer to write up an agreement to that effect.

Zehmer took a restaurant check and wrote on the back of it, "I do hereby agree to sell to W.O. Lucy the Ferguson Farm for $50,000 complete." Lucy told him he had better change it to "We" because Mrs. Zehmer would have to sign it too. Zehmer then tore up what he had written, wrote the agreement quoted above and asked Mrs. Zehmer, who was at the other end of the counter ten or twelve feet away, to sign it. Mrs. Zehmer said she would for $50,000 and signed it. Zehmer brought it back and gave it to Lucy, who offered him $5 which Zehmer refused, saying, "You don't need to give me any money, you got the agreement there signed by both of us."

The discussion leading to the signing of the agreement, said Lucy, lasted thirty or forty minutes, during which Zehmer seemed to doubt that Lucy could raise $50,000. Lucy suggested the provision for having the title examined and Zehmer made the suggestion that he would sell it "complete, everything there," and stated that all he had on the farm was three heifers.

Lucy took a partly filled bottle of whiskey into the restaurant for the purpose of giving Zehmer a drink if he wanted it. Zehmer did, and he and Lucy had one or two drinks together. Lucy said that while he felt the drinks he took, he was not intoxicated, and from the way Zehmer handled the transaction he did not think he was either.

The next day Lucy telephoned to J.C. Lucy and arranged with the latter to take a half interest in the purchase and pay half of the price. On Monday he engaged an attorney to examine the title. The attorney reported favorably, and Lucy wrote Zehmer stating that the title was satisfactory, that he was ready to pay the purchase price in cash and asked when Zehmer would be ready to close the deal. Zehmer replied by mailed letter, asserting that he had never agreed or intended to sell.

Mr. and Mrs. Zehmer were called by the complainants as adverse witnesses. Zehmer testified in substance as follows: He bought this farm more than ten years ago for $11,000. He had had twenty-five offers, to buy it, including several from Lucy, who had never offered any specific sum of money. He had given them all the same answer, that he was not interested in selling it. On the night before Christmas, everybody and his brother came by to have a drink. He took a good many drinks during the afternoon and had a pint of his own. When he entered the restaurant around eight-thirty Lucy was there and he could see that he was "pretty high." He said to Lucy, "Boy, you got some good liquor, drinking, ain't you?" Lucy then offered him a drink. "I was already high as a Georgia pine and didn't have any better sense than to pour another great big slug out and gulp it down, and he took one too."

After they had talked a while Lucy asked whether he still had the Ferguson farm. He replied that he had not sold it and Lucy said, "I bet you wouldn't take $50,000.00 for it." Zehmer asked him if he would give $50,000 and Lucy said yes. Zehmer replied,

"You haven't got $50,000 in cash." Lucy said he did and Zehmer replied that he did not believe it. They argued "pro and con for a long time," mainly about "whether he had $50,000 in cash that he could put up right then and buy that farm."

Finally, said Zehmer, Lucy told him if he didn't believe he had $50,000, "you sign that piece of paper here and say you will take $50,000.00 for the farm." He, Zehmer, "just grabbed the back off of a guest check there" and wrote on the back of it. At that point in his testimony Zehmer asked to see what he had written to "see if I recognize my own handwriting." He examined the paper and exclaimed, "Great balls of fire, I got 'Firgerson' for Ferguson. I have got satisfactory spelled wrong. I don't recognize that writing if I would see it, wouldn't know it was mine."

After Zehmer had, as he described it, "scribbled this thing off," Lucy said, "Get your wife to sign it." Zehmer walked over to where she was and she at first refused to sign but did so after he told her that he "was just needling him [Lucy], and didn't mean a thing in the world, that I was not selling the farm." Zehmer then "took it back over there . . . and I was still looking at the dern thing. I had the drink right there by my hand, and I reached over to get a drink, and he said, 'Let me see it.' He reached and picked it up, and when I looked back again, he had it in his pocket and he dropped a five-dollar bill over there, and he said, 'Here is five dollars payment on it.' I said, 'Hell no, that is beer and liquor talking. I am not going to sell you the farm. I have told you that too many times before.'"

Mrs. Zehmer testified that when Lucy came into the restaurant he looked as if he had had a drink. When Zehmer came in he took a drink out of a bottle that Lucy handed him. She went back to help the waitress who was getting things ready for next day. Lucy and Zehmer were talking but she did not pay too much attention to what they were saying. She heard Lucy ask Zehmer if he had sold the Ferguson farm, and Zehmer replied that he had not and did not want to sell it. Lucy said, "I bet you wouldn't take $50,000 cash for that farm," and Zehmer replied, "You haven't got $50,000 cash." Lucy said, "I can get it." Zehmer said he might form a company and get it, "but you haven't got $50,000.00 cash to pay me tonight." Lucy asked him if he would put it in writing that he would sell him this farm. Zehmer then wrote on the back of a pad, "I agree to sell the Ferguson Place to W.O. Lucy for $50,000.00 cash." Lucy said, "All right, get your wife to sign it." Zehmer came back to where she was standing and said, "You want to put your name to this?" She said "No," but he said in an undertone, "It is nothing but a joke," and she signed it.

She said that only one paper was written, and it said: "I hereby agree to sell," but the "I" had been changed to "We." However, she said she read what she signed and was then asked, "When you read 'We hereby agree to sell to W.O. Lucy,' what did you interpret that to mean, that particular phrase?" She said she thought that was a cash sale that night; but she also said that when she read that part about "title satisfactory to buyer" she understood that if the title was good Lucy would pay $50,000 but if the title was bad, he would have a right to reject it, and that that was her understanding at the time she signed her name.

On examination by her own counsel, she said that her husband laid this piece of paper down after it was signed; that Lucy said to let him see it, took it, folded it and put it in his wallet, then said to Zehmer, "Let me give you $5.00," but Zehmer said, "No, this is liquor talking. I don't want to sell the farm, I have told you that I want my son to have it. This is all a joke." Lucy then said at least twice, "Zehmer, you have sold your farm," wheeled around and started for the door. He paused at the door and said, "I will bring you $50,000.00 tomorrow. No, tomorrow is Sunday. I will bring it to you Monday." She said you could tell that he was drinking, and she said to her husband, "You should have taken him home," but he said, "Well, I am just about as bad off as he is."

The waitress referred to by Mrs. Zehmer testified that when Lucy first came in "he was mouthy." When Zehmer came in they were laughing and joking, and she thought they took a drink or two. She was sweeping and cleaning up for next day. She said she heard Lucy tell Zehmer, "I will give you so much for the farm," and Zehmer said, "You haven't got that much." Lucy answered, "Oh, yes, I will give you that much." Then "they jotted down something on paper . . . and Mr. Lucy reached over and took it, said let me see it." He looked at it, put it in his pocket and in about a minute he left. She was asked whether she saw Lucy offer Zehmer any money and replied, "He had five dollars laying up there, they didn't take it." She said Zehmer told Lucy he didn't want his money "because he didn't have enough money to pay for his property and wasn't going to sell his farm." Both appeared to be drinking right much, she said.

She [the waitress] repeated on cross-examination that she was busy and paying no attention to what was going on. She was some distance away and did not see either of them sign the paper. She was asked whether she saw Zehmer put the agreement down on the table in front of Lucy, and her answer was this: "Time he got through writing whatever it was on the paper, Mr. Lucy reached over and said, 'Let's see it.' He took it and put it in his pocket," before showing it to Mrs. Zehmer. Her version was that Lucy kept raising his offer until it got to $50,000.

The defendants insist that the evidence was ample to support their contention that the writing sought to be enforced was prepared as a bluff or dare to force Lucy to admit that he did not have $50,000; that the whole matter was a joke; that the writing was not delivered to Lucy and no binding contract was ever made between the parties.

It is an unusual, if not bizarre, defense. When made to the writing admittedly prepared by one of the defendants and signed by both, clear evidence is required to sustain it.

In his testimony Zehmer claimed that he "was high as a Georgia pine," and that the transaction "was just a bunch of two doggoned drunks bluffing to see who could talk the biggest and say the most." That claim is inconsistent with his attempt to testify in detail as to what was said and what was done. It is contradicted by other evidence as to the condition of both parties and rendered of no weight by the testimony of his wife that when Lucy left the restaurant, she suggested that Zehmer drive him home. The record is convincing that Zehmer was not intoxicated to the extent of being unable to comprehend the nature and consequences of the instrument he executed, and hence that instrument is not to be invalidated on that ground. It was in fact conceded by defendants' counsel in oral argument that under the evidence Zehmer was not too drunk to make a valid contract.

The evidence is convincing also that Zehmer wrote two agreements, the first one beginning "I hereby agree to sell." Zehmer first said he could not remember about that, then that "I don't think I wrote but one out." Mrs. Zehmer said that what he wrote was "I hereby agree," but that the "I" was changed to "We" after that night. The agreement that was written and signed is in the record and indicates no such change. Neither are the mistakes in spelling that Zehmer sought to point out readily apparent.

The appearance of the contract, the fact that it was under discussion for forty minutes or more before it was signed; Lucy's objection to the first draft because it was written in the singular, and he wanted Mrs. Zehmer to sign it also; the rewriting to meet that objection and the signing by Mrs. Zehmer; the discussion of what was to be included in the sale, the provision for the examination of the title, the completeness of the instrument that was executed, the taking possession of it by Lucy with no request or suggestion by either of the defendants that he give it back, are facts which furnish persuasive evidence that the execution of the contract was a serious business transaction rather than a casual, jesting matter as defendants now contend.

On Sunday, the day after the instrument was signed on Saturday night, there was a social gathering in a home in the town of McKenney at which there were general comments that the sale had been made. Mrs. Zehmer testified that on that occasion as she passed by a group of people, including Lucy, who were talking about the transaction, $50,000 was mentioned, whereupon she stepped up and said, "Well, with the high-price whiskey you were drinking last night you should have paid more. That was cheap." Lucy testified that at that time Zehmer told him that he did not want to "stick" him or hold him to the agreement because he, Lucy, was too tight and didn't know what he was doing, to which Lucy replied that he was not too tight; that he had been stuck before and was going through with it. Zehmer's version was that he said to Lucy: "I am not trying to claim it wasn't a deal on account of the fact the price was too low. If I had wanted to sell $50,000.00 would be a good price, in fact I think you would get stuck at $50,000.00." A disinterested witness testified that what Zehmer said to Lucy was that "he was going to let him up off the deal, because he thought he was too tight, didn't know what he was doing. Lucy said something to the effect that 'I have been stuck before and I will go through with it.'"

If it be assumed, contrary to what we think the evidence shows, that Zehmer was jesting about selling his farm to Lucy and that the transaction was intended by him to be a joke, nevertheless the evidence shows that Lucy did not so understand it but considered it to be a serious business transaction and the contract to be binding on the Zehmers as well as on himself. The very next day he arranged with his brother to put up half the money and take a half interest in the land. The day after that he employed an attorney to examine the title. The next night, Tuesday, he was back at Zehmer's place and there Zehmer told him for the first time, Lucy said, that he wasn't going to sell, and he told Zehmer, "You know you sold that place fair and square." After receiving the report from his attorney that the title was good, he wrote to Zehmer that he was ready to close the deal.

Not only did Lucy actually believe, but the evidence shows he was warranted in believing, that the contract represented a serious business transaction and a good faith sale and purchase of the farm.

In the field of contracts, as generally elsewhere,

> We must look to the outward expression of a person as manifesting his intention rather than to his secret and unexpressed intention. The law imputes to a person an intention corresponding to the reasonable meaning of his words and acts.

At no time prior to the execution of the contract had Zehmer indicated to Lucy by word or act that he was not in earnest about selling the farm. They had argued about it and discussed its terms, as Zehmer admitted, for a long time. Lucy testified that if there was any jesting it was about paying $50,000 that night. The contract and the evidence show that he was not expected to pay the money that night. Zehmer said that after the writing was signed, he laid it down on the counter in front of Lucy. Lucy said Zehmer handed it to him. In any event there had been what appeared to be a good faith offer and a good faith acceptance, followed by the execution and apparent delivery of a written contract. Both said that Lucy put the writing in his pocket and then offered Zehmer $5 to seal the bargain. Not until then, even under the defendants' evidence, was anything said or done to indicate that the matter was a joke. Both of the Zehmers testified that when Zehmer asked his wife to sign he whispered that it was a joke so Lucy wouldn't hear and that it was not intended that he should hear.

The mental assent of the parties is not requisite for the formation of a contract. If the words or other acts of one of the parties have but one reasonable meaning, his undisclosed intention is immaterial except when an unreasonable meaning which he attaches to his manifestations is known to the other party.

> The law, therefore, judges of an agreement between two persons exclusively from those expressions of their intentions which are communicated between them.

An agreement or mutual assent is of course essential to a valid contract but the law imputes to a person an intention corresponding to the reasonable meaning of his words and acts. If his words and acts, judged by a reasonable standard, manifest an intention to agree, it is immaterial what may be the real but unexpressed state of his mind.

So, a person cannot set up that he was merely jesting when his conduct and words would warrant a reasonable person in believing that he intended a real agreement.

Whether the writing signed by the defendants and now sought to be enforced by the complainants was the result of a serious offer by Lucy and a serious acceptance by the defendants or was a serious offer by Lucy and an acceptance in secret jest by the defendants, in either event it constituted a binding contract of sale between the parties.

Defendants contend further, however, that even though a contract was made, equity should decline to enforce it under the circumstances. These circumstances have been set forth in detail above. They disclose some drinking by the two parties but not to an extent that they were unable to understand fully what they were doing. There was no fraud, no misrepresentation, no sharp practice and no dealing between unequal parties. The farm had been bought for $11,000 and was assessed for taxation at $6,300. The purchase price was $50,000. Zehmer admitted that it was a good price. There is in fact present in this case none of the grounds usually urged against specific performance.

Specific performance, it is true, is not a matter of absolute or arbitrary right, but is addressed to the reasonable and sound discretion of the court. But it is likewise true that the discretion which may be exercised is not an arbitrary or capricious one, but one which is controlled by the established doctrines and settled principles of equity; and, generally, where a contract is in its nature and circumstances unobjectionable, it is as much a matter of course for courts of equity to decree a specific performance of it as it is for a court of law to give damages for a breach of it.

The complainants are entitled to have specific performance of the contracts sued on. The decree appealed from is therefore reversed and the cause is remanded for the entry of a proper decree requiring the defendants to perform the contract in accordance with the prayer of the bill.

Reversed and remanded.

Reflection

Lucy v. Zehmer demonstrates that courts determine the existence of an agreement between parties by looking at their outward manifestations. For a contract to exist, there needs to be an agreement between the parties. The law judges that agreement based on the reasonable meaning of parties' outward conduct (outward manifestations) and not their secret inward intent (subjective beliefs).

Thus, the court will not look at whether Zehmer was secretly joking, but at his outward manifestations, which warranted a reasonable person in believing that he intended a real agreement. If you were standing behind Lucy at the restaurant, as an impartial third-party, do you think Zehmer's conduct and words justified Lucy into thinking there was an agreement to sell the farm?

The moral of *Lucy* is that contracts are not joking matters, and courts will bind parties at their word. It would be far too easy to avoid deals if a party could simply claim it was merely joking. How would a court ever prove otherwise? And if contracts can be so easily avoided, how would people be able to rely on them such that commerce could proceed between strangers? The rule must be that contractual intent is measured objectively, as it was in Lucy, if contracts are to have much effect at all.

Discussion

1. In *Lucy*, does the court inquire whether the parties subjectively and secretly intended to contract? Why or why not?

2. Think of any situations where a joke should not be construed as a contract. Can you distinguish that situation from the facts of *Lucy*?

3. Contracts are often referred to as a meeting of the minds. Did the parties have a meeting of the minds in this case? If not, what does that signify about the trope that contracts are a meeting of the minds?

Reading Raffles v. Wichelhaus. A "mistake" is a belief that is not in accord with the facts, an erroneous perception. For example, if a woman has a pretty stone that she thinks is a piece of quartz, but really it is a diamond, that is a mistake. If the woman sells that stone to a pawn broker who also believes the stone is a quartz, the parties have made a mutual mistake, but there is no misunderstanding between them, because they have the same belief about the nature of the stone, however wrong they may be.

A "misunderstanding," on the other hand, is where parties have different beliefs about some material fact. The next case is both very famous and "notoriously cryptic." The *"Peerless"* case is about a misunderstanding so fundamental that it causes a failure of mutual assent.

The essence of the facts are as follows. Wichelhaus agreed to purchase 125 bales of Surat cotton from Raffles, a merchant in Bombay, India. Raffles agreed to deliver the cotton to Liverpool, England via a ship named the Peerless.

Contracts in those days often referenced to a specific ship in order to set the agreed-upon time for delivery. It was commonly understood that a specific ship would sail at a specific time.

The time of delivery can matter a great deal in certain business arrangements. But, in this case, the parties had a misunderstanding that went to the heart of the contract.

Unbeknownst to the parties, there was not one, but two ships named, "Peerless." One of the ships was to set sail in October and the other in December. The seller (Raffles) apparently knew only of the December Peerless, while the buyer (Wichelhaus) had the October Peerless in mind.

This is a classic example of a misunderstanding, where both parties were each correct about their own version of the facts, but they did not share a common understanding.

The famous *Peerless* case is appended below so that students can puzzle over it for themselves. But do not be dismayed if you find it impenetrable, as

commentators no less prestigious than Oliver Wendall Holmes, Samuel Williston, Arthur Corbin, and Grant Gilmore cannot seem to agree on its meaning.

Raffles v. Wichelhaus
2 EWHC Exch J19 (1864) ("Peerless")

DECLARATION.

For that it was agreed between the plaintiff and the defendants, to wit, at Liverpool, that the plaintiff should sell to the defendants, and the defendants buy of
the plaintiff, certain goods, to wit, 125 bales of Surat cotton, guaranteed middling
fair merchant's Dhollorah, to arrive ex "Peerless" from Bombay; and that the cotton
should be taken from the quay, and that the defendants would pay the plaintiff for
the same at a certain rate, to wit, at the rate of 17-d. per pound, within a certain time
then agreed upon after the arrival of the said goods in England.

Averments: that the said goods did arrive by the said ship from Bombay in
England to wit, at Liverpool, and the plaintiff was then and there ready, and willing
and offered to deliver the said goods to the defendants, &c. Breach: that the defendants refused to accept the said goods or pay the plaintiff for them.

Plea. — That the said ship mentioned in the said agreement was meant and
intended by the defendants to be the ship called the " Peerless," which sailed from
Bombay, to wit, in October; and that the plaintiff was not ready and willing and did
not offer to deliver to the defendants any bales of cotton which arrived by the last
mentioned ship, but instead thereof was only ready and willing and offered to deliver
to the defendants 125 bales of Surat cotton which arrived by another and different
ship, which was also called the "Peerless," and which sailed from Bombay, to wit, in
December.

[Procedural posture:] Demurrer, and joinder therein.

[Opinion by Judge] MILWARD, in support of the demurrer.

The contract was 1864 for the sale of a number of bales of cotton of a particular
RAFFLES description, which the plaintiff was ready to deliver. It is immaterial by what
ship the cotton was to arrive, so that it was a ship called the "Peerless." The words "to
arrive ex 'Peerless,'" only mean that if the vessel is lost on the voyage, the contract is to
be at an end. [Pollock, C.B. — It would be a question for the jury whether both parties
meant the same ship called the "Peerless."] That would be so if the contract was for the
sale of a ship called the "Peerless;" but it is for the sale of cotton on board a ship of that
name. [Pollock, C.B. — The defendant only bought that cotton which was to arrive by
a particular ship. It may as well be said, that if there is a contract for the purchase of
certain goods in warehouse A, that is satisfied by the delivery of goods of the same
description in warehouse B.] In that case there would be goods in both warehouses;
here it does not appear that the plaintiff had any goods on board the other "Peerless."
[Martin, B. — It is imposing on the defendant a contract different from that which

he entered into. Pollock, C.B. — It is like a contract for the purchase of wine coming from a particular estate in France or Spain, where there are two estates of that name.] The defendant has no right to contradict by parol evidence a written contract good upon the face of it. He does not impute misrepresentation or fraud, but only says that he fancied the ship was a different one. Intention is of no avail, unless stated at the time of the contract. [Pollock, C.B. — One vessel sailed in October and the other in December.] The time of sailing is no part of the contract.

Mellish (Cohen with him), in support of the plea. — There is nothing on the face of the contract to shew that any particular ship called the "Peerless" was meant; but the moment it appears that two ships called the "Peerless" were about to sail from Bombay there is a latent ambiguity, and parol evidence may be given for the purpose shewing that the defendant meant one "Peerless" and the plaintiff another. That being so, there was no consensus ad idem, and therefore no binding contract.

(He was then stopped by the Court.)

PER CURIAM. There must be judgment for the defendants.

Reflection

There has been much debate over the extent of the circumstances in which a mutual misunderstanding should prevent the formation of a contract. Some argue that a misunderstanding can only occur where the name of a particular thing is misunderstood, while others believe it is where a term has a "double meaning" or only in circumstances where the misunderstood term is "vital enough to justify upsetting the entire arrangement."

A contract should be held nonexistent only when the misunderstanding goes to conflicting and irreconcilable meanings of a material term that could have either, but not both, meanings. For example, imagine you go to an animal shelter and fall in love with a black and white Border Collie. You describe the dog you are hoping to adopt as the black and white dog that weighs around 50 lbs. The employee seems to know exactly the dog you are talking about and draws up the necessary paperwork. You return the next day to pick up your new pup. However, when you arrive, the shelter employee meets you outside with a Dalmatian. This is a mutual misunderstanding. Both you and the shelter employee were correct in your descriptions, meaning no one made a mistake. However, there were two black and white dogs weighing around 50 lbs. in the shelter. In this case, there was no mutual understanding — you and the employee entered a contract, but with different dogs in mind. The black and white dog weighing around 50 lbs. could mean either the Border Collie or the Dalmatian, but not both.

Comments in R2d go into some detail about the academic debate as to when a misunderstanding should defeat the formation of a contract for want of mutual assent. Many scholars argue that R2d's definition of misunderstanding limits the contract formation doctrine too much, therefore leading to conclusions that there was no contract formation in situations where a contract should objectively be found. On the other hand, some scholars argue that the scope of the misrepresentation doctrine should be further increased because contract law should only honor the subjective intention of the parties: if contracts only apply where parties meant the same thing, and did not just say the same thing, the result would be fewer findings of contracts where parties had an actual misunderstanding. R2d apparently tries to strike a balance between these two positions by effectuating the misunderstanding doctrine to (objectively) materially different meanings where (subjectively) neither party had reason to know of the other's meaning.

Discussion

1. In *Lucy*, the court determined there was a contract; whereas in *Peerless*, the court determined there was no contract. Can you distinguish factually between the cases and explain why these different facts should lead to a different legal result?

2. Identify the specific misunderstanding in the *Peerless* case. Can you use this situation to generalize about how the court will treat misunderstandings in general?

Problems

Problem 3.1. **Can Machines Form Mutual Assent?**

Figure 3.2. Travel insurance vending machine in a Japanese airport.
Source: Benzoyl (Flickr), CC BY-SA 2.0.

Sadie Bernstein, a resident of New York City, decided to travel to Miami, Florida to get away for the winter. On December 16, 1951, she went to Newark Airport (just outside of New York City in the State of New Jersey) to purchase an airplane ticket. Just before reaching the ticket counter, Bernstein observed a prominent machine with a well-illuminated display of airplanes flying round and round. The machine was installed by the Fidelity & Casualty Company of New York, an insurance provider. A printed placard on the machine read the following in very large block letters:

DOMESTIC AIRLINE TRIP INSURANCE 25¢ FOR EACH $5,000 MAXI-MUM $25,000.

[This is equivalent to about $2.50 per $50,000 of insurance up to a maximum of $250,000 in today's money.]

Bernstein inserted five quarters ($1.25) into the machine. The machine opened, and from inside its slot, Bernstein removed an insurance policy application form. She used a pen that was affixed to the machine to fill out the form, which included the departure and destination cities and the name of the airline. Bernstein replaced the completed application in the slot and pressed a button labeled "SUBMIT." The machine closed its slot and then printed out a policy that was 22 pages long. The first page of the policy contained a clause titled "Coverage." This provision limited coverage to "civilian scheduled airlines," although Bernstein did not read the policy.

Bernstein then went to the Miami Airlines counter and purchased a ticket for travel from Newark to Miami. Three to four feet from the counter was a large sign that listed which non-scheduled airlines were permitted to conduct business in the terminal. Miami Airlines was listed as a non-scheduled airline, although Bernstein did not notice that sign.

Bernstein boarded her flight on Miami Airlines, which, unfortunately, crashed en route. She subsequently died in the plane crash. Her beneficiary, Marion Lachs, sued to recover the amount of the policy.

In a lawsuit by Lachs against Fidelity to recover the amount of the policy, should a court find that there was mutual assent between Bernstein and Fidelity, despite the use of the vending machine?

See Lachs v. Fid. & Cas. Co. of New York, 118 N.E.2d 555 (N.Y. 1954).

Problem 3.2. Misunderstanding the Triangle

Ernest and Evelyn Chilson owned approximately twenty acres of land. The land, although contiguous, could be easily divided into three distinct units (see figure). The property was divided by Butler Avenue. The largest parcel of land is 17.3 acres and referred to as "Butler North." "Butler South" is approximately 4.3 acres, and finally, a small parcel of land above "Butler North" is called "The Triangle" and is approximately 2.4 acres. The Chilsons originally acquired the property in two separate transactions, then later directed a title agency to prepare one deed for the whole property.

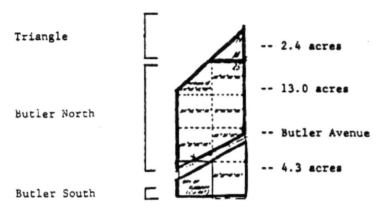

Figure 3.3. Parcel known as "the triangle."

In December 1984, the Chilsons listed Unit 1 and Unit 2 with a broker, seeking a tenant for a long-term lease. Daniel Hill and Craig Shafer saw a sign and inquired about the land with the broker. Hill and Shafer obtained a copy of the appraisal which listed the property as "15 acres of vacant land on the north side of Butler Avenue."

Hill and Shafer inspected the land and submitted a letter of intent proposing to purchase the listed property. The letter of intent described the Triangle and Butler North. Hill and Shafer proposed that the price of the land be subject to an adjustment, depending on the actual acreage to be determined by a survey.

The Chilsons rejected the proposal and insisted that the listing price was a "take it or leave it" offer. The Chilsons also refused throughout the negotiations to include a map of the land or provide any information about the land beyond a simple description.

However, the description did not describe Butler North and the Triangle. The provided description instead described Butler North and Butler South.

Hill and Shafer agreed to purchase the land for the listed price and entered a written contract with the Chilsons. On July 5, 1985, the escrow instructions were signed. When the Chilsons reviewed the escrow instructions, they discovered the error in the description. The Chilsons argued that they always intended to sell Butler North and the Triangle and that the description describing Butler North and Butler South was due to an error.

After discovering the error, the Chilsons prepared an amendment to correct the provided description, but Hill and Shafer refused the amendment. The Chilsons cancelled the escrow, and Hill and Shafer sued for specific performance.

Was there a valid manifestation of mutual assent between the Chilsons and Hill and Shafer?

See *Hill-Shafer Partnership v. Chilson Family Trust*, 165 Ariz. 469 (1990).

Chapter 4

Offers

The manifestation of the offer by the offeror creates the power of acceptance in the offeree. What then is an offer?

Consider the definition of "offer":

> *An offer is the manifestation of willingness to enter into a bargain, so made as to justify another person in understanding that his assent to that bargain is invited and will conclude it.* R2d § 24.

An offer is a proposal to enter a voluntary bargain or exchange, manifested by the offeror (the person who makes the offer) in such a way that the offeree (the person who receives the offer) reasonably believes that they can accept that offer and thereby form a binding contract.

For example, if a random stranger walks up to you on the street and says, "I will buy your house for a million dollars," this is the manifestation of willingness to enter into a bargain. But is it an offer? In other words, are you justified in understanding that, by saying yes, you will reasonably expect that person to pay you a million dollars for that house? No, that would not be a reasonable conclusion under these circumstances.

On the other hand, what if you had a series of business meetings with a lumber company that wanted to buy your farm and use it to cut down trees for lumber? Imagine the company would negotiate and haggle about the price, terms, closing date, title warranties, and all the many details involved in selling acreage for many months, until your business associate finally presents you with a written, signed statement including a definitive price. Would that be an offer? Yes, that probably is an offer.

In contrasting these examples, keep in mind that preliminary negotiations are not required, but notice how the absence of negotiations or indeed any relationship between the parties tends to show that a manifestation was not an offer. The fact that extensive negotiations occurred and resolved into a manifestation of willingness to enter into a bargain, while not itself a prerequisite, tends to make it more justifiable to believe that manifestation invites assent to a bargain.

Rules

A. Preliminary Negotiations

The manifestation of an offer usually does not spring out of nowhere. Moreover, parties often negotiate and bargain before agreeing to a contract in order to clarify their deal and to extract the most value from it.

The ordinary process of contract formation usually begins with "preliminary negotiations." As the name implies, these preliminary negotiations or discussions occur before a contract is formed. Under the common law of contracts, there is usually no contractual liability until contract formation. During preliminary negotiations, the parties remain free to walk away from the deal if they cannot come to terms. (Some scholars, especially Professor Omri Ben Shahar, have argued that contractual liability should not be binary—on or off—in this way, but instead there should be some pre-contractual liability that increases as parties approach a deal. But these suggestions have not been particularly influential on courts, who continue to view the moment of contract formation as the time when contractual liability attaches.)

Preliminary negotiations end when one party proposes a set of final terms. The proposing party is then called the "offeror," and the receiving party is the "offeree." Under common law, the offeree then has two paths forward. The offeree can either accept the terms, thus forming a contract, or reject them. The period of time when the offeree has this power to accept or reject the offer is called the duration of the power of acceptance. An offeree's acceptance is valid only if it is made while the offeree has the power of acceptance.

Preliminary negotiations are colloquially referred to as "bargaining," but the term "bargain" actually has a very different technical meaning under the law of contracts. Under contract law, "bargain" does not mean "haggling" or "negotiating." In fact, lots of contracts are formed without any haggling or negotiating.

For example, when you sign up to use a new app, like Uber, you will sign a contract called something like the Terms of Service. When you agree to these terms by clicking a box marked "I Agree," this act binds you to the terms in that agreement. You cannot haggle or negotiate with Uber to change those terms. You can either agree to Uber's terms—or not use the app. This is an example of a "contract of adhesion." It is a non-negotiable offer. Such contracts of adhesion are generally enforceable even though there was no process of preliminary negotiations between the parties.

Again, neither negotiation nor haggling are required to form a contract. All the law needs is for both parties to manifest mutual assent to terms that contemplate some sort of bargained-for exchange. In the Uber example, the bargained-for exchange is that you get to use the Uber app in exchange for abiding by Uber's terms of service. Even though you did not "bargain" with Uber in the colloquial sense, this is a bargained-for exchange in the legal sense, because both parties are getting something from the deal—you are getting a ride, and Uber is getting paid.

The flip side of this rule is found in the R2d § 26:

A manifestation of willingness to enter into a bargain is not an offer if the person to whom it is addressed knows or has reason to know that the person making it does not intend to conclude a bargain until he has made a further manifestation of assent. R2d § 26.

In other words, a manifestation is not an offer if it reasonably appears to be part of negotiations. For example, if, during negotiations, a lumber man says to a farm owner, "Would you sell your land for $50,000?", that is probably not an offer. The farm owner could not say, "Yes, we have a deal," and thereby create a contract, because the reasonable interpretation of that manifestation is that the lumber man was engaging in preliminary negotiations and not offering. For the same reason, most general advertisements are usually not offers; rather, they are invitations for bids or offers, which is part of preliminary negotiations.

The act of bargaining or negotiating is not necessary for contract formation, but it can be evidence that parties are taking the deal seriously. Evidence regarding the extent of negotiations or the lack thereof may be relevant to determining whether a manifestation is in fact an offer.

In fact, prolonged bargaining is an expected precursor to some kinds of offers, such as purchasing a house or acquiring a corporation. For example, if you went to buy a house, you will probably engage in some bargaining before making an offer. You might ask the seller to include the window treatments, to lower the price, or to close by a certain date.

But, again, not all transactions are subject to this sort of bargaining — and it is very important to remember that the act of bargaining or haggling is not necessary as a matter of law to create a bargained-for exchange.

B. Certainty

Even when a person intends to make an offer, and not merely to engage in preliminary negotiations, he or she may fail to present an acceptable offer because of a lack of certainty.

Even though a manifestation of intention is intended to be understood as an offer, it cannot be accepted so as to form a contract unless the terms of the contract are reasonably certain. R2d § 33(1).

Certainty is the opposite of ambiguity. When an offer is too ambiguous, it cannot be enforced by courts, because courts would not know exactly what the parties intended to be enforced. In fact, the ability of courts to enforce a promise is the test for whether a promise is reasonably certain.

The terms of a contract are reasonably certain if they provide a basis for determining the existence of a breach and for giving an appropriate remedy. R2d § 33(2).

How much detail is required to make an offer certain depends on the circumstances of the transaction. The minimum standard of certainty under common law requires an offer to include the parties, the subject matter, the quantity, and the price. For example, if Maestro offers to give Novice three hours of piano lessons for one hundred dollars, that offer probably meets the common law standard for reasonable certainty.

The Maestro example is an offer even though Maestro did not specify the time for performance. When the contract does not call for a specific time, courts will imply that the time for performance is at a reasonable time, given the circumstances.

Under the UCC, offers for sales of goods may be valid even when lacking a price term. Courts may imply a reasonable price where goods have a clear market value.

C. Advertisements as Offers

Advertisements, also known as general solicitations, present a special problem in the analysis of whether a manifestation is an offer. Most advertisements are not offers, because they lack both the requirements of manifesting an intention to be bound and of proposing reasonably certain terms, but there are cases where advertisements rise to the level of offers that can be accepted.

The principal reason why advertisements are usually not offers is because they are usually interpreted as preliminary negotiations or invitations for offers.

> *Business enterprises commonly secure general publicity for the goods or services they supply or purchase. Advertisements of goods by display, sign, handbill, newspaper, radio or television are not ordinarily intended or understood as offers to sell. The same is true of catalogues, price lists and circulars, even though the terms of suggested bargains may be stated in some detail. R2d § 26 cmt. b.*

Advertisements where the counterparty is not named are rarely offers because whatever good or service is being advertised is probably limited in quantity, so it is not possible for every person who hears the advertisement to accept it as an offer.

Additionally, advertisements are often lacking in essential terms, such as quantity. For example, if an advertisement says, "Jim's Cupcakes — $2 each," how many cupcakes is Jim offering to sell? Moreover, how does an alleged offeree know whether Jim has already sold them all?

Quantity is a very important aspect of sales. Selling one item is one thing, whereas having a dozen or a gross unit (144) on hand is another matter. One store will not reasonably be expected to have an infinite supply of a physical good. If other shoppers buy all Jim's cupcakes before you arrive, he may not have a unit to sell to you. For this reason, the lack of a quantity or a limited quantity term makes the advertisements incomplete and therefore not an offer.

Incompleteness of terms is one of the principal reasons why advertisements and price quotations are ordinarily not interpreted as offers. R2d § 26 cmt. c.

There are a few ways around this, however, such that advertisements can rise to the level of offers. In the famous case of *Lefkowitz v. Great Minneapolis Supply Store*, a store published the following advertisement in a newspaper:

Figure 4.1. Fur coats advertisement in Lefkowitz. Credit: Seth C. Oranburg.

Figure 4.2. Pastel mink scarfs advertisement in Lefkowitz.
Credit Seth C. Oranburg.

In the *Lefkowitz* case below, the advertisement was so specific that it was construed to be an offer. This is the exception that proves the general rule that advertisements are usually not offers. This advertisement was an offer only because it included subject matter (fur coats), price ($1), and quantity (three), and it implied the parties were the store and the first to show up and claim the offer. The limited quantity and the language "first come, first served" made this advertisement an unusual example of an offer that Lefkowitz accepted by showing up on Saturday.

D. Catalogs as Offers

Since quantity is an essential term in an offer, things like catalogs are generally not offers either. A typical catalog will contain a blank order form where a prospective buyer can fill in the item number, quantity, and price. Only when that information is filled in does the order form become an offer. A blank order form lacks certainty and does not manifest an intent to be bound.

What, then, is a catalog, in contract law terminology? Catalogs are usually invitations for orders. When the mail-order company receives a filled-in catalog from a prospective buyer, the company has the option to accept or reject that offer. This is important because the company may have run out of supplies, changed their product lineup, or revised their prices since the catalog was printed and distributed. If catalogs were offers, then mail-order company would risk breaching its promises whenever an order they could not service arrived.

E. Bids and Price Quotes as Offers

The contracting bid process can seem confusing to law students who have not themselves worked in construction and contracting. But the process is actually quite intuitive. When a person, who we will call the "owner," decides to do some major construction project, that person will often try to get the highest quality work done for the lowest price by putting out a "request for proposals" or a "request for bids." This is a sort of advertisement that informs the world that the owner is looking for construction services. Construction service providers known as "general contractors" will then submit bids to do the project on certain terms for a certain cost. But how does the general contractor ("GC") know what to bid? The GC's goal is to organize and oversee the work and to make a profit for this service. So, the GC contract project specialists known as "subcontractors" who will themselves bid on aspects of the job.

For example, Eric wants to add a swimming pool to his back yard. He calls up four local companies that do swimming pool construction and asks them to give bids. The GC at each of the four companies comes to Eric's house and takes measurements. Then the GCs begin calling various subcontractors who will do parts of the work: excavators to remove and haul away the dirt, cement layers to build the foundation, plumbers to install the pipework and masons to create a mosaic border. The subcontractors give their bids to the GC, who adds them up and tacks on some additional profit for the GC and then each GC submits his best bid to the owner, who selects one of the GCs to do the work based on price and perceptions of quality and ability to get the job done on time.

The owner-GC-subcontractor bidding process is important to understand because lawyers often must figure out when in that process were promises made that can be relied upon. For example, if the plumbing subcontractor quotes $10,000 for his work to the GC, and the GC relies on this when submitting his total bid to the owner for $100,000, what should happen if the sub-contractor later refuses to do the work for that price? If binding promises were made, then the owner can sue the GC, and the GC can sue the subcontractor—and even the threat of these lawsuits might impact their behavior. But if either the sub or the GC did not make an offer that was accepted, there would be no liability under contract law.

F. Offers for Rewards

Some offers do not invite a promissory response, meaning, some offers by their terms do not allow acceptance by promising. Rather, these offers only permit acceptance by completing performance.

This may sound abstract, but an example should make it clear and concrete. In 1893, the Carbolic Smoke Ball Company offered a cash reward to any person who inhaled their carbolic smoke ball product for a month, which was advertised to prevent the flu, and yet contracted the flu.

The company put out this offer as a sort of "prove me wrong" test, claiming, "many thousand Carbolic Smoke Balls were sold on these advertisements, but only three persons claimed the reward of £100, thus proving conclusively that this invaluable remedy will prevent and cure the above-mentioned diseases."

Setting aside the fact that the Carbolic Smoke Ball was carcinogenic and in no way prevented or cured any disease, this advertisement is a classic example of an offer for a reward. Such offers for rewards generally can only be accepted by completing the performance contemplated thereby. In this case, the only way to accept the offer and thus earn the reward was by (1) inhaling the Carbolic Smoke Ball for a month and (2) contracting one of the diseases that the product was supposed to prevent.

Offers that can only be accepted by completely performing their terms are called "unilateral offers" or "offers for unilateral contracts." Such offers are subject to special rules of irrevocability, as discussed in the chapter of Duration of the Offer.

G. Reflections on the Offer

An offer is the manifestation of willingness to enter into a bargain. This generally takes the form of a proposal to exchange promises. The element of exchange, or bargain, is required for a manifestation to constitute a contractual offer under common law.

It is important to recognize that this legal definition of "offer" is narrower than the ordinary usage of the term. For example, if Alain says to Berta, "I will drive you to work tomorrow," without more, that is not an offer under contract law, even though it seems to be offer under the ordinary usage. Remember that legal terms have special meaning that does not always accord with the ordinary usage of terms.

The term promise also has a special meaning under contract law. Under contract law, a promise is a commitment to do or not to do a certain thing. This is different from the more general, common meaning of promise. For example, saying "I promise that

Figure 4.3. Carbolic Smoke Ball advertisement. Public domain work.

everything is going to be okay," is probably not actually a promise under common law, because it does not include an intention to do anything specific. Rather, a promise under contract law typically includes a manifestation of intention by the promisor to perform in some manner. For example, "I promise to care for you if you get sick" may be specific enough to constitute a contractual promise — but it is still not an offer, because it does not contemplate an exchange. This is merely a proposal to give a contingent gift. To be an offer, one must say, "I will care for you if you get sick in exchange for $100," or some other terms which contemplate a bargained-for exchange.

In short, offers generally take the form of "I will do X if you do Y." The terms X and Y need to be defined with sufficient certainty that a court can objectively understand and enforce those mutual promises. Once such an offer is made, that creates a power of acceptance for the duration of the offer.

Cases

Reading Lefkowitz v. Great Minneapolis Surplus Store, Inc. Advertisements are generally not offers; rather, advertisements usually are invitations for offer. For example, if Target places an ad in a local magazine that says, "10% off on Xbox games," and Greg Gamer reads the advertisement, should Greg feel guaranteed that the specific game he has in mind will be in stock at the store and available for 10% off? No. First, what games are on sale? The ad is general and not specific enough for Greg to reasonably believe that any specific game is contemplated by the ad; in other words, the subject matter is uncertain. Second, 10% off what? The price is uncertain. Third, for how long will the deal be available? Sales usually do not run forever, but the time for acceptance is uncertain. With such a high level of uncertainty, this ad alone is not an offer that can be accepted.

What if the ad did specify the game, for example, Halo 5? And what if it also stated a price, say $40? This is a more specific ad, to be sure, but it will not be enough to overcome the general rules that advertisements are not intended to be offers but rather are mere invitations for offers. The most significant reason why this more specific ad is still not an offer is because the quantity term is not specified. Quantity is a very important aspect of sales. Selling one game is one thing, whereas having a dozen or a gross unit (144) on hand is another matter. One store will not reasonably be expected to have an infinite supply of a physical good. If other shoppers arrive before Greg, then Target may not have a unit to sell to him. For this reason — the lack of a quantity or a limited quantity term — the ad is still not an offer.

But what about those "doorbuster" sales where there is a guaranteed number of units for sale? What if Target advertised that the first five, ten, or twenty buyers of the new Halo game would also get a limited-edition action figure? In other words, when is the advertisement specific enough to constitute an offer?

The answer to that question is found in the next case. In *Lefkowitz*, the advertisement clearly indicated the price, quantity, subject matter, and manner of acceptance of some good for sale. The key language, "first come, first served" puts the analysis over the top, as this provides a clear means of acceptance in the offer itself.

This ad, therefore, constituted an offer that was available for acceptance.

The case also has a few other lessons about advertisements as offered. For example, when an ad is an offer, the terms of that offer can be changed or retracted only by a similar ad. Read on to better understand when an advertisement is an offer and what are the legal implications of such a "unilateral" offer.

Lefkowitz v. Great Minneapolis Surplus Store, Inc.

251 Minn. 188 (1957)

MURPHY, Justice.

This is an appeal from an order of the Municipal Court of Minneapolis denying the motion of the defendant for amended findings of fact, or, in the alternative, for a new trial. The order for judgment awarded the plaintiff the sum of $138.50 as damages for breach of contract.

This case grows out of the alleged refusal of the defendant to sell to the plaintiff a certain fur piece which it had offered for sale in a newspaper advertisement. It appears from the record that on April 6, 1956, the defendant published the following advertisement in a Minneapolis newspaper:

Saturday 9 A.M. Sharp

3 Brand New Fur Coats Worth to $100.00

First Come First Served $1 Each

On April 13, the defendant again published an advertisement in the same newspaper as follows:

Saturday 9 A.M.

2 Brand New Pastel Mink 3-Skin Scarfs

Selling for $89.50

Out they go Saturday. Each . . . $1.00

1 Black Lapin Stole Beautiful, worth $139.50 . . . $1.00

First Come First Served

The record supports the findings of the court that on each of the Saturdays following the publication of the above-described ads the plaintiff was the first to present himself at the appropriate counter in the defendant's store and on each occasion demanded the coat and the stole so advertised and indicated his readiness to pay the sale price of $1.

On both occasions, the defendant refused to sell the merchandise to the plaintiff, stating on the first occasion that by a "house rule" the offer was intended for women only and sales would not be made to men, and on the second visit that plaintiff knew defendant's house rules.

The trial court properly disallowed plaintiff's claim for the value of the fur coats since the value of these articles was speculative and uncertain. The only evidence of value was the advertisement itself to the effect that the coats were "Worth to $100.00," how much less being speculative especially in view of the price for which they were offered for sale.

With reference to the offer of the defendant on April 13, 1956, to sell the "1 Black Lapin Stole . . . worth $139.50" the trial court held that the value of this article was established and granted judgment in favor of the plaintiff for that amount less the $1 quoted purchase price.

1.

The defendant contends that a newspaper advertisement offering items of merchandise for sale at a named price is a "unilateral offer" which may be withdrawn without notice. Defendant relies upon authorities which hold that, where an advertiser publishes in a newspaper that he has a certain quantity or quality of goods which he wants to dispose of at certain prices and on certain terms, such advertisements are not offers which become contracts as soon as any person to whose notice they may come signifies his acceptance by notifying the other that he will take a certain quantity of them. Such advertisements have been construed as an invitation for an offer of sale on the terms stated, which offer, when received, may be accepted or rejected and which therefore does not become a contract of sale until accepted by the seller; and until a contract has been so made, the seller may modify or revoke such prices or terms.

The defendant relies principally on *Craft v. Elder & Johnston Co.* In that case, the court discussed the legal effect of an advertisement offering for sale, as a one-day special, an electric sewing machine at a named price. The view was expressed that the advertisement was "not an offer made to any specific person but was made to the public generally. Thereby it would be properly designated as a unilateral offer and not being supported by any consideration could be withdrawn at will and without notice." It is true that such an offer may be withdrawn before acceptance. Since all offers are by their nature unilateral because they are necessarily made by one party or on one side in the negotiation of a contract, the distinction made in that decision between a unilateral offer and a unilateral contract is not clear. On the facts before us we are concerned with whether the advertisement constituted an offer, and, if so, whether the plaintiff's conduct constituted an acceptance.

There are numerous authorities which hold that a particular advertisement in a newspaper or circular letter relating to a sale of articles may be construed by the court as constituting an offer, acceptance of which would complete a contract.

The test of whether a binding obligation may originate in advertisements addressed to the general public is "whether the facts show that some performance was promised in positive terms in return for something requested."

The authorities above cited emphasize that, where the offer is clear, definite, and explicit, and leaves nothing open for negotiation, it constitutes an offer, acceptance of which will complete the contract. The most recent case on the subject is *Johnson v. Capital City Ford Co.*, in which the court pointed out that a newspaper advertisement relating to the purchase and sale of automobiles may constitute an offer, acceptance of which will consummate a contract and create an obligation in the offeror to perform according to the terms of the published offer.

Whether in any individual instance a newspaper advertisement is an offer rather than an invitation to make an offer depends on the legal intention of the parties and the surrounding circumstances.

We are of the view on the facts before us that the offer by the defendant of the sale of the Lapin fur was clear, definite, explicit and left nothing open for negotiation. The plaintiff having successfully managed to be the first one to appear at the seller's place of business to be served, as requested by the advertisement, and having offered the stated purchase price of the article, he was entitled to performance on the part of the defendant. We think the trial court was correct in holding that there was in the conduct of the parties a sufficient mutuality of obligation to constitute a contract of sale.

2.

The defendant contends that the offer was modified by a "house rule" to the effect that only women were qualified to receive the bargains advertised. The advertisement contained no such restriction. This objection may be disposed of briefly by stating that, while an advertiser has the right at any time before acceptance to modify his offer, he does not have the right, after acceptance, to impose new or arbitrary conditions not contained in the published offer.

Affirmed.

Reflection

Advertisements are generally not offers — they are invitations for offers. Typically, advertisements are not specific enough to be construed as offers. For an advertisement to be an offer, the advertisement must be so clear and definite that there is nothing left to negotiate.

For example, think about advertisements for Black Friday sales. Stores like Walmart and Target advertise televisions and other electronics for significant discounts that people begin lining up for hours in advance. Say Walmart runs a commercial advertising a huge flat screen television for 80% off its regular price. People camp out all night to try to buy this television, but obviously there is no guarantee that everyone or anyone will leave with that television. Walmart could have only one of that specific television or possibly none of that television in stock. The advertisement was not clear and definite. From the advertisement, it is not clear who, if anyone, will leave with that television. Had the advertisement said, "The first three people to appear at the customer service desk at a specific Walmart on Black Friday with $100 cash in hand will receive this specific flat screen television," the advertisement might be understood differently. See, this advertisement is specific and contains all the essential terms. Anyone who reads the advertisement will understand that the first three people who appear at the customer service desk at that specific Walmart on Black Friday with $100 cash will be able to purchase that specific flat screen.

The advertisement in *Lefkowitz* was so specific and clear that anyone who read the advertisement would understand it to mean that the first person to show up at defendant's store with $1 in hand to purchase the fur coat would be able to leave with that coat. For this reason, the advertisement in *Lefkowitz* was determined to be an offer, which Lefkowitz accepted by showing up at the defendant's store prepared to purchase the coat.

It is also important to note that in a unilateral offer, the advertiser may modify their offer at any point before acceptance. However, the advertiser may not modify or add any additional conditions to their offer after acceptance. In *Lefkowitz*, the defendant attempted to modify the offer after Lefkowitz had accepted the offer. Had Lefkowitz not shown up at the defendant's store ready to purchase the coat, and the defendant ran another advertisement including his "house rules," then the advertisement would have been modified prior to acceptance and the case could have turned out very differently.

Discussion

1. Note the rule of thumb that advertisements are generally not offers. What made the ads in *Lefkowitz* different such that the court found these were offers?

2. Identify several advertisements that you believe are not offers. What about each of these ads makes them not an offer? What specific element(s) of an offer is missing?

3. Try to locate an advertisement that is an offer. What makes this ad different from usual such that it rises to the level of an offer?

4. Great Minneapolis Supply Store told Lefkowitz there was a "house rule" that its ad was only an offer to women. Why did the court find that Lefkowitz, a man, was allowed to accept this offer?

Reading Leonard v. Pepsico, Inc. The following case is at one level a silly story about an advertisement that went too far. Our hapless plaintiff was a student turned entrepreneur who attempted to raise enough money to purchase enough Pepsi points to procure an AV-8B Harrier II jump jet.

Figure 4.4. US AV-8B Harrier II jump jet hovering. Source D. Miller CC-A-2.0

The interesting questions in this case are not about whether the plaintiff got the military fighter plane — he did not — but why he felt so entitled to receive one, and what was the legal basis for the denial of his request to get one? The answer is not merely a simple matter of public policy—although one can imagine good reasons why restricted munitions and military aircraft should not be provided to the public—but rather involves some knowledge of how catalogs and advertisements work in our system of offer and assent. As you read on, think about what is a catalog and ask whether a catalog is an advertisement and, if so, is it an advertisement that rises to the level of an offer? If not, when does an offer first arise from a catalog ordering process?

Leonard v. Pepsico, Inc.

88 F. Supp. 2d 116 (S.D.N.Y. 1999)

KIMBA M. WOOD, District Judge.

Plaintiff brought this action seeking, among other things, specific performance of an alleged offer of a Harrier Jet, featured in a television advertisement for defendant's "Pepsi Stuff" promotion. Defendant has moved for summary judgment pursuant to Federal Rule of Civil Procedure 56. For the reasons stated below, defendant's motion is granted.

I. Background

This case arises out of a promotional campaign conducted by defendant, the producer and distributor of the soft drinks Pepsi and Diet Pepsi. The promotion, entitled "Pepsi Stuff," encouraged consumers to collect "Pepsi Points" from specially marked packages of Pepsi or Diet Pepsi and redeem these points for merchandise featuring the Pepsi logo. Before introducing the promotion nationally, defendant conducted a test of the promotion in the Pacific Northwest from October 1995 to March 1996. A Pepsi Stuff catalog was distributed to consumers in the test market, including Washington State. Plaintiff is a resident of Seattle, Washington. While living in Seattle, plaintiff saw the Pepsi Stuff commercial that he contends constituted an offer of a Harrier Jet.

A. The Alleged Offer

Because whether the television commercial constituted an offer is the central question in this case, the Court will describe the commercial in detail. The commercial opens upon an idyllic, suburban morning, where the chirping of birds in sun-dappled trees welcomes a paperboy on his morning route. As the newspaper hits the stoop of a conventional two-story house, the tattoo of a military drum introduces the subtitle, "MONDAY 7:58 AM." The stirring strains of a martial air mark the appearance of a well-coiffed teenager preparing to leave for school, dressed in a shirt emblazoned with the Pepsi logo, a red-white-and-blue ball. While the teenager confidently preens, the military drumroll again sounds as the subtitle "T-SHIRT 75 PEPSI POINTS" scrolls across the screen. Bursting from his room, the teenager strides down the hallway wearing a leather jacket. The drumroll sounds again, as the subtitle "LEATHER JACKET 1450 PEPSI POINTS" appears. The teenager opens the door of his house and, unfazed by the glare of the early morning sunshine, puts on a pair of sunglasses. The drumroll then accompanies the subtitle "SHADES 175 PEPSI POINTS." A voiceover then intones, "Introducing the new Pepsi Stuff catalog," as the camera focuses on the cover of the catalog.

The scene then shifts to three young boys sitting in front of a high school building. The boy in the middle is intent on his Pepsi Stuff Catalog, while the boys on either side are each drinking Pepsi. The three boys gaze in awe at an object rushing overhead, as the military march builds to a crescendo. The Harrier Jet is not yet visible, but the observer senses the presence of a mighty plane as the extreme winds generated by its flight create a paper maelstrom in a classroom devoted to an otherwise dull physics lesson. Finally, the Harrier Jet swings into view and lands by the side of the school building, next to a bicycle rack. Several students run for cover, and the velocity of the wind strips one hapless faculty member down to his underwear. While the faculty member is being deprived of his dignity, the voiceover announces: "Now the more Pepsi you drink, the more great stuff you're gonna get."

The teenager opens the cockpit of the fighter and can be seen, helmetless, holding a Pepsi. "[L]ooking very pleased with himself," the teenager exclaims, "Sure beats the bus," and chortles. The military drumroll sounds a final time, as the following words appear: "HARRIER FIGHTER 7,000,000 PEPSI POINTS." A few seconds later, the following appears in more stylized script: "Drink Pepsi — Get Stuff." With that message, the music and the commercial end with a triumphant flourish.

Inspired by this commercial, plaintiff set out to obtain a Harrier Jet. Plaintiff explains that he is "typical of the 'Pepsi Generation' . . . he is young, has an adventurous spirit, and the notion of obtaining a Harrier Jet appealed to him enormously." Plaintiff consulted the Pepsi Stuff Catalog. The Catalog features youths dressed in Pepsi Stuff regalia or enjoying Pepsi Stuff accessories, such as "Blue Shades" ("As if you need another reason to look forward to sunny days."), "Pepsi Tees" ("Live in 'em. Laugh in 'em. Get in 'em."), "Bag of Balls" ("Three balls. One bag. No rules."), and "Pepsi Phone Card" ("Call your mom!"). The Catalog specifies the number of Pepsi Points required to obtain promotional merchandise. The Catalog includes an Order Form which lists, on one side, fifty-three items of Pepsi Stuff merchandise redeemable for Pepsi Points. Conspicuously absent from the Order Form is any entry or description of a Harrier Jet. The amount of Pepsi Points required to obtain the listed merchandise ranges from 15 (for a "Jacket Tattoo" ("Sew 'em on your jacket, not your arm.")) to 3300 (for a "Fila Mountain Bike" ("Rugged. All-terrain. Exclusively for Pepsi.")). It should be noted that plaintiff objects to the implication that because an item was not shown in the Catalog, it was unavailable.

The rear foldout pages of the Catalog contain directions for redeeming Pepsi Points for merchandise. These directions note that merchandise may be ordered "only" with the original Order Form. The Catalog notes that in the event that a consumer lacks enough Pepsi Points to obtain a desired item, additional Pepsi Points may be purchased for ten cents each; however, at least fifteen original Pepsi Points must accompany each order.

Although plaintiff initially set out to collect 7,000,000 Pepsi Points by consuming Pepsi products, it soon became clear to him that he "would not be able to buy (let alone drink) enough Pepsi to collect the necessary Pepsi Points fast enough." Reevaluating his strategy, plaintiff "focused for the first time on the packaging materials in the Pepsi Stuff promotion," and realized that buying Pepsi Points would be a more promising option. Through acquaintances, plaintiff ultimately raised about $700,000.

B. Plaintiff's Efforts to Redeem the Alleged Offer

On or about March 27, 1996, plaintiff submitted an Order Form, fifteen original Pepsi Points, and a check for $700,008.50. Plaintiff appears to have been represented by counsel at the time he mailed his check; the check is drawn on an account of plaintiff's first set of attorneys. At the bottom of the Order Form, plaintiff wrote in "1 Harrier Jet" in the "Item" column and "7,000,000" in the "Total Points" column. In a letter accompanying his submission, plaintiff stated that the check was to purchase additional Pepsi Points "expressly for obtaining a new Harrier jet as advertised in your Pepsi Stuff commercial."

On or about May 7, 1996, defendant's fulfillment house rejected plaintiff's submission and returned the check, explaining that:

> The item that you have requested is not part of the Pepsi Stuff collection. It is not included in the catalogue or on the order form, and only catalogue merchandise can be redeemed under this program.
>
> The Harrier jet in the Pepsi commercial is fanciful and is simply included to create a humorous and entertaining ad. We apologize for any misunderstanding or confusion that you may have experienced and are enclosing some free product coupons for your use.

Plaintiff's previous counsel responded on or about May 14, 1996, as follows:

> Your letter of May 7, 1996 is totally unacceptable. We have reviewed the video tape of the Pepsi Stuff commercial . . . and it clearly offers the new Harrier jet for 7,000,000 Pepsi Points. Our client followed your rules explicitly. . . .
>
> This is a formal demand that you honor your commitment and make immediate arrangements to transfer the new Harrier jet to our client. If we do not receive transfer instructions within ten (10) business days of the date of this letter you will leave us no choice but to file an appropriate action against Pepsi. . . .

This letter was apparently sent onward to the advertising company responsible for the actual commercial, BBDO New York ("BBDO"). In a letter dated May 30, 1996, BBDO Vice President Raymond E. McGovern, Jr., explained to plaintiff that:

> I find it hard to believe that you are of the opinion that the Pepsi Stuff commercial ("Commercial") really offers a new Harrier Jet. The use of the Jet was clearly a joke that was meant to make the Commercial more humorous and entertaining. In my opinion, no reasonable person would agree with your analysis of the Commercial.

[Approximately three years of procedural history omitted.]

II. Discussion

[Standard for summary judgment omitted.]

[Choice of law analysis omitted.]

B. Defendant's Advertisement Was Not An Offer

1. Advertisements as Offers

The general rule is that an advertisement does not constitute an offer. The Restatement (Second) of Contracts explains that:

> *Advertisements of goods by display, sign, handbill, newspaper, radio or television are not ordinarily intended or understood as offers to sell. The same is true of catalogues, price lists and circulars, even though the terms of suggested bargains may be stated in some detail. It is of course possible to make an offer by an advertisement directed to the general public (see § 29), but there must ordinarily be some language of commitment or some invitation to take action without further communication.*

Similarly, a leading treatise notes that:

> *It is quite possible to make a definite and operative offer to buy or sell goods by advertisement, in a newspaper, by a handbill, a catalog or circular or on a placard in a store window. It is not customary to do this, however; and the presumption is the other way. . . . Such advertisements are understood to be mere requests to consider and examine and negotiate; and no one can reasonably regard them as otherwise unless the circumstances are exceptional and the words used are very plain and clear.*

An advertisement is not transformed into an enforceable offer merely by a potential offeree's expression of willingness to accept the offer through, among other means, completion of an order form.

In *Mesaros v. United States*, for example, the plaintiffs sued the United States Mint for failure to deliver a number of Statue of Liberty commemorative coins that they had ordered. When demand for the coins proved unexpectedly robust, a number of individuals who had sent in their orders in a timely fashion were left empty-handed. The court began by noting the "well-established" rule that advertisements and order forms are "mere notices and solicitations for offers which create no power of acceptance in the recipient." The spurned coin collectors could not maintain a breach of contract action because no contract would be formed until the advertiser accepted the order form and processed payment. Under these principles, plaintiff's letter of March 27, 1996, with the Order Form and the appropriate number of Pepsi Points, constituted the offer. There would be no enforceable contract until defendant accepted the Order Form and cashed the check.

The exception to the rule that advertisements do not create any power of acceptance in potential offerees is where the advertisement is "clear, definite, and explicit, and leaves nothing open for negotiation," in that circumstance, "it constitutes an offer, acceptance of which will complete the contract." In *Lefkowitz*, defendant had published a newspaper announcement stating: "Saturday 9 AM Sharp, 3 Brand New Fur Coats, Worth to $100.00, First Come First Served $1 Each." Mr. Morris Lefkowitz arrived at the store, dollar in hand, but was informed that under defendant's "house rules," the offer was open to ladies, but not gentlemen. The court ruled that because plaintiff had fulfilled all of the terms of the advertisement and the advertisement was specific and left nothing open for negotiation, a contract had been formed.

The present case is distinguishable from *Lefkowitz*. First, the commercial cannot be regarded in itself as sufficiently definite, because it specifically reserved the details of the offer to a separate writing, the Catalog. The commercial itself made no mention of the steps a potential offeree would be required to take to accept the alleged offer of a Harrier Jet. The advertisement in Lefkowitz, in contrast, "identified the person who could accept." Second, even if the Catalog had included a Harrier Jet among the items that could be obtained by redemption of Pepsi Points, the advertisement of a Harrier Jet by both television commercial and catalog would still not constitute an offer. As the *Mesaros* court explained, the absence of any words of limitation such as "first come, first served," renders the alleged offer sufficiently indefinite that no contract could be formed. "A customer would not usually have reason to believe that the shopkeeper intended exposure to the risk of a multitude of acceptances resulting in a number of contracts exceeding the shopkeeper's inventory." There was no such danger in *Lefkowitz*, owing to the limitation "first come, first served."

The Court finds, in sum, that the Harrier Jet commercial was merely an advertisement. The Court now turns to the line of cases upon which plaintiff rests much of his argument.

2. Rewards as Offers

In opposing the present motion, plaintiff largely relies on a different species of unilateral offer, involving public offers of a reward for performance of a specified act. Because these cases generally involve public declarations regarding the efficacy or trustworthiness of specific products, one court has aptly characterized these authorities as "prove me wrong" cases.

The most venerable of these precedents is the case of *Carlill v. Carbolic Smoke Ball Co.*, a quote from which heads plaintiff's memorandum of law: "[I]f a person chooses to make extravagant promises . . . he probably does so because it pays him to make them, and, if he has made them, the extravagance of the promises is no reason in law why he should not be bound by them."

Long a staple of law school curricula, Carbolic Smoke Ball owes its fame not merely to "the comic and slightly mysterious object involved," but also to its role in developing the law of unilateral offers. The case arose during the London influenza epidemic of the 1890s. Among other advertisements of the time, for Clarke's World Famous Blood Mixture, Towle's Pennyroyal and Steel Pills for Females, Sequah's Prairie Flower, and Epp's Glycerin Jube-Jubes, appeared solicitations for the Carbolic

Smoke Ball. The specific advertisement that Mrs. Carlill saw, and relied upon, read as follows:

> *100 £ reward will be paid by the Carbolic Smoke Ball Company to any person who contracts the increasing epidemic influenza, colds, or any diseases caused by taking cold, after having used the ball three times daily for two weeks according to the printed directions supplied with each ball. 1000 £ is deposited with the Alliance Bank, Regent Street, shewing our sincerity in the matter.*

During the last epidemic of influenza many thousand carbolic smoke balls were sold as preventives against this disease, and in no ascertained case was the disease contracted by those using the carbolic smoke ball.

"On the faith of this advertisement," Mrs. Carlill purchased the smoke ball and used it as directed, but contracted influenza nevertheless. The lower court held that she was entitled to recover the promised reward.

Affirming the lower court's decision, Lord Justice Lindley began by noting that the advertisement was an express promise to pay £ 100 in the event that a consumer of the Carbolic Smoke Ball was stricken with influenza. The advertisement was construed as offering a reward because it sought to induce performance, unlike an invitation to negotiate, which seeks a reciprocal promise. As Lord Justice Lindley explained, "advertisements offering rewards . . . are offers to anybody who performs the conditions named in the advertisement, and anybody who does perform the condition accepts the offer." Because Mrs. Carlill had complied with the terms of the offer, yet contracted influenza, she was entitled to £ 100.

Like *Carbolic Smoke Ball*, the decisions relied upon by plaintiff involve offers of reward.

Other "reward" cases underscore the distinction between typical advertisements, in which the alleged offer is merely an invitation to negotiate for purchase of commercial goods, and promises of reward, in which the alleged offer is intended to induce a potential offeree to perform a specific action, often for noncommercial reasons.

James v. Turilli arose from a boast by defendant that the "notorious Missouri desperado" Jesse James had not been killed in 1882, as portrayed in song and legend, but had lived under the alias "J. Frank Dalton" at the "Jesse James Museum" operated by none other than defendant. Defendant offered $10,000 "to anyone who could prove me wrong." The widow of the outlaw's son demonstrated, at trial, that the outlaw had in fact been killed in 1882. On appeal, the court held that defendant should be liable to pay the amount offered.

In the present case, the Harrier Jet commercial did not direct that anyone who appeared at Pepsi headquarters with 7,000,000 Pepsi Points on the Fourth of July would receive a Harrier Jet. Instead, the commercial urged consumers to accumulate Pepsi Points and to refer to the Catalog to determine how they could redeem their

Pepsi Points. The commercial sought a reciprocal promise, expressed through acceptance of, and compliance with, the terms of the Order Form. As noted previously, the Catalog contains no mention of the Harrier Jet. Plaintiff states that he "noted that the Harrier Jet was not among the items described in the catalog, but this did not affect [his] understanding of the offer." It should have.

Carbolic Smoke Ball itself draws a distinction between the offer of reward in that case, and typical advertisements, which are merely offers to negotiate. As Lord Justice Bowen explains:

> *It is an offer to become liable to any one who, before it is retracted, performs the condition. . . . It is not like cases in which you offer to negotiate, or you issue advertisements that you have got a stock of books to sell, or houses to let, in which case there is no offer to be bound by any contract. Such advertisements are offers to negotiate — offers to receive offers — offers to chaffer, as, I think, some learned judge in one of the cases has said.*

Because the alleged offer in this case was, at most, an advertisement to receive offers rather than an offer of reward, plaintiff cannot show that there was an offer made in the circumstances of this case.

C. An Objective, Reasonable Person Would Not Have Considered the Commercial an Offer

Plaintiff's understanding of the commercial as an offer must also be rejected because the Court finds that no objective person could reasonably have concluded that the commercial actually offered consumers a Harrier Jet.

1. Objective Reasonable Person Standard

In evaluating the commercial, the Court must not consider defendant's subjective intent in making the commercial, or plaintiff's subjective view of what the commercial offered, but what an objective, reasonable person would have understood the commercial to convey.

If it is clear that an offer was not serious, then no offer has been made:

> *What kind of act creates a power of acceptance and is therefore an offer? It must be an expression of will or intention. It must be an act that leads the offeree reasonably to conclude that a power to create a contract is conferred. This applies to the content of the power as well as to the fact of its existence. It is on this ground that we must exclude invitations to deal or acts of mere preliminary negotiation, and acts evidently done in jest or without intent to create legal relations.*

An obvious joke, of course, would not give rise to a contract. On the other hand, if there is no indication that the offer is "evidently in jest," and that an objective, reasonable person would find that the offer was serious, then there may be a valid offer.

[Discussion of whether plaintiff may demand a jury trial omitted.]

3. Whether the Commercial Was "Evidently Done In Jest"

Plaintiff's insistence that the commercial appears to be a serious offer requires the Court to explain why the commercial is funny. Explaining why a joke is funny is a daunting task; as the essayist E.B. White has remarked, "Humor can be dissected, as a frog can, but the thing dies in the process." The commercial is the embodiment of what defendant appropriately characterizes as "zany humor."

First, the commercial suggests, as commercials often do, that use of the advertised product will transform what, for most youth, can be a fairly routine and ordinary experience. The military tattoo and stirring martial music, as well as the use of subtitles in a Courier font that scroll terse messages across the screen, such as "MONDAY 7:58 AM," evoke military and espionage thrillers. The implication of the commercial is that Pepsi Stuff merchandise will inject drama and moment into hitherto unexceptional lives. The commercial in this case thus makes the exaggerated claims similar to those of many television advertisements: that by consuming the featured clothing, car, beer, or potato chips, one will become attractive, stylish, desirable, and admired by all. A reasonable viewer would understand such advertisements as mere puffery, not as statements of fact, and refrain from interpreting the promises of the commercial as being literally true.

Second, the callow youth featured in the commercial is a highly improbable pilot, one who could barely be trusted with the keys to his parents' car, much less the prize aircraft of the United States Marine Corps. Rather than checking the fuel gauges on his aircraft, the teenager spends his precious preflight minutes preening. The youth's concern for his coiffure appears to extend to his flying without a helmet. Finally, the teenager's comment that flying a Harrier Jet to school "sure beats the bus" evinces an improbably insouciant attitude toward the relative difficulty and danger of piloting a fighter plane in a residential area, as opposed to taking public transportation.

Third, the notion of traveling to school in a Harrier Jet is an exaggerated adolescent fantasy. In this commercial, the fantasy is underscored by how the teenager's schoolmates gape in admiration, ignoring their physics lesson. The force of the wind generated by the Harrier Jet blows off one teacher's clothes, literally defrocking an authority figure. As if to emphasize the fantastic quality of having a Harrier Jet arrive at school, the Jet lands next to a plebeian bike rack. This fantasy is, of course, extremely unrealistic. No school would provide landing space for a student's fighter jet, or condone the disruption the jet's use would cause.

Fourth, the primary mission of a Harrier Jet, according to the United States Marine Corps, is to "attack and destroy surface targets under day and night visual conditions." Manufactured by McDonnell Douglas, the Harrier Jet played a significant role in the air offensive of Operation Desert Storm in 1991. The jet is designed to carry a considerable armament load, including Sidewinder and Maverick missiles. As one news report has noted, "Fully loaded, the Harrier can float like a butterfly and sting like a bee — albeit a roaring 14-ton butterfly and a bee with 9,200 pounds of bombs and missiles." In light of the Harrier Jet's well-documented function in attacking and destroying surface and air targets, armed reconnaissance and air interdiction, and offensive and defensive anti-aircraft warfare, depiction of such a jet as a way to get to school in the morning is clearly not serious even if, as plaintiff contends, the jet is capable of being acquired "in a form that eliminates [its] potential for military use."

Fifth, the number of Pepsi Points the commercial mentions as required to "purchase" the jet is 7,000,000. To amass that number of points, one would have to drink 7,000,000 Pepsis (or roughly 190 Pepsis a day for the next hundred years — an unlikely possibility), or one would have to purchase approximately $700,000 worth of Pepsi Points. The cost of a Harrier Jet is roughly $23 million dollars, a fact of which plaintiff was aware when he set out to gather the amount he believed necessary to accept the alleged offer. Even if an objective, reasonable person were not aware of this fact, he would conclude that purchasing a fighter plane for $700,000 is a deal too good to be true.

Plaintiff argues that a reasonable, objective person would have understood the commercial to make a serious offer of a Harrier Jet because there was "absolutely no distinction in the manner" in which the items in the commercial were presented. Plaintiff also relies upon a press release highlighting the promotional campaign, issued by defendant, in which "[n]o mention is made by [defendant] of humor, or anything of the sort." These arguments suggest merely that the humor of the promotional campaign was tongue in cheek. Humor is not limited to what Justice Cardozo called "[t]he rough and boisterous joke . . . [that] evokes its own guffaws." In light of the obvious absurdity of the commercial, the Court rejects plaintiff's argument that the commercial was not clearly in jest.

[Discovery dispute omitted.]

[Discussion of the applicability of the statute of frauds omitted.]

[Discussion of plaintiff's fraud claim omitted.]

III. Conclusion

In sum, there are three reasons why plaintiff's demand cannot prevail as a matter of law. First, the commercial was merely an advertisement, not a unilateral offer. Second, the tongue-in-cheek attitude of the commercial would not cause a reasonable person to conclude that a soft drink company would be giving away fighter planes as part of a promotion. Third, there is no writing between the parties sufficient to satisfy the Statute of Frauds.

For the reasons stated above, the Court grants defendant's motion for summary judgment.

Reflection

Leonard demonstrates how advertisements, especially advertisements for rewards, may or may not be offers. Remember that absent special circumstances, advertisements are generally construed to be an invitation to make an offer. *Lefkowitz* demonstrated when those special circumstances exist. *Leonard*, on the other hand, is a case without special circumstances. Unlike *Lefkowitz*, the commercial was not sufficiently definite and did not include words of limitation like "first come, first serve." Therefore, the advertisement is an invitation to make an offer and not an offer.

Advertisements for rewards can also rise to the status of an offer. These types of offers (called unilateral offers) can only be accepted by completely performing. The plaintiff in *Leonard* tried to argue that the commercial was an advertisement for a reward. The court was unconvinced and determined that the commercial was an invitation to make an offer and the manner of acceptance was for a reciprocal promise through the order form. If it was for a reward, the advertisement would have had to have directed someone to complete performance to receive the reward.

Lastly, the court used the objective reasonable person standard (introduced in *Lucy* in Chapter 3) to determine whether the offer (commercial ad) could be construed seriously. The court determined that an objectively reasonable person would have understood the commercial to be an obvious joke. Therefore, obvious jokes, like the one in the commercial, do not give rise to a contract.

Discussion

1. It may seem obvious to some that the Pepsi commercial was meant in jest, but the court still provided a thorough analysis of whether the ad was serious. Why did the court bother with this analysis on a point that may seem obvious?

2. Why did the *Pepsico* court determine that the ad was in jest and not to be taken seriously?

3. Pepsi provided customers like Leonard an opportunity obtain Pepsi Points they could spend via a catalog. Was the catalog an offer? Why or why not?

4. If you were attorney for Pepsico, would you have identified any legal problems with the advertisement? With the benefit of hindsight, what changes if any would you recommend Pepsico make to its ad to avoid unwanted legal liability?

Reading Academy Chicago Publishers v. Cheever. Even when a person intends to make an offer, and not merely to engage in preliminary negotiations, he or she may fail to present an acceptable offer because of a lack of certainty. Certainty is the opposite of ambiguity. When an offer is too ambiguous, it cannot be enforced by courts, because courts would not know exactly what the parties intended to be enforced.

Cheever highlights a situation where an agreement, although detailed, may have been insufficiently certain for a court to enforce it. Although courts have powers to imply terms and thereby make agreements sufficiently certain in some cases, in others, there is not enough certainty provided by the parties from which a court could create an enforceable obligation.

Academy Chicago Publishers v. Cheever
144 Ill. 2d 24 (1991)

HEIPLE, J

This is a suit for declaratory judgment. It arose out of an agreement between the widow of the widely published author, John Cheever, and Academy Chicago Publishers. Contact between the parties began in 1987 when the publisher approached Mrs. Cheever about the possibility of publishing a collection of Mr. Cheever's short stories which, though previously published, had never been collected into a single anthology. In August of that year, a publishing agreement was signed which provided, in pertinent part:

Agreement made this 15th day of August 1987, between Academy Chicago Publishers or any affiliated entity or imprint (hereinafter referred to as the Publisher) and Mary W. Cheever and Franklin H. Dennis of the USA (hereinafter referred to as Author).

Whereas the parties are desirous of publishing and having published a certain work or works, tentatively titled The Uncollected Stories of John Cheever (hereinafter referred to as the Work):

2. The Author will deliver to the Publisher on a mutually agreeable date one copy of the manuscript of the Work as finally arranged by the editor and satisfactory to the Publisher in form and content.

5. Within a reasonable time and a mutually agreeable date after delivery of the final revised manuscript, the Publisher will publish the Work at its own expense, in such style and manner and at such price as it deems best, and will keep the Work in print as long as it deems it expedient; but it will not be responsible for delays caused by circumstances beyond its control.

Academy and its editor, Franklin Dennis, assumed the task of locating and procuring the uncollected stories and delivering them to Mrs. Cheever. Mrs. Cheever and Mr. Dennis received partial advances for manuscript preparation. By the end of 1987, Academy had located and delivered more than 60 uncollected stories to Mrs. Cheever. Shortly thereafter, Mrs. Cheever informed Academy in writing that she objected to the publication of the book and attempted to return her advance.

Academy filed suit in the circuit court of Cook County in February 1988, seeking a declaratory judgment: (1) granting Academy the exclusive right to publish the tentatively titled, "The Uncollected Stories of John Cheever"; (2) designating Franklin Dennis as the book's editor; and (3) obligating Mrs. Cheever to deliver the manuscript from which the work was to be published. The trial court entered an order declaring, inter alia: (1) that the publishing agreement executed by the parties was valid and enforceable; (2) that Mrs. Cheever was entitled to select the short stories to be included in the manuscript for publication; (3) that Mrs. Cheever would comply with her obligations of good faith and fair dealing if she delivered a manuscript including at least 10 to 15 stories totaling at least 140 pages; (4) Academy controlled the design and format of the work to be published, but control must be exercised in cooperation with Mrs. Cheever.

Academy appealed the trial court's order, challenging particularly the declaration regarding the minimum story and page numbers for Mrs. Cheever's compliance with the publishing agreement, and the declaration that Academy must consult with defendant on all matters of publication of the manuscript.

The appellate court affirmed the decision of the trial court with respect to the validity and enforceability of the publishing agreement and the minimum story and page number requirements for Mrs. Cheever's compliance with same. The appellate court reversed the trial court's declaration regarding control of publication, stating that the trial court erred in considering extrinsic evidence to interpret the agreement regarding control of the publication, given the explicit language of the agreement granting exclusive control to Academy.

The parties raise several issues on appeal; this matter, however, is one of contract and we confine our discussion to the issue of the validity and enforceability of the publishing agreement.

While the trial court and the appellate court agreed that the publishing agreement constitutes a valid and enforceable contract, we cannot concur. The principles of contract state that in order for a valid contract to be formed, an "offer must be so definite as to its material terms or require such definite terms in the acceptance that the promises and performances to be rendered by each party are reasonably certain." Although the parties may have had and manifested the intent to make a contract, if the content of their agreement is unduly uncertain and indefinite no contract is formed.

The pertinent language of this agreement lacks the definite and certain essential terms required for the formation of an enforceable contract. A contract "is sufficiently definite and certain to be enforceable if the court is enabled from the terms and provisions thereof, under proper rules of construction and applicable principles of equity, to ascertain what the parties have agreed to do." The provisions of the subject publishing agreement do not provide the court with a means of determining the intent of the parties.

Trial testimony reveals that a major source of controversy between the parties is the length and content of the proposed book. The agreement sheds no light on the minimum or maximum number of stories or pages necessary for publication of the collection, nor is there any implicit language from which we can glean the intentions of the parties with respect to this essential contract term. The publishing agreement is similarly silent with respect to who will decide which stories will be included in the collection. Other omissions, ambiguities, unresolved essential terms and illusory terms are: No date certain for delivery of the manuscript. No definition of the criteria which would render the manuscript satisfactory to the publisher either as to form or content. No date certain as to when publication will occur. No certainty as to style or manner in which the book will be published nor is there any indication as to the price at which such book will be sold, or the length of time publication shall continue, all of which terms are left to the sole discretion of the publisher.

A contract may be enforced even though some contract terms may be missing or left to be agreed upon, but if the essential terms are so uncertain that there is no basis for deciding whether the agreement has been kept or broken, there is no contract. Without setting forth adequate terms for compliance, the publishing agreement provides no basis for determining when breach has occurred, and, therefore, is not a valid and enforceable contract.

An enforceable contract must include a meeting of the minds or mutual assent as to the terms of the contract. It is not compelling that the parties share a subjective understanding as to the terms of the contract; the parties' conduct may indicate an agreement to the terms of same. *Steinberg v. Chicago Medical School.* In the instant case, however, no mutual assent has been illustrated. The parties did not and do not share a common understanding of the essential terms of the publishing agreement.

In rendering its judgment, the trial court supplied minimum terms for Mrs. Cheever's compliance, including story and page numbers. It is not uncommon for a court to supply a missing material term, as the reasonable conclusion often is that the parties intended that the term be supplied by implication. However, where the subject matter of the contract has not been decided upon and there is no standard available for reasonable implication, courts ordinarily refuse to supply the missing term. No suitable standard was available for the trial court to apply. It is our opinion that the trial court incorrectly supplied minimum compliance terms to the publishing agreement, as the agreement did not constitute a valid and enforceable contract to begin with. As noted above, the publishing agreement contains major unresolved uncertainties. It is not the role of the court to rewrite the contract and spell out essential elements not included therein.

In light of our decision that there was no valid and enforceable contract between the parties, we need not address other issues raised on appeal. For the foregoing reasons, the decisions of the trial and appellate courts in this declaratory judgment action are reversed.

Reversed.

Reflection

The *Cheever* case was hotly contested by lower and higher courts. This contest evidences the natural tendency of many courts to try and make agreements enforceable, especially where there has been performance by the parties. Although the court did not state things in this manner, it appears to me that the greater the amount of performance under a purported contract, the greater the desire of courts to find a contract exists. Otherwise, we must do something else with that performance, such as wrap it in a quasi-contract or repay it using restitution. In cases like this, there is a tension between pragmatism and efficiency on the one hand and rigor and academic honesty on the other.

Discussion

1. The *Cheever* case illustrates a situation where an offer is too indefinite to enforce. What are the minimum requirements for the terms of an offer? What must an offer include for it to be enforceable?

2. How did the lower court attempt to rectify the inadequacies of the contract in *Cheever*? Why did the higher court reject the lower court's approach?

3. If you were the attorney for the publishing company, what advice would you give to ensure future contracts were not unenforceable due to indefiniteness?

Problems

Problem 4.1. Lexus Advertisement

A used car dealership posted an advertisement in the newspaper, advertising a used Lexus for the price of $24,000. However, the newspaper made a typographical and proofreading error. The retail price of the used Lexus was actually $34,000.

Brian Donovan saw the advertisement and attempted to purchase the Lexus for the advertised price. When Donovan appeared at the dealership, the dealership refused to sell him the car for the advertised price, explaining that the newspaper had misprinted the price of the car.

Donovan then sued the dealership for breach of contract.

Was the advertisement an offer? If the advertisement was specific enough to be understood as an offer, would the car dealership be able to modify the offer?

See Donovan v. RRL Corp., 26 Cal. 4th 261, 27 P.3d 702 (2001).

Problem 4.2. Volvo Advertisement

In 1966, Lee Calan Imports, an automobile dealer, advertised a 1964 Volvo Station Wagon for sale in the newspaper. The dealership told the newspaper to advertise the car at $1,795, but the newspaper accidentally listed it at $1,095. Christopher O'Brien saw the advertisement in the newspaper and went to Lee Calan Imports to buy it at the advertised price. However, Lee Calan Imports refused to sell the car at the price in the newspaper.

Did the advertisement constitute an offer on the part of Lee Calan Imports?

See *O'Keefe v. Lee Calan Imports, Inc.*, 262 N.E.2d 758 (Ill. App. Ct. 1970).

Problem 4.3. Definite Commission

RRA is a temporary personnel agency that supplies technical employees to national laboratories and other contractors. The agency pays the employee's wages and benefits, and the contractor pays the agency for supplying the employee. In early 1993, Richard Padilla was hired by RRA.

Soon thereafter, two disputes arose regarding Padilla's compensation by RRA. First, he claimed breach of an oral contract negotiated with Stan Rashkin, a vice president of RRA, to pay him a commission of one to ten percent if he procured additional contracts for RRA. He alleged that he obtained two contracts with a total value of $655,200 but was paid only a $750 finder's fee. Second, he contended that he was paid an hourly wage below that provided by his written contract with RRA.

Defendant contends that there is no contract because the alleged terms are too indefinite. Defendant's argument focuses on the absence of a specific commission rate. Padilla's deposition testimony regarding the compensation terms was as follows:

A: And [Rashkin] asked me what I thought on it, and I said, "Well, to me, I would like to get somewhere between one and ten percent, depending on the size of the contract and how much of a profit margin there was for the company." Because he says, "Oh, yeah, ten percent is pretty high, but it would all have to depend on what—you know, each contract is different." Like I said, depends on the billing rate and how much of a profit that contract allows. Some contracts end up with a lot higher profit rate than other ones do. And I told Stan I understand that if the company don't make much, then I don't make much; but if the company makes a bunch, then I expect to get a lot of it, also. And he agreed to it and—

Q: He agreed to what?

A: To the fact of giving one to ten percent. And I told him, okay, because I know of a couple of contracts that are coming up, and I think I can get the people to come over to RAA. And he said it sounded very good to him, because they were just breaking into a new market at the time, and he could use all the new contracts there that they could muster. Up to that point, they were basically out in Los Alamos. And [Rashkin] told me then that if I brought in a contract that he would get with me afterwards, show me all the paperwork on it, as far as how much it was, getting—actually bringing in, where everything was going to, and then we would negotiate the one to ten percent depending on, you know, how it came out. And I said, "Fine, that way we can look over the figures and I'd *know exactly why you're offering," like I told him, "two, one, eight, ten, whatever."*

To paraphrase, Padilla and Rashkin agreed that if Padilla procured a contract, the two would then review the circumstances surrounding the contract and negotiate a commission of between one and ten percent.

Is this agreement sufficiently definite to be enforceable?

See Padilla v. RRA, Inc., 946 P.2d 1122 (N.M. Ct. App. 1997).

Chapter 5

Termination of the Offer

Contracts are a bit like magic. As a magician conjures a spell by intentionally speaking certain magic words, an ordinary person can invoke a contractual obligation through intentional words as well. Even after studying contract law for a decade, I still find it awesome and powerful that the law allows people to create binding obligations with mere words. Contracts still feel like magic to me.

The first magic moment in contract law is the creation of an offer. As discussed in the previous chapter, preliminary negotiations generally do not have any legal effect. But once an offer is made, the specter of law is invoked. An offer is an obligation waiting to spring into existence. We call this opportunity to create a legal obligation the "power of acceptance."

> *An offer gives to the offeree a continuing power to complete the manifestation of mutual assent by acceptance of the offer. R2d § 35(1).*

But such offers do not wait forever. The offer must either be accepted, in which case it transforms into a binding legal obligation; or the offer is terminated. Once an offer is terminated, it cannot be accepted.

> *A contract cannot be created by acceptance of an offer after the power of acceptance has been terminated in one of the ways listed in § 36. R2d. § 35(2).*

This module is about the termination of the offer while it is still just an offer, such that a contract never comes into being.

When an offer is made by an offeror, that offer creates a power of acceptance in the offeree. The ball, so to speak, is now in the offeree's court. The ways in which the offeree can then accept that offer are discussed in the next module. The question for this module revolves around what might happen after an offer is made but before it is accepted which may terminate the offer, making it unacceptable. The R2d provides the methods of termination of the power of acceptance:

> *An offeree's power of acceptance may be terminated by (a) rejection or counter-offer by the offeree, or (b) lapse of time, or (c) revocation by the offeror, or (d) death or incapacity of the offeror or offeree. R2d § 36(1).*

There are two main categories of actions that will kill an offer before it can mature into a binding contract. The first are affirmative actions taken by the offeror or offeree. For instance, the offeror can revoke the offer, or the offeree can reject it. The second category involves intervening events, such as a lapse of time or the death of the offeree, that terminate the offer without any affirmative action or statement by a party. In either case, an offer, once dead, cannot be unilaterally revived. However, either party is free to make a new offer on the same or similar terms as the old one.

Termination is not a factor once offer has already been accepted. Once an offer is accepted, the offer matures into a contract. A contract is a binding legal instrument. It does not die as easily as offers do. Students would be wise to watch out for fact patterns where, for example, an offeror purports to retract an offer that was already accepted (an invalid retraction), or where an offeree accepts and then changes its mind (an invalid rejection). The second half of this book deals with the interpretation and enforcement of binding contracts. For now, let us return to the making of obligations to understand where obligations are not made even though an offer was pronounced. In other words, we are analyzing whether the power of acceptance was terminated before the offer was accepted.

Rules

A. Rejection

An offeree can terminate an offer and lose the power of acceptance by rejecting the offer.

> *An offeree's power of acceptance is terminated by his rejection of the offer, unless the offeror has manifested a contrary intention.* R2d § 38(1).

Direct rejection, such as saying, "no, I am not interested in that offer," is understood to be where a party makes a clear and unequivocal manifestation, such as a statement that the party does not intend to accept an offer. But there are two complications.

> *A manifestation of intention not to accept an offer is a rejection unless the offeree manifests an intention to take it under further advisement.* R2d § 38(2).

The first complication arises where a party "manifests a contrary intention." This means that the offeree states that he will reject the offer for the present but reconsider it at a future time. For example, the statement, "I am not interested in that offer today, but I will revisit your offer tomorrow," will keep the offer alive.

Whether an offeree manifests a "contrary intention" depends on an analysis of specific facts. For example, if Susan offers to sell her laptop to Bill for $500, and Bill says, "I'm not interested at that price," that is probably a rejection by Bill that terminates the offer. However, if Bill says, "I'm not interested at that price, but let me get back to you after pay day," that might not terminate the offer because Bill has manifested a contrary intention. Bill seems to have manifested an intention to take the offer under further advisement.

Although so far, we have exemplified the manifestation of a rejection in the form of words, a manifestation of rejection can also be formed by action. To put it another way, offers can be rejected either directly or indirectly. Offers are directly rejected when the offeree says "no I am not interested" or other words that clearly reject the offer. However, offers can also be rejected indirectly, through actions.

The second complication arises where a party's actions may constitute an indirect rejection. Some actions by an offeree could reasonably signify an intention not to accept the offer. But these indirect rejections may be subject to different interpretations.

For example, Zeke offers to sell his house to Yolanda. Without affirmatively replying to Zeke, Yolanda buys Wendy's house. Zeke leans that Yolanda bought Wendy's house. Does this constitute an indirect rejection of Zeke's offer to Yolanda?

The answer to that question is not trivial to Zeke, who may not be able to sell his house to someone else while his offer to Yolanda is outstanding. Since Zeke's interests are at issue, the law considers Zeke's reasonable actions in reliance on Yolanda's actions. Since most people only buy one house at a time, it is probably reasonable for Zeke to interpret Yolanda's actions as a rejection of his offer to her. Therefore, Zeke can offer to sell his house to someone else without worrying about contractual liability to Yolanda.

B. Counter-Offer

A counter-offer functions as a rejection. What, then, is a counter-offer?

A counter-offer is an offer made by an offeree to his offeror relating to the same matter as the original offer and proposing a substituted bargain differing from that proposed by the original offer. R2d sec. 39(1).

Notice that the definition of counter-offer has several elements. First, a counter-offer must be an offer. In other words, the counter-offer itself must meet the definition of an offer, as offers were discussed in the previous module.

Second, the counter-offer must relate to the same matter. If Keisha offers to sell Xavier her car, and Xavier responds by offering to mow Keisha's lawn, Xavier's statement is not a counter-offer because it does not relate to Keisha's offer. A counter-offer would instead take the form of Xavier offering to buy Keisha's car for a lower price.

Third, the counter-offer must propose a substitute for the original bargain. If the purported counter-offer and the original offer could both be accepted at once, that is not really a counter-offer at all. For example, Alpha Investors Corporation puts out an advertisement that states, "We will buy all outstanding shares of Alpha stock for a reasonable price." This is probably not an offer but an invitation for offers because advertisements usually are not offers and the price is somewhat indeterminate here. (Although one might argue that a reasonable price for stock is the market price, it turns out that in these sorts of transactions, called "tender offers," the buyer usually pays more than the market price for the stock, and how much more depends on many factors.) Ivan emails Alpha saying, "I will sell half of my shares for $100 each." Alpha replies, "Will you sell your other half for $110 each?" Alpha has not made a counter-offer, because its offer is not a substitute for Ivan's offer; rather, Alpha's offer is a compliment to it. Alpha could both purchase the first half of the shares for $100 and the second half of the shares for $110.

> *An offeree's power of acceptance is terminated by his making of a counter-offer, unless the offeror has manifested a contrary intention or unless the counter-offer manifests a contrary intention of the offeree.* R2d § 39(2).

R2d makes clear that a counter-offer functions as a rejection. This is not the difficult part of the rule. The difficult part of applying the counter-offer rule is determining what is a counter-offer and what is an acceptance. That distinction will be discussed in detail in the next chapter.

C. Lapse of Time

When an offer is made, how long does it last before the offeree can no longer accept it? The offeror is the master of the bargain, so they can specify when the offer will expire. If the offeror says, "you have 3 days to accept the offer," then a specified time was given, and the offer will terminate after 3 days.

What happens if no time was specified? If no time was specified, then the offer lapses after a reasonable time. What constitutes a reasonable amount of time is often a factual question because it can vary depending on the circumstances in a case.

> *An offeree's power of acceptance is terminated at the time specified in the offer, or, if no time is specified, at the end of a reasonable time.* R2d § 41(1).

Generally, when offers are made during a singular conversation, the offer terminates at the end of that conversation. This is known as the "conversation rule."

The conversation rule includes both face-to-face negotiations and discussions over the telephone. It probably applies equally to any other live communication, like FaceTime, Zoom, or VR, but these new technologies have not yet been thoroughly tested in courts.

Contrary intentions will vary based on the circumstances and other specific facts about the parties involved.

D. Revocation

It is often said that the offeror is the master of the bargain. The offeror sets the terms by making the offer. And the offeror can generally revoke that offer at will.

> *An offeree's power of acceptance is terminated when the offeree receives from the offeror a manifestation of an intention not to enter into the proposed contract.* R2d § 42.

Most offers are freely revocable, meaning, the power of acceptance terminates when an offeror revokes an offer. Note that the process of revocation requires the offeree to receive notice of the revocation. Moreover, the revocation is not effective, and the power of acceptance is still available, until the offeree receives actual or constructive notice of revocation.

Actual or express revocation does not require the offeror to use magic words such as "I revoke."

> The word "revoke" is not essential to a revocation. Any clear manifestation of unwillingness to enter into the proposed bargain is sufficient. Thus a statement that property offered for sale has been otherwise disposed of is a revocation. R2d § 42 cmt. d.

For example, Aileen offers to sell her house to Brendan. Before Brendan accepts, Aileen calls Brendan and says to him, "I am feeling really nervous about selling my house, and I might not want to go through with this transaction." The reasonable interpretation of this conversation is that Aileen has revoked her offer, and so Brendan's power of acceptance is terminated.

Constructive notice or indirect communication of revocation occurs where an offeror takes an action that is inconsistent with the offer.

> An offeree's power of acceptance is terminated when the offeror takes definite action inconsistent with an intention to enter into the proposed contract and the offeree acquires reliable information to that effect. R2d § 43.

For example, if Aileen offers to sell her house to Brendan, but, before Brenan accepts, Aileen puts a sign on her property that says "sold," then Aileen has indirectly communicated that the offer is revoked. The revocation is effective when Brendan is informed of the action. For example, if Brendan drives by the house and sees the "sold" sign at 2 p.m. on Tuesday, then his power of acceptance is terminated at 2 p.m. on Tuesday. After that time, Brendan cannot accept Aileen's offer.

E. Revocation of General Offer

Advertisements are usually not offers because they typically are not manifestations of intentions to be bound and because they typically lack material terms. But in the rare cases where advertisements are offers, such as in the case of *Lefkowitz v. Great Minneapolis Supply Store*, then a special rule applies to the revocation of such "general offers."

> Where an offer is made by advertisement in a newspaper or other general notification to the public or to a number of persons whose identity is unknown to the offeror, the offeree's power of acceptance is terminated when a notice of termination is given publicity by advertisement or other general notification equal to that given to the offer and no better means of notification is reasonably available. R2d § 46.

Revoking a general offer requires a general revocation. Even when a revocation is published, it may not be effective immediately, since revocations are effective when received by the offeree.

This situation came up in *Lefkowitz*. Remember that Lefkowitz visited the Great Minneapolis Supply Store twice. The first time, he accepted the offer to purchase a fur coat worth up to $100 for $1. At that time, the store clerk told him that the store had a "house rule" that they would only sell fur coats to women (Lefkowitz was a man). This conversation regarding the house rule occurred after Lefkowitz had accepted the offer, and so a contract to sell him the coat for $1 had already been formed, and the notification of the house rule had no effect on that contract.

But then Lefkowitz came back a second time to accept a second offer to purchase a mink stole for $1. At this second visit, he had actual knowledge of the house rule. Did the clerk have to sell the stole to him?

The court found that Lefkowitz validly accepted this offer, too, because the store did not give general notice about its house rule. The advertisement is a bit hard to read, but it does not anywhere say anything about a house rule to sell only to women. The store failed to give public notice of its house rule, so that rule did not apply to its offer.

Likewise, where an offeror makes an offer via a general solicitation, it may only revoke that offer through reasonable public notice.

F. Irrevocability

Despite the general rule that the offeror is the master of the bargain who can revoke the offer at will, some offers are irrevocable. There are four ways in which an offer can be made irrevocable, which I refer to as:

- option contracts, which result in common law irrevocability;
- merchant's firm offers, which result in statutory irrevocability;
- option quasi-contracts, which result in a equitable irrevocability; and
- the part performance doctrine.

Option Contract-at-Common-Law

Common law irrevocability occurs where the parties enter into what is known as an option contract. An option contract is a special type of contract where one of the promises is to not revoke another offer, and where that promise is supported by another promise in exchange, such as a promise to pay the offeror not to revoke that other offer.

> An option contract is a promise which meets the requirements for the formation of a contract and limits the promisor's power to revoke an offer. R2d § 25.

For example, if Aileen offers to sell her house to Brendan, Brendan might bargain for time to think about her offer. If Brendan says, "I will pay you $100 if you will keep your offer open for one week," and it Aileen accepts Brendan's offer, then the parties are under an option contract which limits Aileen's power to revoke her offer for the period of one week.

Note that option contracts under common law are formed in the same way that contracts are usually formed in common law: option contracts require offer, acceptance during the power of acceptance, consideration, and a lack of defenses to formation. You can thus evaluate whether an option contract is formed in the same way that you would evaluate whether any contract is formed at common law.

The distinct feature about option contracts is not how they are formed but what they do. Option contracts make another offer irrevocable. This effect occurs even if the consideration is not paid. In the example above, if Brendan fails to pay Aileen $100, he has breached his contractual obligation to Aileen, and he is subject to damages for his breach. Whether or not Aileen is still required to perform her mutual obligation of keeping her offer to sell her house open depends on the doctrine of substantial performance and material breach, discussed in the module on performance.

Merchant's Firm Offer under the UCC

The UCC applies to sales of goods. Goods are things that are movable and identifiable at the time of sale. Some special UCC provisions apply to merchants. Merchants are persons who regularly deal in goods of the kind at issue in the transaction. Merchants are presumed to have special skill and knowledge and thus are entitled to special rules regarding how their contracts function.

The firm offer rule is one of the merchant-specific provisions of the UCC.

> *An offer by a merchant to buy or sell goods in a signed writing which by its terms gives assurance that it will be held open is not revocable, for lack of consideration, during the time stated or if no time is stated for a reasonable time, but in no event may such period of irrevocability exceed three months; but any such term of assurance on a form supplied by the offeree must be separately signed by the offeror.* UCC § 2-205.

Statutory law (the UCC) provides that merchants can make their offers irrevocable even without receiving consideration from the offeree. This is different from option contracts at common law, which require both parties to give and get something in exchange. Under common law, an offeree generally pays the offeror to keep the offer open. Under the UCC, however, merchants give binding assurance to keep an offer open even without receiving any compensation for that promise.

Generally, the merchant's firm offer will state for how long it will keep an offer open (meaning, irrevocable). If no time is stated, the offer remains open for a reasonable time, not to exceed three months.

Option Quasi-Contract-at-Equity

As you will learn when studying consideration, courts sometimes enforce promises even when that promise is not supported by a return promise in exchange. Given the general rule that courts at common law only enforce option contracts that are supported by consideration, why should and when do courts at common law make offers irrevocable when nothing is given in exchange for a promise not to revoke an offer?

The core concept is reliance. Reliance — dependance or trust by a person combined with action based on that dependance or trust — occurs where one party reasonably takes some action based on the promise of another. Detrimental reliance refers to a situation where taking that action in reliance worsens the relying party's position.

As you will see when studying consideration, detrimental reliance can serve as a substitute for or alternative to consideration. In other words, where one party reasonably and detrimentally relied on the promise of another, courts may enforce that promise even where it was not given in exchange for anything of value.

This equitable concept also applies to the formation of option contracts. Recall that options contracts, like all contracts at law, require consideration or bargained-for exchange, meaning a promise not to revoke an offer is only enforceable if the promisor receives something in exchange for that promise.

For example, if Aileen offers to sell her house to Brendan and says, "I will give you one week to think about it," she is not legally bound to this promise. Aileen's promise to keep her offer open for a week is unsupported by consideration. She is not receiving anything in exchange. Therefore, as a matter of law, courts will not require her to keep that promise. She can sell the house to someone else or take it off the market before the week's end without incurring liability to Brendan. Her promise to keep the offer open is unenforceable for want of consideration.

But what if Brendan takes some detrimental action in reasonable reliance on Aileen's offer? For example, imagine that Brendan responds by mortgaging his own house to raise the cash to pay for Aileen's. Acquiring that mortgage takes his time, reduces his credit score, and costs him closing costs. If Aileen refuses to sell her house to Brendan, then Brendan is worse off because he now has a mortgage he would not have otherwise obtained. This is an example of Brendan's detrimental reliance. When detrimental reliance is reasonable, courts may enforce the promise that caused the reliance even where there is no consideration for that promise. In his hypo, the question would be whether a reasonable person in Brendan's situation would have obtained a mortgage based on Aileen's promise to keep her offer open for one week.

I refer to this situation as a quasi-contract or an option contract at equity to distinguish it from the standard case of a classical option contract at law, which is supported by consideration. The distinction is important, because courts are required to enforce contracts at law, but they only enforce promises under contracts at equity where justice so requires. In other words, Brendan is virtually sure to win in litigation if he pays Aileen in exchange for her promise to keep her offer open. But Brendan's success in court is much less certain where he has relied on but not paid for her promise.

The Part Performance Doctrine

Most offers can be accepted either by promising to perform or by actually performing. For example, if you neighbor says, "I will give you $20 to mow my law by Friday," you can say, "OK, I will do that," or you can simply mow the law on Thursday. In either case, you have accepted the contract and are thus entitled to $20.

But some offers cannot be accepted by promising. In technical terms, some offers do not invite a promissory acceptance. Such offers are called offers for unilateral contracts or unilateral offers — unilateral meaning "one way" and referring to the one way (performance) that such offers can be accepted.

A typical example of a unilateral offer is an offer for a reward. For example, Susan posts a sign that says, "LOST DOG $1,000 REWARD IF FOUND AND RETURNED." How can you accept this offer? Susan is not inviting you to call her and promise to find her dog. She only wants to pay you if you actually return her dog to her. This is an offer than can only be accepted by performance.

Another example is a bar's trivia contest. The bar makes the offer, "FREE BEER FOR WINNER OF THE CONTEST." You cannot accept this offer by promising to win the contest and then demanding your free beer. Rather, the reasonable interpretation is that you might earn the highest score in the contest, and then you can collect your prize of free beer. This is also an example of a unilateral offer.

A third example is the classic case of *Carbolic Smoke Ball*. The Carbolic Smoke Ball company made an offer in a newspaper to pay cash to anyone who used their product as indicated and then contracted influenza. The only way to accept this offer and claim the prize was to actually use the product for one month and then get the flu. This is yet another example of an offer for a unilateral contract.

Note that in all these cases of unilateral contract, the offeree must begin performance before forming a contract. Indeed, the only way to form the contract is by completing performance. If the offer is revocable by the offeror any time before the contract is formed, this creates room for some mischief on the part of the offeror. In the lost dog example, what if Susan saw you walking down the street with her dog and then called out, "I revoke" right before you arrived at her house? If you spent the night playing trivia in a bar only for the bar to close before finishing the contest, are you denied your free beer? If the Carbolic Smoke Ball company published a revocation of its offer after you had purchased and inhaled its noxious product for three weeks, are you out of luck?

The law has developed the part performance doctrine to deal with this potential for offeror mischief in the case of unilateral offers.

> *Where an offer invites an offeree to accept by rendering a performance and does not invite a promissory acceptance, an option contract is created when the offeree tenders or begins the invited performance or tenders a beginning of it.* R2d § 45(1).

When an offeree begins performance of a unilateral offer, that offer become irrevocable for a reasonable time for the offeree to complete performance. This doctrine prevents Susan from revoking when you are at her doorstep, prevents the bar from ending the contest just before you win free beer, and prevents Carbolic Smoke Ball from denying rewards to people who purchased and used their product.

G. Death or Incapacity of the Offeror or Offeree

Unlike an indirect revocation, which is only effective where the offeree knew or should have known about the revocation, and unlike an indirect rejection, where the offeror should have known about the rejection, the death or incapacity of an offeror or offeree terminates an offer even if the other party has no notice of this event.

> *An offeree's power of acceptance is terminated when the offeree or offeror dies or is deprived of legal capacity to enter into the proposed contract.* R2d § 48.

This rule, although still followed in most jurisdictions, is out of sync with the other rules regarding termination of the power of acceptance, which all turn on reasonable notice of the termination. It appears that this rule is a holdover from a now-outdated notion that contracts require a subjective meeting of the minds. Obviously, a subjective meeting of the minds is impossible if one of those minds is now dead or incapacitated. Modern contract law generally uses an objective standard, asking how a reasonable person would interpret manifestations, but this rule does not fit with that reasoning.

Perhaps the rule remains good law because it seems unfair to hold an estate liable for offers made by a decedent that were not accepted during the decedent's lifetime. But this rule is on shaky ground. Some state legislatures have overturned it with statutes that allow banks and collection agencies to accept offers after the death of the offeror. And courts have refused to obey this rule on equitable grounds.

Since it seems possible that this rule is eroding, lawyers can make arguments why this rule should not be followed. For example, if the application of the death-of-offeree rule means that a widow does not receive a payout from an insurance company, the widow's attorney might present facts that tend to show this result is unfair, and that argument might prevail.

H. Reflection on Duration of the Offer

Offers are ephemeral. They quickly mature into contracts or decay into nothing. Offers have a natural half-life, in the sense that they lapse and decay into non-offers after some reasonable time. But offers may also be terminated by the offeror or the offeree. The offeror is the master of the bargain and generally can revoke it unless some basis for irrevocability applies. The offeree can also terminate the offer by giving the offeror reasonable basis for relying on the offeree's non-acceptance.

When an offer is terminated by the offeror or offeree, such termination is effective upon notice to the other party. This notice can be actual, such as where the offeror calls up the offeree and informs her that the deal is off, or constructive, such as where the offeree learns that the offeror concluded the bargain with someone else. This timing matters when the offeree accepts the offer before the offeror revokes it, as discussed in the section on the Mailbox Rule in the chapter on acceptance.

The exception to this timing rule regards death or incapacity of the offeror or offeree. Such death or incapacity immediately terminates the offer, even where there is no notice to the other party. This is theoretically out of sync with the modern objective view of contract formation. But the law evolves slowly, and this vestige of the subjective view of contract formation remains on the books for now.

To recap, offers create a power of acceptance in the offeree when received by that offeree. This power of acceptance terminates when the offeree receives a revocation or when the offeror receives a rejection or counter-offer. This power of acceptance also automatically terminates when the offer lapses or when the offeror or offeree dies or becomes incapacitated. Once the power of acceptance is terminated, the offer can no longer be accepted. But, so long as the offer is alive, it can be accepted as soon as the offeree sends an acceptance, as you will learn in the next lesson.

Cases

Reading Smaligo v. Fireman's Fund Insurance Co. Direct rejection may be easy to identify where a party makes a clear and unequivocal manifestation, such as a statement that the party does not intend to accept an offer. The harder case, however, arises where a party's actions may constitute an indirect rejection. The *Smaligo* case illustrates a situation where a party may have indirectly rejected an offer to settle a lawsuit by taking an action that may be considered inconsistent with entertaining a settlement offer. As you read this case, think about what sorts of actions the plaintiffs (the Smaligos) might have taken that would still have kept the settlement offer open, and what other actions they could have taken that would manifest their intention to terminate the offer.

Smaligo v. Fireman's Fund Insurance Co.

432 Pa. 133 (1968)

[Elizabeth Smaligo was a high school graduate who had also attended night classes at Duquesne University. She was employed as a secretary by Westinghouse Electric Corporation from 1949 until October 1962, when she was admitted to Western Psychiatric Hospital and diagnosed as schizophrenic at the age of 37. Elizabeth was later admitted to Mayview State Hospital and was still committed at the time of her death. She was permitted to visit her home on weekends and holidays. On March 27, 1967, during a weekend stay with her parents, Elizabeth was struck and killed by a hit-and-run driver.

Michael and Mary Smaligo, Elizabeth's parents, made a claim against their insurance company under the terms of the Uninsured Motorist Provisions of an automobile liability policy that had been issued to them by that company wherein that company had agreed to pay "all sums which the insured or his legal representative shall be legally entitled to recover as damages."

The company refused to pay the $9,750.00 asked by the Smaligos in settlement.

On July 27, 1967, the company notified the Smaligos' counsel by a letter that stated:]

> We [Fireman's Insurance Fund] concede that there is a settlement value to the case but that it is not worth $9,750, as demanded by you. In an effort to avoid further expenses and time to both, I will now make an offer to conclude this claim on an amicable basis and for the sum of $7,500, which you may convey to your clients. If the offer of $7,500 is not acceptable, I would then suggest that your arbitration papers be prepared as we have no intention of increasing this offer, feeling that it is fair and just to all parties concerned.

On August 30, 1967, Smaligos' counsel made a demand for arbitration to the American Arbitration Association. A hearing was held on December 18, 1967, which resulted in the arbitrator awarding only $243.

The Smaligos argued that there was an offer and acceptance of a settlement in the amount of $7,500. However, we are constrained to agree with the reasoning of the lower court that, when the Smaligos filed for arbitration of the dispute, they rejected the offer of settlement. The letter quoted offering the $7,500 clearly stated that the company was "now" offering the same and that if it is not acceptable then Smaligos should proceed to arbitration.

By proceeding to arbitration, the Smaligos showed the offer was not acceptable and such conduct clearly showed that the Smaligos did not intend to accept the offer nor take it under further advisement.

Reflection

Smaligo illustrates how an offer is indirectly rejected based on conduct inconsistent with the offer.

R2d § 38 states:

> A manifestation of intention not to accept an offer is a rejection unless the offeree manifests an intention to take it under further advisement.

In this case, the insurance company clearly offered the Smaligos $7,500 and that if the Smaligos found this unacceptable, they could proceed with arbitration, but they would not be increasing the offer. The Smaligos chose to proceed with arbitration, therefore rejecting the offer from the insurance company. The Smaligos made it clear that they found the amount unacceptable and showed no intent to take the offer under further advisement.

The important takeaway from this case is that offers can be indirectly rejected. Offers can be rejected by a manifestation of intent not to accept.

Discussion

1. How can offers be rejected? Can you distinguish between an express versus an implied rejection?

2. Why should rejection terminate the power of acceptance? Consider how a rejection impacts the offeror and what a reasonable offeror might due upon receiving a rejection.

3. Why did the Smaligos' filing for arbitration implicitly reject the Insurance Fund's offer to settle the case? What else might the Smaligos have done to avoid terminating their power of acceptance?

Reading Yaros v. Trustees of University of Pennsylvania. When an offer is made, how long does it last before the offeree can no longer accept it? The offeror is the master of the bargain, so they can specify when the offer will expire. If the offeror says, "you have 3 days to accept the offer," then a specified time was given, and the offer will terminate after 3 days.

What happens if no time was specified? If no time was specified, then the offer lapses after a reasonable time. What constitutes a reasonable amount of time is often a factual question because it can vary depending on the circumstances in a case. As you read the *Yaros* case below, pay attention to how the court determined what a reasonable amount of time should have been, given the situation and whether offers always end at the end of conversations. This case also introduces the "conversation rule" while simultaneously providing an exception to it.

Yaros v. Trustees of University of Pa.

742 A.2d 1118 (Pa. Super. Ct. 1999)

ORIE MELVIN, J.:

This is an appeal from an Order entered February 22, 1999, granting appellee Dr. Nancy Yaros's Motion to Enforce Settlement against appellant, the Trustees of the University of Pennsylvania ("University"). For the reasons that follow, we affirm.

The record reveals Dr. Yaros brought a negligence action against the University after she fell at one of its ice skating rinks. Trial was held before the Honorable Paul Ribner. At trial, attorney Richard P. Haaz represented Dr. Yaros. Counsel for the University was John Orlando. Also present was Erika Gross, who was the liability administrator for the University. Testimony began on January 26, 1998. On that date, the University offered Dr. Yaros a settlement offer of $750,000.00. Attorney Haaz informed Attorney Orlando that Dr. Yaros would accept $1.5 million in settlement up until the time she testified, after which she would not settle for any amount. The trial continued, two defense witnesses took the stand, and then Dr. Yaros testified. No settlement was reached at that time.

On January 29, 1998, after the conclusion of testimony, the University offered Dr. Yaros $750,000.00 in settlement. Attorney Orlando made the offer to Attorney Haaz during a ten minute recess prior to closing arguments. At the close of the conversation Attorney Orlando told Attorney Haaz "you've got to get back to me." When he made this statement, Attorney Orlando looked at the clock and placed his palms sideward. No time limitations regarding the offer were communicated, nor was it indicated that the offer was only open until closing arguments began. Attorney Haaz stated he would talk to his client now. After the offer was made Attorney Haaz left the courtroom to speak to his client. Attorney Orlando also left the courtroom to go to the men's restroom. Attorney Haaz returned to the courtroom without Dr. Yaros, who was in the restroom. Attorney Haaz asked the trial court for two minutes to speak to his client before closings, to which the court agreed. At that time Attorney Orlando assumed Attorney Haaz had not discussed the offer with Dr. Yaros.

Upon Dr. Yaros's return, Attorney Haaz did not confer with her and closing arguments commenced immediately. Earlier that day, Judge Ribner informed both counsel he expected closing arguments to be finished by 5:00 p.m. so he could charge the jury the next day. During the University's closing, Dr. Yaros authorized Attorney Haaz to accept the offer. After the University ended its closing, Attorney Haaz gave his rebuttal. At a sidebar conference following closings Attorney Haaz stated Dr. Yaros accepted the University's settlement offer. Attorney Orlando replied by stating, "I don't know if it's still there, judge." The next day, prior to jury deliberations Dr. Yaros orally moved to enforce the settlement. Judge Ribner denied the motion pending evidentiary hearings on the matter and the jury's verdict. The jury came back with a defense verdict. Following trial, Dr. Yaros filed a Motion for Post-Trial Relief and a Motion to Enforce Settlement. One evidentiary hearing was held before Judge Ribner. However, upon his retirement the case was reassigned to the Honorable Sandra Mazer Moss, who conducted hearings on January 12 and 15, 1999. On February 22, 1999, Judge Mazer Moss granted Dr. Yaros's Motion to Enforce Settlement. This timely appeal followed.

On appeal, the University raises several allegations of error in connection with the trial court's enforcement of the settlement. It presents the following issues for our review:

1. Whether the Trial Court erred in granting [Dr. Yaros's] Motion to Enforce Settlement, which overturns a unanimous jury verdict for [the University], even though the Trial Court failed to apply the proper legal standard for determining whether there was a valid and enforceable settlement agreement between the parties?

2. Whether the Trial Court erred in granting [Dr. Yaros's] Motion to Enforce Settlement, even though, as a matter of law, [Dr. Yaros's] conduct constituted a rejection of the settlement offer?

3. Whether the Trial Court erred in granting [Dr. Yaros's] Motion to Enforce Settlement, even though, as a matter of law, [Dr. Yaros] did not accept the settlement offer within a reasonable time under the circumstances, and therefore allowed the offer to lapse?

4. Whether the Trial Court's factual finding that [Dr. Yaros] accepted the University's offer within a reasonable period of time was against the weight of the evidence, capricious and erroneous as a matter of law?

We first address the University's contention the trial court failed to apply the proper legal standard in determining whether there was a valid and enforceable settlement. Initially, we note the University's first claim on appeal challenges the trial court's conclusions of law. When reviewing questions of law, our scope of review is plenary. Thus, we are free to draw our own inferences and reach our own conclusions. "If a trial court erred in its application of the law, [we] will correct the error."

The trial court found the University's offer was not withdrawn and Dr. Yaros accepted it within a reasonable amount of time under the circumstances. In analyzing whether this was a valid and enforceable settlement agreement the trial court relied upon the standards set forth in *Vaskie v. West American Ins. Co.*, wherein this Court stated:

> Under such circumstances, i.e. where an offer does not specify an expiration date or otherwise limit the allowable time for acceptance, it is both hornbook law and well-established in Pennsylvania that the offer is deemed to be outstanding for a reasonable period of time.

The University asserts the above legal standard is only a general rule. It maintains the "conversation rule" as stated in Restatement (Second) Contracts § 41, comment d governs. That comment provides as follows:

> d. Direct negotiations. Where the parties bargain face to face or over the telephone, the time for acceptance does not ordinarily extend beyond the end of the conversation unless a contrary intention is indicated. A contrary intention may be indicated by express words or by the circumstances. For example, the delivery of a written offer to the offeree, or an expectation that some action will be taken before acceptance, may indicate that a delayed acceptance is invited.

Our Court has adopted the legal standard enunciated in comment d; *Textron, Inc. v. Froelich* (stating "an oral offer ordinarily terminates at the end of the conversation"); and *Boyd v. Merchants' and Farmers' Peanut Co.* (stating "[w]hen an offer is made to another orally and he goes away without accepting it, it would seem that ordinarily the offer would be considered as having lapsed").

In *Textron*, the Court acknowledged that this standard does not preclude the possibility that an oral offer continues past the conversation and noted the general rule that if no time is specified, the offer terminates at the end of a reasonable amount of time. Furthermore, the Court stated while there may be times when a judge could find as a matter of law that an oral offer terminates with the end of the conversation, if there is any doubt as to what is a reasonable interpretation, the decision should be left to the factfinder. The University insists that because of the face-to-face nature of the negotiations, the offer terminated at the end of the conversation between counsel or at the very latest at the beginning of closing arguments.

Because the parties' counsel conducted face-to-face negotiations it appears comment d initially provides the more on point legal standard; however, this does not affect the trial court's ultimate decision. The offer by the University clearly extended beyond the end of counsels' conversation, during the court recess when Attorney Haaz walked out of the courtroom to speak with his client about the settlement offer. A contrary intention was clearly indicated by Attorney Orlando when he ended the conversation with Attorney Haaz by stating "get back to me." Thus, the time for acceptance by Dr. Yaros extended beyond the end of the conversation between the parties' attorneys. The question that then arises is how long was the offer open. The University maintains it intended the offer was only open until the beginning of closing arguments, and such intention was clear. It submits that although Attorney Orlando did not articulate explicitly a definite time limit for Dr. Yaros's acceptance, its intention was manifested by the fact closing arguments were imminent, the established pattern of including an event condition with a settlement offer, and the verbal and non-verbal expressions used.

The enforceability of settlement agreements is determined according to principles of contract law. "[I]n the case of a disputed oral contract, what was said and done by the parties as well as what was intended by what was said and done by them are questions of fact." We find preposterous the University's assertion that its intention regarding the time limitation of the offer was clear. The trial court made a factual determination that no time or event conditions were ever placed on the settlement offer.

Here, the duration of the offer was not even clear to its trial counsel Attorney Orlando or its risk manager, Erika Gross. After Dr. Yaros accepted the offer Attorney Orlando stated, "I don't know if it's still there, judge." Certainly, if Attorney Orlando, the offeror, was unclear of whether the offer was still open after closing arguments were complete, it's incredulous to argue the offeree, Dr. Yaros, was clearly aware that the offer would lapse once closing arguments began. Moreover, we reject the University's claim that verbal and non-verbal conduct made the time limitation of the offer apparent. The University argues Attorney Orlando's statement "you've got to get back to me" can only be interpreted as "you've got to get back to me with an answer as soon as possible — which is, when we both come back into the courtroom: you from your discussion with your client and I from the Men's Room, so we can conclude this negotiation in the next few minutes before closings." We will not reject the trial court's findings in favor of such a strained interpretation of the statement, "you've got to get back to me," or conduct like Attorney Haaz's statement that he needed two minutes to speak with his client and Attorney Orlando's non-verbal act of looking at the clock and "put[ting] [his] palms sidewards."

Additionally, the University makes much of the fact that Dr. Yaros had earlier during the trial imposed an event condition on a settlement offer. During trial Attorney Haaz informed Attorney Orlando that Dr. Yaros would accept a settlement in a certain dollar amount only up until the time she testified. The University now maintains this established a pattern of including an event condition with a settlement offer. While the prior course of dealings between the parties is instructive, in this case it cuts against the University's argument. In the parties' prior course of dealings, Dr. Yaros and her counsel explicitly informed the University of the event condition. There was no such explanation when the University made its offer just prior to closing arguments. Moreover, the offer remained open during the course of several witnesses' testimony. Under such circumstances, the prior course of dealing between the parties did not establish closing argument was an event which would terminate the offer.

The University next argues Dr. Yaros's conduct constituted a rejection of the offer. Specifically, it maintains that because Attorney Haaz did not confer with Dr. Yaros when she returned to the courtroom just prior to closings and because Dr. Yaros participated in closing and rebuttal arguments without accepting the offer, it was justified in inferring she had in fact rejected the offer. The trial court found Dr. Yaros never rejected the offer. The court further rebuffed the University's contention that it could infer its offer had been rejected when closing arguments commenced.

An offer is rejected when the offeror is justified in inferring from the words or conduct of the offeree that the offeree intends not to accept the offer or to take it under further advisement. In *Smaligo*, an insurance company made a settlement offer informing the offeree plaintiffs that proceeding forward with the case would be viewed as a rejection. The plaintiffs proceeded to arbitration. This Court agreed with the trial court that plaintiffs' action clearly showed that they did not intend to accept the offer. Unlike *Smaligo*, this is not a situation where the offeree was placed on notice that certain conduct would constitute a rejection of the offer. While an offeree need not be put on specific notice that certain conduct will be viewed by the offeror as a rejection of the offer, not all conduct can justify an offeror in inferring that the offer has been rejected. In this case we can find no error in the trial court's finding that the University was not justified in inferring that proceeding to closing arguments would constitute a rejection of the settlement offer.

There is no per se rule that commencing with closing arguments constitutes a rejection of a settlement offer. Nor do we wish to create one here. It would produce a situation where an offeror would have the unfair advantage of unilaterally asserting after the offer has been accepted that an unspecified, undefined and uncommunicated event at trial constituted a rejection. Moreover, we agree with Dr. Yaros's observation that since the University believed she had not had an opportunity to consult with her counsel and was unaware of the settlement offer, it would not be justified in inferring that proceeding to closing arguments constituted a rejection of the offer. How the University could interpret the actions of Dr. Yaros and Attorney Haaz as a rejection of its offer when the University was under the impression Dr. Yaros was unaware of the offer at that time is beyond our understanding.

The University finally argues the settlement offer lapsed because, as a matter of law, Dr. Yaros did not accept it within a reasonable amount of time. It submits the trial court's factual finding that Dr. Yaros accepted the offer within a reasonable amount of time was against the weight of the evidence. Where an offer does not specify an expiration date or otherwise limit the allowable time for acceptance, the offer is deemed to be outstanding for a reasonable period of time. In *Vaskie*, this Court examined the issue of whether reasonableness is a question of law or of fact:

> *What is a reasonable time is ordinarily a question of fact to be decided by the jury and is dependent upon the numerous circumstances surrounding the transaction. Such circumstances as the nature of the contract, the relationship or situation of the parties and their course of dealing, and usages of the particular business are all relevant.*

However, there are situations where the question of what is a reasonable time for acceptance may be decided by the court as a matter of law. As stated in *Boyd*:

> *What is a reasonable time for acceptance is a question of law for the court in such commercial transactions as happen in the same way, day after day, and present the question upon the same data in continually recurring instances; and where the time taken is so clearly reasonable or unreasonable that there can be no question of doubt as to the proper answer to the question. Where the answer to the question is one dependent on many different circumstances, which do not continually recur in other cases of like character, and with respect to which no certain rule of law could be laid down, the question is one of fact for the jury.*

After holding numerous evidentiary hearings, the trial court treated this issue as a question of fact, finding the time period was reasonable under the circumstances. The University believes this is a question of law because trials happen in the same manner every day in the sense that the significant events of trial such as opening arguments, the presentation of evidence, and closing arguments proceed in the same manner in every trial. While trials do commence in the same manner, "the course and nature of settlement negotiations varies greatly from case to case." There are individual circumstances distinct to this case, such as when and how the offer was made, which will not necessarily continually recur in other cases. Thus, we believe the trial court was correct in treating this as a question of fact.

As a reviewing court we will not disturb the findings of a trial judge sitting as the finder of fact unless there is a determination that those findings are not based upon competent evidence. In reviewing the trial court's findings, the victorious party is entitled to have the evidence viewed in the light most favorable to him and all the evidence must be taken as true and all unfavorable inferences rejected. Moreover, the trial court's decision should not be overturned unless the trial court's factual findings were capricious or against the weight of the evidence.

In support of its contention that a reasonable amount of time to accept the offer had lapsed, the University rehashes the same arguments we have already addressed.

The University maintains, although it did not articulate explicitly a definite time limit for acceptance, it limited the duration of the offer through its words and body language. As we have already found such conduct would not put Dr. Yaros on notice of any event condition on the offer, we will not discuss it further.

The University also submits the seventy minutes Dr. Yaros took to accept the offer was unreasonable in light of the fact the offer occurred during trial. It maintains there is an urgency that accompanies a response when an offer is made during the course of trial, and in such a context the actual amount of minutes from offer to acceptance is irrelevant. In effect, the University maintains where an offer is made immediately before closing arguments it is unreasonable for the offer to stay open beyond the commencement of closings, which in this case occurred approximately ten minutes after the offer was made.

In this regard the University makes much of the trial court's finding that closing arguments are not significant trial court events, instead arguing that "academic research, the wisdom of modern trial practitioners and more than two thousand years of jurisprudential history" require us to vacate the trial court's order. The University's argument is misplaced because the trial court made its observation regarding the significance of closings to address the University's argument that a rejection could be inferred when Dr. Yaros participated in closings. Whether or not closing arguments are significant trial events does not support the University's contention that the occurrence of closing arguments automatically causes a settlement offer to lapse. There are many significant events during the course of a trial. Settlement offers are accepted at all stages of trial. Even assuming a closing argument is a significant trial event, such an occurrence does not necessarily determine whether an offeree accepted an offer within a reasonable period of time. It is but one consideration.

Here, the trial court found the offer was accepted within a reasonable amount of time under the circumstances. We will not disturb that finding. Under the facts of this case, we cannot say the trial court erred in finding Dr. Yaros accepted the offer within a reasonable amount of time or such a finding was against the weight of the evidence. In conclusion, we find no abuse of discretion or error of law in the trial court's enforcement of the settlement.

Order affirmed.

Reflection

Yaros features a particularly interesting discussion on whether an offer ordinarily lapses at the end of a conversation. The general rule is that an offer ends along with the conversation that started it, unless circumstances indicate otherwise. If a Dunder Mifflin sales representative calls you and asks whether you'd like to purchase 10 reams of paper for a special discount of 20%, you cannot necessarily call back next week and expect that deal to still be available. But, of course, it all depends on the circumstances. If that is the third time in as many weeks that the rep called you with the same special price, a court would probably consider it reasonable if you called back an hour after the third call to accept the offer.

The *Yaros* court likewise held that, although the "conversation rule" is the good default rule, not all offers end at the end of conversations. In this case, a face-to-face meeting between an authorized agent of a University and a Professor included the University's offer of employment to the Professor and ended with the University's agent saying, "get back to me." The University tried to argue that, as a matter of law, their offer terminated at the end of the meeting. But the court was unconvinced. "Get back to me" is at least unclear, so summary judgment (a civil procedure standard that allows a court to decide a case as a matter of law without presenting conflicting facts to a jury) was not appropriate. Moreover, it was possible for a reasonable jury to find that the University's agent expressed an intention that was contrary to the default rule. Therefore, the court did not reverse the jury's ruling that the Professor's acceptance was within a reasonable amount of time.

The case also nicely reflects R2d § 41's reasoning. The rule for when an offer lapses is that it terminates at the time specified in the offer, or if unspecified, it terminates at the end of a reasonable time. A reasonable time may be until the end of a meeting or phone call, but this is not necessarily the end of an offer. A party who wishes to avoid contractual liability for an offer should make it clear when the offer has expired. Otherwise, there is room to argue that an acceptance was made within a reasonable time.

Discussion

1. What is the "conversation rule"? Is this rule based on formal legal principles, or a realistic understanding of parties' likely intentions?

2. What facts in the *Yaros* case indicate whether the conversation rule applies here? What you learn from this specific case about when the conversation rule applies more generally?

3. When the conversation rule does not apply, what other events or happenings aside from the end of a conversation should cause an offer to lapse?

Problems

Problem 5.1. The Prisoners' Rejection and the Master Plan

In early 1978, prisoners at the Washington State Reformatory filed a class action on behalf of all present and future Reformatory inmates, alleging that the conditions of their confinement were unconstitutional. A trial date was set for January 15, 1981. As often happens on the eve before trial, the parties sought to reach a last-minute agreement before the trial began, and this was apparently effective. On January 13, the parties gave notice of a mutual settlement, and the trial was cancelled. On January 19, a proposed consent decree was issued by the Washington State Reformatory. The proposed consent decree (a type of settlement that functions as a contract and which must be approved by a judge) provided that the Reformatory would reduce its population from 865 to 656 over the course of two years.

However, there was an error in the consent decree. The Reformatory's plan provided that the Reformatory's population reduction would be accomplished by March 1, 1983, instead of April 1, 1983. On February 13, 1981, the state submitted a revised consent decree, listing April 1, 1983, as the deadline for the reduction. On February 26, the prisoners moved for approval of the consent decree with the March 1 date intact. The state moved for modification of the decree to incorporate the April 1 date.

On March 4, 1981, the magistrate denied both the state's and the prisoners' motions, finding there had been no meeting of the minds with respect to a key term of the agreement and therefore no contract had been formed.

On May 15, 1981, the prisoners filed a notice stating that they accepted the offer of settlement embodied in the proposed decree submitted by the state on February 13, which was the decree that listed April 1 as the deadline for reduction, not March 1.

Did the prisoners reject the decree that listed April 1 as the deadline for the reduction when they moved to approve the master plan with the March 1 deadline?

See Collins v. Thompson, 679 F.2d 168 (9th Cir. 1982).

Problem 5.2. **A MINI Lapse**

MINI is a British automotive marque that is now owned by the German automotive company BMW. BMW designed, manufactured, sold, and serviced MINI cars through its dealer network. Mini Works, a company that is not in BMW's dealer network, sold, and serviced pre-owned MINI cars. BMW contacted Mini Works and offered to refrain from filing a lawsuit seeking monetary relief if Mini Works agreed in writing to cease and desist using MINI trademarks. BMW's letter stated:

> It is our client's hope that this matter can be amicably resolved and that it will have your cooperation in discontinuing use of BMW's trademarks. Specifically, BMW requests that you:
>
> (1) Promptly drop "MINI" from your trade name and domain names;
>
> (2) Cease and desist any and all other trademark use of MINI marks on your websites or elsewhere;
>
> (3) Countersign and return the acknowledgement on page 4 of this letter, by June 21, 2007.
>
> If your company meets BMW's request to cease and desist, then BMW will consider the matter closed and will not seek monetary or other relief regarding this matter from you or your company. We look forward to your response by June 21.

On July 3, 2007, Mini Works signed and returned the acknowledgement. BMW sued Mini Works trying to enforce the settlement agreement, since Mini Works continued to infringe on its trademarks. Mini Works argued that BMW's offer expired on its own terms, and they could not have accepted it.

Did BMW's offer lapse by the time that Mini Works returned the letter?

See BMW of N.A., LLC v. Mini Works, LLC, 166 F. Supp. 3d 976 (D. Ariz. 2010).

Problem 5.3. **Docked Out Settlement**

Jason Varney is a master dock builder and was the star of a cable television show called "Docked Out." He is also the president and sole shareholder of plaintiff Varney Entertainment Group, Inc. (collectively, "Varney"). Avon Plastics Inc. manufactures products used to build docks.

In 2016, Varney and Avon entered into a written Endorsement Agreement, under which Mr. Varney agreed to promote Avon's brand and products and allow Avon to use his name and likeness for two years in exchange for payment. The contract allowed Avon to terminate the contract early if "Docked Out" was no longer broadcast on television. It also contained a prevailing party attorney fee provision (meaning, the losing party in any litigation must pay the winning party's attorney fees).

Midway through the contract term, "Docked Out" was cancelled. Avon then unilaterally terminated the agreement and stopped paying Varney. Varney challenged the termination because "Docked Out" reruns remained available for viewing on the internet. A debate between the parties ensued regarding the meaning of the contractual term regarding "broadcast." Varney claimed that reruns counted as broadcasting while Avon argued that they did not. The parties were unable to resolve their differences, and Avon refused to pay Varney any more money. Varney responded by suing Avon for $250,000, which is the amount Varney claimed Avon still owed under the Endorsement Agreement.

Just before the lawsuit went to trial, Varney sent Avon a settlement offer in the form a letter in which Varney offered to voluntarily dismiss his lawsuit in exchange for Avon paying Varney $190,000. Three days later, before Avon replied, Varney sent a second letter in which he "clarified . . . that his offer is contingent on Avon entering into a stipulated judgment in favor of Varney," effectively stating that Varney was the prevailing party in the suit. The next day, Avon initiated a wire transfer on a Monday for $190,000 exactly, and then Varney voluntarily dismissed its suit.

Varney accepted the wire transfer and then sued Avon for $60,000 in attorney's fees. Avon refused to pay these fees, arguing that it accepted Varney's initial offer to settle, and further arguing that the common meaning of settlement does not contemplate that either party wins, therefore Varney is not entitled to attorney's fees. Varney counter-argued that his second letter implicitly revoked his first offer and replaced it with his second offer, so that Avon's acceptance of the first offer was ineffective, and that Avon accepted his second offer to pay the settlement plus attorney's fees.

How should a court rule on the question of whether Avon owes Varney attorney's fees?

See Varney Ent. Group, Inc. v. Avon Plastics, Inc., 275 Cal. Rptr. 3d 394 (Cal. App. 4th Dist. 2011).

Chapter 6

Acceptance

When an offer to contract is made, that offer creates a power of acceptance in the offeree. The power of acceptance does not last forever; rather, it can be terminated pursuant to the methods discussed in the lesson on duration of the offer. But, so long as that power exits, an offeree can create a contract by sending an acceptance to the offeror.

A valid acceptance will complete the process of contract formation, instantaneously transforming a mere offer into a binding contract. This lesson is about determining whether and when that magic moment of contract formation occurs.

Sometimes it is easy to determine when an offer is accepted. In a simple offer with few terms, a simple "I agree" or "I accept" can seal the deal. For example, if Aaron says to Benjamin, "Will you commit to purchasing my Honda Civic next Tuesday for $10,000 cash?", and if Benjamin immediately replies, "I do," that simple offer was simply accepted.

In the real world of commerce, however, offers are often quite complex. They may contain various terms, conditions, representations, and warranties. In situations that involve more complex terms, it is more likely that the offeror's manifestation of the offer does not exactly match the offeree's purported acceptance. For example, if Caitlin says to Deltona, "Will you commit to purchasing my Honda Civic next Tuesday for $10,000 cash?," and if Deltona replies, "I'll bring the cash on Wednesday," we now have to analyze whether Deltona's response was an acceptance, which creates a contract, or a counter-offer, which rejects the original offer and replaces it with a new offer that the original offeror (Caitlin in this case) can accept or reject.

The most significant challenge in dealing with the concept of acceptance is distinguishing acceptance from counter-offer. This distinction is critical because an acceptance turns an offer into a contract, whereas a counter-offer terminates the original offer. This distinction is especially challenging because the common law and the UCC define acceptance differently.

As you learned in the lesson on duration of the offer, an offer can only be accepted while the offeree has the power of acceptance, and that power can be terminated by several methods. The analysis of whether an offer is alive at the time of acceptance is preliminary to determining whether a manifestation is an acceptance or a counter-offer, so review that prior lesson before moving on to this one.

There is one quirky timing issue that is worth mentioning at the outset of this lesson, which involves the difference in timing between sending and receiving information. Recall that offers become effective when received by the offeree. This makes sense: how could a person manifest acceptance of an offer of which he or she is not aware? Likewise, rejection and counter-offer operate as termination of the offer when they are received by the offeror, and revocation terminates the offer when received by the offeree. Yet acceptance is different. An acceptance is effective as soon as it is sent.

The rules that acceptances are effective when sent means that an acceptance can supersede a previously sent rejection. For example, if an offeree put a letter containing a rejection into the overnight mail, and later that same day, the offeree also mails an acceptance, then the acceptance occurs before the rejection, and the offer is accepted.

This quirky timing issue used to come up more often when people sent offers, acceptances, and rejections by mail, which could take days to arrive. These timing rules regarding offer, duration of the offer, and acceptance, are generally grouped together into what is known at the Mailbox Rule.

Rules

A. Acceptance Under the Common Law: The Mirror Image Rule

The Mirror Image Rule is a common law rule that requires the offeree's acceptance to "mirror" the offer by matching its terms exactly. This rule allowed the offeror to be the master of the offer and to set all the terms. The offeree would then have to match all the terms exactly in the acceptance. To put this another way, the acceptance must comply with terms of the offer.

> *(1) Acceptance of an offer is a manifestation of assent to the terms thereof made by the offeree in a manner invited or required by the offer.*
>
> *(2) Acceptance by performance requires that at least part of what the offer requests be performed or tendered and includes acceptance by a performance which operates as a return promise.*
>
> *(3) Acceptance by a promise requires that the offeree complete every act essential to the making of the promise.* R2d § 50.
>
> *An acceptance must comply with the requirements of the offer as to the promise to be made or the performance to be rendered.* R2d § 58.

Under common law, the offeree cannot change any of the terms when accepting. A purported acceptance which changes terms or qualifies or conditions the acceptance on any change or addition to the terms is not an acceptance but rather a counter-offer.

An acceptance which requests a change or addition to the terms of the offer is not thereby invalidated unless the acceptance is made to depend on an assent to the changed or added terms. R2d § 61.

A reply to an offer which purports to accept it but is conditional on the offeror's assent to terms additional to or different from those offered is not an acceptance but is a counter-offer. R2d § 59.

In the past, courts applied the Mirror Image Rule strictly and required the terms of the offer and acceptance to match exactly. For example, in the 1867 case of *Myers v. Smith*, the offeror wrote an offer to sell malt "delivered on the boat at Weedsport." The offeree responded by letter accepting and stating that the malt was to be "deliverable by boat on Weedsport." The words "delivered" and "deliverable" were not synonymous and deemed different enough that it was a "manifest variance of the terms of the offer." The Myers court found that the use of the word deliverable in the purported acceptance made that a counter-offer, such that no contract was formed.

Modern Mirror Image Rule Example: P & W Railroad. Modern courts do not apply the Mirror Image Rule so strictly. Rather, modern courts tend to recognize that a contract exists despite minor differences between the offer and acceptance. The acceptance must be definite and unequivocal, but an inconsequential change in terms will generally be ignored.

The modern common law approach to the Mirror Image Rule is found in the case on *Rhode Island Department of Transportation v. Providence & Worcester Railroad Company*, below. In that case, a railroad company wanted to sell some land it owned on which there were some railroad tracks. Pursuant to a state statute, the railroad company was required to offer the land to the State of Rhode Island first, before selling that land to anyone else, because the state has what is called the Right of First Offer.

Providence & Worcester Railroad Company wrote to the Rhode Island State Department of Transportation, offering to sell the land for $100,000. Critically, in that offer letter, the railroad company said that it would fulfill its obligation to remove the tracks from the property before the sale. Apparently, the railroad company had no such obligation, and, moreover, the state wanted to use the tracks. The director of transportation for the State of Rhode Island wrote back to the railroad company, purporting to accept the offer while saying, "Of course, you understand that certain wording in the Real Estate Sales Agreement relating to 'buyer' and obligations concerning the removal of track would be inappropriate to the purpose of the State's purchase."

To summarize, the offer included the seller's promise to remove railroad tracks at its own expense, and the purported acceptance told the seller not to bother and to leave the tracks in place. Was this an acceptance or a counter-offer?

Under the strict, traditional version of the Mirror Image Rule, this is a counter-offer, because it qualifies the purported acceptance with a change in terms. But when you think about the change, was this really a problem for the offeror? Did this really depose the offeror from its lofty position as master of the bargain?

The *P & W RR* court reasoned,

> When an offeree, in its acceptance of an offer, absolves the offeror of a material obligation, the "rules of contract construction and the 'rules of common sense'" preclude construing that absolution as an additional term that invalidates the acceptance.

Following this so-called rule of common sense, the court reasoned that the reference to removing the tracks was immaterial because it conferred a clear benefit to the seller, who could thereby avoid the cost of removing the tracks. This was a change in terms by the offeree, but, since the change benefitted the offeror, it still constituted a valid acceptance.

In addition, the seller had written the buyer's name wrong in the offer, and the buyer corrected this in its acceptance. The seller again tried to argue that this change violated the Mirror Image Rule. This second argument proved even weaker than the first. The name of the buyer was changed out of an obvious necessity. Moreover, the state also made it clear that it was making a positive acceptance by stating in their letter that they accepted the offer to purchase the land.

While the *P & W RR* case is often cited as authority that the strict version of the mirror image rule does not apply in general, take a minute to think about what might have really been going on in this case. Why, do you think, did the railroad company argue that the state's reply was not a valid acceptance? Why did the railroad company not want to sell the land to the state?

Recall that the railroad company only offered to sell its land to the state because a state statute gave the state the right of first offer. I believe that the railroad company was trying to find a loophole whereby it met its statutory obligation in a technical sense yet was still able to sell the land to someone else. I think the court saw through this ruse and bent the Mirror Image Rule to prevent this perceived injustice. For this reason, I am not sure that the case is as generally applicable as some others believe it to be. I am particularly skeptical that courts would always find that a change in terms by the offeree that benefits the offeror does not violate the Mirror Image Rule, if only for the reason that courts are poorly equipped to determine what changes benefit the offeror and which detriment the offeror.

In my opinion, the court's holding that the change in the buyer's name did not violate the Mirror Image Rule more closely reflects the modern view that the mirror image rule does not need to be strictly adhered to. Today, the Mirror Image Rule is subject to common sense, and minor differences regarding immaterial terms that have no bearing on the original offer will not defeat acceptance. Especially in cases where it would be unfair to strictly apply the Mirror Image Rule, courts are willing to recognize valid acceptances when there are minor discrepancies about immaterial matters between the offer and acceptance.

B. Acceptance Under the UCC: Battle of the Forms

Under the common law, if the offeree did not accept every single term in the contract, or if the offeree attempted to add or change a term, then no binding contract was formed. The common law rule is called the "Mirror Image Rule." The UCC, however, expressly rejects the Mirror Image Rule and adopts what is known as the "Battle of the Forms."

Battle of the Forms refers to the common situation in which one party makes an offer, to which the offeree responds with slightly different terms, and then the parties proceed with the transaction without ever signing any final contract. The UCC formed the rule so that contracts can still be created via the exchange of nonmatching forms. The rule was created in recognition that parties may have intended to enter a contract even though the forms they exchanged were not the mirror image of each other.

> *A definite and seasonable expression of acceptance or a written confirmation which is sent within a reasonable time operates as an acceptance even though it states terms additional to or different from those offered or agreed upon, unless acceptance is expressly made conditional on assent to the additional or different terms.* UCC § 2-207(1).

The "Battle of the Forms" rule is only applied in cases where there was "definite and reasonable acceptance." For example, if a grocery store owner makes an offer to a peach farmer for the purchase of 15 dozen peaches for $250, and the peach farmer responds with an offer expressing that he would sell ten dozen peaches for $250, Battle of the Forms would not apply. The famer and store owner expressly and substantially disagreed on the quantity of peaches, a core term of the contract.

If the acceptance does not seek to change terms in the offer, but rather purports to add additional terms that were not in the original offer, the result depends on whether both parties are "merchants." Merchants are people or companies that commonly transact regarding the goods involved in this transaction. For example, a peach farmer and a grocer are both merchants with regards to peaches. The UCC applies different rules to merchants and non-merchants.

If either party is not a merchant, then the additional terms are "knocked out." The terms that do not match are knocked out of the agreement so that the contract only contains the mutually agreed-upon terms. The additional terms are mere proposals to modify the contract, which can be accepted or not by the other party. Any remaining gaps in the contract are filled by the UCC's default terms.

> *[If either party is not a merchant, then the] additional terms are to be construed as proposals for addition to the contract.* UCC § 2-207(2).

If the parties are merchants, however, and if there are additional terms included in the acceptance of the offer, those terms do become a part of the final contract unless: (1) the original offer specifically said that no terms can be added, (2) the new terms materially alter the contract, or (3) the offeror objects to the new terms within a reasonable time.

> *Between merchants such terms become part of the contract unless: (a) the offer expressly limits acceptance to the terms of the offer; (b) they materially alter it; or (c) notification of objection to them has already been given or is given within a reasonable time after notice of them is received.* UCC § 2-207(2).

The merchants' version of the Battle of the Forms is sometimes called the Last Shot Rule because the merchant who send the last form (who takes the last shot at defining the terms) wins the battle. This Last Shot Rule should be contrasted with the Knock-Out Rule, which applies to non-merchants under the UCC.

Merchants' Battle of the Forms Example: Flender v. Tippins. The 2003 case of *Flender Corporation v. Tippins International Incorporation*, below, illustrates a common application of the merchant's Battle of the Forms. Tippins mailed a Purchase Order to Flender for the purchase of some custom-made gear drive assemblies, which are goods. Tippins's Purchase Order included an arbitration clause which specified that any dispute under the contract must be submitted to arbitration in Vienna, Austria, and be governed by Austrian law. Flender did not sign Tippins's Purchase Order; rather, Flender made and shipped the good and included in the shipment its Invoice. Flender's Invoice included a clause which specified that any dispute must be heard in Chicago, Illinois.

Thus, there are different terms in the offer and the acceptance. The Purchase Order, which is the order, specified arbitration in Vienna, Austria. The Invoice, which accompanied the acceptance, specified litigation in Chicago, Illinois. How should the court resolve this dispute?

First, it is important to recognize that the Mirror Image Rule does not apply because this contract is formed under the UCC. If the Mirror Image Rule applied, as it does at common law, there would be no contract, because the offer and acceptance are different. But the UCC permits formation where offer and acceptance differ, so we can continue with the analysis pursuant to the Battle of the Forms.

Second, it is worth noting that Flender and Tippins are merchants. If Flender and Tippins were not merchants, then the UCC requires the court to "knock out" the non-matching terms. The difference regarding arbitration in Vienna versus litigation in Chicago is quite apparent. If the parties are not merchants, the UCC applies the Knock-Out Rule to such different terms.

But Flender and Tippins are merchants, so we need to continue the analysis one step further. Recall that, under the UCC, where both parties are merchants, the Last Shot Rule applies, such that additional or changed terms become part of the contract unless they materially alter it. The court thus needs to determine whether an agreement to litigate disputes in Chicago is materially different from an agreement to arbitrate disputes in Vienna.

In Flender, the trial court found, and the appellate court agreed, that the terms were quite different. Litigating in Chicago under Illinois law is materially different from arbitrating in Vienna under Austrian law. Therefore, the exception to the Last Shot Rule applies, and the term was knocked out.

Upon finding that the parties' final contract had no term regarding forum selection or choice of law, the court allowed a Pennsylvania court to hear the case because Tippins had headquarters in Pittsburgh.

C. The Mailbox Rule

The Mailbox Rule comes into play where contracts are formed via correspondence. This rule only applies where there is some time delay between sending and receiving information about a proposed contract. The Mailbox Rule does not apply, for example, when two people are negotiating during a conversation. There is no significant time delay in that case, and the Conversation Rule applies instead.

Today most correspondence is via email, which is virtually instantaneous. Courts seem mixed about whether the Mailbox Rule applies to email. Most seem to apply the Mailbox Rule to email, even though email is instantaneous whereas traditional mail is not. Other courts will treat email like a conversation. As new forms of communication arise — such as text messages, Slack conversations, and deal negotiations in a virtual reality session — the applicability of the Mailbox Rule will likely be called into question. But, for now, bar examiners are still like to test on quirky timing issues involving time-delayed correspondence, so let us review the basics.

The Mailbox Rule is a rule about the timing of three things: the creation of offers, the termination of offers, and the acceptance of offers. Acceptance is only valid if it occurs before the offer is terminated, so timing matters. As a general rule:

- Offers, revocations, rejections, counter-offers, and other communications that terminate an offer are effective when received by the other party.
- Acceptance is effective when sent, regardless of when or even whether it reaches the other party.

The R2d explains that an acceptance takes effect as soon as it is dispatched in a manner that irrevocably puts the acceptance out of the offeree's control:

> *Unless the offer provides otherwise, an acceptance made in a manner and by a medium invited by an offer is operative and completes the manifestation of mutual assent as soon as put out of the offeree's possession, without regard to whether it ever reaches the offeror.* R2d § 63(a).

The Mailbox Rule has a few additional quirks. First, an offeror can make an offer that does not permit acceptance by mail. The Mailbox Rule simply does not apply to an offer that cannot be accepted by mail.

Second, the Mailbox Rule does not apply to acceptance under an option contract:

> *An acceptance under an option contract is not operative until received by the offeror. R2d § 63(b).*

Acceptances under an option contract are commonly subject to a definitive time limit, and courts reason that the party who holds the option assumes the risk that the acceptance does not arrives before that time limit expires.

Setting aside the exception for option contracts, most Mailbox Rule problems can be resolved simply by remembering that, where there is a delay between sending and receipt of deal documents, everything is effective upon receipt, except for acceptances, which are valid upon sending. If you remember the rule that acceptances are effective when they are sent, and everything else is effective when received, then you can work out virtually any Mailbox Rule problem.

Mailbox Rule Hypo: Gallaway. The mailbox rule seems simple but can be made complex by unusual facts. For example, consider the following Mailbox Rule problem.

On Friday, January 1, 2021, Gallaway posts an advertisement in a local newspaper that he is selling his car. He does not state a price but provides a mailing address to write to for more information. Hernandez writes to Gallaway on Tuesday, January 5 offering to pay $10,000 for the car. Gallaway receives Hernandez's offer on Thursday, January 7. Gallaway replies on Friday, January 8 with a letter to Hernandez saying that he would take $12,000. Over the weekend, Gallaway has a change of heart. First thing Monday morning, he sends a FedEx same-day letter saying simply "I accept your offer for $10,000," which Hernandez receives that same day (Monday, January 11). Gallaway's second letter (proposing $12,000 for the car) arrives in Hernandez's mailbox on Wednesday, January 13. On Friday, January 15, Hernandez sends a note to Gallaway saying simply, "I accept"; Gallaway receives that note on Tuesday, January 19. On Wednesday, Gallaway drives the car to Hernandez and demands $12,000. What is Hernandez required to pay, if anything?

Let us analyze this situation. The first message, Gallaway's advertisement, is not an offer but rather an invitation for offers because it lacks the essential term of price. Plus, a general advertisement is ordinarily not construed as an offer but as an invitation for offers. The second message, Hernandez's first letter, seems to be an offer, which became valid and created the power of acceptance when Gallaway received it. Gallaway's first response is a counter-offer and thus a rejection, which would be effective and would terminate Gallaway's power of acceptance when Hernandez received it. However, Gallaway sent a second letter, which appears to be an acceptance, before Hernandez received the first letter. This second letter was therefore an effective acceptance by Gallaway since acceptances are effective when sent. The acceptance occurred before Gallaway's power of acceptance was terminated. In other words, this second letter constituted a valid acceptance and formed a binding contract as soon as it was sent.

The rest of the letters are effectively invalid. When Hernandez received Gallaway's offer to sell for $12,000, that was not a valid offer because Gallaway already had a pre-existing duty to sell the car to Hernandez for $10,000. Even though Hernandez appeared to accept this offer when he replied, "I accept," a contract for the car was already formed by that point.

D. Reflections on Acceptance

This introduction to Mutual Assent may have at times seemed a little abstract at first. That is because the doctrine of mutual assent is best understood by exploring its specific elements, offer and acceptance, which we did after reviewing the general concepts. As the doctrine gets more specific, it should also become clearer. At the conclusion of that study, however, see if you can reconstruct the abstraction of mutual assent with a newfound appreciation for its purpose: mutual asset reflects the goal of contract law to effectuate the intent of the parties.

Yet this goal of enforcing two parties' original mutual intentions is in tension with the realities of contract law. Intentions can be obscure. Ephemeral memories of past feelings give courts little guidance on how they should rule today. Contracts must be clear and predictable if they are to govern the actions of two parties. For this reason, objective evidence—such as written terms, eyewitness testimony, or an expert in the trade—is preferred over testimony evidence of a party's subjective perspective. In other words, although mutual assent is a subjective state of meeting of the mind, courts will look for objective evidence that the parties expressed a common understanding, and that outward expression is what mutual assent entails.

Cases

Reading P & W Railroad. The Mirror Image Rule is a common law rule that requires the offeree's acceptance to "mirror" the offer by matching its terms exactly. This rule allowed the offeror to be the master of the offer and to set all the terms. The offeree would then have to match all the terms exactly in their acceptance. Thus, it is clear where a valid acceptance is made, since the terms match. For a simple example, imagine a form on which the offeror typed up the offer and provided a place for the offeree to sign. Signing that document would be an acceptance, since that manifests agreement to all the terms. However, if material terms were crossed out (like quantity and price) and written in with pen or even deleted from the original document, that "acceptance" would not be a mirror image of the offer. Under the common law, that purported acceptance would be a counter-offer.

Some courts in the past strictly applied this rule and required the terms of the offer and acceptance to match exactly. In the 1867 case, *Myers v. Smith*, 48 Barb. 614 (N.Y. Sup. Ct. 1867), the offeror wrote an offer to sell malt "delivered on the boat at Weedsport." The offeree responded by letter accepting and stating that the malt was to be "deliverable by boat on Weedsport." The words "delivered" and "deliverable" were not synonymous and deemed different enough that it was a "manifest variance of the terms of the offer."

The *P & W RR* case is an example of how modern courts interpret the mirror image rule. Pay attention to how the court deals with the certainty that definite and unequivocal acceptances provide versus its unfairness.

State Department of Transportation v. Providence & Worcester Railroad Co.

674 A.2d 1239 (R.I. 1996) ("P & W RR")

LEDERBERG, Justice.

This case arose following the sale of a parcel of land by the defendant, Providence and Worcester Railroad Co. (P & W or the railway company), to the codefendant, Promet Corp. (Promet). The conveyance was declared "null and void" by an amended judgment of the Superior Court that ordered P & W to convey the parcel to the plaintiff, the State of Rhode Island Department of Transportation (state), for the purchase price of $100,000. The state was ordered to pay prejudgment interest on the purchase price, and P & W was required to reimburse Promet for interest on the purchase price and for property taxes that Promet paid while it was in possession of the parcel. The state appealed from the requirement that it pay interest on the purchase price; P & W appealed from the Superior Court's findings that the state was entitled to purchase the property and that P & W had to reimburse Promet for property taxes and for interest on the purchase price. Promet filed a brief in support of the amended Superior Court judgment. For the reasons recited below, we sustain in part and reverse in part the judgment of the Superior Court.

In 1985, P & W owned a 6.97-acre parcel of waterfront property in East Providence, Rhode Island. Railroad tracks were situated on the property, but the property was, and remains, otherwise unimproved. The railroad tracks at one time ran from the former Union Station through a tunnel, and over a bridge. At that point the tracks reached the subject property where they split to form a Y, one of whose arms directed rail traffic north, and the other traveled south on what is known as the

Bristol secondary track. The railroad company had acquired this property in 1982 from the Consolidated Rail Corporation (Conrail) as part of P & W's purchase of all Conrail's Rhode Island freight operations.

The property, however, was acquired by P & W subject to an order of the Special Court under the Regional Rail Reorganization Act of 1973. That order required P & W to "guarantee rail service [on the property] for four years from the date" of conveyance on May 1, 1982, and stipulated that P & W could "not seek to abandon or discontinue rail service . . . for such four-year period." It is undisputed that P & W never petitioned the Interstate Commerce Commission (ICC) to abandon or to discontinue rail service pursuant to the provisions [of a federal statute regarding the termination of rail services].

On December 12, 1985, P & W entered into a purchase and sale agreement with Promet for the sale of the subject property at the price of $100,000. Although the tracks were still suitable for rail use, the property was not being used for rail purposes, or any other uses at the time of the transaction. The terms of the purchase and sale agreement expressly made the agreement "subject to a 30 day option in the State of Rhode Island to purchase the premises," as required by [Rhode Island's statute governing the sale of rail properties], which provided:

> "All rail properties within the state offered for sale by any railway corporation after April 9, 1976 shall be offered for sale to the state in the first instance at the lowest price at which the railway corporation is willing to sell. The railway corporation shall notify the state in writing if it desires to offer for sale any rail properties. The state shall have a period of not more than thirty (30) days from receipt of the notification to accept the offer."

On November 20, 1985, Joseph Arruda (Arruda), assistant director for planning for the State Department of Transportation, wrote to P & W's agent, Joseph DiStefano (DiStefano). In that letter, Arruda referred to an October 22, 1985 meeting he had attended with DiStefano and principals of Promet at which "it was mentioned that Promet Property and P & W were discussing the sale of abandoned railroad properties." Arruda claimed that "the state must be given first option to acquire" the property and stated that "[i]f, in fact, P & W is pursuing the sale of any railroad property in this area, we would sincerely appreciate being notified at the earliest possible date." On December 12, 1985, DiStefano wrote to Arruda, stating:

> Dear Mr. Arruda:
>
> You are hereby notified, pursuant to Section 39-6.1-9 of the Rhode Island General Laws, that this company proposes to sell a certain parcel of land situated at East Providence, Rhode Island . . . for $100,000 with a closing to be held on January 17, 1986.
>
> Pursuant to statute, the State of Rhode Island has a period of thirty (30) days from the date of this notification within which to accept this offer to sell under the same terms and conditions as outlined in the enclosed Real Estate Sales Agreement.

If the State's rights are not exercised within such period, we shall deem ourselves free to sell the property to Promet Corp. in accordance with the terms of the enclosed Real Estate Sales Agreement.

This notice is sent to you although this company is of the opinion that the property in question is not covered by [Rhode Island's statute governing the sale of rail properties].

On January 7, 1986, Herbert DeSimone (DeSimone), director of transportation for the state, accepted the offer in writing. In his letter to DiStefano, DeSimone wrote, "Of course, you understand that certain wording in the Real Estate Sales Agreement relating to 'buyer' and obligations concerning the removal of track would be inappropriate to the purpose of the State's purchase." The closing between P & W and Promet had been originally scheduled for January 17, 1986, but the parties rescheduled several times, finally agreeing to April 14, 1986, at 10 a.m. The reason for rescheduling the closing date was to allow the state and Promet's engineers to determine whether the property could accommodate Promet's development plans while preserving the state's rail options. Such a plan proved to be impossible.

On April 11, 1986, the state filed a complaint in Superior Court, claiming that P & W was refusing to convey title to the property to the state but was going to "convey title to said land to the Promet Corporation on Monday, April 14, 1986 at 8:30 A.M. in derogation of the State's statutory rights." The state sought a temporary restraining order to enjoin the conveyance to Promet, but the Superior Court justice denied the state's request, indicating that the state had protected its rights and that P & W would be proceeding at its own risk.

Some minutes before 10 a.m. on April 14, 1986, Arruda appeared on behalf of the state at DiStefano's office and tendered a check for $100,000. Arruda was informed that P & W had already delivered the deed to the property to Promet earlier that morning. The closing between P & W and Promet had taken place at a location and time (8:30 a.m. instead of 10 a.m.) different from those originally scheduled, and P & W had taken no affirmative steps to inform the state of these changes.

The state filed its amended complaint on December 9, 1986, naming both P & W and Promet as defendants, praying that the deed to Promet be declared null and void. Promet filed two counterclaims and a request for jury trial. The counterclaims were later severed, and the parties waived by stipulation the demand for a jury trial. The trial was held before a justice of the Superior Court on November 15, 1991, and January 30, 1992. At trial, P & W and Promet argued that the subject property was not "rail property" subject to the statute because it was not being used for rail purposes at the time of the conveyance. The railroad company and Promet further argued that the state had waived any rights it possessed under the statute by having failed to tender payment for the property within the thirty days prescribed [by Rhode Island's statute governing the sale of rail properties].

In his decision issued from the bench, the trial justice found that the property in question is "rail property" within the meaning of [Rhode Island's statute governing the sale of rail properties], that it was dedicated for railroad use, and that it was available for rail purposes. The trial justice found "some of the testimony given by defendant's witness disingenuous when he made the comment that there was no function in 1986 for rail property uses, when that was exactly the same condition when the Special Court order was entered into in 1982, which specifically says that no abandonment or discontinue of rail use service should take place for a four-year period after the conveyance." The trial justice further found that the state had validly accepted P & W's offer within the thirty-day period and that the state was not required to tender payment at that time. Rather, the trial justice determined that the state had a "reasonable time" in which to pay for the property, and he indicated that such reasonable time coincided with the various closing dates scheduled by P & W and Promet.

The trial justice issued an amended judgment on March 17, 1994. In that judgment, the trial justice declared the deed from P & W null and void and ordered that the property be transferred to the state. In addition, the trial justice ordered P & W to repay to Promet the purchase price of $100,000 plus interest and to reimburse Promet for real estate taxes that Promet had paid on the property, plus interest on that amount. Finally, the amended judgment required the state to pay P & W the $100,000 purchase price plus interest.

On April 14, 1994, the state appealed that portion of the amended judgment that required the state to pay P & W the interest on the $100,000 purchase price. The railroad company filed its notice of appeal on April 20, 1994.

Did the State's January 7, 1986 Letter Constitute a Valid Acceptance of P & W's Offer?

The trial justice found that on December 12, 1985, P & W extended an option to the state to purchase the subject property and that the January 7, 1986 letter from DeSimone to DiStefano was "a valid exercise of [Rhode Island's statute governing the sale of rail properties] option." The finding of a trial justice sitting without a jury in respect to the formation of a contract is entitled to great weight, and this Court will not disturb such a finding unless the trial justice "misconceived material evidence or was otherwise clearly wrong." On appeal, P & W asserted that no contract for the sale of the subject parcel existed because the state's January 7, 1986 letter did not constitute a valid acceptance of P & W's December 12, 1985 offer. In support of its assertion, P & W argued that the January 7 letter in fact proposed additional terms to the agreement. The letter from DeSimone to DiStefano provided in pertinent part:

> *Pursuant to [Rhode Island's statute governing the sale of rail properties], I am writing to you on behalf of the State of Rhode Island to exercise its right to accept the offer to purchase 6.9 acres of land.*
>
> *Of course, you understand that certain wording in the Real Estate Sales Agreement [referring to the agreement between P & W and Promet] relating to 'buyer' and obligations concerning the removal of track would be inappropriate to the purpose of the State's purchase.*

Please contact Mr. Joseph F. Arruda of this department to arrange for a meeting to revise the existing offer to conform the State's acceptance.

P & W argued that "[a]s a matter of law, [the state's] letter was nothing more than an invitation to meet and attempt to reach agreement on the terms of the sale." We disagree.

This Court has held that a valid acceptance "must be definite and unequivocal," and that an "acceptance which is equivocal or upon condition or with a limitation is a counteroffer and requires acceptance by the original offeror before a contractual relationship can exist." It is not equivocation, however, "if the offeree merely puts into words that which was already reasonably implied in the terms of the offer." It is further the case that "an acceptance must receive a reasonable construction" and that "the mere addition of a collateral or immaterial matters [sic] will not prevent the formation of a contract."

The state's letter of acceptance points out that the name of the buyer in the original agreement would have to be changed. In our opinion, this statement simply reflected the obvious necessity to replace "the state" for "Promet" as the named buyer in the deed. Moreover, the letter's reference to P & W's obligation to Promet to remove tracks from the property as "inappropriate to the purpose of the State's purchase" did not add any terms or conditions to the contract but, instead, constituted a clear benefit to P & W. In pointing out that the "wording" that obligated P & W to remove tracks would be "inappropriate" in an agreement between P & W and the state, the state, in fact, relieved P & W from the obligation and expense it otherwise would have incurred in selling the property to Promet.

When an offeree, in its acceptance of an offer, absolves the offeror of a material obligation, the "rules of contract construction and the 'rules of common sense'" preclude construing that absolution as an additional term that invalidates the acceptance. Moreover, DeSimone explicitly and unequivocally stated, "I am writing to you on behalf of the State of Rhode Island to exercise its right to accept the offer to purchase 6.9 acres of land," and requested the meeting with Arruda in order "to revise the existing offer to conform the State's acceptance."

Therefore, we concur, with the trial justice who found that the state validly accepted the option extended to it by P & W. Because the contract was valid, we need not address P & W's contention that the parcel was not rail property within the meaning of [Rhode Island's statute governing the sale of rail properties].

[Discussion of whether the state had to pay interest on the purchase price of the property omitted.]

In conclusion, therefore, we sustain the state's appeal, and we deny and dismiss the appeal of P & W. We affirm the amended judgment of the Superior Court except that we vacate the requirement that the state pay interest to P & W on the purchase price of the property. The papers in this case may be returned to the Superior Court with direction to enter judgment consistent with this opinion.

Reflection

The *P & W RR* court recognized that a contract existed despite minor differences between the offer and acceptance. The rule for valid acceptance is that it must be definite and not open to more than one interpretation (unequivocal). If the acceptance includes additional terms, limitations or conditions, then it is not a "mirror image" of the offer and is instead a counter-offer.

The court reasoned that the state did not add any new terms or conditions that invalidated the acceptance. The name of the buyer was changed out of an obvious necessity and the reference to removing the tracks was immaterial because it conferred a clear benefit to P & W. Moreover, the state also made it clear that it was making a positive acceptance by stating in their letter that they accepted the offer to purchase the land.

The court's decision reflects the modern view that the Mirror Image Rule does not need to be strictly adhered to. The minor differences are usually immaterial matters or terms that have no major bearing on the original offer. Imagine if P & W was allowed to get out of the contract because the state said that they did not have to pay the expense of ripping up the railway tracks. It would be unfair if the Mirror Image Rule was strictly applied since the offer and the acceptance did not match exactly. Therefore, courts are willing to recognize valid acceptances when there are minor discrepancies about immaterial matters between the offer and acceptance.

Discussion

1. What is the "Mirror Image Rule"? Cite to the R2d provision that contains this rule and then explain that provision in your own words.

2. What is the purpose of the Mirror Image Rule? Why should an acceptance mirror an offer? Consider what advantages this provides to private parties, to society generally, and to the courts.

3. What are some problems with the strict application of the Mirror Image Rule? Think of some situations where the strict application would lead to unjust results, and explain why those results are unjust.

4. Consider whether or to what extent the *P & W RR* court followed the Mirror Image Rule. Why should courts follow this rule strictly, and when should they relax it?

Reading Flender v. Tippins. Under the common law, if the offeree did not accept every single term in the contract, no binding contract was formed (the "Mirror Image Rule"). However, the UCC expressly rejects the mirror image rule and adopts what is known as the "Battle of the Forms."

The Battle of the Forms refers to the common situation in which one party makes an offer, to which the offeree responds with its own counter-offer, and then the parties proceed with the transaction without ever signing any final contract. The UCC formed the rule so that contracts can still be created via the exchange of nonmatching forms. The rule was created in recognition that parties may have intended to enter a contract even though the forms they exchanged were not the mirror image of each other.

The Battle of the Forms is only applied in cases where there was "definite and reasonable acceptance." For example, if a grocery store owner makes an offer to a peach farmer for the purchase of 15 dozen peaches for $250, and the peach farmer responds with an offer expressing that he would sell ten dozen peaches for $250, Battle of the Forms would not apply. The famer and store owner expressly and substantially disagreed on the quantity of peaches, a core term of the contract.

Where there is an offer with a "definite and reasonable expression of acceptance" that contains different terms, the "Knock-Out Rule" applies: the terms that do not match are knocked out of the agreement so that the contract only contains the agreed-upon terms. Any remaining gaps in the contract are filled by the UCC's default terms. The Knock-Out Rule only applies where there are express conflicting terms. Where a contract is silent as to a term, the new term will be considered an "additional term."

If the acceptance does not seek to change terms in the offer, but rather purports to add additional terms that were not in the original offer, the result depends on whether both parties are "merchants," which are people or companies that deal in the kinds of goods involved in this transaction. If the parties are not merchants, then the additional terms are "knocked out." If the parties are merchants, however, and there are additional terms in the acceptance, those terms become part of the contract unless (1) the original offer specifically said that no terms can be added, (2) the new terms materially alter the contract, or (3) the offeror objects to the new terms within a reasonable time.

There is an exception to "Battle of the Forms," which is known as "The Proviso Clause." If the acceptance of an offer is expressly made conditional on assent to different or additional terms, then the acceptance does not operate as an actual acceptance and no contract is formed. A proviso clause forces Battle of the Forms to act as the Mirror Image Rule — offers must be accepted "as is," meaning the acceptance and offer must have all the same terms.

Flender represents a traditional "Battle of the Forms" scenario. In the case, two companies, Flender and Tippins, both use their own preprinted forms for the purchase of goods. Both parties proceeded with performance even though both parties' forms contained arbitration clauses designating vastly different locations for disputes to be resolved. In this case, the court uses the Knock-Out Rule so that the agreement only contains agreed upon terms.

Flender Corp. v. Tippins International, Inc.

830 A.2d 1279 (Pa. Super. 2003)

JOHNSON, J.

This matter arose out of a "battle of the forms" in which the two contracting parties attempted to impose differing terms of the purchase of goods. Tippins, a Pittsburgh based company, engaged in the construction of a steel rolling mill in the Czech Republic. Tippins sought to purchase gear drive assemblies from Flender Corporation for installation at the new facility.

In January 1998, Tippins mailed a purchase order to Flender specifying terms of sale. The form required that the parties' disputes under any resulting contract be submitted to arbitration. The order stated Tippins's terms as follows:

> *"Tippins['s] purchase order is expressly limited to acceptance of 'Standard General Conditions Nova Hut Purchase Order' and special conditions of purchase, which take precedence over any terms and conditions written on the back of the purchase order."*

The "Standard General Conditions Nova Hut Purchase Order" included the arbitration clause at issue here, requiring that all claims or disputes arising out of the contract must be submitted to arbitration before the International Chamber of Commerce in Vienna, Austria and be governed by Austrian law.

Moreover, the order limited the form of Flender's acceptance as follows: "AS PART OF THIS OFFER TO PURCHASE GOODS OR SERVICES THE ATTACHED ACKNOWLEDGMENT FORM OF THE PURCHASE ORDER 'MUST' BE SIGNED AND RETURNED.... [NEITHER] TIPPINS NOR ANY OF ITS AFFILIATES RECOGNIZES ANY OTHER DOCUMENT AS AN ACKNOWLEDGMENT."

Flender did not sign the attached acknowledgment form or issue any other written acceptance of Tippin's offer, but instead manufactured and shipped the finished drive assemblies. Flender's invoice, which accompanied the drive assemblies, provided "Conditions of Sale and Delivery" that attached conditions to Flender's acceptance of Tippins's order. Flender's conditions provided as follows:

> *"[T]hese terms and conditions will govern all quotations covering purchase orders for and sales of Seller's products and are the sole terms and conditions on which the order of buyer will be accepted. Seller's acceptance of Buyer's order will not constitute an acceptance of printed provisions on Buyer's order form which are inconsistent with or additional to these terms and conditions unless specifically accepted in writing by the Seller. Buyer's agreement and Buyer's form containing inconsistent, or material terms shall not be deemed a specific objection to any terms hereof."*

The invoice did not, however, require that Tippins accept these additional terms for the parties to form a binding contract. The invoice did provide a mechanism for dispute resolution. The dispute resolution clause required that "exclusive jurisdiction and venue of any dispute arising out of or with respect to this Agreement or otherwise relating to the commercial relationships of the parties shall be vested in the Federal and/or State Courts located in Chicago, Illinois."

Tippins accepted and installed the gear drives, but, subsequently, failed to pay the balance due on the shipment. Flender then commenced this action in the Court of Common Pleas of Allegheny County seeking to recover an amount outstanding of $238,663.15, plus $76,372.16 in service charges.

In the trial court, Tippins filed preliminary objection to Flender's complaint, arguing that the parties' contract of sale required that Flender submit its claim to arbitration in Vienna, Austria.

The Honorable Ronald W. Folino, denied Tippins's objections, reasoning that the arbitration clause on which Tippins relied had been "knocked out" because it was materially different from the dispute resolution clause in Flender's invoice.

Tippins raised the following question for review:

Did the Trial Court err in ruling that neither Flender's nor Tippins's forum selection provision became a part of their contract thus finding that the appropriate forum for Flender to bring this action was in Pennsylvania?

Section 2207(a) provides that an expression of acceptance may operate to accept an offer, even if it contains terms additional to or different from those stated in the offer. Thus, mere non-conformance between competing forms will not undermine the formation of a contract, so long as the parties demonstrate their mutual assent to essential terms. Under such circumstances, a written contract is deemed to exist consisting of the essential terms of the offer, to which the offeree's response has established its agreement. The formation of a written contract is defeated only where the offeree responds with different or additional terms and "explicitly communicates his or her unwillingness to proceed with the transaction" unless the offeror accepts those terms.

In this case, Flender, through its course of conduct and subsequent invoice, accepted the essential terms of Tippin's offer. Although the invoice provided terms that did not appear in Tippins's offer, Flender did not communicate its unwillingness to proceed without them or condition the transaction on Tippins's acceptance of those terms.

Consequently, we agree with Tippins that the parties did form a written contract under section 2207(a). The dispute provision in Flender's acceptance, requiring resolution of the parties' disagreements in state or federal courts in Chicago, is clearly at odds with and quite "different" from the clause in Tippins offer requiring arbitration of disputes before the International Chamber of Commerce in Vienna. By operation of the rule, we adopt today, those provisions are both, quite clearly, "knocked out." Neither became a part of the parties' contract. Accordingly, the trial court did not err in refusing to compel arbitration in response to Tippins's preliminary objections.

For the foregoing reasons, we affirm the trial court's order.

Order AFFIRMED.

Reflection

Flender is a great example of the Battle of the Forms. Flender and Tippins exchanged pre-printed forms for the purchase of goods. Both forms included dispute resolution clauses that expressly designated different locations. Even though the forms contained competing clauses, the court found a "definite and reasonable expression of acceptance" from the parties' course of performance and, therefore, course to apply the Battle of the Forms.

Since the dispute resolution clauses provided by both parties were clearly at odds with each other, the court applied the "knock out" rule and removed the clauses from both forms. The court "knocked out" all competing terms to simplify the contract to just the terms that were agreed upon. The court then utilized the UCC gap filler to decide where litigation should take place.

Discussion

1. The R2d adopts the Mirror Image Rule, but the UCC does not. Beyond generally observing that the R2d and UCC rules are different, can you specifically articulate all the ways in which they are different? Write a table comparing the elements of the two rules.

2. Why does the UCC do away with the Mirror Image Rule? Is there anything unique about contracts involving sales of goods that would obviate the need for this rule?

3. Why does the UCC provide special acceptance rules for merchants? What makes contracts for sales of goods between merchants different from sales of goods generally? Note the merchant-specific rules on your table.

Problems

Problem 6.1. Primo Ladders

Taylor, a housepainter, sent a text message to the Primo Ladder Company ordering Model No. 35E, a 35-foot aluminum extension ladder with safety harness, for $325. Primo Ladder replied by text stating, "We accept your offer. Model 35E is no longer available. We have shipped Model 40E to you at no extra cost, payment due on delivery." Taylor texts back, "I do not want the 40E, it's too long for my truck." Primo responds, "Product has already shipped, we demand payment on delivery." Taylor refused to accept delivery of the ladder, and Primo sued Taylor for breach of contract.

Under UCC § 2-207, was a binding contract formed by Primo's "acceptance?"

What if Primo's initial text message had stated: "We accept. Model 35E has been shipped to your address, payment due upon delivery. Any and all disputes must be resolved by arbitration."

Would this communication "operate as an acceptance" under UCC § 2-207(1)? Was a contract formed by the exchange of these communications?

Problem 6.2. **An Earnest Letter**

Erneste Ardente made a bid of $250,000 for William & Katherine Horan's residential property. After the bid was deemed acceptable, Ardente received and executed the purchase and sale agreement. Ardente's attorney returned the agreement to the Horans along with a check for $20,000 and a letter which read:

> My Clients are concerned that the following items remain with the real estate: a) dining room set and tapestry wall covering in dining room; b) fireplace fixtures throughout; c) the sun parlor furniture. I would appreciate your confirming that these items are part of the transaction, as they would be difficult to replace.

After receiving the letter, the Horans refused to sell the enumerated items and did not sign the purchase and sale agreement. Ardente sued, seeking specific performance for the property.

Was Ardente's letter a counter-offer or a valid acceptance?

See Ardente v. Horan, 366 A.2d 162 (1976).

Problem 6.3. **Conditional Acceptance of a Court Order**

Mr. Jameel Ibrahim lost a lawsuit in the United States Court of Federal Claims, which dismissed his complaint against the United States for an alleged breach of an implied-in-law contract. The "contract" Ibrahim refers to is a child support order from the state court system of New Jersey.

On January 23, 2019, Ibrahim sent a twelve-page letter to various officials of the State of New Jersey, cabinet secretaries, and the Supreme Court of the United States, titled "Conditional Acceptance for the Value/Agreement/Counter Offer to Acceptance of Offer." In the letter, Ibrahim alleged that he had "received [these parties'] offer and accept[ed]" it, subject to conditions set forth in the rest of the letter — for the most part, demanding that the recipients justify the existence of various governmental agencies and practices. The letter asserts that failure to do so would result in "default," and in turn, an obligation to pay Ibrahim $3.5 million in damages.

Did Ibrahim's "Conditional Acceptance" letter constitute a valid acceptance of the state's child support order, and, if so, on what terms?

See Ibrahim v. United States, 799 Fed. App'x 865 (Fed. Cir. 2020).

Module III

Consideration and Alternatives to Consideration

Contract liability is voluntary. A person must choose to take on a contractual responsibility. The general idea is that when a person chooses to take on such a contractual liability, that person is doing so because they value what is gained from the contract more than what must be given up in exchange. For example, if I agree to sell you my car for $10,000, that is strong evidence that I value $10,000 more than I value the car; otherwise, why would I sell it for that price?

The theory goes that society is made to be better when people engage in voluntary transactions like this. In the car example, I valued $10,000 more than a car, and you valued a car more than $10,000; otherwise, we would not each agree to make this exchange. After the exchange, you have increased your total value and so have I. So long as we did not make anyone else worse off in the process, we have just increased the total welfare of society, simply by moving some property to new owners.

But contracts only make society better when some conditions are met. One condition is that you have rationally chosen to exchange your money for that car, and that this transaction was not thrust upon you. If I visit your house in the dead of night and paint the exterior without your permission, then send you a bill for $5,000, it is not clear that you valued house paint more than $5,000. This transaction was thrust upon you, and it may not reflect what you value.

The consideration doctrine is a sort of failsafe that ensures contract parties at least thought they would become better off as the result of entering into a binding contract. In brief, the modern formulation of the consideration doctrine states that every contract must include a bargained-for exchange. The presence of such consideration—the fact that the parties are each getting something in exchange for their promises — is evidence that both parties thought that the contract would make themselves better off. The first question, then, is what counts as consideration? And second, should courts enforce some promises that lack this element of bargained-for exchange in the interest of fairness, justice, or the public interest?

Chapter 7
Consideration

To be enforceable at law, contracts must feature some sort of exchange. Typically, contracts involve an exchange of promises. Consideration is what is given in exchange for the offeror's promise.

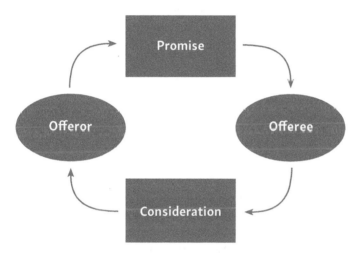

Figure 7.1. Consideration is what the offeree promises the offeror in exchange for the offeror's promise to the offeree.

Consideration is simply an extension of the definition of contract that you learned earlier. The "set of promises" described in the Restatement's definition of what is a contract is the offeror's promise, on the one hand, and the offeree's consideration for that promise, on the other.

> *A contract is a promise or a set of promises for the breach of which the law gives a remedy, or the performance of which the law in some way recognizes as a duty.* R2d § 1.

Consideration ensures that both parties to a contract are getting something from the deal. This accords with the economic notion that people are rational and self-interested such that they will make decisions that they believe will make themselves better off. When two people make each other better off through a transaction, without making anyone else worse off in the process, society itself is better off. Those two rational people have exchanged some goods, services, properties, ideas, or other things so that they now belong to the people who value them more.

Imagine that Francis owns an apple orchard, and Benjamin owns an orange grove. The apple orchard produces more applies than Francis wants to eat, and the orange grove produce more oranges than Benjamin wants to eat. The leftover fruits rot on the ground and go to waste.

But apples ripen in September, while oranges are ready for harvest in May. Francis and Benjamin cannot simply exchange apples for oranges in a barter system because they do not have the fruits at the same time. Instead, they need to make binding promises to each other if they are to trade.

Contract law allows Francis and Benjamin to bind each other to a set of promises. Francis offers to give half her apple harvest to Benjamin when it is ready, and Benjamin agrees to give Francis half of his oranges when he picks them. Both parties can rely on each other to perform their obligations because otherwise they can sue one another for breach. Contract law thus enables Francis to have and eat Benjamin's oranges in May, and Benjamin can deliver those oranges and then rest assured that he will have Francis's apples in September (or he can sue for the value of those apples). Instead of rotting on the ground, both parties enjoy the fruits of this agreement. This represents a benefit to both parties, and harms no one, and thus society is improved by this transaction.

When people repeat this process of bargained-for exchange on a large scale over time, society allocates goods and services to their place of highest value. Even with the same amount of stuff, human society is better off thanks to the ability to make trades over time. Law generally seeks to improve social welfare, and contract law evolved to enforce voluntary agreements in which people think they will make themselves better off, because that tends to increase social welfare in the long term. Hence, the consideration exists to limit the scope of legal enforcement of voluntary promises to promises that people make in the expectation of receiving some benefit.

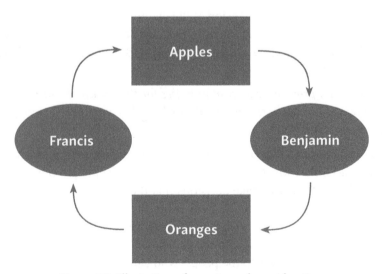

Figure 7.2. Illustration of promise and consideration.

Although this explains why courts require consideration, it does not explain what exactly consideration is. When does a party truly attempt to improve itself through an exchange of promises, and when are those promises given for other reasons? Courts have two different theories to explain what consideration is: the older benefit/detriment theory, and the modern bargained-for exchange theory. Courts still discuss both theories in their reasoning, and the theories overlap substantially in terms of their results, but there are some critical differences and some reasons why the bargained-for exchange theory is preferred because it produces better legal results.

Rules

A. The Historical Benefit/Detriment Theory

Historically, there have been two alternative theories that attempt to explain what consideration is or why the law should require it. The first, and older, is the benefit/detriment theory. It asks whether the promisor incurs a benefit, or whether the promisee incurs a detriment, to evaluate whether consideration is present such that a binding contract may be formed. This historic test is now disfavored by modern courts and has largely been replaced by the bargained-for exchange test of consideration. However, the doctrine is varied, and courts still cleave to the old language. For this reason, law students should read and understand the historic case of *Hamer v. Sidway*, which is perhaps the most famous articulation of the benefit/detriment test in practice. Despite the name of the case, the facts revolve around an uncle named Willian E. Story and his nephew named Willian E. Story the Second.

> . . . 'William E. Story agreed to and with William E. Story, 2d, that if he would refrain from drinking liquor, using tobacco, swearing, and playing cards or billiards for money until he should become twenty-one years of age, then he, the said William E. Story, would at that time pay him, the said William E. Story, 2d, the sum of $5,000 for such refraining, to which the said William E. Story, 2d, agreed,' and that he 'in all things fully performed his part of said agreement.'

The uncle died before the nephew turned 21, but the nephew fulfilled the promise anyway. The administrator of the uncle's estate refused to pay the nephew, claiming that the nephew did not render consideration for the uncle's promise. The administrator reasoned that the nephew benefitted from abstaining from liquor, tobacco, swearing, cards, and billiards, and that the uncle received no personal benefit from his nephew's abstinence. The court applied the benefit/detriment test to determine whether the nephew gave consideration in exchange for his uncle's promise:

> The exchequer chamber in 1875 defined 'consideration' as follows: 'A valuable consideration, in the sense of the law, may consist either in some right, interest, profit, or benefit accruing to the one party, or some forbearance, detriment, loss, or responsibility given, suffered, or undertaken by the other.'

The court found that the nephew did indeed incur a detriment, because he gave up his legal rights:

> *It is sufficient that [the nephew] restricted his lawful freedom of action within certain prescribed limits upon the faith of his uncle's agreement.*

The nephew did not have to suffer or end up worse off because of this bargain in order to incur a detriment under this test; rather, merely giving up one's legal rights is enough to pass as a detriment. The nephew incurred a detriment, the court reasoned, so he gave consideration for the promise. The court acknowledged that the benefit/detriment test requires either a detriment to the promisee or a benefit to the promisor. Upon find this detriment to the promisee, the court did not have to opine on whether the promisor benefitted; but, in dicta, it stated:

> *We see nothing in this record that would permit a determination that the uncle was not benefited in a legal sense.*

This famous case of *Hamer v. Sidway* shows how the benefit/detriment theory is applied to determine whether there is consideration. But the case also shows why the rule is problematic. From the economic perspective of increasing social welfare, how does requiring a person to incur a detriment help ensure that enforceable contracts make society better off?

The benefit/detriment theory is also problematic because pain and pleasure are somewhat subjective. The court could not ask the uncle whether he benefitted from his nephew's abstinence because the uncle was dead at the time of the trial. And whether the nephew suffered or enjoyed his abstinence from intoxicating liquors is also a subjective matter that is both hard to discover and difficult to enforce generally. The theory is difficult to apply, and courts have generally replaced it with a new theory that is both easier to objectively measure and more likely to result in an increase in social welfare.

B. The Modern Bargained-For Exchange Theory

Most modern courts have moved away from the benefit/detriment test and toward the bargained-for exchange test. The R2d clearly adopts this modern test.

> *To constitute consideration, a performance or a return promise must be bargained for.* R2d § 71(1).

In this more modern test, the question is whether the contract is the result of both parties' desire to receive something from the transaction. This does not require bargaining per se, meaning, the parties do not have to haggle or dicker over terms. Rather, the test simply looks at whether promises are given in exchange for one another.

> *A performance or return promise is bargained for if it is sought by the promisor in exchange for his promise and is given by the promisee in exchange for that promise.* R2d § 71(2).

The bargained-for exchange test is flexible and inclusive. It includes a wide variety of actions that can count as consideration. The promise and the consideration in exchange for that promise can be affirmative actions, forbearance, promises, other acts, and anything that alters some legal relationship.

> *The performance may consist of (a) an act other than a promise, or (b) a forbearance, or (c) the creation, modification, or destruction of a legal relation.* R2d § 71(3).

The consideration does not even have to flow to the original promisor. If a promisor bargains for the promisee to give consideration to a third party, that still counts as consideration.

> *The performance or return promise may be given to the promisor or to some other person. It may be given by the promisee or by some other person.* R2d § 71(4).

This modern test fits better with the law and economics approach to contract law, which justifies enforceable agreements on that basis that they generally make the world more valuable by allocating property to the person who values it more.

The bargained-for exchange test is flexible enough to apply in cases where the benefit/detriment test would fail. In the case of *Pennsy Supply, Inc. v. American Ash Recycling Corp.*, American Ash had a business of converting hazardous waste into useful material. Businesses would pay American Ash to remove their waste and by-products, then American Ash would process the material and give the resulting recycled product, which it called AggRite, away for free. American Ash thus avoided the cost of disposing the hazardous waste and, hopefully, made a profit by charging more to remove the hazardous materials then it spent recycling, storing, and advertising the resulting recycled AggRite.

Pennsy Supply agreed to take about 11,000 tons of AggRite from American Ash and use it in a paving project. Pennsy used the product correctly. Unfortunately, the pavement developed extensive cracking within three months of its use. Pennsy then asked American Ash to remediate the defective work under the theory that American Ash owed Pennsy an implied warranty that the product would not crack and fail so quickly.

In courses focusing on the law of Sales, you will learn that contracts for sales of goods usually include implied warranties such as this. For present purposes, simply note that sales of goods include implied warranties of "merchantability," meaning fitness for the ordinary purchase for which such goods are used, *see* UCC § 2-314, and "fitness for a particular purpose," meaning the buyer's special purposes if the seller has reason to know of them, *see* UCC § 2-315. Although courts sometimes use these terms interchangeably, serious UCC scholars regard that as a seriously inexcusable confusion. *See, e.g.,* 1 James J. White & Robert S. Summers, Uniform Commercial Code at 527 (1995). In this case, the AggRite should be warrantied for its ordinary use in making pavement that would not crack, but this warranty only applies if American Ash "sold" the AggRite to Pennsy and did not give it away as a gift.

Returning to our facts, the pavement made of AggRite cracked, and American Ash refused to fix the pavement, claiming that there was no contract because it had merely given Pennsy a gift, since it did not charge any money for the AggRite. Pennsy sued.

The trial court applied the benefit/detriment test and agreed with American Ash. It found that American Ash gave Pennsy a conditional gift. The trial court reasoned that, since the parties did not discuss disposal costs during any part of the bargaining process, American Ash did not give away the AggRite with the intent to avoid disposal costs. Hauling away the AggRite was simply Pennsy's only way to receive the gift of the product.

The appellate court disagreed for two reasons. First, it found that American Ash did seek people to haul away its AggRite. It advertised the material for free and would have otherwise paid to dispose of it. The trial court mistakenly thought that since the material was free, it was a gift. But the material had a negative value. It was a "bad," not a "good." It was made of hazardous waste that was expensive to eliminate. But removing a negative thing from American Ash, Pennsy gave American Ash a benefit. Therefore, under the benefit/detriment test, there was a benefit to the promisor, and therefore, there was consideration for the promise.

Second, the appellate court applied the bargain theory of consideration. It found that the trial court misunderstood and misapplied the theory where it found that there was no bargain because the parties did not have a bargaining process. This was an error. There is no requirement for a bargaining process. What is required is that both parties seek something in exchange. The appellate court reasoned that, in this case, American Ash sought removal of hazardous waste from its property, and Pennsy sought paving material. Both parties expected to get something from this exchange, and therefore, there was consideration for the promise.

This case shows how the benefit/detriment test and the bargained-for exchange test overlap and can arrive at the same result. But it also shows that the benefit/detriment test can be difficult to apply, and the bargained-for exchange test is both easier to determine objectively and more analytically straightforward. This shows why courts have moved toward the bargained-for exchange theory of consideration.

C. Gratuitous Promises Are Not Supported by Consideration

Gratuitous means given or done for free. Gratuitous, as in the word gratuity, is synonymous with free, gratis, complementary voluntary, unpaid, without charge, and pro bono. Likewise, a gratuitous promise is a promise to give a gift, to volunteer, to do something for nothing. Contractual promises require consideration, which is something in exchange for the promise. By definition, a gratuitous promise seeks nothing in return. By this definition, therefore, gratuitous promises are not supported by consideration.

D. Conditional Gifts Are Not Supported by Consideration

Consideration is usually easy to spot where both parties to a contract are expecting and wanting to get some benefit from that transaction. But there are cases where consideration appears to be present but is truly absent. Professor Williston provided a famous example of such a situation where consideration is absent.

In Williston's example, a benevolent man promises a tramp (a homeless person) that if the tramp goes to the corner store, the tramp may purchase a new coat on the benevolent man's account. Is there consideration for the promise?

At first blush, it looks like there might be consideration: under the benefit/detriment theory, the promisee incurs a detriment by going into a store she would otherwise not have gone to. The tramp might reason the walk was the price she paid for the promise of the coat. But, according to Professor John Murray, this is not the kind of detriment that counts as consideration:

> If the promisor made the promise for the purpose of inducing the detriment, the detriment induced the promise. If, however, the promisor made the promise with no particular interest in the detriment that the promisee had to suffer to take advantage of the promised gift or other benefit, the detriment was incidental or conditional to the promisee's receipt of the benefit. Even though the promisee suffered a detriment induced by the promise, the purpose of the promisor was not to have the promisee suffer the detriment because she did not seek that detriment in exchange for her promise.

John Edward Murry, Jr., Murray on Contracts § 60 (3d ed. 1990). Applying Murray's conception of detriment, one must ask, did the benevolent man want the tramp to walk to the store? Was the purpose of the promise of the coat to induce the tramp to suffer the walk? That does not seem to be the most reasonable interpretation of the situation. The benevolent man likely did not care about the tramp's walk. Rather, walking to the store was the only way for the tramp to purchase the coat. The walk was merely the condition necessary to obtain the promise.

Under the bargained-for exchange theory, is there consideration? Now we see that the coat is obviously a gift, not an exchange. The benevolent man gets nothing of value. He is just giving charity. The tramp is not giving anything of value, she simply needs to walk to the corner to obtain the gift waiting for her. We can draw the bargained-for exchange diagram and quickly see that the tramp offers no consideration in exchange for the promise of the coat.

This is another example of how the using bargained-for exchange test makes consideration easier to determine than under the benefit/detriment test.

Distinguishing true consideration from a mere conditional gift is one of the more common ways the problems with consideration appear in contract doctrine. As you evaluate consideration problems, think carefully about how you would distinguish a rationally bargained-for exchange from a mere conditional promise.

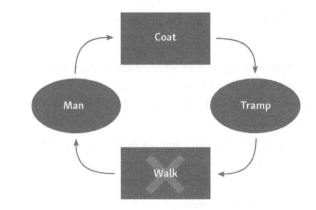

Figure 7.3. Illustrating a lack of consideration.

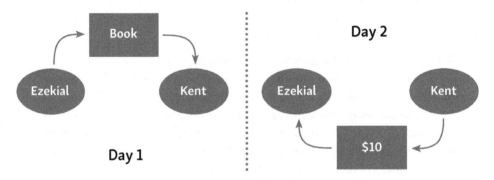

Figure 7.4. Illustration of "past consideration."

E. "Past Consideration" Is Not Consideration

Consideration must induce the promisor to give the promise to the promisee in exchange for the consideration. If the consideration has already been given to the promisor, then it cannot serve to further induce him. Therefore, there is no such thing as "past consideration." Sometimes the term is used to refer to a moral obligation to repay someone, but promises to repay someone for a benefit previously received is governed by the doctrine of promissory restitution.

For example, if Ezekial gives Kent a book on Day 1 as a gift, and then on Day 2, Kent promises to repay Ezekial $10 for the book, Kent's promise obviously is not intended to induce Ezekial to give the book the Kent. Ezekial already gave Kent the book for free, and Kent already possesses and owns the book. If we diagram this situation, it looks quite different from situations where we find consideration.

There are situations where a promise to pay for a benefit previously received can be binding. But such situations do not form contracts-at-law. Rather, they are potentially enforceable promises pursuant to the equitable doctrine of promissory restitution. Moreover, such promises are only enforced when and to the extent that justice requires. In general, promises to pay for past benefits are not enforceable, and you will learn about the special and rare exceptions to that rule.

F. Illusory Promises Are Not Consideration

Illusory promises are promises that do not actually have to be performed by the promisor. If Nancy says to Drew, "If you pay me $20, I promise to drive you to the airport tomorrow, provided that I feel up to it," that is an illusory promise, because Nancy reserves total control on whether she fulfills her promise or not. There is the illusion of a promise, since Nancy spoke the words "I promise," but in reality, she did not commit herself to perform any task. In the terms of the R2d, Nancy has reserved a choice of alternative performance:

> *A promise or apparent promise is not consideration if by its terms the promisor or purported promisor reserves a choice of alternative performances unless (a) each of the alternative performances would have been consideration if it alone had been bargained for, or (b) one of the alternative performances would have been consideration and there is or appears to the parties to be a substantial possibility that before the promisor exercises his choice events may eliminate the alternatives which would not have been consideration. R2d § 77.*

There is, however, a doctrine which can serve to bind a promisor to what would otherwise be an illusory promise. The duty of good faith and fair dealing requires that contractual parties act in good faith to produce the fruits of their mutual agreement. A famous case authored by Justice Cardozo, *Wood v. Lucy, Lady Duff-Gordon*, 222 N.Y. 88 (1917), excerpted in Chapter 16 below, dealt with precisely this issue.

Lady Duff-Gordon (1863–1935) was a leading British fashion designer who survived the sinking of the RMS Titanic in 1912. She was also booked to sail on the RMS Lusitania, a cruise ship that was sunk by a German submarine in 1915 as a precursor to the First World War, but she cancelled her trip due to illness.

Around the time when the Lusitania set sail, Duff-Gordon offered to hire a certain Otis T. Wood, an American advertising agent, to help her turn her vogue into money, on the following terms:

> *[Wood] was to have the exclusive right, subject always to [Duff-Gordon's] approval, to place her indorsements on the designs of others. He was also to have the exclusive right to place her own designs on sale, or to license others to market them. In return, she was to have one-half of "all profits and revenues" derived from any contracts he might make. The exclusive right was to last at least one year from April 1, 1915, and thereafter from year to year unless terminated by notice of ninety days.*

Today, we would call Duff-Gordon an "influencer," and Wood was her P.R. man. Their deal clearly included his exclusive right to her indorsements, yet Duff-Gordon violated this promise by placing her indorsements on other things without Wood's

Figure 7.5. Lady Duff-Gordon on the deck of the Titanic, Library of Congress (1900).
Public domain work.

knowledge, and she did not share profits with him. Wood sued Duff-Gordon for damages, and the issue upon which the case turned was whether Duff-Gordon's promise to give Wood an exclusive is supported by a promise from Wood in exchange.

Duff-Gordon argued that Wood's promise was illusory. Wood did not promise her anything, she reasoned, because the contract did not specify that Wood had to make any efforts to locate and suggest items for Duff-Gordon to endorse. Since Wood did not really bind himself to do anything for her, Duff-Gordon was equally free from contractual obligations to him.

Cardozo did not agree with this reasoning:

> *A promise may be lacking, and yet the whole writing may be "instinct with an obligation," imperfectly expressed. If that is so, there is a contract.*

If the contract does not have a term in which Wood makes a binding promise to Duff-Gordon, where can we find such an obligation? Cardozo finds it in the circumstances surrounding the deal. Wood created a business for the purpose of placing such indorsements as Duff-Gordon approved, which tends to show he intended to commit to this work.

> *The plaintiff [Wood] goes on to promise that he will account monthly for all moneys received by him, and that he will take out all such patents and copyrights and trademarks as may in his judgment be necessary to protect the rights and articles affected by the agreement.*

Cardozo finds that these promises are nonsensical without the implication that Wood shall make his best efforts to place Duff-Gordon's indorsements. One should not assume that business transactions, especially ones supported by formal written contracts prepared by lawyers and signed by the parties, are intended to be merely optional. Rather, one should presume that the parties intended to both make good faith efforts to bring about the fruits of the agreement.

If a party does indeed have total freedom to perform or not perform a promise at its own discretion, then that is an illusory promise that cannot constitute consideration. But courts will look for that obligation in law and facts:

> *A limitation on the promisor's freedom of choice need not be stated in words. It may be an implicit term of the promise, or it may be supplied by law.* R2d § 77 cmt. d.

The doctrine of good faith and fair dealing implies limits on parties' freedom not to perform their obligations. This makes some obligations that would otherwise be illusory into binding promises that can constitute valid consideration.

G. Nominal Consideration Is Not Consideration

Courts do not generally inquire about the value of consideration. There is no obligation that the consideration be worth the same or more than the promise. In fact, the point of contract law is to allow parties to decide for themselves what they value and how much they value it. It is antithetical to this purpose for courts to police bargains based on how the judges value components of the parties' exchange.

> *If the requirement of consideration is met, there is no additional requirement of . . . equivalence in the values exchanged.* R2d § 79(b).

Parties are free to agree to exchanges of unequal values. Moreover, many things have no fixed or general sense of market value or price. Beauty is in the eye of beholder, and valuation is left to private parties because they in the best position to evaluate their own transaction.

Although courts generally do not inquire about the value of consideration, they may question whether gross inadequacy of consideration implies that the consideration is just a sham. Parties who are aware of the consideration doctrine may attempt to make a gratuitous promise binding by claiming in writing that it was for good and valuable consideration where that is in fact not the case. Or parties may offer some relatively tiny amount of payment as consideration for a promise in order to obtain the pretense of consideration through mere formality. Such tiny amounts are called nominal consideration, and nominal consideration is not sufficient to enforce a contract-at-law.

For example, in the historic 1861 case of *Schnell v. Nell*, 17 Ind. 29 (1861), a widower wanted to honor his deceased wife's desire to bequeath $200 to each of three heirs. To accomplish this, the widower wrote contracts by which he agreed to pay them $200 each, and the writing recited three forms of consideration for this payment:

1. A promise, on the part of the plaintiffs, to pay him one cent.

2. The love and affection he bore his deceased wife, and the fact that she had done her part, as his wife, in the acquisition of property.

3. The fact that she had expressed her desire, in the form of an inoperative will, that the persons named therein should have the sums of money specified.

The court held, first, that one cent is nominal consideration with regards to a promise to pay $200. It is obvious that no one desires $0.01 more than $200. This was a sham, and courts are not mindless wooden sticks.

Second, the court held that love and affection is not consideration, for two reasons. First, the wife had died, so her love and affection was in the past. As discussed earlier, "past consideration" is not consideration. Second, even present or future love and affection of a wife is not consideration to pay a third party. Consideration must be a thing of tangible value, not a moral obligation or a sense of endearment.

Third, his wife's desire is also not consideration. His wife failed to make a valid will. An invalid will is meaningless and valueless, so it cannot constitute consideration. The fact that Schnell now venerates the memory of his deceased wife is not valid consideration to pay any third person money.

H. Reflections on Consideration

The consideration doctrine notoriously troubles law students, but, in reality, it is rarely a problem in most commercial agreements. The debate on the doctrine is primarily an academic one. This module has shown you how to evaluate whether the element of consideration is present in a contract. Perhaps the best way to do this evaluation is by remembering the common situations in which consideration is likely to be absent. Illusory promises, gratuitous promises, and the like are common scenarios where consideration must be examined more closely. These situations are rare in real life contracting, but obnoxiously common on the bar exam, so a wise student will learn to watch out for red flags that are meant to signal the necessity of a consideration analysis. If consideration is found lacking, all hope is not lost. A contract may still be enforceable based on some alternative to consideration, as the next module explores.

Cases

Reading Hamer v. Sidway. Historically, there have been two alternative theories that attempt to explain what consideration is or why the law should require it. The first, and older, theory is best understood as the benefit/detriment test. It asks whether the promisor incurs a benefit, or whether the promisee incurs a detriment, to evaluate whether consideration is present such that a binding contract may be formed. This historic test is now disfavored by modern courts and has largely been replaced by the bargained-for exchange test of consideration. However, the doctrine is varied, and courts still cleave to the old language. For this reason, and because the case is a hallmark of the classic contract law canon, students should read and remember the facts of the historic case of *Hamer v. Sidway*, which is perhaps the most famous articulation of the benefit/detriment test in practice.

Hamer v. Sidway

124 N.Y. 538, 27 N.E. 256 (1891)

PARKER, J., The question which provoked the most discussion by counsel on this appeal, and which lies at the foundation of plaintiff's asserted right of recovery, is whether by virtue of a contract defendant's testator, William E. Story, became indebted to his nephew, William E. Story, 2d, on his twenty-first birthday in the sum of $5,000.

The trial court found as a fact that 'on the 20th day of March, 1869, William E. Story agreed to and with William E. Story, 2d, that if he would refrain from drinking liquor using tobacco, swearing, and playing cards or billiards for money until he should become twenty-one years of age, then he, the said William E. Story, would at that time pay him, the said William E. Story, 2d, the sum of $5,000 for such refraining, to which the said William E. Story, 2d, agreed,' and that he 'in all things fully performed his part of said agreement.'

The defendant contends that the contract was without consideration to support it and is therefore invalid. He asserts that the promisee, by refraining from the use of liquor and tobacco, was not harmed, but benefited; that that which he did was best for him to do, independently of his uncle's promise, — and insists that it follows that, unless the promisor was benefited, the contract was without consideration, — a contention which, if well founded, would seem to leave open for controversy in many cases whether that which the promisee did or omitted to do was in fact of such benefit to him as to leave no consideration to support the enforcement of the promisor's agreement. Such a rule could not be tolerated and is without foundation in the law.

Courts will not ask whether the thing which forms the consideration does in fact benefit the promisee or a third party, or is of any substantial value to anyone. It is enough that something is promised, done, forborne, or suffered by the party to whom the promise is made as consideration for the promise made to him. In general, a waiver of any legal right at the request of another party is a sufficient consideration for a promise. Any damage, or suspension, or forbearance of a right will be sufficient to sustain a promise.

Pollock in his work on Contracts, after citing the definition given by the exchequer chamber, says:

'The second branch of this judicial description is really the most important one. "Consideration" means not so much that one party is profiting as that the other abandons some legal right in the present or limits his legal freedom of action in the future, as an inducement for the promise of the first.'

Now, applying this rule to the facts before us, the promisee used tobacco, occasionally drank liquor, and he had a legal right to do so. That right he abandoned for a period of years upon the strength of the promise of the testator that for such forbearance he would give him $5,000. We need not speculate on the effort which may have been required to give up the use of those stimulants. It is sufficient that he restricted his lawful freedom of action within certain prescribed limits upon the faith of his uncle's agreement, and now, having fully performed the conditions imposed, it is of no moment whether such performance actually proved a benefit to the promisor, and the court will not inquire into it; but, were it a proper subject of inquiry, we see nothing in this record that would permit a determination that the uncle was not benefited in a legal sense.

Few cases have been found which may be said to be precisely in point, but such as have been, support the position we have taken. In Shadwell v. Shadwell, an uncle wrote to his nephew as follows:

My dear Lancey: I am so glad to hear of your intended marriage with Ellen Nicholl, and, as I promised to assist you at starting, I am happy to tell you that I will pay you 150 pounds yearly during my life and until your annual income derived from your profession of a chancery barrister shall amount to 600 guineas, of which your own admission will be the only evidence that I shall receive or require. Your affectionate uncle, CHARLES SHADWELL.

It was held that the promise was binding and made upon good consideration.

In *Lakota v. Newton*, the complaint averred defendant's promise that:

If you [meaning the plaintiff] will leave off drinking for a year I will give you $100.

Plaintiff's assent thereto, performance of the condition by him, and demanded judgment therefor. Defendant demurred, on the ground, among others, that the plaintiff's declaration did not allege a valid and sufficient consideration for the agreement of the defendant. The demurrer was overruled.

In *Talbott v. Stemmons*, the step-grandmother of the plaintiff made with him the following agreement:

I do promise and bind myself to give my grandson Albert R. Talbott $500 at my death if he will never take another chew of tobacco or smoke another cigar during my life, from this date up to my death; and if he breaks this pledge he is to refund double the amount to his mother.

The executor of Mrs. Stemmons demurred to the complaint on the ground that the agreement was not based on a sufficient consideration. The demurrer was sustained, and an appeal taken therefrom to the court of appeals, where the decision of the court below was reversed. In the opinion of the court it is said that:

The right to use and enjoy the use of tobacco was a right that belonged to the plaintiff, and not forbidden by law. The abandonment of its use may have saved him money, or contributed to his health; nevertheless, the surrender of that right caused the promise, and, having the right to contract with reference to the subject matter, the abandonment of the use was a sufficient consideration to uphold the promise.

Abstinence from the use of intoxicating liquors was held to furnish a good consideration for a promissory note in *Lindell v. Rokes*. The order appealed from should be reversed, and the judgment of the special term affirmed, with costs payable out of the estate. All concur.

Reflection

Hamer v. Sidway explains the benefit/detriment test. The benefit/detriment test suggests that for there to be adequate consideration, the contract must either benefit the promisor or detriment the promisee. If the contract does not benefit the promisor or detriment the promisee, the contract is without consideration and is therefore invalid. Adequate consideration can consist of "some right, interest, profit, or benefit accruing to the one party, or some forbearance, detriment, loss, or responsibility given, suffered, or undertaken by the other."

In *Hamer v. Sidway*, the nephew promised to forbear from drinking, swearing, smoking, and some gambling until his 21st birthday. He did forbear from these activities, and it does not matter how much he had to suffer because of it, because he restricted his legal freedom to do so. The nephew restricted his legal freedom of action in the future based on the inducement of his uncle's promise. However, the benefit/detriment test is often disfavored by courts, since it leaves room for controversy in many cases as to whether the promisee either did or did not do something that was to his benefit, therefore leaving no consideration to support the enforcement of the promisor's agreement. For the most part, courts apply a more modern test, the bargained-for exchange test, to evaluate whether a contract is supported by consideration.

Discussion

1. Why do courts require consideration?

2. What is the role of (i) inducement and (ii) exchange in (a) the benefit/detriment test as articulated in *Hamer* and (b) the modern consideration test (R2d § 71)?

3. Evaluate the facts of *Hamer* under the bargained-for exchange test of consideration. Is the result the same?

4. The *Hamer* court makes analogy to several cases including *Lakota* and *Talbott*. What is similar about these three cases? Can you identify any distinctions that the court glossed over?

———————

Reading Pennsy Supply, Inc. v. American Ash Recycling Corp. Most modern courts and the R2d have moved away from the benefit/detriment test and toward the bargained-for exchange test. In this modern test (R2d § 71), the question is whether the contract is the result of both parties' desire to receive something from the transaction. This does not require bargaining per se, meaning, the parties do not have to haggle or dicker over terms. Rather, the test simply looks at whether promises are given in exchange for one another. This modern test fits better with the law and economics approach to contract law, which justifies enforceable agreements on the basis that they generally make the world more valuable by allocating property to the person who values it more.

But the bargained-for exchange test is not perfect. The *Pennsy* case highlights one of the challenges in applying this test where the contract is not for a typical good. In the following case, the contract is instead for the removal of a "bad": hazardous waste. Fortunately, the bargained-for exchange test proves flexible enough to accommodate this circumstance, demonstrating one way in which it proves superior to the benefit/detriment test in terms of its ability to distinguish socially beneficial bargains from ones that should not necessarily be enforced by courts.

Pennsy Supply, Inc. v. American Ash Recycling Corp.

895 A.2d 595 (Pa. Super. Ct. 2006).

ORIE MELVIN, J.:

Appellant, Pennsy Supply, Inc. ("Pennsy"), appeals from the grant of preliminary objections in the nature of a demurrer [Pennsylvania's version of a motion to dismiss] in favor of Appellee, American Ash Recycling Corp. of Pennsylvania ("American Ash"). We reverse and remand for further proceedings.

The trial court summarized the allegations of the complaint as follows:

> The instant case arises out of a construction project for Northern York High School (Project) owned by Northern York County School District (District) in York County, Pennsylvania. The District entered into a construction contract for the Project with a general contractor, Lobar, Inc. (Lobar). Lobar, in turn, subcontracted the paving of driveways and a parking lot to [Pennsy].
>
> The contract between Lobar and the District included Project Specifications for paving work which required Lobar, through its subcontractor Pennsy, to use certain base aggregates. The Project Specifications permitted substitution of the aggregates with an alternate material known as Treated Ash Aggregate (TAA) or AggRite.
>
> The Project Specifications included a "notice to bidders" of the availability of AggRite at no cost from [American Ash], a supplier of AggRite.

The Project Specifications also included a letter to the Project architect from American Ash confirming the availability of a certain amount of free AggRite on a first come, first served basis.

Pennsy contacted American Ash and informed American Ash that it would require approximately 11,000 tons of AggRite for the Project. Pennsy subsequently picked up the AggRite from American Ash and used it for the paving work, in accordance with the Project Specifications.

Pennsy completed the paving work in December 2001. The pavement ultimately developed extensive cracking in February 2002. The District notified . . . Lobar as to the defects and Lobar in turn directed Pennsy to remedy the defective work. Pennsy performed the remedial work during summer 2003 at no cost to the District.

The scope and cost of the remedial work included the removal and appropriate disposal of the AggRite, which is classified as a hazardous waste material by the Pennsylvania Department of Environmental Protection. Pennsy requested American Ash to arrange for the removal and disposal of the AggRite; however, American Ash did not do so. Pennsy provided notice to American Ash of its intention to recover costs.

Pennsy also alleged that the remedial work cost it $251,940.20 to perform and that it expended an additional $133,777.48 to dispose of the AggRite it removed.

On November 18, 2004, Pennsy filed a five-count complaint against American Ash alleging breach of contract (Count I); breach of implied warranty of merchantability (Count II); breach of express warranty of merchantability (Count III); breach of warranty of fitness for a particular purpose (Count IV); and promissory estoppel (Count V). American Ash filed demurrers to all five counts. Pennsy responded and also sought leave to amend should any demurrer be sustained. The trial court sustained the demurrers by order and opinion dated May 25, 2005 and dismissed the complaint. This appeal followed.

Pennsy raises three questions for our review:

(1) Whether the trial court erred in not accepting as true . . . [the] Complaint allegations that (a) [American Ash] promotes the use of its AggRite material, which is classified as hazardous waste, in order to avoid the high cost of disposing [of] the material itself; and (b) [American Ash] incurred a benefit from Pennsy's use of the material in the form of avoidance of the costs of said disposal sufficient to ground contract and warranty claims.

(2) Whether Pennsy's relief of [American Ash's] legal obligation to dispose of a material classified as hazardous waste, such that [American Ash] avoided the costs of disposal thereof at a hazardous waste site, is sufficient consideration to ground contract and warranty claims.

[(3) Promissory estoppel question omitted.]

"Preliminary objections in the nature of a demurrer test the legal sufficiency of the complaint." [A demurrer is an older term in civil procedure for what is now more commonly known as a motion to dismiss.]

When reviewing the dismissal of a complaint based upon preliminary objections in the nature of a demurrer, we treat as true all well-pleaded material, factual averments and all inferences fairly deducible therefrom. Where the preliminary objections will result in the dismissal of the action, the objections may be sustained only in cases that are clear and free from doubt. To be clear and free from doubt that dismissal is appropriate, it must appear with certainty that the law would not permit recovery by the plaintiff upon the facts averred. Any doubt should be resolved by a refusal to sustain the objections. Moreover, we review the trial court's decision for an abuse of discretion or an error of law.

In applying this standard to the instant appeal, we deem it easiest to order our discussion by count.

Count I raises a breach of contract claim. "A cause of action for breach of contract must be established by pleading (1) the existence of a contract, including its essential terms, (2) a breach of a duty imposed by the contract and (3) resultant damages." While not every term of a contract must be stated in complete detail, every element must be specifically pleaded. Clarity is particularly important where an oral contract is alleged.

Instantly, the trial court determined that "any alleged agreement between the parties is unenforceable for lack of consideration." The trial court also stated, "the facts as pleaded do not support an inference that disposal costs were part of any bargaining process or that American Ash offered the AggRite with an intent to avoid disposal costs." Thus, we understand the trial court to have dismissed Count I for two reasons related to the necessary element of consideration: one, the allegations of the Complaint established that Pennsy had received a conditional gift from American Ash, and two, there were no allegations in the Complaint to show that American Ash's avoidance of disposal costs was part of any bargaining process between the parties.

It is axiomatic that:

> *Consideration is an essential element of an enforceable contract.*
>
> *Consideration consists of a benefit to the promisor or a detriment to the promisee.*
>
> *Consideration must actually be bargained for as the exchange for the promise.*
>
> *It is not enough, however, that the promisee has suffered a legal detriment at the request of the promisor. The detriment incurred must be the "quid pro quo", or the "price" of the promise, and the inducement for which it was made.... If the promisor merely intends to make a gift to the promisee upon the performance of a condition, the promise is gratuitous, and the satisfaction of the condition is not consideration for a contract. The distinction between*

such a conditional gift and a contract is well illustrated in Williston on Contracts, where it is said:

> *If a benevolent man says to a tramp, — "If you go around the corner to the clothing shop there, you may purchase an overcoat on my credit," no reasonable person would understand that the short walk was requested as the consideration for the promise, but that in the event of the tramp going to the shop the promisor would make him a gift.*

Whether a contract is supported by consideration presents a question of law. The classic formula for the difficult concept of consideration was stated by Justice Oliver Wendell Holmes, Jr.:

> *The promise must induce the detriment and the detriment must induce the promise.*

As explained by Professor Murray:

> *If the promisor made the promise for the purpose of inducing the detriment, the detriment induced the promise. If, however, the promisor made the promise with no particular interest in the detriment that the promisee had to suffer to take advantage of the promised gift or other benefit, the detriment was incidental or conditional to the promisee's receipt of the benefit. Even though the promisee suffered a detriment induced by the promise, the purpose of the promisor was not to have the promisee suffer the detriment because she did not seek that detriment in exchange for her promise.*

This concept is also well summarized in AMERICAN JURISPRUDENCE:

> *As to the distinction between consideration and a condition, it is often difficult to determine whether words of condition in a promise indicate a request for consideration or state a mere condition in a gratuitous promise. An aid, though not a conclusive test, in determining which construction of the promise is more reasonable is an inquiry into whether the occurrence of the condition would benefit the promisor. If so, it is a fair inference that the occurrence was requested as consideration. On the other hand, if the occurrence of the condition is no benefit to the promisor but is merely to enable the promisee to receive a gift, the occurrence of the event on which the promise is conditional, though brought about by the promisee in reliance on the promise, is not properly construed as consideration.*

Upon review, we disagree with the trial court that the allegations of the Complaint show only that American Ash made a conditional gift of the AggRite to Pennsy. In paragraphs 8 and 9 of the Complaint, Pennsy alleged:

> *American Ash actively promotes the use of AggRite as a building material to be used in base course of paved structures, and provides the material free of charge, in an effort to have others dispose of the material and thereby avoid incurring the disposal costs itself. . . . American Ash provided the AggRite to*

Pennsy for use on the Project, which saved American Ash thousands of dollars in disposal costs it otherwise would have incurred.

Accepting these allegations as true and using the Holmesian formula for consideration, it is a fair interpretation of the Complaint that American Ash's promise to supply AggRite free of charge induced Pennsy to assume the detriment of collecting and taking title to the material, and critically, that it was this very detriment, whether assumed by Pennsy or some other successful bidder to the paving subcontract, which induced American Ash to make the promise to provide free AggRite for the project. Paragraphs 8–9 of the Complaint simply belie the notion that American Ash offered AggRite as a conditional gift to the successful bidder on the paving subcontract for which American Ash desired and expected nothing in return.

We turn now to whether consideration is lacking because Pennsy did not allege that American Ash's avoidance of disposal costs was part of any bargaining process between the parties. The Complaint does not allege that the parties discussed or even that Pennsy understood at the time it requested or accepted the AggRite that Pennsy's use of the AggRite would allow American Ash to avoid disposal costs. However, we do not believe such is necessary.

The bargain theory of consideration does not actually require that the parties bargain over the terms of the agreement. . . . According to Holmes, an influential advocate of the bargain theory, what is required [for consideration to exist] is that the promise and the consideration be in "the relation of reciprocal conventional inducement, each for the other."

Here, as explained above, the Complaint alleges facts which, if proven, would show the promise induced the detriment and the detriment induced the promise. This would be consideration. Accordingly, we reverse the dismissal of Count I. [Discussion of Counts II, III, IV (Breach of Warranty — Sales) and V (Promissory Estoppel) omitted.]

For all of the foregoing reasons, we reverse the trial court's order granting the demurrers and dismissing the Complaint and remand for further proceedings. Jurisdiction relinquished.

Reflection

The *Pennsy* case is an example of a court using both the benefit/detriment test and the bargained-for exchange test. The benefit/detriment test states that "[c]onsideration consists of a benefit to the promisor or a [legal] detriment to the promisee." Here, there is both a benefit and detriment, though both do not need to be present. The promisor (American Ash) benefited by saving thousands of dollars in disposal costs. A legal detriment is something that the promisee is not obligated to do. Thus, Pennsy collecting and taking title to the AggRite was the detriment.

The court also applied the bargained-for exchange test. That test states "[c]onsideration must actually be bargained for as the exchange for the promise." The type of bargain required for consideration is not negotiating or bartering over terms but that "[t]he promise must induce the detriment and the detriment must induce the promise." In other words, a bargain induces (persuades/encourages) the other's response, and the other person is induced by it and acts on that inducement.

One way to tell the difference between a gratuitous promise (condition) and consideration is whether the occurrence of that condition would benefit the promisor. Unlike the Tramp Hypothetical, where the walk around the corner was merely incidental to obtaining the overcoat, taking the AggRite was not. The promisor did not benefit from the promisee walking around the corner nor was his promise motivated by it. In *Pennsy*, American Ash benefited and induced others to get rid of the AggRite by offering it free of charge to avoid the disposal costs. Pennsy was induced by American Ash and acted on that inducement by taking and collecting the material thereby suffering a legal detriment.

Discussion

1. How does the *Pennsy* court distinguish between a conditional gift and a promise supported by consideration? Why did the court find that AggRite offered its aggregate as part of a bargained-for exchange and not as a conditional gift?

2. Would this case have come out differently if the court had applied the benefit/detriment test and not the bargained-for exchange test? Why or why not?

3. Does the court discuss whether justice and equity require treating AggRite's manifestation as an offer? Why does the court include or omit a discussion about justice and equity?

Problems

Problem 7.1. An Aunt's Promise

Dougherty, a boy of eight years, received from his aunt a promissory note for $3,000, payable at her death or before. While visiting her nephew, the aunt saw how well her nephew was progressing in school and decided that she wanted to help take care of the child since she loved him very much. The aunt had the boy's guardian draft a promissory note for her. The aunt handed a note to her nephew, which read:

> *You have always done for me, and I have signed this note for you. Now, do not lose it. Someday it will be valuable.*

Following the aunt's death, Dougherty sought to recover for the note.

Was there adequate consideration to form an enforceable contract?

See Dougherty v. Salt, 125 N.E. 94 (N.Y. 1919).

Problem 7.2. Betty and the Benefit

M.J.D., Inc. ("MJD") applied to Bank for a loan to pay off its debt. The Bank approved the loan subject to a guaranty (a contract where one person agrees to pay the debt of the other if they fail to do so) by the Small Business Administration ("SBA"), a federal government agency. The SBA approved the loan but required the principals, Melton Meadors, Jay Judd, Harold Ducote, and Ducote's wife to sign a guaranty on the SBA form. On the application, the guarantors had been "Melton E. Meadors — a single person, Jay A. Judd & Wife, Harold A. Ducote, Jr., & Wife."

At the signing, the three principals and their wives were all present, including Betty Meadors, Meadors' wife. The SBA was not present. All six — the three principals and their wives — signed the guaranty form. MJD defaulted on the loan, and SBA was to take over the guaranteed portion of the loan. The United States sued to collect the deficiency from the guarantors, including Betty Meadors.

Applying both the benefit-detriment test and bargained-for-exchange test, did Betty Meadors receive consideration from the SBA for her signature on the guaranty form?

See United States v. Meadors, 753 F.2d 590 (7th Cir. 1985).

Problem 7.3. Shifting Sands

Peter was on a guided tour through the Sahara Desert when a sandstorm suddenly appeared. In the chaos of the storm, Peter got separated from his tour group. After the storm abated, Peter found himself lost in the desert. He wandered for two full days in the baking sun, growing weak and very thirsty, when he finally happened upon a village in the desert. Peter urgently ran up to the first person he saw, who was a man named Merzouga, and asked desperately for water. Merzouga said to Peter, "If you walk through my village and over the last dune beyond it, you will find a stream of clean water. If you promise to send me and my family $1,000 upon your return to America, then you may go there and drink as much water as you like." Peter agreed and shook Merzouga's hand, then walked through the village and over the dune, where he found a cold, clear stream. Peter drunk a great deal of water and refreshed himself.

Later that day, a search party found Peter and took him back to his tour group, which later returned to America. When he arrived, Peter remembered his promise to Merzouga, but he felt that $1,000 was much too high a price, and so he decided not to pay Merzouga anything.

As a matter of law, has Peter formed a contract with Merzouga? If so, what is Peter's obligation under that agreement?

Chapter 8

Promissory Estoppel

When gratuitous promises foreseeably and actually cause the promisee to rely on the promise, and where that reliance is detrimental to the promisee, the doctrine of promissory estoppel may require enforcement of that promise, even where it not supported by consideration.

Before going over the elements of promissory estoppel — which is the legal term for a promise that is enforceable because it reasonably and foreseeably induces action or forbearance by the promisee — it is worth noting that situations involving promissory estoppel at first blush appear similar to cases where consideration may be found. After all, consideration is something given in exchange for a promise, often a promise to do something in the future. How is a promise supported by consideration different from a gratuitous promise reasonably inducing action or forbearance?

A simple litmus test for distinguishing between a promise supported by consideration and a gratuitous promise is whether the promisor actually wants the action or forbearance to occur because that action or forbearance is anticipated to produce a valuable economic benefit to the promisor. If the action or forbearance is not sought after by the promisor for its own sake but is merely a condition or means by which the promisee can receive a gift, then that promise is probably not supported by consideration.

Recall that the consideration doctrine is fundamentally based on economic principles. By requiring a bargained-for exchange as a prerequisite to contractual enforceability, the law recognizes that contracts are primarily a means by which two or more parties attempt to make themselves better off by agreeing to make some exchange in the future or to pay for its value. If people are the best judge of what they value (and noting that this assumption is essential to the claim that a free society increases social welfare), then contract law, with its consideration doctrine, is the instrument by which people can reliably promise to make each other better off.

But even contract law, which many would consider to be the area of law most aligned with economic thinking, is not ruled by concerns of efficiency alone. Like all the law, notions of justice and fairness must also be considered. For example, if a six-year-old boy agrees to trade his valuable Micky Mantle autographed baseball card for an ice cream on a hot day, there may be mutual assent and consideration, but a judge should not enforce the agreement regardless. Not only does the child lack legal capacity to incur binding obligations, but also there seems something unfair about the trade. The many defense doctrines evolved to account for these negative situations, where the legal elements of contract formation are met but justice and fairness demand that the agreement be nullified anyway.

On the flip side, there are positive situations, where the formal legal elements of contract formation are not met, yet justice and fairness compel courts to find a binding obligation anyway. These situations are the subject of this Chapter, and the doctrines that evolved to handle these positive circumstances are generally referred to as the estoppel doctrines. The Restatement provides the modern formulation of the doctrine of equitable estoppel:

> *A promise which the promisor should reasonably expect to induce action or forbearance on the part of the promisee or a third person and which does induce such action or forbearance is binding if injustice can be avoided only by enforcement of the promise. The remedy granted for breach may be limited as justice requires.* R2d § 90(1).

Note that this doctrine requires three elements: a promise, reliance, and detriment, as illustrated in this figure:

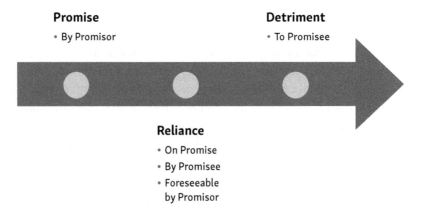

Figure 8.1. Promissory estoppel elements illustrated.

First, we will explore the theory and purpose of the doctrine of equitable estoppel. Then, we will analyze its elements in more detail.

Rules

A. Theory of Promissory Estoppel

The word estoppel comes from the French word for stop, and it essentially means that a court will stop a party from denying that an enforceable promise exists. Estoppel doctrines are found in many areas of law, and the estoppel doctrines that apply to contract law are commonly referred to as alternatives to consideration, because they stop parties from arguing that a lack of consideration renders a promise unenforceable. The doctrine of promissory estoppel will stop a promisor from arguing its promise is unenforceable due to lack of consideration where the promisee foreseeably, actually, and detrimentally relied on that promise.

Recall from the chapter on Consideration the story of Williston's tramp. In this illustration, a benevolent man says to a tramp, "If you walk to the store on the corner, you may purchase a coat on my account." Although this looks at first blush like a promise supported by consideration — namely, the promisor's coat in exchange for the promisee's walk — a closer evaluation reveals that there is no consideration in this illustration. Ask yourself, does the benevolent man really want the tramp to take a walk? Is that man bargaining for the tramp's walk because it is something the man desires? No. The walk is simply necessary to obtain the gift of a coat. This is an illustration of what Williston calls a conditional gift, where the walk is the condition, and the coat is the gift.

The benevolent man's promise is thus unenforceable as a matter of law because it lacks consideration. But it may be enforceable under the doctrine of promissory estoppel. To see how, we will extend the hypothetical. Imagine now that the tramp has camped on the front steps of the ostensibly benevolent man's apartment building, and that the store is not right around the next street corner but rather halfway across town. The man knows that the tramp must pack up and remove her camp in order to walk to the store without risking the loss of her few material possessions. Perhaps the man even offers the coat to lure the tramp away from his premises, although we may never know his subjective and hidden reasons for his supposed benevolence. The promise then induces the tramp to pack up and trek across town; meanwhile, the man calls the store and tells its clerk not to use his account for the tramp. The tramp arrives at the store only to be turned away empty-handed, and then she returns to the man's apartment to find the steps barricaded so she can no longer camp there. Cold and without shelter, the tramp then proceeds to find some alternative encampment.

Let's imagine further that the tramp sues the man for breaching his promise to give her a coat. Can she prove they had a contract at law? No, for the reasons we just discussed: the man received no consideration, and gratuitous promises and promises to give conditional gifts are unenforceable as a matter of law for want of consideration. But she may have a case under the doctrine of promissory estoppel.

Why should the law distinguish between the first case, where the man was acting benevolently, from the second case, where the man was acting for his self-interest? In the first case, the man does not intent to exploit the tramp's faith in the law. But, in the second case, the ostensibly benevolent man is relying on the tramp's trust in the legal process to persuade her to take an action that is detrimental to her. That law incorporates safeguards against its exploitation.

B. Promise Reasonably Inducing Action or Forbearance

The first element of promissory estoppel is, of course, a promise. Recall that all contractual obligations stem from promises. Therefore, there can be no contractual duty where there is no promise. But what sort of promise is sufficient for its enforcement pursuant to the doctrine of promissory estoppel?

The law requires that a promise reasonably induce action or forbearance if it is to be sufficient for enforcement per promissory estoppel. This means that the promisor actually or reasonably should have expected that its promise may cause a reasonable person to take some action or commit to some inaction.

Note that this definition uses the word "reasonable" in several places. First, the promisor's promise is not judged on some subjective mindset, but rather, the promisor's promise is judged on what a reasonable promisor would think about the likely result of that promise upon the promisee. If a reasonable promisor would think that a reasonable promisee would rely on the promise, then that is a promise reasonably inducing action or forbearance.

Under this analysis, it does not matter whether the actual promisor actually thought that its promise would induce reliance. One reason that this subjective standard is not required is because it is so hard to prove what an individual actually and subjectively thought. People may even lie or misconstrue their prior mindset where it avoids some obligation which they do not desire. But, if the promisor happens to actually intend its promise to cause reliance, and if the promisor admits that in a manner admissible in court, then the promisor's subjective intention to induce the promisee's action or forbearance is sufficient to establish this element.

Second, the promisee's reliance is likewise judged from the perspective of a reasonable person. The judge or jury asks the question, would a reasonable person rely on the promisor's promise, to determine whether the promise reasonably induces action or forbearance. If the promisee in questions happens to be especially gullible, or unusually cynical, that generally does not impact the analysis of whether a reasonable person would rely on the promise.

However, the reasonable promisee is not judged in a vacuum; rather, the court should consider how a reasonable promisee in the position of the actual promisee would reasonably respond. For example, if the promisee is the promisor's adult grandson, it is likely to be more reasonable for that promise to reasonably induce reliance than if the parties were total strangers. On the other hand, if the promisor is a notorious liar and trickster, then a reasonable promisee is less likely to rely on the promise.

The 1898 case of *Ricketts v. Scothorn*, below, illustrates this case. Katie Scothorn was the granddaughter of a certain Andrew D. Ricketts. Grandpa Ricketts promised Granddaughter Scothorn that, if Scothorn stopped working, then Ricketts would pay for her living expenses. Ricketts' promise was proved by a writing signed by his own hand, which said:

> *May the First, 1891. I promise to pay to Katie Scothorn on demand, $2,000,*
> *to be at 6 per cent. per annum. J.C. Ricketts.*

You should notice straight away that this promise lacks considerations. By its terms, Scothorn must do nothing in exchange for Rickett's $2,000. As you will later learn in the chapter on the Parol Evidence Rule, a final written agreement excludes any evidence of prior negotiations or discussion, so, as a technical matter, any understanding that Scothorn would quit work in exchange for Ricketts' money is excluded from this analysis. Since the promise lacks consideration, it is unenforceable as a matter of law.

Problems did not arise until Grandpa Ricketts died. Upon his death, the executor of his estate, Andrew D. Ricketts, refused to continue to support Scothorn.

But as a matter of equity, the promise could be enforced pursuant to the doctrine of promissory estoppel. Here, the legal question is whether Grandpa Ricketts should have reasonably expected that Granddaughter Scothorn would rely on his promise. The answer seems to be a clear "yes." Not only did the parties enjoy a special relationship of trust and confidence that made reliance on one another more reasonable, but Scothorn also actually relied on the promise by quitting her job. In fact, Ricketts' express intention was to motivate Scothorn to quit her job. Therefore, there was foreseeable reliance on the promise.

C. Reliance on the Promise

The second element of promissory estoppel is whether the promisee actually relied on the promise. This is typically not a difficult inquiry because the common law defines reliance broadly in this context: the promisor is affected by any foreseeable reliance by the promisee upon the promise. Foreseeable is broader than intended or foreseen by the promisor. The legal question is whether the promisee's reliance was reasonably foreseeable; that is, foreseeable by a reasonable person in the promisor's position.

1. Legal Enforceability of Contracts by Mutual Assent

Legal resolutions are preferred over equitable ones. A plaintiff seeking enforcement should generally argue, first, that there is a binding contract as a matter of law and, arguendo (in the alternative), that there is an equitably enforceable promise. In other words, equitable analysis regarding promissory estoppel (detrimental reliance) should usually be preceded by legal analysis including whether the parties engaged in offer, acceptance (during the power of acceptance), and consideration. For rules regarding offers, see R2d Ch. 2, Topic 3. For rules regarding duration of the offer, see R2d Ch. 2, Topic 4. For rules regarding acceptance, see R2d Ch. 2, Topic 5. For rules regarding consideration, see R2d Ch. 4, Topic 1.

Note that even where mutual assent with consideration is objectively present, there might be some defenses showing that mutual assent was invalid or voidable. For example, a party who lacks capacity cannot form mutually binding obligations. *See*

R2d Ch. 2. Some otherwise valid agreements are unenforceable unless their material terms are evidenced by a writing signed by the party to be charged. *See* R2d Ch. 5. Contracts formed pursuant to a material mistake may be voidable when the mistaken party does not bear the risk of that mistake. *See* R2d Ch. 6. Additional grounds for voidability exist where that mistake was induced by the other party's misrepresentation. *See* R2d Ch. 7 Topic 1. When mutual assent was induced by an improper threat or undue influence, the contract may be voidable on these grounds as well. *See* R2d Ch. 7 Topic 2. And courts will not enforce obligations that are "unconscionable" as a matter of public policy. *See* R2d Ch. 8.

2. Analysis of Equitable Enforceability of Contracts by Promissory Estoppel

As the name implies, promissory estoppel requires, as a preliminary matter, a promise. In fact, all contractual obligations stem from promises. Without a promise, there cannot be any contractual remedy, although other areas of law including property, tort, and restitution may provide remedies in those cases where contract law does not.

The promise must meet two qualifications or elements for promissory estoppel to apply. First, the promisor must reasonably foresee that the promise will induce reliance; and second, the promisee must actually rely on the promise in a foreseeable manner.

You can think of these elements in an alternative way. You might instead think of promissory estoppel as requiring two manifestations: a promise, and an action or forbearance in reliance on that promise. The promise and the action do not have to be the same, but they must be related. It must be reasonably foreseeable by the promisor for the promise to potentially cause the action. The action must therefore be reasonable in light of the promise.

Although the doctrine of promissory estoppel is flexible, there must be a reasonable relationship between the promise and the action in reliance thereon. For example, in *Coffman Industries, Inc. v. Gorman-Taber Co.*, 521 S.W.2d 763 (Mo. Ct. App. 1975), an insurance company orally promised to pay a subcontractor if the subcontractor dropped its suit against a general contractor who was the insurance company's client. The court found that the subcontractor's action to drop the case was reasonably in reliance on the insurance company's promise to pay the subcontract. And in *Katz v. Danny Dare, Inc.*, 610 S.W.2d 121 (Mo. Ct. App. 1980), an employee was injured on the job. In exchange for retiring immediately instead of collecting unemployment, the company orally promised to pay the employee a pension. The employee retired, and the court found that his action was reasonably induced by the company's promise. In cases like these, the relationship between the promise and the action may seem obvious, but attorneys still need to prove that relationship and argue that it is reasonable.

Even if the elements of promissory estoppel are technically met, the case is not over. Winning a case on the basis of promissory estoppel is an uphill battle. As an equitable remedy, promissory estoppel is granted only where justice requires it. Even if the elements of the claim are met, a court can still refuse to enforce the promise, when doing so would be unjust or unfair.

3. Promise to Give Charity

In some jurisdictions, charitable subscriptions (promises to give charity or to otherwise donate money to non-profit organizations and good causes) are enforceable even without proof of actual reliance. R2d states:

> A charitable subscription or a marriage settlement is binding under Subsection (1) without proof that the promise induced action or forbearance. R2d § 90(2).

Other jurisdictions do not distinguish charitable subscripts in this way. In *Maryland National Bank v. United Jewish Appeal Federation of Greater Washington, Inc.*, below, a certain Milton Polinger pledged to give $200,000 to the United Jewish Appeal (UJA), a charitable organization, for its general-purpose fund. Polinger died before paying UJA, and his executor, the bank, refused to pay the pledge on the ground that it was unenforceable for want of consideration. The court first decided whether it would adopt the R2d approach to this issue.

The *UJA* court declined to adopt the R2d approach, instead cleaving to its precedent of requiring actual reliance for promissory estoppel even in cases of charities, because some obligations are better left to the internal conscience:

> Indeed, considering the number of these (charitable) institutions, erected and maintained by private munificence alone, the cases are very rare in which subscribers have refused compliance with their engagements. Instances may occur in which parties, feeling themselves released in consequence of a failure of expectations reasonably entertained at the time of making the subscription, might avail themselves of legal defenses, without justly forfeiting the good opinion of those who embarked with them in the enterprise. The propriety, however, of employing such means of resisting payment the parties must determine for themselves.

For its position, the R2d argues that courts do favor charitable subscriptions and, for that matter, marriage settlements as the two types of promises that do not require substantial reliance to be enforceable.

> American courts have traditionally favored charitable subscriptions and marriage settlements, and have found consideration in many cases where the element of exchange was doubtful or nonexistent.

It is a bit odd that both the *UJA* court and the R2d commentors each claim that precedent supports their own position, where both position are opposite to each other. Both cite substantial authority for their claims, too. This goes to show that the law is sometimes hard to determine objectively.

D. Justice Requires Enforcing the Promise

The third and final element of promissory estoppel is the positive requirement to enforce the promise for the sake of justice. This is a very loose standard that is hard to illustrate because it is designed by its very nature to be ultimately flexible. Courts sitting in equity can consider almost any factors when determining what justice requires. For example, if a wealthy and powerful man seeks to enforce a promise by an impoverished and infirm vagabond, the court can consider their difference in status when deciding whether to enforce the vagabond's promise. This should not be a factor when evaluating contracts-at-law, because such contractual promises must be kept. The court has much more discretion when rendering decisions based on estoppel and other equitable doctrines.

Defining when justice requires enforcing a promise is no less a task than defining what is justice itself. The question of what is justice has persisted at least since Plato and Aristotle in ancient Greece, and it will not be resolved here. For present purposes, we will escape to Justice Stewart's approach in *Jacobellis v. Ohio*, 378 U.S. 184 (1964), and define justice as "I know it when I see it." Students are encouraged to think creatively about how arguments for and against justice might apply in any situation involving a request for an equitable remedy.

E. Reflections on Promissory Estoppel

The consideration doctrine is meant to ensure that courts enforce only voluntary bargains. However, the doctrine is perhaps too rigid. In economic terms, we would say that this generates false positives and false negatives. On the one hand, the consideration doctrine generates false positives by making contracts enforceable where they only have the trappings and external appearance of a voluntary exchange. If a robber puts a gun to a grandmother's head and demands that she sign a paper under which she shall give one million dollars to the robber in exchange for letting her live, that does have the appearance of a contract supported by consideration, but in truth, the robber exerted duress (wrongful pressure) on the grandmother such that she did not make a free and voluntary decision.

On the other hand, the consideration doctrine generates false negatives by making contracts unenforceable where the formal elements of bargained-for exchange are missing. When a waitress brings a hamburger to a hungry man, who eats it quickly, and then the man says he will pay $10 tomorrow for that hamburger, that promise is gratuitous. The man got the hamburger without making a return promise, so we cannot say that his promise to pay induced the waitress to bring the hamburger. There is no consideration in this example. But clearly, the parties entered into a valuable and voluntary exchange, where one got food he wanted, and the other was to get paid the fair value of the food.

Since the rigid consideration doctrine is both over- and under-inclusive, the law has developed equitable exceptions to reduce the harmful effects of false positives and false negatives. On the one hand, the defense against formation and the excuse doctrines ameliorate some of the false positive. On the other hand, the alternatives to consideration resolve some of the false negatives. Although these doctrines make contract law more complex, they also make the law fairer and more in line with people's reasonable expectations.

The next chapter regards Promissory Restitution, another exception from the consideration doctrine. The difference between these equitable doctrines is, primarily, that promissory estoppel requires one person's promise to induce another's action, whereas promissory restitution involves a gratuitous promise to pay for a past benefit. In other words, the promise in promissory estoppel is prospective or forward-looking, while promissory restitution is retrospective or backward-looking.

Cases

> *Reading Rickets v. Scothorn.* The doctrine of promissory estoppel developed under common law during the 19th century primarily to deal with contracts that were unenforceable for want of consideration. The case of *Ricketts v. Scothorn* illustrates the development of this doctrine, which is now also found in R2d § 90.

Ricketts v. Scothorn

57 Neb. 51, 77 N.W. 365 (1898)

SULLIVAN, J.

In the district court of Lancaster county the plaintiff, Katie Scothorn, recovered judgment against the defendant, Andrew D. Ricketts, as executor of the last will and testament of John C. Ricketts, deceased. The action was based upon a promissory note, of which the following is a copy: "May the first, 1891. I promise to pay to Katie Scothorn on demand, $2,000, to be at 6 per cent. per annum. J.C. Ricketts." In the petition the plaintiff alleges that the consideration for the execution of the note was that she should surrender her employment as bookkeeper for Mayer Bros. and cease to work for a living. She also alleges that the note was given to induce her to abandon her occupation, and that, relying on it, and on the annual interest, as a means of support, she gave up the employment in which she was then engaged. These allegations of the petition are denied by the administrator.

The material facts are undisputed. They are as follows: John C. Ricketts, the maker of the note, was the grandfather of the plaintiff. Early in May — presumably on the day the note bears date — he called on her at the store where she was working. What transpired between them is thus described by Mr. Flodene, one of the plaintiff's witnesses:

> A. *Well, the old gentleman came in there one morning about nine o'clock, probably a little before or a little after, but early in the morning, and he unbuttoned his vest, and took out a piece of paper in the shape of a note; that is the way it looked to me; and he says to Miss Scothorn, "I have fixed out something that you have not got to work any more." He says, none of my grandchildren work, and you don't have to.*
>
> Q. *Where was she?*
>
> A. *She took the piece of paper and kissed him, and kissed the old gentleman, and commenced to cry.*

It seems Miss Scothorn immediately notified her employer of her intention to quit work, and that she did soon after abandon her occupation. The mother of the plaintiff was a witness and testified that she had a conversation with her father, Mr. Ricketts, shortly after the note was executed. In the note, he informed her that he had given the note to the plaintiff to enable her to quit work; that none of his grandchildren worked, and he did not think she ought to. For something more than a year the plaintiff was without an occupation, but in September, 1892, with the consent of her grandfather, and by his assistance, she secured a position as bookkeeper with Messrs. Funke & Ogden.

On June 8, 1894, Mr. Ricketts died. He had paid one year's interest on the note, and a short time before his death expressed regret that he had not been able to pay the balance. In the summer or fall of 1892 he stated to his daughter, Mrs. Scothorn, that if he could sell his farm in Ohio he would pay the note out of the proceeds. He at no time repudiated the obligation. We quite agree with counsel for the defendant that upon this evidence there was nothing to submit to the jury, and that a verdict should have been directed peremptorily for one of the parties.

The testimony of Flodene and Mrs. Scothorn, taken together, conclusively establishes the fact that the note was not given in consideration of the plaintiff pursuing, or agreeing to pursue, any particular line of conduct. There was no promise on the part of the plaintiff to do, or refrain from doing, anything. Her right to the money promised in the note was not made to depend upon an abandonment of her employment with Mayer Bros., and future abstention from like service. Mr. Ricketts made no condition, requirement, or request. He exacted no quid pro quo. He gave the note as a gratuity, and looked for nothing in return.

So far as the evidence discloses, it was his purpose to place the plaintiff in a position of independence, where she could work or remain idle, as she might choose. The abandonment of Miss Scothorn of her position as bookkeeper was altogether voluntary. It was not an act done in fulfillment of any contract obligation assumed when she accepted the note. The instrument in suit, being given without any valuable consideration, was nothing more than a promise to make a gift in the future of the sum of money therein named. Ordinarily, such promises are not enforceable, even when put in the form of a promissory note.

It has often been held that an action on a note given to a church, college, or other like institution, upon the faith of which money has been expended or obligations incurred, could not be successfully defended on the ground of a want of consideration. In this class of cases the note in suit is nearly always spoken of as a gift or donation, but the decision is generally put on the ground that the expenditure of money or assumption of liability by the donee on the faith of the promise constitutes a valuable and sufficient consideration. It seems to us that the true reason is the preclusion of the defendant, under the doctrine of estoppel, to deny the consideration. Such seems to be the view of the matter taken by the supreme court of Iowa in the case of *Simpson Centenary College v. Tuttle*:

> *Where a note, however, is based on a promise to give for the support of the objects referred to, it may still be open to this defense [want of consideration], unless it shall appear that the donee has, prior to any revocation, entered into engagements, or made expenditures based on such promise, so that he must suffer loss or injury if the note is not paid. This is based on the equitable principle that, after allowing the donee to incur obligations on the faith that the note would be paid, the donor would be estopped from pleading want of consideration.*

And in the case of *Reimensnyder v. Gans*, which was an action on a note given as a donation to a charitable object, the court said: "The fact is that, as we may see from the case of *Ryerss v. Trustees*, a contract of the kind here involved is enforceable rather by way of estoppel than on the ground of consideration in the original undertaking." It has been held that a note given in expectation of the payee performing certain services, but without any contract binding him to serve, will not support an action. But when the payee changes his position to his disadvantage in reliance on the promise, a right of action does arise.

Under the circumstances of this case, is there an equitable estoppel which ought to preclude the defendant from alleging that the note in controversy is lacking in one of the essential elements of a valid contract? We think there is. An estoppel *in pais* is defined to be "a right arising from acts, admissions, or conduct which have induced a change of position in accordance with the real or apparent intention of the party against whom they are alleged." Mr. Pomeroy has formulated the following definition:

> *Equitable estoppel is the effect of the voluntary conduct of a party whereby he is absolutely precluded, both at law and in equity, from asserting rights which might, perhaps, have otherwise existed, either of property, of contract,*

or of remedy, as against another person who in good faith relied upon such conduct, and has been led thereby to change his position for the worse, and who on his part acquires some corresponding right, either of property, of contract, or of remedy.

According to the undisputed proof, as shown by the record before us, the plaintiff was a working girl, holding a position in which she earned a salary of $10 per week. Her grandfather, desiring to put her in a position of independence, gave her the note, accompanying it with the remark that his other grandchildren did not work, and that she would not be obliged to work any longer. In effect, he suggested that she might abandon her employment, and rely in the future upon the bounty which he promised. He doubtless desired that she should give up her occupation, but, whether he did or not, it is entirely certain that he contemplated such action on her part as a reasonable and probable consequence of his gift.

Having intentionally influenced the plaintiff to alter her position for the worse on the faith of the note being paid when due, it would be grossly inequitable to permit the maker, or his executor, to resist payment on the ground that the promise was given without consideration. The petition charges the elements of an equitable estoppel, and the evidence conclusively establishes them. If errors intervened at the trial, they could not have been prejudicial. A verdict for the defendant would be unwarranted. The judgment is right and is affirmed.

Reflection

In *Ricketts*, the promissory note was a clear and definite promise. The grandfather would have reasonably expected to induce his granddaughter to give up her job by his words and actions. The granddaughter relied on his promise and quit the job she had. The court found that allowing the executor to resist payment would be grossly inequitable, and therefore, enforced the promise under the doctrine of promissory estoppel.

Discussion

1. Promissory estoppel is a very fact-specific doctrine. What specific facts in the *Ricketts* case convinced the court that promissory estoppel was appropriate here?

2. What is the purpose of the consideration doctrine? Were the purposes underlying the consideration doctrine served here?

3. Does it matter whether Ms. Scothorn was worse off or better off for having not worked for some time? How does *Ricketts* compare with *Hamer*?

Reading Conrad v. Fields. This case is a more recent illustration of how courts today still use this doctrine when a person relies on a promise to their detriment. In this case, Walker R. Fields offered to pay for Marjorie Conrad's legal education. Legal questions involve whether that promise was supported by consideration and, if not, whether it should be enforceable as a matter of justice under the doctrine of promissory estoppel.

As you read this case, pay attention to how it compares and contrasts with *Ricketts*. Do the courts use the same rules and tests? Which material facts are different, and what circumstances are similar?

Conrad v. Fields

2007 WL 2106302 (Minn. Ct. App. July 24, 2007)

PETERSON, Judge.

This appeal is from a judgment and an order denying posttrial motions. The judgment awarded respondent damages in the amount of the cost of her law-school tuition and books based on a determination that the elements of promissory estoppel were proved with respect to appellant's promise to pay for the tuition and books. We affirm the judgment and grant in part and deny in part respondent's motion to strike appellant's brief and appendix.

Facts

Appellant Walter R. Fields and respondent Marjorie Conrad met and became friends when they were neighbors in an apartment complex in the early 1990's. Appellant started his own business and became a financially successful businessman. Appellant built a $1.2 million house in the Kenwood neighborhood in Minneapolis and leased a Bentley automobile for more than $50,000 a year. Appellant is a philanthropic individual who has sometimes paid education costs for others.

In the fall of 2000, appellant suggested that respondent attend law school, and he offered to pay for her education. Respondent, who had recently paid off an $11,000 medical bill and still owed about $5,000 for undergraduate student loans, did not feel capable of paying for law school on her own. Appellant promised that he would pay tuition and other expenses associated with law school as they became due. Appellant quit her job at Qwest, where she had been earning $45,000 per year, to attend law school. Appellant admitted at trial that before respondent enrolled in law school, he agreed to pay her tuition.

Respondent testified that she enrolled in law school in the summer of 2001 as a result of appellant's "inducement and assurance to pay for [her] education." Appellant made two tuition payments, each in the amount of $1,949.75, in August and

October 2001, but he stopped payment on the check for the second payment. At some point, appellant told respondent that his assets had been frozen due to an Internal Revenue Service audit and that payment of her education expenses would be delayed until he got the matter straightened out. In May 2004, appellant and respondent exchanged e-mail messages about respondent's difficulties in managing the debts that she had incurred for law school. In response to one of respondent's messages, appellant wrote, "to be clear and in writing, when you graduate law school and pas[s] your bar exam, I will pay your tuition." Later, appellant told respondent that he would not pay her expenses, and he threatened to get a restraining order against her if she continued attempting to communicate with him.

Respondent brought suit against appellant, alleging that in reliance on appellant's promise to pay her education expenses, she gave up the opportunity to earn income through full-time employment and enrolled in law school. The case was tried to the court, which awarded respondent damages in the amount of $87,314.63 under the doctrine of promissory estoppel. The district court denied appellant's motion for a new trial or amended findings. This appeal followed.

Decision

The district court's "[f]indings of fact, whether based on oral or documentary evidence, shall not be set aside unless clearly erroneous, and due regard shall be given to the opportunity of the trial court to judge the credibility of the witnesses." In applying this rule, "we view the record in the light most favorable to the judgment of the district court." If there is reasonable evidence to support the district court's findings of fact, this court will not disturb those findings. While the district court's findings of fact are reviewed under the deferential "clearly erroneous" standard, this court reviews questions of law de novo.

"Promissory estoppel implies a contract in law where no contract exists in fact." "A promise which the promisor should reasonably expect to induce action or forbearance on the part of the promisee or a third person and which does induce such action or forbearance is binding if injustice can be avoided only by enforcement of the promise." Restatement (Second) of Contracts § 90(1) (1981).

The elements of a promissory estoppel claim are (1) a clear and definite promise, (2) the promisor intended to induce reliance by the promisee, and the promisee relied to the promisee's detriment, and (3) the promise must be enforced to prevent injustice. Judicial determinations of injustice involve a number of considerations, "including the reasonableness of a promisee's reliance."

"Granting equitable relief is within the sound discretion of the trial court. Only a clear abuse of that discretion will result in reversal." But:

> The court considers the injustice factor as a matter of law, looking to the reasonableness of the promisee's reliance and weighing public policies (in favor of both enforcing bargains and preventing unjust enrichment). When the facts are taken as true, it is a question of law as to whether they rise to the level of promissory estoppel.

I.

Appellant argues that respondent did not plead or prove the elements of promissory estoppel. Minnesota is a notice-pleading state that does not require absolute specificity in pleading and, instead, requires only information sufficient to fairly notify the opposing party of the claim against it.

Paragraph 12 of respondent's complaint states, "That as a direct and approximate result of the negligent conduct and breach of contract conduct of [appellant], [respondent] has been damaged. . . ." But the complaint also states:

> 4. *That in 2000, based on the assurance and inducement of [appellant] to pay for [respondent's] legal education, [respondent] made the decision to enroll in law school at Hamline University School of Law (Hamline) in St. Paul, Minnesota which she did in 2001.*

> 5. *That but for the inducement and assurance of [appellant] to pay for [respondent's] legal education, [respondent] would not have enrolled in law school. [Appellant] was aware of this fact.*

Paragraphs four and five of the complaint are sufficient to put appellant on notice of the promissory estoppel claim.

At a pretrial deposition, respondent testified that negligence and breach of contract were the only two causes of action that she was pleading. Because promissory estoppel is described as a contract implied at law, respondent's deposition testimony can be interpreted to include a promissory-estoppel claim.

In its legal analysis, the district court stated:

> *The Court finds credible [respondent's] testimony that [appellant] encouraged her to go to law school, knowing that she would not be able to pay for it on her own. He knew that she was short on money, having helped her pay for food and other necessities. He knew that she was working at Qwest and would need to quit her job to go to law school. He offered to pay for the cost of her going to law school, knowing that she had debts from her undergraduate tuition. He made a payment on her law school tuition after she enrolled. [Respondent] knew that [appellant] was a wealthy philanthropist, and that he had offered to pay for the education of strangers he had met in chance encounters. She knew that he had the wealth to pay for her law school education. She knew that [ ] he was established in society, older than she, not married, without children, an owner of a successful company, an owner of an expensive home, and a lessor of an expensive car. Moreover, [appellant] was a friend who had performed many kindnesses for her already, and she trusted him. [Appellant's] promise in fact induced [respondent] to quit her job at Qwest and enroll in law school, which she had not otherwise planned to do.*

> *The circumstances support a finding that it would be unjust not to enforce the promise. Upon reliance on [appellant's] promise, [respondent] quit her*

job. She attended law school despite a serious health condition that might otherwise have deterred her from going.

These findings are sufficient to show that respondent proved the elements of promissory estoppel.

Appellant argues that because he advised respondent shortly after she enrolled in law school that he would not be paying her law-school expenses as they came due, respondent could not have reasonably relied on his promise to pay her expenses to her detriment after he repudiated the promise. Appellant contends that the only injustice that resulted from his promise involved the original $5,000 in expenses that respondent incurred to enter law school. But appellant's statement that he would not pay the expenses as they came due did not make respondent's reliance unreasonable because appellant also told respondent that his financial problems were temporary and that he would pay her tuition when she graduated and passed the bar exam. This statement made it reasonable for respondent to continue to rely on appellant's promise that he would pay her expenses.

II. [Court's discussion of appellant's misplaced reliance on *Olson v. Synergistic Techs. Bus. Sys., Inc.* omitted.]

III. [Discussion of statute of frauds omitted.]

IV. [Discussion of damages omitted.]

V.

Appellant argues that because respondent received a valuable law degree, she did not suffer any real detriment by relying on his promise. But receiving a law degree was the expected and intended consequence of appellant's promise, and the essence of appellant's promise was that respondent would receive the law degree without the debt associated with attending law school. Although respondent benefited from attending law school, the debt that she incurred in reliance on appellant's promise is a detriment to her.

VI. [Discussion of civil procedure omitted.]

Affirmed; motion granted in part.

Reflection

Both *Ricketts* and *Conrad* exemplify successful arguments for applying the doctrine of promissory estoppel where there is a lack of consideration. The basic elements to prove a promissory estoppel claim are: (1) a clear and definite promise, (2) the promisor should reasonably expect to induce reliance by the promisee, (3) the promisee relied to the promisee's detriment, and (4) the promise must be enforced to prevent injustice. Elements three and four are often combined, but either formulation works.

In Conrad, the defendant promised to pay tuition and other expenses associated with law school as they became due. He encouraged her to go to law school at his expense knowing she did not have the money and would have to quit her job to attend. She relied on his promise by enrolling in law school and assuming the debt. The trial court found that it would be unjust to enforce the promise, and the Minnesota court of appeals affirmed.

Discussion

1. Reasonable reliance is a key element of any promissory estoppel claim. Did Conrad reasonably rely on Fields' promise? List specific facts that tend to show her reliance was reasonable. Then list other facts or considerations tending to show it was unreasonable for her to rely on Fields' promise. Can you weight and balance the facts to determine which are more compelling?

2. *Conrad* applied the bargained-for exchange test. Would this case have come out differently under the benefit/detriment test? Did Marjorie Conrad incur a detriment? Did Walter R. Fields incur a benefit?

Reading Otten v. Otten. This case focuses on Wife's claim that Husband's promise to pay her $4,500 is not sufficient consideration for her promise to relinquish her legal right to $7,800 in past due child support. Wife is correct, but Husband may still merit enforcement of Wife's promise under the doctrine of promissory estoppel. *Otten* illustrates the limits of promissory estoppel and its element of foreseeable reliance.

Although foreseeable reliance is a flexible principle, it is not merely a blank check for the plaintiff to rubber stamp. The divorce settlement case of *Otten v. Otten*, 632 S.W.2d 45 (Mo. App. 1982), circumscribes the limits of foreseeable reliance.

In 1976, Husband and Wife divorced, and their divorce decree granted Wife $200 per month for child support. In 1981, Husband filed to modify the decree on the ground that one of the children had become emancipated. Wife responded that Husband owed her $7,800, which amounted to over three years, in unpaid child support. The court found that Husband had been delinquent, and it ordered garnishment of Husband's bank account. The bank disbursed that sum (plus thirty dollars) to Wife.

Husband appealed, alleging that Wife called Husband's attorney prior to the court's order, offering to settle the dispute for $4,500 cash, and $100 monthly child support thereafter; and that after consulting Husband, Husband's attorney advised Wife that Husband could deliver $1,000 cash immediately and $3,500 via a stipulated promissory note, in exchange for Wife withdrawing her claims; and that Wife orally agreed to this settlement. The appeal turns on whether her oral promise to abide by the settlement is enforceable. Courts will consider both legal and equitable enforceability.

Otten v. Otten

632 S.W.2d 45 (1982)

WASSERSTROM, Judge.

This is a suit to specifically enforce an alleged settlement agreement. The trial court sustained defendant's motion to dismiss, and plaintiff appeals. We affirm.

In 1976, as part of a decree dissolving the marriage between the parties, the wife (defendant here) was granted $200 per month as a single sum for the support of two minor children. On January 13, 1981, the husband (plaintiff here) filed a motion to modify the decree on the ground that one of the children had become emancipated. The next day, January 14, 1981, the wife filed execution for $7,800 which she alleged to be accrued in unpaid child support and ordered garnishment on Third National Bank. The garnishment papers were served upon the bank on January 16, 1981. The bank paid $7,830 into court, and disbursement of that sum to the wife was ordered by the court on February 26, 1981.

On March 2, 1981, the husband filed his petition in the present case. He alleged that the wife had called his attorney on January 21, 1981, offering to settle all questions with respect to back child support for the sum of $4,500 and further offering that the decree of divorce be amended to provide child support on and after February 1, 1981, of only $100. The petition further alleged that the attorney told the wife he would have to consult his client; and that after consultation, the attorney advised the wife that the husband could raise $1,000 in cash immediately and would deliver to her his note for $3,500 in full satisfaction of back child support payments. The petition goes on to allege that the wife then stated that she would accept the proposal and would stop in the attorney's office the following Wednesday to pick up the check for $1,000 and the $3,500 note and that she would at that time sign a stipulation for modification of the decree. The husband alleges that he performed his part of the agreement by executing his check and note and by signing the agreed stipulation.

Paragraph 8 of the petition then proceeds to allege as follows: "Relying to his detriment upon the fact that a compromise agreement had been reached, and the respondent would upon the following Wednesday, her next day off, stop by petitioner's attorney's office and execute Exhibit B and pick up her promissory note and check in full settlement of all back child support payments, borrowed a substantial sum of money in order to meet business obligations incurred by him and relying upon the fact that a compromise agreement had been made satisfying the judgment for all child support payments due respondent through January 31, 1981 caused said loan proceeds to be temporarily deposited in a business account in his name alone at Third National Bank, Sedalia, Missouri." The petition goes on to allege that the wife, in violation of her agreement said to have been orally agreed on January 26, 1981, caused execution and garnishment to be issued on January 14, 1981.

The petition concludes with a prayer that the wife be ordered to specifically perform the January 26 agreement by executing the Stipulation and that the court order the clerk of the court to return to the husband the sum of $7,800 paid into court by Third National Bank.

On the same day that the petition was filed, the trial court entered a temporary order for escrow of the $7,830 paid in by Third National Bank. Thereafter the wife filed her motion to dismiss the petition on the ground that it failed to state a cause of action. The court sustained that motion on the grounds that (1) the facts did not show an accord and satisfaction; and (2) there was no valid consideration for the alleged compromise agreement.

The husband's sole point on this appeal is that the court erred in dismissing his petition as an unsatisfied accord "because the contractual obligation alleged in the appellant's petition was a bilateral contract and not a full accord and satisfaction."

I.

The law is unclear as to whether an accord can be enforced where it is not followed by a completed satisfaction. The general texts show a conflict of authority on this point.

One eminent legal writer [Williston] states that there is strangely little authority upon the matter and the few cases on the point contain reasoning which is not very full or satisfactory. This writer goes on to say that:

> As a court of law cannot give adequate relief, and as the promise of temporary forbearance necessarily included in the accord gives equity jurisdiction of the matter, there seems good reason for equity to deal with the whole matter by granting specific performance.

Some Missouri cases contain dicta bearing on this question. However, no Missouri holding squarely in point has been found. For purposes of this opinion we shall assume, without holding, that an agreement embodied in an accord is a proper subject for specific performance, even though the accord be not followed with a completed satisfaction.

II.

The trial court stated as an alternative ground for its ruling that: "It is clear upon the face of the pleadings there is no valid consideration for the alleged compromise agreement."

The wife devotes the bulk of her brief to an argument supporting that conclusion. The husband has omitted giving this court the benefit of his views as to wherein consideration may be found. Nevertheless we shall consider: (a) whether consideration need be shown by the petition; and (b) whether any consideration has been shown or can be reasonably inferred from the allegations made in this petition.

A.

An accord and satisfaction will not be given effect unless founded upon a sufficient consideration. Moreover the party relying upon the alleged contract of settlement is obligated to plead the matter of consideration.

B.

The first possible basis upon which to claim consideration would be the husband's promise to pay $4,500. That must be considered, however, in the light of the fact that the wife was claiming $7,800 in past due child support. Nowhere in his petition does the husband deny that he was delinquent in the amount of $7,800. An agreement on his part to pay the partial sum of $4,500 out of a total undisputed amount due of $7,800 cannot be acceptable consideration.

Nor can the husband's promise to pay $100 child support on and after February 1, 1981, be accepted as legal consideration. The husband was already under a continuing obligation to pay $200 per month. Even though one of the children may have become emancipated, that did not automatically result in a reduction of the $200 figure. The law in this state is clear that when support is awarded for more than one child in a single lump sum for all of them, the same total amount continues for the remaining child or children even after the emancipation of any one of the children, until reduction of that amount by court order. Furthermore, the reduction of child support is not a valid subject of contract between the parents.

The only remaining basis upon which the requirement of consideration might possibly be satisfied would have to rest upon the allegations of paragraph 8 of the petition, in which the husband alleged that he had borrowed money for his general business purposes and in reliance upon the wife's promises had deposited the borrowed sum in Third National Bank. Those allegations seem to represent an effort on the part of the husband to bring himself within the theory of promissory estoppel, set forth in Restatement (Second) of Contracts Section 90 (1981).

That doctrine, which permits a promise without consideration to be enforced if the elements of estoppel are present, has been adopted in this state.

However, such a promise will be enforced only where the promisor should have expected or reasonably foreseen the action which the promisee claims to have taken in reliance upon the promise. Thus, Comment b to Section 90 of the Restatement (Second) of Contracts states:

> The promisor is affected only by reliance which he does or should foresee.

Henderson, *Promissory Estoppel and Traditional Contract Doctrine*, 78 Yale L.J. 343, 346 (1969), puts the matter this way:

> In short, Section 90 states the proposition that, in situations where traditional consideration is lacking, reliance which is foreseeable, reasonable, and serious will require enforcement if injustice cannot otherwise be avoided.

In all of the Missouri cases involving the application of promissory estoppel, the facts clearly showed that the promisor should have and in fact clearly did foresee the precise action which the promisee took in reliance. Thus in *Coffman Industries, Inc. v. Gorman-Tabor Co., supra*, the opinion states: "Fidelity should reasonably have expected that its promise of payment would induce the change of position by

Gorman-Tabor." And in *Katz v. Danny Dare, Inc.*, the opinion states: "It is conceded Dare intended that Katz rely on its promise of a pension. . . ."

In the present case the nature of the situation would not impel a reasonable expectation by the wife that the oral agreement allegedly made by her would lead the husband to borrow money for his business and deposit it in Third National Bank. Nor does the husband's petition allege any special facts which would support a conclusion that the wife expected or should have foreseen such borrowing and deposit by the husband. Accordingly, the present case is not within the doctrine of promissory estoppel.

The husband has not carried the burden of pleading consideration for the alleged contract of settlement. The trial court therefore properly sustained the motion to dismiss.

Affirmed.

All concur.

Discussion

1. The court finds that Ms. Otten's offer to settle the lawsuit was not supported by consideration. Why? Cite and use the definition in the R2d when analyzing this issue.

2. Mr. Otten argues that Mrs. Otten's promise to settle the lawsuit is enforceable on the basis of promissory estoppel. List the elements of promissory estoppel and explain whether Mr. Otten meets each of them.

3. Unlike contracts-at-law, contracts-at-equity need only be enforced to the extent that justice requires. Were there any facts or circumstances in this case that may have led the court to decide that justice did not need to enforce Mrs. Otten's promise to Mr. Otten?

Reading Maryland National Bank v. United Jewish Appeal Federation of Greater Washington, Inc. In some jurisdictions, charitable subscriptions (promises to donate money to non-profit organizations and good causes) are enforceable even without consideration. Other jurisdictions do not distinguish charitable subscripts in this way. The following case carefully decides whether to accord an equitable exception to the consideration doctrine for charitable subscriptions unsupported by consideration.

As you read this case, decide for yourself whether charitable subscriptions should be subject to or excepted from the consideration doctrine.

Maryland National Bank v. United Jewish Appeal Federation of Greater Washington, Inc.

286 Md. 274 (1979)

ORTH, Judge.

The issue in this case is whether a pledge to a charitable institution survives the death of the pledgor and is an enforceable obligation of his estate.

I

Milton Polinger pledged $200,000 to the United Jewish Appeal Federation of Greater Washington, Inc. (UJA) for the year 1975. He died on 20 December 1976. His last will and testament was admitted to probate in the Orphans' Court for Montgomery County and letters were issued to Melvin R. Oksner and Maryland National Bank as personal representatives. At the time of Polinger's death, $133,500 was unpaid on his pledge.

The personal representatives disallowed the claim for the balance of the pledge. UJA filed a petition praying that the claim be allowed and moved for summary judgment. The personal representatives answered and filed a cross-motion for summary judgment. The court granted UJA's motion for summary judgment, denied the personal representatives' motion for summary judgment, allowed UJA's claim against the estate in the amount of $133,500, and assessed the costs against the personal representatives. The personal representatives noted an appeal to the Court of Special Appeals and petitioned this Court to issue a writ of certiorari to that court before decision by it. We did so.

II

The facts before the court were undisputed in material part. They showed the nature of UJA and its relationship with its beneficiaries. UJA, chartered in the District of Columbia, is a public non-profit corporation. In general, its objective is to solicit, collect and receive funds and property for the support of certain religious, charitable, philanthropic, scientific and educational organizations and institutions, and it enjoys tax exempt status federally and in Maryland, Virginia and the District of Columbia. Based on monies received and pledged, it makes allocations to tax exempt organizations. No formal commitment agreement is executed with respect to the allocations, but UJA undertakes to pay pursuant to the allocation and the beneficiary organizations "go ahead to act as though they are going to have the money and they spend it." In other words, UJA makes allocations to various beneficiary organizations based upon pledges made to it, and the beneficiary organizations incur liabilities based on the allocations. Historically 95% of the pledges are collected over a three-year period, and allowance for the 5% which may be uncollected is made in determining the amount of the allocations. So, according to Meyer Brissman, Executive Vice-President Emeritus of UJA: "We always pay (the allocated amount). I don't know of any case where we haven't paid." Pledges to "emergency funds" are not paid on the basis of an allocation by UJA. All monies actually collected on those pledges are paid to the emergency funds.

The facts before the court showed the circumstances surrounding the pledge of Polinger with which we are here concerned. It was evidenced by a card signed by Polinger under date of 9 November 1974. It recited:

> *In consideration of the obligation incurred based upon this pledge, I hereby promise to pay to the United Jewish Appeal the amount indicated on this card.*

The amount indicated as his "1975 pledge" was $100,000 for "UJA including local, national and overseas," and $100,000 for "Israel Emergency Fund."

UJA organized a "mission" to Israel in the fall of 1974. The mission was in no sense a tour. It was at the time of the missile crisis in Israel, and the members of the mission were to meet with Golda Meir, then Prime Minister, and with other government leaders to be briefed on the problems the country faced. It was to be involved with "people in the troubled settlements." Certain community leaders, including Polinger, went on the mission. Polinger had been active in the affairs of UJA and had regularly made substantial contributions to it.

"Pre-solicitation" is a process whereby it is determined who can be expected to make large pledges and specifically who will likely substantially increase their pledges of previous years. Pre-solicitation is part of a well-conceived plan to obtain large contributions. It leads to a "high-pressure meeting" at which, according to Brissman,

> *(T)here is no question that the technique is the interchange and people knowing everyone else in the room, and if this one is thinking of a need of being so great as to be willing to do something unusual, the others thought it was similarly important for them to demonstrate it.*

The idea is that "if somebody thought it was important enough to give more than he gave before, (others would think) that they ought to give more, and they (give) more money.... (W)e get together and discuss reactions to what they have seen, what the needs are, and people sometimes make a speech before they decide what they are going to say about the money, and it is a free-flowing thing, and nobody knows in advance what anybody is going to say, but some of the people are talked to one by one privately to condition them to make some kind of a special response to influence the group. The whole purpose of fund raising is to get an example."

Polinger was selected to be an example on the Israel mission. He had pledged $65,000 for 1973. He had "participated willingly" in such a meeting in connection with the 1974 fund raising campaign and had pledged $150,000. He was one of those it was "felt was ready to do something unusual...." He was pre-solicited by three or four individuals and went up to two hundred thousand dollars for 1975. It was agreed that his pledge would be made in a "caucus" at the King David Hotel in Jerusalem. The caucus was held and Polinger "came into the caucus," as Brissman said, "so we could announce all the gifts and influence other people of different levels." Polinger was to be a "pacesetter."

There were about thirty men at the caucus. About four of them had pledged an amount as large as $200,000 before Polinger made his announcement. Brissman thought that "there was an emotional impact that develops when a man has seen things that influence him to believe that there is something desperate and earth-shaking going on and he could do something about it beneficially, and he responds." When Polinger said he would give $200,000, he indicated that he wanted everybody to give as much as they could. He thought he was giving the greatest amount that he possibly could find himself able to so do. Of course, Polinger was only one of many people who spoke and made a pledge. Whether anyone in fact increased his pledge because of Polinger was never discussed at the meeting, and Brissman was unable to say whether anyone was influenced by Polinger's pledge.

> It is just a dynamics of an involvement where after two weeks of being together night and day in a setting of that kind after a major war, meeting with individuals who lived through three or four such wars, that everybody is strung out and you are like a family, and in the process of interchange, speeches are made, and maybe somebody made a gift of $5,000.00 influenced people just as much as the man who gave $200,000.00 because of what the money meant in their view of this person's ability to give.

> It is just not the biggest number, but it is the concept of response to a need that these people are reacting to. And I don't know that you verbalize it in that way necessarily, but it does come out that one influences another in the interchange, because you are going around a room and everybody is talking about how they were moved by what they were into. So there is no question one influences another.

Brissman was asked "whether aside from the specific group of people who were present in Israel with Mr. Polinger, are there any other people here in the Washington area or anywhere else that you are aware of who made pledges, gifts, or increased gifts as a result of Mr. Polinger's gift?" He could not say. He could only give the procedure followed:

> I solicited personally hundreds of people, some face to face, some by telephone, some by appointment with two or three people talking to an individual. And frequently I, personally, and I know of others who do likewise, start to tell people what kind of response we are getting when we get to the question of what is a standard for giving, or what you ought to consider as your share, and in the process I have used Milton Polinger as an example talking to individuals. They know who Milton is. And I would tell them what Milton had done in 1973 and in 1974 in trying to get them to respond in some way to move further ahead in their extension as far as they can, because we are talking of stretching. If you can give so much, can you give a little but more type of thing, and I frequently would use Milton as an illustration.

> There is no question in my mind when I do it I know others do it, and I have seen at the time that we are talking about people reporting on the mission

to others who were not there, soliciting gifts at meetings or in individual con-frontations, telling what happened at the mission, and they would go down line by line everybody who made gifts, they had a list in front of them as a tool.

So it was used. There is no question about it. I cannot tell you this one increased his gift only because of that one's response, but it is part of a package. That is how you raise money.

III

We find that the law of Maryland with regard to the enforcement of pledges or subscriptions to charitable organizations is the rule thus expressed in the Restatement of Contracts § 90 (1932):

A promise which the promisor should reasonably expect to induce action or forbearance of a definite and substantial character on the part of the prom-isee and which does induce such action or forbearance is binding if injustice can be avoided only by enforcement of the promise.

We reach this conclusion through opinions of this Court in four cases, *Gittings v. Mayhew; Erdman v. Trustees Eutaw M.P. Ch.; Sterling v. Cushwa & Sons;* and *American University v. Collings.*

Gittings concerned the building of an Atheneum. The subscription contract authorized the calling of payment of installments by the subscribers when a certain amount had been pledged. The amount was reached, installments were called for and paid, contracts to erect the building were made and the Atheneum was completed. It was in these circumstances that the Court said:

In whatever uncertainty the law concerning voluntary subscriptions of this character may be at this time, in consequence of the numerous decisions pronounced upon the subject, it appears to be settled, that where advances have been made, or expenses or liabilities incurred by others, in consequence of such subscriptions, before notice of withdrawal, this should, on general principles, be deemed sufficient to make them obligatory, provided the advances were authorized by a fair and reasonable dependence on the subscriptions. . . . The doctrine is not only reasonable and just, but consistent with the analogies of the law.

This statement of the law appeared to be *Obiter dictum* in *Gittings*, but if it were, it became the law in *Erdman*.

Erdman dealt with a suit on a promissory note whereby there was a promise to pay the Eutaw Methodist Protestant Church the sum of $500 four years after date with interest. The consideration for the note was a subscription contract made with the trustees of the church for the purpose of paying off a building debt, which had been incurred for the erection of a new church building. It had been entered on the books of the church, the trustees had subsequently borrowed $2,000 on that subscription and other subscriptions to pay off the indebtedness for the erection of the church building. The Court held that in such circumstances the subscription contract was a valid and binding one and constituted a sufficient consideration to support the note, observing that "(t)he policy of the law, to sustain subscription contracts of the character of the one here in question, is clearly stated by this court, and by other appellate courts, in a number of cases." The only Maryland case cited was *Gittings*.

The holding in *Gittings* was said to be "that as the party had authorized others by the subscription to enter into engagements for the accomplishment of the enterprise, the law requires that he should save them harmless to the extent of his subscription." *Erdman*. One case in another appellate court was discussed, *Trustees v. Garvey*, and two cited as to like effect, *McClure v. Wilson* and *United Presbyterian Church v. Baird*.

In *Garvey* the court noted that:

> *As a matter of public policy, courts have been desirous of sustaining the legal obligation of subscriptions of this character, and in some cases . . . have found a sufficient consideration in the mutuality of the promises, where no fraud or deception has been practiced. But while we might be unwilling to go to that extent and might hold that a subscription could be withdrawn before money had been expended or liability incurred, or work performed on the strength of the subscriptions, and in furtherance of the enterprise, the church trustees had, on the faith of the subscriptions, borrowed money, relying on the subscription as a means of payment and incurred a specific liability.*

Thus, it seems that *Erdman* made law of the dictum in *Gittings*, but that law was that charitable subscriptions to be enforceable require reliance on the subscriptions by the charity which would lead to direct loss to the organization or its officers if the subscriptions were not enforced.

This principle of the law was applied in *Sterling*. In that case pledges were made to support a failing bank, to restore confidence in it and protect its depositors and creditors, to comply with demands of the bank commissioner so as to keep the bank open and to prevent impairment of its capital. There were, therefore, substantial considerations for the subscriptions. "Not only was every subscription expressly made in consideration of the agreement of other subscribers, who have fulfilled their pledges, but a prior subscription agreement was to be, and was, in fact, released to the specified extent, when the new one became binding, and consent of the bank commissioner to the continued functioning of the bank was thereby induced." In such circumstances, the Court declared: "The sufficiency of such considerations cannot be doubted."

Gittings and *Erdman* were referred to in *American University v. Collings* as cases "which hold that where one has made a subscription and thereby authorized the entering into engagements to accomplish the purpose for which the subscription was made, the subscription was upon a valuable consideration." The Court carefully pointed out that "(in those) cases, however, the promisee had actually incurred obligations relying upon the promises," but that in the case it was considering there was no claim "that any such obligations had been entered into." The case turned on the finding that the pledge was testamentary in nature.

In summary, the rule announced in *Gittings*, referred to in *Collings* and applied in *Erdman* and *Sterling*, is in substance the rule set out in § 90 of the Restatement of Contracts (1932). It is the settled law of this State.

IV

UJA would have us "view traditional contract law requirements of consideration liberally" in order to maintain what it believes to be a judicial policy of favoring charities. We deeply appreciate the fact that private philanthropy serves a highly important function in our society. This was well expressed by the Court some hundred and twenty-five years ago in observing that the maintenance of charitable institutions was "certainly of the highest merit":

> *Whether projected for literary, scientific or charitable purposes, they address themselves to the favorable consideration of those whose success in life may have enabled them, in this way, to minister to the wants of others, and at the same time promote their own interests, by elevating the character of the community with whose prosperity their fortunes may be identified.*

But we are not persuaded that we should, by judicial fiat, adopt a policy of favoring charities at the expense of the law of contracts which has been long established in this state. We do not think that this law should be disregarded or modified so as to bestow a preferred status upon charitable organizations and institutions.

It may be that there are cases in which judgments according to the law do not appear to subserve the purposes of justice, but this, ordinarily, the courts may not remedy. "It is safer that a private right should fail, or a wrong go unredressed, than that settled principles should be disregarded in order to meet the equity of a particular case." *Gittings*. If change is to be made it should be by legislative enactment, as in the matter of the tax status of charitable organizations.

In advocating its position, UJA points to this statement in *Gittings*:

> *In some cases, the courts, in furtherance of what they deemed a recognized public policy, have felt themselves warranted in relaxing, to some extent, the rigor of the common law, and have held the subscribers liable, when, perhaps, upon strict principles, there was not a legal consideration for the contract.*

That this was no more than an observation and not an adoption of the principle was made manifest by the further comments of the Court:

> *Indeed, considering the number of these (charitable) institutions, erected and maintained by private munificence alone, the cases are very rare in which subscribers have refused compliance with their engagements. Instances may occur in which parties, feeling themselves released in consequence of a failure of expectations reasonably entertained at the time of making the subscription, might avail themselves of legal defenses, without justly forfeiting the good opinion of those who embarked with them in the enterprise. The propriety, however, of employing such means of resisting payment the parties must determine for themselves. Upon that portion of the present case, therefore, so much contested at the bar, we decline expressing any opinion.*

In *Collings* the Court noted that American University had cited cases from other jurisdictions which, the educational institution stated, "represents the general trend of judicial authority, and it is in accordance with the better reasoned opinion, that contracts for subscriptions or donations to churches or charitable or kindred institutions which have been duly accepted are based upon a valid consideration because of the mutual obligations of other subscribers."

But the Court also observed Professor Williston's criticism of this view. In any event, as we have indicated, the Court had no occasion to decide whether the pledge involved in Collings was given for a valid consideration.

Restatement (Second) of Contracts (Tent. Draft No. 2, 1965) proposes changes in §90. It would read:

> *A promise which the promisor should reasonably expect to induce action or forbearance on the part of the promisee or a third person and which does induce such action or forbearance is binding if injustice can be avoided only by enforcement of the promise. The remedy granted for breach may be limited as justice requires.*

This deletes from the existing section the qualification "of a definite and substantial character" with regard to the inducement of action or forbearance and has the inducement of forbearance apply to "a third person" as well as the promisee. It also adds the discretionary limitation as to the remedy. Comment c to the proposed Section concerns "(c)haritable subscriptions, marriage settlements, and other gifts." It begins:

> *One of the functions of the doctrine of consideration is to deny enforcement to a promise to make a gift. Such a promise is ordinarily enforced by virtue of the promisee's reliance only if his conduct is foreseeable and reasonable and involves a definite and substantial change of position which would not have occurred if the promise had not been made.*

This reflects the previous section and the Maryland rule. The comment then notes that "(i)n some cases, however, other policies reinforce the promisee's claim." It states:

American courts have traditionally favored charitable subscriptions and marriage settlements and have found consideration in many cases where the element of exchange was doubtful or nonexistent. Where recovery is rested on reliance in such cases, a probability of reliance is likely to be enough, and no effort is made to sort out mixed motives or to consider whether partial enforcement would be appropriate.

Illustration 7 is of a charitable subscription:

> *A orally promises to pay B, a university, $100,000 in five annual installments for the purposes of its fund-raising campaign. The promise is confirmed in writing by A's agent, and two annual installments are paid before A dies. The continuance of the fund-raising campaign by B is sufficient reliance to make the promise binding on A and his estate.*

Section 90 of the tentative draft No. 2 of the Restatement (Second) of Contracts, 1965, has not been adopted by the American Law Institute, and we are not persuaded to follow it.

"Cases throughout the country clearly reflect a conflict between the desired goal of enforcing charitable subscriptions and the realities of contract law. The result has been strained reasoning which has been the subject of considerable criticism." *Salsbury v. Northwestern Bell Telephone Company*. When charitable subscriptions, even though clearly gratuitous promises, have been held either contracts or offers to contract, the "decisions are based on such a great variety of reasoning as to show the lack of any really sufficient consideration." Williston on Contracts. "Very likely, conceptions of public policy have shaped, more or less subconsciously, the rulings thus made. Judges have been affected by the thought that 'defenses of (the) character (of lack of consideration are) breaches of faith towards the public, and especially towards those engaged in the same enterprise, and an unwarrantable disappointment of the reasonable expectations of those interested.'" *Allegheny College v. National Chautauqua County Bank*. Therefore, "(c)ourts have . . . purported to find consideration on various tenuous theories. . . . (The) wide variation in reasoning indicates the difficulty of enforcing a charitable subscription on grounds of consideration. Yet, the courts have generally striven to find grounds for enforcement, indicating the depth of feeling in this country that private philanthropy serves a highly important function in our society." J. Calamari & J. Perillo, The Law of Contracts, § 6–5 (1977). Some courts have forthrightly discarded the facade of consideration and admittedly held a charitable subscription enforceable only in respect of what they conceive to be the public policy. See, for example, *Salsbury v. Northwestern Bell Telephone Company*; *More Game Birds in America, Inc. v. Boettger*.

We are not convinced that such departure from the settled law of contracts is in the public interest. A charitable subscription must be a contract to be enforceable, unless we characterize it as some other type of agreement, unknown to established contract law, for which a valid consideration is not essential. We said in *Broaddus v. First Nat. Bank*:

> It is unnecessary at this time to cite authorities in this state and elsewhere to the effect that every contract must be supported by a consideration; and this must be regarded as one of the elementary principles of the law of contract.

And, we recently cited *Broaddus* in *Peer v. First Fed. S. & L. Ass'n*, in asserting, after noting several other requirements of a valid contract: "Finally, the agreement must be supported by sufficient consideration." We abide by that principle in determining the validity of the charitable subscriptions.

V

When the facts concerning the charitable subscription of Polinger are viewed in light of the Maryland law, it is manifest that his promise was not legally enforceable. There was no consideration as required by contract law. The incidents on which Gittings indicated a charitable pledge was enforceable, and on which Erdman and Sterling held the subscriptions in those cases were enforceable are not present here. The consideration recited by the pledge card was "the obligation incurred based upon this pledge." But there was no legal obligation incurred in the circumstances. Polinger's pledge was not made in consideration of the pledges of others, and there was no evidence that others in fact made pledges in consideration of Polinger's pledge. No release was given, nor binding agreement made by the UJA on the strength of Polinger's pledge. The pledge was not for a specific enterprise; it was to the UJA generally and to the Israel Emergency Fund. With respect to the former, no allocation by UJA to its beneficiary organization was threatened or thwarted by the failure to collect the Polinger pledge in its entirety, and, with respect to the latter, UJA practice was to pay over to the Fund only what it actually collected, not what was pledged. UJA borrowed no money on the faith and credit of the pledge. The pledge prompted no "action or forbearance of a definite and substantial character" on the part of UJA. No action was taken by UJA on the strength of the pledge that could reasonably be termed "definite and substantial" from which it should be held harmless. There was no change shown in the position of UJA made in reliance on the subscription which resulted in an economic loss, and, in fact, there was no such loss demonstrated. UJA was able to fulfill all of its allocations. Polinger's pledge was utilized as a means to obtain substantial pledges from others. But this was a technique employed to raise money. It did not supply a legal consideration to Polinger's pledge. On the facts of this case, it does not appear that injustice can be avoided only by enforcement of the promise.

To summarize, there was no specific goal prompting the pledge such as existed in Gittings, Erdman and Sterling with a mutual awareness of future reliance on the subscription. UJA did not enter into binding contracts, incur expenses or suffer liabilities in reliance on the pledge. UJA's function was to serve as a conduit or clearinghouse to collect gifts of money from many sources and to funnel them into various charitable organizations. It did, of course, plan for the future, in that it estimated the rate of cash flow based on the pledges it received and told its beneficiaries to expect certain amounts. In so doing, however, it expressly did not incur liabilities in reliance on specific pledges. It seems that none of the organizations to which it allocated money would have legal rights against UJA in the event of failure to pay the allocation, and, in any event, UJA, cognizant of the past history of collections, made due allowance for the fact that a certain percentage of the pledges would not be paid.

We hold that Polinger's pledge to UJA was a gratuitous promise. It had no legal consideration, and under the law of this State was unenforceable. The Orphans' Court for Montgomery County erred in allowing the claim for the unpaid balance of the subscription, and its order of 5 January 1979 is vacated with direction to enter an order disallowing the claim filed by UJA.

ORDER OF 5 JANUARY 1979 OF THE ORPHANS' COURT FOR MONTGOMERY COUNTY VACATED;

CASE REMANDED TO THAT COURT WITH DIRECTION TO ENTER AN ORDER DISALLOWING THE CLAIM FILED BY THE UNITED JEWISH APPEAL FEDERATION OF GREATER WASHINGTON, INC.;

COSTS TO BE PAID BY APPELLEE.

Reflection

The issue in *UJA* is whether a pledge to a charitable institution survives the death of the pledgor and is an enforceable obligation of his estate. When Polinger died, $133,500 of his pledge remained unpaid.

In contract law, where advances have been made, or expenses or liabilities incurred by others, in consequence of such subscriptions, before notice of withdrawal, this should, on general principles, be deemed sufficient to make them obligatory, provided the advances were authorized by a fair and reasonable dependence on the subscriptions.

Polinger's pledge was not supported by consideration. The consideration recited by the pledge card was "the obligation incurred based upon this pledge. . . ." But there was no legal obligation incurred in the circumstances. Polinger's pledge was not made in consideration of the pledges of others, and there was no evidence that others in fact made pledges in consideration of Polinger's pledge. No allocation by UJA to its beneficiary organization was threatened or thwarted by the failure to collect the Polinger pledge in its entirety, and, with respect to the latter, UJA practice was to pay over to the Fund only what it actually collected, not what was pledged. There was no change shown in the position of UJA made in reliance on the subscription which resulted in an economic loss, and, in fact, there was no such loss demonstrated. UJA was able to fulfill all of its allocations.

When looking at whether or not a charitable donation should be enforced, it is important to consider whether injustice can be avoided only by enforcement of the promise. On the facts of this case, it does not appear that injustice can be avoided only by enforcement of the promise. UJA did not enter into binding contracts, incur expenses or suffer liabilities in reliance on the pledge.

Discussion

1. The *UJA* court declines to follow the R2d approach. Why? Which, in your opinion, is the right approach?

2. Would the case have come out differently if the court applied the R2d approach? Analyze the claim based on R2d § 90.

3. The R2d gives special preferences to promises to give charity and promises to give alimony. Why are these two categories of promises singled out?

Problems

Problem 8.1. Escaped Bull

Martin Fitzpatrick owned a small farm in Vermont on which lived a prized bull. Somehow, in September 1860, that bull escaped Fitzpatrick's farm and wandered across Chittenden, Vermont, eventually arriving upon a pasture owned by Bishop Boothe in Pittsford, Vermont, about 11 miles away. Boothe then cared for the bull by providing for its food and shelter while he attempted to determine who owned the bull, but he was not able to quickly ascertain the owner.

In November, Boothe determined that Fitzpatrick owned the bull, and the two men met in Pittsford. At the meeting, Fitzpatrick said that the bull was indeed his, and that he would pay for its care, but could not drive it away until the winter ended. Boothe kept the bull through the winter, and Fitzpatrick drove him home in Spring.

Boothe sent Fitzpatrick a bill for the cost of the care. The amount charged was reasonable, but Fitzpatrick refused to pay.

What is Fitzpatrick's best legal argument for why he does not have to pay Boothe?

What is Boothe's counterargument for why Fitzpatrick must pay him?

Which party is more likely to prevail if this case was brought to court?

See Boothe v. Fitzpatrick, 36 Vt. 681 (1864).

Problem 8.2. **Plantations Steel**

Plantations Steel Co. ("Plantations") manufactured steel reinforcing rods for use in concrete construction. The company was the employer of Edward J. Hayes. In January 1972, Hayes planned to retire the next year. Approximately one week before his actual retirement, Hayes spoke to Hugo R. Mainelli, Jr., an officer and stakeholder of Plantations. Mainelli said that he would "take care" of Hayes. There was no mention of a sum of money or a percentage of salary that Hayes would receive. Nor was there any formal authorization from other shareholders or formal provision for a pension for employees other than unionized employees. Hayes was not a union member. Hayes received $5,000 per year as part of his pension.

Mainelli testified that his father had authorized the first payment "as a token of appreciation for the many years of Hayes' service." It was implied that that check would continue on an annual basis and would continue as long as Mainelli was still around. After retirement, Hayes would visit the company thanking and discussing with Mainelli the payments he was receiving. He also asked how long they would continue so he could plan his retirement. Hayes testified that he would not have retired had he not expected to receive a pension. After he stopped working for Plantations, he sought no other employment.

The payments stopped in 1976 when the Mainellis, including Hugo Mainelli, Jr. and his father, lost the company in a takeover by the DiMartino family. Hayes sued Plantations for three years that he did not receive the pension payment.

Under R2d § 90, does Hayes have an affirmative claim of promissory estoppel for the lack of consideration?

See Hayes v. Plantations Steel Co., 438 A.2d 1091 (R.I. 1982).

Chapter 9

Promissory Restitution

Restitution is a body of law regarding the return of wrongful gains. The common law of restitution dates back to at least the thirteenth century. The concept of restitution goes back even further. Pomponius Mela, a Roman geographer who died in the year 45 A.D., wrote, "It is by nature fair that nobody should enrich himself at the expense of another." The Roman law of condictio authorized recovery by the plaintiff of a certain object or money in the hands of the defendant. Today, the law of restitution provides a plaintiff the means to recover in the amount of the defendant's wrongful gain, also known as unjust enrichment: "A person who has been unjustly enriched at the expense of another is required to make restitution to the other."

For example, Robert was driving down the highway when a truck going the opposite direction crossed the centerline and crashed into Robert's car. The collision knocked Robert unconscious and badly injured him. While Robert was unconscious, paramedics took him to a hospital, which treated his injuries. Robert woke up in the hospital several days later, and he checked out several days after that. The hospital billed Robert's medical insurance sixty thousand dollars for his treatment. By mistake, the insurance company sent a check for this amount to Robert, not to the hospital. If Robert cashes that check, he is unjustly enriched by sixty thousand dollars. The law of unjust enrichment should require him to make restitution by disgorging the sixty thousand dollars to the hospital.

Note that in the example above, there was no promise made by Robert to the hospital; after all, he was unconscious when the hospital rendered services to him, and he did not make a promise to pay after the fact. Since there is no promise in this example, there is no contract law claim. Contracts is the law of enforceable promises, so there cannot be a contract claim without a promise.

What if Robert, on his way out of the hospital, had promised to pay for the services he previously received? As you learned in the previous module, this promise is gratuitous. Robert has already received the benefit of hospital services, so his promise to pay for the services cannot be made in order to induce the hospital to serve him. This is an example of "past consideration," which is an oxymoron, since for a promise to count as consideration, must be made to induce the other party to perform in the future. Since Robert's promise to pay the hospital lacks consideration, it is unenforceable as a matter of contract law.

But there is an intermediate doctrine which straddles the borders of contract law and restitution law: promissory restitution. Promissory restitution essentially provides a means for a plaintiff to enforce a defendant's promise where the defendant promises to make restitution. In the second version Robert's case, when Robert left the hospital, he effectively promised to make restitution for the hospital's services. This promise, though unsupported by consideration, tends to show that it would be fair for Robert to pay the amount he promised for the services rendered.

It is the defendant's promise that puts such circumstances within the ambit of contract law. Once we have established a relevant promise, we must then consider when that promise occurred, because timing of the promise distinguishes promissory restitution from promissory estoppel. Promissory restitution is found in R2d § 86, where it is called Promise for Benefit Received. As this heading implies, promissory restitution is where a benefit is rendered first, and then later, the beneficiary promises to pay for that benefit. Note that the promise to pay for a benefit already rendered is a gratuitous promise. Such a promise to pay cannot be given to obtain the benefit, since the benefit was already obtained when such promise was made. Sometimes such a promise is called "past consideration," but this term is an oxymoron.

Under the R2d approach, there cannot be such a thing as past consideration. Consideration is given to secure a promise in the future, so "past consideration" cannot exist under this usage of the term. At best, such a promise creates a moral obligation to pay, but the law does not enforce mere moral obligations, only legal ones. A moral obligation needs something more to be enforceable — if nothing more was required, this would eviscerate the consideration doctrine. These promises amount to promises to give a gift, and such promises are generally unenforceable, because gifts are not promised in order to obtain something of value in return. That something more is justice or fairness. According to R2d § 86, such a gratuitous promise to pay for a benefit previously received is only enforceable to the extent necessary to prevent injustice. The series of cases below illustrates several common scenarios where justice requires such enforcement, but the law has room for creative arguments that new circumstances also merit this special treatment. Again, the category of cases where an otherwise gratuitous promise to pay for a benefit previously received is called promissory restitution:

> *A promise made in recognition of a benefit previously received by the promisor from the promisee is binding to the extent necessary to prevent injustice.*
> R2d § 86(1).

Recall that consideration is found where, at the moment of contract formation, both parties agree to give something in order to get something of value, simultaneously.

When this timing is off — either because the thing of value was already received in the past (invoking the possibility of promissory restitution), or because the promise proximately causes some action or forbearance in the future (invoking the possibility of promissory estoppel) — then the lack of consideration will make the promise unenforceable unless some equitable exception applies. Read on to discover the specific cases and general principles under which these exceptions are likely to be applied by courts of law.

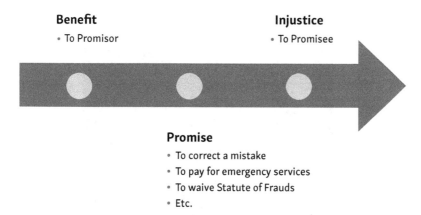

Figure 9.1. Illustration of the elements of promissory restitution as they occur across time.

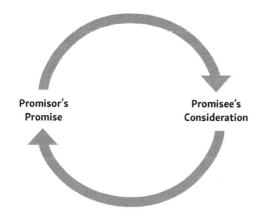

Figure 9.2. The exchange of promises happens simultaneously at the moment of contract acceptance.

Rules

A. Promise to Pay for Benefit Received

Most cases in which there is a promise unsupported by consideration will result in a court finding there is no contract and no enforceable promise. The general rule is that a promise is enforceable under contract law only when consideration is given in exchange for that promise. A simple promise to pay for a benefit received, without more, does not justify any deviation for this rule.

The classic case of *Mills v. Wyman*, below, took place in Hartford, Connecticut, in 1825. A 25-year-old man named Levi Wyman returned to port in Hartford from a sea voyage sick, poor, and in distress. Daniel Mills found him and cared for him at his own expense, until Levi died. Upon learning that Mills cared for his son, Levi's father,

Figure 9.3. The Sick Man by Laurits Andersen Ring (1902).
Public domain work.

Seth Wyman, wrote a letter to Mills promising to pay for the expense of his care. Yet Wyman never paid, and Mills sued.

The court found this was a garden variety example of an unenforceable promise to pay for a past benefit. The promise was made to compensate the stranger for a benefit that happened in the past. Without more, such promises will not be enforced for want of consideration. The promisor (Seth Wyman) did not seek to induce some kind of action, and the promisee (David Mills) was not induced, so there was no consideration, and the case was dismissed in the lower court.

Perhaps Wyman had a moral obligation to pay Mills. But the question is not whether he ought to pay Mills. The question is whether he is legally obligated to do so. The court explained that courts of law do not enforce these so-called moral obligations.

> *If moral obligation, in its fullest sense, is a good substratum for an express promise, it is not easy to perceive why it is not equally good to support an implied promise. What a man ought to do, generally he ought to be made to do, whether he promise or refuse. But the law of society has left most of such obligations to the interior forum, as the tribunal of conscience has been aptly called.*

When Seth Wyman failed to keep this promise, that may be a violation of some kind of moral obligation or duty. But moral obligation is not consideration. There needs to be something more. The next several topics will demonstrate what plus factors courts typically recognize as valid bases for enforcement of promises without consideration.

B. Promise to Correct a Mistake

In all cases of promissory restitution, the promise to pay for some benefit occurs after the benefit occurs. In such cases, it is impossible for the prospect of the benefit to induce the promisee to pay for it. Time flows in only one direction, and events in the future cannot influence intentions in the past. Events in the future, however, can evidence what intentions a person would have had in the past. For example, if Husband says to Wife, "I cooked you steak for dinner tonight. Would you promise to clean up afterwards?" Wife then says that she agrees. What might we deduce about Wife's intentions and preferences? It seems that Wife might have agreed to exchange her cleaning up after dinner in return for a steak dinner.

Perhaps Husband was originally mistaken. He thought Tuesday was steak night, but Tuesday was actually soup night. The couple have a course of dealing under which they've established that when Husband cooks the correct meal, Wife cleans up afterwards. If Husband cooks the wrong meal, on the other hand, Wife has no legal obligation to clean up afterwards. She may have a moral obligation to help Husband, but not a legal one. But, when Husband makes a mistake (cooks the wrong meal) and Wife still promises to "pay" for it (clean up afterwards), her promise functions as a substitute for consideration. By making that promise, Wife indicates that she would have wanted that bargain in the first place. The bargain does not appear thrust upon her. Rather, even though there was not an offer that contemplated both a promise and its consideration, as we normally find in cases involving consideration, we have evidence that both parties determined that the bargain would make each of them better off. This is similar to consideration, which evidences that parties entered into a deal to make themselves better off. And this is likewise evidence of a voluntary agreement. Therefore, it may satisfy the consideration requirement by substituting for it.

A similar situation occurred in *Drake v Bell*, below. Drake hired a contractor to fix issues she was having with her house. The contractor accidentally repaired Drake's neighbor, Bell's, house without Bell's knowledge. The repairs significantly improved Bell's house. After the repairs were completed, Bell orally agreed to pay the contractor for the improvements. Read on to determine whether Bell's oral promise should be binding.

C. Promise to Pay for Emergency Services and Necessaries

As a policy matter, society wants to encourage people to help each other in times of need and struggle. At such times, it may be impossible to formally contract. For example, if a man comes across an unconscious woman lying in the street, that woman lacks the capacity to contract. Yet the man wraps her in a blanket and drives her 100 miles to the nearest hospital. When the woman wakes up, she feels indebted to the man. As a contract matter, she owes no legal obligation, because contracts are voluntary and cannot be thrust upon people. People who were incapacitated at the time of formation incur only voidable obligations. When she awakes, she only has a moral obligation to repay him for his time and trouble.

If the story ends here, the man will not be able to sue the woman for the services he rendered, at least not under contract law. Otherwise, imagine the unintended consequences if simply rendering emergency services entitled a man to be paid what he deemed to be the value for them. A man could go about looking for incapacitated people, dress them in fine silk robes, hire expensive personal care nurses, inject them with gold-plated IVs, then later supply an incredible bill for these unwanted services. This would have the undesirable effect of over-encouraging this kind of behavior. There needs to be some sort of plus factor before the law will enforce such a bargain.

That plus factor arises where the beneficiary actually promises to pay for the services. Obviously, the promise cannot always happen at the time of the emergency — people may not be thinking about the formalities of legal obligation while their house is burning down or when they push someone out of the way of a speeding railcar — so consideration may be wanting in these emergency situations. However, a promise to pay for these emergency services after the emergency has passed can be a substitute for consideration. By later agreeing to pay for emergency services rendered, the promisor implies that the value received is worth what is given in exchange. Although the law usually holds that "past consideration" is not consideration, here, in situations where present consideration was impossible due to an emergency, the court may retroactively apply the promise to pay as if it was made before the emergency services were rendered in order to induce that service.

In the case of *Webb v. McGowin*, below, Joe Webb and J. Greeley McGowin were working in the W.T. Smith Lumber Company in Alabama. Webb was working on the upper floor, where his job was to drop pine blocks, which weighted about 75 pounds, onto the ground floor below in order to clear the upper floor. While throwing one such block of wood, Webb saw McGowin below him. Webb realized that if he released the block, it could kill McGowin. To divert the heavy block that he was already throwing, Webb contorted himself and fell along with the block to the ground below. Webb thus saved McGowin, but in the process, he seriously injured himself and, indeed, crippled himself for life such that he was no longer able to work.

Afterwards, McGowin promises to care for Webb for the rest of Webb's life by providing him $15 every two weeks. McGowin made this payment for almost nine years, and then he died. The executor of McGowin's estate, however, refused to continue payments, on the basis that McGowin's promise to pay was unsupported by consideration. Webb sued.

The court opinion is well worth reading because it illustrates several other circumstances where promises without consideration may still be enforceable, including the famous case of the escaped bull. The court concludes that McGowin's executor must pay Webb in this case — even though there is clearly no consideration, because McGowin made a promise to pay Webb for a benefit (saving his life) that he received in the past. The court reasoned that since Webb acted in the face of an emergency, where there was no time to bargain, and since McGowin later recognized the value of

Figure 9.4. William Arthur Cooper, Lumber Industry (1934). Credit Smithsonian American Art Museum. Public domain work.

Webb's action by promising to pay for it, then this promise should be enforceable to the extent that McGowin himself received the benefit of Webb's action.

As a thought experiment, imagine what Webb and McGowin would have agreed upon if time stopped just as Webb began to drop the block of wood upon McGowin. In this freeze-frame image, Webb says to McGowin, "Will you pay me $15 every two weeks if I cripple myself in order to save your life?" If you were McGowin, what would you say? It seems theoretically reasonable to agree to this bargain, and, moreover, McGowin actually agreed to it by promising later to make such payments. Although the parties did not actually strike a bargain, the resulting exchange of promises seems to be a reasonable approximation of the bargain the parties could have struck had they had the opportunity to do so. This seems to make the court more comfortable in enforcing Webb's promise, even though did not result from an actual bargain.

D. Promise to Pay for a Past Gift

The *Mills* case establishes the basic rule that promises to pay for past gifts are unenforceable. For example, if I give my mother an iPhone as a birthday present, and a week later, she calls me and says that I should not have spent so much on her and so she will pay me back the purchase price, this promise is unenforceable. In fact, this situation is a simple example of "past consideration," which is not consideration at all.

Not all gifts are true gifts, however. Sometimes, especially in business situations, parties offer something for free with the intention of gaining more business later. For example, a contractor might offer to a homeowner a "free estimate" on the cost to repair a roof. This is not a true gift in the sense that the contractor is not looking to give charity to the homeowner. Rather, the contractor is hoping that the homeowner will hire it to repair the roof. The free estimate is not a true gift but rather a loss leader, a strategy in which a seller gives away something for free or sells it for less than it is worth in order to attract more business in the future.

The notion that not all gifts are truly given freely is ancient. Black's Law Dictionary points out that the term "gratuitous gift" appears redundant, but in fact, this is a more specific use of the concept of gift. A gratuitous gift is a very old term, which originated in Roman law as the *donum gratuitum*. The fact that a seemingly redundant term survived for well over a thousand years implies that the term has utility beyond what first meets the eye. The persistence of the term gratuitous gift implies there might be such a thing as a non-gratuitous gift, that is, some sort of gift that is intended to produce some benefit for the giftor.

We are familiar with the concept in modern language. We might say that a gift comes "with strings attached," meaning, you might be expected to do something in return for accepting such a gift. If one is looking for something in exchange, then one is not really giving a donum gratuitous, a gratuitous gift, but rather a *largitio*, which is a gift for self-interested motives.

While American law does not use these Latin terms, it likewise distinguishes between truly gratuitous gifts from gifts given for self-interested motives. A promise to pay for a truly gratuitous gift that was given in the past is unenforceable; again, this is the classic definition of "past consideration," which is not consideration at all. But a promise to pay for a gift previously given for self-interested motives may be enforceable. Therefore, lawyers must conceptually distinguish between *gratuitum* and *largitio*, even if they need not use those Latin terms.

The law generally assumes that family members give *gratuitum,* true gifts, to each other. The default presumption, due to the love and bonds of the family, is that, for example, a grandfather who offers to pay for his granddaughter's law school does so unsupported by consideration. Of course, there are exceptions to this general rule. A man might say to his son, I will pay you $5 to mow the lawn. This clearly has the form of a contract and may easily override the presumption that family members give gifts to one another. Family members may also make contracts together.

In the business world, on the other hand, where strangers engage in arms-length transactions, the presumption is flipped. Courts assume that commercial activities are contracts and bargaining, not gifts. A construction worker who agrees to "help out" his boss by working on Sunday probably expects to be paid for his work, and not to give a gift of his time out of love for his boss. Of course, there are exceptions to this rule, too. Corporations may give charity to causes that do not directly or indirectly benefit the corporation, such as the CEO of a restaurant chain who promises to drive

Figure 9.5. Peter Jungen (on the right) presents a gift to ambassador Philip D. Murphy (on the left). Credit Raimond Spekking (2013). CC BY-SA 4.0.

all the food left over at the end of the day to the local food bank. While uncommon, businesses can also make promises to give gratuitous gifts.

The key point to remember is that the law recognizes that there are things which look like gifts in the business world, but they are not gifts in the pure sense. Sometimes referred to as loss leaders, one way a firm can gain new business is by giving a trial of its services for free. The purpose of giving the free trial is not to give charity. The purpose of the trial is to entice the buyer to sign up for the service or to permanently purchase the product. The free trial is not a pure gift — it comes with some expectations or strings attached.

When a gift is given with the hope of receiving something in return — when a gift is *largitio* and not *gratuitum* — then it can form the basis of an enforceable promise if the person who benefits from the gift-that-is-not-really-a-gift promises to pay for it. Again, the party who receives the so-called gift is only obligated to pay for it if that receiving party actually promises to pay. One cannot simply thrust a contractual obligation upon another, because contract law requires voluntary agreement to be bound by terms. But, when a person who receives a "gift" with strings attached and then offers to pay for that gift, that promise will be binding as a matter of promissory estoppel.

E. Promise to Pay for an Unpaid Contract

The doctrine of consideration provides some protection against enforcement of unwitting or casual promises. The law does not want parties running to court for every trifling grievance, because that would tax the court's limited bandwidth and stall or prevent the legal system from resolving more important debates. Moreover, contract law is not intended to police morality; rather, contract law is intended to encourage economically beneficial transactions. Concerns regarding public morality are more properly reserved for publicly elected legislatures to decide; moreover, many moral issues are left to the interior forum, meaning, one's conscience. For this reason, courts will generally not enforce promises that are not bargained-for in exchange for something else in return. This principle is known as the consideration doctrine.

However, there are exceptions to the consideration doctrine, and the common theme behind the seemingly myriad exceptions are that they also require some plus factor which shows that the parties would have intended to make a bargain, had the circumstances been different.

Once such case can occur where one party did in fact form a binding contractual bargain, and that party performed its contractual obligations, but that party did not receive whatever it expected in exchange or return for its performance. In some subset of such cases, the party's performance benefitted a third party. And in some subset of those cases, the third party promises to pay for the benefit it received pursuant to someone else's unfulfilled contractual obligation. We can refer to this situation as a promise to pay for an unpaid contract.

Although the law disfavors enforcement of promises to pay for past benefits received, because those look like gratuitous promises to pay for gifts, this situation is different because courts feel more confident that the performing party was not simply trying to bestow some benefit upon another person. Rather, the contract shows that the completion of that promise was done for good reason, as part of a voluntary exchange.

Moreover, the goal of contract law is not to force parties into litigation but to encourage parties to work things out. This doctrine encourages third party beneficiaries to resolve contractual disputes before the parties go to litigation.

The classic case of *Edson v. Poppe*, below, is a famous example of this situation, although the Restatement illustrates the facts a bit differently from how the judge presents them in his 1910 opinion. We will interpret the facts as the Restatement did in 1982, because that will give us a better idea of how the modern law functions with regard to promises to pay for benefits conferred pursuant to contract.

William Poppe owned land on which George F. Edson rented and lived. Poppe urged Edson to build a well on the land, and Edson contracted with a digger to build it. The well was built, but the tenants were unable to pay the digger. The landlord, Poppe, seeing how the well improved the value of his land, then agreed to pay the digger for the reasonable value of the well, which was $250. But then he failed to pay, and Edson sued Poppe for the value of the well.

The Restatement's version of the facts does not entirely make sense because, in this version of the story, Edson did not expend money or resources, but rather hired a digger to do the work. Why, then would Edson want or be entitled to sue Poppe?

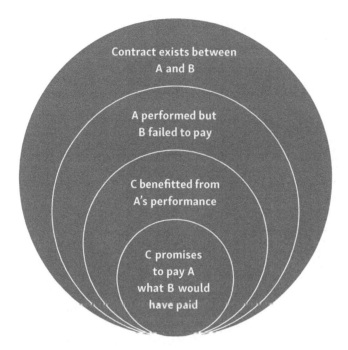

Figure 9.6. Stacked Venn diagram showing the circumstance where promise to pay for another's contract will be enforceable under promissory estoppel.

And, if such a suit was successful, what damages would Edson be entitled to where he now enjoys a well that cost him nothing?

The Restatement's version must not be an accurate illustration of what actually unfolded in the case. My reading of this case is that Edson did the digging himself, and Poppe promised to pay him for the work. In that actual case, as I read it, Edson and Poppe had a verbal agreement, but it was not an enforceable contract because they did not agree on price until after the Edson completed the work. Poppe then ratified the price term by agreeing to pay $250 after the work was completed.

As far as I can tell, there was no third party in the actual case. There was no third-party digger and no contract between Edson and said digger. But, for purposes of understanding what the Restatement presents as the rule regarding promises to pay for benefits conferred by another's unpaid contract, let us proceed with the probably inaccurate but useful assumption that there was some third-party digger in the case who did not get paid by Edson for his work pursuant to a contract with Edson to build a well on Poppe's land.

Poppe argued that he did not have to pay because his promise was gratuitous, and therefore unenforceable, because it was unsupported by consideration. He reasoned that he simply promised to pay for a benefit received; that is, his promise was supported by "past consideration," which is not actually consideration at all, and therefore, he did not have to perform what he promised to do.

Figure 9.7. Հայերեն: Ջրհոր Գյումրիում (Well in Gyumri, Armenia) by Sununa (2019), CC-ASA4.

According to the Restatement's illustration, the court found that Poppe's promise was enforceable because his promise was pursuant to Edson's contract. The existence of some contract shows that the benefit was not thrust upon Poppe, but rather that he would have bargained for it had the circumstances been different. In other words, Poppe's promise to pay the digger when Edson was unable to do so, combined with the fact that Poppe benefitted from the digger's work by improving Poppe's land, constates a plus factor that makes Poppe's promise enforceable on the basis of promissory restitution.

This particular exemption is on shaky ground, because it is not clearly supported by case law. Remember that the Restatement is only a treatise about the law, which is supposed to say what the law is. The Restatement does not have the power to change the law, only to restate it. Some scholars have challenged this principle of moral obligation as a basis for contract recovery, and courts may not accept it.

In my opinion, this case is not really about promissory restitution at all. Rather, to the extent there really was a third-party digger at all, *Edson v. Poppe* is either an implied delegation of the duty to pay the digger from Edson to Poppe or a novation whereby Poppe took Edson's place as the obligor in a contract where the digger was the obligee.

In any event, the common law does seem susceptible to finding promissory restitution where one party promises to pay for another's unpaid contract, at least where the party who promises to pay received a benefit from that contract.

F. Promise to Pay for an Unenforceable Contract

There are many reasons why a promise turns out to be unenforceable. Parties who intended to contract may have failed to include enough definition in the terms of the agreement for a court to enforce it. The contract may be of a sort which requires a signed writing to be enforceable, and it lacks such a writing. The contract may have emerged from a mistake about the nature of the subject matter. Even changed circumstances after a valid formation can excuse an obligation and make it unenforceable.

Although the general legal rule is that gratuitous promises are unenforceable, the common law provides an exception and enforces promises to pay for otherwise unenforceable contracts. This is similar to the rule that a promise to pay for the benefit received pursuant to another's unpaid contract is enforceable. The law wants parties to keep their obligations and looks for plus factors that overcome the general presumption against enforcement of gratuitous promises.

In the 1909 case of *Muir v. Kane*, below, M. Francis Kane and his wife Ida Kane orally agreed to pay B.L. Muir & Co. for Muir's assistance in selling a parcel of real estate that the Kanes owned. This was, in effect, a commission for the sale of real estate. Muir succeeded in finding a purchaser, Paul Bush, and then the parties executed a formal written agreement in which the parties agreed that Muir would receive $200 from the sale proceeds as its commission.

At the time, the State of Washington had a statue that required commission for the sale of real estate to be in writing. The Kanes refused to pay the commission and made two arguments: first, the original oral agreement to pay the commission was unenforceable because it was not in writing; and, second, the later written agreement to pay the commission was not a contract because it lacked consideration. The second argument was predicated on the notion that past consideration is not actually consideration at all; and since Muir had already fully rendered its services at the time that the Kanes promised in writing to pay Muir for Muir's work, the Kanes' written promise to pay Muir was a gratuitous promise.

The court disagreed. Although the original oral agreement was unenforceable due to the statutory requirement of a writing, it was still a valid contract formed by offer and acceptance with consideration for a promise. The later writing revived that earlier obligation and made it enforceable.

> *The court, it will be observed, makes a distinction between contracts formerly good but on which the right of recovery has been barred by the statute, and*

*those contracts which are barred in the first instance because of some legal
defect in their execution, holding that the former will furnish a consideration
for a subsequent promise to perform, while the latter will not.*

In general, mere moral obligations are not enforceable as a matter of contract
law. But, here, where the parties first created a valid contract, and then that contract
became unenforceable due to some legal principle or changed circumstances, the
original promisee can effectively revive the legal obligation.

G. Reflections on Promissory Restitution

Alternatives to consideration evolved over time, punching holes in the consideration
doctrine until, some have argued, the consideration doctrine should be abandoned
like a piece of old Swiss cheese. Yet consideration remains the law of the R2d,
UCC and in most states. Perhaps during your career, you will be the lawyer who
successfully argues for its demise in your jurisdiction. But for now, the best way to
learn about this requirement of bargained-for exchange and the exceptions to this
rule is by looking at the various paths that equitable precedent has carved through
the legal doctrine.

For pedagogical reasons, this Chapter features more cases than typical. The cases
are short and illustrate specific instances where judges felt comfortable eschewing
the requirement of consideration because justice and fairness demanded it. You will
need to recognize where similar circumstances come up in the future and analogize
those situations to the ones in the cases in this chapter to make specific arguments
that a promise should be enforceable without consideration. Going back to
our cheese analogy, this is like following an existing path through the Swiss cheese
that is the requirement of consideration that well established precedent has punched
through it.

But locating a closely analogous case and taking its same route to its same conclusion
is only the first step toward mastering the estoppel doctrines. Next you must
seek to understand what is common about the equitable exceptions so you can argue
that a relatively novel contracting circumstance likewise merits relief from the legal
requirement of consideration "where justice so requires." Make no mistake that this
general form of argument based on principles is more complex and requires higher
order thinking that merely arguing by analogy. In fact, many top law students find
this challenge inspiring, because lawyers have considerably more freedom in making
equitable arguments, allowing your creative cognition and procedural knowledge
skills to shine.

The equitable (or fairness) exceptions to the consideration doctrine are grouped
into two main categories, promissory restitution (promise for a benefit received),
which you have just learned; and promissory estoppel (promise reasonably inducing
action or forbearance), which is the subject of the last Chapter.

Note that both equitable doctrines have a critical similarity: Both require promises. There is no contractual liability without a promise. There are other legal areas, such as the doctrines of restitution and unjust enrichment, under which an aggrieved party may assert a claim for damages without alleging a promise. But such claim alleges, at best, a quasi-contract, meaning, something that looks like a contract but is not a contract as a matter of law. You may study the law of restitution in other courses, but it is beyond the scope of contract law and therefore beyond the scope of this book and this course. For now, you need to note that no promise means no contract and therefore no contract liability, even under the equitable alternative to consideration doctrines.

Cases

> **Reading Mills v. Wyman.** Establishing whether there is promissory restitution starts with determining whether there was a promise. In the case below, a father promised to compensate a stranger that took care of his dying adult son. The promise was made to compensate the stranger for a benefit that happened in the past. The promisor (the father) did not seek to induce some kind of action, and the promisee (the stranger) was not induced, so there was no consideration, and the case was dismissed in the lower court. If there was no consideration, then there needed to be an alternative — one based on a sense of fairness and justice.
>
> If the father failed to keep this promise, wouldn't it feel like a violation of some kind of moral obligation or duty? But can moral obligation alone be an alternative to consideration? As you read the *Mills* case below, determine whether moral obligation alone can be an alternative to consideration or if there needs to be something more.

Mills v. Wyman

20 Mass. 207 (1825)

PARKER C. J.

General rules of law established for the protection and security of honest and fair-minded men, who may inconsiderately make promises without any equivalent, will sometimes screen men of a different character from engagements which they are bound *in foro conscientiæ* [before the tribunal of conscience] to perform. This is a defect inherent in all human systems of legislation. The rule that a mere verbal promise, without any consideration, cannot be enforced by action, is universal in its application, and cannot be departed from to suit particular cases in which a refusal to perform such a promise may be disgraceful.

The promise declared on in this case appears to have been made without any legal consideration. The kindness and services towards the sick son of the defendant were not bestowed at his request. The son was in no respect under the care of the defendant. He was twenty-five years old, and had long left his father's family. On his return from a foreign country, he fell sick among strangers, and the plaintiff acted the part of the good Samaritan, giving him shelter and comfort until he died. The defendant, his father, on being informed of this event, influenced by a transient feeling of gratitude, promises in writing to pay the plaintiff for the expenses he had incurred. But he has determined to break this promise, and is willing to have his case appear on record as a strong example of particular injustice sometimes necessarily resulting from the operation of general rules.

It is said a moral obligation is a sufficient consideration to support an express promise; and some authorities lay down the rule thus broadly. However, upon examination of the cases, we are satisfied that the universality of the rule cannot be supported, and there must have been some preexisting obligation, which has become inoperative by positive law, to form a basis for an effective promise. The cases of debts barred by the statute of limitations, of debts incurred by infants, of debts of bankrupts, are generally put for illustration of the rule.

Express promises founded on such preexisting equitable obligations may be enforced. There is a good consideration for them. They merely remove an impediment created by law to the recovery of debts honestly due, but which public policy protects the debtors from being compelled to pay. In all these cases there was originally a quid pro quo; and according to the principles of natural justice the party receiving ought to pay; but the legislature has said he shall not be coerced. Then comes the promise to pay the debt that is barred, the promise of the man to pay the debt of the infant, of the discharged bankrupt to restore to his creditor what by the law he had lost. In all these cases there is a moral obligation founded upon an antecedent valuable consideration.

These promises therefore have a sound legal basis. They are not promises to pay something for nothing. Not naked pacts; but the voluntary revival or creation of obligation which before existed in natural law, but which had been dispensed with. It was not for the benefit of the party obliged solely, but principally for the public convenience.

If moral obligation, in its fullest sense, is a good substratum for an express promise, it is not easy to perceive why it is not equally good to support an implied promise. What a man ought to do, generally he ought to be made to do, whether he promise or refuse. But the law of society has left most of such obligations to the interior forum, as the tribunal of conscience has been aptly called. Is there not a moral obligation upon every son who has become affluent by means of the education and advantages bestowed upon him by his father, to relieve that father from pecuniary embarrassment? To promote his comfort and happiness, and even to share with him his riches, if thereby he will be made happy? And yet such a Son may, with impunity, leave such a father in any degree of penury above that which will expose the community in which he dwells, to the danger of being obliged to preserve him from absolute want. Is not a wealthy father under strong moral obligation to advance the interest of an obedient, well disposed son? To furnish him with the means of acquiring and maintaining a becoming rank in life, to rescue him from the horrors of debt incurred by misfortune? Yet the law will uphold him in any degree of parsimony, short of that which would reduce his son to the necessity of seeking public charity.

Without doubt there are great interests of society which justify withholding the coercive arm of the law from these duties of imperfect obligation. As they are called; imperfect, not because they are less binding upon the conscience than those which are called perfect, but because the wisdom of the social law does not impose sanctions upon them.

A deliberate promise, in writing, made freely and without any mistake, one which may lead the party to whom it is made into contracts and expenses, cannot be broken without a violation of moral duty. But if there was nothing paid or promised for it, the law, perhaps wisely, leaves the execution of it to the conscience of him who makes it. It is only when the party making the promise gains something, or he to whom it is made loses something, that the law gives the promise validity. And in the case of the promise of the adult to pay the debt of the infant, of the debtor discharged by the statute of limitations or bankruptcy, the principle is preserved by looking back to the origin of the transaction, where an equivalent is to be found. An exact equivalent is not required by the law; for there being a consideration, the parties are left to estimate its value: though here the courts of equity will step in to relieve from gross inadequacy between the consideration and the promise.

These principles are deduced from the general current of decided cases upon the subject, as well as from the known maxims of the common law. The general position, that moral obligation is a sufficient consideration for an express promise, is to be limited in its application, to cases where at some time or other a good or valuable consideration has existed.

A legal obligation is always a sufficient consideration to support either an express or an implied promise; such as an infant's debt for necessaries, or a father's promise to pay for the support and education of his minor children. But when the child shall have attained to manhood, and shall have become his own agent in the world's business, the debts he incurs, whatever may be their nature, create no obligation upon the father; and it seems to follow, that his promise founded upon such a debt has no legally binding force.

The cases of instruments under seal and certain mercantile contracts, in which considerations need not be proved, do not contradict the principles above suggested. The first import a consideration in themselves, and the second belong to a branch of the mercantile law, which has found it necessary to disregard the point of consideration in respect to instruments negotiable in their nature and essential to the interests of commerce.

The opinions of the judges had been variant for a long course of years upon this subject, but there seems to be no case in which it was nakedly decided, that a promise to pay the debt of a son of full age, not living with his father, though the debt were incurred by sickness which ended in the death of the son, without a previous request by the father proved or presumed, could be enforced by action.

It has been attempted to show a legal obligation on the part of the defendant by virtue of our statute, which compels lineal kindred in the ascending or descending line to support such of their poor relations as are likely to become chargeable to the town where they have their settlement. But it is a sufficient answer to this position, that such legal obligation does not exist except in the very cases provided for in the statute, and never until the party charged has been adjudged to be of sufficient ability thereto. We do not know from the report any of the facts which are necessary to create such an obligation. Whether the deceased had a legal settlement in this commonwealth at the time of his death, whether he was likely to become chargeable had he lived, whether the defendant was of sufficient ability, are essential facts to be adjudicated by the court to which is given jurisdiction on this subject. The legal liability does not arise until these facts have all been ascertained by judgment, after hearing the party intended to be charged.

For the foregoing reasons we are all of opinion that the nonsuit directed by the Court of Common Pleas was right, and that judgment be entered thereon for costs for the defendant.

Reflection

Mills demonstrates that, in general, a promise based on moral obligation to compensate for a benefit already received cannot be enforced without a preexisting obligation. In other words, moral obligation alone is insufficient to be an alternative to consideration. It needs to be based on something that is already recognized as legal consideration like a preexisting legal duty. One of the examples the court used was, if someone filed for bankruptcy, the law could discharge certain debts and they would not have to pay the debt back. However, if that same person decided to pay it back, out of a sense of moral obligation, then it could be enforced by law because it was once supported by consideration. The debtor had a legal duty to pay back his creditor, but the law allowed the forgiveness of the debt due to public policy. Though the debtor revived the promise out a sense of moral obligation, it is supported by the preexisting legal duty to pay back the creditor.

Arguably, the father was morally obligated to pay the stranger what he had promised. But since the stranger helped the son in the past without the inducement of the father's words and actions, it cannot be consideration. Moral obligation alone cannot be an alternative to consideration, therefore, the court cannot enforce the promise.

Discussion

1. The *Mills* court case found that Seth Wyman (the father of Levi Wyman) did not have to pay Daniel Mills (the caregiver of Levi Wyman). Do you think this is the right result? Justify your opinion by making a policy argument.

2. The *Mills* court determined that Seth Wyman's promise to Daniel Mills lacked consideration. What specific facts led the *Mills* court to this holding, and what have you learned generally about what is consideration from this case?

3. Would the case have come out differently if Levi Wyman was an unemancipated minor? Why?

Reading Drake v. Bell. Contracts are usually enforceable as a matter of law only where both parties were mutually induced to perform an exchange. But promises could alternatively be enforceable on the basis of equity, even where there is no inducement, pursuant to the doctrine of promissory restitution. Restitution refers to the return of ill-gotten gains or the disgorgement of unjust enrichment. Promissory restitution is where one party makes a promise to return some money or property that it is not entitled to hold. By definition, promissory restitution cannot induce a material transfer that already occurred; as mentioned above, time flows in only one direction, and events in the future cannot influence intentions in the past.

In *Drake v Bell*, Bell received valuable home improvements from Drake that were not bargained for. Bell later promises to pay Drake. The *Drake* court finds Bell's promise enforceable under the doctrine of promissory estoppel. What makes the *Drake* case different from the *Mills* case, where a father's promise to pay a stranger for previously rendered care of his son was deemed unenforceable?

Drake is distinguishable from *Mills* because David Mills gave care out of pure charity, expecting nothing in return, whereas the contractor in *Drake* performed his work because he believed he was to be paid for it. In other words, the promise to pay the contractor related to a prior legal obligation. Chancellor Kent said:

> *It is an unsettled point whether a moral obligation is of itself a sufficient consideration for a promise, except in those cases in which a prior legal obligation or consideration had once existed.*

In *Drake*, there was consideration for the promise to repair Drake's house, so consideration had once existed with regard to the promise Bell made. This distinguishes *Drake* from *Mills*, where there was never any consideration.

Figure 9.8. Old House in Rector Street (from Scene of Old New York), Henry Farrer (1870). Public domain work.

Note that this obligation still required a voluntary promise from Bell. He would not have to pay for the repairs if he did not promise to do so. Bell was not obligated to pay the contractor for the repairs, even though the repairs improved his house, because those repairs were thrust upon him, without his manifestation of assent to pay for them. However, when Bell promised to pay the contractor for the repairs, the contract became binding. Bell's promise to pay the contractor was not solely based on a moral obligation; Bell reaped a benefit from the contractor's repairs to his house, and the contractor performed those repairs pursuant to a contract supported by consideration; therefore, Bell's promise was supported by consideration and is binding.

Drake v. Bell

55 N.Y.S. 945 (App. Div. 1899)

GAYNOR, J.

The defendant was under no legal obligation to pay for the work. Nor is there any question of acceptance as of a chattel, for there was nothing capable of being rejected or taken away. Did, then, his promise bind him? Lord Mansfield with his keen perception, broad mind, and aversion to alleged rules of law resting on misunderstood or inadvertent remarks of judges, instead of on foundations of reason and justice, said in *Hawkes v. Saunders*, that:

> *Where a man is under a moral obligation, which no court of law or equity can enforce, and promises, the honesty and rectitude of the thing is a consideration.*

Buller, J., said in the same case:

> *If such a question were stripped of all authority it would be resolved by inquiring whether law were a rule of justice, or whether it was something that acts in direct contradiction to justice, conscience and equity.*

If the rule so plainly stated by Lord Mansfield, that a moral obligation was of itself sufficient consideration for a subsequent promise, had been followed, the sole question in each case would be whether there was a moral obligation to support the promise. That would resolve the present case for the plaintiff. But it has not been always followed. I have examined the cases on the subject in England and here from the beginning. They are irreconcilable, and it would be no use to cite and review them.

But notwithstanding much stray remark by judges may be cited to the contrary, it seems to me that a promise to pay for antecedent value received by the promisor from the promisee binds, although there was never any obligation to pay which could be enforced. Why not? Such a case is not one of mere moral obligation resting on no consideration received, if there can be any such abstract moral obligation. The case is one of moral obligation created by a past valuable consideration derived from another.

For instance, a promise after coming of age to pay a debt incurred during infancy, and which cannot be enforced, or by a woman after coming discovers to pay a like debt incurred while covert, is binding. On the other hand, a subsequent promise by a father to pay for the care of his adult son while sick among strangers, or of a son to pay for like care of his father, is not binding. *Mills v. Wyman.* The distinction is that in the former class of cases there was past valuable consideration to the promisor, while in the latter not. The promise in the one class is not a naked pact, for it is not to pay something for nothing, while in the other class just that is the case.

[Case law] is construed to mean that only a subsequent promise which revives an obligation formerly enforceable either at law or in equity, but which has grown extinct, is binding. "But a mere moral or conscientious obligation, unconnected with any prior legal or equitable claim, is not enough," is the rule reduced from the said note in a number of cases. And yet the same opinions say that the moral obligation "to pay a debt contracted during infancy or coverture, and the like," is sufficient to support a subsequent promise; as though in such cases the moral obligation rested on a prior legal or equitable claim, which it does not. Such is true though of a promise to pay a debt barred by the statute of limitations or by a discharge in bankruptcy, which all of the cases hold to be binding.

The actual decisions most worthy of attention (not feeling bound by mere general remarks of judges and their citation) make two classes. In one of them the promise is held binding because based on a former obligation enforceable at law or in equity, which obligation it revives; in the other because the promisor though never under any such obligation nevertheless received an antecedent valuable consideration, Hence the rule seems to be that a subsequent promise founded on a former enforceable obligation, or on value previously had from the promisee, is binding.

It does not seem to me there is any actual decision in this state opposed to this. Some decisions may seem to be until something more than the head note and bare opinion are considered. The actual decision cannot be broader than the actual facts.

The promise in *Frear v. Hardenbergh*, was by the owner of land to pay a trespasser in possession the value of his improvements if the owner prevailed in his action of ejectment then pending. The plaintiff had entered knowing that he had no title, and it was held that no moral obligation for the promise could arise out of the willful trespass.

The language of the opinion in *Eastwood v. Kenyon* is very large, but the point decided does not seem controlling of cases like the present one. After coming of age the woman promised to pay back moneys expended by her father's executor for her benefit upon her real property during her infancy. Having afterwards become covert, her husband promised to pay the same. An action against him on his promise was not sustained, the opinion saying:

> *If the ratification of the wife while sole was relied on, then a debt from her would have been shown, and the defendant could not have been charged in his own right without some further consideration, as of forbearance after marriage, or something of that sort.*

The debt was the wife's, and while the husband was liable for it by the common law in an action against both of them, he was not liable in an action against him in his own right on his said assumpsit. The point is technical.

Chancellor Kent does not confine the validity of such promises to cases of past legal obligation, but extends it to cases of the existence of a prior consideration. He says it is an unsettled point whether a moral obligation is of itself "a sufficient consideration for a promise, except in those cases in which a prior legal obligation or consideration had once existed."

I do not pretend that this question is free from doubt, but to use the words of Chief Justice Marshall, "I do not think that law ought to be separated from justice where it is at most doubtful", and that has no doubt influenced me some in reaching a conclusion.

Judgment for the plaintiff.

Reflection

This case illustrates that a subsequent promise founded on a former enforceable obligation is binding — however, a subsequent promise founded solely on moral obligation, unconnected to any other legal claim, is not binding.

At first, Bell was not obligated to pay the contractor for the work, even though the repairs improved his house. However, when Bell promised to pay the contractor for the repairs, the contract became binding. Bell's promise to pay the contractor was not solely based on a moral obligation; Bell reaped a benefit from the contractor's repairs to his house, therefore, his promise was supported by consideration and is binding.

Discussion

1. How does the court distinguish *Drake* from *Mills*? Do you agree with this distinction?

2. Why does the *Mills* court argue that the *Frear* case referenced in its opinion is not on point?

3. What have you learned about when promissory restitution applies based on the distinctions between *Drake* on the one hand and *Mills* and *Frear* on the other?

———————

Reading Webb v. McGowin. As a policy matter, society wants to encourage people to help each other in times of need and struggle. At such times, it may be impossible to formally contract. For example, if a man comes across an unconscious woman lying in the street, that woman lacks the capacity to contract. Yet the man wraps her in a blanket and drives her 100 miles to the nearest hospital. When the woman wakes up, she feels indebted to the man. As a legal matter, she owes no legal obligation, because contracts are voluntary and cannot be thrust upon people. People who were incapacitated at the time of formation incur only voidable obligations. When she awakes, she only has a moral obligation to repay him for his time and trouble.

If the story ends here, the man will not be able to sue the woman for the services he rendered. Otherwise, imagine the unintended consequences if simply rendering emergency services entitled a man to be paid what he deemed to be the value for them. A man could go about looking for incapacitated people, dress them in fine silk robes, hire expensive personal care nurses, and inject them with gold-plated IVs, then later supply an incredible bill for these unwanted services. This would have the undesirable effect of over-encouraging this kind of behavior. There needs to be some sort of plus factor before the law will enforce such a bargain.

Webb v. McGowin

27 Ala. App. 82 (1936)

BRICKEN, Presiding Judge.

This action is in assumpsit. [Assumpsit comes from the present active infinitive of the Latin verb *assumere*, meaning, "he has undertaken." In this historical context, it means that the plaintiff has filed an action to recover money owed due to an implied promise. The modern significance is that this is essentially an equitable pleading, meaning, the plaintiff seeks justice to remedy some unjust enrichment or failed quasi-contractual obligation.]

The complaint as originally filed was amended. The demurrers to the complaint as amended were sustained. [A demurrer is a historical civil procedure that is closely related to a modern motion to dismiss. If the defendant's demurrer is granted, then the plaintiff's case is dismissed.]

Because of this adverse ruling by the court the plaintiff took a nonsuit. [A voluntary nonsuit is where the plaintiff dismisses its own case without a court order to do so. Plaintiffs may have some opportunity to refile the claim. The specific rules regarding nonsuit are governed by Fed. R. Civ. Pro. 41 and similar provisions in state civil procedure codes.]

The assignment of errors on this appeal are predicated upon said action or ruling of the court.

A fair statement of the case presenting the questions for decision is set out in appellant's brief, which we adopt.

"On the 3d day of August, 1925, appellant while in the employ of the W.T. Smith Lumber Company, a corporation, and acting within the scope of his employment, was engaged in clearing the upper floor of mill No. 2 of the company. While so engaged he was in the act of dropping a pine block from the upper floor of the mill to the ground below; this being the usual and ordinary way of clearing the floor, and it being the duty of the plaintiff in the course of his employment to so drop it. The block weighed about 75 pounds.

As appellant was in the act of dropping the block to the ground below, he was on the edge of the upper floor of the mill. As he started to turn the block loose so that it would drop to the ground, he saw J. Greeley McGowin, testator of the defendants, on the ground below and directly under where the block would have fallen had appellant turned it loose. Had he turned it loose it would have struck McGowin with such force as to have caused him serious bodily harm or death. Appellant could have remained safely on the upper floor of the mill by turning the block loose and allowing it to drop, but had he done this the block would have fallen on McGowin and caused him serious injuries or death. The only safe and reasonable way to prevent this was for appellant to hold to the block and divert its direction in falling from the place where McGowin was standing and the only safe way to divert it so as to prevent its coming into contact with McGowin was for appellant to fall with it to the ground below. Appellant did this, and by holding to the block and falling with it to the ground below, he diverted the course of its fall in such way that McGowin was not injured. In thus preventing the injuries to McGowin appellant himself received serious bodily injuries, resulting in his right leg being broken, the heel of his right foot torn off and his right arm broken. He was badly crippled for life and rendered unable to do physical or mental labor.

On September 1, 1925, in consideration of appellant having prevented him from sustaining death or serious bodily harm and in consideration of the injuries appellant had received, McGowin agreed with him to care for and maintain him for the remainder of appellant's life at the rate of $15 every two weeks from the time he sustained his injuries to and during the remainder of appellant's life; it being agreed that McGowin would pay this sum to appellant for his maintenance. Under the agreement McGowin paid or caused to be paid to appellant the sum so agreed on up until McGowin's death on January 1, 1934. After his death the payments were continued to and including January 27, 1934, at which time they were discontinued. Thereupon plaintiff brought suit to recover the unpaid installments accruing up to the time of the bringing of the suit.

The material averments of the different counts of the original complaint and the amended complaint are predicated upon the foregoing statement of facts."

In other words, the complaint as amended averred in substance: (1) That on August 3, 1925, appellant saved J. Greeley McGowin, appellee's testator, from death or grievous bodily harm; (2) that in doing so appellant sustained bodily injury crippling him for life; (3) that in consideration of the services rendered and the injuries received by appellant, McGowin agreed to care for him the remainder of appellant's life, the amount to be paid being $15 every two weeks; (4) that McGowin complied with this agreement until he died on January 1, 1934, and the payments were kept up to January 27, 1934, after which they were discontinued.

The action was for the unpaid installments accruing after January 27, 1934, to the time of the suit.

The principal grounds of demurrer to the original and amended complaint are: (1) It states no cause of action; (2) its averments show the contract was without consideration; (3) it fails to allege that McGowin had, at or before the services were rendered, agreed to pay appellant for them; (4) the contract declared on is void under the statute of frauds.

1. The averments of the complaint show that appellant saved McGowin from death or grievous bodily harm. This was a material benefit to him of infinitely more value than any financial aid he could have received. Receiving this benefit, McGowin became morally bound to compensate appellant for the services rendered. Recognizing his moral obligation, he expressly agreed to pay appellant as alleged in the complaint and complied with this agreement up to the time of his death; a period of more than 8 years.

Had McGowin been accidentally poisoned and a physician, without his knowledge or request, had administered an antidote, thus saving his life, a subsequent promise by McGowin to pay the physician would have been valid. Likewise, McGowin's agreement as disclosed by the complaint to compensate appellant for saving him from death or grievous bodily injury is valid and enforceable.

Where the promisee cares for, improves, and preserves the property of the promisor, though done without his request, it is sufficient consideration for the promisor's subsequent agreement to pay for the service, because of the material benefit received.

In *Boothe v. Fitzpatrick*, the court held that a promise by defendant to pay for the past keeping of a bull which had escaped from defendant's premises and been cared for by plaintiff was valid, although there was no previous request, because the subsequent promise obviated that objection; it being equivalent to a previous request. On the same principle, had the promisee saved the promisor's life or his body from grievous harm, his subsequent promise to pay for the services rendered would have been valid. Such service would have been far more material than caring for his bull. Any holding that saving a man from death or grievous bodily harm is not a material benefit sufficient to uphold a subsequent promise to pay for the service, necessarily rests on the assumption that saving life and preservation of the body from harm have only a sentimental value. The converse of this is true. Life and preservation of the body have material, pecuniary values, measurable in dollars and cents. Because of this, physicians practice their profession charging for services rendered in saving life and curing the body of its ills, and surgeons perform operations. The same is true as to the law of negligence, authorizing the assessment of damages in personal injury cases based upon the extent of the injuries, earnings, and life expectancies of those injured.

In the business of life insurance, the value of a man's life is measured in dollars and cents according to his expectancy, the soundness of his body, and his ability to pay premiums. The same is true as to health and accident insurance.

It follows that if, as alleged in the complaint, appellant saved J. Greeley McGowin from death or grievous bodily harm, and McGowin subsequently agreed to pay him for the service rendered, it became a valid and enforceable contract.

2. It is well settled that a moral obligation is a sufficient consideration to support a subsequent promise to pay where the promisor has received a material benefit, although there was no original duty or liability resting on the promisor.

In the case of *State ex rel. Bayer v. Funk,* the court held that a moral obligation is a sufficient consideration to support an executory promise where the promisor has received an actual pecuniary or material benefit for which he subsequently expressly promised to pay.

The case at bar is clearly distinguishable from that class of cases where the consideration is a mere moral obligation or conscientious duty unconnected with receipt by promisor of benefits of a material or pecuniary nature. Here the promisor received a material benefit constituting a valid consideration for his promise.

3. Some authorities hold that, for a moral obligation to support a subsequent promise to pay, there must have existed a prior legal or equitable obligation, which for some reason had become unenforceable, but for which the promisor was still morally bound. This rule, however, is subject to qualification in those cases where the promisor, having received a material benefit from the promisee, is morally bound to compensate him for the services rendered and in consideration of this obligation promises to pay. In such cases the subsequent promise to pay is an affirmance or ratification of the services rendered carrying with it the presumption that a previous request for the service was made.

Under the decisions above cited, McGowin's express promise to pay appellant for the services rendered was an affirmance or ratification of what appellant had done raising the presumption that the services had been rendered at McGowin's request.

4. The averments of the complaint show that in saving McGowin from death or grievous bodily harm, appellant was crippled for life. This was part of the consideration of the contract declared on. McGowin was benefited. Appellant was injured. Benefit to the promisor or injury to the promisee is a sufficient legal consideration for the promisor's agreement to pay.

5. Under the averments of the complaint the services rendered by appellant were not gratuitous. The agreement of McGowin to pay and the acceptance of payment by appellant conclusively shows the contrary.

6. [Discussion regarding the statute of frauds omitted.]

The cases of *Shaw v. Boyd* and *Duncan v. Hall* are not in conflict with the principles here announced. In those cases the lands were owned by the United States at the time the alleged improvements were made, for which subsequent purchasers from the government agreed to pay. These subsequent purchasers were not the owners of the lands at the time the improvements were made. Consequently, they could not have been made for their benefit.

From what has been said, we are of the opinion that the court below erred in the ruling complained of; that is to say, in sustaining the demurrer, and for this error the case is reversed and remanded.

Reversed and remanded.

242

Reflection

Webb illustrates that, sometimes, a material benefit received in the past can be consideration if there was a subsequent promise for it and it was for emergency services or necessaries. Moral obligation alone cannot be sufficient consideration unless there was a prior legal or equitable obligation. In this case, a moral obligation did not stand alone; McGowin received a material benefit from the promisee.

Webb had saved McGowin's life without any inducement. McGowin subsequently promised to pay Webb for saving his life. Thus, there is no consideration, and the court must look towards alternatives. Here, unlike *Mills*, the case did not rest upon only a moral obligation to carry out the promise. McGowin materially benefited because he was saved from death or serious bodily injury. Therefore, because McGowin made a subsequent promise to compensate for a material benefit, the promise between McGowin's estate and Webb is binding.

Discussion

1. The *Webb* court distinguishes this case from ones where "the consideration is a mere moral obligation." What consideration does the court here find? Does it find it under the benefit/detriment test or the bargained-for exchange test?

2. Would a modern court applying the R2d approach find consideration in this case? Why or why not?

3. If it were possible to freeze time at the very moment where Webb had the choice to injure himself in order to save McGowin's life, what do you think the parties would have bargained to do? Would McGowin have traded his life in exchange for lifetime payments to Webb? Does your answer to the question tend to support or refute the holding in *Webb*?

Reading Haynes Chemical Corp. v. Staples & Staples. A gift is defined as the voluntary transfer of property to another without compensation. By definition, one does not expect something in return for a gift. One does not give a gift in order to get some sort of consideration in exchange. True gifts are, therefore, gratuitous, that is, they are given without any expectation of exchange.

But this usage of gift as *donum gratuitum* is not necessarily how the term is used in commercial circumstances. Consider a situation where you get a "free $10 Amazon gift card" answering a "brief 73-question marketing survey." Is the marketing firm truly looking to give away Amazon gift card cards, and the survey is simply the means of acquiring that gift? Or is something else going on beyond what is nominally being said? The situation appears to be closer to a bargain than to a gift, because the marketing company wants (and is willing to "pay") for your information, and you are only completing the survey to get the gift card. This represents an exchange, distinguishable from gifts between friends. In fact, the presumption that parties are giving each other gifts generally does not apply to such commercial relationships.

In the *Haynes Chemical* case, two commercial parties entered into a relationship where an advertising firm agreed to produce a trial advertising campaign for another company. If the company was not pleased with the campaign, it could have simply dismissed the advertising firm without incurring liability. But, instead, the company expressed a great deal of pleasure with the advertising product. The company even insisted on paying the advertising firm for the work. But, after some changes in management, the company ended up refusing to pay.

On the one hand, the trial advertising campaign was given without the support of consideration. There was no express agreement that the company would pay for the campaign. In this sense, the campaign was a gift. On the other hand, businesses like this do not usually give pure gratuitous gifts to each other. The commercial context implies that there were some strings attached, or at least some hopes that this work would generate future business. But even that hope is not enough to make the company pay for the advertisement. After all, how much would a court charge? It is still too uncertain. But then, when the recipient of such a "gift" promises to pay a specific amount for it, that promise may function as a substitute for consideration.

Haynes Chemical Corp. v. Staples & Staples

133 Va. 82 (1922)

WEST, J., delivered the opinion of the court.

The defendant in error, Staples & Staples, Incorporated, hereinafter called the plaintiff, recovered a judgment against the plaintiff in error, Haynes Chemical Corporation, hereinafter called the defendant, in the law and equity court of the city of Richmond for the sum of $707.09, with interest from February 28, 1921, till paid. The case is here upon a writ of error to that judgment.

The plaintiff and defendant are both corporations duly chartered under the laws of the state of Virginia.

The defendant is engaged in the manufacture and sale of an insecticide product known as "Preventol."

The plaintiffs are engaged in the advertising business, styling themselves as, "Advertising Counsellors," who advise the manufacturers of the country as to how to market their products; there being over 100 of these advertising agencies in this country. A manufacturer desiring to put a product upon the market, selects an agent, and directs him to map out plans for marketing his product. The agent's remuneration for handling the advertising campaign usually consists of a commission of 15 percent on the space which the manufacturer buys and is paid by the publishers. The cost of drawings, displays, and matters of that kind is invariably paid for by the manufacturer of the goods.

In August, 1919, C.P. Hasbrook, treasurer and a director of the defendant corporation, had an interview with H.L. Staples, president, and J.W. Fawcett, vice president, of the plaintiff corporation, and commissioned them to prepare an advertising plan for the defendant, showing them how to put "Preventol" on the market, promising them their plans would receive the heartiest consideration on the part of his people, and, if satisfactory, the advertising under such plan would go to them. The plaintiff does not submit plans in competition, and no notice of competition was given it until its plans had been perfected and submitted.

Acting under instructions of Director Hasbrook, the plaintiff proceeded to make the plans without expectation of payment therefor, if satisfactory, as in that event the plaintiff would be selected to handle the campaign and make his commission out of the publishers; and if unsatisfactory, it would be entitled to nothing, provided, in either event, a decision in good faith was made on the merits of the plan. Later, Hasbrook requested the plaintiff to speed up the plan, and on October 12, 1919, Staples and Fawcett presented the plan to C.P. Hasbrook treasurer and director, L.G. Larus, director, and Roger Topp, vice president and general manager of the defendant corporation, all three of whom expressed themselves as satisfied with the campaign plan in all respects.

Hasbrook and Larus left the room stating that Topp, as general manager, was the man to sell, and would have the last say; and at their suggestion the plans were left at defendant's office for their study. Later Hasbrook attended a meeting of the board of directors of his company in New York, taking with him the proxy of Larus. Having no notice of the meeting, no representative of the plaintiff was present to explain the plan, nor was the plan itself, the sketches, statistics, merchandise data, or results of trade investigations there. At the close of the meeting, Hasbrook telegraphed Topp:

> *Our president deems it necessary to have a New York agent. Advise Staples.*

The plaintiff, on condition of a fair decision, on its merits, had spent a large sum of money to produce a satisfactory plan, and there is nothing in the telegram to indicate that the plan was not satisfactory. Later Topp said to Staples and Fawcett, in discussing what happened at the New York meeting:

> *It looks like you got the rough end of the poker; however, you did a good job; your work was fine; and we feel you ought to be recompensed, and we would like for you to send us a bill for your expenses.*

The bill was sent, but not paid, and this suit was brought to collect it.

The defendant's assignments of error are to the action of the court:

(1) In refusing certain instructions asked for by the defendant;

(2) In granting certain instructions;

(3) In overruling defendant's motion to set aside the verdict of the jury;

(4) In entering judgment upon the verdict.

The instructions granted by the court were as follows:

Instruction No. 1:

> *"The court instructs the jury that if they believe from all the evidence that the defendant requested the plaintiff to devise and submit a plan of advertising to them, and it was known to the defendant that the costs and expenses were connected with the work to be done by the plaintiff, and no express agreement was made between the parties with reference to payment for the services of the plaintiff, then the jury may infer from the evidence an implied contract on the part of the defendant to reimburse the plaintiff for such expenses in connection with getting up the advertising plan as were reasonably within the contemplation of the parties."*

Instruction No. 2:

> *"The court instructs the jury that if they believe from the evidence that the plaintiff performed certain work at the instance and request of the defendant, and thereafter the defendant acknowledged liability to the plaintiff for the expenses incident thereto and promised to pay the same, they shall find for the plaintiff in whatever amount they deem reasonable under all the circumstances of the case for such expenses."*

Instruction No. 3:

> *"The court instructs the jury that if they believe from the evidence that the defendant did no more than to agree that the plaintiff should devise and submit to it for its acceptance a plan for an advertising campaign, then the defendant is not liable to the plaintiff for any expenses incurred in and about getting up the plan to submit to the defendant."*

Instruction No. 4:

> *"The court instructs the jury that if they believe from the evidence that it was understood between the parties the plaintiff was merely to offer plans or specifications or a plan for advertising the product of the defendant for sale, and whether such specifications or plan were offered in competition with others or not, then the defendant is not liable for the expense of getting up such a plan unless accepted by it."*

Instruction No. 5:

> *"The court instructs the jury that where one party requests of another an opportunity of submitting an offer, then unless it be in the minds of both parties and understood and agreed at that time that the party making the offer*

is to be reimbursed for his expenses in submitting the same, then the law does not raise an implied contract for such reimbursement unless the jury shall further believe that there is a custom and usage equally within the knowledge of both parties and with reference to which they can be necessarily presumed to have contracted, calling for such reimbursement."

Instructions numbered 1 and 2 were given by the court at the request of the plaintiff; instruction numbered 3 was given by the court of its own motion, after refusing instructions offered by the defendant; instruction numbered 4 was given by the court in lieu of instruction "B," as requested by the defendant; and instruction numbered 5 was given at the request of the defendant.

Where one renders services for another at the latter's request, the law, in the absence of an express agreement, implies a promise to pay what those services are reasonably worth, unless it can be inferred from the circumstances that those services were to be rendered without compensation.

It plainly appears from the evidence that the primary consideration which moved the plaintiff to prepare the advertising plan was the assurance of the representative of the defendant corporation that his people would give the plan heartiest consideration, which meant nothing less than a full and fair consideration of the plans and specifications upon their merits, by the proper authorities of that corporation.

The record shows that the board of directors, which, according to the present contention of the defendant, was alone authorized to pass upon them, never gave the plaintiff an opportunity to present its plans, and, without seeing them, and without regard to their merits, gave the contract to another agency, because the president of the company felt they should have a New York agent. In view of such conduct on the part of the defendant, it cannot be "inferred from the circumstances" that the services of the plaintiff, so far as concerns the expenses incurred by it, were to be rendered without compensation, and we are of opinion that the law implies a promise to pay any reasonable amounts expended by the plaintiff in complying with the request of the defendant to prepare the plans.

A person cannot request another to pay out money, or perform services for him, upon his agreement to render certain services for that person, and then, after the money is paid, or the services performed, refuse to keep his agreement and escape liability for the amount of money or labor so expended at his request.

It is said by the Supreme Court of Massachusetts in *Williams v. Bemis*:

The defendant having refused to perform [the contract], the party paying the money or rendering the services in pursuance thereof, may treat it as a nullity, and recover the money or value of the services under the common counts

There is evidence that the vice president and general manager of the defendant corporation, after the contract was awarded the New York agent, said to the vice president of the plaintiff company that they had considered the matter, and felt that the plaintiff should be compensated, and asked him to send bill for expenses.

The defendant contends that a subsequent express promise does not create any new cause of action, and is without consideration, except in those cases where the circumstances are such that an implied promise to pay arises under the law, and relies with confidence on a line of cases of which the following is representative: *Stout v. Humphrey*, where it is said:

> *An express promise, therefore, as it should seem, can only revive a prece-dent good consideration, which might have been enforced at law through the medium of an implied promise, had it not been suspended by some positive rule of law, but can give no original right of action if the obligation on which it is founded never could have been enforced at law, though not barred by any legal maxim or statute provision.*

In the case of *Beaumont v. Reeve*, the rule is thus stated, and it is quoted by Mr Chitty in the text of his work on contracts (volume 1, p. 54):

> *An express promise cannot be supported by a consideration from which the law would not imply a promise, except where the express promise does away with a legal suspension or bar of a right of action which, but for such suspen-sion or bar, would be valid.*

In our view, there is nothing in this line of cases which should deprive the plain-tiff of its right to a recovery, as there was an implied promise to pay the amount expended at the defendant's request.

The defendant questions the authority of Hasbrook to bind the corporation by a contract of this nature.

It appears from the evidence that Hasbrook was treasurer and director, Larus, director, and Roger Topp, vice president and general manager of the defendant cor-poration, all of whom resided in Richmond, and that they constituted three of the five stockholders of the corporation, the remaining two, including the president, being residents of New York.

The general manager had full authority and was in active charge of the business of the company and was made vice president to increase his authority.

Hasbrook requested the work to be done, and promised that the plans would have the heartiest consideration of his people, and that, if approved, the defendant would be given the contract.

The plans were in preparation for several months, during which time it is pre-sumed that he informed the proper officials of his company as to the agreement he had made with the defendant, as he sent defendants a request to speed up the plans. When completed, the plans and specifications were submitted to these three gentle-men, all of whom received and inspected them, without any suggestion from the vice president that Hasbrook had exceeded his authority in the premises. All three declared the plans satisfactory. Hasbrook and Larus, upon leaving, informed Staples that Topp, vice president and general manager, was the man they would have to sell; that he would have the last say. There is nothing in the record to show that any member of the board of directors at the New York meeting question Hasbrook's authority. On the contrary, his telegram intimates that the board had no objection to the plans, but the president felt the contract ought to go to a New York agent.

In *Winston v. Gordon*, this court held:

> *An act of an agent from which he derives no personal benefit, but which is done in good faith for the benefit of his principal, and which was apparently necessary and would redound to his benefit, will be held to have been ratified and acquiesced in, and be thereby rendered valid upon slight evidence.*

And it is said:

> *This doctrine . . . is as applicable to corporations as to other principals.*

The contract under consideration, entered by one director, was within the charter powers of the corporation, and was made, the circumstances tend to show, with the knowledge and consent of the vice president and general manager and another director of the company.

In *Am. B.H.O.S. Mach. Co. v. Burlack*, the court said: "There are so-called corporations which for all practical purposes, when they do business, cannot be reached at all, if we are not permitted to treat the only known or accessible embodiment in any other way than according to the character the manager may see fit for the occasion to assume. He is possessed of full authority to talk and act where there is anything to be gained, but he is not the proper man to talk or act when there is anything to be lost; and yet the principal, for all practical purposes, if not often in reality, is represented in no other way except by a name, so that a species of legerdemain is carried on — 'now you see it, and now you don't.' The ordinary business world is becoming tired with, if not vexed at, this sort of jugglery, and thinks that the true principles of evidence and of agency are not so narrow or so rigid that they may not be made to reach such cases."

Admitting that the making of the contract was irregular in its inception, those who governed the corporation will be held, by their conduct, to have waived such irregularity, and the corporation is estopped to rely on it as a defense to this action.

We find no error in the instructions granted of which the defendant can complain; and are of the opinion that the jury were fully and fairly instructed, and that there is no error in the court's refusal to grant instructions.

Upon the record we are unable to say that the verdict of the jury is plainly wrong, or without evidence to support it.

For the foregoing reasons the judgment complained of will be affirmed.

Affirmed.

Reflection

In *Haynes Chemical*, the plaintiff made plans to advertise the defendant's product without expectation of payment. If the plaintiff was chosen to run the campaign, then they would receive payment. However, the plaintiff's advertising plan was not selected.

The telegraph informing the plaintiff that the director wished to hire a New York agent made no mention of the plan being unsatisfactory. After the plaintiff was informed that it was not selected to run the campaign, the chemical company reached out to the plaintiff, letting it know that they realized the amount of money spent on the campaign and wished to reimburse it for the cost. The plaintiff submitted its bills but was not reimbursed.

In this case, the intention that moved the plaintiff to create the advertising plan was not to receive immediate payment but for the company to honestly consider their plan. However, after the plaintiff was not selected to run the campaign, the defendant made the promise to reimburse the plaintiff.

A person cannot request another to pay out money, or perform services for him, upon his agreement to render certain services for that person, and then, after the money is paid, or the services performed, refuse to keep his agreement and escape liability for the amount of money or labor so expended at his request.

The chemical company requested that the advertising firm create an advertising plan in exchange for its consideration. However, the firm did not consider the plaintiff's plan since the director decided that the company must use an advisor from New York instead. For this reason, the chemical company cannot escape liability for the money and labor that had been expended, since the company did not full-heartedly consider the plaintiff's campaign.

Discussion

1. What did Haynes Chemical promise to Staples & Staples? Did this promise contemplate receiving anything in exchange in the future, or was the promise given in recognition of something done in the past?

2. The court finds that Haynes Chemical made a contract with Staples & Staples. Would a modern court applying R2d reach the same result? If so, cite the R2d provision that mirrors the rule in *Haynes Chemical*. If not, cite the correlated R2d provision and analyze how it would come out differently under the R2d.

3. Do business corporations typically give gifts to each other? How does the answer to this question impact the court's interpretation of Haynes's promise to Staples?

4. Would this case have been decided differently if the companies were small, family-run businesses where the owners were longtime friends or if the prom-

ises were between family relations who have a long history of giving freely to each other?

5. What are jury instructions? How can jury instructions impact the disposition of a case? Why might jury instructions be litigated upon appeal?

————————

Reading Edson v. Poppe. The entire doctrine of promissory restitution requires much of the same elements that are required for a contract-at-law. In both cases, there must be a promise to do something, and a promise to do something in return. But that is where the similarities begin to break down. When promises mutually induce each other, we call the return promise consideration. But what happens where the promise and the return promise are separated by time, such that it is logically and chronologically impossible for the return promise to induce the performance of the original promise? For example, if I serve you a hamburger and you eat it, and any promise to pay me for that hamburger is not motivated by your desire to incentivize me to cook a hamburger for you. The hamburger has already been cooked, served, and eaten! In truth, all you have done in this scenario is to make a gratuitous promise to me. You may feel morally obligated to follow through on this promise, but absent other circumstances, you are probably not legally required to do so.

One of the other circumstances that can raise a moral obligation to a legal liability is where the original promise was completed pursuant to some other contract. Where a contract formed the basis of a parties' actions, we may feel more confident that the performing party was not simply trying to thrust some benefit upon another person. Rather, the contract shows that the completion of that promise was done for good reason, as part of a voluntary exchange.

Unfortunately, contracts do not always work out. The promisee may prove unable to pay the consideration. The promisee may dispute whether the performance meets the criteria required by the agreement. Or the promisee may claim that it no longer wants or needs to pay for the performance because of changed circumstances.

In some of these instances, where one party's side of a contract was performed, yet the other side was not ready to perform, a third party who was not part of the original contract but who benefitted from it may feel a moral obligation to pay for the performance. A moral obligation is not enough to make for an enforceable agreement, but when the beneficiary manifests a desire to pay for that benefit, that manifestation may constitute a promise that can be binding upon the promisor.

The *Edson* case is a famous example of this situation. Tenants on property ordered a valuable well to be built. The well was built, but the tenants refused to pay. The landlord, seeing how the well improved the value of his land, then agreed to pay for the well. Just like the person who had already eaten the hamburger, the landlord has already received the well, and in both those cases, any promise to pay is gratuitous. But the difference between the scenarios is that the well was constructed pursuant to a valid contract. That may give courts confidence that the well digger was not simply trying to thrust unwanted benefits on landowners.

Edson v. Poppe

124 N.W. 441 (S.D. 1910)

McCOY, J.

The plaintiff recovered judgment upon the verdict of a jury in the circuit court. The case was tried upon the following complaint: That the defendant at all the times hereinafter named was the owner of the following described premises situated in Turner county, S.D., to wit (describing the land). That at all the times herein named George Poppe was in possession of said premises as the tenant of defendant. During the year 1904 this plaintiff, at the instance and request of said George Poppe, drilled and dug upon said premises a well 250 feet deep, and obtained water in said well, and placed casing therein. The reasonable value of the digging and casing of said well was and is the sum of $250 and said well was and is a valuable improvement upon the said premises, and greatly adds to the value thereof. It has been used by the occupants of said premises since the said digging thereof.

Accordingly, with the knowledge and consent of defendant; that on or about the 5th day of August, 1905, the defendant, at the said premises, after having examined the said well, and in consideration of the said well to him, and of the improvement it made upon said premises, expressly ratified the acts of his said tenant in having said well drilled. He then and there promised and agreed to pay plaintiff the reasonable value of the digging and casing of the said well as aforesaid.; Defendant has since refused, and still refuses, to pay plaintiff anything for said well. Wherefore, etc.

To the said complaint, defendant made the following answer: Denies generally and specifically each and every allegation in said complaint, except such as is hereinafter specifically admitted. Defendant admits that he is the owner of the said premises as stated in the complaint. At the opening of the trial, and upon the offer of testimony on the part of plaintiff, defendant objected to the introduction of any evidence. For the reason that the complaint did not state a cause of action, in that the consideration alleged in the contract is a past consideration, and no consideration for any promise, if any was made, and no consideration for the promise alleged. The objection was overruled, and defendant excepted. This ruling of the trial court is assigned and now urged as error, but we are of the opinion that the ruling of the learned trial court was correct.

It seems to be the general rule that past services are not a sufficient consideration for a promise to pay therefor, made at a subsequent time, and after such services have been fully rendered and completed; but in some courts a modified doctrine of moral obligation is adopted, and it is held that a moral obligation, founded on previous benefits received by the promisor at the hands of the promisee, will support a promise by him. The authorities are not so clear as to the sufficiency of past services, rendered without previous request, to support an express promise; but, when proper distinctions are made, the cases as a whole seem to warrant the statement that such a promise is supported by a sufficient consideration if the services were beneficial, and were not intended to be gratuitous.

In *Drake v. Bell*, a mechanic, under contract to repair a vacant house, by mistake repaired the house next door, which belonged to the defendant. The repairing was a benefit to the latter, and he agreed to pay a certain amount therefor. It was held that the promise rested upon sufficient consideration. Gaynor, J., says: "The rule seems to be that a subsequent promise, founded on a former enforceable obligation, or on value previously had from the promisee, is binding."

In *Glenn v. Savage*, it was held that an act done for the benefit of another without his request is deemed a voluntary act of courtesy, for which no action can be sustained, unless after knowing of the service the person benefited thereby promises to pay for it.

In *Boothe v. Fitzpatrick*, it is held that if the consideration, even without request, moves directly from the plaintiff to the defendant, and inures directly to the defendant's benefit, the promise is binding though made upon a past consideration. In this case the court held that a promise by defendant to pay for the past keeping of a bull, which had escaped from defendant's premises and been cared for by plaintiff, was valid, although there was no previous request, but that the subsequent promise obviated that objection; it being equivalent to a previous request.

The allegation of the complaint here is that the digging and casing of the well in question inured directly to the defendant's benefit, and that, after he had seen and examined the same, he expressly promised and agreed to pay plaintiff the reasonable value thereof. It also appears that said well was made under such circumstances as could not be deemed gratuitous on the part of plaintiff, or an act of voluntary courtesy to defendant. We are therefore of the opinion that, under the circumstances alleged, the subsequent promise of defendant to pay plaintiff the reasonable value for digging and casing said well was binding, and supported by sufficient consideration. We are also of the opinion that the instructions based on this complaint, and in particular as to the validity of the subsequent promise of defendant, properly submitted the issues to the jury.

At the close of plaintiff's evidence, and again at the close of all the evidence on both sides, defendant moved for a directed verdict. Both motions were overruled. Defendant excepted, and now assigns such rulings as error; but, as the evidence is not contained in the abstract on which these motions were based, the assignment cannot be considered. Neither can we consider assignments of error based on evidence or objections to evidence not shown by the abstract.

Finding no error in the record, the judgment of the circuit court is affirmed.

Reflection

Edson demonstrates when a third person subsequently promises to pay for the benefit received under another's contract, that promise can be binding. Here, Poppe received a material benefit that was not intended to be gratuitous. He then subsequently promised to compensate Edson for the benefit. Therefore, the subsequent promise is binding.

Discussion

1. The *Edson* court references the *Drake* and *Boothe* cases. Does it use these cases as authority for rules, as factual analogies, as distinctions, or something else?

2. The defense is based on the claim "that the complaint did not state a cause of action, in that the consideration alleged in the contract is a past consideration." Explain what this means

3. In *Mills*, the court found there was no enforceable promise; in *Edson*, the court found there was. Can you distinguish the key facts of these cases such that the same rule applies to both, even though it produces different results?

Reading Muir v. Kane. There are many reasons why a promise turns out to be unenforceable. Parties who intended to contract may have failed to include enough definition in the terms of the agreement for a court to enforce it. The contract may be of a sort which requires a signed writing to be enforceable, and it lacks such a writing. The contract may have emerged from a mistake about the nature of the subject matter. Even changed circumstances after a valid formation can excuse an obligation and make it unenforceable.

In the *Muir* case, a man owed a debt. But the collection of this debt became unenforceable because of the passage of time. Recognizing the unfairness of this situation, the debtor renewed his promise to pay the debt. Note that the renewed promise was not supported by consideration. When he made the renewed promise, the debtor already had received the loan. He did not make this promise in order to get a loan, but rather in recognition of his moral obligation to repay it.

In general, mere moral obligations are not enforceable as a matter of contract law. But, here, where the parties first created a valid contract, and then that contract became unenforceable due to some legal principle or changed circumstances, the original promisor can effectively revive the legal obligation.

Muir v. Kane

55 Wash. 131 (1909)

FULLERTON, J.

The respondent brought this action to recover of the appellants the sum of $200, alleged to be due pursuant to a written agreement executed and delivered to him by the appellants, whereby they agreed to pay him the sum of $200 for his services in selling for appellants a certain tract of real property.

Issue was taken on the complaint, and a trial had thereon which resulted in a judgment in his favor for the amount claimed to be due. The case was tried by the court sitting without a jury. No question is raised as to the correctness of the facts found, but the case is here on the question whether these facts justify the judgment of the court.

The court's findings of fact are as follows:

"(1) That now and at all times herein referred to the plaintiff is and was doing a general real estate business in Seattle, Wash., under the firm name and style of B.L. Muir & Co., being the sole owner thereof.

"(2) That now and at all times concerned herein the defendants are and were husband and wife.

"(3) That on or about the 21st day of November, 1906, the defendants made, executed, and delivered to the plaintiff their written agreement, agreeing to pay said plaintiff $200 for his services in selling for them a certain parcel of real estate; said agreement being in words and figures, to wit:

> M. Francis Kane and Ida Kane, his wife, agree to sell and Paul Bush agrees to buy the following described real estate situated in the county of King, state of Washington, to wit: South 40 feet of lot 1, block 17, J.H. Nagle's addition to the city of Seattle, for the sum of nine thousand six hundred dollars ($9,600) the purchaser having paid the sum of five hundred dollars ($500) the receipt of which is hereby acknowledged, as earnest money and part payment for said land, the same to be held in trust by B.L. Muir & Co. until the sale is closed or canceled and the balance of said purchase price shall be paid as follows, or as soon after said dates respectively as the title to said real estate is shown to be marketable, to wit: Three thousand dollars ($3,000) on or before the 22nd day of Nov., 1906, at 1 p. m.; nineteen hundred dollars ($1,900) on or before the 22nd day of Nov., 1907, at 1 p. m.; four thousand dollars ($4,000) according to certain mortgage to be executed due in three years from date. The purchaser agrees to pay interest at the rate of six percent, payable semiannually on all deferred payments. The vendor agrees to furnish an abstract of title made by a reliable abstract company for said real estate, showing a marketable title of record in the vendor free from encumbrances to date of conveyance, except the street assessments amount to about two hundred dollars ($200) and if over $200 the surplus to be deducted from the

nineteen hundred payment which the purchaser assumes and agrees to pay as a part of the above named purchase price, and the vendor further agrees to transfer said property to the purchaser by a good and sufficient warranty deed to the said vendee or his assigns and pay two hundred dollars ($200) of the purchase price to B.L. Muir & Co., for services rendered. The purchaser shall have one day's time after the delivery of said abstract for examination of same, and in case the abstract shall show a marketable title in the vendor, this sale shall be completed, and if the said title is not marketable and cannot be made so, then B.L. Muir & Co. shall refund to the said vendee the above named earnest money, and the sale shall be canceled, the deposit of $500 to be paid to Mrs. Ida Kane in the event of the purchaser failing to comply with this agreement.

Witness our hands this 21st day of November 1906. Signed and delivered in the presence of B.L. Muir. M. Francis Kane. [Seal.] Ida Kane. [Seal.] Paul Bush. [Seal.]'

"(4) That the plaintiff did make the sale referred to in said written contract and which sale was accepted by the defendants, but they have since failed, neglected, and refused to pay the aforesaid two hundred dollars ($200) commission allowed, although the same is long past due and still the property of the plaintiff."

The statut e governing contracts for commissions for buying or selling real estate provides that any agreement authorizing an employee, as an agent, or broker, to sell or purchase real estate for compensation or a commission, shall be void unless the agreement, contract, or promise or some note or memorandum thereof be in writing.

The appellants contend that the writing relied upon by the respondent is insufficient under the statute; that it is not an agreement authorizing the respondent to sell the real property described for compensation or commission, nor does it authorize or employ the respondent to sell real estate at all. Manifestly, if the writing sued upon was intended as an agreement authorizing the respondent to sell real estate of the appellants, it is faulty in the particulars mentioned, and so far, deficient as not to warrant a recovery even if a sale had been made thereunder. But we do not understand that this is the question presented by the record. This writing was not intended as an agreement authorizing the respondent to sell the real property mentioned. In fact, it was executed after that service had been performed, and is an agreement in writing to pay a fixed sum for a past service, not a service to be performed in the future.

The question for determination is its validity as a promise to pay for a past service. Looking to the instrument itself, there is nothing on its face that in any manner impugns its validity. It is a direct promise to pay a fixed sum of money for services rendered. Prima facie, therefore, it is legal and valid; and, if it is illegal at all, it is because the actual consideration for the promise, which was alleged and proven, rendered the promise illegal. This consideration was the sale of real property for the appellants by the respondent acting as a broker without a written agreement authorizing the service, and it is thought that, because the statute declares an agreement for such a service void unless in writing, the service furnishes no consideration for the subsequent promise, since the service must either have been founded upon an invalid agreement or was voluntary.

There are cases which maintain this doctrine. In *Bagnole v. Madden*, the precise question was presented. There the plaintiff had been orally authorized by the defendant to sell a parcel of real estate owned by the defendant. A purchaser was found, and a contract of sale entered. The defendant thereupon executed a written agreement, and delivered the same to the plaintiff, wherein she promises to pay him $50 for his services. In an action brought upon the writing, the court held that she could not recover because of the invalidity of the original oral contract authorizing the services; it being in violation of the statute declaring such agreement void unless in writing.

The case was rested on a decision of the Court of Errors and Appeals, which announced the same doctrine, but upon a state of facts not quite the same; the subsequent promise to pay being oral instead of in writing. During its opinion in the latter case the court said: "It is clear that if a contract between two parties be void, and not merely voidable, no subsequent express promise will operate to charge the party promising, even though he has derived the benefit of the contract. Yet, according to the commonly received motion respecting moral obligations, and the force attributed to a subsequent express promise, such a person ought to pay. An express promise, therefore, as it should seem, can only revive a precedent good consideration which might have been enforced at law through the medium of an implied promise had it not been suspended by some positive rule of law, but can give no original right of action if the obligation on which it is founded never could have been enforced at law, though not barred by any legal maxim or statute provision."

The court, it will be observed, makes a distinction between contracts formerly good, but on which the right of recovery has been barred by the statute, and those contracts which are barred in the first instance because of some legal defect in their execution, holding that the former will furnish a consideration for a subsequent promise to perform, while the latter will not. It has seemed to us that this distinction is not sound. The moral obligation to pay for services rendered as a broker in selling real estate under an oral contract where the statute requires such contract to be in writing is just as binding as is the moral obligation to pay a debt that has become barred by the statute of limitations; and there is no reason for holding that the latter will support a new promise to pay while the former will not.

There is no moral delinquency that attaches to an oral contract to sell real property as a broker. This service cannot be recovered for because the statute says the promise must be in writing, not because it is illegal in itself. It was not intended by the statute to impute moral turpitude to such contracts. The statute was intended to prevent frauds and perjuries, and, to accomplish that purpose, it is required that the evidence of the contract be in writing; but it is not conducive to either fraud or perjury to say that the services rendered under the void contract or voluntarily will support a subsequent written promise to pay for such service. Nor is it a valid objection to say there was no antecedent legal consideration.

The validity of a promise to pay a debt barred by the statute of limitations is not founded on its antecedent legal obligation. There is no legal obligation to pay such a debt, if there were there would be no need for the new promise. The obligation is moral solely, and, since there can be no difference in character between one moral obligation and another, there can be no reason for holding that one moral obligation will support a promise while another will not.

Our attention has been called to no case, other than the New Jersey case above cited, where the facts of the case at bar are presented. A case in point on the principle involved, however, is *Ferguson v. Harris*. Certain persons without authority from the defendant had ordered lumber and used it in the erection of a building on the defendant's separate property; she being a married woman. Subsequently she gave her promissory note therefor, and, when an action was brought upon the note, she sought to defend on the ground of want of consideration. It was conceded that there was never any legal obligation on the part of the defendant to pay for the lumber, but that her obligation was wholly moral. It was thereupon urged that such an obligation was insufficient to support the promise.

Speaking upon this question, the court said: "All of the authorities admit that where an action to recover a debt is barred by the statute of limitations, or by a discharge in bankruptcy, a subsequent promise to pay the same can be supported by the moral obligation to pay the same, although the legal obligation is gone forever; and I am unable to perceive any just distinction between such a case and one in which there never was a legal, but only a moral, obligation to pay. In the one case the legal obligation is gone as effectually as if it had never existed, and I am at a loss to perceive any sound distinction in principle between the two cases. In both cases, at the time the promise sought to be enforced is made there is nothing whatever to support it except the moral obligation, and why the fact that, because in the one case there was once a legal obligation, which, having utterly disappeared, is as if it had never existed, should affect the question, I am at a loss to conceive. If in the one case the moral obligation, which alone remains is sufficient to afford a valid consideration for the promise, I cannot see why the same obligation should not have the same effect in the other."

The remark made by Lord Denman in *Eastwood v. Kenyon*, that the doctrine for which I am contending "would annihilate the necessity for any consideration at all, inasmuch as the mere fact of giving a promise creates a moral obligation to perform it," is more specious than sound, for it entirely ignores the distinction between a promise to pay money which the promisor is under a moral obligation to pay, and a promise to pay money which the promisor, is under no obligation, either legal or moral, to pay. It seems to me that the cases relied upon to establish the modern doctrine, so far as my examination of them has gone, ignore the distinction pointed out in the note to *Comstock v. Smith*, above cited, between an express and an implied promise resting merely on a moral obligation, for, while such obligation does not seem to be sufficient to support an implied promise, yet it is sufficient to support an express promise.

To the same effect is *Anderson v. Best*, wherein it was said: "The distinction sought to be made between considerations formerly good but now barred by statute, and those barred by statute in the first instance, is not substantial, and is not sustained by the cases."

Believing, as we do, that the better rule is with the cases holding the moral obligation alone sufficient to sustain the promise, it follows that the judgment appealed from should be affirmed. It is so ordered.

RUDKIN, C. J., and GOSE, CHADWICK, and MORRIS, JJ., concur.

Reflection

The issue for determination in the *Muir* case regards the validity of a promise to pay for a past service. *Muir* states the rule that where an action to recover a debt is barred by the statute of limitations, a subsequent promise to pay the same can be supported by the moral obligations to pay the same. However, the legal obligation is gone forever.

In the *Muir* case, the consideration was the sale of real property for the appellants by the respondent acting as a broker. However, there was no written agreement authorizing such service, and the statute of limitations declares an agreement for such a service void unless in writing. For this reason, the service furnished no consideration for the subsequent promise.

The validity of a promise to pay a debt barred by the statute of limitations is not founded on its antecedent legal obligation. There is no legal obligation to pay such a debt; if there were, there would be no need for the new promise. The obligation is moral solely, and, since there can be no difference in character between one moral obligation and another, there can be no reason for holding that one moral obligation will support a promise while another will not.

The main takeaway from *Muir* is that where an action to recover a debt is barred by the statute of limitations, a subsequent promise to pay the same can be supported by the moral obligation to pay the same, but the legal obligation is gone forever.

Discussion

1. What does the *Muir* court mean when it states that moral obligation alone may be sufficient to sustain a promise?

2. The statute at issue, which requires contracts promising real estate commission to be evidenced by a signed writing, is a type of statute of frauds. What purpose does the statute serve here? In other words, why should courts require real estate commissions to be evidenced by signed writings?

3. The *Muir* opinion cites long provisions from cases that distinguish consideration formerly good but now barred from "consideration" that was never good. Can you apply this distinction to *Mills* and to the other cases in this chapter?

4. Is there any doubt that the seller agreed to pay the real estate commission? Does the clear and substantial nature of the promise seem to have any impact on the court's willingness to enforce it? Should that be a factor?

Problems

Problem 9.1. **IRAC Edson**

Under R2d, promises without consideration are generally unenforceable; however, the doctrine of promissory restitution makes promises to pay for a past benefit received enforceable where some plus factor applies. *Edson* is a classic case where the court found that justice required promissory restitution — but why? And, noting that *Edson* was decided even before the first Restatement of Contracts, would it still be so decided under R2d? In other words, what was the plus factor in *Edson*, and does this factor "count" under R2d? Answer this question using the IRAC writing paradigm; that is, first write the issue regarding this particular element of promissory estoppel: "Whether Edson merits enforcement of Poppe's promise based on promissory restitution, where . . . ?" Include key material facts after the where clause. Second, write and cite the key rules from the R2d needed to answer this question (including the rule for promissory restitution) before analyzing the facts of this case under those rules. Finally, conclude whether Edson merits promissory restitution.

Problem 9.2. **Annihilation of Consideration**

The opinion in *Muir* defends its holding against the claim by Lord Denman in *Eastwood* that the doctrine espoused in *Muir* "would annihilate the necessity for any consideration at all, inasmuch as the mere fact of giving a promise creates a moral obligation to perform it." The *Muir* court retorts that Denman's remark "is more specious than sound, for it entirely ignores the distinction between a promise to pay money which the promisor is under a moral obligation to pay, and a promise to pay money which the promisor, is under no obligation, either legal or moral, to pay." What do you make of these competing rationales for two competing doctrines? Discuss, first, whether it is easy and readily possible to distinguish between promises made pursuant to a moral obligation and promises made pursuant no obligation; and second, whether the doctrine should be as *Muir* argues it should, that is, whether promises made pursuant to moral obligations should be enforceable? Does the *Muir* doctrine "annihilate" the consideration doctrine?

Module IV

Defenses

Almost all legal rules tend to be both under-inclusive and over-inclusive at once. On the one hand, rules are under-inclusive where the law leaves out persons or situations that are appropriate for a given status or remedy. In contract law, the rule requiring consideration can be under-inclusive by not permitting courts to enforce some promises that should be enforced for reasons of justice and fairness. The law has evolved the equitable alternatives to consideration, promissory restitution and promissory estoppel, as solutions to the problem of under-inclusion. Equity solves the problem of under-inclusion by allowing courts to enforce certain promises that do not form contracts as a matter of law.

On the other hand, rules are over-inclusive where the law includes persons or situations who are not appropriate for a given status or remedy. In contract law, the rule requiring contractual promises to be enforced where there is offer, acceptance and consideration can be over-inclusive by mandating courts to enforce unjust or unfair promises. The defense doctrines, which are the subject of this module, are the solution to the problem of over-inclusion. Defenses solve the problem of over-inclusion by allowing courts to refuse to enforce certain contractual promises.

The defense doctrines can be grouped into four or five conceptual categories. While this casebook identifies four categories, it is worth mentioning that a potential fifth group of defenses are the incapacity or lack of capacity defenses. This category is notable because it reflects a paternalism that is not generally present in contract law. The goal of the capacity defenses is to protect people who cannot protect themselves — although it does so by removing such vulnerable people's freedom to contract. Infants, people under guardianship, the mentally ill, and the intoxicated may benefit from these defenses after they engage in disadvantageous contracts, but the capacity defenses also serve to discourage others from contracting with them in the first place.

Capacity to contract was discussed in the introductory module because the mental capacity to form intentions to be bound and the physical capacity to manifest such intentions is prerequisite to the ability to engage in contracting by mutual assent. R2d § 12 sets forth this principle:

> *(1) No one can be bound by contract who has not legal capacity to incur at least voidable contractual duties. Capacity to contract may be partial and its existence in respect of a particular transaction may depend upon the nature of the transaction or upon other circumstances.*
>
> *(2) A natural person who manifests assent to a transaction has full legal capacity to incur contractual duties thereby unless he is (a) under guardianship, or (b) an infant, or (c) mentally ill or defective, or (d) intoxicated.*

Since we already studied and learned these concepts, we will not repeat that lesson. But at this point in our study of contract-law defenses, it bears mentioning that some treat the capacity not as a prerequisite to contracting but as a defense against formation. Litigators and trial-minded attorneys have a good reason for grouping incapacity along with the other defenses: defendants must plead incapacity as an affirmative defense in response to the plaintiff's complaint, pursuant to Federal Rule of Civil Procedure 8(c). Many states have similar rules of civil procedure.

This book does not rely on students' knowledge of civil procedure, since many students are learning that topic presently or will learn it in the future. Accordingly, this book generally does not emphasize procedural matters like when a defense must be pled or who bears the burden of proving it. For present purposes, simply note that affirmative defenses, including the defenses of incapacity and other defenses against contract formation found in this module, are asserted by the defendant in the defendant's answer to the plaintiff's complaint. The defendant bears the burden of alleging new facts that tend to prove the defense, and the defendant also bears the burden of proving those facts to be true by a preponderance of the evidence.

But aside from this quirk of civil procedure, others, including the author of this casebook, consider capacity to assent as preliminary to mutual assent, which is why the discussion on incapacity was found in a prior module and not this one: since capacity to contract is a prerequisite to mutual assent, this book already discussed capacity in its introductory chapter, and so the capacity defenses will not be reiterated in detail in this module. But students might note that some other books and treatises treat incapacity as a defense and not as a prerequisite to mutual assent.

In this casebook and the R2d, the first group of defenses, called the Statute of Frauds, deals with cautioning parties against making enforceable obligations and channeling those obligations into forms which are easier for courts to assess. The Statute of Frauds is literally a statutory requirement for certain kinds of contracts to be evidenced by a signed writing. This makes these kinds of contracts seem more serious to parties, while it also requires parties to create some kind of paper record for such serious contracts that courts can later review to determine whether and to what extent those contracts create obligations.

The second group of defenses involves mistakes. Mistakes, in the contract law sense, are situations where one or both parties had an inaccurate belief regarding some material fact. For example, if two collectors believe they are buying and selling a rare baseball card, but it is in fact a common card, there is a mutual mistake that could provide a basis for asserting a defense. In the case of a mistake, one party did not lead the other into having an erroneous belief; in fact, one party may not even be aware of the other's mistake. In these cases, a party may have been negligent, but there is no affirmative bad faith or intentional effort to trick or fool the other party.

The third group of defenses regard misrepresentations and coercions. These situations involve some inappropriate act by one party or the other, and they rise in levels of severity. A misrepresentation is an assertion that is not in accord with the facts, where one party causes the other to have a mistaken belief through its words, conduct, or, in rare cases, through silence where there is a duty to speak. Innocent or negligent misrepresentations are less likely to be grounds for avoiding a contract than a deliberate or fraudulent misrepresentation. Worse than misrepresentation is duress, where one party threatens the other. Duress involving economic threats are less likely to be grounds for avoiding a contract than threats of physical violence. Worse still is undue influence, where one party who dominates and controls another uses its power to force the other into agreeing to a contract. Such cases of undue influences are most likely to be grounds for avoiding a contract where the parties have a special relationship of responsibility, trust, and confidence, such as an adult child who is the sole caregiver for an infirm, elderly parent.

Although the second and third groups of defenses can be distinguished by whether the parties acted innocently or culpably, both groups are similar in that in both cases, the harm falls upon one or the other of the parties. In both of these cases, the contract may be avoidable because there was not true mutual assent. One party then seeks to avoid the contract because it made that party worse off than expected. In other words, the harm of the error or bad act is internalized.

The fourth group of defenses deals with external harm. The defenses of unconscionability and public policy deal with contracts that may result from mutual assent between the parties, but which are bad for the rest of society to enforce. For example, a contract to hire a hit man may be based on mutual assent and consideration, but courts will not require parties to carry out or pay for these contracts because that would be abhorrent to justice.

Finally, some consider misunderstanding to be a defense to contract formation, but I argue that misunderstanding is better understood as a failure of mutual assent. Misunderstanding occurs when two parties both believe something that is true, and it appears to each other that both mean their manifestation of that concept to mean the same thing, but, in reality, there are two versions of the truth such that the parties are both correct but do not believe the same thing. This is not a mistake, because a mistake only occurs where one or more parties has an inaccurate belief about reality.

A misunderstanding occurs where all the parties have an accurate belief, but it is not the same belief. This is not a defense but rather a case where mutual assent did not occur at all.

Chapter 10

The Statute of Frauds

A statute of frauds is, literally, a statute. It is a law passed by a legislative body, which happens to impact the enforceability of contracts. A statute of frauds creates an affirmative defense where a party can avoid certain types of contracts where they are not evidenced by a signed writing.

The British Parliament passed the original statute of frauds, titled the English Act for Prevention of Frauds and Perjuries, in 1677. It required courts to see some writing signed by the party to be charged (which generally means the party against whom enforcement of the contract is sought) that evidenced a contract — although not necessary the contract itself — prior to courts granting judgment for breach of agreements regarding certain matters.

Statutes of frauds caught on in America, and most states have some version of the original statute of frauds on the books. In fact, many states have not only one but many statutes of frauds. Any statute that requires an enforceable contract to be in writing can be deemed a statute of frauds. Such statutes can appear in different places within one state's legal code. For example, Pennsylvania's statute of frauds requiring real estate leases to be in writing is codified in the Pennsylvania Landlord-Tenant Act at 68 P.S. § 250.202; and Pennsylvania's statute of frauds requiring sales of goods for more than $500 to be in writing is codified in the Pennsylvania Uniform Commercial Code at 13 P.S. § 2201(a). Most states do not put all writing requirements into a single statute, but simply add writing requirements to the statutes covering the transactions in question.

Requiring a signed writing provides three functions. First, it creates evidence of contracting, which makes lawsuits easier to adjudicate or dismiss. Second, it cautions contract parties, who should realize that signing or sealing a formal writing is likely to bind them as to the terms therein. Third, it promotes the use of forms of agreements, which are standardized signed writings that reflect common issues that arise in specific types of transactions.

You will typically be alerted that a statute of frauds issue may come up when one party does not want to be subject to a contract, and that contract is either entirely oral or has some potential defect in its writing. When you spot an issue like this, ask three analytical questions to determine whether the statute of frauds forbids enforcement of that contract.

1. Does the statute of frauds in this jurisdiction require a signed writing for this general class of contract?

2. Is there a signed writing that satisfies the statute?

3. If there is no memorandum, do the specific facts suggest an equitable exception to the statute of frauds?

Each state must enact its own version of the statute of frauds. That process led to three main varieties of the statute of frauds in the various states. You can tell which style of statute of frauds applies in your jurisdiction by reading it and paying attention to the specific language.

- Some provide that "no action shall be brought" on the contract or the contract "shall not be enforced" in the absence of a writing signed by the party to be charged.

- Some declare contracts "void" in the absence of a writing signed by the party to be charged.

- Some make contracts "voidable" by the party to be charged where there is no evidence of a signed writing by that party.

Despite these variations in statutory language, the interpretation and enforcement of them is quite similar across the states. In general, all statutes of frauds have the same effect:

A statute of frauds forbids enforcement of a contract unless there is a written memorandum or an applicable exception.

Understanding this effect makes analyzing statute of frauds problems easy. There is a straightforward three step process to analyzing every statute of frauds situation.

Rules

A. Classes of Contracts Requiring Signed Writing (MYLEGS)

According to the Restatement (Second) of Contracts (R2d), most American states have adopted a statute of frauds which covers six classes of contracts. The acronym "MYLEGS" is often used to represent these six classes:

1. Marriage

2. Year-long (or longer)

3. Land

4. Executorship

5. Goods for more than $500

6. Suretyship

Note that this is just shorthand and does not fully explain that nature of these classes of contracts. Marriage, for example, refers not to the marriage contract itself but rather to a contract where one party agrees to marry another in return for some consideration under that contract. The next section will clarify what the terms in the acronym mean. Note that the acronym is out of order from R2d § 110, for the sake of making it easy to remember.

Many states require additional categories of transactions to be evidenced by a writing to be enforceable. For example, Texas requires a signed writing for an agreement to pay a commission on the sale of mineral rights in the land. *See* Tex. Bus. & Com. Code § 26.01(b)(7)(D) (2001). On the other hand, many states do not require the traditional categories to be in writing. For example, Louisiana does not require a signed writing for sales of goods. *See* La. Rev. Stat. § 10:8-113 (2016). Check the state legal codes to determine whether a certain type of contract requires evidence of its existence in the form of a signed writing.

Once you have located the statute of frauds in a jurisdiction, you can read it to determine which of the typical classes of contracts are covered by it. The most common classes of contracts that require a signed writing are ones that involve sales of Land and ones that cannot be completely performed within one Year.

The statute of frauds effectively requires additional proof of a contract that falls into one of the classes that it covers.

R2d § 110 lists the five classes of contracts that were included in the English Statute of Frauds (1677). Although the English Statute was repealed in 1954, except for the suretyship and land contract provisions, many American states still require a signed writing to evidence five classes of contracts that were subject to the original statute of frauds.

(a) *a contract of an executor or administrator to answer for a duty of his decedent (the Executor-administrator provision);*

(b) *a contract to answer for the duty of another (the Suretyship provision);*

(c) *a contract made upon consideration of marriage (the Marriage provision);*

(d) *a contract for the sale of an interest in land (the Land contract provision);*

(e) *a contract that is not to be performed within one Year from the making thereof (the one-year provision).*

   R2d § 110(1).

R2d was revised in 1981, after the Uniform Commercial Code, Article 2 — Sales was adopted in almost every American state. Accordingly, R2d includes the UCC's requirement for evidence of a signed writing where there is

(f) *a contract for the sale of Goods for the price of $500 or more (UCC § 2-201).* R2d § 110.

These classes may overlap. In other words, a contract may be subject to a statute of frauds for multiple reasons. For example, if a landowner agrees to sell a tract of land, with closing to occur in 366 days, then that contract is subject to two provisions of the traditional statute of frauds: the Land provision and Year-long provision.

1. Executor/Administrator

An executor (or executrix) of an estate is an individual appointed to administer the estate of a deceased person. The executor must understand and honor the decedent's will, if one exists, and represent the estate in court as necessary. While performing this duty, the executor generally obligates the estate to make payment to creditors or provide awards to inheritors. These ordinary-course transactions, where the executor is only obligating the estate and not the executor himself, are not subject to the statute of frauds executor provision

> *A contract of an executor or administrator to answer personally for a duty of his decedent is within the Statute of Frauds if a similar contract to answer for the duty of a living person would be within the Statute as a contract to answer for the duty of another.* R2d § 111.

The executor provision only comes up in unusual circumstances where the executor agrees to be personally liable. For example, Sam is appointed executor of Dan, who recently died. When Dan died, he owed Carl $10,000. Sam strikes a bargain with Carl by promising to personally guarantee that the estate will pay Carl $5,000 if he agrees to write off the rest of the debt. Sam's promise is within the executor provision because he is personally liable for the remainder of the debt. Sam would likely take on the debt because he is the main beneficiary of the estate and would have assumed the debt of the estate anyway. This is also a way to speed up probate.

On the other hand, if Sam simply promises Carl that the estate will pay $5,000 now instead of Carl waiting for the estate to go through probate, then the agreement is not within the executor provision because Sam is not personally liable for that obligation.

2. Suretyship

Surety is a guarantee that the obligation of another will be performed. This commonly occurs, for example, where a parent co-signs on the lease of a child. The parent thereby provides surety to the landlord that the monthly rent will be paid.

> *A contract is not within the Statute of Frauds as a contract to answer for the duty of another unless the promisee is an obligee of the other's duty, the promisor is a surety for the other, and the promisee knows or has reason to know of the suretyship relation.* R2d § 112.

The requirement that suretyship agreements be evidenced with a writing signed by the person who gives the surety provides a cautionary function. The reasoning is that the surety will think twice about taking on another's obligation before signing a formal document. It also provides an evidentiary function. Since the motivation of the surety is essentially gratuitous, courts demand a higher burden of proof to show that surety was actually given.

3. Marriage

Marriage itself is a commonly misunderstood topic under the statue of frauds. When people get married, it is commonly referred to as the bond of matrimony. In some cultures, such marital bonds were actually represented by a formal contract. For example, under Jewish law, the marriage itself must be evidenced by a traditional marriage contract called a "ketubah." But this is a contract formalizing the marriage itself, which is distinguishable from a contract that is made upon consideration of marriage.

But when you read the Restatement carefully, you will realize it is not actually talking about marriage contracts. The marriage class of contracts is confusing because it does not refer to marriage contracts themselves. Rather, this class refers to contracts in which marriage or a promise to marry is given in exchange for something else.

> *A promise for which all or part of the consideration is either marriage or a promise to marry is within the Statute of Frauds, except in the case of an agreement which consists only of mutual promises of two persons to marry each other.* R2d § 124.

For example, Joe wants to marry Anita, but Anita is worried that if she leaves her father's house, then no one will take care of her ailing father. Joe induces Anita to marry him by promising her that if she marries him, he will hire a live-in nurse to care for Anita's father. This contract is within the statute of frauds under the marriage provision.

On the other hand, if Joe promises to marry Anita and she promises to marry him, that agreement is not within the statute of frauds. Mutual promises to marry were within the words of the English statute but were not within the statutory purpose and were soon excluded by judicial interpretation. A number of American statutes explicitly exclude such promises from the marriage provision.

Moreover, a promise is not within the Statute merely because it is conditional on marriage, or because marriage is contemplated by the promisor or the promisee or both. The marriage or promise to marry must be bargained for and given in exchange for the promise.

4. Land

The land provision is found in most statutes of frauds and is usually uncomplicated. Anytime one person sells real estate to another, it must be evidenced by a writing signed by the party to be charged.

> *A promise to transfer to any person any interest in land is within the Statute of Frauds.* R2d 125(1).

This gets tricky, however, when land is leased.

Figure 10.1. A stylized Jewish marriage contract or "Ketubah." Note that such a marriage contract, which recognizes a union, is distinct from a contract made upon consideration of marriage, which creates a duty upon consummation of marriage.

Statutes in most states except from the land contract and one-year provisions of the Statute of Frauds short-term leases and contracts to lease, usually for a term not longer than one year. R2d § 125(4).

The language in the Restatement leaves some clarity to be desired. It effectively means that short-term leases usually are not within the statute of frauds, where short-term means one year or less. Therefore, leases for one year or less generally do not require evidence of a signed writing to be enforceable.

The original English Statute of Frauds specifically excepted leases "not exceeding the term of three years from the making thereof." Most modern state statutes of frauds reduce the term to one year and eliminate the words "from the making thereof." The usual result is to validate an oral lease or contract to lease for a one-year term even though it was made before the term begins.

Check the specific language of the statute of frauds in the applicable jurisdiction to determine what constitutes a short-term lease that is excepted from the statute of frauds. Note that even if a contract for the transfer of interest in land does not fall within a given state's land-sale provision, it could still fall within the state's provision regarding contracts not to be performed within a year.

Year

The one-year (or more) provision covers only those contracts whose performance cannot possibly be completed within a year.

> *Where any promise in a contract cannot be fully performed within a year from the time the contract is made, all promises in the contract are within the Statute of Frauds until one party to the contract completes his performance. R2d § 130(1).*

For example, Sally contracts with AT&T for 18 months of cellular phone service at a price of $40 per month. This contract is within the one-year (or more) provision because it cannot possibly be performed within one year. There is no way that 18 months of service can be provided in less than 365 days.

Note that enforceability of a contract under the one-year provision does not turn on the actual course of subsequent events, nor on the expectations of the parties as to what could happen. If Allstate promises to insure Brian's house against fire for five years in exchange for weekly premiums, the contract is not within the statute of frauds, because the house could burn down at any time, even within the first year. If Brian's house burns down only a month after he entered into the insurance contract, and if the insurer promptly pays, then the contract will be fully performed in less than one year. Since this is possible — regardless of whether it is probable — then this insurance contract is not subject to the statute of frauds one-year provision.

Likewise, the traditional view is that a contract for lifetime employment or free beer for life is not subject to the statute of frauds one-year provision because a person could die within a year from the making thereof — although a minority of jurisdiction have recently deviated from this traditional view and now treat such agreements as falling within the one-year category.

Contracts of uncertain duration are simply excluded; the one-year (or more) provision covers only those contracts whose performance cannot possibly be completed within a year.

Additionally, the law excludes from the one-year provision any contract where one party has fully performed its obligation. This is sometimes called the full performance on one side exception:

> *When one party to a contract has completed his performance, the one-year provision of the Statute does not prevent enforcement of the promises of other parties. R2d 130(2).*

For example, if Farmer Fred promises to deliver three shipments of peaches to Grocer Georgia in six months, one year, and eighteen months, this contract appears to be within the statute of frauds because Farmer Fred cannot perform his obligation within one year. But if Grocer Georgia pays Farmer Fred in full up front, then Grocer Georgia performed her side of the bargain at the time the parties made the contract. This full and immediate performance by Grocer Georgia places this contract within an exception to the one-year provision such that a signed writing is not required for this agreement, at least not pursuant to the one-year provision of the statute of frauds.

Goods

The Uniform Commercial Code (UCC) is a model statute that has been adopted in whole or in part by almost every U.S. jurisdiction. It will usually be found in a different section of the state code than the other statute of frauds provisions. The model statute amounts to a few basic principles.

First, sales of goods for $500 or more shall be evidenced by a signed writing.

> Except as otherwise provided in this section a contract for the sale of goods for the price of $500 or more is not enforceable by way of action or defense unless there is some writing sufficient to indicate that a contract for sale has been made between the parties and signed by the party against whom enforcement is sought or by his authorized agent or broker. UCC § 2-201(1).

Second, merchants (who are people that deal professionally in that type of good) are not subject to the signed writing requirement where one issued a confirmation to the other. This is called the "merchant's exception" to the sale of goods. This reflects commercial realities which might be new to many law students. Parties do not always make a formal contract before beginning performance.

Diamond merchants, for example, are famous for shipping valuable stones to prospective buyers without requiring any formal agreement. If the prospective buyer keeps the stone, the merchants follow up by sending a confirmation memorandum, which contains the terms of the sale. Such a confirmation memorandum is sufficient against the sender, that is, such a memo will evidence that the diamond merchant intended to sell the stone on the terms provided therein. Even though such a memo is not a contract in a formal sense, it is enough to satisfy the statute of frauds under the UCC merchant's exception rule.

> Between merchants if within a reasonable time a writing in confirmation of the contract and sufficient against the sender is received and the party receiving it has reason to know its contents, it satisfies the requirements of subsection (1) against such party unless written notice of objection to its contents is given within 10 days after it is received. UCC § 2-201(2).

Third, there are three additional exceptions that apply to sales of goods between merchants and non-merchants alike: the "special manufacture exception," the "party admission exception," and the "goods accepted exception." Read the model statute below carefully for the details of how these exceptions operate.

> A contract which does not satisfy the requirements of subsection (1) but which is valid in other respects is enforceable if the goods are to be specially

*manufactured for the buyer and are not suitable for sale to others in the
ordinary course of the seller's business and the seller, before notice of repudiation
is received and under circumstances which reasonably indicate that
the goods are for the buyer, has made either a substantial beginning of their
manufacture or commitments for their procurement.* UCC § 2-201(3)(a).

The special manufacture exception is based on the rationale that specially manufacturing
goods for a specific buyer is evidence that the manufacturer and the buyer
formed a contract.

*A contract which does not satisfy the requirements of subsection (1) but
which is valid in other respects is enforceable if the party against whom
enforcement is sought admits in his pleading, testimony or otherwise in court
that a contract for sale was made, but the contract is not enforceable under
this provision beyond the quantity of goods admitted.* UCC § 2-201(3)(b).

The party admission exception likewise shows that alternative evidence can be
produced in the absence of a signed writing that still shows a contract was formed.
When a party admits a contract was formed, there is little basis for a court to deny its
existence on merely formalistic grounds.

*A contract which does not satisfy the requirements of subsection (1) but
which is valid in other respects is enforceable with respect to goods for which
payment has been made and accepted or which have been received and
accepted.* UCC § 2-201(3)(c).

The goods accepted exception once again shows how there can be other and perhaps
better evidence of contract formation, even where there is no signed writing
to prove the contract was formed. When a party accepts and pays for goods, that is
evidence that the party wanted the benefit of that bargain.

B. Satisfaction of the Statute of Frauds

If it has been determined that the contract must be evidenced by a signed writing
because it falls into one of the classes covered by the statute of frauds, then the
inquiry turns to whether there is some writing that satisfies the statute of frauds.
If no such writing exists, then the alleged contract is unenforceable, unless there is
some exception in law or equity.

Please note that my recommendation that you analyze statute of frauds issues in
this way — i.e., (1) does the transaction fall within the statue of frauds, (2) is there a
writing satisfy the statute, and if not, (3) is there an exception — and is not absolute.
You could (and should) come to the same result if you first looked at whether there
was an exception and only performed the sufficient-writing analysis if no exception
applies. The order of operations I offer here is to ensure that students taking law
school exams touch on all the possible issues raised by the examiner in order to score
a maximum number of points.

The rationale for this order of operations is that many transactions in the real world are evidenced by sufficient writings, whether they fall within the statute of frauds or not. Moreover, in the real world, it can be confusing whether a contract falls within the law of one state or another, and the two states can have different statutes of frauds and thus different requirements for when a signed writing is required. In these cases, it might be much easier to simply determine that there is a sufficient writing and therefore no further statute of frauds analysis is necessary.

On an exam, the examiner will usually provide some hints as to whether the complete three-step statute of frauds analysis suggested above is required. If the prompt says that the parties entered into a signed written agreement, it is probably not necessary to spend a lot of time analyzing the statute of frauds issue. On the other hand, if the prompt specifically says there was no written agreement, that is probably a hint that statute of frauds issues should at least be considered.

Whichever path you take should lead to the right result so long as you follow the rules outlined in the module. But it is worth reminding you that the most confusing aspect of satisfying the statute of frauds is that the contract itself is not required. A party does not have to produce a formal written and signed agreement in order to have a court enforce its terms. The party seeking enforcement of the contract must only produce a memorandum that is sufficient under law. As the following sections make clear, the requisites of such a memorandum are less strenuous than one might expect.

1. Memorandum

The previous material regarded when a signed writing is required. There are six classes of contracts, represented by the acronym MYLEGS, that typically require a signed writing to be enforceable. R2d identifies two common law exceptions, one that applies generally and one that applies only to sales of land. The UCC provides four additional exceptions that only apply to sales of goods.

Once it has been determined that a contract requires a signed writing to be enforceable, the question turns to whether there is such a writing. In other words, is the statute of frauds satisfied?

> *Unless additional requirements are prescribed by the particular statute, a contract within the Statute of Frauds is enforceable if it is evidenced by any writing, signed by or on behalf of the party to be charged, which (a) reasonably identifies the subject matter of the contract, (b) is sufficient to indicate that a contract with respect thereto has been made between the parties or offered by the signer to the other party, and (c) states with reasonable certainty the essential terms of the unperformed promises in the contract.* R2d § 131.

To put this more simply, a sufficient memorandum must identify the subject matter, indicate a contract was formed, state its essential terms, and be signed by the party who denies the contract. Instead of memorizing this list, think about why this rule exists, based on the fundamental purpose of the statute.

The primary purpose of the statute of frauds is to require reliable evidence of the existence and terms of a contract. This prevents enforcement through fraud or perjury of contracts never in fact made. To accomplish this purpose, courts require a memorandum that makes successful fraud unlikely. This does not necessarily require written production of all the terms of the contract.

The memorandum may be a written contract, but any writing, formal or informal, may be sufficient. A memorandum may be a will, a notation on a check, a receipt, a pleading, or an informal letter. Neither delivery to the party to be charged nor communication of the memorandum is essential. Even a diary entry in a private ledger can serve as a memorandum for the purpose of satisfying the statute of frauds.

The cases below give examples of an insufficient memorandum. As you read the first of those, *Sterling v. Taylor*, think about why the memorandum was not sufficient. The case also provides a thorough review and discussion of the general requisites of a memorandum that will help you better understand how the rule stated above is applied by courts. The second case, *Howard Const. Co. v. Jeff-Cole Quarries, Inc.*, is famous for its in-depth discussion of the rationale for the memorandum requirement, and it provides another illustration of how this doctrine is applied in practice.

2. Several Writings

Parties may create several writings that relate to a single transaction. Complex agreements, for example regarding corporate mergers, typically require many documents. Even simple transactions may generate several writings. A frequent scenario is where a buyer might make an offer to purchase a specific thing in one writing, and the seller responds with another writing simply offering to sell at a higher price. The seller's reply might describe that thing in detail, but those details are incorporated by reference to the buyer's writing. R2d allows incorporation of multiple writings so long as the court can determine they are in fact related.

> *The memorandum may consist of several writings if one of the writings is signed and the writings in the circumstances clearly indicate that they relate to the same transaction.* R2d § 132.

Where two or more documents are signed by the party to be charged, they may be read together even though neither contains any reference to the other. The question whether they constitute a sufficient memorandum is substantially the same as if they had been incorporated in a single document. A sufficient connection between the papers is established simply by a reference in them to the same subject matter or transaction.

The upshot is this:

> *The memorandum required by the statute [of frauds] may be pieced together out of separate writings, some signed and some unsigned, provided they all clearly refer to the same transaction.*

3. Signature

Recall that the statute of frauds requires a signed writing for certain classes of contract. What does "signed" mean? One might think this requires an actual pen-and-ink signature, but one's "John Hancock" is not actually required.

> *The signature to a memorandum may be any symbol made or adopted with an intention, actual or apparent, to authenticate the writing as that of the signer.* R2d § 134.

For the purposes of satisfying the statute of frauds, there must be a memorandum that sufficiently evidences the contract to be enforced and is signed by the party to be charged. "Signed" for R2d and UCC purposes is not limited to the traditional form of signature. While the name of the signer, handwritten in ink, is clearly a "signature" for the purpose of this statute, other symbols may count as a signature that satisfies that statute of frauds. Initials, a thumbprint or an arbitrary code sign may be used as a signature. The signature may be written in pencil, typed, printed, made with a rubber stamp, or impressed into the paper. Signed copies may be made with carbon paper or by photographic process.

Most states have adopted some form of the Uniform Electronic Transactions Act (UETA), which defines an electronic signature as "an electronic sound, symbol, or process attached to or logically associated with a record and executed or adopted by a person with the intent to sign the record." In addition, the Electronic Signature in Global and National Commerce (eSIGN) Act of 2000 lays out the guidelines for the use of electronic signatures in interstate commerce. According to the eSIGN Act, a contract or signature "may not be denied legal effect, validity, or enforceability solely because it is in electronic form." In other words, electronic signatures and records are just as good as their paper equivalents.

Like the UCC, the UETA and ESIGN act as overlay statutes. They fill in the gaps that the common law of contracts does not address, and in some cases, they modify the common law by statute. As to what courts recognize as a signature, UETA and ESIGN replace certain paper requirements with an electronic record or an electronic signature.

4. Loss or Destruction of a Memorandum

The statute of frauds requires creation of a signed writing for certain classes of contracts to be enforceable. But it does not actually require that signed writing to be presented to the court. Recall that the statute of frauds is not a rule of evidence but rather a rule that requires the creation of evidence. It is laxer with regard to the preservation and presentation of that evidence in court.

> *The loss or destruction of a memorandum does not deprive it of effect under the Statute.* R2d § 137.

Although the statute of frauds was designed to create evidence, it is not itself a rule of evidence. If the memorandum that evidenced a contract was lost or destroyed, the fact of its existence and contents may be shown by an unsigned copy or by oral evidence.

This rule shows how the statute of frauds is eroded by various doctrines that make its satisfaction easier.

C. Exceptions to the Statute of Frauds

The statute of frauds has been criticized for creating more fraud than it prevents. By requiring a signed writing to enforce an agreement, some actual agreements become unenforceable.

To cope with this problem, courts at common law have applied the doctrine of promissory estoppel to enforce certain agreements that fall within the statute of frauds and were not evidenced by a signed writing. This equitable exception applies generally to all classes of contract subject to the statute of frauds under common law.

More specifically, common law also developed a specific exception to the land sale provision. In addition, the Uniform Commercial Code includes four exceptions that are specific to the requirement of a signed writing in sales of goods.

1. Promissory Estoppel

The promissory estoppel doctrine is familiar to students who have already studied consideration. Consideration — the requirement that enforceable promises must not be gratuitous — is required as an element in the formation of contracts. But common law provides several exceptions where consideration is not required. Promissory estoppel, which is also called detrimental reliance, occurs where one party takes an action to its detriment in reliance on a promise being kept.

In such cases, courts can "estop" (prevent) a party from arguing the contract did not exist because there was no consideration for its promise thereunder. Virtually the same rule applies to enforce promises that would otherwise be unenforceable for the lack of written evidence. In such cases, the detrimental act taken in reliance is evidence of the promise itself.

> *A promise which the promisor should reasonably expect to induce action or forbearance on the part of the promisee or a third person and which does induce the action or forbearance is enforceable notwithstanding the Statute of Frauds if injustice can be avoided only by enforcement of the promise. The remedy granted for breach is to be limited as justice requires.* R2d § 139(1).

More recently, courts have applied virtually the same standard to justify enforcement of contracts that would otherwise be unenforceable for want of a signed writing:

> *In determining whether injustice can be avoided only by enforcement of the promise, the following circumstances are significant: (a) the availability and adequacy of other remedies, particularly cancellation and restitution;*

(b) the definite and substantial character of the action or forbearance in relation to the remedy sought; (c) the extent to which the action or forbearance corroborates evidence of the making and terms of the promise, or the making and terms are otherwise established by clear and convincing evidence; (d) the reasonableness of the action or forbearance; (e) the extent to which the action or forbearance was foreseeable by the promisor. R2d § 139(2).

Like all equitable doctrines, application of the promissory estoppel exception to the statute of frauds requires a fact-specific inquiry. The following cases illustrate how courts have applied this doctrine. As you read the cases, think carefully about how the factors above weighed in the court's decision below. On an exam, you may likewise be asked to evaluate how a set of facts would be analyzed under this doctrine.

Note that Second Restatement was a bit ambitious in drafting this rule, as it takes a minority position. Most states do not yet recognize the broad exception of the R2d. Rather, most states still follow the narrower exception found in the First Restatement, which creates a smaller exception to the statute of frauds only where the party detrimentally relied on a promise that a writing existed or would be created.

The case of *McIntosh v. Murphy* provides a useful review of the statute of frauds, including its purpose, before discussing the promissory estoppel exception to the statute of frauds. In that case, an employer in Hawaii allegedly promised a man who lived in California a year of employment in return for his moving to Hawaii. There is a useful discussion about whether the contract falls under the one-year provision, and there is also discussion about whether an exception applies. The court found that justice required enforcement of the promise, because the employee acted in reasonable reliance and suffered a significant detriment based on the employer's promise. But the case also features a vigorous dissent. I recommend reading the dissent because it shows how such a fact-specific inquiry can come out differently. Moreover, the dissent reminds us that application of equitable exceptions can eviscerate the purpose of the statute of frauds, and so they must be applied carefully and infrequently.

Another case below, *Stearns v. Emery-Waterhouse*, was decided by a unanimous opinion and thereby illustrates a more clear-cut application of the doctrine. In that case, an employer allegedly induced an employee to move from around Boston, Massachusetts to Portland, Maine, by promising long-term employment. The employee already owned property in Maine, and he travelled from Boston to Portland in about two hours by car. Today, a bus ticket from Boston, MA to Portland, ME costs about $15. Under these facts, the court found that the employee did not reasonably, substantially and detrimentally rely on the employer's promise of long-term employment. Law students should read *McIntosh* and *Stearns* in detail and work out how to distinguish one from the other based on the facts, as the court did, because this illustrates when the equitable exception to the statute of frauds will apply and when it will not.

2. Part Performance of Land Transactions

The *McIntosh* and *Stearns* cases illustrate how the doctrine of promissory estoppel can make contracts enforceable, even where there is no signed writing. The promissory estoppel exception applies to all classes of the statute of frauds. Indeed, the promissory estoppel exception even applies to the doctrine of consideration. One might say that the promissory estoppel exception is very broad.

The part performance exception, however, is more limited. The part performance doctrine generally applies only to sales of land. Land is a special kind of property called real property — distinguishable from personal property and intellectual property — for which the law has developed many special doctrines. R2d recognizes that sales of land are special and provides a special exception to the statute of frauds such that sales of land can be enforced without a signed writing where the party to be charged partly performed his, her, or its obligations in the land sale transaction.

> *A contract for the transfer of an interest in land may be specifically enforced notwithstanding failure to comply with the Statute of Frauds if it is established that the party seeking enforcement, in reasonable reliance on the contract and on the continuing assent of the party against whom enforcement is sought, has so changed his position that injustice can be avoided only by specific enforcement.* R2d § 129.

Enforcement of contracts for transfers in interest in land, without a signed writing, is justified on the ground that repudiation after "part performance" amounts to a "virtual fraud." Courts are vested with equitable powers to dispense justice based on a promisee's reliance. This reliance may be reasonable where the promisor took actions consistent with the contract. A court may estop such a promisor from disavowing a contract where it is clear from the promisor's behavior that the promisor believed a contract existed. But this equitable power is to be exercised with caution in the light of all the circumstances, as its over-use would undermine the purpose of the statute of frauds.

For example, Sarah orally agrees to sell, and Betty orally agrees to buy Blackacre. Prior to the closing, and with Sarah's consent, Betty takes possession of the land, pays some of the price, builds a house on the land and occupies it. Two years later, as a result of a dispute over the amount still to be paid, Sarah repudiates the agreement. Betty may obtain a decree of specific performance to enforce the oral agreement to transfer Blackacre.

3. Merchant Exceptions for Goods Transactions

UCC Article 2 deals with sales of goods and provides many special rules for transactions in goods. It has also developed special exceptions to the statute of frauds where the parties to the transaction are experienced and therefore should be able to fend for themselves. These so-called "big boy" clauses are common in securities regulation as well. The UCC identifies a class of people called merchants to whom special rules apply because these merchants can fend for themselves to a greater extent than ordinary people can.

> *Between merchants if within a reasonable time a writing in confirmation of the contract and sufficient against the sender is received and the party receiving it has reason to know its contents, it satisfies the requirements of subsection (1) against such party unless written notice of objection to its contents is given within 10 days after it is received.* UCC § 2-201(2).

A "merchant" is "a person who deals in goods of the kind or otherwise by his occupation holds himself out as having knowledge or skill peculiar to the practices or goods involved in the transaction or to whom such knowledge or skill may be attributed by his employment of an agent or broker or other intermediary who by his occupation holds himself out as having such knowledge or skill." UCC § 2-104(1).

When two people who both qualify as merchants, because they both ordinarily deal in goods of the kind involved in the contract at issue, there is an exception to the statute of frauds where one merchant provides a confirmation to the other. This can be as simple as an email that says, "thank you for your order" and outlines the nature and quantity of goods sold and the prices for each. If the merchants have reason to know and understand the contents of an even simpler confirmation, that confirmation will also suffice as an exception to the statute of frauds provision for the sale of goods.

The challenge, however, is in determining whether a person is a "merchant." Although the official comment to the UCC provides an expansive definition of merchant, courts have taken a narrower view.

For example, in *Cook Grains, Inc. v. Fallis*, 239 Ark. 962 (1965), a soybean farmer allegedly agreed to sell and deliver 5,000 bushels of soybeans at a cost of $2.54 per bushel to a soybean dealer. The soybean dealer introduced evidence that they entered into a verbal agreement that delivery was to be made between September and November 1963. Following this discussion, the dealer mailed a proposed written contract to the farmer which provided that the farmer had sold 5,000 bushels of soybeans to the grain company. The dealer signed the contract, but the farmer did not. Nor did the farmer send a written objection to this proposed contract.

The farmer failed to deliver the soybeans. When the dealer sued to enforce this agreement, the farmer denied that there was a contract and further defended on the grounds that the action was barred by the statute of frauds since he had not signed any writing. In turn, the grain company argued that the sale fell within the merchant's exception, U.C.C. § 2-201(2). Thus, in order to determine whether the merchant's exception applied to this transaction, the Arkansas Supreme Court first had to determine whether this farmer was a "merchant."

The *Cook Grains* court affirmed the lower court's holding that this farmer was not a merchant. The court acknowledged the merchant definition in § 2-104, but reasoned that in construing a statute, its words must be given their plain and ordinary meaning. The court relied on general dictionary definitions and concluded that, in its plain and ordinary meaning, a farmer is "one devoted to the tillage of the soil," not a professional trader as contemplated by UCC § 2-104.

Cook Grains has been criticized for ignoring the Code's special merchant definition and, instead, relying on pre-Code definitions of merchant. But it is not the only court to apply a narrow definition of "merchant" and thereby limit this exception to the statute of frauds. Practitioners should be careful not to rely too heavily on the merchant's exception where there is any doubt as to whether one of the parties fits the plain-English meaning of a merchant of a certain type of goods.

a. Special Manufacture

Remember that the statute of frauds is designed to create evidence by requiring a signed writing in order to avoid disputes later. However, the UCC recognizes that a signed writing is not the only evidence of a contract. Sometimes actions speak louder than words. If one party produces a good that is specially designed for the buyer, then the court can infer the special manufacture of that good as evidence that the parties agreed to buy and sell it.

> *A contract which does not satisfy the requirements of subsection (1) but which is valid in other respects is enforceable if the goods are to be specially manufactured for the buyer and are not suitable for sale to others in the ordinary course of the seller's business and the seller, before notice of repudiation is received and under circumstances which reasonably indicate that the goods are for the buyer, has made either a substantial beginning of their manufacture or commitments for their procurement.* UCC § 2-201(3)(a).

The UCC does not require a signed writing for the sale of "specially manufactured" goods. The rationale behind this is, essentially, *res ipsa loquitur*, the thing speaks for itself. The existence of a thing specifically manufactured for a particular buyer is itself evidence of a contract for the sale of that thing.

The term "specially manufactured" refers to the nature of the particular goods in question and whether they are specially made for a particular buyer. For example, in *Company Image Knitware, Ltd. v. Mothers Work, Inc.*, 2006 PA Super 272 (2006) ("*CIK*"), the question presented was whether goods were "specially manufactured." The test for whether goods are specially manufactured or not is:

> *whether the manufacturer could sell the goods in the ordinary course of his business to someone other than the original buyer. If with slight alterations the goods could be so sold, then they are not specially manufactured; if, however, essential changes are necessary to render the goods marketable by the seller to others, then the exception does apply.*

CIK agreed to manufacture maternity garments in Mexico according to the standards set and approved by Mothers Work regarding fabric, color, style, and pattern, and Mothers Work agreed to pay CIK a set price. The record clearly established that all fabric, findings and garments were specially manufactured for Mothers Work. The colors had to be very specific and exact; the fabric had to have specific content, hand feel and processing; the findings had to be manufactured to match the colors of the fabric; the garments had to have a certain feel; and the sizes of the garments were manufactured to fit American women. The garments and fabric were not suitable for market re-sale in the ordinary course of CIK's business. The court found that these were specially manufactured goods.

The reason for this exception is that a seller would not likely produce a strange or distinctive good unless there was an order in hand. The costs to a seller who mistakenly manufactures specialty goods is higher than a manufacturer who makes ordinary goods because the former cannot be resold as easily as the latter. Think about how much you would pay for a leather notepad with someone else's monogram embossed on it versus for a plain leather notepad. Most people would prefer to carry a plain pad than one with someone else's name on it. For this reason, the erroneously monogrammed pad is worth less on the open market than the plain pad. Likewise, specialty manufactured goods are worth less on the open market than ordinary goods. Therefore, a seller bears a higher error cost when erroneously manufacturing specialty goods than ordinary goods and should for this reason be less likely to make them erroneously.

The exception does not ask whether those goods were "specially made" in the usual course of the seller's business. If a good was produced for a specific buyer, then the seller must show some unusual or special feature of the good that could attest to its character as specially made for a particular buyer.

The crucial inquiry is whether the manufacturer could sell the goods in the ordinary course of his business to someone other than the original buyer. If with slight alterations the goods could be so sold, then they are not specially manufactured; if, however, essential changes are necessary to render the goods marketable by the seller to others, then the exception does apply.

b. Party Admission

A party who admits that a contract for the sale of goods exists is effectively estopped under the UCC from asserting that it cannot be enforced.

> *A contract which does not satisfy the requirements of subsection (1) but which is valid in other respects is enforceable if the party against whom enforcement is sought admits in his pleading, testimony or otherwise in court that a contract for sale was made, but the contract is not enforceable under this provision beyond the quantity of goods admitted.* UCC § 2-201(3)(b).

The seemingly uncontroversial provision becomes more contentious with regard to involuntary admissions. Courts are split as to whether a party can be involuntarily forced to admit that a contract has been made.

Most courts hold that involuntary admissions are proper. They reason is that the statute of frauds serves only an evidentiary function, and that this function is satisfied by an admission that a contract has been made.

c. Complete Performance

The statute of frauds is not a rule of evidence per se. Rather, it is usually described as a rule that requires the creation of evidence; namely, the statute of frauds requires the creation of evidence of an agreement in the form of a signed writing. This is supposed to prevent fraud by one party who claims the other agreed to do something or who claims that it does not have to do something. In those cases, the court can look at the writing to determine what the parties agreed to do.

However, the UCC recognizes that there is other evidence of what goods parties agreed to buy and sell. When a person accepts payment for goods, that evidences the person wanted to sell those goods for that price. When a person accepts a delivery of goods, that evidences the person wanted to buy those goods. Accordingly, the UCC provides the "part performance" exception where the party to be charged has accepted payment for or paid for goods.

> *A contract which does not satisfy the requirements of subsection (1) but which is valid in other respects is enforceable with respect to goods for which payment has been made and accepted or which have been received and accepted (Sec. 2-606).* UCC § 2-201(3)(c).

A seller can enforce an oral contract for the sale of goods to the extent that a buyer has received and accepted the goods. A buyer can enforce an oral contract for sale to the extent that the seller has accepted payment for the goods. In both these cases, the action of accepting goods or payment serves as evidence that the contract exists.

Notably, the part performance exception only applies to the goods that were actually paid for or delivered. If the seller delivers 1,000 reams of paper, which the buyer accepts and pays for, the seller cannot later deliver 9,000 more reams of paper and claim there was a contract for the sale of 10,000 reams.

D. Reflections on the Statute of Frauds

This chapter has shown how state statutes make certain classes of contracts unenforceable unless evidenced by a writing signed by the party to be charged. The first step in analyzing a statute of frauds problem is to determine whether the contract at issue falls within one of the classes of contracts that requires a signed writing. If it does, the next question is whether an exception applies. The doctrine of promissory estoppel applies as an equitable exception to any statute of frauds provisions, whereas the part performance exception only applies to contracts regarding transfers of interests in land. The UCC also provides four exceptions to the statute of frauds for contracts regarding the sale of goods for more than $500.

If the contract falls within the statute of frauds, and an exception does not apply, then the inquiry turns to whether the statute of fraud was satisfied. Satisfaction of the statute of frauds requires production of a memorandum that is signed by the party to be charged. Memorandum means any writing that reasonably identifies the subject matter of the contract, indicates that the parties agreed to be bound under it, and states with reasonable certainty the essential terms of that contract. Signed has a very broad meaning in this context and includes any symbol intended to signify acceptance of an agreement. Thanks to the UETA, this includes electronic signatures. The party to be charged is the party who is denying the existence or enforceability of the agreement. The memorandum does not have to remain in existence at the time of trial, so long as evidence that it once existed is produced.

Cases

Reading McIntosh v. Murphy. The statute of frauds was established for three purposes: (1) cautioning parties against entering into serious agreements; (2) evidencing those agreements so they can be properly enforced by courts; and (3) channeling certain types of agreements into certain forms and modes that are easier to adjudicate. This is meant as a defense shield or bulwark against people fraudulently claiming that there is a serious agreement where none actually exist.

However, the statute of frauds can also itself create the opportunity for fraud. For example, where one party promises to put an agreement in writing, that party may fail to do so to ensure the contract is unenforceable if that party chooses not to document and enforce it. The law has created an exception to this instance, such that where a party promises to memorialize a contract in writing, the other party can evidence reliance on that promise that justifies an exemption to the statute of frauds.

A more general exception to the statute of frauds comes from reliance on the promise more generally. Even where a party does not rely specifically on the other's promise to memorialize a contract in writing, the aggrieved party can still attempt to enforce that contract on the basis of reasonable reliance. The *McIntosh* case illustrates where one party relied on the oral promise of another. The court must first establish whether the contract falls within the statute of frauds. Finding that it does, the court then goes on to determine whether an equitable exception applies. Read on to learn how courts will apply R2d § 139 to determine whether equity requires enforcement of contracts that are not evidenced in writing.

McIntosh v. Murphy provides a useful review of the statute of frauds, including its purpose, before discussing the promissory estoppel exception to the statute of frauds. The dissent is also included because it shows how such a fact-specific inquiry can come out differently. Moreover, the dissent reminds us that application of equitable exceptions can eviscerate the purpose of the statute of frauds, and so they must be applied carefully and infrequently. The subsequent case, *Stearns v. Emery-Waterhouse*, was decided by a unanimous opinion and thereby illustrates a more clear-cut application of the doctrine.

McIntosh v. Murphy

52 Haw. 29, 469 P.2d 177 (1970)

This case involves an oral employment contract which allegedly violates the provision of the Statute of Frauds requiring "any agreement that is not to be performed within one year from the making thereof" to be in writing in order to be enforceable. In this action the plaintiff-employee Dick McIntosh seeks to recover damages from his employer, George Murphy and Murphy Motors, Ltd., for the breach of an alleged one-year oral employment contract.

While the facts are in sharp conflict, it appears that defendant George Murphy was in southern California during March, 1964 interviewing prospective management personnel for his Chevrolet-Oldsmobile dealerships in Hawaii. He interviewed the plaintiff twice during that time. The position of sales manager for one of the dealerships was fully discussed but no contract was entered.

In April 1964 the plaintiff received a call from the general manager of Murphy Motors informing him of possible employment within thirty days if he was still available. The plaintiff indicated his continued interest and informed the manager that he would be available. Later in April, the plaintiff sent Murphy a telegram to the effect that he would arrive in Honolulu on Sunday, April 26, 1964.

Murphy then telephoned McIntosh on Saturday, April 25, 1964 to notify him that the job of assistant sales manager was available and work would begin on the following Monday, April 27, 1964. At that time McIntosh expressed surprise at the change in job title from sales manager to assistant sales manager but reconfirmed the fact that he was arriving in Honolulu the next day, Sunday. McIntosh arrived on Sunday, April 26 1964 and began work on the following day, Monday, April 27, 1964.

As a consequence of his decision to work for Murphy, McIntosh moved some of his belongings from the mainland to Hawaii, sold possessions, leased an apartment in Honolulu and obviously forwent any other employment opportunities. In short, the plaintiff did all those things which were incidental to changing one's residence permanently from Los Angeles to Honolulu, which is approximately 2200 miles. McIntosh continued working for Murphy until July 16, 1964, approximately two and one-half months, at which time he was discharged on the grounds that he was unable to close deals with prospective customers and could not train the salesmen.

At the conclusion of the trial, the defense moved for a directed verdict arguing that the oral employment agreement was in violation of the Statute of Frauds, there being no written memorandum or note thereof. The trial court ruled that as a matter of law the contract did not come within the Statute, reasoning that Murphy bargained for acceptance by the actual commencement of performance by McIntosh, so that McIntosh was not bound by a contract until he came to work on Monday, April 27, 1964. Therefore, assuming that the contract was for a year's employment, it was performable within a year exactly to the day and no writing was required for it to be enforceable.

Alternatively, the court ruled that if the agreement was made final by the telephone call between the parties on Saturday, April 25, 1964, then that part of the weekend which remained would not be counted in calculating the year, thus taking the contract out of the Statute of Frauds. With commendable candor the trial judge gave as the motivating force for the decision his desire to avoid a mechanical and unjust application of the Statute.

The case went to the jury on the following questions: (1) whether the contract was for a year's duration or was performable on a trial basis, thus making it terminable at the will of either party; (2) whether the plaintiff was discharged for just cause; and (3) if he was not discharged for just cause, what damages were due the plaintiff.

The jury returned a verdict for the plaintiff in the sum of $12,103.40. The defendants appeal to this court on four principal grounds, three of which we find to be without merit. The remaining ground of appeal is whether the plaintiff can maintain an action on the alleged oral employment contract in light of the prohibition of the Statute of Frauds making unenforceable an oral contract that is not to be performed within one year.

I. Time of Acceptance of the Employment Agreement

The defendants contend that the trial court erred in refusing to give an instruction to the jury that if the employment agreement was made more than one day before the plaintiff began performance, there could be no recovery by the plaintiff. The reason given was that a contract not to be performed within one year from its making is unenforceable if not in writing.

The defendants are correct in their argument that the time of acceptance of an offer is a question of fact for the jury to decide. But the trial court alternatively decided that even if the offer was accepted on the Saturday prior to the commencement of performance, the intervening Sunday and part of Saturday would not be counted in computing the year for the purposes of the Statute of Frauds. The judge stated that Sunday was a non-working day and only a fraction of Saturday was left which he would not count. In any event, there is no need to discuss the relative merits of either ruling since we base our decision in this case on the doctrine of equitable estoppel which was properly briefed and argued by both parties before this court, although not presented to the trial court.

II. Enforcement by Virtue of Action in Reliance on the Oral Contract

In determining whether a rule of law can be fashioned and applied to a situation where an oral contract admittedly violates a strict interpretation of the Statute of Frauds, it is necessary to review the Statute itself together with its historical and modern functions. The Statute of Frauds, which requires that certain contracts be in writing in order to be legally enforceable, had its inception in the days of Charles II of England. Hawaii's version of the Statute is found in HRS § 656-1 and is substantially the same as the original English Statute of Frauds.

The first English Statute was enacted almost 300 years ago to prevent "many fraudulent practices, which are commonly endeavored to be upheld by perjury and subornation of perjury". Certainly, there were compelling reasons in those days for such a law. At the time of enactment in England, the jury system was quite unreliable, rules of evidence were few, and the complaining party was disqualified as a witness so he could neither testify on direct-examination nor, more importantly, be cross-examined. The aforementioned structural and evidentiary limitations on our system of justice no longer exist.

Retention of the Statute today has nevertheless been justified on at least three grounds: (1) the Statute still serves an evidentiary function thereby lessening the danger of perjured testimony (the original rationale); (2) the requirement of a writing has a cautionary effect which causes reflection by the parties on the importance of the agreement; and (3) the writing is an easy way to distinguish enforceable contracts from those which are not, thus channeling certain transactions into written form.

In spite of whatever utility the Statute of Frauds may still have, its applicability has been drastically limited by judicial construction over the years in order to mitigate the harshness of a mechanical application. Furthermore, learned writers continue to disparage the Statute regarding it as "a statute for promoting fraud" and a "legal anachronism."

Another method of judicial circumvention of the Statute of Frauds has grown out of the exercise of the equity powers of the courts. Such judicially imposed limitations or exceptions involved the traditional dispensing power of the equity courts to mitigate the "harsh" rule of law. When courts have enforced an oral contract despite the Statute, they have utilized the legal labels of "part performance" or "equitable estoppel" in granting relief. Both doctrines are said to be based on the concept of estoppel, which operates to avoid unconscionable injury.

Part performance has long been recognized in Hawaii as an equitable doctrine justifying the enforcement of an oral agreement for the conveyance of an interest in land where there has been substantial reliance by the party seeking to enforce the contract. Other courts have enforced oral contracts (including employment contracts) which failed to satisfy the section of the Statute making unenforceable an agreement not to be performed within a year of its making. This has occurred where the conduct of the parties gave rise to an estoppel to assert the Statute.

It is appropriate for modern courts to cast aside the raiments of conceptualism which cloak the true policies underlying the reasoning behind the many decisions enforcing contracts that violate the Statute of Frauds. There is certainly no need to resort to legal rubrics or meticulous legal formulas when better explanations are available. The policy behind enforcing an oral agreement which violated the Statute of Frauds, as a policy of avoiding unconscionable injury, was well set out by the California Supreme Court. In *Monarco v. Logreco*, a case which involved an action to enforce an oral contract for the conveyance of land on the grounds of 20 years performance by the promisee, the court said:

> *The doctrine of estoppel to assert the statute of frauds has been consistently applied by the courts of this state to prevent fraud that would result from refusal to enforce oral contracts in certain circumstances. Such fraud may inhere in the unconscionable injury that would result from denying enforcement of the contract after one party has been induced by the other seriously to change his position in reliance on the contract.*

In seeking to frame a workable test which is flexible enough to cover diverse factual situations and provide some reviewable standards, we find very persuasive section 139 of the Second Restatement of Contracts. That section specifically covers those situations where there has been reliance on an oral contract which falls within the Statute of Frauds. Section 139 states:

> *(1) A promise which the promisor should reasonably expect to induce action or forbearance on the part of the promisee or a third person and which does induce the action or forbearance is enforceable notwithstanding the Statute of Frauds if injustice can be avoided only by enforcement of the promise. The remedy granted for breach is to be limited as justice requires.*
>
> *(2) In determining whether injustice can be avoided only by enforcement of the promise, the following circumstances are significant: (a) the availability and adequacy of other remedies, particularly cancellation and restitution; (b) the definite and substantial character of the action or forbearance in relation to the remedy sought; (c) the extent to which the action or forbearance corroborates evidence of the making and terms of the promise, or the making and terms are otherwise established by clear and convincing evidence; (d) the reasonableness of the action or forbearance; (e) the extent to which the action or forbearance was foreseeable by the promisor.*

We think that the approach taken in the Restatement is the proper method of giving the trial court the necessary latitude to relieve a party of the hardships of the Statute of Frauds. Other courts have used similar approaches in dealing with oral employment contracts upon which an employee had seriously relied. This is to be preferred over having the trial court bend over backwards to take the contract out of the Statute of Frauds. In the present case the trial court admitted just this inclination and forthrightly followed it.

There is no dispute that the action of the plaintiff in moving 2200 miles from Los Angeles to Hawaii was foreseeable by the defendant. In fact, it was required to perform his duties. Injustice can only be avoided by the enforcement of the contract and the granting of money damages. No other remedy is adequate. The plaintiff found himself residing in Hawaii without a job.

It is also clear that a contract of some kind did exist. The plaintiff performed the contract for two and one-half months receiving $3,484.60 for his services. The exact length of the contract, whether terminable at will as urged by the defendant, or for a year from the time when the plaintiff started working, was up to the jury to decide.

In sum, the trial court might have found that enforcement of the contract was warranted by virtue of the plaintiff's reliance on the defendant's promise. Naturally, each case turns on its own facts. Certainly, there is considerable discretion for a court to implement the true policy behind the Statute of Frauds, which is to prevent fraud or any other type of unconscionable injury. We therefore affirm the judgment of the trial court on the ground that the plaintiff's reliance was such that injustice could only be avoided by enforcement of the contract.

Affirmed.

Dissent

ABE, J., dissenting

The majority of the court has affirmed the judgment of the trial court; however, I respectfully dissent.

I.

Whether alleged contract of employment came within the Statute of Frauds:

As acknowledged by this court, the trial judge erred when as a matter of law he ruled that the alleged employment contract did not come within the Statute of Frauds; however, I cannot agree that this error was not prejudicial as this court intimates.

On this issue, the date that the alleged contract was entered into was all important and the date of acceptance of an offer by the plaintiff was a question of fact for the jury to decide. In other words, it was for the jury to determine when the alleged one-year employment contract was entered into and if the jury had found that the plaintiff had accepted the offer more than one day before plaintiff was to report to work, the contract would have come within the Statute of Frauds and would have been unenforceable.

II.

This court holds that though the alleged one-year employment contract came within the Statute of Frauds, nevertheless the judgment of the trial court is affirmed "on the ground that the plaintiff's reliance was such that injustice could only be avoided by enforcement of the contract."

I believe this court is begging the issue by its holding because to reach that conclusion, this court is ruling that the defendant agreed to hire the plaintiff under a one-year employment contract. The defendant has denied that the plaintiff was hired for a period of one year and has introduced into evidence testimony of witnesses that all hiring by the defendant in the past has been on a trial basis. The defendant also testified that he had hired the plaintiff on a trial basis.

Here on one hand the plaintiff claimed that he had a one-year employment contract; on the other hand, the defendant claimed that the plaintiff had not been hired for one year but on a trial basis for so long as his services were satisfactory. I believe the Statute of Frauds was enacted to avoid the consequences this court is forcing upon the defendant. In my opinion, the legislature enacted the Statute of Frauds to negate claims such as has been made by the plaintiff in this case. But this court holds that because the plaintiff in reliance of the one-year employment contract (alleged to have been entered into by the plaintiff but denied by the defendant) has changed his position, "injustice could only be avoided by enforcement of the contract." Where is the sense of justice?

Now assuming that the defendant had agreed to hire the plaintiff under a one-year employment contract and the contract came within the Statute of Frauds, I cannot agree, as intimated by this court, that we should circumvent the Statute of Frauds by the exercise of the equity powers of courts. As to statutory law, the sole function of the judiciary is to interpret the statute and the judiciary should not usurp legislative power and enter into the legislative field. Thus, if the Statute of Frauds is too harsh as intimated by this court, and it brings about undue hardship, it is for the legislature to amend or repeal the statute and not for this court to legislate.

Reflection

McIntosh involved a man who moved from California to Hawaii to take a job. He sold many of his possessions to make this long-distance transition. The court seems to make much about the 2200-mile move. This implies that the case could have come out differently if the move was only 200 or 20 miles. But this raises the question, how far a move is far enough to constitute substantial reliance?

The court also seems to gloss over that fact that most terms of employment are at will. Is it reasonable to expect that a sales job will last for a year, regardless of performance on the job? There is not much discussion about McIntosh's job performance. Should his quality matter?

Perhaps the answers to these questions are found by evaluating the procedural posture. The Supreme Court decision you read follows a jury verdict. Courts are reluctant to set aside jury verdicts, especially on matters of fact. Whether or not McIntosh substantially and reasonably relied is very much a fact-specific question. The court even says, "each case turns on its own facts." Perhaps the Supreme Court's deference to the jury finding implies that court presumed the jury found McIntosh's reliance was substantial and that he was not fired for cause.

Discussion

1. What is the purpose of the statute of frauds? Discuss how the underlying purpose of the statute was implicated in this case and whether or not its purpose would be served by allowing Defendant to avoid the contract.

2. The promissory estoppel exception to the statute of frauds works similarly to the promissory estoppel exception to the requirement of consideration. Compare R2d §§ 90 and 139. How are they similar? How are they different?

3. The equitable exception to the statute of frauds implicitly recognizes that the statute can sometimes create injustice. Can you think of some situations where requiring a signed writing might perpetuate injustice instead of preventing fraud?

Reading Stearns v. Emery-Waterhouse Co. Although the *McIntosh* court suggests that employment agreements will be treated favorably to the employee-plaintiff, there are cases where the employee does not merit the equitable exception to the statute of frauds. The *Stearns* case, also about an employment offer resulting in a long-distance move, comes out differently than *McIntosh*, even though the court applies the same rule. As you consider the facts of this case, consider how they can be distinguished from *McIntosh* such that the result should also differ.

Stearns v. Emery-Waterhouse Co.

596 A.2d 72 (Me. 1991)

ROBERTS, J.

Emery-Waterhouse Co. appeals from a judgment of the Superior Court awarding damages to Timothy B. Stearns for breach of an oral contract to employ Stearns for a definite term greater than one year. The court held Emery-Waterhouse estopped to assert its defense under the statute of frauds, by the extent of Stearns's detrimental reliance on the oral contract. Because Stearns did not produce clear and convincing evidence of fraud on the part of his employer, we hold that enforcement of the oral contract was barred by the statute of frauds. Accordingly, we vacate the judgment.

Emery-Waterhouse is a Portland hardware wholesaler that also franchises "Trustworthy" hardware stores throughout the Northeast and owns several such stores. In December, 1984 the Employer's president, Charles Hildreth, met with Timothy Stearns in Massachusetts to discuss hiring him to run the Employer's retail stores.

Stearns was managing a Sears-Roebuck & Company store in Massachusetts, had done retail marketing for Sears for twenty-seven years and was fifty years old. He was earning approximately $99,000 per year, owned his home in Massachusetts, and also owned property in Maine. Stearns had some dissatisfactions with Sears but was concerned about retaining his Sears job security and was aware that his age would make it hard to find another marketing job. After the initial meeting Stearns came to

Maine, inspected some stores, and met with Hildreth in Portland. The substance of this second meeting was disputed, but the jury found that Hildreth gave Stearns an oral contract of employment until age fifty-five with a guaranteed salary of $85,000 per year. This contract was never reduced to writing.

Stearns resigned from Sears, moved to Maine, and became Emery-Waterhouse's director of retail sales. His employer retained Stearns in this position at $85,000 for nearly two years. In December 1986, Hildreth advised Stearns that he was being removed, but Stearns was given a different job as the national accounts manager the next day. Stearns remained in this new position at an annual salary of $68,000 for six months. Hildreth then succeeded in his efforts to acquire a national marketing firm, eliminated Stearns's position as a result, and terminated his employment before he reached age fifty-five.

Stearns eventually filed a complaint in the Superior Court for breach of contract. The court denied summary judgment based on the possibility that the employer might be estopped to assert its defense under the statute of frauds by Stearns's detrimental reliance. At trial, the court held that such an estoppel applied. The jury established the oral contract and breach by special findings and the court assigned damages in equity pursuant to Restatement (Second) of Contracts § 139. Following the denial of its post-trial motions Emery-Waterhouse brought this appeal.

The appeal presents a question of first impression in Maine: whether an employee may avoid the statute of frauds based solely upon his detrimental reliance on an employer's oral promise of continued employment. Other jurisdictions have divided on this question. Some have permitted avoidance based on theories of promissory estoppel, or part performance. Others have rejected such an avoidance as contrary to the policy of the statute, or as unsupported by sufficient evidence to verify the oral promise. Stearns contends that our case law permits him to avoid the statute of frauds under the promissory estoppel theory of section 139 of the Restatement (Second) of Contracts. We disagree.

In *Chapman v. Bomann*, we adopted promissory estoppel as a substitute for consideration, Restatement (Second) of Contracts § 90, but did not decide whether it would permit a direct avoidance of the statute of frauds. Chapman involved an oral promise to make a writing satisfying the statute of frauds that was ancillary to a contract for the sale of land. We considered whether this ancillary promise could be enforced under the equitable principle that the statute of frauds may not itself become an instrument of fraud. Focusing on the conduct of the defendant, we concluded that an actual, subjective intention to deceive can estop the operation of the statute. In addition, an oral, ancillary promise may be enforced if the circumstances show objectively that "a fraud, or a substantial injustice tantamount to a fraud" would result from strict application of the statute. Thus, although we invoked the rubric of promissory estoppel, our decision in Chapman actually applied an equitable estoppel and extended it only to an ancillary promise to make a writing.

We affirm that equitable estoppel, based upon a promisor's fraudulent conduct, can avoid application of the statute of frauds and that this principle applies to a fraudulent promise of employment. But we decline Stearn's invitation to accept promissory estoppel as permitting avoidance of the statute in employment contracts that require longer than one year to perform. Although section 139 of the Restatement may promote justice in other situations, in the employment context it contravenes the policy of the Statute to prevent fraud. It is too easy for a disgruntled former employee to allege reliance on a promise, but difficult factually to distinguish such reliance from the ordinary preparations that attend any new employment. Thus, such pre-employment actions of reliance do not properly serve the evidentiary function of the writing required by the statute. An employee who establishes an employer's fraudulent conduct by clear and convincing evidence may recover damages for deceit, or may avoid the statute of frauds and recover under an oral contract. The policy of the statute commands, however, that the focus remains upon the employer's conduct rather than upon the employee's reliance.

For similar reasons we reject the part performance doctrine as an avenue for avoidance of the statute of frauds in the employment context. We have recognized in other circumstances that a promisor's acceptance of partial performance may estop a defense under the statute on the ground of equitable fraud.

Under this doctrine, our focus has been upon the conduct of the promisor. Moreover, an employee's preparations to begin a new assignment generally convey no direct benefit to an employer so it is particularly inappropriate to remove from an employer the protections of the statute. An employee can recover for services actually performed in quantum meruit. But to enforce a multi-year employment contract an employee must produce a writing that satisfies the statute of frauds or must prove fraud on the part of the employer.

Stearns has neither alleged nor proved fraud on the part of Emery-Waterhouse. Stearns does not dispute that he was adequately compensated for the time that he actually worked. We conclude that his action for breach of contract is barred by the statute of frauds. Our holding renders it unnecessary to address the employer's other contentions on appeal.

The entry is:

Judgment vacated.

Case remanded with direction to enter judgment for the defendant. Because of the novel question presented, no costs are awarded to either party.

All concurring.

Reflection

The *Stearns* court concludes simply, "to enforce a multi-year employment contract an employee must produce a writing that satisfies the statute of frauds or must prove fraud on the part of the employer." This does not appear to be the same standard that *McIntosh* employed. The *McIntosh* court did not require a finding of fraud to enforce that employment agreement. Did both courts truly follow R2d § 139? Or is one court more accurate about the rule?

The R2d does not specially require that fraud is an element of the exception. Rather, the R2d's wording is broader: "the promise . . . is enforceable notwithstanding the Statute of Frauds if injustice can be avoided only by enforcement of the promise." While fraud by the employer can show injustice, this is not a necessary element in all cases. Thus, the *Stearns* court seems to take this doctrine further than the R2d contemplates.

Discussion

1. What are the factual distinctions between *McIntosh* and *Stearns*? Do you think these factual distinctions are sufficient to produce a different legal result?

2. The *Stearns* court seems to add a new requirement for the promissory estoppel exception to the statute of frauds, such that fraud by one party is required to prevent the statute of frauds from barring enforcement of the contract by the other. Do you agree with this addition? Explain your reasoning in terms of public policy.

Reading Sterling v. Taylor. The primary purpose of the statute of frauds is to require reliable evidence of the existence and terms of a contract. This prevents enforcement through fraud or perjury of contracts never in fact made. To accomplish this purpose, courts require a memorandum that makes successful fraud unlikely. This does not necessarily require written production of all the terms of the contract.

The memorandum may be a written contract, but any writing, formal or informal, may be sufficient. A memorandum may be a will, a notation on a check, a receipt, a pleading, or an informal letter. Neither delivery to the party to be charged nor communication of the memorandum is essential. Even a diary entry in a private ledger can serve as a memorandum for the purpose of satisfying the statute of frauds.

The case below gives an example of an insufficient memorandum. As you read the *Sterling v. Taylor* case, think about why the memorandum was not sufficient. The case also provides a thorough review and discussion of the general requisites of a memorandum that will help you better understand how the rule stated above is applied by courts.

Sterling v. Taylor
40 Cal. 4th 757 (2007)

CORRIGAN, J.

The statute of frauds provides that certain contracts "are invalid, unless they, or some note or memorandum thereof, are in writing and subscribed by the party to be charged. . . ." In this case, the Court of Appeal held that a memorandum regarding the sale of several apartment buildings was sufficient to satisfy the statute of frauds. Defendants contend the court improperly considered extrinsic evidence to resolve uncertainties in the terms identifying the seller, the property, and the price.

We reverse, but not because the court consulted extrinsic evidence. Extrinsic evidence has long been held admissible to clarify the terms of a memorandum for purposes of the statute of frauds. Statements to the contrary appear in some cases, but we disapprove them. A memorandum serves only an evidentiary function under the statute. If the writing includes the essential terms of the parties' agreement, there is no bar to the admission of relevant extrinsic evidence to explain or clarify those terms. The memorandum, viewed in light of the evidence, must be sufficient to demonstrate with reasonable certainty the terms to which the parties agreed to be bound. Here, plaintiffs attempt to enforce a price term that lacks the certainty required by the statute of frauds.

I. Factual and Procedural Background

In January 2000, defendant Lawrence Taylor and plaintiff Donald Sterling discussed the sale of three apartment buildings in Santa Monica owned by the Santa Monica Collection partnership (SMC). Defendant was a general partner in SMC. Plaintiff and defendant, both experienced real estate investors, met on March 13, 2000, and discussed a series of transactions including the purchase of the SMC properties. At this meeting, plaintiff drafted a handwritten memorandum entitled "Contract for Sale of Real Property."

The memorandum encompasses the sale of five properties; only the SMC properties are involved here. They are identified in the memorandum as "808 4th St.," "843 4th St.," and "1251 14th St.," with an aggregate price term of "approx. 10.468 × gross income[,] estimated income 1.600.000, Price $16,750.00." Although defendant had given plaintiff rent rolls showing the income from the properties, neither man brought these documents to the March 13 meeting. Plaintiff dated and initialed the memorandum as "Buyer," but the line he provided for "Seller" was left blank. Plaintiff contends the omission was inadvertent. Defendant, however, asserts he did not sign the document because he needed approval from a majority of SMC's limited partners.

On March 15, 2000, plaintiff wrote to defendant, referring to the properties by street address only, and stating "[t]his letter will confirm our contract of sale of the above buildings." The letter discussed deposits plaintiff had given to defendant and noted "our agreement that the depreciation allocation and tax benefits will be given to me no later than April 1, 2000, since I now have equitable tittle [sic]." Price terms were not mentioned. Both parties signed the letter, defendant beneath the handwritten notation "Agreed, Accepted, & Approved."

Plaintiff claims the March 13 memorandum was attached to the March 15 letter, which defendant annotated and signed in his presence. Defendant insists nothing was attached to the March 15 letter, which he did not sign until March 30. According to defendant, his signature reflected only an accommodation to acknowledge the deposits he had received from plaintiff.

On April 4, 2000, defendant sent plaintiff three formal purchase agreements with escrow instructions, identifying the properties by their legal descriptions. SMC was named as the seller and the Sterling Family Trust as the buyer. The price terms totaled $16,750,000. Defendant signed the agreements as a general partner of SMC. Plaintiff refused to sign. Defendant claims plaintiff telephoned on April 28, saying the purchase price was unacceptable.

Plaintiff asserts that after reviewing the rent rolls, he determined the actual rental income from the SMC buildings was $1,375,404, not $1,600,000 as estimated on the March 13 memorandum. Plaintiff claims he tried to have defendant correct the escrow instructions, but defendant did not return his calls. Plaintiff wanted to lower the price to $14,404,841, based on the actual rental income figure and the 10.468 multiplier noted in the memorandum.

Plaintiff did not ask for the $16,750.00 purchase price stated in the memorandum. He admits that he "accidentally left off one zero" when he wrote down that figure. Defendant also acknowledges that the price recorded on the memorandum was meant to be $16,750,000.

Defendant returned plaintiff's uncashed deposit checks on May 23. The parties conducted further negotiations in December 2000 and January 2001. Defendant provided additional rent rolls, but no agreement was reached.

In March 2001, the trustees of the Sterling Family Trust sued Taylor, SMC, and related entities, alleging breach of a written contract to sell the properties for a total price of $14,404,841. The March 13 memorandum and the March 15 letter were attached to the complaint as the "Purchase Agreement." The complaint included causes of action for breach of the implied covenant of good faith and fair dealing, specific performance, declaratory relief, an accounting, intentional misrepresentation, and imposition of a constructive trust.

Defendants sought summary judgment, claiming that no contract was formed, the alleged contract violated the statute of frauds, and plaintiffs could not prove fraud. Defendants contended the memorandum and letter did not satisfy the statute because they established no agreement on price, failed to sufficiently identify either the contracting parties or the properties, and were not signed by Taylor and Christina Development. The trial court granted summary judgment. It ruled that the price term was too uncertain to be enforced and the writings did not comply with the statute of frauds. The court also concluded that the undisputed facts disclosed neither a fraudulent intent on defendant's part nor damages to plaintiff, thus foreclosing the misrepresentation claim.

The Court of Appeal reversed as to the contract causes of action but remanded for entry of summary adjudication in defendants' favor on the fraud claim. The court held that Taylor's name and signature on the writings submitted by plaintiffs satisfied the statute of frauds. It also deemed the identification of the properties by street address sufficient, in light of extrinsic evidence specifying the city and state. Likewise, the court held that the price terms in the March 13 memorandum, while ambiguous, could be clarified by examining extrinsic evidence. It concluded that defendants' evidence raised a triable issue as to whether the parties had agreed on a formula for determining the purchase price. The court further ruled that the fraud claim failed because plaintiffs could not prove damages. Only the contract claims are at issue in this appeal.

II. Discussion

Defendants contend the Court of Appeal improperly considered extrinsic evidence to establish essential contract terms. They insist the statute of frauds requires a memorandum that, standing alone, supplies all material elements of the contract. Plaintiffs, on the other hand, argue that extrinsic evidence is routinely admitted for the purpose of determining whether memoranda comply with the statute of frauds.

Both sides of this debate find support in California case law, sometimes in the same opinion. Part A of our discussion explains that plaintiffs' view is correct. The statute of frauds does not preclude the admission of evidence in any form; it imposes a writing requirement, but not a comprehensive one. In part B, however, we conclude that defendants are nevertheless entitled to judgment. The Court of Appeal properly considered the parties' extrinsic evidence, but erroneously deemed it legally sufficient under the statute of frauds to establish the price sought by plaintiffs.

A. The Memorandum Requirement of the Statute of Frauds

The statute of frauds does not require a written contract; a "note or memorandum ... subscribed by the party to be charged" is adequate. We [in a prior case] observed that "[a] written memorandum is not identical with a written contract; it is merely evidence of it and usually does not contain all of the terms." Indeed, in most instances it is not even necessary that the parties intended the memorandum to serve a contractual purpose.

A memorandum satisfies the statute of frauds if it identifies the subject of the parties' agreement, shows that they made a contract, and states the essential contract terms with reasonable certainty. "Only the essential terms must be stated, 'details or particulars' need not [be]. What is essential depends on the agreement and its context and also on the subsequent conduct of the parties."

This court recently observed that the writing requirement of the statute of frauds

"serves only to prevent the contract from being unenforceable; it does not necessarily establish the terms of the parties' contract." Unlike the parol evidence rule, which "determines the enforceable and incontrovertible terms of an integrated written agreement," the statute of frauds "merely serve[s] an evidentiary purpose."

As the drafters of the Second Restatement of Contracts explained: "The primary purpose of the Statute is evidentiary, to require reliable evidence of the existence and terms of the contract and to prevent enforcement through fraud or perjury of contracts never in fact made. The contents of the writing must be such as to make successful fraud unlikely, but the possibility need not be excluded that some other subject matter or person than those intended will also fall within the words of the writing. Where only an evidentiary purpose is served, the requirement of a memorandum is read in the light of the dispute which arises and the admissions of the party to be charged; there is no need for evidence on points not in dispute."

Thus, when ambiguous terms in a memorandum are disputed, extrinsic evidence is admissible to resolve the uncertainty. Extrinsic evidence can also support reformation of a memorandum to correct a mistake.

Because the memorandum itself must include the essential contractual terms, it is clear that extrinsic evidence cannot supply those required terms. It can, however, be used to explain essential terms that were understood by the parties but would otherwise be unintelligible to others. Two early cases from this court demonstrate that a memorandum can satisfy the statute of frauds, even if its terms are too uncertain to be enforceable when considered by themselves.

In *Preble v. Abrahams*, a written agreement for the sale of land described the property to be sold as "forty acres of the eighty-acre tract at Biggs." The court observed: "An agreement not in writing for the sale and purchase of real estate is void. And the description of the property in the written agreement is so entirely uncertain as to render the instrument inoperative and void, unless we can go beyond the face of it to ascertain its meaning."

To give effect to the agreement, the *Preble* court relied on extrinsic evidence that another buyer had purchased one 40-acre tract and the defendant had agreed to purchase the remainder. "We think the evidence makes the subject-matter sufficiently certain, and that is all that is necessary." Professor Pomeroy says:

> It is not strictly accurate to say that the subject-matter must be absolutely certain from the writing itself, or by reference to some other writing. The true rule is, that the situation of the parties and the surrounding circumstances, when the contract was made, can be shown by parol evidence, so that the court may be placed in the position of the parties themselves; and if then the subject-matter is identified, and the terms appear reasonably certain, it is enough.

In *Brewer v. Horst and Lachmund Co.*, a contract was memorialized by two telegrams employing a form of shorthand notation so arcane that "[i]f there were nothing to look to but the telegrams, the court might find it difficult, if not impossible, to determine the nature of the contract, or that any contract was entered into between the parties." The defendant contended the telegrams were an insufficient "note or memorandum" to satisfy the statute of frauds.

The *Brewer* court disagreed, stating: "[T]he court is permitted to interpret the memorandum (consisting of the two telegrams) by the light of all the circumstances under which it was made; and if, when the court is put into possession of all the knowledge which the parties to the transaction had at the time, it can be plainly seen from the memorandum who the parties to the contract were, what the subject of the contract was, and what were its terms, then the court should not hesitate to hold the memorandum sufficient. Oral evidence may be received to show in what sense figures or abbreviations were used; and their meaning may be explained as it was understood between the parties."

Reading the telegrams "by the light of the circumstances surrounding the parties," the Brewer court concluded it was clear that they referred to a contract for the purchase of 296 bales of hops on terms understood by the parties. The facts of Brewer were adapted by the drafters of the Restatements as an illustration of a sufficient memorandum for purposes of the statute of frauds.

Despite this venerable authority, conflicting statements appear in other California cases: The sufficiency of a writing to satisfy the statute of frauds cannot be established by evidence which is extrinsic to the writing itself. The preeminent qualification of a memorandum under the statute of frauds is 'that it must contain the essential terms of the contract, expressed with such a degree of certainty that it may be understood without recourse to parol evidence to show the intention of the parties. The whole object of the statute would be frustrated if any substantive portion of the agreement could be established by parol evidence. Unless the writing, considered alone, expresses the essential terms with sufficient certainty to constitute an enforceable contract, it fails to meet the demands of the statute.

Defendants rely on these and similar cases to argue that the Court of Appeal improperly considered extrinsic evidence to determine the meaning of essential but imperfectly stated terms in the memorandum drafted by plaintiff Sterling.

To clarify the law on this point, we disapprove the statements in California cases barring consideration of extrinsic evidence to determine the sufficiency of a memorandum under the statute of frauds. The purposes of the statute are not served by such a rigid rule, which has never been a consistent feature of the common law.

Corbin observes:

> *Judicial dicta abound to the effect that the writing must contain all of the "essential terms and conditions" of the contract, and it is often said that these must be so clear as to be understood "without any aid from parol testimony." But the long course of judicial decision shows that "essential terms and conditions" is itself a term of considerable flexibility and that the courts do not in fact blind themselves by excluding parol testimony when it is a necessary aid to understanding.*

Some confusion is attributable to a failure to keep clearly in mind the purpose of the statute and the informal character of the evidence that the actual words of the statute require; some is no doubt due to differences in the attitude of the judges as to the beneficence of the statute and the wisdom of its existence. Further, there are differences in the strictness of judicial requirements as to the contents of the memorandum. It is believed that sometimes these apparent differences can be explained by the degree of doubt existing in the court's mind as to the actual making and performance of the alleged contract. The better and the more disinterested is the oral testimony offered by the plaintiff, the more convincing the corroboration that is found in the surrounding circumstances, and the more limited the disputed issue because of admissions made by the defendant, the less that should be and is required of the written memorandum.

Williston offers similar counsel:

> In determining the requisites and meaning of a "note or memorandum in writing," courts often look to the origin and fundamental purpose of the Statute of Frauds. In fact, a failure to do so will often result in a futile preoccupation with the numerous and conflicting precepts and decisions involving the clauses providing for a note or memorandum, and a corresponding failure to see the forest for the trees.

The Statute of Frauds was not enacted to afford persons a means of evading just obligations; nor was it intended to supply a cloak of immunity to hedging litigants lacking integrity; nor was it adopted to enable defendants to interpose the Statute as a bar to a contract fairly, and admittedly, made. In brief, the Statute "was intended to guard against the perils of perjury and error in the spoken word." Therefore, if after a consideration of the surrounding circumstances, the pertinent facts and all the evidence in a particular case, the court concludes that enforcement of the agreement will not subject the defendant to fraudulent claims, the purpose of the Statute will best be served by holding the note or memorandum sufficient even though it is ambiguous or incomplete.

The governing principle is: "That is certain which can be made certain." We hold that if a memorandum includes the essential terms of the parties' agreement, but the meaning of those terms is unclear, the memorandum is sufficient under the statute of frauds if extrinsic evidence clarifies the terms with reasonable certainty and the evidence as a whole demonstrates that the parties intended to be bound. Conflicts in the extrinsic evidence are for the trier of fact to resolve, but whether the evidence meets the standard of reasonable certainty is a question of law for the court.

We emphasize that a memorandum of the parties' agreement is controlling evidence under the statute of frauds. Thus, extrinsic evidence cannot be employed to prove an agreement at odds with the terms of the memorandum. This point was made in *Beazell v. Schrader*. There, the plaintiff sought to recover a 5 percent real estate broker's commission under an oral agreement. The escrow instructions, which specified a 1.25 percent commission, were the "memorandum" on which the plaintiff relied to comply with the statute.

However, he contended the instructions incorrectly reflected the parties' actual agreement, as shown by extrinsic evidence. The *Beazell* court rejected this argument, holding that under the statute of frauds, "the parol agreement of which the writing is a memorandum must be one whose terms are consistent with the terms of the memorandum." Thus, in determining whether extrinsic evidence provides the certainty required by the statute, courts must bear in mind that the evidence cannot contradict the terms of the writing.

B. The Sufficiency of This Memorandum

As noted above, it is a question of law whether a memorandum, considered in light of the circumstances surrounding its making, complies with the statute of frauds. Accordingly, the issue is generally amenable to resolution by summary judgment. We independently review the record to determine whether a triable issue of fact might defeat the statute of frauds defense in this case.

A memorandum of a contract for the sale of real property must identify the buyer, the seller, the price, and the property. Defendants contend the memorandum drafted by plaintiff Sterling fails to adequately specify the seller, the property, or the price.

The Court of Appeal correctly held that the seller and the properties were sufficiently identified. The parties themselves displayed no uncertainty as to those terms before their dispute over the price arose. It is a "cardinal rule of construction that when a contract is ambiguous or uncertain the practical construction placed upon it by the parties before any controversy arises as to its meaning affords one of the most reliable means of determining the intent of the parties." The same rule governs the interpretation of a memorandum under the statute of frauds.

The memorandum referred to "Seller Larry Taylor, & Christina Development." Defendants argue that the omission of the actual owner of the properties, SMC, is fatal. However, they do not dispute Taylor's authorization to act as SMC's agent, or his actual performance of that role. A contract made in the name of an agent may be enforced against an undisclosed principal, and extrinsic evidence is admissible to identify the principal. If a term is stated in a memorandum with sufficient certainty to be enforced, it satisfies the statute of frauds. Therefore, the reference to Taylor was adequate, regardless of the apparently mistaken inclusion of Christina Development.

Similarly, while the properties were identified in the memorandum only by street address, neither party displayed any confusion over their actual location. The purchase agreements Taylor prepared included full legal descriptions, and when Sterling received those agreements he did not object that he wanted to buy buildings on 4th and 14th Streets in Manhattan rather than Santa Monica. In any event, the better view has long been that extrinsic evidence may be consulted to locate property described in imprecise terms, even though a memorandum with a more complete description would be preferable.

As defendants forthrightly conceded in the trial court, "[t]he problem here is the price term." The Court of Appeal concluded that the lines in the memorandum stating "approx. 10.468 × gross income[,] estimated income 1.600.000, Price $16,750.00" were ambiguous, given the use of the modifier "approx." before the multiplier, the omitted zero in the price, and the uncertain meaning of "gross income." The court then considered Sterling's testimony that "approx." was meant to modify the total price, not the multiplier; that the missing zero was merely an error; and that "gross income" was used by the parties to refer to actual gross annual income. It decided that this evidence, if accepted by the trier of fact, could establish an agreement to determine the price based on a formula, which would be binding under *Carver v. Teitsworth*. In *Carver*, a bid for either a specified price or $1,000 over any higher bid was deemed sufficiently certain.

In this court, plaintiffs also cite *Cal. Lettuce Growers v. Union Sugar Co.* to show that a price term may be calculated from a formula. There, a price formula was derived from industry custom and the parties' past practice. Plaintiffs contend the parties here negotiated a 10.468 multiplier to be applied to the actual gross rental income from the buildings in March 2000, as indicated by the fact that Taylor gave Sterling rent rolls before their March 13 meeting.

The Court of Appeal erred by deeming Sterling's testimony sufficient to establish his interpretation of the memorandum for purposes of the statute of frauds. Had Taylor testified that the parties meant to leave the price open to determination based on a rental income figure that was yet to be determined, this would be a different case. Then, the "admissions of the party to be charged" might have supported a reasonably certain price term derived from a negotiated formula. Here, however, Taylor insists the price was meant to be $16,750,000, and Sterling agrees that was the number he intended to write down, underlined, as the "Price."

$16,750,000 is clearly an approximate product of the formula specified in the memorandum, applied to the income figure stated there. On the other hand, Sterling's asserted price of $14,404,841 cannot reasonably be considered an approximation of $16,750,000. It is instead an approximate product of the formula applied to an actual income figure not found in the memorandum. The writing does not include the term "actual gross income," nor does it state that the price term will vary depending on proof or later agreement regarding the actual rental income from the buildings. In effect, Sterling would employ only the first part of the price term ("approx. 10.468 × gross income") and ignore the last parts ("estimated income 1.600.000, Price $16,750.00"). He would hold Taylor to a price that is 10.468 times the actual rental income figure gleaned from the rent rolls, but only "approximately" so because of Sterling's computational errors.

Thus, two competing interpretations of the memorandum were before the court. Taylor's is consistent with the figures provided in the memorandum, requiring only the correction of the price by reference to undisputed extrinsic evidence. Sterling's price is not stated in the memorandum, and depends on extrinsic evidence in the form of his own testimony, disputed by Taylor, that the parties intended to apply the formula to actual gross rental income instead of the estimated income noted in the memorandum. Even if the trier of fact were to accept Sterling's version of the parties' negotiations, the price he seeks is not reflected in the memorandum; indeed, it is inconsistent with the price term that appears in the memorandum. Under these circumstances, we conclude the evidence is insufficient to establish Sterling's price term with the reasonable certainty required by the statute of frauds.

The statute of frauds demands written evidence that reflects the parties' mutual understanding of the essential terms of their agreement, when viewed in light of the transaction at issue and the dispute before the court. The writing requirement is intended to permit the enforcement of agreements actually reached, but "to prevent enforcement through fraud or perjury of contracts never in fact made." The sufficiency of a memorandum to fulfill this purpose may depend on the quality of the extrinsic evidence offered to explain its terms. In *Preble*, the memorandum failed to describe the property to be sold with any certainty, but extrinsic evidence established that the parties could only have been referring to the portion of a tract that was not sold to another buyer. Similarly, in *Brewer*, telegrams that were otherwise inscrutable demonstrated an ascertainable agreement when the court considered the circumstances of the transaction and the parties' understanding of the terms employed.

Here, unlike in the *Preble* and *Brewer* cases, the extrinsic evidence offered by plaintiffs is at odds with the writing, which states a specific price and does not indicate that the parties contemplated any change based on actual rental income. Therefore, the evidence is insufficient to show with reasonable certainty that the parties understood and agreed to the price alleged by plaintiffs. The price terms stated in the memorandum, considered together with the extrinsic evidence of the contemplated price, leave a degree of doubt that the statute of frauds does not tolerate. The trial court properly granted defendants summary judgment.

III. Disposition

The judgment of the Court of Appeal is reversed with directions to affirm the trial court judgment in its entirety.

Reflection

In *Sterling*, the parties disputed the purchase price, and the court found that price to be ambiguous. Later, in the chapters on contract interpretation, you will learn that courts have tools known as the Canons of Construction to resolve ambiguities in a document. Courts may also take evidence such as parties' and experts' testimonies to determine how a contract should be interpreted. You will also learn about the so-called policy canon that an unresolvable ambiguity should be construed against the drafter. All of these legal tools can be employed by courts to dis-ambiguate a contract and resolve a dispute by assessing damages for breach.

But the *Sterling* court did not engage in this interpretive activity. Instead, the court focused on the preliminary question of whether there was any enforceable contract at all. This reflects a certain jurisprudential stance. Some courts would be more apt to construe the legal meaning of the writing and thus find the contract was enforceable in this case. Yet this court chose not to imply an agreement where the parties did not expressly write out what price they would pay for a rental property. Although *Sterling* accords with principles in the R2d, a court with a different perspective could have resolved the case differently. It is important for law students and junior lawyers to recognize that, given a complex enough set of rules such as we find in contract law, courts have more freedom than might be initially apparent to uphold contracts — or not. Careless drafting puts parties at risk of judicial discretion.

Discussion

(1) Although the Statute of Frauds does not require an entire contract to be written, it does require written evidence of material terms. What are material terms in general?

(2) In *Cheever*, the trial court found that, although the contract lacked essential terms, the court could discover and imply those terms, thus making the contract enforceable. By noting that the decision was eventually reversed, can you reason why the court in *Sterling* did not take it upon itself to determine what the price term should be in that case?

Reading Howard Construction Co. v. Jeff-Cole Quarries, Inc. This case provides an in-depth discussion of the rationale for the memorandum requirement. This is a case regarding the sale of goods, so it discusses whether a contract falls with the statute of frauds because it is for a sale of goods for five hundred dollars or more. It also discusses how the UCC rule applies to the evaluation of whether a memorandum satisfies the writing requirement.

But the UCC does not itself provide the equitable exception to this writing requirement. Rather, this is another application of the common law, which applies to all contracts cases unless specifically preempted by statute. Read the case to understand why courts have this requirement to better understand when courts will find it has been satisfied.

Howard Construction Co. v. Jeff-Cole Quarries, Inc.

669 S.W.2d 221 (Mo. Ct. App. 1983)

NUGENT, J.

This case arose out of an action brought by Howard Construction Company (hereinafter "Howard Construction" or "Plaintiff") against Jeff-Cole Quarries, Inc. (hereinafter "Jeff-Cole" or "Defendant"), seeking damages on a breach of contract theory (Count I), or in the alternative, a promissory estoppel theory (Count II). The trial court granted summary judgment in favor of defendant on both Counts. Plaintiff contends on appeal that the trial court (1) erred in granting defendant's motion for summary judgment as to Count I because defendant failed to meet the burden of proof under Rule 74.04 and (2) erred in finding that the statute of frauds barred Count I of plaintiff's complaint. We affirm the judgment.

Howard Construction was the successful bidder on a Missouri Highway Department project to construct a portion of Highway 54. Before Howard Construction was awarded the contract, it received from Jeff-Cole a typewritten document entitled "Proposal" which referred to the Missouri Highway Project and listed descriptions, quantities and prices on types of rock needed for the project. The proposal contains six separate entries including a base type and asphaltic types of rock. It was dated November 21, 1972, and was signed by Harry Adrian, president of Jeff-Cole. The bid letting for the highway project took place in December, 1972, and Howard Construction was awarded the contract. Within a few weeks after the bid letting, the general superintendent of Howard Construction, Glenn Moore, met with Harry Adrian at defendant's office. The foregoing facts are not in dispute.

The parties do disagree, however, as to what occurred at that meeting. Plaintiff contends that Glenn Moore and Harry Adrian reached an oral agreement at the meeting and that Glenn Moore altered the typewritten prices on the proposal in his own handwriting to reflect the agreement that was reached. Plaintiff relies on Glenn Moore's deposition which reads as follows:

> Q: *Now, this particular document appears to have some figures written on it. Do you know anything about the various figures that are written in over the typing?*
>
> A: *Yes, sir.*
>
> Q: *What are those figures?*
>
> A: *Those is [sic] after we got the job I went to Jeff Cole's office and sat down with them. And those are the prices we came up with.*
>
> Q: *All right, when you say you sat down with them, are you talking about Roger Adrian and Harry Adrian?*
>
> A: *I'm talking about Harry Adrian.*
>
> . . . .
>
> Q: *Whose handwriting are those figures in if you know?*
>
> A: *They are mine.*
>
> Q: *You after discussion with Harry Adrian, changed —*
>
> A: *We agreed on those prices that's [sic] written in.*

Although defendant admits in its pleadings that discussions ensued between Jeff-Cole and Howard Construction, defendant denies that any agreement was ever reached in those discussions. Thus, the only disputed fact is whether the parties ever arrived at an agreement for the sale of asphaltic rock.

After the meeting between Mr. Moore and Mr. Adrian, at which the proposal was altered, Howard Construction, on January 12, 1973, mailed a purchase order to Jeff-Cole. It contained essentially the same items, quantities and prices listed on the altered proposal. The only other written document is a formal contract dated June 12, 1973, for the sale of base rock signed by agents of both parties. The subject matter of the contract, a base rock, is of the same description, quantity and price as the second entry on the altered proposal and the first entry on the purchase order. The contract, however, does not refer to any of the other types of rock which the proposal and the purchase order listed.

On appeal, Howard Construction first claims that defendant failed to meet the burden of proof under Rule 74.04 and that the trial court's grant of summary judgment was therefore in error. Howard Construction contends that a genuine issue exists as to a material fact because the parties dispute whether or not they ever entered into an agreement for the sale of asphaltic rock.

Summary judgment is authorized where, but only where, the "pleadings, depositions, and admissions on file, together with the affidavits, if any, show that there is no genuine issue as to any material fact and that any party is entitled to a judgment as a matter of law." Rule 74.04(c). (As no affidavits were filed in this case, the record before us consists of the pleadings, the three documents they incorporate [the proposal, the purchase order, and the contract], and the deposition of Glenn Moore.) The reviewing court, as well as the trial court, must view the record on a motion for summary judgment in the light most favorable to the party against whom the motion was filed, [Citations omitted]. Viewed in this light, the record indicates that the factual question whether the parties ever reached an agreement is indeed disputed.

Jeff-Cole contends, however, that summary judgment was properly granted because this dispute does not involve material facts, "i.e., those which have legal probative force as to a controlling issue." Defendant argues that the dispute over whether an agreement was reached does not involve material facts because even if the court accepts as true plaintiff's assertion that an oral agreement was reached, the statute of frauds bars enforcement of that agreement.

If the contract for the sale of asphaltic rock is indeed unenforceable because of the statute of frauds, then the issue whether the oral contract was made is not a material issue of fact which would preclude the entry of summary judgment for Jeff-Cole.

Subsections (1) and (2) of § 400.2-2014 [Missouri's adoption of the UCC] read:

> *(1) Except as otherwise provided in this section a contract for the sale of goods for the price of five hundred dollars or more is not enforceable by way of action or defense unless there is some writing sufficient to indicate that a contract for sale has been made between the parties and signed by the party against whom enforcement is sought or by his authorized agent or broker. A writing is not insufficient because it omits or incorrectly states a term agreed upon but the contract is not enforceable under this paragraph beyond the quantity of goods shown in such writing.*

> *(2) Between merchants if within a reasonable time a writing in confirmation of the contract and sufficient against the sender is received and the party receiving it has reason to know its contents, it satisfies the requirements of subsection (1) against such party unless written notice of objection to its contents is given within ten days after it is received.*

Subsection (1) sets forth the basic rules for satisfying the statute of frauds in a contract for the sale of goods for $500 or more. The Official Comment to the Uniform Commercial Code establishes "three definite and invariable requirements" as to the writing. First, the memorandum must evidence a contract for the sale of goods; second, it must be "signed," a word which includes any authentication which identifies the party to be charged; and third, the memorandum must specify a quantity.

Subsection (2) eliminates the signature requirement when both parties are merchants. If the merchant sending the confirmatory memorandum has met the requirements of the subsection and if the merchant receiving the writing does not give any notice of objection within ten days of its receipt, then the confirmatory writing need not be signed by the receiving merchant in order to satisfy the statute of frauds. Courts have, however, required that the writing be signed by the sender in order to be "sufficient against the sender." The confirmatory memorandum must also state a quantity term and must be sufficient to indicate that a contract for sale has been made. Thus, in order for a writing to satisfy the requirements of subsection (2) it must meet the basic requirements of subsection (1) except that the confirmatory memorandum under subsection (2) need not be signed by the party to be charged; only the signature of the sender is required.

The primary requirement under both subsections (1) and (2) is that the writing evidence an agreement between the parties. Although the language of the two subsections differs in that subsection (1) requires "some writing sufficient to indicate that a contract for sale has been made" and subsection (2) requires "a writing in confirmation of the contract and sufficient against the sender," courts have found that the §2-201(2) confirmatory memorandum must satisfy the "sufficient to indicate" requirement of §2-201(1).

The official comment to U.C.C. §2-201 explains that

> All that is required for a writing to sufficiently indicate that a contract for sale has been made is that the writing afford a basis for believing that the offered oral evidence rests on a real transaction.

One writer has suggested that the spirit of the comments seems to be that "sufficient to indicate" is roughly equivalent to "more probably than not." J. White, *supra*, at 62. In other words, if it is more probable than not that the writing evidences a deal between the parties, then the writing should be found sufficient.

Case law on the "sufficient to indicate" requirement arises from interpretations of both §2-201(1) and (2). Most courts have required that the writing indicate the consummation of a contract, not mere negotiations. Thus, a writing which contained language indicating a tentative agreement has been found insufficient to indicate that a contract for sale had been made. *Arcuri v. Weiss*, 184 A.2d 24, 26 (Pa. Super. 1962) (check inscribed with "tentative deposit on tentative purchase" held insufficient because it indicated no final commitment had been made). Writings which do not contain words indicating that a binding or completed transaction has occurred have been found insufficient. Some courts have required that the writings completely acknowledge the evidence of an agreement. Even those courts giving a liberal interpretation to the requirement that the writing evidence an agreement have insisted that the terms of the writing at least must allow for the inference that an agreement had been reached between the parties.

The Kansas Supreme Court, however, in *SW Engineering Co, Inc. v. Martin*, held that a mere price list afforded "a substantial basis for the belief that it rest[ed] on a real transaction." In that case, employees of the buyer and seller met and discussed the sale of a generator. The seller's employee listed the generator, various accessories, and their prices on a piece of paper on which he also handprinted his name and his company's name. The seller later refused to deliver the generator, and the buyer purchased a substitute for $27,541. The buyer sued for the difference in price, and the seller contended that the contract was unenforceable because of the statute of frauds. The Kansas Supreme Court held for the buyer and found that the writing met the statutory requirements.

The court's finding that the writing evidenced a contract has been severely criticized. That criticism stems from the fact that "[t]he memorandum before the court — on its face nothing more than a price list — was proof not of agreement, but, at most, only of negotiations." Finding such writing sufficient plants the seeds for allowing the statute of frauds to be satisfied by any evidence of mere negotiations.

While U.C.C. § 2-201 was indeed designed to eliminate much of the rigidity produced by prior interpretations of the statute of frauds, it retained some safeguards against fraudulent commercial practices. The requirement that the writing indicate that a contract for sale has been made is one of those safeguards. The words "as per our agreement," "in confirmation of," or "sold to buyer," would indicate that the parties had reached an agreement. Even the terms of the writing itself might be so specific and favorable to the party against whom the writing is offered that the court at least could draw the inference that an agreement had been reached. Such writings would deter fraudulent assertions that a contract had been agreed upon where in fact only negotiations had taken place. The price list which the Kansas Supreme Court found sufficient to indicate that a contract had been made, however, contained no such words or terms. Thus, the decision in *SW Engineering* has been criticized as one that substantially weakens the protection offered by the statute of frauds. and as a "case that may go too far."

In the case at bar, the writings are similar to the document in *SW Engineering*. We hold that they do not satisfy the requirements of U.C.C. § 2-201(1) or (2) because the writings, considered either separately or together, do not even allow for the inference that an agreement had been reached between the parties for the sale of asphaltic rock.

Although the typewritten proposal was signed by an agent of Jeff-Cole (prior to the handwritten alterations made thereon by plaintiff's agent) and states specific quantity terms, no words on the writing allow for the inference that any agreement was reached between the parties and therefore it does not by itself meet the primary requirement of either § 2-201(1) or (2). Viewed in the light most favorable to the plaintiff, the unaltered proposal could be no more than an offer by Jeff-Cole.

Assuming that the typewritten proposal was an offer, neither the alterations made on the proposal by Glenn Moore nor the purchase order sent by Howard Construction to Jeff-Cole could constitute an acceptance. Although U.C.C. § 2-207 rejects the common law mirror image rule and converts many common law counteroffers into acceptances, no contract is formed when the acceptance diverges significantly as to a material term. The handwritten alterations made by Glenn Moore on the proposal and the terms of the purchase order sent by Howard Construction to Jeff-Cole diverge significantly from the terms of the unaltered proposal — Jeff-Cole's offer. For example, Jeff-Cole's unaltered proposal lists Item No. 390-90.00, temporary surfacing, at $1.55 a ton for 150 tons. Howard Construction altered the price to $1.85 a ton. Similar alterations were made by Howard Construction as to each of the terms listed on Jeff-Cole's proposals. These price changes constitute significant divergences of material terms and therefore neither the handwritten alterations made on the typewritten proposal, nor the purchase order is an acceptance under § 2-207(1).

Because the price terms of the alterations and the purchase order radically differ from the price terms of the unaltered proposal, they could indeed constitute a counteroffer. The only writing evidencing an acceptance of this counter-offer, however, is the formal contract between Jeff-Cole and Howard Construction for the sale of base rock. That contract is void of any reference to the asphaltic types of rock which were also listed on the proposal and the purchase order. Thus, the writings when taken together do not evidence a contract for the sale of asphaltic rock. At best, they evidence negotiations for the sale of asphaltic rock and a separate and completed contract for the sale of base rock.

Although Howard Construction concedes that the handwritten alterations on the proposal were made by Glenn Moore (Howard Construction's agent) after the proposal was signed by Jeff-Cole's agent, Howard Construction appears to argue that the proposal as altered reflects an agreement reached by the parties and thus satisfies § 2-201(1). Plaintiff argues that Glenn Moore's deposition, in which he asserted that he and Harry Adrian "agreed on those prices that's written in," tends to prove that an agreement was reached. While such evidence is indeed relevant to the issue of whether an agreement was reached between the parties (and would prevent the grant of summary judgment in favor of Jeff-Cole were it not for the bar of the statute of frauds), it is not relevant to the issue of whether the writing itself reflects an agreement.

Howard Construction confuses the parol evidence rule with the statute of frauds requirements. The parol evidence rule presupposes a contract has been made and is concerned only with what the terms of that contract are. Thus, the parol evidence rule provides that a written agreement, incomplete on its face, may be supplemented or explained by testimony concerning a prior or contemporaneous agreement, if such parol evidence is consistent with the written agreement. Such evidence is inadmissible, however, in determining whether the statute of frauds requirements have been met. In fact, the major purpose of the writing requirement is to prevent claims of agreement where none has been made. The statute of frauds requirement does not presuppose that an agreement has been made as does the parol evidence rule. We thus disagree with Howard Construction's premise that Mr. Moore's statements in his deposition should be considered in determining whether the writing satisfies the statute of frauds. To permit such evidence on this issue would result in the anomalous sequence of allowing proof of an oral contract before the determination has been made that the writing itself is sufficient to remove the bar of the statute of frauds.

Thus, the determination of whether the altered proposal satisfies the statute of frauds requirement that the writing at least allow for the inference that an agreement was reached, must be made by looking solely to the writing itself. In so doing, we find that the proposal as altered by Glenn Moore's handprinted figures does not contain any terms which indicate that an agreement had been reached. The altered proposal is similar to the typewritten proposal in that neither contains terms from which the inference can be drawn that an agreement was reached between the parties. At best, the altered proposal may allow for the inference that the parties had negotiated.

Howard Construction next contends that the purchase order sent by them to Jeff-Cole is a confirmatory memorandum which meets the requirements of § 2-201(2). The requirement under § 2-201(1) that the writing evidence an agreement applies with equal force to § 2-201(2). The purchase order thus fails to meet the requirements of § 2-201(2) for the same reason that the proposal (in its typewritten and altered form) failed to meet the requirements of § 2-201(1). It does not indicate that an agreement had been made. The purchase order, like the proposal, is void of any terms on its face which indicate or would allow us to infer that an agreement was ever reached between the parties. Nor does the fact that the terms of the purchase order correspond to the terms of the altered proposal create any basis on which we can make such an inference, either. As we stated above, the altered proposal, at best, reflects nothing more than negotiations. It does not indicate that an agreement was ever reached between the parties for the sale of asphaltic rock.

None of the writings, whether analyzed separately or in conjunction with each other allows for the inference that an agreement was reached between Jeff-Cole and Howard Construction. The primary requirement under § 2-201(1) and (2) that the writing evidence a contract has thus not been satisfied. The statute of frauds therefore bars further evidence of the alleged agreement and bars enforcement of the same as a matter of law. Because the alleged oral contract for the sale of asphaltic rock is unenforceable as a matter of law under the statute of frauds, we hold that the trial court's grant of summary judgment in favor of Jeff-Cole was proper.

Howard Construction's contention that the statute of frauds should not bar Count I of its complaint because the "defendant has performed in part," is without merit. U.C.C. § 2-201(3)(c) provides:

> *(3) A contract which does not satisfy the requirements of subsection (1) but which is valid in other respects is enforceable . . .*
>
> *(c) with respect to goods for which payment has been made and accepted or which have been received and accepted. . . .*

The exception to the writing requirement in this subsection limits enforceability to the goods that the buyer has received and accepted or paid for.

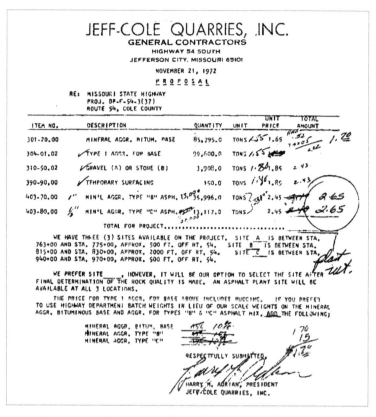

Figure 10.2. Exhibit A in Howard Const. Co.: The Proposal.

This subsection validates a divisible contract only for as much of the goods as have been delivered and paid for. Only the base rock — the subject matter of the formal contract — was delivered and paid for. No asphaltic rock — the subject matter of the alleged oral contract — was ever delivered or paid for. The delivery of the base rock can only be deemed complete performance of the parties' separate contract for the sale of base rock. Thus, the statute of frauds still bars enforcement of Howard Construction's alleged oral contract for the sale of asphaltic rock.

We do not consider whether the trial court erred in granting summary judgment in favor of defendant as to Count II because plaintiff failed to preserve the issue for appeal. Even if plaintiff's first point on appeal includes an allegation of error as to Count II, no argument was presented in the brief concerning promissory estoppel.

Accordingly, we affirm the judgment of the trial court.

All concur.

KENNARD, J., Concurring and Dissenting.

I agree with the majority that extrinsic evidence is admissible to resolve the meaning of an ambiguity in a written memorandum required by the statute of frauds as evidence of an agreement, and that conflicts in the evidence are for the trier of fact to resolve. The majority, however, goes astray when it takes it upon itself to resolve

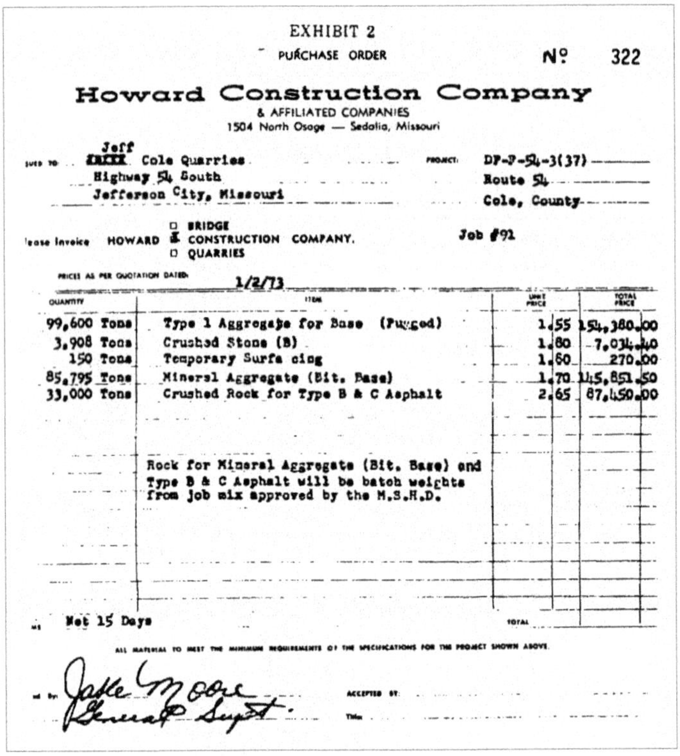

EXHIBIT 2

PURCHASE ORDER № 322

Howard Construction Company

& AFFILIATED COMPANIES
1504 North Osage — Sedalia, Missouri

Jeff Cole Quarries
Highway 54 South
Jefferson City, Missouri

PROJECT: DP-P-54-3(37)
Route 54
Cole, County

Please Invoice HOWARD ☐ BRIDGE ☒ CONSTRUCTION COMPANY. ☐ QUARRIES

Job #91

PRICES AS PER QUOTATION DATED: 1/2/73

QUANTITY	ITEM	UNIT PRICE	TOTAL PRICE
99,600 Tons	Type 1 Aggregate for Base (Pugged)	1.55	154,380.00
3,908 Tons	Crushed Stone (B)	1.80	7,034.40
150 Tons	Temporary Surfa cing	1.80	270.00
85,795 Tons	Mineral Aggregate (Bit. Base)	1.70	145,851.50
33,000 Tons	Crushed Rock for Type B & C Asphalt	2.65	87,450.00
	Rock for Mineral Aggregate (Bit. Base) and Type B & C Asphalt will be batch weights from job mix approved by the M.S.H.D.		

Net 15 Days TOTAL

ALL MATERIAL TO MEET THE MINIMUM REQUIREMENTS OF THE SPECIFICATIONS FOR THE PROJECT SHOWN ABOVE.

Jake Moore
General Supt.

ACCEPTED BY:
Title:

Figure 10.3. Exhibit B in Howard Const. Co.: The Purchase Order.

an existing conflict in the evidence. In my view, the ambiguity in the language of the memorandum at issue should be resolved by the trier of fact.

I.

In January 2000, plaintiff Donald Sterling and defendant Lawrence N. Taylor, both of whom are experienced real estate investors, discussed the proposed sale of three apartment buildings in Santa Monica owned by a partnership in which defendant was the general partner. On March 13, 2000, they met again. At the meeting, plaintiff (the prospective buyer) prepared a brief handwritten memorandum entitled "Contract for the Sale of Real Property." As relevant here, the memorandum identified properties at "808 4th St.," "843 4th St.," and "1251 14th St." This is immediately followed by "approx 10.468 × gross income [¶] estimated income 1.600.000, Price $ 16,750,000." The memorandum was initialed by plaintiff, but was not signed by defendant. Two days later, on March 15, 2000, plaintiff sent defendant a letter that confirmed the contract of sale but did not mention the price. Defendant signed the letter below the handwritten notation, "Agreed, Accepted, & Approved." The parties dispute whether the March 13 memorandum was attached to the March 15 letter.

The issue is whether the document entitled "Contract for the Sale of Real Property" is a memorandum sufficient to satisfy the statute of frauds. That statute provides that contracts for, among other things, the sale of real estate are invalid unless evidenced by a note or memorandum signed by the party to be charged. Plaintiff here claims that the memorandum meets the requirements of the statute of frauds because extrinsic evidence he offered clarifies that the agreed price was $14,404,841 — determined by applying the formula in the memorandum of multiplying the actual rent times 10.468. Plaintiff's extrinsic evidence includes the "Contract for Sale of Real Property," the letter dated March 15, 2000, confirming the buildings' sale signed by defendant, and defendant's having given plaintiff information showing the actual rent received. Defendant maintains that the price is the figure $16,750,000 expressed in the memorandum.

The trial court granted defendant's motion for summary judgment. The Court of Appeal, concluding there was a triable issue of material fact as to whether the parties had agreed to a formula for determining the purchase price, reversed.

II.

The parties' dispute here centers on whether the price description in the memorandum is ambiguous so that extrinsic evidence is admissible to clarify its meaning and satisfy the statute of frauds. Regarding price the memorandum states: "approx. 10.468 × gross income [¶] estimated income 1.600.000, Price $16,750,000." Plaintiff claims that the word "approx." modified the entire statement, not just "10.468 × gross income," and that the parties understood the term "gross income" to mean actual annual gross rental income. In other words, plaintiff's position is that the memorandum sets forth a formula for determining the actual price — 10.468 multiplied by actual annual gross rental income, which results in a price of $14,404,841 — and that the reference to "Price $16,750,000" is an estimate of the actual price, determined by application of the formula just mentioned, albeit using a somewhat inaccurate estimate of gross annual rental income. Defendant disagrees, contending that the memorandum's mention of "Price $16,750,000" reflects the actual purchase price agreed upon by the parties. Both have a point.

As the Court of Appeal observed, the language in the memorandum is ambiguous; that is, it can reasonably be read as each party proposes. To accept plaintiff's argument would give meaning to the language in the disputed statement of "10.468 × gross income [¶] estimated 1.600.000." To accept defendant's argument would give meaning to the term "Price $16,750,000." Which view should be accepted is a determination to be made by the trier of fact, based on its consideration of the extrinsic evidence presented. Either way, the trier of fact's resolution would result in a specific purchase price: one arrived at through application of a formula expressed in the memorandum, the other through acceptance of the figure $16,750,000 mentioned in the memorandum.

The majority, however, simply adopts defendant's view instead of leaving it to the trier of fact to resolve the conflict in the evidence. In accepting defendant's view, the majority rejects plaintiff's view as attempting to alter rather than explain the terms of the memorandum. I disagree.

Apparently based on its own evaluation of the evidence, which as discussed above is conflicting, the majority takes it upon itself to decide that the agreed price was

$16,750,000 and then concludes that any extrinsic evidence presented by plaintiff would be inconsistent with that figure. The majority reasons that plaintiff is looking only to the first part of the memorandum's price description of "approx. 10.468 × gross income," while ignoring the last part stating "estimated income 1.600.000, Price $16,750,000." This is both a misapprehension of plaintiff's view and a failure to appreciate that defendant's view too is not free from ambiguity.

Plaintiff's position that the memorandum sets forth a formula for determining the price does not ignore the memorandum's reference to "estimated income 1.600.000, Price $16,750,000." According to plaintiff, the memorandum's stated price is itself an estimate, for it is the product of the estimated income of 1.600.000 times 10.468, while the actual price is to be determined by using the formula 10.468 multiplied by the actual gross income, resulting in a price of $14,404,841. Defendant's view that the actual price is $16,750,000 finds support in the memorandum's mention of "Price $16,750,000" but it ignores the memorandum's formula that plaintiff relies on. Unlike the majority, I see no reason to reject plaintiff's position as a matter of law when the purchase terms in the memorandum are ambiguous and are as reasonably susceptible to plaintiff's position as to defendant's. I would leave it to the trier of fact to resolve the ambiguity.

Unlike the majority, I would affirm the judgment of the Court of Appeal.

WERDEGAR, J., concurred.

Appellants' petition for a rehearing is denied April 18, 2007. GEORGE, C.J., did not participate therein. KENNARD, J., and WERDEGAR, J., were of the opinion that the petition should be granted.

Reflection

This case involved a vigorous dissent that reflects the general debate on the statute of frauds. On the one hand, legal rules provide guidance for merchants so they can rest assured that contracts will be enforced when formalities are followed. On the other hand, equitable bases for the prevention of injustice introduce uncertainties into the commercial arrangement. There is always a balance between efficiency on the one hand and fairness on the other. The statute of frauds is meant to give courts the power to dismiss a contract claim early in the proceedings before the parties have spent much time and money in litigation. This promotes legal and judicial efficiency. But the law is not only about efficient results in general. It must also consider what is fair and right in a specific instance.

Discussion

1. The UCC makes it easier for merchants to satisfy the statute of frauds than the R2d does for ordinary people. What policy reasons might justify a rule that effectively makes it easier for merchants to enforce contracts among each other?

2. The dissent argues that the majority overreached its judicial authority where it determined what the contract itself means. According to the dissent, who should resolve such matters of factual inquiry? Why should appellate courts not resolve such inquiries?

3. Take a look at the parties' writing. What do you think they intended? Are you able to determine based on the writing what the parties intended to exchange?

———————

Reading Crabtree v. Elizabeth Arden Sales Corp. The next case demonstrates how a court might assemble various writings into a single memorandum that satisfies the statute of frauds. In the case of *Crabtree v. Elizabeth Arden Sales Corp*, below, Nate L. Crabtree accepted a sales job offer from Elizabeth Arden, a cosmetics company. The terms of employment, including matters such as base pay and commissions, were written on some payroll cards. Today, a payroll card refers to something that looks and feels like a credit or debit card; but when the case was decided in 1953, a payroll card was more like a promissory note where the employer instructed its bank how much money to transfer to an employee.

In this case, the employer's sales manager wrote and signed several cards indicating a salary increase to its employee Mr. Crabtree with the phrase "2 years to make good" written on them. When the employer refused to honor its promise to pay Mr. Crabtree his raise, he sued, and the employer defended on the basis that the contract was within the statute of frauds pursuant to the one year provision.

The company first argued that it could not perform within a year. But this argument failed. Two years to make good was a maximum, and not a minimum, so the contract could theoretically be performed within one year. Therefore, the employment contract was not within the statute of frauds.

But even if the contract was within the statute of frauds, the court found the statue was satisfied by the payroll cards. Courts will find the statute of frauds is satisfied even where a memorandum of a contract gives assurance that the contract to be enforced was in fact made and provides evidence of its terms. That memorandum may consist of several separate documents, even though not all of them are signed and even though no one of them is itself a sufficient memorandum. At least one must be signed by the party to be charged, and the documents and circumstances must be such that the documents can be read together as "some memorandum or note" of the agreement. Explicit incorporation by reference is unnecessary, but if the connection depends on evidence outside the writings, the evidence of connection must be clear and convincing.

Crabtree v. Elizabeth Arden Sales Corp.

305 N.Y. 48 (1953)

FULD, J.

In September of 1947, Nate Crabtree entered preliminary negotiations with Elizabeth Arden Sales Corporation, manufacturers and sellers of cosmetics, looking toward his employment as sales manager. Interviewed on September 26th, by Robert P. Johns, executive vice-president and general manager of the corporation, who had apprised him of the possible opening, Crabtree requested a three-year contract at $25,000 a year. Explaining that he would be giving up a secure well-paying job to take a position in an entirely new field of endeavor which he believed would take him some years to master he insisted upon an agreement for a definite term. And he repeated his desire for a contract for three years to Miss Elizabeth Arden, the corporation's president. When Miss Arden finally indicated that she was prepared to offer a two-year contract, based on an annual salary of $20,000 for the first six months, $25,000 for the second six months and $30,000 for the second year, plus expenses of $5,000 a year for each of those years, Crabtree replied that that offer was "interesting". Miss Arden thereupon had her personal secretary make this memorandum on a telephone order blank that happened to be at hand:

EMPLOYMENT AGREEMENT WITH NATE CRABTREE

Date Sept. 26-1947 6: PM
At 681-5th Ave

* * *

Begin   20000.
6 months   25000.
6 months   30000.
5000. per year
Expense money
(2 years to make good)
Arrangement with
    Mr Crabtree
  By Miss Arden
Present   Miss Arden
   Mr John
   Mr Crabtree
   Miss OLeary

A few days later, Crabtree "phoned Mr. Johns and telegraphed Miss Arden"; he accepted the "invitation to join the Arden organization", and Miss Arden wired back her "welcome". When he reported for work, a "pay-roll change" card was made up and initialed by Mr. Johns, and then forwarded to the payroll department. Reciting that it was prepared on September 30, 1947, and was to be effective as of October 22d, it specified the names of the parties, Crabtree's "Job Classification" and, in addition, contained the notation that "This employee is to be paid as follows:

First six months of employment

$20,000. per annum
Next six months of employment
25,000. per annum
After one year of employment
30,000. per annum
Approved by RPJ [initialed]"

After six months of employment, Crabtree received the scheduled increase from $20,000 to $25,000, but the further specified increase at the end of the year was not paid. Both Mr. Johns and the comptroller of the corporation, Mr. Carstens, told Crabtree that they would attempt to straighten out the matter with Miss Arden, and, with that in mind, the comptroller prepared another "pay-roll change" card, to which his signature is appended, noting that there was to be a "Salary increase" from $25,000 to $30,000 a year, "per contractual arrangements with Miss Arden". The latter, however, refused to approve the increase and, after further fruitless discussion, plaintiff left defendant's employ and commenced this action for breach of contract.

At the ensuing trial, defendant denied the existence of any agreement to employ plaintiff for two years, and further contended that, even if one had been made, the statute of frauds barred its enforcement. The trial court found against defendant on both issues and awarded plaintiff damages of about $14,000, and the Appellate Division, two justices dissenting, affirmed. Since the contract relied upon was not to be performed within a year, the primary question for decision is whether there was a memorandum of its terms, subscribed by defendant, to satisfy the statute of frauds.

Each of the two payroll cards the one initialed by defendant's general manager, the other signed by its comptroller unquestionably constitutes a memorandum under the statute. That they were not prepared or signed with the intention of evidencing the contract, or that they came into existence subsequent to its execution, is of no consequence, [Citations omitted]; it is enough, to meet the statute's demands, that they were signed with intent to authenticate the information contained therein and that such information does evidence the terms of the contract. Those two writings contain all the essential terms of the contract the parties to it, the position that plaintiff was to assume, the salary that he was to receive except that relating to the duration of plaintiff's employment. Accordingly, we must consider whether that item, the length of the contract, may be supplied by reference to the earlier unsigned office memorandum, and, if so, whether its notation, "2 years to make good", sufficiently designates a period of employment.

The statute of frauds does not require the "memorandum . . . to be in one document. It may be pieced together out of separate writings, connected with one another either expressly or by the internal evidence of subject-matter and occasion." Where each of the separate writings has been subscribed by the party to be charged, little if any difficulty is encountered. Where, however, some writings have been signed, and others have not as in the case before us there is basic disagreement as to what constitutes a sufficient connection permitting the unsigned papers to be considered as part of the statutory memorandum. The courts of some jurisdictions insist that there be a reference, of varying degrees of specificity, in the signed writing to that unsigned, and, if there is no such reference, they refuse to permit consideration of the latter in determining whether the memorandum satisfies the statute. That conclusion is based upon a construction of the statute which requires that the connection between the writings and defendant's acknowledgment of the one not subscribed, appear from examination of the papers alone, without the aid of parol evidence. The other position which has gained increasing support over the years is that a sufficient connection between the papers is established simply by a reference in them to the same subject matter or transaction. The statute is not pressed "to the extreme of a literal and rigid logic", [Citations omitted], and oral testimony is admitted to show the connection between the documents and to establish the acquiescence, of the party to be charged, to the contents of the one unsigned.

The view last expressed impresses us as the more sound, and, indeed although several of our cases appear to have gone the other way, [Citations omitted], this court has on a number of occasions approved the rule, and we now definitively adopt it, permitting the signed and unsigned writings to be read together, provided that they clearly refer to the same subject matter or transaction.

The language of the statute "Every agreement . . . is void, unless . . . some note or memorandum thereof be in writing, and subscribed by the party to be charged", Personal Property Law, § 31-does not impose the requirement that the signed acknowledgment of the contract must appear from the writings alone, unaided by oral testimony. The danger of fraud and perjury, generally attendant upon the admission of parol evidence, is at a minimum in a case such as this. None of the terms of the contract are supplied by parol. All of them must be set out in the various writings presented to the court, and at least one writing, the one establishing a contractual relationship between the parties, must bear the signature of the party to be charged, while the unsigned document must on its face refer to the same transaction as that set forth in the one that was signed. Parol evidence to portray the circumstances surrounding the making of the memorandum serves only to connect the separate documents and to show that there was assent, by the party to be charged, to the contents of the one unsigned. If that testimony does not convincingly connect the papers, or does not show assent to the unsigned paper, it is within the province of the judge to conclude, as a matter of law, that the statute has not been satisfied. True, the possibility remains that, by fraud or perjury, an agreement never in fact made may occasionally be enforced under the subject matter or transaction test. It is better to run that risk, though, than to deny enforcement to all agreements, merely because the signed document made no specific mention of the unsigned writing. As the United States Supreme Court declared, in sanctioning the admission of parol evidence to establish the connection between the signed and unsigned writings. "There may be cases in which it would be a violation of reason and common sense to ignore a reference which derives its significance from such (parol) proof. If there is ground for any doubt in the matter, the general rule should be enforced. But where there is no ground for doubt, its enforcement would aid, instead of discouraging, fraud."

Turning to the writings in the case before us the unsigned office memo, the payroll change form initialed by the general manager Johns, and the paper signed by the comptroller Carstens it is apparent, and most patently, that all three refer on their face to the same transaction. The parties, the position to be filled by plaintiff, the salary to be paid him, are all identically set forth; it is hardly possible that such detailed information could refer to another or a different agreement. Even more, the card signed by Carstens notes that it was prepared for the purpose of a "Salary increase per contractual arrangements with Miss Arden". That certainly constitutes a reference of sorts to a more comprehensive "arrangement," and parol is permissible to furnish the explanation.

The corroborative evidence of defendant's assent to the contends of the unsigned office memorandum is also convincing. Prepared by defendant's agent, Miss Arden's personal secretary, there is little likelihood that that paper was fraudulently manufactured or that defendant had not assented to its contents. Furthermore, the evidence as to the conduct of the parties at the time it was prepared persuasively demonstrates defendant's assent to its terms. Under such circumstances, the courts below were fully justified in finding that the three papers constituted the "memorandum" of their agreement within the meaning of the statute.

Nor can there be any doubt that the memorandum contains all of the essential terms of the contract. Only one term, the length of the employment, is in dispute. The September 26th office memorandum contains the notation, "2 years to make good". What purpose, other than to denote the length of the contract term, such a notation could have, is hard to imagine. Without it, the employment would be at will, [Citations omitted], and its inclusion may not be treated as meaningless or purposeless. Quite obviously, as the courts below decided, the phrase signifies that the parties agreed to a term, a certain and definite term, of two years, after which, if plaintiff did not "make good", he would be subject to discharge. And examination of other parts of the memorandum supports that construction. Throughout the writings, a scale of wages, increasing plaintiff's salary periodically, is set out; that type of arrangement is hardly consistent with the hypothesis that the employment was meant to be at will. The most that may be argued from defendant's standpoint is that "2 years to make good", is a cryptic and ambiguous statement. But, in such a case, parol evidence is admissible to explain its meaning. Having in mind the relations of the parties, the course of the negotiations and plaintiff's insistence upon security of employment, the purpose of the phrase or so the trier of the facts was warranted in finding was to grant plaintiff the tenure he desired.

The judgment should be affirmed, with costs.

Reflection

Transactions are often documented in a series of writings, not just one bound stack of paper. R2d § 132 specifically contemplates this:

> *The memorandum may consist of several writings if one of the writings is signed and the writings in the circumstances clearly indicate that they relate to the same transaction.*

This first issue to resolve where dealing with multiple writings is thus to determine whether they do indeed relate to the same transaction. In the *Crabtree* case, the transaction regarded Crabtree's employment. Salary, expenses, and benefits are all reasonably related to a party's employment. In this case, the court did not have a hard time determining that the memorandum evidencing the employment agreement consisted of several writings, since they all pertained to common employment matters.

But this analysis is not always so simple. In *Dorman v. Cohen*, 66 A.D.2d 411, , 413 N.Y.S.2d 377 (1979), industrial consultants agreed to provide services for a five-year term. That would clearly be within the stature of frauds one-year provision, so a signed writing is required. There was a writing in the form of a letter from and signed by Cohen that stipulated that Cohen would pay Dorman $1,000 a month for five years. Cohen stopped paying after less than a year, and Dorman sued.

Dorman presented a signed writing as evidence of breach. But that writing clearly stated that both parties had the right to break the agreement at any time. Under these terms, Cohen had the right to cancel, so there was no breach.

Dorman then presented a second writing, consisting of a letter Dorman sent Cohen saying, "I would not want to enter into this unless it was, as you said, over a five year period." Dorman presents this as evidence that Cohen could not break the contract. But Dorman was mistaken, because Dorman's own writing and signature are insufficient against the party to be charged because they do not show that Cohen agreed to this term. Unlike the situation in *Crabtree*, where Defendant wrote and signed all the memoranda at issue, in *Dorman*, the defendant actually refused to sign for an "unbreakable" term. In the words of the *Dorman* court:

> *To permit the unsigned document prepared by the plaintiff to serve as a portion of the requisite memorandum would open the door to evils the Statute of Frauds was designed to avoid.*

The *Dorman* court further distinguished its case from *Crabtree*:

> *The Court of Appeals [in* Crabtree*] specifically noted that the writings relied on to constitute the memorandum sufficient to satisfy the Statute of Frauds contained all of the essential terms of the contract. These writings consisted of two payroll cards of defendant, each subscribed by an officer of defendant, and an unsigned office memorandum of defendant bearing in pertinent part the notation "2 years to make good."*

It was noted respecting the subscribed writings — the two receipts — that "it is enough to meet the statute's demands, that they were signed with intent to authenticate the information contained therein and that such information does evidence the terms of the contract. Those two writings contain all of the essential terms of the contract . . . except that relating to the duration of plaintiff's employment"

The missing term was supplied by [the Crabtree*] defendant's unsigned memorandum which was viewed as clearly evincing the fact that the parties agreed to a definite term of two years after which if plaintiff did not "make good," he would be subject to discharge Thus the Court of Appeals concluded that the danger of fraud or perjury attendant upon the admission of parol evidence was at a minimum because "[none] of the terms of the contract are supplied by parol. All of them must be set out in the various writings presented to the court, and at least one writing, the one establishing a contractual relationship between the parties, must bear the signature of the party to be charged, while the unsigned document must on its face refer to the same transaction as that set forth in the one that was signed"*

In our case the two writings, one signed and one unsigned, do not set forth all of the essential terms of the contract; the signed writing does not authenticate plaintiffs' version of the contract to the effect that defendants have no right of termination; the signed writing contains information which clearly does not evidence, indeed it contradicts, the terms of the contract alleged by plaintiff, to wit, a five-year contract with no right of termination on defendants' part; and, finally, the second of the two writings was issued unilaterally by the plaintiff and is not a writing of defendant or one whose issuance was controlled by defendant in any manner.

This is an excellent illustration of the art of distinction. By factually distinguishing *Dorman* from *Crabtree*, the court justified reaching a different result.

Discussion

1. As you will soon learn, the definition of "signed" for the purposes of a memorandum that satisfies the statute of frauds is quite broad. Given the rule that multiple writings can be aggregated when they are signed by the party to be charged, is there some risk that one party incurs a contractual risk it did not expect by producing additional documentation? If so, how would this impact incentives to properly document transactions?

2. How can a court determine whether multiple documents all refer to the same transaction?

3. If one party does not want a document integrated into an existing agreement, how would you advise that party to conduct itself to avoid that liability?

Reading Barwick v. Government Employee Insurance Co. Barwick v. GEICO, below, deals with a car insurance policy that was issued over the internet. As part of the online application process, the applicant waived medical benefits coverage and electronically signed to that effect. At that time, applicable law said that medical benefits coverage could only be rejected "in writing." However, that jurisdiction had also adopted the UETA prior to the date of the application. The question is whether the online application constituted a signed writing. *Barwick* discusses the meaning of "writing" with respect to replacing the writing requirement with an electronic record or contract.

Barwick v. Government Employee Insurance Co.

2011 Ark. 128 (2011)

COURTNEY HUDSON HENRY, Associate Justice

Appellant Dustin Barwick brings this appeal from an order entered by the Benton County Circuit Court granting summary judgment and dismissing his claim for medical benefits under an automobile insurance policy issued by appellee Government Employee Insurance Co., Inc. (GEICO). For reversal, appellant contends that the circuit court erred in ruling that an electronically generated record containing an electronic signature meets the requirement that a rejection of no-fault coverage be "in writing.". . . Although this case was originally filed with the court of appeals, we assumed jurisdiction pursuant to Ark. Sup.Ct. R. 1-2(b)(1) and (6), as the appeal involves an issue of first impression and a question of statutory interpretation. We find no error and affirm.

On June 14, 2009, Lucy Sheets, who subsequently married appellant, purchased automobile insurance coverage online at GEICO's website. On January 5, 2010, a vehicle struck appellant, who was then a named insured on the policy. Appellant presented a claim to GEICO for the payment of $6284 in medical expenses that he incurred as a result of the accident. GEICO denied liability on the ground that Ms. Barwick had rejected coverage for medical benefits when she applied online for the purchase of insurance. On March 16, 2010, appellant then filed suit against GEICO, claiming entitlement to medical benefits in the sum of $5000, the minimum amount of coverage required.

In its answer to the complaint, GEICO asserted that Ms. Barwick specifically rejected coverage for medical benefits as indicated by the online application and by her electronic signature, which GEICO claimed was valid under the Uniform Electronic Transactions Act (UETA).

On April 12, 2010, appellant moved for summary judgment, contending that Ms. Barwick's electronic signature on the application did not qualify as a written rejection of coverage as required by section 23-89-203. GEICO responded with its own motion for summary judgment, in which it argued that the Arkansas Code gives legal effect to electronic records, signatures, and contracts and that Ms. Barwick's electronic signature on the form satisfied the "in writing" requirement.

In support of its motion, GEICO submitted excerpts from Ms. Barwick's deposition, and the "Arkansas Information and Option Form," completed by Ms. Barwick online. The form indicated that she rejected both medical benefits and medical-payments coverage, and it bore an electronic signature of her name. In her deposition, Ms. Barwick acknowledged that she completed the form on the website and that she did not select coverage for medical benefits. She also testified that she signed the application electronically. Ms. Barwick stated, however, that she had not physically signed any written document provided by GEICO rejecting medical-benefits coverage.

After a hearing, and upon consideration of the parties' briefs, the circuit court granted GEICO's motion for summary judgment, ruling that the online rejection of coverage and electronic signature satisfied the statutory requirement for a rejection to be in writing under section 23-89-203. Appellant filed a timely appeal from the order of summary judgment entered on August 9, 2010.

In this appeal, appellant contends that a rejection of coverage must be in writing in accordance with section 23-89-203 and that pressing a button on a computer is not a "writing" that is contemplated by the terms of the statute. Relying on the settled principle of law that a general statute does not apply when a specific one governs the subject matter, he argues that section 23-89-203, which specifically applies to insurance claims, takes precedence over the provisions in the UETA.

While appellant does not dispute that a contract may be entered into electronically pursuant to the UETA, appellant asserts that the ability to form a contract by electronic medium should not be confounded with the statutory requirement that a rejection of coverage must be in writing. In support of the circuit court's decision, GEICO asserts that section 23-89-203 and the provisions of the UETA are not in conflict and that the plain language of the UETA permits an electronic record to satisfy the requirements of section 23-89-203. In the alternative, GEICO contends that appellant should be estopped from questioning the validity of the electronic rejection of coverage because he is also seeking to benefit from the insurance policy that Ms. Barwick obtained online.

This case is before us on cross-motions for summary judgment concerning a question of statutory interpretation. A circuit court may grant summary judgment only when it is clear that there are no genuine issues of material fact to be litigated and that the party is entitled to summary judgment as a matter of law. Normally, we determine if summary judgment is proper based on whether evidentiary items presented by the moving party leave a material fact unanswered, viewing all evidence in favor of the nonmoving party. Here, however, the facts are not in dispute, and the circuit court decided the case purely as a matter of statutory interpretation.

The question of the correct application and interpretation of an Arkansas statute is a question of law, which this court decides de novo. We are not bound by the circuit court's decision; however, in the absence of a showing that the circuit court erred, its interpretation will be accepted as correct. The basic rule of statutory construction is to give effect to the intent of the General Assembly. Reviewing issues of statutory interpretation, we first construe a statute just as it reads, giving the words their ordinary and usually accepted meaning in common language. When the language of a statute is plain and unambiguous and conveys a clear and definite meaning, there is no need to resort to rules of statutory construction. Our court also strives to reconcile statutory provisions to make them consistent, harmonious, and sensible.

The coverage involved in this case is no-fault coverage that is mandated by the General Assembly to be offered to prospective insureds. Section 23-89-202 sets out the required minimum benefits that automobile liability-insurance policies must include for medical and hospital benefits, income disability benefits, and accidental death benefits. As pertinent here, the statute provides that every automobile liability-insurance policy covering any private-passenger motor vehicle issued or delivered in this state shall provide minimum medical and hospital benefits to the named insured for all reasonable and necessary expenses incurred within twenty-four months after the accident up to an aggregate of $5000 per person. However, section 23-89-203(a) states that the "named insured shall have the right to reject in writing all or any one (1) or more coverages enumerated in § 23-89-203." Thus, these statutes encompass the mandatory offering of no-fault coverage accompanied by the right to reject such coverage in writing.

Along with forty-seven other states, Arkansas adopted the UETA in 2001. The provisions of the UETA must be construed and applied to facilitate electronic transactions consistent with other applicable law; to be consistent with reasonable practices concerning electronic transactions and with the continued expansion of those practices; and to effectuate its general purpose to make uniform the law with respect to the subject of this chapter among states enacting it.

In terms of scope, the UETA applies to electronic records and electronic signatures relating to a transaction. However, it does not apply to transactions under certain articles of the Uniform Commercial Code and to those governed by a law concerning the creation and execution of wills, codicils, or testamentary trusts. Also, a transaction subject to the act is subject to other applicable substantive law. Arkansas Code Annotated section 25-32-107 provides as follows:

(a) A record or signature may not be denied legal effect or enforceability solely because it is in electronic form.

(b) A contract may not be denied legal effect or enforceability solely because an electronic record was used in its formation.

(c) If a law requires a record to be in writing, an electronic record satisfies the law.

(d) If a law requires a signature, an electronic signature satisfies the law.

As defined in the UETA, "electronic record" means a record created, generated, sent, communicated, received, or stored by electronic means. An "electronic signature" means an electronic sound, symbol, or process attached to or logically associated with a record and executed or adopted by a person with the intent to sign the record.

The issue in this case is whether an electronically generated record satisfies the requirement of section 23-89-203 that a rejection of coverage for medical benefits must be memorialized in writing. In our view, the meaning of section 25-32-107(c) could not be more straightforward when it states that "[i]f a law requires a record to be in writing, an electronic record satisfies the law." We perceive no conflict between these two statutory provisions, and they can be read harmoniously to mean that an electronic record fulfills the requirement of a written rejection of coverage. In the present case, Ms. Barwick rejected coverage for medical benefits when she completed the online application for insurance. She also expressed her intention to forego those benefits with her electronic signature. We hold that the electronic record memorializing her rejection of coverage qualifies as a written rejection of benefits under section 23-89-203. Accordingly, we affirm the circuit court's grant of summary judgment. In light of our holding, it is not necessary for us to address GEICO's estoppel argument.

Affirmed.

Reflection

Forty-seven states, the District of Columbia, Puerto Rico and the U.S Virgin Islands have all adopted the UETA. (Illinois, New York, and Washington have not adopted the UETA, but they have similar legislation.) This uniform rule has thus been highly effective at harmonizing the law regarding electronic transactions across the country. This is especially important where electronic transactions tend to be interstate due to the nature of the internet. The UETA makes electronic signatures an effective means of creating a signed memorandum.

In addition, the federal government adopted the ESIGN act, which likewise provides that electronic signatures have the same status as ink signatures under federal law. Both UETA and ESIGN have many nuances, including rules about notice and intent. But, for present purposes, the upshot is that electronic signatures generally are treated like ink signatures in the vast majority of U.S. transactions.

However, both the UETA and ESIGN Acts were enacted in the early 2000s. The internet and ecommerce have changed since then. We now have concepts like blockchain records and ring signatures. People are now starting to conduct business in the metaverse, a Web3 development in which people can meet in virtual reality. Just as UETA and ESIGN accommodated early web-based transactions and digital commerce, revisions to these rules may soon be required to clarify and harmonize the law of Web3-based transactions and virtual commerce.

Discussion

1. If you send an email that contains your name in the metadata, but you do not write you name in the email, have you "signed" the email due to the metadata that shows you sent it?

2. If you write your name at the bottom of an email, is that a signature? How might courts determine whether the sender of an email intended it to constitute a signature?

3. Are text messages "signed"?

Problems

Problem 10.1. Perpetuating Frauds

The equitable exception to the statute of frauds implicitly recognizes that the statute can sometimes create injustice. Can you think of some situations where requiring a signed writing might perpetuate fraud instead of preventing fraud? In other words, could someone use the requirement of a signed writing to defraud another? Discuss a hypothetical situation to illustrate your reasoning.

Problem 10.2. Frauds Policy

The *Stearns* court concludes simply, "to enforce a multi-year employment contract an employee must produce a writing that satisfies the statute of frauds or must prove fraud on the part of the employer." This does not appear to be the same standard that *McIntosh* or the R2d employ, in that *Stearns* seems to add a new requirement for the promissory estoppel exception to the statute of frauds, such that fraud by one party is required to prevent the statute of frauds from barring enforcement of the contract by the other. Do you agree with this addition? Explain your reasoning in terms of public policy.

Problem 10.3. UCC Frauds

The UCC makes it easier for merchants to satisfy the statute of frauds than the R2d does for ordinary people. What policy reasons might justify a rule that effectively makes it easier for merchants to enforce contracts among each other? Do you agree with this distinction for merchants? Make sure to cite the rules and describe their differences in your discussion of the policy reasons for such differences.

Problem 10.4. Text Signatures

If you send an email that contains your name in the metadata, but you do not write your name in the email, have you "signed" the email due to the metadata that shows you sent it? Likewise, are text messages "signed"? Is it even possible to "sign" a text message pursuant to the UETA?

Chapter 11

Mistake

A mistake is a belief that is not in accord with the facts, as defined in the R2d:

A mistake is a belief that is not in accord with the facts. R2d § 151.

This seemingly simple statement needs to be unpacked, because the terms have special meaning under the law.

First, what is a belief? A belief is a state of mind about the truth of something or that something exists. A belief is not a prediction about the future. For example, I may believe that you own a fertile cow, or that the stone I found is a quartz, or that the law permits me to build a home on some parcel of land. On the other hand, it is not precisely accurate to say that you "believe" a cow will become infertile next winter. Rather, you should say that you "predict" as much. One cannot hold beliefs about uncertainties about the future; therefore, one cannot make a mistake when the future turns out differently. It is technically correct and legally appropriate to describe that as a prediction that turned out to be wrong.

The second word which merits sifting through is "facts." Facts are known or can be proven to be known truths. For example, it is a fact that the world is round. Scientists have empirically and theoretically demonstrated this fact. Or a watchmaker might claim that a piece of quartz crystal cut into a specific shape and in a certain piezo-electric material to which a specific voltage is applied will oscillate 32,768 times per second. (This is how quartz watches keep the time, by the way.) If you observed that piece of quartz yet were convinced that it would oscillate much faster under those conditions, then you would have been mistaken.

You can be mistaken about legal facts. For example, you may earnestly and reasonably believe that a corporation is only allowed to raise $1.07 million dollars pursuant to Crowdfunding Regulations, but in fact the Securities and Exchange Commission recently issued a new rule that raised the limit to $5 million. If you had checked the recent press releases, perhaps you would have realized this change in the nature of the world, but while you are unaware of it, you are holding a mistaken belief regarding a legal fact.

However, you cannot be mistaken about things that are not verifiable. If John says, I feel happier today than yesterday, it is not possible that John has made a mistake. John's happiness is not something that can be proven to be true, so it cannot be a mistake, either.

The classic case of *Wood v. Boynton*, below, teaches us what is a mistake and, perhaps more importantly, what is not a mistake as defined by contract law. Ms. Wood visited Mr. Boynton's jewelry store to get a pin mended. While there, she showed him a stone she found. The stone was the size of a canary bird's egg and the color of straw. Neither party knew what kind of stone it was, but someone told Wood it was a topaz. The parties agreed to buy and sell the stone for one dollar, and they consummated the transaction on the spot. There were no other witnesses.

The stone turned out to be a valuable but uncut and thus unrecognizable diamond, and not a topaz of very small value. This is literally the story of the diamond in the rough, disguised from the casual eye. Upon learning the true nature of what she sold, Wood demanded Boynton rescind the transaction. He refused, and Wood sued Boynton to avoid the contract on the ground of mistake. These facts gave the court a perfect opportunity to discuss what is a mistake, and why a mistake did not occur here.

In common speech, we might say that Wood made a mistake in the sense she engaged in an improvident or foolish action by selling an uncut diamond. But improvidence is not how contract law defines mistake; under contract law, a mistake is a belief not in accord with the facts.

What did the parties believe here? Wood believed she had a mysterious stone of unknown value, and Boynton believed the same. Neither party knew or claimed to know the true nature of the stone. Wood did not believe she had a topaz; she only knew that she had an uncut stone that may have some value. As the *Wood* court explained:

> There is no pretense of any mistake as to the identity of the thing sold. It was produced by the plaintiff and exhibited to the vendee before the sale was made, and the thing sold was delivered to the vendee when the purchase price was paid.

Perhaps Wood was mistaken about the value of the mysterious stone. But parties typically bear the risks of their own mistakes with regards to the value of things. The value of a thing is different from the nature of a thing. Here, neither party knew the true value of the stone, and so each took the risk of paying too much or selling for too little, and each bore the potential reward of paying too little or selling for too much. When parties take risks in this manner, courts should not void the contract where one party ends up being wrong, because that would eviscerate virtually all contracts regarding things whose value is uncertain.

Wood's contract defense of mistake fails in her case. If you think this result is unfair, consider the court's analysis of what should happen if the roles were reversed: "Suppose the appellant had produced the stone, and said she had been told that it was a diamond, and she believed it was, but had no knowledge herself as to its character or value, and Mr. Boynton had given her $500 for it, could he have rescinded the sale if it had turned out to be a topaz or any other stone of very small value? Could Mr. Boynton have rescinded the sale on the ground of mistake? Clearly not."

The lesson from *Wood v. Boynton* is that the defense of mistake is narrower than common use of the term mistake might lead students to initially believe. This is yet another reminder that students of the law must make special effort to confirm the legal meaning of terms in rules and contracts, since the legal meaning can differ from the ordinary meaning in material ways. In this case, since Wood thought she was selling a stone of uncertain value, and Boynton thought he was buying a stone of uncertain value, the parties were not mistaken about the material facts of the transaction. Therefore, Wood could not avail herself of the mistake doctrine, because no mistakes were made.

Now that we have worked through the peculiar legal meaning of terms that are central to the legal analysis of a contractual mistake, let us develop the categories of mistake that are analyzed differently under the law.

Rules

A. Unilateral Mistake

A unilateral mistake is where only one party to a transaction is mistaken as to a material fact of that transaction, while the other's belief is accurate. For example, if I believe that I am the legal owner of two acres of land, where in fact I have legal rights to three acres, I am mistaken about how much land I own. If I offer to sell you "all the land I have" for a price of $200,000, and you neither know nor make any efforts to learn how much land I have, then I have made a mistake. If this mistake results in harm to me — for example, perhaps I would have sold three acres for $300,000, so I am harmed by $100,000 — then I may attempt to use the defense of unilateral mistake to avoid this contract.

Whether one will be entitled to the mistake defense, however, requires a much more thorough discussion. As should be apparent at the outset, the law should not encourage ignorance of such matters in order to give a mistaken party a second chance to get a better deal, as that would be unfair to other parties while it undermines faith in contracts generally.

Illustration of Unilateral Mistake: DePrince v. Starboard Cruise Services, Inc. The recent case of *DePrince v. Starboard Cruise Services, Inc.* illustrates a unilateral mistake. Thomas DePrince was traveling aboard a Starboard cruise ship when he visited the ship's jewelry boutique and indicated his interest in purchasing a large loose diamond. The boutique's manager called his corporate office, which in turn contacted the corporation's diamond broker in New York. The broker emailed the following prices to the corporate office, which forwarded the communication to the boutique, who then presenting this information to Mr. DePrince:

> *EC 20.64 D VVS2 GIA VG G NON selling price $235,000*
>
> *EC 20.73 E VVS2 GIA EX EX FNT selling price $245,000*

The manager, who was authorized to transact on behalf of Starboard, then agreed to sell the first stone to DePrince for $235,000. DePrince paid with his credit card, and the manager promised that Starboard would ship the stone to him. But this manager, who had never dealt with such a large diamond before, made a critical mistake.

Unbeknownst to the Starboard boutique's manager, diamond traders quote prices in per-carat terms. In this case, the first stone was 20.64 carat, and the per-carat price was $235,000, so the total price should have been $4,850,400. In other words, the manager made a four-and-a-half-million-dollar mistake.

When Starboard corporation discovered the error, it immediately notified DePrince of the error and reversed the charge to his card. But DePrince did not want his money back; rather, he wanted Starboard to keep its promise and consummate the transaction. DePrince sued Starboard to enforce the contract, and Starboard defended on the ground of unilateral mistake.

The court of appeals upheld the jury verdict that Starboard should be excused. The jury, the trial judge, and the court of appeals all agreed that the elements of unilateral mistake were met, as described in R2d § 153:

> *Where a mistake of one party at the time a contract was made as to a basic assumption on which he made the contract has a material effect on the agreed exchange of performances that is adverse to him, the contract is voidable by him if he does not bear the risk of the mistake under the rule stated in § 154, and*
>
> *(a) the effect of the mistake is such that enforcement of the contract would be unconscionable, or*
>
> *(b) the other party had reason to know of the mistake or his fault caused the mistake.*

The court did not need to focus on subparagraph (a) regarding unconscionability, because Starboard presented sufficient evidence that DePrince knew of the mistake yet kept silent about it. Key facts supporting the court's decision to grant the defense of mistake included the fact that DePrince's partner, Mr. Crawford, who was with him at the time of the sale, was a certified gemologist. This tends to show that DePrince should have known that Starboard's manager was making a mistake.

Additionally, Crawford called DePrince's sister, who was a graduate gemologist, to discuss the price. The sister advised that something was wrong because a diamond of that size should cost millions of dollars. This provided further evidence that DePrince knew of Starboard's mistake.

As for the other elements, the mistake clearly had a material impact on the transaction, where Starboard sold a diamond for one-twentieth of its value. There was nothing in the parties' contract showing that Starboard had the risk of this mistake, although a seller is typically responsible for pricing its goods correctly. But, here, a jury found that DePrince knowingly took advantage of Starboard's material mistake, and therefore, granting the defense of mistake was appropriate.

B. Mutual Mistake

A mutual mistake is where both parties share the same mistake as to a material fact of the transaction. For example, if we both believe that we are buying and selling a 2004 Dodge Ram Pickup 1500 vehicle identified by vehicle identification number (VIN) 1D7HU18D54S747050, and instead my agent inadvertently transfers a 2004 Chevrolet Tracker with VIN 2CNBJ134146900067, then we have both made the same mistake by identifying the wrong vehicle for this transaction. One of us is likely to be harmed by this. In this example, the Dodge Ram has an estimated value of $6,000, while the Chevy Tracker has an estimated value of $5,000. In this hypothetical, the buyer is likely to be harmed by over-paying for the vehicle. The party who is harmed by the mutual mistake may attempt to employ the mistake defense.

The rule governing the defense of mutual mistake is found in R2d § 152(1):

> *Where a mistake of both parties at the time a contract was made as to a basic assumption on which the contract was made has a material effect on the agreed exchange of performances, the contract is voidable by the adversely affected party unless he bears the risk of the mistake under the rule stated in § 154. R2d § 152.*

For reasons that will hopefully become more apparent as you study this chapter, courts are more likely to grant the defense of mutual mistake than of unilateral mistake. The defense of unilateral mistake requires either unconscionability or that the other party had reason to know about or caused the mistake. But the defense of mutual mistake does not require this element, making it easier to prove.

Courts still will not grant this defense where one party should have borne the risk of mistake. The rule regarding when a party bears the risk of mistake is found in R2d § 154:

> *A party bears the risk of a mistake when (a) the risk is allocated to him by agreement of the parties, or (b) he is aware, at the time the contract is made, that he has only limited knowledge with respect to the facts to which the mistake relates but treats his limited knowledge as sufficient, or (c) the risk*

is allocated to him by the court on the ground that it is reasonable in the circumstances to do so. R2d § 154.

Risk allocation by agreement occurs where the parties expressly provide who shall bear that risk. This is a question of contract interpretation, which is the subject of the module on Interpretation. For example, imagine a contract that provides A will sell Blueacre to B via a quitclaim deed. Unlike a general or special warranty deed, a quitclaim deed is a legal instrument that provides no protections for the buyer. The buyer, B, has assumed the risk that A's title to Blueacre is defective.

Conscious ignorance occurs when a party does not expressly agree to take a risk, but where that party knows his knowledge of material facts is limited, and that party assumes the risk of mistake regarding those facts. For example, imagine a contract in which C and D agree to buy and sell Greenacre. During negotiations, D, the buyer, requests to include a condition that buyer can cancel the contract if the surveyor's report is wrong, but C, the seller, refuses to include this condition. If D signs the contract without first verifying the surveyor's report, then D has accepted the risk of mistake with regards to that report.

Risks are allocated by courts where it is reasonably clear that one party should bear the risk of mistake. For example, a homebuilder who contracts to build a house generally bears the risk that the subsoil conditions are normal. Additionally, if the seller is an ordinary person and the buyer is a sophisticated and powerful corporation, such as a car dealer like CarMax Corporation, the court may determine that the powerful and knowledgeable party bears the risk of mistakes with regard to price and will refuse to grant the defense to such a powerful counterparty.

Illustration of Mutual Mistake: Sherwood v. Walker. Mutual mistake is famously illustrated by the 1887 case of *Sherwood v. Walker*, which is also known as the case of the fertile cow. Hiram Walker & Sons agreed to sell a cow named Rose 2d of Aberlone to Theodore C. Sherwood for five and a half cents per pound. Rose weighed in at 1,420 pounds, and Sherwood tendered $80 for her. But Walker refused to deliver Rose to Sherwood, and Sherwood sued for the cow.

Walker defended on the ground that the parties assumed Rose was a barren cow and would not breed. But both parties were mistaken. Rose turned out to be with calf. A fertile cow is worth ten times more than a barren cow. Therefore, Walker argued, the parties made a mutual mistake, where they thought they were transacting regarding a barren cow, but were transacting regarding a fertile cow.

Sherwood counter-argued that the parties made a contract for Rose 2d, and Rose 2d is indeed what the parties agreed to buy and sell. Whether Rose was barren or fertile was of no moment, argued Sherwood. To Sherwood, his case was analogous to *Wood v. Boynton*, where the parties transacted regarded a stone of uncertain nature, and so there was no mistake when that stone turned out to be a diamond and not a topaz.

The *Sherwood* court thus had to answer the question of whether the contract was for a barren cow, or for Rose 2d. That court determined that the contract was for a barren cow, and it reasoned as follows: "The parties would not have made the contract of sale except upon the understanding and belief that [Rose 2d] was incapable of breeding, and of no use as a cow. It is true she is now the identical animal that they thought her to be when the contract was made; there is no mistake as to the identity of the creature. Yet the mistake was not of the mere quality of the animal, but went to the very nature of the thing. A barren cow is substantially a different creature than a breeding one. There is as much difference between them for all purposes of use as there is between an ox and a cow that is capable of breeding and giving milk. If the mutual mistake had simply related to the fact whether she was with calf or not for one season, then it might have been a good sale; but the mistake affected the character of the animal for all time, and for her present and ultimate use. She was not in fact the animal, or the kind of animal, the defendants intended to sell or the plaintiff to buy. She was not a barren cow, and, if this fact had been known, there would have been no contract. The mistake affected the substance of the whole consideration, and it must be considered that there was no contract to sell or sale of the cow as she actually was. The thing sold and bought had in fact no existence. She was sold as a beef creature would be sold; she is in fact a breeding cow, and a valuable one."

Scholars have puzzled for over a century as to what distinguishes *Sherwood* from *Wood*. Even at the time, *Sherwood* included a strenuous descent. The dissenting judge would put the risk of mistake with the parties; otherwise, many such contracts could likewise be rescinded.

The dissent reasoned: "If the owner of a Hambletonian horse had speeded him, and was only able to make him go a mile in three minutes, and should sell him to another, believing that was his greatest speed, for $300, when the purchaser believed he could go much faster, and made the purchase for that sum, and a few days thereafter, under more favorable circumstances, the horse was driven a mile in 2 Minn. 13 sec., and was found to be worth $20,000, I hardly think it would be held, either at law or in equity, by any one, that the seller in such case could rescind the contract. The same legal principles apply in each case."

The dissent takes the position that promises out to be kept, and courts should be very reluctant to employ defenses, saying:

> It is not the duty of courts to destroy contracts when called upon to enforce them, after they have been legally made.

This case highlights the tensions behind the mistake defense: if contracts are easily voidable due to a mistake by one or both parties, then contracts cease to be useful devices for shifting the risk of unforeseen events or conscious ignorance.

C. Mistranscription

Mistranscriptions, also known as "scrivener's errors," occur where contracts are recorded incorrectly. For example, in a purchase and sale agreement for a house, the broker leaves off a zero, such that the sale agreement is for $100,000 instead of $1,000,000. These types of mistranscription mistakes are the easiest for courts to fix, at least where the document is easy to fix. The process of fixing a mistaken document is called reformation. Courts are generally quite willing to reform a document where the parties had an actual meeting of the minds that was simply not recorded properly. Doing so does not challenge essential principles of contract law unless some third party was harmed.

D. Reflections on Mistake

Mistakes occur when one or both parties has a belief that is not in accord with the facts. When only one party has a mistaken belief, and the other party has a correct or no belief about that matter, that is a unilateral mistake. When both parties share the same mistaken belief, that is a mutual mistake. When the mistake occurs in the final written memorialization of an agreement, that is called a Mistranscription.

Applying the mistake defense requires balancing two policies underlying contract law that can be at odds with each other. On the one hand, it seems unfair to impose a contractual obligation upon a party who entered that obligation with a mistaken belief about a material fact. On the other hand, if we allow parties to escape obligations when they make mistakes, that encourages carelessness. Unilateral mistake is especially problematic, because our society generally believes that capable people should bear the risk of their own mistakes. For this reason, the unilateral mistake defense is rarely granted.

Mutual mistake is granted somewhat more readily. When a mutual mistake occurs in the formation process, reasonable questions arise about whether mutual assent was really present. Mutual assent is a foundational element of contracting in a free society, so the lack of mutual assent strikes at the very foundation of enforceable obligations. When parties do not agree as to a fundamental point, and where neither party is at fault for this failure, a court should be inclined to void a transaction based on such a mistake. Mistranscription does not always require avoidance of the contract; in cases where there is a mere typo, the court may reform the correct to simply correct the error.

Some people will classify a misunderstanding as a type of mistake — although I believe this is a misclassification. A misunderstanding is where two people have correct beliefs about a material fact of the transaction, but those beliefs are not shared. For me, this is not a mistake at all, since a mistake is a belief that is not in accord with the facts, and as just explained, a misunderstanding is where parties have accurate beliefs that are just divergent from each other's. For example, imagine that there are two cargo ships sailing from Bombay, India, to Surrey, England, and both, ironically, are named "The Peerless." One of these "Peerless" ships is due to leave in October, while the other plans to depart in December. I bargain with you to ship some cotton on the Peerless. I am not aware that there are two ships, and, instead, I think only of the October Peerless. In this sense, I am not mistaken, as the October Peerless exists. As you bargain with me, you have in mind the December Peerless; through no fault of your own, you are not aware of any other ship. Once again, you are not mistaken, since you hold a belief that is in accord with the facts. However, we do not have the same belief. This situation, which some scholars mistakenly call a mistake, is really a failure of mutual assent. Although we manifested signs that implied we had a meeting of the minds, in fact we never did agree as to mean the same thing at the same time. The contract does not need to be excused because it never really existed. This is a misunderstanding, but not a mistake.

Fifth, still others will group misrepresentations in the same category as mistakes. Once again, I think this is inaccurate as a matter of doctrine and unhelpful as a matter of practice. As you will read in the next chapter, a misrepresentation is an assertion that is not in accord with the facts. In other words, a misrepresentation occurs when a person speaks or acts in a misleading manner. Although a misrepresentation can cause a mistake — I can have an inaccurate belief about the facts because you lied to me about those facts — it is more helpful to focus on the deception and its wrongfulness, instead of on the inaccurate belief and who bears its risk. That wrongful conduct changes the analysis, whereas the mistake doctrine is used where erroneous thinking is the result of neither party's overt fault. The next chapter will discuss such affirmative and voluntary actions that can give rise to a defense against contractual formation.

Cases

Reading Wood v. Boynton. Imagine you have a beanie baby collection that you want to sell. You don't know how much they're worth, but you go to a shop anyways. The shop owner doesn't know how much they're worth either, but you decide to sell for $20. Later you find out they were actually worth $20,000. Can you use the defense of mistake? What was your belief that was not in accord with the facts? The next case discusses a similar situation where Ms. Wood sold a stone for $1, but the stone was actually an expensive diamond.

Wood v. Boynton

64 Wis. 265 (1885)

TAYLOR, J.

This action was brought in the circuit court for Milwaukee county to recover the possession of an uncut diamond of the alleged value of $1,000. The case was tried in the circuit court and, after hearing all the evidence in the case, the learned circuit judge directed the jury to find a verdict for the defendants. The plaintiff excepted to such instruction, and, after a verdict was rendered for the defendants, moved for a new trial upon the minutes of the judge. The motion was denied, and the plaintiff duly excepted, and, after judgment was entered in favor of the defendants, appealed to this court.

The defendants are partners in the jewelry business. On the trial it appeared that on and before the 28th of December, 1883, the plaintiff was the owner of and in the possession of a small stone of the nature and value of which she was ignorant; that on that day she sold it to one of the defendants for the sum of one dollar. Afterwards it was ascertained that the stone was a rough diamond, and of the value of about $700. After learning this fact, the plaintiff tendered the defendants the one dollar, and ten cents as interest, and demanded a return of the stone to her. The defendants refused to deliver it, and therefore she commenced this action.

The plaintiff testified to the circumstances attending the sale of the stone to Mr. Samuel B. Boynton, as follows: "The first time Boynton saw that stone he was talking about buying the topaz, or whatever it is, in September or October. I went into his store to get a little pin mended, and I had it in a small box, — the pin, — a small ear-ring; . . . this stone, and a broken sleeve-button were in the box. Mr. Boynton turned to give me a check for my pin. I thought I would ask him what the stone was, and I took it out of the box and asked him to please tell me what that was. He took it in his hand and seemed some time looking at it. I told him I had been told it was a topaz, and he said it might be. He says, 'I would buy this; would you sell it?' I told him I did not know but what I would. What would it be worth? And he said he did not know; he would give me a dollar and keep it as a specimen, and I told him I would not sell it; and it was certainly pretty to look at. He asked me where I found it, and I told him in Eagle. He asked about how far out, and I said right in the village, and I went out. Afterwards, and about the 28th of December, I needed money pretty badly, and thought every dollar would help, and I took it back to Mr. Boynton and told him I had brought back the topaz, and he says, 'Well, yes; what did I offer you for it?' and I says, 'One dollar;' and he stepped to the change drawer and gave me the dollar, and I went out."

In another part of her testimony, she says: "Before I sold the stone, I had no knowledge whatever that it was a diamond. I told him that I had been advised that it was probably a topaz, and he said probably it was. The stone was about the size of a canary bird's egg, nearly the shape of an egg, — worn pointed at one end; it was nearly straw color, — a little darker." She also testified that before this action was commenced, she tendered the defendants $1.10, and demanded the return of the stone, which they refused. This is substantially all the evidence of what took place at and before the sale to the defendants, as testified to by the plaintiff herself. She produced no other witness on that point.

The evidence on the part of the defendant is not very different from the version given by the plaintiff, and certainly is not more favorable to the plaintiff. Mr. Samuel B. Boynton, the defendant to whom the stone was sold, testified that at the time he bought this stone, he had never seen an uncut diamond; had seen cut diamonds, but they are quite different from the uncut ones; "he had no idea this was a diamond, and it never entered his brain at the time." Considerable evidence was given as to what took place after the sale and purchase, but that evidence has very little if any bearing upon the main point in the case. This evidence clearly shows that the plaintiff sold the stone in question to the defendants, and delivered it to them in December, 1883, for a consideration of one dollar. The title to the stone passed by the sale and delivery to the defendants.

How has that title been divested and again vested in the plaintiff? The contention of the learned counsel for the appellant is that the title became vested in the plaintiff by the tender to the Boyntons of the purchase money, with interest, and a demand of a return of the stone to her. Unless such tender and demand revested the title in the appellant, she cannot maintain her action. The only question in the case is whether there was anything in the sale which entitled the vendor (the appellant) to rescind the sale and so revest the title in her. The only reasons we know of for rescinding a sale and revesting the title in the vendor so that he may maintain an action at law for the recovery of the possession against his vendee are (1) that the vendee was guilty of some fraud in procuring a sale to be made to him; (2) that there was a mistake made by the vendor in delivering an article which was not the article sold, — a mistake in fact as to the identity of the thing sold with the thing delivered upon the sale.

This last is not in realty a rescission of the sale made, as the thing delivered was not the thing sold, and no title ever passed to the vendee by such delivery. In this case, upon the plaintiff's own evidence, there can be no just ground for alleging that she was induced to make the sale she did by any fraud or unfair dealings on the part of Mr. Boynton. Both were entirely ignorant at the time of the character of the stone and of its intrinsic value. Mr. Boynton was not an expert in uncut diamonds, and had made no examination of the stone, except to take it in his hand and look at it before he made the offer of one dollar, which was refused at the time, and afterwards accepted without any comment or further examination made by Mr. Boynton. The appellant had the stone in her possession for a long time, and it appears from her own statement that she had made some inquiry as to its nature and qualities. If she chose to sell it without further investigation as to its intrinsic value to a person who was guilty of no fraud or unfairness which induced her to sell it for a small sum, she cannot repudiate the sale because it is afterwards ascertained that she made a bad bargain.

There is no pretense of any mistake as to the identity of the thing sold. It was produced by the plaintiff and exhibited to the vendee before the sale was made, and the thing sold was delivered to the vendee when the purchase price was paid. Suppose the appellant had produced the stone, and said she had been told that it was a diamond, and she believed it was, but had no knowledge herself as to its character or value, and Mr. Boynton had given her $500 for it, could he have rescinded the sale if it had turned out to be a topaz or any other stone of very small value? Could Mr. Boynton have rescinded the sale on the ground of mistake? Clearly not, nor could he rescind it on the ground that there had been a breach of warranty, because there was no warranty, nor could he rescind it on the ground of fraud, unless he could show that she falsely declared that she had been told it was a diamond, or, if she had been so told, still she knew it was not a diamond.

It is urged, with a good deal of earnestness, on the part of the counsel for the appellant that, because it has turned out that the stone was immensely more valuable than the parties at the time of the sale supposed it was, such fact alone is a ground for the rescission of the sale, and that fact was evidence of fraud on the part of the vendee. Whether inadequacy of price is to be received as evidence of fraud, even in a suit in equity to avoid a sale, depends upon the facts known to the parties at the time the sale is made. When this sale was made the value of the thing sold was open to the investigation of both parties, neither knew its intrinsic value, and, so far as the evidence in this case shows, both supposed that the price paid was adequate. How can fraud be predicated upon such a sale, even though after-investigation showed that the intrinsic value of the thing sold was hundreds of times greater than the price paid? It certainly shows no such fraud as would authorize the vendor to rescind the contract and bring an action at law to recover the possession of the thing sold. Whether that fact would have any influence in an action in equity to avoid the sale we need not consider.

We can find nothing in the evidence from which it could be justly inferred that Mr. Boynton, at the time he offered the plaintiff one dollar for the stone, had any knowledge of the real value of the stone, or that he entertained even a belief that the stone was a diamond. It cannot, therefore, be said that there was a suppression of knowledge on the part of the defendant as to the value of the stone which a court of equity might seize upon to avoid the sale. The following cases show that, in the absence of fraud or warranty, the value of the property sold, as compared with the price paid, is no ground for a rescission of a sale. However unfortunate the plaintiff may have been in selling this valuable stone for a mere nominal sum, she has failed entirely to make out a case either of fraud or mistake in the sale such as will entitle her to a rescission of such sale so as to recover the property sold in an action at law.

The judgment of the circuit court is affirmed.

Reflection

The *Wood* case is an introduction to what a mistake is not. In this case, there was no mistake as to the identity of the thing being sold. It might be tempting to say that

Wood and Boynton believed the stone to be a topaz when in fact it was an uncut diamond. But that is not exactly what happened in their transaction. There is no mistake as to the identity of the thing sold, because both buyer and seller exchanged a stone of uncertain value. As the court stated, "[b]oth were entirely ignorant at the time of the character of the stone and of its intrinsic value." Wood intended to sell a stone of uncertain value for $1, and that is what she indeed sold. Boynton intended to buy a stone of uncertain value for $1, and that was what he indeed bought.

As a counterfactual hypothetical, let's imagine what it would look like to have a mistake in this case. A mistake in the *Wood* case could have occurred because Wood had two stones, Stone A and Stone B. If she meant to sell Stone A, but, by accident, Wood sold stone B in the place of A, that would have been a mistake as to the identity of the thing sold. If only Wood had the intention to sell that stone, while Boynton intended to purchase any stone, that would have been Wood's unilateral mistake. If Boynton likewise intended to buy Stone A, and ended up with Stone B instead, the parties would have made a mutual mistake.

The law does provide some limited grounds for rescinding a contract on the basis of such a mutual mistake. But Wood cannot back out of a bargain because it later turns out the thing she sold of uncertain value was more valuable than she had presumed.

In deciding for Boynton, the court mainly focuses on Wood's assumption of the risk. Wood had the stone in her possession for a long time, and she made some inquiry as to its nature. She chose to sell it without further investigation into the stone's true value. Boynton was not guilty of fraud against her. Under these facts, Wood assumed the risk that the stone of uncertain value was actually quite valuable. She cannot back out of the bargain because it later turned out the thing she sold of uncertain value was in fact worth something.

Therefore, there was no mistake in this case, and Wood assumed the risk when she sold a stone of uncertain value.

Discussion

1. The court finds that there was no mistake in this case, so that defense is unavailable as a definitional matter. What is the definition of mistake and why do the circumstances in this case not reflect a mistake by either party?

2. Defenses are granted to ensure that contract law does not create injustice. What injustice does the plaintiff seek to remedy by avoiding the contract? Why does the court determine that it is not unjust to enforce the contract?

3. Neither of the parties in this case was an expert in gemology. Did this lack of expertise seem to impact the court's decision? Should courts consider whether a party is an expert or not in determining whether there has been a mistake?

> *Reading DePrince v. Starboard Cruise Services, Inc.* As previously stated, a mistake is a belief that is not in accord with the facts. A unilateral mistake occurs when a mistake of one party at the time a contract was made as to a basic assumption on which he made the contract has a material effect on the agreed exchange of performances that is adverse to him. The contract is voidable by him if he does not bear the risk of the mistake. This next case focuses on who bears that risk of mistake.

DePrince v. Starboard Cruise Services, Inc.

271 So. 3d 11 (Fla. 3d Dist. App. 2018)

LUCK, J.

[On February 11, 2013, Thomas DePrince, a passenger aboard a cruise ship, visited the ship's jewelry boutique, operated by Starboard, where he indicated his interest in purchasing a fifteen to twenty carat loose diamond. DePrince specified he wanted an emerald cut, high quality, color D, E, or F diamond with a G.I.A. certificate. The shipboard jewelry store did not have such a diamond, so the store's manager, Mr. Rusan, e-mailed Starboard's corporate office.

The corporate office reached out to Starboard's diamond vendor in California. The vendor in California then called a diamond broker in New York for its available inventory. The diamond broker then sent a list of diamonds available with the desired specifications. The list provided a per-carat price and net price for each diamond. The vendor in California then selected two diamonds from the inventory listing and electronically mailed the corporate office the following information:

> *These prices are ship sailing prices based on the lowest tier diamond margin we have. Let me know if you have any questions.*
>
> *EC 20.64 D VVS2 GIA VG G NON selling price $235,000*
>
> *EC 20.73 E VVS2 GIA EX EX FNT selling price $245,000*

The corporate office forwarded this information back to the ship. Mr. Rusan presented the information to DePrince and his partner, Mr. Crawford.

Neither the contact or the corporate office nor Mr. Rusan had ever sold a large loose diamond before and did not realize that the quoted price was per carat. Mr. Crawford, who was a certified gemologist, asked the opinion of DePrince's sister, a graduate gemologist. The sister warned that something was not right because the price for a diamond of that size should be in the millions and recommended not buying the diamond.

Disregarding his sister's advice, DePrince contracted with Starboard to purchase the 20.64 carat diamond for the quoted $235,000 price, paying with his American

Express credit card. Starboard discovered that the $235,000 price was per carat and immediately notified DePrince of the error and reversed the charges to his credit card.

DePrince then filed a complaint seeking to enforce the parties' contract.

The trial court initially granted summary judgment in favor of Starboard on June 20, 2014, based on Starboard's defense of unilateral mistake. The trial court used a "four-prong test to establish unilateral mistake." The court held that in order to rescind an otherwise-valid contract based on a unilateral mistake, the party seeking to avoid the contract must show:

(1) The mistake was induced by the party seeking to benefit from the mistake

(2) There is no negligence or want of due care on the part of the party seeking to return to the status quo

(3) Denial of release from the agreement would be inequitable, and

(4) The position of the opposing party has not so changed that granting the relief would be unjust.

The court concluded that there was a genuine issue of material fact on the inducement prong because "knowledge of an error is markedly different than inducement of that error." As an example of inducement, the court quoted the test for fraudulent inducement, and explained:

We do not hold that the burden to establish inducement for purposes of the first prong of a unilateral mistake defense is the same as proving the elements for a fraudulent inducement defense, but merely use fraudulent inducement by way of example to demonstrate that inducement requires some type of action, not mere knowledge. In fact, the burden of proof cannot be the same because such a requirement would render the unilateral mistake of fact defense completely obsolete by requiring a party seeking to avoid a contract on that basis to prove fraudulent inducement, which is itself sufficient to render a contract voidable by the aggrieved party.

The court also concluded that there was a genuine issue of material fact on the negligence prong. "[W]hether Starboard made a reasonable and understandable mistake or acted negligently in its handling of the sale is a disputed issue of fact." Based on this, the court reversed the summary judgment for Starboard and remanded for further proceedings because there remained genuine issues of material fact to be resolved.

The case went to trial on April 4, 2016, on DePrince's claim for breach of contract and Starboard's defense of unilateral mistake. The parties did not dispute that they entered into an agreement; the only issue was whether Starboard was excused from that agreement because it made a unilateral mistake.

The trial court instructed the jury on the elements of the unilateral mistake affirmative defense, including inducement: "To establish this defense Starboard must prove . . . the mistake was induced by the party, here Mr. DePrince, seeking to benefit from the mistake. Inducement may occur through misrepresentations, statements or omissions which cause the contracting party to enter into a transaction."

The jury found that Starboard should be excused from performing under the contract because it committed a unilateral mistake. The trial court denied DePrince's motion for directed verdict on the unilateral mistake affirmative defense and entered judgment for Starboard consistent with the jury's verdict.

The case was remanded for a new trial because the trial court's jury instruction on inducement prong of the unilateral mistake test was inconsistent. The trial court defined inducement to include DePrince's omission of information about the price of the diamond, even though inducement had previously been defined as "some type of action, not mere knowledge."

The District Court of Appeal held that inducement is not an element of a unilateral mistake defense to enforce a contract, that the jury was property instructed on the element of unilateral mistake and that sufficient evidence supported the jury's finding that all required elements for rescission of a contract on the basis of unilateral mistake had been met.]

Reflection

A unilateral mistake occurs when a mistake of one party at the time a contract was made as to a basic assumption on which he made the contract has a material effect on the agreed exchange of performances that is adverse to him.

In this case, Starboard made a mistake by not realizing that the quoted price of the diamond was per carat, not for the entire diamond. Starboard sold the diamond to DePrince for less than a twentieth of the actual cost of the diamond. The price of the diamond is fundamental to the contract and materially affects the agreed exchange of performances. Had Starboard not made this mistake, they never would have agreed to sell the uncut diamond for that price. In this case, Starboard, the party who made the mistake, bears the brunt of the mistake. Starboard sold the uncut diamond for less than a twentieth of the actual cost and is therefore responsible for the difference in the cost.

Starboard is a great example of a unilateral mistake. Starboard made a mistake as to a basic assumption on which the contract was made that materially affected the agreed exchange of performances and adversely affected the seller, the party that made the mistake.

Discussion

1. Generally, the party seeking to avoid a contract on the grounds of mistake is the party making the mistake. In *DePrince*, Starboard Cruise Services is looking to avoid the contract. What is Starboard's mistake? Evaluate this purported mistake based on the R2d's definition of "mistake" and confirm whether this is a mistake for which the law can grant a remedy.

2. Mistakes are only actionable where they relate to a material aspect of the transaction. Was the mistake in *DePrince* material? Explain.

3. A party only merits the defense of mistake where it did not bear the risk of mistake. Did Starboard bear the risk of its mistake in this case? Why or why not?

Reading Sherwood v. Walker. The following case of the barren cow is perhaps the most famous case in the history of the mistake doctrine. The facts of *Sherwood* are that the defendant (Walkers) was in the business of importing and breeding polled Angus cattle. The plaintiff (Sherwood) was a banker and wanted to purchase some of their stock but could find none that suited him. Later, he met with one of the defendants and was informed that the cows he was about to look at were probably barren and would not breed. When the cow turned out the be fertile, the economics of the deal turned out to be different. The question became, can one party avoid the deal, given the mutual mistake about the nature of the cow?

Sherwood v. Walker

66 Mich. 568 (1887)

MORSE, J.

Replevin [procedure where seized goods can be returned to the owner dependent on the lawsuit] for a cow. Suit commenced in justice's court; judgment for plaintiff; appealed to circuit court of Wayne county, and verdict and judgment for plaintiff in that court. The defendants bring error, and set out 25 assignments of the same. . . . It appears from the record that both parties supposed this cow was barren and would not breed, and she was sold by the pound for an insignificant sum as compared with her real value if a breeder. She was evidently sold and purchased on the relation of her value for beef, unless the plaintiff had learned of her true condition, and concealed such knowledge from the defendants. Before the plaintiff secured the possession of the animal, the defendants learned that she was with calf, and therefore of great value, and undertook to rescind the sale by refusing to deliver her.

The question arises whether they had a right to do so. The circuit judge ruled that this fact did not avoid the sale and it made no difference whether she was barren or not. I am of the opinion that the court erred in this holding. I know that this is a close question, and the dividing line between the adjudicated cases is not easily discerned. But it must be considered as well settled that a party who has given an apparent consent to a contract of sale may refuse to execute it, or he may avoid it after it has been completed, if the assent was founded, or the contract made, upon the mistake of a material fact, — such as the subject-matter of the sale, the price, or some collateral fact materially inducing the agreement; and this can be done when the mistake is mutual.

If there is a difference or misapprehension as to the substance of the thing bargained for; if the thing actually delivered or received is different in substance from the thing bargained for, and intended to be sold, — then there is no contract; but if it be only a difference in some quality or accident, even though the mistake may have been the actuating motive to the purchaser or seller, or both of them, yet the contract remains binding. "The difficulty in every case is to determine whether the mistake or misapprehension is as to the substance of the whole contract, going, as it were, to the root of the matter, or only to some point, even though a material point, an error as to which does not affect the substance of the whole consideration." It has been held, in accordance with the principles above stated, that where a horse is bought under the belief that he is sound, and both vendor and vendee honestly believe him to be sound, the purchaser must stand by his bargain, and pay the full price, unless there was a warranty.

It seems to me, however, in the case made by this record, that the mistake or misapprehension of the parties went to the whole substance of the agreement. If the cow was a breeder, she was worth at least $750; if barren, she was worth not over $80. The parties would not have made the contract of sale except upon the understanding and belief that she was incapable of breeding, and of no use as a cow.

It is true she is now the identical animal that they thought her to be when the contract was made; there is no mistake as to the identity of the creature. Yet the mistake was not of the mere quality of the animal, but went to the very nature of the thing. A barren cow is substantially a different creature than a breeding one. There is as much difference between them for all purposes of use as there is between an ox and a cow that is capable of breeding and giving milk. If the mutual mistake had simply related to the fact whether she was with calf or not for one season, then it might have been a good sale, but the mistake affected the character of the animal for all time, and for its present and ultimate use. She was not in fact the animal, or the kind of animal, the defendants intended to sell or the plaintiff to buy. She was not a barren cow, and, if this fact had been known, there would have been no contract.

The mistake affected the substance of the whole consideration, and it must be considered that there was no contract to sell or sale of the cow as she actually was. The thing sold and bought had in fact no existence. She was sold as a beef creature would be sold; she is in fact a breeding cow, and a valuable one. The court should have instructed the jury that if they found that the cow was sold, or contracted to be sold, upon the understanding of both parties that she was barren, and useless for the purpose of breeding, and that in fact she was not barren, but capable of breeding, then the defendants had a right to rescind, and to refuse to deliver, and the verdict should be in their favor.

The judgment of the court below must be reversed, and a new trial granted, with costs of this court to defendants.

Reflection

Sherwood demonstrates a way to determine whether there is a mutual mistake between parties. This court expands on the rule for mistake that was established in *Wood*. Recall that in *Wood*, the parties were found not to be mistaken as to the nature of the thing sold, namely, a stone of uncertain value. In *Sherwood*, there is no mistake as to the identity of the creature: it is the same cow. Yet the *Sherwood* court looks to the nature of the cow. If mutual assent to a bargain was made upon the mutual mistake of a material fact (such as the subject matter of the sale or the price) that materially induced the agreement, then the contract is void. The mistake must go to the substance of the contract, and this is where the difficulty arises under the rule in *Sherwood*.

The court held that a barren cow was not just a quality of the animal but went to the very nature of the thing. "A barren cow is substantially a different creature than a breeding one." The court also believed that the parties would not have contracted for the sale except on the understanding and belief that the cow was incapable of breeding. "The mistake affected the character of the animal for all time, and for its present and ultimate use." The cow would have been sold for around $750 if not barren, as opposed to the $80, and this went to the substance of the whole agreement.

The court's distinction between whether the mistake went to the substance of the contract or to its quality can be confusing since what affects its value also affects its consideration. R2d's rule on mutual mistake makes less of a distinction and instead states that the mistake must have been "as to a basic assumption on which the contract was made" and that it had a material effect.

Discussion

1. In *Wood*, the court found there was no mistake; in *Sherwood*, the court found there was. Can you distinguish the cases on their facts such that you can apply the same rule and arrive at different results?

2. In a case regarding the purchase and sale of a farm animal, who should bear the risk of mistake that the animal is not as expected, the rancher or the purchaser?

3. Orthodox Jews only eat meat from cows whose lungs do not have blemishes. Such blemishes are only observable after slaughtering the animal. If a rancher sells to a Jewish butcher a cow that both believe to be unblemished (*glatt*), but the cow turns out to have lesions in its lungs, is this a mistake? Is this a mistake that merits avoidance of the contract?

Problems

Problem 11.1. **A Mistaken Dream**

After landing her dream job, Lauren decided to buy herself a car to celebrate. Lauren did months of online research before she went to a used car lot to look at the cars in person.

Lauren had decided that she wanted to purchase a used Volkswagen Beetle listed for $4,700 at Trevor's Used Car Dealership. Based on her research, Lauren knew that a used Volkswagen Beetle with approximately 50,000 miles should cost closer to $10,000 than $5,000.

Kierstin had just started working at Trevor's Used Car Dealership three days before Lauren arrived at the dealership to look at used cars. Kierstin's boss sent her an email that listed the prices of all the new cars on the lot that Kierstin needed to tag. Kierstin had misread the email and mislabeled the cars. The $4,700 price tag was supposed to be placed on the Volkswagen Passat with almost 100,000 miles that was parked next to the Beetle.

Lauren moved forward with purchasing the Beetle from Trevor's Used Car Dealership even though she knew that the car should be sold for nearly $5,000 more than it was listed. Kierstin drew up all the paperwork, and she and Lauren entered a contract for the sale of the car.

Kierstin's boss, Shannon, arrived at the dealership later that afternoon and while reviewing the paperwork, realized that Kierstin had listed the car at the wrong price and immediately called Lauren to rectify the error.

Is the contract for the sale of the Volkswagen Beetle voidable based on the theory of unilateral mistake?

Problem 11.2. **A Foundational Mistake**

In the summer of 1995, Jesse and Barbara Darnell expressed an interest in buying a home from Magdalene Myers. They both made preparations to sell and purchase the house. The Darnells received a copy of the Seller's Disclosure of Real Property Condition Report ("Seller's Disclosure"). In it, Myers answered that she was not aware of "any water leakage, accumulation, or dampness within the basement or crawl space." She also answered that there were not "any repairs or other attempts to control any water or dampness problem in the basement or crawl space."

The Darnells and Myers met to negotiate the price, and Myers brought, unsolicited, a handwritten list of amenities. The list included a "[n]ew pump in crawl space to remove whatever water comes in when we have a hard rain." The Darnells did not end negotiations, because they believed that water only came in through the crawl space after a hard rain and that it normally wasn't a problem because the sump pump prevented accumulation. The parties agreed on a price.

The Darnells had the home inspected, and the inspector noticed a "moisture problem" in the crawl space that should be fixed. The Darnells put all of their money into the house and decided to forgo the repairs for another year, which the inspector thought would be fine. In the inspector's report, the "Structural" section indicated the moisture as a "major deficiency," but it did not indicate the intensity of the water problem or whether the moisture had caused any actual damage to the structure of the house. The crawl space was not readily accessible, and a pre-printed paragraph stated: "If there is an inaccessible basement or crawl space, there is a possibility that past or present . . . rot exists in this area. Since no visual inspection can be made, it is not possible to make a determination of this damage if it exists."

The Darnells read the contradictory report and signed an agreement of sale with no renegotiation because of the crawl space or moisture. The day after they moved in, the Darnells noticed water problems underneath a carpet on the first floor. They called someone to do another inspection and discovered that the structural framing in the crawl space was so severely deteriorated from water that three-quarters of the structural members were no longer capable of holding up the house. They were advised to leave the house and have not been able to return since. The Darnells sued Myers for rescission of the agreement of sale and argued, among others, the defense of mistake.

Under R2d, what is the mistake and what type of mistake should the Darnells argue for in court? Under R2d, do the Darnells have a viable defense of mistake?

See Darnell v. Myers, 1998 WL 294012 (Del. Ch. 1998).

Problem 11.3. **A Policy Mistake**

OneBeacon America Insurance Company and Pennsylvania General Insurance Company (collectively, "OneBeacon") issued a car insurance policy to Leasing Associates, Inc. and LAI Trust (collectively "LAI"), a vehicle leasing agency. LAI then leased a vehicle insured under this policy to Capform, Inc., which had its own insurance coverage from Travelers. Capform, Inc. drove the vehicle negligently and struck a pedestrian in an accident that resulted in a vehicle liability suit that Capform settled for $1,000,000, which is the limit under the OneBeacon insurance policy. Citing the OneBeacon/LAI policy, Capform demanded that OneBeacon reimburse Travelers $1,000,000, the policy's limit. The OneBeacon/LAI policy defines an "insured" to include:

> a. *You for any covered auto.*

> b. *Anyone else while using with your permission a covered auto you own.*

Although OneBeacon acknowledges that this language may be read to extend coverage to LAI's lessees, it says that neither it nor LAI intended that coverage. Accordingly, OneBeacon asked the district court to reform the policy in light of "mutual mistake." OneBeacon asked the court to reform the insurance policy to match the parties' intent that it would cover only those lessees who had specifically applied for, and been approved for, coverage under the OneBeacon policy.

Is OneBeacon entitled to reform the insurance policy due to a scrivener's errors (mistranscription mistake)?

See OneBeacon Am. Ins. Co. v. Travelers Indem. Co., 465 F.3d 38 (1st Cir. 2006)

Chapter 12

Misrepresentation, Duress, and Undue Influence

Contract law is based on free will; that is, parties should be liable for contractual promises that were freely made. This is often referred to as "private ordering" or "freedom of contract." By that same logic, parties likewise should not be liable for contracts they did not freely make. This module is really about this "freedom from contract." When a party has seemingly manifested an intention to be bound by contractual terms, but that manifestation was predicated on fraud or coerced by threat, there may not be any true intention to be bound.

To put it another way, contract law is predicated on the presumption that the bargaining process is authentic. This presumption fails to hold true in two main situations. First, when a party is induced to make a contract by a misinterpretation (an assertion that is not in accord with the facts), that party may have the right to void the contract. You may recall from the prior chapter that a mistake is a belief that is not in accord with the facts. When such a mistake by one party occurs because of the other party's assertion that is not in accord with the facts, the aggrieved party generally argues for the stronger defense of misrepresentation, as opposed to the relatively weak and rarely granted defense of mutual mistake.

For example, in the case of *Wood v. Boynton*, the seller of a pretty stone mistakenly thought it was a topaz when it fact it was a diamond. She was unable to use the defense of mistake to void the contract, because both parties had assumed the pretty stone was of an uncertain nature, so no mistake had really been made. But what if the buyer had told the seller that the buyer was a gemologist (an expert in the nature of stones) and further told the seller that the stone was a topaz? In this case, the seller could attempt to employ the stronger defense of misrepresentation in her effort to void the contract, and she would have a greater chance of prevailing under this set of facts than the actual case where the buyer did not make an assertion about the nature of the stone.

The case for avoiding a contract is even stronger where one party coerced the other's nominal assent through duress. Duress includes improper threats and physical compulsion, such that one party has no reasonable alternative to manifesting assent. For example, if E says to F, "Sign this contract promising to sell me Blackacre for $100 or I will shoot you dead right here and now," then F's signature on that contract does not reflect F's manifestation of intent to be bound. Rather, it reflects F's desire not to be murdered. Such coerced assent should be deemed invalid.

When the parties are in a special relationship of trust, such that one party has power over the other, we characterize such coercion as undue influence. While the behaviors involved in duress and undue influence are similar, undue influence may allow a party to avoid a contract that does not rise to the level of physical compulsion or improper economic threat. The reason for the lower standard of bad conduct required for the undue influence defense is because the special relationship of trust or power creates a duty for the trusted or powerful party to act with greater case toward the less powerful one.

What ties all the defenses in this chapter together is that they all evidence a lack of mutual assent. Remember that judges are not mindless wooden sticks, and the law is not some dull mechanical instrument. Lawyers must be prepared to look beyond the superficial appearance of things and to make arguments that in actuality the assumptions that underpin contractual obligations are missing in certain cases.

Rules

A. Misrepresentation

> *A misrepresentation is an assertion that is not in accord with the facts.*
> R2d § 159.

Misrepresentation commonly takes the form of spoken or written words, but misrepresentation can also stem from actions or even from inaction where there is some duty to act or speak. A misrepresentation is any assertion that is not true. And an assertion, in turn, is communication, as defined in Black's Law Dictionary:

> *Assertion. A person's speaking, writing, acting, or failing to act with the intent of expressing a fact or opinion; the act or an instance of engaging in communicative behavior.*

A misrepresentation is therefore any false communication. But not every misrepresentation is ground for avoiding a contract. A misrepresentation must be either fraudulent or material to be ground for avoiding a contract.

1. Fraudulent Misrepresentation

Fraudulent misrepresentations, which occur when a party deliberately intends a false assertion to induce the other party to manifest assent to a bargain, are perhaps the most intuitive form of misrepresentation.

> *A misrepresentation is fraudulent if the maker intends his assertion to induce a party to manifest his assent and the maker (a) knows or believes that the assertion is not in accord with the facts, or (b) does not have the confidence that he states or implies in the truth of the assertion, or (c) knows that he does not have the basis that he states or implies for the assertion. R2d § 162(1).*

The hallmarks of a fraudulent misrepresentation under contract law are statements that are both consciously false and intended to mislead another. This knowing deception is described by courts as "scienter." This term derives for the Latin verb *sciō*, meaning "know." The English term science comes from the same root: *scientia* is Latin for "knowledge." The modern legal usage of term scienter indicates knowledge of wrongdoing, and that knowledge of wrongdoing is at the heart of fraud.

2. Material Misrepresentation

A misrepresentation does not have to be fraudulent to be ground for avoiding a contract. And innocent misrepresentation can support a defense, provided that misrepresentation is material:

> *A misrepresentation is material if it would be likely to induce a reasonable person to manifest his assent, or if the maker knows that it would be likely to induce the recipient to do so.* R2d § 162(2).

As a reminder, a misrepresentation is any false communication, whether the speaker or writer intended to deceive or not. If deception was not intended — if there is no scienter — then the question is whether the misrepresentation is material.

For example, if Ivan honestly published an advertisement to sell "one genuine authentic original Babe Ruth rookie card," because that is what Ivan thought he owned; if James agreed to purchase it for $7,000; and if the card turns out to be a fake or a reprint; then, Ivan has made a misrepresentation whether or not he believed the card to be authentic.

If Ivan was unaware, his misrepresentation is ground for James to refuse to pay for the card, and thus avoid the contract, if Ivan's misrepresentation concerns a material aspect of the transition. In the case of a Babe Ruth rookie card, the authenticity of the card is material because it is core to the value of the card. James would not have paid $7,000 for a reprint. When a party would not have agreed to the contract but for the misrepresentation, then that misrepresentation is material.

As you might imagine, courts are more willing to void a contract based on the defense of fraudulent misrepresentation than on innocent misrepresentation; in fact, an innocent misrepresentation must be material if it is to be used as a defense against contract enforcement.

Proving fraud is difficult, because it requires the aggrieved party to prove by a preponderance of the evidence in a court of law that the other party knew or believed its assertion was not in accord with the facts and intended that assertion to mislead the aggrieved party into making the contract. This scienter can be difficult to prove, because subjective states of mind can be difficult for courts to probe. This is why contract law generally does not concern itself with subjective or hidden intentions. And the law recognizes that parties do not always keep records of their knowledge, especially where they are making assertions that do not comport with this knowledge. For these and other reasons, parties who seek to avoid a contract based on the misrepresentation defense often plead material misrepresentation in addition to fraudulent misrepresentation.

3. Concealment as Misrepresentation

Although an assertion usually comes in the form of an affirmative statement, the law will sometimes recognize concealment or even silence as a potentially fraudulent misrepresentation. Concealment commonly occurs when one parties takes action to hide something from the other, such as painting over a defect.

> *Action intended or known to be likely to prevent another from learning a fact is equivalent to an assertion that the fact does not exist.* R2d § 160.

For example, if the seller of a house knows that there is a crack in the foundation of the house, and so the seller paints over a crack in the basement so the defect is not obvious to buyers, this probably constitutes the sort of concealment that rises to the level of a fraudulent assertion. Again, misrepresentation by concealment requires some affirmative act.

4. Silence as Misrepresentation

There are also rare cases where inaction and silence constitute a misrepresentation. Silence as misrepresentation only arises where one party has a duty to inform the other. Such a duty can arise from four different situations, as described in R2d § 161:

> *A person's non-disclosure of a fact known to him is equivalent to an assertion that the fact does not exist in the following cases only: (a) where he knows that disclosure of the fact is necessary to prevent some previous assertion from being a misrepresentation or from being fraudulent or material; (b) where he knows that disclosure of the fact would correct a mistake of the other party as to a basic assumption on which that party is making the contract and if non-disclosure of the fact amounts to a failure to act in good faith and in accordance with reasonable standards of fair dealing; (c) where he knows that disclosure of the fact would correct a mistake of the other party as to the contents or effect of a writing, evidencing or embodying an agreement in whole or in part; or (d) where the other person is entitled to know the fact because of a relation of trust and confidence between them.*

Non-disclosure cases are harder to prove, however, because parties generally do not have a duty to disclose all the facts about a deal. In fact, parties often use their informational advantage to secure a better deal. For an omission to rise to the level of a fraudulent assertion, the failure to disclosure this fact must amount to a failure to act in good faith and in accordance with reasonable standards of fair dealing.

5. Conclusion: Misrepresentation

There are fifteen sections in R2d dedicated to explaining the defense of misrepresentation. This book reproduced and explicated the key rules; but, given the broad scope and technical nature of this section, I recommend students to read all these rules and comments for themselves.

Here are some tips on how to analyze a misrepresentation scenario:

First, state the ISSUE. For example,

> The ISSUE is whether [Buyer] can avoid the contract regarding [Term] because [Seller] misrepresented, where [Seller] asserted [Assertion] but [Fact] is true.

Second, cite RULES including R2d § 159's definition of misrepresentation plus any other rules you need to analyze whether the misrepresentation meets the definition of misrepresentation. Remember to include,

> *A misrepresentation is an assertion that is not in accord with the facts.* R2d § 159.

R2d § 159 cmt. c. defines the meaning of "fact":

> *Facts include past events as well as present circumstances but do not include future events.*

Only fraudulent or material misrepresentation makes a contract voidable:

> *If a party's manifestation of assent is induced by either a fraudulent or a material misrepresentation by the other party upon which the recipient is justified in relying, the contract is voidable by the recipient.* R2d § 164.

Third, ANALYZE whether Fact meets the legal definition of a fact and not an opinion, prediction, or puffery. Distinguish Assertion from Fact — the difference or dis-accord between Assertion and Fact is Misrepresentation.

Identify Misrepresentation as fraudulent (i.e., intentional) and/or material. *See* R2d § 162. Any misrepresentation that is neither fraudulent nor material cannot make a contract voidable and should be set aside. Explain how Misrepresentation induced Buyer to contract with Seller.

Fourth, CONCLUDE whether Buyer merits the defense of misrepresentation, including whether Seller acted in accord with the standards of good faith and fair dealing. Answer the question: can Buyer avoid the contract?

B. Duress

The legal term "duress" appears not to come directly from Latin but rather from even older Proto-Indo-European languages in which deru or dreu means "firm" and specifically refers to the hardness, solidity, and steadfastness of objects made from wood. For example, the Sanskrit word *dru* means tree. In Greek, *doru* is the wooden shaft of a spear. The Celtic word *druid* literally means "tree-knower" or "strong-seer," and this word evolved into the Old French *druide*.

The term became more abstract in Latin, in which *durus* means "hard." In the 14th century, Old French added the *-esse*, as in "essence," which modifies an adjective into a noun, as in largesse (grants) or fortress (strong place). The root is also present in the legal term "laches," which comes from the Old French *lachesse*, meaning lawlessness or negligence. The modern legal term laches refers to a civil defense where the defendant claims that the plaintiff unreasonably and negligently delayed in filing a claim, thus prejudicing the defendant and potentially equitably estopping the plaintiff from making the belated claim.

In modern American law usage, duress more specifically deals with an inappropriate use of strength. When one person uses its strength to compel another to manifest assent to a contract, that assent may be voidable by the victim under the doctrine of duress. The victim must show, however, that the compulsion represents an inappropriate or unfair use of strength that leaves the victim with no reasonable alternative to manifesting assent.

In a sense, duress is similar to coercion, meaning, using force to cause a party to manifest assent that it would not have otherwise manifested; however, the term coercion tends to reference forcible constraint by government, law or authority, whereas duress tends to refer to power dynamics between private people. Contact law is generally about private ordering, that is, the relationship between private people, and thus duress is the most appropriate way to refer to one person's improper use of power over another to compel the other's manifestation of assent.

Duress takes two forms: physical and economic. Physical duress involves improper threats of violence and physical harm. Economic duress involves improper threats of financial harm. A milder form of unfair persuasion includes undue influence, which only justifies a contractual defense where the persuading party has a special control, dominion, and responsibility over the persuaded party. All three can result in the victim avoiding a contract, provided that the elements of a defense are met.

1. Physical Compulsion

Duress by physical compulsion is to literally turn the screws on someone. The phrase turn the screws refers to an archaic torture device called a thumbscrew, which was a tool used to extract confessions. This simple device consisted of three bars. The upper and lower bars were fixed in place, while the middle bar would rise and lower upon the turning of a screw. The inquisitor would place the victim's thumbs below the middle bar and then tighten it down upon the digits, causing excruciating pain and potentially crushing the thumbs, causing lasting damage. The inquisitor would only let up the pressure when the victim confessed to a crime and admitted to some blame or responsibility.

You can imagine that one might manifest agreement to some contractual terms in order to escape certain torture like the thumbscrews. But such a manifestation is not based on the a person's willful desire to make themselves better off, but rather to escape from immediately from pain. This is not what contract law considers to be a true manifestation of assent, as R2d explains:

> If conduct that appears to be a manifestation of assent by a party who does not intend to engage in that conduct is physically compelled by duress, the conduct is not effective as a manifestation of assent. R2d § 174.

Figure 12.1. Thumbscrew used in France to make prisoners confess to crimes or to otherwise reveal information. Credit Wellcome Trust, Science Museum A67686, CC-A 4.0.

This first rule relates to physical compulsion, and it is usually obvious. For example, physically forcing a person's hand to sign a document or literally twisting someone's arm until they consent to some terms produce invalid manifestations of assent.

Duress need not be immediate. It may also come in the form a threat of some physical violence in the future. In these cases, the question is whether the threat leaves the victim without any reasonable alternative but to consent to the agreement:

> *If a party's manifestation of assent is induced by an improper threat by the other party that leaves the victim no reasonable alternative, the contract is voidable by the victim.* R2d § 175(1).

This test is evaluated subjectively, meaning, the question is whether the victim felt it had a reasonable alternative — not whether a reasonable person would have felt it had an alternative. For example, in the historic case of *Parmentier v. Pater*, 13 Or. 121 (1885), Louis Parmentier wrote a note acknowledging a debt of $6,000 (worth about a quarter of a million dollars today) owed by Claude Pater was cancelled. Five days later, Mr. Parmentier committed suicide. The decedent's wife, Elizabeth Parmentier, sued for the debt. Mr. Pater produced the signed cancellation note, and Mrs. Parmentier defended that note on the basis that Mr. Pater improperly threatened Mr. Parmentier.

In court, Ms. Parmentier admitted that she told her husband not to fear Pater and that Pater could not hurt him. But her husband was so distressed by Pater's threats that he could not eat or sleep. The court found,

> Louis Parmentier was evidently a weak person, and the appellant apparently was pushing an advantage he seemed to have had over him, which, it may be inferred, resulted in the cancellation of the obligation. I do not believe that the relinquishment of a debt under such circumstances is valid, whether the party relinquishing it is insane or not. At least, a jury might properly conclude that it was enforced against the will of the party.

The court found that Mr. Pater knowingly took advantage of Mr. Parmentier's suicidal insanity and leveraged his fragile condition to extract unconscionable terms. The court discusses how such as "eggshell" defendant can merit protection under the law of contract:

> It was a restraint or fear incited by threats that an impending calamity would befall the unfortunate Parmentier unless he complied with the demands of the appellant. The threats may have been vague, and the danger remote; but they were just as effectual in the accomplishment of their purpose as a double-barrel shot-gun would have been, if loaded and leveled at the party's head. They created all the agitation and consternation in the mind of the victim that the appellant could have desired. It resulted in an apparent absolution of the appellant from the obligation of his debt; at least, the jury might have so inferred from the evidence and circumstances. I am not able to discover any difference between wrongful means resorted to in order to compel a party to do something against his will. It is no more wicked, in my opinion, to put a person in prison, or deprive him of a limb, than to scare him to death, by any artifice or chicanery that may be employed; the inequity of the act consists in compelling a person to do what he does not want to do. Any course calculated to excite alarm, which is resorted to by one party in order to coerce another to do an act detrimental to his rights, and advantageous to the former, is unlawful; and I do not think the law should make any distinction between means that are adopted in order to secure such ends.

When one party induces another's manifestation of assent through threats knowing that they make the victim fear for its life, those manifestations are invalid, even where the victim is unusually vulnerable or fragile.

> If a party's manifestation of assent is induced by one who is not a party to the transaction, the contract is voidable by the victim unless the other party to the transaction in good faith and without reason to know of the duress either gives value or relies materially on the transaction. R2d § 175(2).

Moreover, a threat can be improper even where it does not rise to the level of life-threatening. R2d provides a list of improper threats, which extend significantly beyond the metaphorical thumbscrews or gun-to-the-head situation:

A threat is improper if (a) what is threatened is a crime or a tort, or the threat itself would be a crime or a tort if it resulted in obtaining property, (b) what is threatened is a criminal prosecution, (c) what is threatened is the use of civil process and the threat is made in bad faith, or (d) the threat is a breach of the duty of good faith and fair dealing under a contract with the recipient. R2d 176(1).

A threat can be deemed improper based on its results or ends as well:

A threat is improper if the resulting exchange is not on fair terms, and (a) the threatened act would harm the recipient and would not significantly benefit the party making the threat, (b) the effectiveness of the threat in inducing the manifestation of assent is significantly increased by prior unfair dealing by the party making the threat, or (c) what is threatened is otherwise a use of power for illegitimate ends. R2d § 176(2).

In summary, duress may occur where one party induces the other's purported manifestation of assent through an improper threat. Threats can be improper based on means (e.g., threatening violence) or ends (e.g., to punish and economically harm someone out of pure malicious vindictiveness).

2. Economic Threat

Economic coercion, such as where G threatens to arrange a boycott against H's stores unless H promises to sell goods to G for a discount, may be ground for the duress defense. Although cases voiding a contract based on economic are rare, the duress doctrine does seem to include cases where there was no physical or unlawful threat, but merely an "improper" or wrongful threat.

For example, Galtaco Redlaw Castings Corporation agreed to produce automotive brake assemblies for Kelsey-Hayes Company. During the performance of a three-year "requirements" contract (a contract in which Kelsey-Hayes agreed to purchase as much as it required from Galtaco, without specifying a specific quantity), Kelsey-Hayes agreed to two price increases resulting from the Galtaco's financial difficulties. Kelsey-Hayes had no economic choice other than to pay more for Galtaco's products, since it could not find an alternate source supplier, and since declining the Galtaco's offer would have had the effect of shutting down Kelsey-Hayes's operations. In other words, the supplier's offer to either sell at a higher price or not to sell at all did not really present an option to the buyer, who would cease to exist if it did not take the offer. The court found that faced with the imminent shutdown of its operations, the manufacturer may have had no alternative other than agreeing to the supplier's "requests" for price increases.

Economic duress cases succeed when they involve two businesses who deal at arm's length from another. More commonly, successful economic duress defenses may occur where one party uses its overwhelmingly greater market power or influence to extract money or to punish, embarrass, and ruin a less powerful party.

C. Undue Influence

While the duress defense may be invoked by parties who are at arm's length, the undue influence defense may only be invoked where parties are in a special relationship of trust or power. While undue influence is a milder form of persuasion than duress, the defense is available where the power dynamic between the parties is sufficiently skewed against the victim.

> *Undue influence is unfair persuasion of a party who is under the domination of the person exercising the persuasion or who by virtue of the relation between them is justified in assuming that that person will not act in a manner inconsistent with his welfare.* R2d § 177(1).

Such relationships include parent and child, husband and wife, clergyman and parishioner, physician and patient, and lawyer and client. The defense may be raised where one party takes substantial advantage of its position of domination over the other to extract unreasonable terms:

> *If a party's manifestation of assent is induced by undue influence by the other party, the contract is voidable by the victim.* R2d § 177(2).

The defense of undue influence will fail where the aggrieved party had no good reason to believe that the other party would act only in the interests of the aggrieved party's welfare.

> *If a party's manifestation of assent is induced by one who is not a party to the transaction, the contract is voidable by the victim unless the other party to the transaction in good faith and without reason to know of the undue influence either gives value or relies materially on the transaction.* R2d § 177(3)

For example, Adam is the owner of Goldacre, a valuable parcel of land. While taking a break at work, Adam mentions to Brian, a co-worker in another department with whom Adam is not particularly well acquainted, of Adam's desire to sell Goldacre. Brian urges Adam to make a contract to sell to Goldacre to Candy, Brian's lover, at a price that is well below its fair value. Adam is thereby induced to make the contract. Brian's conduct does not amount to misrepresentation, because he made no assertions as to the value of Goldacre. His behavior is not duress, because Adam had reasonable alternatives other than selling Goldacre to Candy. And Brian's behavior is not undue influence, because Adam has no good reason to believe that Brian will only act in favor of Adam's welfare.

If, on the other hand, Brian was not a mere acquaintance of Adam, but Brian was instead Adam's trusted uncle who had given Adam business advice over a course of many years, and if Adam had reasonably come to trust and rely upon Brian's advice, then the defense of undue influence may be available to Adam.

D. Reflections on Misrepresentation, Duress, and Undue Influence

The foundational principal of freedom to contracts means that people should be allowed to enter into binding agreements. For this reason, courts are hesitant to disturb agreements that reflect the intent of the parties. But there are cases where what appears to be mutual intent is no more than window dressing.

When a party's consent to be bound is founded on fraudulent or material misrepresentations, duress, or undue influence, the court should allow the aggrieved party to void the contract.

While courts are quite hesitant to deny enforcement of commercial contracts that are formed at arm's length, courts are more likely to void agreements in which a party took advantage of a special relationship of trust or power to extract unfair terms. Courts are split on whether one party has the duty to correct the others' mistake. When there is a mutual mistake, courts will consider which party bears the risk of that mistake.

The reason for the misrepresentation and coercion defenses is they help prevent contract law from being used as a weapon by one party upon another. Lying, cheating, threatening, and forcing contractual "consent" undermines the fundamental contracts principle of mutual assent and voluntary private ordering.

Cases

Reading Barrer v. Women's National Bank. Under R2d § 159, a misrepresentation is an assertion not in accord with the facts. A deliberate lie will always be an assertion, while concealment and non-disclosure may be in certain circumstances outlined in R2d §§ 160 & 161. Once a misrepresentation has been identified, it needs to be material or fraudulent under R2d § 162.

The case below is about an innocent material misrepresentation which is when a person fails to disclose something unintentionally. As you read the case below, pay attention to how the court organizes its rules and analysis for determining whether there is an innocent material misrepresentation.

Barrer v. Women's National Bank
761 F.2d 752 (1985)

HARRY T. EDWARDS, Circuit Judge.

The appellant, Lester A. Barrer, brought this action against Women's National Bank ("the Bank" or "WNB") for damages he allegedly sustained as the result of the Bank's eleventh-hour decision to rescind a loan agreement. WNB defended and moved for summary judgment on the ground that Barrer had made innocent material misrepresentations in his loan application that justified the Bank's avoidance of the contract. The magistrate found that Barrer had made five material representations to the Bank that were not in accord with the facts and, on that basis, granted WNB's motion for summary judgment. We find that the magistrate failed to apply the correct legal test for determining when an innocent material misrepresentation permits the rescission of a contract, and that there are material issues of fact that make summary judgment inappropriate. Accordingly, we reverse and remand for further proceedings consistent with this opinion.

I. Background

A. Factual Background

On June 24, 1981, Lester Barrer's personal home was sold at a tax sale by the Internal Revenue Service ("IRS") because of his inability to pay certain employment taxes. The taxes were owed by Barrer's closely-held corporation, Today News Service, Inc., and had been asserted against him personally as a 100 percent penalty pursuant to 26 U.S.C. § 6672 (1982). At the tax sale, Barrer's home was purchased by Edward L. Curtis, Jr., for $16,326, subject to the underlying mortgage. The Internal Revenue Code provides for the redemption of real property within 120 days of a tax sale upon payment to the purchaser of the purchase price plus interest. Barrer accordingly was advised by the IRS that he could redeem his home by delivering $17,400, in cash or its equivalent, to the IRS or to Curtis on or before October 22, 1981.

On October 20, 1981, Barrer went to WNB to discuss a personal loan for the redemption amount. Apparently, on the previous day, Barrer had approached one other bank about the possibility of a loan; however, he had been advised by the President of that bank that it would not be possible to process an application for a loan in the amount sought by Barrer in such a short period of time. Barrer indicated in his deposition statement that he waited until the last minute to seek a bank loan because he had been involved in serious negotiations over the sale of his business and had expected to close on the sale before October 20, 1981, and that he had intended to use the proceeds from that sale to redeem his house.

At WNB, Barrer spoke with Emily Womack, the President of the Bank, with whom he had a professional acquaintance. Barrer's corporation published the Women Today Newsletter, a periodical to which the Bank subscribed and which, according to Barrer's deposition statement, had published an article on the Bank. Barrer's corporation also maintained an account with the Bank. Womack gave Barrer a loan application form, which he completed and returned to her the next day, October 21, along with certain supporting documents, including those concerning the tax sale and his efforts to sell the business.

Barrer evidently explained to Womack that he had experienced severe financial difficulties since his wife and long-time professional collaborator died of cancer in 1978. At his deposition, Barrer testified that he told Womack that, for a period after his wife died, he lost his motivation to work and that the business they had jointly owned and managed suffered serious economic reverses as a consequence. Those reverses led to Today News Service, Inc.'s inability to pay its employment taxes and ultimately to the tax sale of Barrer's home. Womack sympathized with Barrer's plight and expressed to one of her bank officers the hope that they could help him.

On October 21, Barrer and Womack reviewed his loan application line by line. With reference to his home mortgage, Barrer told her that his house was worth approximately $130,000 and that Columbia First Federal Savings and Loan Association ("Columbia") held a $65,000 mortgage on it. When asked whether his mortgage payments were up-to-date, Barrer recalls replying that he "thought" he was two months behind. By contrast, Womack testified that Barrer said he was current. In fact, Barrer was six months behind. Barrer explained that he thought his obligation to pay his mortgage ceased at the time of the tax sale and that he did not realize that he was responsible for more than the two months' mortgage payments that had been due before the sale.

Because Barrer's mortgage payments were in arrears, Columbia had begun foreclosure proceedings — also a fact that Barrer did not disclose to Womack. In his deposition statement, Barrer accounted for this failure by stating that on October 21, 1981, he did not know that Columbia had initiated foreclosure proceedings.

On the liability side of the loan application, Barrer revealed that he had borrowed $40,000 from friends and relatives. Barrer testified that he explained to Womack that he had borrowed this sum to ease the financial difficulties he had encountered since his wife's death.

Barrer also disclosed the $38,000 tax liability which was the cause of the tax sale. He did not indicate, however, a contingent liability for an additional $11,000 in employment taxes owed by his corporation which had not, at that time, been asserted against him personally under 26 U.S.C. §6672. Barrer seems to argue both that this $11,000 was included in the $38,000 figure, and that because the $11,000 tax liability had not been assessed against him personally it was not a contingent liability that he was obligated to reveal.

Nor did Barrer list as a contingent liability a $5,300 debt owed by his wife's estate to IBM. The Bank argues that this debt should have been revealed because Barrer had demonstrated, by requesting the probate court to charge the obligation to him, that he thought himself responsible for the debt. Barrer contends that because the probate court ultimately ruled that the obligation belonged to the estate, his failure to list the amount on the loan application was not a misrepresentation.

Finally, Barrer did not indicate on the loan application that he had approximately $1,500 in unsatisfied judgments pending against him. However, he answered in the affirmative to a specific question on the application form which inquired whether he was "a defendant in any suits or legal actions." Barrer also stated at his deposition that he told Womack that he owed small amounts arising out of these lawsuits. He said that he explained to her that these debts involved disputes over medical bills and that he expected his major medical insurance to cover most of them.

After Barrer and Womack finished discussing the content of the completed loan application form and Barrer's financial situation, Womack indicated that, in order for the Bank to grant the loan, the IRS would have to agree to subordinate its claim with respect to Barrer's house to that of WNB. On October 22, 1981, the last redemption day, Barrer obtained the subordination agreement from the IRS and delivered it to the Bank. Barrer then executed a collateral note for $17,400, payable in 90 days at 15 percent interest, which gave the Bank the right to a security interest in his house. The Bank's Vice President, Emma Carrera, gave Barrer a cashier's check, payable to him, for the loan amount. Prior to granting the loan, neither Womack nor Carrera obtained a credit report on Barrer and neither officer phoned Columbia about the status of his mortgage.

That afternoon, Barrer delivered the endorsed check to the IRS in accordance with the required redemption procedure and returned home, believing that his home had been saved.

In the meantime, the tax sale purchaser, Curtis, phoned WNB and spoke with Carrera. According to her deposition, their conversation was as follows:

> *He stated that he had some information that he thought would be of interest to me on the loan that the bank had made to Mr. Barrer. I told him at that time that I could not discuss any loan with him in regards to who it was or what it was for. He said he didn't want me to do any discussing, but he just wanted to tell me some facts.*

> *He then told me he was the purchaser of the property at the tax sale. He couldn't believe that a bank would make a loan to a man who was in the credit position that he was in; that there were liens and judgments and so forth against him and at that time, I signaled for my secretary to bring me the file on Mr. Barrer.*

> *I quickly looked through the file and found there wasn't a credit report in the file. At that time I told her to pull a credit report on him, which she did, and brought it to me within just a couple of minutes.*

> *In the meantime, Mr. Curtis was continuing to talk. He had mentioned something about some kind of code that says that a person who buys a property at a tax sale cannot interfere with the owner's right to redeem, but that he didn't feel he was doing that just by informing the bank of Mr. Barrer's situation.*

> *He put me on a conference call with a gentleman who identified himself as an official of the mortgage company [Columbia] that held the mortgage on Mr. Barrer's property. He [Mr. Ford] asked me at that time who, in his organization, had given us a credit report.*

> *. . . I . . . answer[ed] him . . . that it was my understanding that all of the savings and loan associations required a written request for credit rating [sic] on any of the mortgages that they held and it had always been, to my knowledge, their policies not to give a reference by phone.*

[Mr. Ford] said at that point he thought it was important that we know that Mr. Barrer's mortgage was six months in arrears and they were prepared to go to foreclosure on the property. He excused himself and Mr. Curtis stayed on the line.

[Mr. Curtis] said that he had knowledge that IRS had not made an agreement with Mr. Barrer to repay the balance of the taxes; that they were ready to go back to another tax sale as soon as this $17,400 was paid.

Based on the information furnished by Curtis, Ford, and the credit report, the Bank decided to stop payment on the cashier's check. The Bank's counsel called Barrer later that day to inform him that the check would not be honored. When Curtis, to whom the IRS had turned over the check, presented it for payment the Bank refused to cash it. Barrer, therefore, did not effect the redemption of his home within the statutory period and Curtis became the owner.

B. Procedural History

Barrer filed suit against the Bank in District Court to recover damages to compensate him for the loss of $94,000 equity in his home — the difference between the market value of the house and the balance due on the mortgage — that he allegedly suffered as a result of the Bank's rescission of the loan agreement. Barrer also claimed punitive damages for the embarrassment he endured and the rent he has been required to pay Curtis in order to remain in his home.

The case was referred to a magistrate for pretrial proceedings. On the Bank's motion for summary judgment, the magistrate found that Barrer did not disclose the following five material facts to the Bank: (1) that he was six months delinquent in mortgage payments, (2) that Columbia had begun foreclosure procedures, (3) that Barrer had at least an $11,000 contingent liability to the IRS in addition to his $38,000 actual liability, (4) that he had a contingent liability to IBM of approximately $5,000, and (5) that he had approximately $1,500 in unsatisfied judgments pending against him. The magistrate purported to rely on the law of innocent material misrepresentation to hold that these disclosure omissions justified WNB's rescission of the loan contract. On that basis, he granted summary judgment in favor of the Bank. This appeal followed.

II. Analysis

[A. Standards for Summary Judgment omitted.]

B. Elements of Innocent Material Misrepresentation

It is well established that misrepresentation of material facts may be the basis for the rescission of a contract, even where the misrepresentations are made innocently, without knowledge of their falsity and without fraudulent intent. The rationale supporting this rule, which has its origins in equity, is that, as between two innocent parties, the party making the representation should bear the loss. Stated another way, the rule is based on the view that "one who has made a false statement ought not to benefit at the expense of another who has been prejudiced by relying on the statement." This rule may be employed "actively," as in a suit at equity or law for rescission and restitution, or "passively," as a defense to a suit for breach of contract.

It is generally understood that four conditions must be met before a contract may be avoided for innocent misrepresentation. The recipient of the alleged misrepresentation must demonstrate that the maker made an assertion: (1) that was not in accord with the facts, (2) that was material, and (3) that was relied upon (4) justifiably by the recipient in manifesting his assent to the agreement. District of Columbia law adds a fifth condition, i.e., that the recipient relied to his detriment.

Unfortunately, the applicable precedent does not elaborate on the meaning of these conditions. In trying to give them content, we have found that the Restatement (Second) of Contracts ("Restatement (Second)") provides helpful guidance concerning the first four conditions.

1. Misrepresentation

Section 159 of the Restatement (Second) defines a misrepresentation as "an assertion that is not in accord with the facts." Comment c explains that an "assertion must relate to something that is a fact at the time the assertion is made in order to be a misrepresentation. Such facts include past events as well as present circumstances but do not include future events." Comment d observes that a person's state of mind is a fact and that an assertion of one's opinion constitutes a misrepresentation if the state of mind is other than as asserted.

According to section 161, the only non-disclosures that may be considered assertions of fact for purposes of misrepresentation analysis are non-disclosures of facts known to the maker where the maker knows that disclosure: (a) is necessary to prevent a previous assertion from being a misrepresentation or from being fraudulent or material, (b) would correct a mistake of the other party as to a basic assumption on which that party is making the contract, if non-disclosure amounts to a failure to act in good faith and in accordance with reasonable standards of fair dealing, or (c) would correct a mistake of the other party as to the contents or effect of a writing. The section also provides that where the other person is entitled to know the non-disclosed facts because a relation of trust and confidence exists between the parties, non-disclosure is equivalent to an assertion of facts.

2. Materiality

In section 162, comment c, the Restatement (Second) explains that a misrepresentation is material "if it would be likely to induce a reasonable person to manifest his assent." The court in *Cousineau v. Walker* elaborated on the materiality requirement, noting that it is a mixed question of law and fact that asks whether the assertion is one to which a reasonable person might be expected to attach importance in making a choice of action. A material fact is one that could reasonably be expected to influence a person's judgment or conduct concerning a transaction.

The justification for the materiality requirement is that it is believed to encourage stability in contract relations. It prevents parties who become disappointed at the outcome of their bargain from seizing upon any insignificant discrepancy to void the contract.

3. Reliance

Section 167 requires that the misrepresentation be causally related to the recipient's decision to agree to the contract—that it have been an inducement to agree. Inducement, as comment a explains, is shown through actual reliance. Comment a goes on to state that this reliance need not, however, be the sole or predominant factor influencing the recipient's decision. Comment b indicates that circumstantial evidence is often important in determining whether there was actual reliance.

4. Justifiability of Reliance

Section 172 of the Restatement (Second) provides that a recipient's fault in not knowing or discovering the facts before making the contract does not make his reliance unjustified unless it amounts to a failure to act in good faith and in accordance with reasonable standards of fair dealing.

While section 169 suggests that reliance on an assertion of opinion often is not justified, section 168(2) and the accompanying comment d make clear that in some situations the recipient may reasonably understand a statement of opinion to be more than an assertion as to the maker's state of mind. Where circumstances justify it, a statement of opinion may also be reasonably understood as carrying with it an assertion that the maker knows facts sufficient to justify him in forming it.

5. Detriment

Because the Restatement (Second) does not require a showing of detriment for rescission, it does not define it. We think that, in the innocent material misrepresentation context, a recipient is appropriately considered to have relied to his detriment where he receives something that is less valuable or different in some significant respect from that which he reasonably expected.

C. Application of Legal Standards

Application of the foregoing principles to the facts of this case requires that the case be remanded for trial. The magistrate tested Barrer's alleged misrepresentations against only two of the five elements necessary for rescission—he asked only if the representations were in accord with the facts and if they were material. In making this inquiry, the magistrate failed to consider the legal distinctions between assertions of fact and nondisclosure and between assertions of fact and statements of opinion. He neglected to investigate whether the Bank actually relied on the representations in deciding to make the loan; whether that reliance, if it existed, was justifiable; and whether the Bank relied to its detriment. Furthermore, the magistrate incorrectly concluded that there were no legally probative, material issues of fact in dispute.

1. Elements the Magistrate Failed to Consider

Initially, assuming for a moment that Barrer actually "misrepresented" certain facts, the materiality of the representations is hardly obvious. After deciding which representations meet the legal definition of misrepresentation, the trial court must determine with regard to each individual misrepresentation whether it was "likely to induce a reasonable [bank] to manifest [its] assent" to the loan agreement. If no single misrepresentation is found to be material, the court may consider, after ascertaining the assertions upon which WNB justifiably relied, whether those assertions are material when taken together.

All five alleged "misrepresentations" also raise serious factual questions as to whether the Bank actually and justifiably relied on them. Womack's expressed sympathy for Barrer combined with the fact that the loan was issued in a very short time, without either a credit check, which was obtainable in minutes, or an inquiry into the status of Barrer's mortgage, and the fact that the loan was withdrawn only when the Bank was placed in an embarrassing position by the tax sale purchaser — all these circumstances could suggest that the Bank was not very interested in the particulars of Barrer's financial condition. Indeed, it was clear from the loan application that Barrer did admit that he was experiencing financial difficulties, yet WNB chose to make no further inquiry into the details of these problems. These facts could be construed to show that Womack's sympathy for Barrer's predicament was the real inducement for the loan. If the trial court finds that the Bank actually relied on Barrer's alleged "misrepresentations," it nonetheless must proceed to decide whether that reliance was justified.

The trial court must also determine whether the Bank's reliance on Barrer's alleged "misrepresentations" caused it any detriment. Did WNB receive as its benefit of the bargain something less valuable or significantly different from what it reasonably expected? In addition, the trial court should consider whether the subordination agreement, in combination with the right to a security interest in Barrer's house granted by the collateral note, fully satisfied the Bank's expectations.

The magistrate also made individual errors with respect to the five representations. These errors are outlined below.

2. Delinquency in Mortgage Payments

Barrer and Womack disagree over whether he told her that he "thought" he was two months behind in his mortgage payments or whether he said that he was current. Because this case is before us on appeal from the magistrate's grant of summary judgment for the Bank, we must accept Barrer's statement of the facts. The Bank argues that even if Barrer's version is accepted, a misrepresentation still occurred because Barrer was actually six months behind. The Bank's position is not necessarily correct.

Barrer's statement that he "thought" he was in arrears by two months initially raises the factual question whether he made any misrepresentation. On the surface, the fact asserted by Barrer was his state of mind — what he thought. No finding was made below that Barrer's state of mind was other than what he declared. On remand, before it may determine that this statement constituted a misrepresentation, the court must find either that Barrer misstated his thoughts, in accordance with the rule laid out in section 159, comment d of the Restatement (Second), or that Barrer's statement could reasonably have been understood as carrying with it an assertion that Barrer knew sufficient facts that justified him in forming his opinion, in accordance with section 168(2).

When evaluating the materiality of this particular representation, the court should keep in mind the concession made by WNB's counsel at oral argument—that by itself this representation might not be sufficient to justify summary judgment.

3. Failure to Disclose Mortgage Foreclosure Proceedings

Although the Bank evidently did not ask Barrer directly whether his mortgage was being foreclosed upon, it contends that he had an obligation to volunteer that information and that his failure to do so is tantamount to a misrepresentation. Barrer argues that he had no duty to reveal the existence of the foreclosure proceedings because he did not know about them. The Bank maintains that he must have known, because before Barrer applied for the loan his teen-age daughter signed for a certified letter from Columbia notifying him of the foreclosure.

The magistrate erred in finding on summary judgment that this non disclosure is equivalent to a misrepresentation. The Restatement (Second) provides that a non-disclosure may be considered an assertion of fact for purposes of misrepresentation analysis only if the non-disclosed fact is known to the maker and if certain other conditions are met. Because there exists a material issue of fact as to whether Barrer knew that Columbia had begun to foreclose, summary judgment was inappropriate.

4. $11,000 Contingent Liability

The magistrate also erred in finding on summary judgment that Barrer's alleged failure to list as a personal contingent liability an $11,000 tax debt owed to the IRS by his corporation constituted a misrepresentation. First, summary judgment is precluded by the existence of a factual dispute over whether this $11,000 was included in the $38,000 tax liability that Barrer did list. Barrer seems to contend that at least some of this amount was included in the $38,000 figure; the Bank seems to dispute this contention. Second, there is a mixed question of law and fact as to whether the IRS had, at the time of the loan application, taken any action to assert the $11,000 tax debt owed by Today News Service, Inc., against Barrer personally and, if not, whether the corporation's liability may be considered Barrer's contingent liability. If the $11,000 tax debt could not at that time have been considered Barrer's liability, his failure to list such a debt was not a misrepresentation.

5. $5,300 Debt Owed to IBM

The magistrate found that Barrer's failure to reveal as a personal liability a $5,300 debt owed to IBM for equipment purchased by his wife was a misrepresentation. We disagree as a matter of law. Although Barrer asked the probate court handling his wife's estate to charge him with the debt, the court refused, ruling that the debt was hers alone. Contrary to the Bank's protestations, it makes no difference to the determination whether a misrepresentation occurred that Barrer asked the probate court to charge him with the debt before, and the court refused after, Barrer submitted the loan application. A misrepresentation is "an assertion that is not in accord with the facts." The fact is that a court decided that this debt never legally belonged to Barrer. Barrer's thoughts or wishes on the matter are irrelevant. He made no legal misrepresentation to the Bank on this subject.

6. $1,500 in Judgments

Finally, the magistrate determined that Barrer's failure to list $1,500 in judgments that were outstanding against him constituted a misrepresentation. This issue should not have been resolved on summary judgment. Barrer disclosed on the loan application that he was a defendant in some lawsuits. Furthermore, in his deposition he stated that he had informed Womack that he owed some small judgments arising out of these suits and that he expected his health insurance to cover most of them. Accepting Barrer's version of the facts, as we must in reviewing a grant of summary judgment, he revealed both his defendant status and the existence of judgments against him. It is true that he did not list them on the application form. Because, however, Barrer contends that he adequately disclosed these debts in connection with the question concerning lawsuits and in his discussion with Womack, there exists a dispute over whether he actually revealed these debts; consequently the magistrate should not have resolved this issue on summary judgment. On remand, two factual questions must be decided. First, what information concerning these judgments did Barrer give to Womack? Second, was that information sufficient to give the Bank notice of them? If it was sufficient, then Barrer made no misrepresentation.

III. Conclusion

The magistrate both failed to utilize the correct legal test for determining when an innocent material misrepresentation permits the rescission of a contract and to recognize that this case presents disputed material issues of fact that render summary judgment inappropriate. We reverse and remand for further proceedings consistent with this opinion.

Reflection

Barrer is an example of how to analyze a case of innocent misrepresentation. In an innocent misrepresentation, the assertion must be material and justifiably relied on by the recipient in manifesting his assent to the agreement. In Washington, D.C., the recipient also had to rely to their detriment.

In its analysis of the rules, the court first defined misrepresentation and determined that the assertion may be a non-disclosure. The assertion must be material enough to reasonably induce a person to manifest their assent. An assertion of an opinion is not normally something that can be justifiably relied upon but may under certain circumstances. The additional requirement of detrimental reliance is determined on whether the recipient received something less in value than reasonably expected.

The court believed the magistrate did not distinguish between statements of nondisclosure and statements of opinion and this was a factual dispute that needed to be resolved in a trial court. Even assuming Barrer's statements were misrepresentations, there was also a factual dispute over whether the Bank justifiably relied on the misrepresentations and whether there was a detriment suffered. Only when all these elements are met can a contract be voided by the Bank, therefore, the case was remanded consistent with the court's analysis.

Discussion

1. What are each of the purported misrepresentations in the *Barrer* case? For each, apply the R2d definition of "misrepresentation" to confirm whether each is in fact a misrepresentation under the legal definition.

2. The trial court in *Barrer* failed to consider whether the misrepresentations were material. For each misrepresentation, analyze whether each was material and/or fraudulent.

3. The defense of misrepresentation is said to be "stronger" than the defense of mistake, in the sense that courts are more likely to permit avoidance of a contract on the ground of misrepresentation than mistake. Why might courts be more willing to grant the misrepresentation defense than the mistake defense? Present your opinion in terms of a policy analysis.

Reading Nigro v. Lee. The next case is an example of an instance where one party accuses the other of making a fraudulent misrepresentation. To analyze whether this argument should prevail, you must deconstruct the elements of misrepresentation and ensure there was in fact a statement that was not in accord with facts, and, moreover, that the statement had a material influence on the decision contract.

Nigro v. Lee

63 A.D.3d 1490 (N.Y. App. Div. 2009)

PETERS, J.P.

Appeal from an order of the Supreme Court (Devine, J.), entered April 1, 2008 in Albany County, which, among other things, granted defendants' motion for summary judgment dismissing the complaint.

In 2006, defendant Maxwell Lee initiated an eBay auction sale of a 1995 Mercedes Benz owned by his mother, defendant Alice Aizhen Lee. Defendants' eBay advertisement described the car as "gorgeous," with three minor blemishes in the form of a missing master key, CD cartridge and spare tire, represented that the seller was the sole owner of the vehicle and cautioned that "[t]he vehicle is [being] sold as it is and conditions are disclosed to the best of my knowledge." Plaintiff, a New York resident, purchased the vehicle which was delivered to him from Nevada, where defendants reside, on July 30, 2006. Upon its arrival, plaintiff began experiencing difficulties with the automobile. He had an inspection performed, which revealed that the car had been damaged in an accident and had been painted, the upholstery was stained, the undercoating was worn out and parts were rusted, and that body work would cost $1,741.66. He also received estimates for electrical and sensory repairs exceeding $7,495, repairs to the throttle that exceeded $3,931 and a new catalytic converter costing approximately $1,100. Plaintiff communicated his dissatisfaction to defendants and, although they refunded a portion of the purchase price, plaintiff commenced this action to rescind the contract or, in the alternative, to recover damages for defendants' fraudulent misrepresentations regarding the condition of the vehicle. Supreme Court granted defendants' motion for summary judgment dismissing the complaint and denied plaintiff's cross motion for summary judgment. Plaintiff appeals and we affirm.

Supreme Court properly dismissed plaintiff's cause of action for breach of warranty. Under the UCC, any description of the goods, or affirmation of fact or promise relating to the goods, which is made part of the basis of the bargain creates an express warranty that the goods shall conform to such description, affirmation or promise. On the other hand, "a statement purporting to be merely the seller's opinion or commendation of the goods does not create a warranty". Here, defendants' advertisement made no promises or affirmations of fact as to the condition or quality of the electrical or sensory systems, throttle or catalytic converter. While the advertisement did describe the car as "gorgeous," this generalized expression was merely the seller's opinion of the car and constitutes "no more than 'puffery,' which should not have been relied upon as an inducement to purchase the vehicle," particularly in light of the fact that this was a used car transaction.

Plaintiff next asserts that defendants fraudulently misrepresented that the car was gorgeous and virtually unblemished despite their knowledge that it had been used extensively, had been in an accident and was in need of significant repairs. In order to establish fraud, "'a party must establish that a material misrepresentation, known to be false, has been made with the intention of inducing its reliance on the misstatement, which caused it to reasonably rely on the misrepresentation, as a result of which it sustained damages'".

As to the element of reliance, "'if the facts represented are not matters peculiarly within the party's knowledge, and the other party has the means available to him [or her] of knowing, by the exercise of ordinary intelligence, the truth . . . of the representation, he [or she] must make use of those means, or he [or she] will not be heard to complain that he [or she] was induced to enter into the transaction by misrepresentations'".

Here, all of the deficiencies that plaintiff has alleged could have been easily discovered by routine investigation. Plaintiff could have contacted defendants to inquire about the vehicle or its history (as defendants' advertisement specifically invited prospective purchasers to do), procured a vehicle history report (as recommended on eBay's Web site) or hired a mechanic in Nevada to inspect and/or examine the car before purchasing it. Instead, plaintiff made no attempt to ascertain the true condition or history of the vehicle prior to his purchase. Further, there can be no doubt that plaintiff could have ascertained the true facts with reasonable diligence, inasmuch as a mechanical examination of the vehicle and vehicle history report — steps which plaintiff took only after delivery of the vehicle — revealed exactly those conditions of which plaintiff now complains. Plaintiff's claim that he was prevented from inspecting the vehicle simply because it was located in Nevada is insufficient to defeat defendants' summary judgment motion, plaintiff failed to prove that his reliance on those representations was justifiable and, therefore, his causes of action sounding in fraud were properly dismissed.

ORDERED that the order is affirmed, with costs.

Reflection

Nigro is a case that demonstrates how an opinion is ordinarily not an assertion and how some jurisdictions have different standards for reliance. When a seller is trying to sell something, they will use favorable language to describe it expressing their opinion. This is often called "puffery" or "sales talk" and is not considered to be an assertion for the purposes of a misrepresentation.

This case also contradicts what was stated in *Barrer* which was quoting R2d § 172 where "[a] recipient's fault in not knowing or discovering the facts before making the contract does not make his reliance unjustified unless it amounts to a failure to act in good faith and in accordance with reasonable standards of fair dealing." However, the court here found that if the recipient has the means available to find out the truth, by the exercise of ordinarily intelligence, then that person must make use of those means, otherwise there is no inducement. Thus, since the buyer could have the car inspected before buying it, they cannot rescind the contract due to fraudulent misrepresentation. This is just one example of how R2d cannot reflect all jurisdictions and it's important to remain aware of the different rules.

Discussion

1. What are the various assertions that Lee claims were misrepresentations? For each of these, confirm that each meets the legal definition of misrepresentation as found in R2d, and then classify each misrepresentation as (i) an affirmative misrepresentation, (ii) concealment, or (iii) misrepresentation by silence.

2. Did these two parties have a relationship of trust and confidence such that one party had an obligation to speak lest silence be a misrepresentation? Or was this an arm's length transaction where neither party had an affirmative duty to disclose additional information?

3. Did Plaintiff reasonably rely on Defendant's assertions?

> *Reading Quebodeaux v. Quebodeaux.* The following case exhibits both duress and undue influence. I selected this case because the threats by one party are so egregious that they would likely constitute duress even if the parties did not have a special relationship. But you may also notice in the case caption that the parties have the same last name. The parties in this case are husband and wife. In such a relationship, a defense of undue influence might also be raised. As you read this case, think about why the court voided this contract on the basis of duress and not undue influence.

Quebodeaux v. Quebodeaux

102 Ohio App. 3d 502 (1995)

SLABY, Judge.

Anthony Quebodeaux appeals from a trial court order granting Merry Quebodeaux her motion for relief from judgment. We affirm.

Anthony and Merry sought a dissolution of their eleven-year marriage. The dissolution petition included a separation agreement signed by both parties. This agreement gave custody of the couple's two sons to Anthony and the couple's daughter to Merry. Although Merry's annual income was less than half of Anthony's, the agreement stated that Merry would not receive spousal support. Similarly, the agreement did not require either party to pay child support.

The trial judge extensively questioned Merry about the terms of the separation agreement. Merry stated that she consented to the terms. Despite having "some distinct reservations" about the agreement, the trial judge ordered the dissolution pursuant to the terms specified in the agreement.

About two months later, Merry moved for relief from judgment, alleging that she had entered into the separation agreement while under duress. She further claimed that Anthony had misrepresented his financial status.

After a lengthy hearing, the trial court granted Merry's motion and found that Merry had not entered into the agreement freely. The court also found that Anthony had failed to report his financial interest in a house. The parties had leased the house for approximately one and one-half years prior to the dissolution. Anthony bought the house after the dissolution petition was filed. The court found that he received credit for the lease payments, which were made from the parties' joint checking account, against the price of the house.

Anthony appeals, assigning three errors.

Assignments of Error I and II

I. The trial court erred to the prejudice of [Anthony] when it permitted Marily Zeidner to testify to general aspects of the battered woman syndrome, where there was no testimony from an expert indicating that [Merry] suffered from the syndrome.

II. The trial court erred and abused its discretion when it granted [Merry's] motion for relief from the separation agreement pursuant to Civ.R. 60(B)(5) and found that [Merry] had been coerced into signing the separation agreement, where [Merry's] testimony regarding abuse was not corroborated and where [Merry] failed to present sufficient evidence as a matter of law that she signed the separation agreement under duress.

Anthony argues that the trial court abused its discretion in finding that Merry signed the separation agreement while under duress and by invalidating the agreement on that basis. Anthony contests the admissibility of the hearing testimony of Marilyn Zeidner, an assistant director of a local battered woman shelter. He notes that Zeidner never observed Merry prior to the dissolution and that her testimony concerned only general aspects of battered woman syndrome. He also argued that *State v. Koss* limit the admissibility of evidence of battered woman syndrome to criminal proceedings in which the woman seeks to use the syndrome as a defense.

In her motion, Merry asserted that she signed the separation agreement while under duress. Three elements are necessary to establish duress; first, that one side involuntarily accepted the terms of another; second, that circumstances permitted no other alternative; and third, that the opposite party's coercive acts caused those circumstances. *Blodgett v. Blodgett.*

We find that the trial court did not abuse its discretion in granting Merry's motion for relief from judgment. The agreement was drafted by Anthony and his attorney. Merry testified that Anthony threatened to take all three of the children from her unless she assented to the agreement:

> "Q. Why did you give those answers [indicating consent to the separation agreement] to Judge Basinski?"
>
> "A. Because I had to tell him that. I mean. I didn't have any choice but to tell him that."
>
> "Q. Tell us why you are saying that."
>
> "A. Because Tony told me, as long as I signed everything and did what he said, that he would let me keep [their daughter]. And, if I gave him a hard time, that he would leave and take the kids with him, and I wouldn't have any of them. And that he would have me declared as unfit."

Merry also testified to repeated acts of actual and threatened abuse by Anthony during the marriage. She repeatedly stated her belief that she had no alternative to signing the agreement, believing that she stood to lose her children otherwise. Based on the foregoing, the trial court did not abuse its discretion in finding that Merry signed the agreement while under duress.

We reject Anthony's argument regarding testimony on the battered woman syndrome. The court was not required to find that Merry was suffering from battered woman syndrome as a prerequisite to determining that she was under duress. Indeed, the trial court's journal entry specifically declined to acknowledge Merry as a victim of battered woman syndrome. Accordingly, any error in admitting Zeidner's testimony was harmless.

Anthony's first and second assignments of error are overruled.

Assignment of Error III

[Discussion regarding trial court's abuse of discretion omitted.]

Anthony's third assignment of error is overruled. . . .

Reflection

Quebodeaux is a great example of a duress case. There are three elements necessary to establish a duress case; first, the one side involuntarily accepted the terms of another; second, that circumstances permitted no other alternative; and third, that the opposite party's coercive acts caused those circumstances.

The first element is that one side involuntarily accepted the terms of another. In this case, Merry involuntarily agreed to Anthony's terms. Merry did not want to agree to her ex-husband's terms, but felt that she had to.

The second element is that the circumstances permitted no other alternative. Merry had no choice but to agree to Anthony's terms. Had Merry not agreed to the terms, Anthony was going to have Merry deemed an unfit mother and take all three children away.

Finally, the opposite party's coercive acts must have caused those circumstances. Merry did not want to agree to Anthony's terms, but she had no alternatives and had to agree to his terms, or else she risked losing all three of her children.

Why didn't the court characterize Merry's defense as undue influence? Perhaps the reason is the parties, although married at the time in a technical sense, were undergoing a bitter divorce at the time. While in a typical situation, a wife should be entitled to rely on her husband, under these circumstances, perhaps the court found it unreasonable for Merry to rely on Anthony looking out for her best interests.

It is also important to note that in addition to physical duress, there is also what is called economic duress. However, economic duress is very rarely found to be a basis for avoidance of a contract, whereas physical duress commonly is.

Discussion

1. Duress can arise due to physical compulsion or an improper threat. List all the potential instances of compulsion and all the potential threats. For each threat, analyze where it was improper pursuant to R2d § 175.

2. In general, contract law considers objective manifestations. But in the case of duress, there is a subjective test for inducement. Explain that subjective test in general and then apply it to the specific facts of *Quebodeaux*. In other words, how did Mr. Quebodeaux's threat to Mrs. Quebodeaux make Mrs. Quebodeaux feel and think?

3. Why does contract law generally take an objective approach, and why does it take a subject approach with regards to the duress doctrine?

Problems

Problem 12.1. Motor Home Misrepresentation

In early January 2004, John Powers, III attended a motor home show in Tucson, Arizona where he and Damon Rapozo, a salesman for Guaranty RV, Inc. discussed Powers purchasing a Country Coach, Inc. (Country Coach) motor home from Guaranty.

Powers had certain specifications that he wanted in a motor home, including an engine sufficiently powerful to tow a large trailer. On January 21, 2004, Rapozo sent Powers a proposal for a Country Coach Intrigue motor home with a C-13 Caterpillar 525 hp engine.

Because Powers had heard of instances in which large engines in motor homes overheated, he specifically asked for an assurance that the C-13 engine would not overheat in the Intrigue. In response, Rapozo emailed Jeff Howe, an employee with Country Coach, the following:

> Hi Jeff,
>
> I have a customer ready to fly up and order a new Intrigue Serenade. He wants a letter from CC that states the C-13 will not overheat in the Intrigue, then he said he will fly up. Is that possible?
>
> Damon

Howe forwarded Rapozo's email to Bently Buchanan, Country Coach's chassis engineering manager, who replied via email as follows:

> The cooling system for each power train installation is required to be tested by the engine manufacturer. The cooling system consists of a radiator, charge air cooler, transmission cooler, hydraulic oil cooler, air conditioning condenser, hydraulic pump, hydraulic motor and the cooling fan. Recently we successfully completed this testing for our C-13 installation on our Magna

and Affinity chassis. This same cooling system will be used on your Intrigue with the C-13. The only difference between our Magna/Affinity installation and the Intrigue is the engine access door. On our Magnas and Affinities the doors have "hidden horizontal louvers" cut into them. On Intrigues we install a door which has a perforated aluminum panel on it. These louvers and perforations aid in engine compartment heat dissipation. Whereas I have faith that our cooling package installation on the C-13 Intrigue will be successful, the effect that the different door has on cooling is unknown at this time. Because our cooling system equipment is the same on all chassis with the C-13, we are not required to test our Intrigue installation.

Rapozo then transmitted Buchanan's response to Powers. On July 19, 2004, Powers and Guaranty executed the purchase documents for the 2004 Intrigue for a sales price of $344,382.00. The Intrigue overheated during its initial drive from the lot in Oregon to Arizona, and repeatedly thereafter.

On July 18, 2005, Powers filed a complaint against Country Coach and Guaranty alleging, among other things, fraudulent inducement to contract.

Should the court void the agreement on the basis of fraudulent misrepresentation?

See Powers v. Guar. RV, Inc., 229 Ariz. 555, 562, 278 P.3d 333, 340 (Ct. App. 2012).

Problem 12.2. **The Blodgetts Under Duress**

Nancy and William Blodgett were married in Connecticut on November 22, 1975. William signed an antenuptial agreement the day before their marriage; Nancy did not sign the agreement until December 31, 1975. Shortly after they married, the Blodgetts moved to Ohio.

On November 10, 1975, William entered into an agreement to purchase the assets of Roberts Cartage, Inc., later known as Roberts Express, Inc. William ran the company, and Nancy assisted in its operations by performing at various times duties such as clerical work, delivering freight, dispatching drivers and sales. The company prospered and was sold to Roadway Services, Inc. in 1984 for $6,000,000 in cash, $3,000,000 in incentives if certain profit goals were reached by 1989 and $3,000,000 for a non-competition provision between William Blodgett and Roadway Services.

Nancy and William separated in February 1986, and in April 1986, Nancy filed a complaint for divorce. The trial court granted the divorce in January 1988. With regard to property division, the trial court found the $6,000,000 proceeds from the sale of Roberts Express to be a marital asset. The non-competition and incentive payments were found to be non-marital assets and solely the property of William. Nancy's share of the marital assets, including the sale of Roberts Express, was set at $3,100,000. Because of tax consequences, the trial court ordered that Nancy be paid $2,765,000 if she signed a satisfaction of judgment within forty-five days of the trial court's judgment entry, filed on January 29, 1988.

Both parties appealed the distribution of assets. Nancy contended that the incentive and non-competition payments should have been treated as marital assets. William appealed the trial court's refusal to enforce the antenuptial agreement. While her appeal was pending, Nancy requested the court of appeals to order that $2,765,000 be released to her from escrow, and the same amount to William.

On May 11, 1988, Nancy signed and executed the satisfaction of judgment. In return, $2,765,000 was released from escrow, and William executed a deed to the family home.

The next day, William filed a motion to dismiss Nancy's appeal based on her execution of the satisfaction of judgment, which he claimed had terminated her right to appeal. The court of appeals took the motion under advisement, indicating it would rule on the motion prior to its decision on the merits.

In order for Nancy to use the excuse of duress, what elements must she be able to prove?

See Blodgett v. Blodgett, 551 N.E.2d 1249 (Ohio 1990).

Problem 12.3. Undue Bequest

Florence Goldman, a widow in her eighties, sued August Bequai, an attorney and long-time friend of Goldman's family. Goldman alleges that Bequai fraudulently induced her to convey to him substantially all of her property shortly after the death of her husband. Goldman brought claims against Bequai for fraud and deceit, breach of fiduciary obligation, tortious conversion, and legal malpractice; and against Bequai's wife, Mary Ryan Bequai, for breach of fiduciary obligation. After permitting limited discovery, the District Court ruled that Goldman's claims against appellee were barred by the three-year statute of limitations in the District of Columbia. The trial court rejected Goldman's contentions that the running of the limitations period should have been equitably tolled.

In response to the ruling, Goldman brought a new claim for recission of the agreement to convey her property to Bequai under the defense of undue influence. Her complaint seeking recission based on this defense included the following facts:

Florence Goldman's husband died on October 31, 1985, after a long bout with Alzheimer's and Parkinson's diseases. For several years prior to her husband's death, Goldman cared for him at home. During much of her husband's illness and for some time thereafter, Goldman was under the care of a psychiatrist, who treated her for depression stemming from the strain and grief she experienced because of her husband's declining health. As part of this therapy Goldman was treated with antidepressant drugs, which she alleges had a negative effect on her cognitive processes.

Goldman's Complaint described August Bequai as a long-time friend whom she regarded as almost a member of her family. Bequai in turn described Goldman's husband as a "surrogate father," and stated that both Mr. and Mrs. Goldman often referred to him as their "good son."

Bequai is an attorney and has written several books about white-collar crime and served as an adjunct professor or lecturer at several universities. Goldman alleged in her complaint that during her husband's illness and after his death, she looked to Bequai as her "adviser and attorney" in her financial affairs.

In January 1986, three months after her husband's death, Goldman conveyed to Bequai joint tenancy with a right of survivorship in a condominium in Bethesda, Maryland, and in a partnership interest in property at 423 Massachusetts Avenue, N.W., in Washington, DC. Ten dollars ($10) was given in consideration for the transfer of each property. Goldman had no legal counsel or independent advice of any sort, and she alleges that Bequai did not fully explain the nature of the transactions to her. There were no witnesses to the transactions other than the notary, whose commission apparently had expired several months prior to the signing of the deeds.

The Massachusetts Avenue property was sold in January 1990, and the proceeds attributable to the Goldman/Bequai partnership share were distributed to them. Both Bequai and Goldman were represented at the closing by Robert Pollock, an attorney hired by Bequai. Goldman, however, described Pollock as "a flunky who did [Bequai's] bidding."

After the sale of the Massachusetts Avenue property, Bequai accompanied Goldman to the bank, where both placed their proceeds in investment accounts that were opened that day. Bequai placed his money in an account he owned jointly with his wife. Goldman placed her share in a joint account with Bequai.

In her deposition, appellant stated that, at least as early as 1986, she, her son (Dennis Goldman), and Bequai had discussed starting a business that would employ both Goldman and her son. Dennis Goldman stated in an affidavit that Bequai had said that he needed to be listed as an owner of the Massachusetts Avenue property in order adequately to represent the Goldmans' interests during negotiations over the sale of the property, and that Bequai told him that the transfer "would be temporary, and solely for the limited purpose of inflating his financial worth on paper" while he looked for a business in which to invest. Florence Goldman stated that Bequai told her that he needed to be a part owner in order to "participate fully" in negotiations for the sale of the property, and to locate a suitable business opportunity for himself and the Goldmans. Goldman further stated that:

> He said that it was necessary in order to represent me that he had to have his name on the property as a half owner. But all the proceeds from whatever I had, except to live on, would be going into the business and a future for my son and a future for me. That's what we were building on.

According to Goldman, "this is why we let him do this, not ever realizing that I was relinquishing my full interest." Goldman stated that it was her understanding that the purpose of the documents she signed conveying a joint tenancy in her properties to Bequai was: "To give him stature in negotiating for the business for the three of us." At several points in her deposition, Goldman stated that she relied on Bequai's representations and so did not read the documents she signed.

In August 1987, at Bequai's dictation, Goldman hand wrote a power of attorney authorizing her son to represent her "in all matters pertaining to the sale" of the Massachusetts Avenue property. The purpose of this power of attorney was ostensibly to allow Dennis Goldman to attend partnership meetings concerning the sale of the property. Florence Goldman indicated that Bequai suggested to her that it would be too much of a strain for her to attend these meetings herself.

Goldman stated in her deposition that her "first inklings" that Bequai had "deceived" her came in June of 1990, after she received the money for the sale of the Massachusetts Avenue property: "His name was on my half. His name was on everything I had: my checking account, my savings account. The other half he put in his name and his wife's name and I couldn't understand that."

It appears that there was also a disagreement between Dennis Goldman and Bequai at about this time. Both men stated that they formerly were very close friends, and Bequai had employed Dennis Goldman for some time as an administrative member of his legal practice. However, in middle to late 1990, the two had an argument stemming at least in part from Bequai's handling of Florence Goldman's finances. As a result of this quarrel, Bequai dismissed Dennis Goldman from his employ.

Should the court rescind the agreement under which Goldman bequeathed her property to Bequai based on the defense of undue influence?

See Goldman v. Bequai, 19 F.3d 666 (D.C. Cir. 1994).

Module V

Interpretation

Up until now, contracts class has focused on whether a contract was formed. In other words, we analyzed whether parties owed any legal obligations to each other under contract law. Now, we assume some contract was duly formed and ask, what does this contract mean? What legally enforceable obligations do these parties have to each other under this agreement?

To put it another way, we are going to learn the different interpretive techniques that courts apply when attaching meaning to contractual obligations. Perhaps the most famous case study involves the meaning of the word "chicken." The *Frigaliment* case involves an agreement for the purchase and sale of chicken from a U.S. company to a Swiss corporation. The dispute arose when the seller delivered stewing chickens. The buyer claimed the seller should have delivered frying chickens. The legal question presented is, therefore, what is the meaning of chicken?

The *Frigaliment* court refers to a classic quotation from Oliver Wendell Holmes regarding the meaning of a contract:

> *The making of a contract depends not on the agreement of two minds in one intention, but on the agreement of two sets of external signs — not on the parties' having meant the same thing but on their having said the same thing.*

The analysis of contractual meaning thus begins with the question, what did both parties say? In *Frigaliment*, both parties said "chicken," but did they mean frying chickens, stewing chickens, or either?

The *Frigaliment* case is famous not only for its subject matter, but also because it established a framework for thinking about seven sources of contract evidence, and which take priority. The point of reading this case is not to define chickens per se but to understand how courts determine the parties' mutual intent through their words and actions. The lessons learned through this case are also found throughout this module.

Chapter 13

Classifying Contractual Evidence

When two parties agree they have formed a contract but disagree about that contract requires each to do, the debate usually centers around the parties' varied interpretations of their agreement. For example, in the *Frigaliment* case, both parties agreed they formed a contract to buy and sell chicken, but the buyer argued they meant frying chickens, whereas the seller argued they meant any chickens. Whose meaning prevails? How should court determine the prevailing meaning? This is the central question of contract interpretation.

> *Interpretation of a promise or agreement or a term thereof is the ascertainment of its meaning.* R2d § 200.

R2d defines interpretation of a promise or agreement as the ascertainment of its meaning. This is somewhat of an obvious rule, and it does not answer the critical question of *how* such meaning is determined. There are two general ways to arrive at the meaning of a contract: on the one hand, courts can focus on the writing itself, on the words of the agreement, and make an objective determination. Or courts could take a more subjective approach by asking what did the parties actually intend their agreement to mean.

This objective/subjective dichotomy runs all the way through contract law analysis, but it is perhaps more in evidence here. The more modern R2d has taken a relatively subjective approach based on legal realism, although some courts still cleave to the objective approach supported by legal formalism.

A court following R2d will usually consider both intrinsic and extrinsic evidence in determining contractual meaning. In other words, the judge will not only consider what she or he thinks a word means, the judge should also obtain evidence about how the parties used that term to understand how they meant it in the context of this agreement.

Admitting extrinsic evidence regarding what the parties said or did, or how a term is used in society or trade, can help courts better understand what parties meant. But this open inquiry means that contractual disputes must be resolved through depositions, hearings, testimony, and other expensive and time consuming fact finding.

For reasons of judicial efficiency, many jurisdictions continue to hold to a more objective theory, which accords with the Four Corners Rule, the approach that courts should look primarily to the words of the contract, and, in many cases, exclude evidence of what the parties did or said that could change the obvious written meaning of a contract.

Rules

A. Evidence of Contractual Meaning

Courts generally agree that interpretation of a contract requires ascertainment of the parties' meaning. But courts go about this process in different ways. Depending on whether the court takes an objective or subjective approach, that court will be more or less eager to consider different types of evidence. There are seven sources of evidence of the contractual meaning of written agreements, which can be divided into two general categories:

Intrinsic evidence, which is evidence that comes directly from written agreements, and

Extrinsic evidence, evidence that comes from outside of the written agreement.

1. Intrinsic Evidence

The types of intrinsic evidence are:

1. Common or trade usage of written terms,
2. Defined terms that are spelled out in the agreement or via express references to external definitions, and
3. Reasonable meaning in context of the parties' purpose of the agreement.

2. Extrinsic Evidence

The types of extrinsic evidence are:

4. Course of performance, how the parties dealt with each other under this agreement,
5. Course of dealing, how the parties dealt with each other under similar prior agreements,
6. Usage of trade, how people in this trade or practice commonly act in this situation, and
7. Preliminary negotiations, what the parties discussed prior to entering to a signed writing, but which were not included in that writing.

Although all these forms of evidence may be considered in certain situations, courts generally prefer intrinsic evidence over extrinsic evidence: where written evidence of contractual intent exists, that is usually regarded as a better indicator than parties' memory or testimony alone.

On the other end of the spectrum from written terms is evidence regarding preliminary negotiations. Preliminary negotiations are often considered the least reliable source of evidence of contractual meaning and may even be inadmissible in a court of law pursuant to the Parol Evidence Rule.

Within this spectrum, courts have significant freedom to focus on intrinsic evidence or to consider a range of extrinsic evidence. Courts that prefer the objective approach tend to focus on intrinsic evidence such as the written words parties used. Courts that take the subjective approach tend to admit a wider range of extrinsic evidence that helps the court better understand the parties' true intentions. The cases in this chapter are intended to help you evaluate which approach is better and to articulate why.

B. Conflicting Evidence

Whose meaning prevails when two parties to a contract have a misunderstanding, that is, they do not attach the same meaning to a particular term in a contract? If the misunderstanding is fundamental, the parties may not really have a contract or agreement at all. Recall the case about the Two Ships Peerless, where the buyer referred to the October Peerless and the seller referred to the December Peerless. Both ships existed, and the contractual term "ex rel Peerless" referred to real vessels — but the parties did not have the same ship in mind when using the semantic label "Peerless."

Words in the English language are often symbols about more abstract ideas, mental states and concepts. Words are extremely contingent upon their context to derive meaning. For example, the word "cleave" can mean to join with or to separate from, depending on its context. If two parties agree, in writing, to "cleave," have they agreed to join or separate?

Good contract drafting can avoid this problem by clarifying ambiguities in advance of finalizing a written agreement, but even the best efforts can fall short. For example, in the Canadian case of *Rogers Communications Inc. v. Aliant Inc.*, one Canadian utilities corporation agreed to string the other's cable lines across its utility poles in exchange for an annual fee of $9.60 per pole. Rogers thought they had a five-year fixed-rate deal, but Aliant disagreed, arguing that the second comma in the termination clause means that Aliant had the right to cancel the agreement at any time with one years' notice:

> *This agreement shall continue in force for a period of five years from the date it is made, and thereafter for successive five year terms, unless and until terminated by one year prior notice in writing by either party.*

To clarify the comma conflict: Rogers believed that the above clause means that the agreement shall continue for at least five years, whereas Aliant believed that the above clause means that either party can cancel the agreement at any time with one years' notice. Whose meaning prevails? (You can research the case heard by the Canadian Radio-Television and Telecommunications Commission to find out.)

This is not a mere exercise in grammar and punctuation. If Aliant is right, Rogers will pay an extra $2 million per year to use its utility poles. How would you feel if you were the lawyer whose comma cost your client $2 million?

Moreover, how should courts evaluate this term? Should it apply strict rules of grammar? Can you locate any grammar rule which clearly states how to understand this term? Might there be a contrary rule elsewhere? Consider that some style manuals prefer a terminal comma, while others avoid it, and still others suggest either is appropriate so long as a writing is internally consistent.

What if one party spoke primarily English and the other primarily spoke French? Should courts consider the nature of the parties when determining whether to strictly construe terms according to grammatical rules? What if the grammar or verbiage at issue is used differently in different regions or countries?

Does the Restatement seem to honor the written agreement such that its objective meaning is paramount? Or does the Restatement seem to leave the door open for the parties to introduce evidence that the contract does not actually mean what it appears to say?

> Where the parties have attached the same meaning to a promise or agreement or a term thereof, it is interpreted in accordance with that meaning. R2d § 201(1).

R2d focuses the judicial inquiry on what the parties intended to mean, thus inviting at least some subjective inquiry into what the actual parties thought. This approach is based on R2d's foundations in legal realism. R2d implicitly recognizes that words are merely symbols and representations of mental states.

Moreover, according to the Restatement, the mental states of mutual understanding and mutual assent — where both parties actually agree to be bound by contractual terms — is the polestar of contractual interpretation. To search for contractual meaning is to inquire into what the parties actually intended. To effectuate this purpose, the Restatement would permit or even require courts to review extrinsic evidence that may be relevant to what the parties thought and intended at the time of contractual formation.

As you study contract interpretation, you might see how the tensions in contract law manifest themselves most clearly when courts are called upon to decide how written language reflects human intention. Sociology teaches that languages is important to culture, and contract law shows also how culture is important to understanding language. Culture regards the customs and institutions of a social group, which can be as widespread as 20th century popular culture or as localized as the Alaskan Inuktitut fishing traditions in the 1970s. If a court interprets a contract based on widespread meaning, it may not reflect the intentions of the specific people involved in the deal.

For example, the Inuit culture has a strong tradition of sharing food. In this culture, a family member who uses another's fishing boat might be expected to share the catch with the family; whereas in popular culture, the borrower might be expected to clean the boat and fill it with gasoline but not to exchange fish.

Over the course of this chapter, you might think about how you would answer the above questions while learning the R2d's approach and its rationale. This thinking should help you articulate reasons why a court should adopt your client's position, whether that be to understood terms in the context of the commercial circumstances in which they were formed. Do you think R2d strikes the right balance between the goals of enforcing the intention of the parties, maintaining judicial efficiency, and creating reasonable certainty in the enforcement of contracts?

C. Evidence Regarding Circumstances

R2d takes a subjective approach to contract interpretation; that is, R2d authorizes and perhaps requires courts to consider extrinsic evidence such as the circumstances in which a contract was formed. The R2d's philosophy is founded in legal realism, which recognizes that the meaning of words depends on their context. Thus, even when determining the meaning of intrinsic evidence such as the dictionary meaning of a commonly used term or the grammatical significance of a comma, a court can and perhaps should look to the principal purpose of the parties.

> *Words and other conduct are interpreted in the light of all the circumstances, and if the principal purpose of the parties is ascertainable it is given great weight.* R2d § 202.

How might parties signify their purpose in writing a contract? Parties often write recitals at the beginning of a contract that explain the reasons for entering into it. But even where parties do not write down their intentions, courts following the R2d subjectivist approach can hear extrinsic evidence that sheds light on the parties' intent.

For example, in *Spaulding v. Morse*, 322 Mass. 149 (1947), George D. Morse and Ruth D. Morse got divorced. In 1946, they signed a divorce settlement agreement, pursuant to which George provide for their son Richard D. Morse thus:

> *Beginning May 1, 1947, [George D. Morse shall pay] the sum of one hundred dollars ($100) per month until such time, if any, as the beneficiary enters college, and, thereupon, and for a period not to exceed four (4) years thereafter, to pay the sum of twenty-two hundred dollars ($2,200) per year.*

World War II interrupted Richard's plans to go to college. Instead, Richard joined the U.S. Army the day after he completed high school. George claimed this absolved him of his duty to pay, but Richard's trustee, Wickliffe J. Spaulding, disagreed. Spaulding made an objectivist, formalist argument: the agreement says George shall pay, so he should pay. George, and the court, disagreed.

George successfully argued that the court should take the whole circumstance into account. He produced evidence that Ruth wanted George to provide for Richard's education, and this was unnecessary and indeed impossible while Richard was at war under the custody of the Army. The court reasoned this was correct because writing must be evaluated in context:

> *Every instrument in writing is to be interpreted, with a view to the material circumstances of the parties at the time of the execution, in the light of the pertinent facts within their knowledge and in such manner as to give effect to the main end designed to be accomplished.*
>
> *The instrument is to be so construed as to give effect to the intent of the parties as manifested by the words used illumined by all the attendant factors, unless inconsistent with some positive rule of law or repugnant to other terms of the instrument. An omission to express an intention cannot be supplied by conjecture.*
>
> *But if the instrument as a whole produces a conviction that a particular result was fixedly desired although not expressed by formal words, that defect may be supplied by implication and the underlying intention may be effectuated, provided it is sufficiently declared by the entire instrument.*

Extrinsic evidence is not the only source of context. The contract itself can provide clues to its context. Just as words should not be severed from reality, one part of a writing should not be severed from another, so that any disputed terms in a writing are understood in the context of the whole writing:

> *A writing is interpreted as a whole, and all writings that are part of the same transaction are interpreted together.* R2d § 202(2).

Interpreting a writing as a whole means that terms used in one place should have the same meaning as the same terms used in another place. Does this reflect how people actually use words? If you were drafting a contract, should you get a thesaurus and choose varied words to make the contract more interesting to read? Or should you get a dictionary and choose the best word to effect your meaning and use it consistently?

R2d's inclusive approach does not mean, however, that words are unimportant. Rather, the language of an agreement is usually the best evidence of its meaning:

> *Unless a different intention is manifested, where language has a generally prevailing meaning, it is interpreted in accordance with that meaning.* R2d § 202(3)(a).

What does it mean to say that language has a generally prevailing meaning? Does this mean that words have an objective meaning? Which words could you look up in a dictionary and thereby find a clear meaning? For example, look up the definition of the words "execute," "tender," and "cleave." Discuss whether you are able to understand those words out of context based on their generally prevailing meaning.

It seems that meaning changes depending on the time and location. The word "pop" had a different meaning in England in 1070 than it does in America today. Although the word originated from the Middle English verb "poppen," when meant to strike or thrust, it has evolved to denote a onomatopoeic sound ("pop goes the weasal"), soda products, and a style of music.

Is there a common usage of a term throughout the United States, and if so, is that the meeting that should be applied? Or should courts look to how parties used words specially in their own circumstances? Or perhaps if words were used in a unique way in a particular geography or location, should that be the way we interpret the words in this agreement? Courts may answer these questions differently when ordinary people form agreements without realizing they are saying the same words but attached a different meaning to them. When parties are part of a technical trade, however, courts can look to usage of trade as evidence of what those parties probably intended:

> *Technical terms and words of art are given their technical meaning when used in a transaction within their technical field.* R2d § 202(3)(b).

Technical usage is often different from ordinary usage. For example, in contract law, the word "execute" means to sign a written enforceable agreement. In criminal law, execute means to carry out a sentence of death on a legally condemned person. The meaning attributed to the word "execute" should be different if used among contract lawyers than if used among criminal lawyers.

Parties also develop their own language as they work together in furtherance of mutual goals.

> *Where an agreement involves repeated occasions for performance by either party with knowledge of the nature of the performance and opportunity for objection to it by the other, any course of performance accepted or acquiesced in without objection is given great weight in the interpretation of the agreement.* R2d § 202(4).

According to R2d, contracts gain meaning as parties act pursuant to them. Once the contract has been formed and the parties begin performing their obligations under it, their actions that occur after the formation of the contract shed light on the meaning that they intended when they wrote the agreement.

With so many different sources of evidence of contractual meaning, it is possible for evidence to conflict. The R2d's final rule on interpretation suggests that courts should attempt to find the meaning that is as consistent as possible with as much of the evidence as possible.

> *Wherever reasonable, the manifestations of intention of the parties to a promise or agreement are interpreted as consistent with each other and with any relevant course of performance, course of dealing, or usage of trade.* R2d § 202(5).

It would be nice if parties' performance of a contract were always consistent with prevailing meaning. But how should a court prioritize evidence that is inconsistent? The answer to that question may be found in the next Restatement provision, which regards the priority of these sources of contractual meaning.

D. Hierarchy of Evidence

Although courts prefer to determine the meaning of an agreement that accords will all the evidence, this is not always possible. For example, in the case of *Nānākuli Paving & Rock Co. v. Shell Oil Co.*, below, the two parties had a contract for the purchase and sale of asphalt, which is made of oil and used to pave roads. The contract said the price of the asphalt should be "Shell's posted price at time of delivery." This verbiage seems pretty clear, but it does not reflect what the parties actually did, nor did it reflect industry standards. Instead, Shell previously offered price protection to Nānākuli, meaning, Shell would charge Nānākuli the price it posted at the time Nānākuli made the order, not when Shell made the delivery.

This conflict between paper and practice came to a head during the oil crisis of the 1970s. The price of oil multiplied exponentially between when Nānākuli placed an order and when Shell delivered it. Shell's new sales manager refused to give price protection, citing the plain meaning of their agreement, and Nānākuli sued.

In deciding whether the parties intended for price protection to be incorporated into their contract, a court must apply some standards of preference between conflicting evidence. Both R2d and UCC offer similar advice about how to prioritize evidence. R2d begins:

> *In the interpretation of a promise or agreement or a term thereof, the following standards of preference are generally applicable.* R2d § 203.

The first rule is to give effect to all terms. Nothing in a written contract should be deemed superfluous or inconsequential:

> *An interpretation which gives a reasonable, lawful, and effective meaning to all the terms is preferred to an interpretation which leaves a part unreasonable, unlawful, or of no effect.* R2d § 203(a).

For example, if a contract between a shipyard and a boat captain says, "Vessel to be loaded promptly" and also says "Vessel to be loaded in turn," the captain might try to argue that loaded promptly means his vessel get loaded first. But the shipyard should successfully counter-argue that is the wrong interpretation because it makes the phrase regarding in turn superfluous and unnecessary. Rather, the correct interpretation is that the vessel shall be loaded in turn, and then it shall be loaded promptly.

When considering a written contract, intrinsic evidence should be prioritized over extrinsic evidence:

> *Express terms are given greater weight than course of performance, course of dealing, and usage of trade, course of performance is given greater weight than course of dealing or usage of trade, and course of dealing is given greater weight than usage of trade.* R2d § 203(b).

In *Citizens Nat'l Bank v. L.L. Glascock, Inc.*, 243 So. 2d 67 (Miss. 1971), an architect agreed to supervise construction of a bank in exchange for a stated fee. The architect claimed that he was also entitled to additional pay for supplemental work not within the terms of the contract because it is customary within the trade for an architect to order additional work. The bank disagreed and refused to pay more than the contract price. The *Citizens* court sided with the bank and against the architect, stating:

> We are of the opinion that the written contract expresses the agreement of the parties and that it prevails over custom. Courts do not have the power to make contracts where none exist, nor to modify, add to, or subtract from the terms of one in existence.

Courts' emphasis and reliance on a written contract extends to terms in the contract that are more specific or otherwise more obviously something the parties thought about.

> Specific terms and exact terms are given greater weight than general language. R2d § 203(c).

In general, this rule means that handwritten changes to a contract are more persuasive than pre-printed terms. But there are logical and reasonable limits to this general rule. For example, in *United States Fidelity & Guar. Co. v. First Nat'l Bank*, 244 S.C. 436 (1964), a banker drew up a check and imprinted on it an amount using the bank's automated check writing machine. The borrower then handwrote a different amount on the check. Although the general rule is that specific terms control over general ones, and that handwriting is more influential than pre-printed terms, the *First National* court did not apply that rule in this case because it found that the handwriting could be fraudulent.

The rule prioritizing specific over general terms also extends to specifically negotiated provisions. Contracts often contain boilerplate, which is standard language that is often pre-printed on a form. Boilerplate is usually non-negotiable. But evidence that the parties specifically negotiated and changed the boilerplate is also persuasive:

> Separately negotiated or added terms are given greater weight than standardized terms or other terms not separately negotiated. R2d § 203(d).

It is sometimes said that handwritten terms are more persuasive than typewritten terms, and typewritten terms are more persuasive than pre-printed terms. For example, a typewritten line can be deleted by parties drawing a line through it. But, as the *First Nat'l* case shows, courts will look for evidence that the party who contests the added term actually produced it; otherwise, it would be too easy for a party to commit fraud by unilaterally modifying a written agreement in its own favor.

> **UCC Priorities in Interpretation.** The UCC, which governs sales of goods and which supersedes the common law when they conflict, essentially agrees with the R2d's priorities in interpretation. This book does not typically repeat UCC provisions where they are harmonious with the common law, but these provisions are reproduced here because this section of the UCC provides useful explanation that might apply even when dealing in contracts not for goods.
>
> First, the UCC defines "course of performance":
>
> > A "course of performance" is a sequence of conduct between the parties to a particular transaction that exists if: (1) the agreement of the parties

with respect to the transaction involves repeated occasions for perfor-
mance by a party; and (2) the other party, with knowledge of the nature
of the performance and opportunity for objection to it, accepts the per-
formance or acquiesces in it without objection. UCC § 1-303(a).

A simple way to remember course of performance is that is involves the same parties in the same deal. This is the best source of extrinsic evidence because it shows how these parties actually behaved under the contract at issue.

Course of dealing involves how these parties behaved under a prior deal:

A "course of dealing" is a sequence of conduct concerning previous trans-
actions between the parties to a particular transaction that is fairly to be
regarded as establishing a common basis of understanding for interpret-
ing their expressions and other conduct. R2d § 1-303(b).

Course of dealing evidence is only available where the parties have contracted multiple times. In such cases, how parties previously interpreted a similar term under a different contract can shed light on how they probably intended that same term under the contract at issue.

Moving beyond the specific parties in this dispute, courts also inquire into how the trade generally interprets or uses a disputed term:

A "usage of trade" is any practice or method of dealing having such regu-
larity of observance in a place, vocation, or trade as to justify an expec-
tation that it will be observed with respect to the transaction in question.
The existence and scope of such a usage must be proved as facts. If it is
established that such a usage is embodied in a trade code or similar rec-
ord, the interpretation of the record is a question of law. UCC § 103(c).

The UCC is even more subjectivist and liberal in its admission of extrinsic evidence than the R2d. Under the UCC, courts virtually always consider extrinsic evidence:

A course of performance or course of dealing between the parties or
usage of trade in the vocation or trade in which they are engaged or of
which they are or should be aware is relevant in ascertaining the mean-
ing of the parties' agreement, may give particular meaning to specific
terms of the agreement, and may supplement or qualify the terms of the
agreement. A usage of trade applicable in the place in which part of the
performance under the agreement is to occur may be so utilized as to
that part of the performance. UCC 1-303(d).

Regarding prioritization of evidence, the UCC approach is not substantially different from the R2d approach. In both cases, intrinsic evidence is more persuasive than extrinsic evidence. Even the most subjectivist courts still appreciate the gravity of a signed written contract.

Except as otherwise provided in subsection (f), the express terms of an
agreement and any applicable course of performance, course of dealing,

or usage of trade must be construed whenever reasonable as consistent with each other. If such a construction is unreasonable: (1) express terms prevail over course of performance, course of dealing, and usage of trade; (2) course of performance prevails over course of dealing and usage of trade; and (3) course of dealing prevails over usage of trade. UCC § 1-303(e).

The UCC does place special emphasis on the parties' course of performance. When one party repeatedly behaves in a manner inconsistent with the written contract, that may constitute its waiver or modification of that term. For example, in the *Nānākuli* case, Shell Oil gave price protection to Nānākuli several times, even though the written agreement did not contemplate price protection. This seems to be why the *Nānākuli* court found that Nānākuli merited price protection even after Shell refused to freely give it.

Subject to Section 2-209, a course of performance is relevant to show a waiver or modification of any term inconsistent with the course of performance. UCC § 1-303(f).

Under both the UCC and the R2d, courts consider the context of a contract when determining its meaning. Context includes the commercial context in which it was made. For example, carpenters commonly refer to boards as "two-by-fours" when virtually everyone in that industry knows such lumber measures 1.5 inches wide by 3.5 inches tall. A professional carpenter would thus probably fail if suing a lumber supplier for providing these commonly sized boards.

But trade usage can be inadmissible where one party has no reason to know of the specific trade usage, or where such evidence would otherwise be unfair or prejudicial:

Evidence of a relevant usage of trade offered by one party is not admissible unless that party has given the other party notice that the court finds sufficient to prevent unfair surprise to the other party. UCC § 1-303(g).

The R2d and UCC approaches have more similarities than differences. Moreover, both are generally consistent with the hierarchy of evidence of contractual meaning presented at the beginning of this chapter:

1. Common usage
2. Defined terms
3. Reasonable meaning
4. Course of performance
5. Course of dealing
6. Usage of trade
7. Preliminary negotiations

Cases

Reading Frigaliment Importing Co., Ltd., v. B.N.S. International Sales Corp. The *Frigaliment* case involves an agreement for the purchase and sale of chicken from a U.S. company to a German company. The dispute arose when the seller delivered stewing chickens. The buyer claimed the seller should have delivered frying chickens. The legal question presented, therefore, is what is the meaning of chicken?

Figure 13.1. Gallina Poulle, Albert Flamen (1659). CC0 1.0.

In studying this case, please make sure to identify all the different strategies that the court uses to determine the meaning of chicken. In particular, try to list all the various sources of evidence that a court could consider when determining the meaning of contractual terms. Then explain which sources of evidence take priority over which others, and be prepared to discuss why this prioritization of evidence of contractual meaning makes sense.

Frigaliment Importing Co., Ltd., v. B.N.S. International Sales Corp

190 F. Supp. 116 (S.D.N.Y. 1960)

FRIENDLY, J.

The issue is, what is chicken? Plaintiff says "chicken" means a young chicken, suitable for broiling and frying. Defendant says "chicken" means any bird of that genus that meets contract specifications on weight and quality, including what it calls "stewing chicken" and plaintiff pejoratively terms "fowl". Dictionaries give both meanings, as well as some others not relevant here. To support its, plaintiff sends a number of volleys over the net; defendant essays to return them and adds a few serves of its own. Assuming that both parties were acting in good faith, the case nicely illustrates Holmes' remark "that the making of a contract depends not on the agreement of two minds in one intention, but on the agreement of two sets of external signs — not on the parties' having meant the same thing but on their having said the same thing." The Path of the Law, in Collected Legal Papers, p. 178. I have concluded that plaintiff has not sustained its burden of persuasion that the contract used "chicken" in the narrower sense.

The action is for breach of the warranty that goods sold shall correspond to the description, New York Personal Property Law, McKinney's Consol. Laws, c. 41, § 95. Two contracts are in suit. In the first, dated May 2, 1957, defendant, a New York sales corporation, confirmed the sale to plaintiff, a Swiss corporation, of

> US Fresh Frozen Chicken, Grade A, Government Inspected, Eviscerated 2½–3 lbs. and 1½–2 lbs. each all chicken individually wrapped in cryovac, packed in secured fiber cartons or wooden boxes, suitable for export
>
> 75,000 lbs. 2½–3 lbs. . . . . @$33.00
>
> 25,000 lbs. 1½–2 lbs. . . . . @$36.50
>
> per 100 lbs. FAS New York, scheduled May 10, 1957 pursuant to instructions from Penson & Co., New York.

The second contract, also dated May 2, 1957, was identical save that only 50,000 lbs. of the heavier "chicken" were called for, the price of the smaller birds was $37 per 100 lbs., and shipment was scheduled for May 30. The initial shipment under the first contract was short but the balance was shipped on May 17. When the initial shipment arrived in Switzerland, plaintiff found, on May 28, that the 2½–3 lbs. birds were not young chicken suitable for broiling and frying but stewing chicken or "fowl"; indeed, many of the cartons and bags plainly so indicated. Protests ensued. Nevertheless, shipment under the second contract was made on May 29, the 2½–3 lbs. birds again being stewing chicken. Defendant stopped the transportation of these at Rotterdam.

This action followed. Plaintiff says that, notwithstanding that its acceptance was in Switzerland, New York law controls; defendant does not dispute this, and relies on New York decisions. I shall follow the apparent agreement of the parties as to the applicable law.

Since the word "chicken" standing alone is ambiguous, I turn first to see whether the contract itself offers any aid to its interpretation. Plaintiff says the 1½–2 lbs. birds necessarily had to be young chicken since the older birds do not come in that size, hence the 2½–3 lbs. birds must likewise be young.

This is unpersuasive — a contract for "apples" of two different sizes could be filled with different kinds of apples even though only one species came in both sizes. Defendant notes that the contract called not simply for chicken but for "US Fresh Frozen Chicken, Grade A, Government Inspected." It says the contract thereby incorporated by reference the Department of Agriculture's regulations, which favor its interpretation; I shall return to this after reviewing plaintiff's other contentions.

The first hinges on an exchange of cablegrams which preceded execution of the formal contracts. The negotiations leading up to the contracts were conducted in New York between defendant's secretary, Ernest R. Bauer, and a Mr. Stovicek, who was in New York for the Czechoslovak government at the World Trade Fair. A few days after meeting Bauer at the fair, Stovicek telephoned and inquired whether defendant would be interested in exporting poultry to Switzerland. Bauer then met with Stovicek, who showed him a cable from plaintiff dated April 26, 1957, announcing that they "are buyer" of 25,000 lbs. of chicken 2½–3 lbs. weight, Cryovac packed, grade A Government inspected, at a price up to 33¢ per pound, for shipment on May 10, to be confirmed by the following morning, and were interested in further offerings. After testing the market for price, Bauer accepted, and Stovicek sent a confirmation that evening. Plaintiff stresses that, although these and subsequent cables between plaintiff and defendant, which laid the basis for the additional quantities under the first and for all of the second contract, were predominantly in German, they used the English word "chicken"; it claims this was done because it understood "chicken" meant young chicken whereas the German word, "Huhn," included both "Brathuhn" (broilers) and "Suppenhuhn" (stewing chicken), and that defendant, whose officers were thoroughly conversant with German, should have realized this. Whatever force this argument might otherwise have is largely drained away by Bauer's testimony that he asked Stovicek what kind of chickens were wanted, received the answer "any kind of chickens," and then, in German, asked whether the cable meant "Huhn" and received an affirmative response. Plaintiff attacks this as contrary to what Bauer testified on his deposition in March, 1959, and also on the ground that Stovicek had no authority to interpret the meaning of the cable. The first contention would be persuasive if sustained by the record, since Bauer was free at the trial from the threat of contradiction by Stovicek as he was not at the time of the deposition; however, review of the deposition does not convince me of the claimed inconsistency. As to the second contention, it may well be that Stovicek lacked authority to commit plaintiff for prices or delivery dates other than those specified in the cable; but plaintiff cannot at the same time rely on its cable to Stovicek as its dictionary to the meaning of the contract and repudiate the interpretation given the dictionary by the man in whose hands it was put. Plaintiff's reliance on the fact that the contract forms contain the words "through the intermediary of:", with the blank not filled, as negating agency, is wholly unpersuasive; the purpose of this clause was to permit filling in the name of an intermediary to whom a commission would be payable, not to blot out what had been the fact.

Plaintiff's next contention is that there was a definite trade usage that "chicken" meant "young chicken." Defendant showed that it was only beginning in the poultry trade in 1957, thereby bringing itself within the principle that "when one of the parties is not a member of the trade or other circle, his acceptance of the standard must be made to appear" by proving either that he had actual knowledge of the usage or that the usage is "so generally known in the community that his actual individual knowledge of it may be inferred." Here there was no proof of actual knowledge of the alleged usage; indeed, it is quite plain that defendant's belief was to the contrary. In order to meet the alternative requirement, the law of New York demands a showing that "the usage is of so long continuance, so well established, so notorious, so universal and so reasonable in itself, as that the presumption is violent that the parties contracted with reference to it, and made it a part of their agreement."

Plaintiff endeavored to establish such a usage by the testimony of three witnesses and certain other evidence. Strasser, resident buyer in New York for a large chain of Swiss cooperatives, testified that "on chicken I would definitely understand a broiler." However, the force of this testimony was considerably weakened by the fact that in his own transactions the witness, a careful businessman, protected himself by using "broiler" when that was what he wanted and "fowl" when he wished older birds. Indeed, there are some indications, dating back to a remark of Lord Mansfield, *Edie v. East India Co.*, 2 Burr. 1216, 1222 (1761), that no credit should be given "witnesses to usage, who could not adduce instances in verification." While Wigmore thinks this goes too far, a witness' consistent failure to rely on the alleged usage deprives his opinion testimony of much of its effect. Niesielowski, an officer of one of the companies that had furnished the stewing chicken to defendant, testified that "chicken" meant "the male species of the poultry industry. That could be a broiler, a fryer or a roaster", but not a stewing chicken; however, he also testified that upon receiving defendant's inquiry for "chickens", he asked whether the desire was for "fowl or frying chickens" and, in fact, supplied fowl, although taking the precaution of asking defendant, a day or two after plaintiff's acceptance of the contracts in suit, to change its confirmation of its order from "chickens," as defendant had originally prepared it, to "stewing chickens." Dates, an employee of Urner-Barry Company, which publishes a daily market report on the poultry trade, gave it as his view that the trade meaning of "chicken" was "broilers and fryers." In addition to this opinion testimony, plaintiff relied on the fact that the Urner-Barry service, the Journal of Commerce, and Weinberg Bros. & Co. of Chicago, a large supplier of poultry, published quotations in a manner which, in one way or another, distinguish between "chicken," comprising broilers, fryers and certain other categories, and "fowl," which, Bauer acknowledged, included stewing chickens. This material would be impressive if there were nothing to the contrary. However, there was, as will now be seen.

Defendant's witness Weininger, who operates a chicken eviscerating plant in New Jersey, testified "Chicken is everything except a goose, a duck, and a turkey. Everything is a chicken, but then you have to say, you have to specify which category you want or that you are talking about." Its witness Fox said that in the trade "chicken" would encompass all the various classifications. Sadina, who conducts a food inspection service, testified that he would consider any bird coming within the classes of "chicken" in the Department of Agriculture's regulations to be a chicken. The specifications approved by the General Services Administration include fowl as well as broilers and fryers under the classification "chickens." Statistics of the Institute of American Poultry Industries use the phrases "Young chickens" and "Mature chickens," under the general heading "Total chickens." And the Department of Agriculture's daily and weekly price reports avoid use of the word "chicken" without specification.

Defendant advances several other points which it claims affirmatively support its construction. Primary among these is the regulation of the Department of Agriculture, 7 C.F.R. §70.300–70.370, entitled, "Grading and Inspection of Poultry and Edible Products Thereof." and in particular 70.301 which recited:

Chickens. The following are the various classes of chickens:

    (a) Broiler or fryer . . .

    (b) Roaster . . .

    (c) Capon . . .

    (d) Stag . . .

    (e) Hen or stewing chicken or fowl . . .

    (f) Cock or old rooster . . .

Defendant argues, as previously noted, that the contract incorporated these regulations by reference. Plaintiff answers that the contract provision related simply to grade and Government inspection and did not incorporate the Government definition of "chicken," and also that the definition in the Regulations is ignored in the trade. However, the latter contention was contradicted by Weininger and Sadina; and there is force in defendant's argument that the contract made the regulations a dictionary, particularly since the reference to Government grading was already in plaintiff's initial cable to Stovicek.

Defendant makes a further argument based on the impossibility of its obtaining broilers and fryers at the 33¢ price offered by plaintiff for the 2½–3 lbs. birds. There is no substantial dispute that, in late April, 1957, the price for 2½–3 lbs. broilers was between 35 and 37¢ per pound, and that when defendant entered into the contracts, it was well aware of this and intended to fill them by supplying fowl in these weights. It claims that plaintiff must likewise have known the market since plaintiff had reserved shipping space on April 23, three days before plaintiff's cable to Stovicek, or, at least, that Stovicek was chargeable with such knowledge. It is scarcely an answer to say, as plaintiff does in its brief, that the 33¢ price offered by the 2½–3 lbs. "chickens" was closer to the prevailing 35¢ price for broilers than to the 30¢ at which defendant procured fowl. Plaintiff must have expected defendant to make some profit — certainly it could not have expected defendant deliberately to incur a loss.

Finally, defendant relies on conduct by the plaintiff after the first shipment had been received. On May 28 plaintiff sent two cables complaining that the larger birds in the first shipment constituted "fowl." Defendant answered with a cable refusing to recognize plaintiff's objection and announcing "We have today ready for shipment 50,000 lbs. chicken 2½–3 lbs. 25,000 lbs. broilers 1½–2 lbs.," these being the goods procured for shipment under the second contract, and asked immediate answer "whether we are to ship this merchandise to you and whether you will accept the merchandise." After several other cable exchanges, plaintiff replied on May 29 "Confirm again that merchandise is to be shipped since resold by us if not enough pursuant to contract chickens are shipped the missing quantity is to be shipped within ten days stop we resold to our customers pursuant to your contract chickens grade A you have to deliver us said merchandise we again state that we shall make you fully responsible for all resulting costs." Defendant argues that if plaintiff was sincere in thinking it was entitled to young chickens, plaintiff would not have allowed the shipment under the second contract to go forward, since the distinction between broilers and chickens drawn in defendant's cablegram must have made it clear that the larger birds would not be broilers. However, plaintiff answers that the cables show plaintiff was insisting on delivery of young chickens and that defendant shipped old ones at its peril. Defendant's point would be highly relevant on another disputed issue — whether if liability were established, the measure of damages should be the difference in market value of broilers and stewing chicken in New York or the larger difference in Europe, but I cannot give it weight on the issue of interpretation. Defendant points out also that plaintiff proceeded to deliver some of the larger birds in Europe, describing them as "poulets"; defendant argues that it was only when plaintiff's customers complained about this that plaintiff developed the idea that "chicken" meant "young chicken." There is little force in this in view of plaintiff's immediate and consistent protests.

When all the evidence is reviewed, it is clear that defendant believed it could comply with the contracts by delivering stewing chicken in the 2½–3 lbs. size. Defendant's subjective intent would not be significant if this did not coincide with an objective meaning of "chicken." Here it did coincide with one of the dictionary meanings, with the definition in the Department of Agriculture Regulations to which the contract made at least oblique reference, with at least some usage in the trade, with the realities of the market, and with what plaintiff's spokesman had said. Plaintiff asserts it to be equally plain that plaintiff's own subjective intent was to obtain broilers and fryers; the only evidence against this is the material as to market prices and this may not have been sufficiently brought home. In any event it is unnecessary to determine that issue. For plaintiff has the burden of showing that "chicken" was used in the narrower rather than in the broader sense, and this it has not sustained.

This opinion constitutes the Court's findings of fact and conclusions of law. Judgment shall be entered dismissing the complaint with costs.

Reflection

According to R2d, "Interpretation of a promise or agreement or a term thereof is the ascertainment of its meaning." R2d § 200. But, by studying *Frigaliment*, you have found that there is an inherent tension in contract interpretation in cases where a party challenges the meaning of a term written in an agreement. Should a court consider evidence that tends to show that a contract does not mean what it seems to say? The question of whether or not to admit such evidence turns out to have a great deal of bearing on the result of the contract interpretation process.

In contract law, everything written within the "four corners" of the agreement is called "intrinsic evidence," whereas "extrinsic evidence" is everything relating to a contract but not appearing on the face of the contract because it comes from other sources, such as statements between the parties or the circumstances surrounding the agreement. When all the evidence is clearly in accord, there is no need for interpretation; and when the written terms are obviously unclear, courts should look to facts and circumstances to derive the parties' intended meaning. The more challenging issue arises where there is a conflict between what the parties wrote about what they promised to do and what they actually did.

Such tensions in a contract or between what a contract says and what parties do can result in an "ambiguity," which Black's Law Dictionary defines as "doubtfulness or uncertainty of meaning or intention, as in a contractual term or statutory provision; indistinctness of signification, esp. by reason of doubleness of interpretation." Contract law further distinguishes between "patent ambiguity" and "latent ambiguity." A patent ambiguity, also known as an intrinsic ambiguity or, in Latin, an *ambiguitas patens*, is an ambiguity that clearly appears on the face of a document; a patent ambiguity arises from the contract language itself.

A latent ambiguity, on the other hand, does not readily appear in the language of a document, but instead arises when the document's terms are applied to specific circumstances during the time for performance of the agreement. Such circumstances are termed "extrinsic evidence" of contractual intent. For example, in the case of *Raffles v. Wichelhaus*, which we studied in Chapter 3, the contract discussed shipment of cotton on the ship "Peerless." An objective judge reading this contract might find it perfectly clear, but when it came time to ship the cotton, it turned out that two ships of the same name were to sail from the same harbor at different times. This latent ambiguity only came to light when the terms of the contract were to be operationalized.

Courts vary on their willingness to consider extrinsic evidence where the terms of a contract facially appear clear. Some courts take a "formalist" or "objectivist" approach, which often connects with a "conservative" or "Willistonian" jurisprudence, and which will generally not permit extrinsic evidence where there is no patent ambiguity. Other courts take a "realist" or "subjectivist" approach, which often connects with a "liberal" or "Corbinian" jurisprudence, and they will more readily admit extrinsic evidence that tends to show a latent ambiguity. The R2d apparently attempts to walk a fine line between these two positions: in the provision titled "Whose Meaning Prevails," the R2d would admit extrinsic evidence of a latent ambiguity where one party can show that the other had reason to know of some meaning other than what the document purports to intrinsically mean. R2d § 201(2)(b).

The famous *Frigaliment* case was decided before the R2d was established, but it takes a similar approach. Judge Friendly asks, "what is chicken?" He recognizes that one party intends "frying chickens," whereas the other meant "broiling chickens," but he does not begin the analysis by inquiring why they held these different meanings. Rather, Judge Friendly begins with the dictionaries, which "give both meanings." Upon thus finding that the term chicken is patently ambiguous with regard to what kind of chicken, Judge Friendly then proceeds to entertain extrinsic evidence. It is not clear what the judge would have done had some universal dictionary offered a singular definition, but one suspects that he would have agreed with the R2d comment that "ordinarily a party has reason to know of meanings in a general usage" and therefore thrown the book, so to speak, at whichever party was attesting to be ignorant of such a clearly established term.

Discussion

1. Generally, courts apply the plain meaning to a contractual term. Why did the court not apply the plain meaning of "chicken" in this case? What does its reasoning indicate about the plain meaning rule in general?

2. What constitutes an ambiguity? Should courts hear evidence that tends to show a term is latently ambiguous, or should courts only admit extrinsic evidence where a term is patently ambiguous?

Reading Nānākuli Paving & Rock Co. v. Shell Oil Co. Nānākuli is a difficult case to read for the same reason that so many contracts cases are difficult: because the subject matter of these cases are commercial transactions that are foreign to most law students. The parties — and the opinions resolving their disputes — tend to use specific and technical terms that have special meaning for those in the field.

While this may be frustrating, it is also necessary. To many judges, contract interpretation is the art and science of determining what the parties actually intended when they entered into an agreement. Courts use the language of the parties and their trade to understand what intentions they had when they formed their agreement. To do this requires judges, attorneys, and law students to understand language and terminology that is sometimes unfamiliar to them.

The key term in this case is "price protection." This means that the seller will not raise the price for some period of time. Generally, price protection benefits a buyer. This concept is not as strange as it might at first seem. Many credit cards offer price protection, which means that if the price of an item drops within some period of time (usually 90 days) after a purchase, the buyer can get the lower price.

Nānākuli is one of two local road paving companies on the island of Honolulu, and thus the buyer of raw asphalt from Shell Oil, which is one of the largest corporations on earth. Nānākuli is arguing that it is entitled to price protection with regard to its purchase of asphalt. Nānākuli claims that the price should not exceed the seller's posted price at the time the buyer committed to use the asphalt in a paving project.

Figure 13.2. Roads are often paved with refined bitumen, which is derived from crude oil. Thus, the cost of paving roads varies with the price of oil, and the short-term volatility of oil prices presents challenging for pricing contracts for long-term construction projects such as paving roads.
Photo credit Seth C. Oranburg.

The contract, however, says otherwise. The seller, Shell — a corporation that is now worth over $100 billion — argues that the court should interpret its agreement with Nānākuli according to the plain meaning of their agreement. The parties' written contract clearly states in the writing that the contract price shall be "Shell's Posted Price at time of delivery." This is not ambiguous. Posted price means the price that Shell is charging on that day. The posted price can change, either up or down.

Nānākuli attempts to enter two types of evidence in support of its claim: trade usage and course of performance. As you read this case, pay attention to the arguments each party uses to argue for or against the admission of this evidence. Those are the same kinds of arguments that law students and lawyers might make. Also, consider why the court accepted Nānākuli's argument in the end. Why did this court ignore the plain meaning of the contract? How might this reasoning impact whether courts are likely to accept extrinsic evidence that changes the meaning of written terms?

Nānākuli Paving & Rock Co. v. Shell Oil Co.

664 F.2d 772 (9th Cir. 1981)

HOFFAN, J.

Appellant [Plaintiff] Nānākuli Paving and Rock Company (Nānākuli) initially filed this breach of contract action against appellee [Defendant] Shell Oil Company (Shell) in Hawaiian State Court in February, 1976.

Nānākuli, the second largest asphaltic paving contractor in Hawaii, had bought all its asphalt requirements from 1963 to 1974 from Shell under two long-term supply contracts; its suit charged Shell with breach of the later 1969 contract.

The jury returned a verdict of $220,800 for Nānākuli on its first claim, which is that Shell breached the 1969 contract in January, 1974, by failing to price protect Nānākuli on 7200 tons of asphalt at the time Shell raised the price for asphalt from $44 to $76.

Nānākuli's theory is that price-protection, as a usage of the asphaltic paving trade in Hawaii, was incorporated into the 1969 agreement between the parties, as demonstrated by the routine use of price protection by suppliers to that trade, and reinforced by the way in which Shell actually performed the 1969 contract up until 1974.

Price protection, appellant claims, required that Shell hold the price on the tonnage [of asphalt] Nānākuli had already committed [to use in performance of government paving contracts] because Nānākuli had incorporated that price into bids put out to or contracts awarded by general contractors and government agencies.

The District Judge set aside the verdict and granted Shell's motion for judgment notwithstanding the verdict of the jury, which decision we vacate. We reinstate the jury verdict because we find that, viewing the evidence as a whole, there was substantial evidence to support a finding by reasonable jurors that Shell breached its contract by failing to provide protection for Nānākuli in 1974. We do not believe the evidence in this case was such that, giving Nānākuli the benefit of all inferences fairly supported by the evidence and without weighing the credibility of the witnesses, only one reasonable conclusion could have been reached by the jury.

Nānākuli offers two theories for why Shell's failure to offer price protection in 1974 was a breach of the 1969 contract. First, it argues, all material suppliers to the asphaltic paving trade in Hawaii followed the trade usage of price protection and thus it should be assumed, under the U.C.C., that the parties intended to incorporate price protection into their 1969 agreement. This is so, Nānākuli continues, even though the written contract provided for price to be "Shell's Posted Price at time of delivery," free on board (F.O.B.) Honolulu [meaning, buyer accepts and takes legal responsibility for the asphalt when it arrives at port in Honolulu].

Its proof of a usage that was incorporated into the contract is reinforced by evidence of the commercial context, which under the U.C.C. should form the background for viewing a particular contract. The full agreement must be examined in light of the close, almost symbiotic relations between Shell and Nānākuli on the island of Oahu, whereby the expansion of Shell on the island was intimately connected to the business growth of Nānākuli. The U.C.C. looks to the actual performance of a contract as the best indication of what the parties intended those terms to mean. Nānākuli points out that Shell had price protected it on the two occasions of price increases under the 1969 contract other than the 1974 increase. In 1970 and 1971 Shell extended the old price for four and three months, respectively, after an announced increase. This was done, in the words of Shell's agent in Hawaii, in order to permit Nānākuli's to "chew up" tonnage already committed at Shell's old price.

Nānākuli's second theory for price protection is that Shell was obliged to price protect Nānākuli, even if price protection was not incorporated into their contract, because price protection was the commercially reasonable standard for fair dealing in the asphaltic paving trade in Hawaii in 1974. Observance of those standards is part of the good-faith requirement that the Code imposes on merchants in performing a sales contract. Shell was obliged to price protect Nānākuli in order to act in good faith, Nānākuli argues, because such a practice was universal in that trade in that locality.

Shell presents three arguments for upholding the judgment n.o.v. or, on cross appeal, urging that the District Judge erred in admitting certain evidence. First, it says, the District Court should not have denied Shell's motion in limine to define trade, for purposes of trade usage evidence, as the sale and purchase of asphalt in Hawaii, rather than expanding the definition of trade to include other suppliers of materials to the asphaltic paving trade. Asphalt, its argument runs, was the subject matter of the disputed contract and the only product Shell supplied to the asphaltic paving trade. Shell protests that the judge, by expanding the definition of trade to include the other major suppliers to the asphaltic paving trade, allowed the admission of highly prejudicial evidence of routine price protection by all suppliers of aggregate.

Shell's second complaint is that the two prior occasions on which it price protected Nānākuli, although representing the only other instances of price increases under the 1969 contract, constituted mere waivers of the contract's price term, not a course of performance of the contract. A course of performance of the contract, in contrast to a waiver, demonstrates how the parties understand the terms of their agreement.

Shell cites two U.C.C. Comments in support of that argument: (1) that, when the meaning of acts is ambiguous, the preference is for the waiver interpretation, and (2) that one act alone does not constitute a relevant course of performance.

Shell's final argument is that, even assuming its prior price protection constituted a course of performance and that the broad trade definition was correct and evidence of trade usages by aggregate suppliers was admissible, price protection could not be construed as reasonably consistent with the express price term in the contract, in which case the Code provides that the express term controls.

We hold that the judge did not abuse his discretion in defining the applicable trade, for purposes of trade usages, as the asphaltic paving trade in Hawaii, rather than the purchase and sale of asphalt alone, given the unusual, not to say unique, circumstances:

- the smallness of the marketplace on Oahu;
- the existence of only two suppliers on the island;
- the long and intimate connection between the two companies on Oahu, including the background of how the development of Shell's asphalt sales on Oahu was inextricably linked to Nānākuli's own expansion on the island;

- the knowledge of the aggregate business on the part of Shell's Hawaiian representative, Bohner;

- his awareness of the economics of Nānākuli's bid estimates, which included only two major materials, asphalt and aggregate;

- his familiarity with realities of the Hawaiian marketplace in which all government agencies refused to include escalation clauses in contract awards and thus pavers would face tremendous losses on price increases if all their material suppliers did not routinely offer them price protection; and

- Shell's determination to build Nānākuli up to compete for those lucrative government contracts with the largest paver on the island, Hawaiian Bitumuls (H.B.), which was supplied by the only other asphalt company on the islands, Chevron, and which was routinely price protected on materials.

We base our holding on the reading of the Code Comments as defining trade more broadly than transaction and as binding parties not only to usages of their particular trade but also to usages of trade in general in a given locality. This latter seems an equitable application of usage evidence where the usage is almost universally practiced in a small market such as was Oahu in the 1960's before Shell signed its 1969 contract with Nānākuli.

Additionally, we hold that, under the facts of this case, a jury could reasonably have found that Shell's acts on two occasions to price protect Nānākuli were not ambiguous and therefore indicated Shell's understanding of the terms of the agreement with Nānākuli rather than being a waiver by Shell of those terms.

Lastly we hold that, although the express price terms of Shell's posted price of delivery may seem, at first glance, inconsistent with a trade usage of price protection at time of increases in price, a closer reading shows that the jury could have reasonably construed price protection as consistent with the express term.

We reach this holding for several reasons. First, we are persuaded by a careful reading of the U.C.C., one of whose underlying purposes is to promote flexibility in the expansion of commercial practices and which rather drastically overhauls this particular area of the law. The Code would have us look beyond the printed pages of the contract to usages and the entire commercial context of the agreement in order to reach the "true understanding" of the parties.

Second, decisions of other courts in similar situations have managed to reconcile such trade usages with seemingly contradictory express terms where the prior course of dealings between the parties, trade usages, and the actual performance of the contract by the parties showed a clear intent by the parties to incorporate those usages into the agreement or to give to the express term the particular meaning provided by those usages, even at times varying the apparent meaning of the express terms.

Third, the delineation by thoughtful commentators of the degree of consistency demanded between express terms and usage is that a usage should be allowed to modify the apparent agreement, as seen in the written terms, as long as it does not totally negate it. We believe the usage here falls within the limits set forth by commentators and generally followed in the better reasoned decisions.

The manner in which price protection was actually practiced in Hawaii was that it only came into play at times of price increases and only for work committed prior to those increases on non-escalating contracts. Thus, it formed an exception to, rather than a total negation of, the express price term of "Shell's Posted Price at time of delivery."

Our decision is reinforced by the overwhelming nature of the evidence that

- price protection was routinely practiced by all suppliers in the small Oahu market of the asphaltic paving trade and therefore was known to Shell;
- that it was a realistic necessity to operate in that market and thus vital to Nānākuli's ability to get large government contracts and to Shell's continued business growth on Oahu; and
- that it therefore constituted an intended part of the agreement, as that term is broadly defined by the Code, between Shell and Nānākuli.

I. History Of Nānākuli-Shell Relations Before 1973

[This section may be summarized as follows: Nānākuli and Shell had been working together closely since the early 1960s. In fact, Nānākuli painted its trucks "Shell white" and placed the Shell logo on its trucks and its stationery to symbolize the closeness of their relationship. In 1969, the parties signed a long term (seven year) supply agreement. That agreement is the subject of this case.]

II. Trade Usage Before And After 1969

[This section may be summarized as follows: in 1969 in Oahu, Hawaii, the majority of paving contracts were between a few paving companies like Nānākuli on the one hand and government agencies on the other. None of the agencies allowed escalation clauses—which would increase the amount paid to paving companies if the price of input materials like asphalt goes up. Without price protection, paving companies could find themselves paying more for asphalt than they would receive under the government contracts for paving. Therefore, price protection was an economic necessity and a nearly universal practice.]

III. Shell's Course Of Performance Of the 1969 Contract

[This section may be summarized as follows: Nānākuli made several orders of asphalt from Shell under their 1969 contract. The original price was $35 per ton of asphalt. From the inception of that agreement until the events that gave rise to this lawsuit, Shell raised its price of asphalt only two times: in 1970 and 1971, Shell raised its price to $40 and $44. Both times, Nānākuli complained about the price increase, and after negations with Shell's Hawaiian Representative, Bohner, Shell price protected Nānākuli by holding its price constant for several months after announcing a price increase. Shell argued that this evidenced its good faith under the contract, but Nānākuli argued this evidenced that Nānākuli reasonably relied on Shell's price protection.]

[Shell sent its customers, including Nānākuli, a] November 25, 1970, letter setting out "Shell's New Pricing Policy" at its Honolulu and Hilo terminals. The letter explained the elimination of price protection: "In other words, we will no longer guarantee asphalt prices for the duration of any particular construction projects or for the specific lengths of time. We will, of course, honor any existing prices which have been committed for specific projects for which we have firm contractual commitments." The letter requested a supply contract be signed with Shell within 15 days of the receipt of an award by a customer.

[Nānākuli's Vice President] Smith's reading of this was that Nānākuli's supply contract with Shell was a firm contractual commitment by Shell and that no further contract was needed. "We felt that this letter was unapplicable (sic) to our supply contract, that we already had a contractual commitment with Shell Oil Company which was not to end before 1975." [Nānākuli did not comply with the letter.]

IV. Shell-Nānākuli Relations, 1973-74

Two important factors form the backdrop for the 1974 failure by Shell to price protect Nānākuli: the Arab oil embargo and a complete change of command and policy in Shell's asphalt management. . . .

[Shell's Hawaiian Representative] Bohner testified to a big organizational change at Shell in 1973 when asphalt sales were moved from the construction sales to the commercial sales department. In addition, by 1973 the top echelon of Shell's asphalt sales had retired. Lewis and Blee, who had negotiated the 1969 contract with Nānākuli, were both gone. Their duties were taken over by three men: Fuller in San Mateo, California, District Manager for Shell Sales, Lawson, and Chippendale, who was Shell's regional asphalt manager in Houston. When the philosophy toward asphalt pricing changed, apparently no one was left who was knowledgeable about the peculiarities of the Hawaiian market or about Shell's long-time relations with Nānākuli or its 1969 agreement, beyond the printed contract.

[On December 31, 1973, Shell informed Nānākuli of a price increase to $76 per ton of asphalt.] On January 4, 1974, [Nānākuli's Vice President] Smith called [Shell's Hawaiian representative] Bohner, as he had done before at times of price increases, to ask for price protection, this time on 7200 tons. Bohner told Smith that he would have to get in touch with the mainland, but he expected that the response would be negative. . . . Smith wrote several letters in January and February asking for price protection. After getting no satisfaction, he finally flew to California to meet with Lawson, Fuller, and Chippendale. Chippendale, from the Houston office, was acknowledged by the other two to be the only person with authority to grant price protection. All three Shell officials lacked any understanding of Nānākuli and Shell's long, unique relationship or of the asphaltic trade in Oahu. They had never even seen Shell's contracts with Nānākuli before the meeting. When apprised of the three and their seven-year duration, Fuller remarked on the unusual nature of Nānākuli's relations with Shell, at least within his district. Chippendale felt it was probably unique for Shell anywhere. Smith testified that Fuller admitted to knowing nothing, beyond the printed page of Nānākuli's agreement with Shell, of the background negotiation or Shell's past pricing policies toward Nānākuli . . . Fuller testified that Shell would not act without written proof of Shell's past price protection of Nānākuli.

We conclude that the decision to deny Nānākuli price protection was made by new Houston management without a full understanding of Shell's 1969 agreement with Nānākuli or any knowledge of its past pricing practices toward Nānākuli. If Shell did commit itself in 1969 to price protect Nānākuli, the Shell officials who made the decisions affecting Nānākuli in 1974 knew nothing about that commitment. Nor did they make any effective effort to find out. They acted instead solely in reliance on the 1969 contract's express price term, devoid of the commercial context that the Code says is necessary to an understanding of the meaning of the written word. Whatever the legal enforceability of Nānākuli's right, Nānākuli officials seem to have acted in good faith reliance on its right, as they understood it, to price protection and rightfully felt betrayed by Shell's failure to act with any understanding of its past practices toward Nānākuli.

V. Scope of Trade Usage

The validity of the jury verdict in this case depends on four legal questions. First, how broad was the trade to whose usages Shell was bound under its 1969 agreement with Nānākuli: did it extend to the Hawaiian asphaltic paving trade or was it limited merely to the purchase and sale of asphalt, which would only include evidence of practices by Shell and Chevron? Second, were the two instances of price protection of Nānākuli by Shell in 1970 and 1971 waivers of the 1969 contract as a matter of law or was the jury entitled to find that they constituted a course of performance of the contract? Third, could the jury have construed an express contract term of Shell's posted price at delivery as reasonably consistent with a trade usage and Shell's course of performance of the 1969 contract of price protection, which consisted of charging the old price at times of price increases, either for a period of time or for specific tonnage committed at a fixed price in non-escalating contracts? Fourth, could the jury have found that good faith obliged Shell to at least give advance notice of a $32 increase in 1974, that is, could they have found that the commercially reasonable standards of fair dealing in the trade in Hawaii in 1974 were to give some form of price protection?

We approach the first issue in this case mindful that an underlying purpose of the U.C.C. as enacted in Hawaii is to allow for liberal interpretation of commercial usages. The Code provides, "This chapter shall be liberally construed and applied to promote its underlying purposes and policies."

No U.C.C. cases have been found on this point, but the court's reading of the Code language is similar to that of two of the best-known commentators on the U.C.C.:

> *Under pre-Code law, a trade usage was not operative against a party who was not a member of the trade unless he actually knew of it or the other party could reasonably believe he knew of it.*

White and Summers add:

> *This view has been carried forward by 1-205(3) . . . . (U)sage of the trade is only binding on members of the trade involved or persons who know or should know about it. Persons who should be aware of the trade usage doubtless include those who regularly deal with members of the relevant trade, and also members of a second trade that commonly deals with members of a relevant trade (for example, farmers should know something of seed selling).*

Using that analogy, even if Shell did not "regularly deal" with aggregate supplies, it did deal constantly and almost exclusively on Oahu with one asphalt paver. It therefore should have been aware of the usage of Nānākuli and other asphaltic pavers to bid at fixed prices and therefore receive price protection from their materials suppliers due to the refusal by government agencies to accept escalation clauses. . . .

The Comment explains:

> *The ancient English tests for "custom" are abandoned in this connection. Therefore, it is not required that a usage of trade be "ancient or immemorial," "universal" or the like. . . . (F)ull recognition is thus available for new usages and for usages currently observed by the great majority of decent dealers, even though dissidents ready to cut corners do not agree.*

The Comment's demand that "not universality but only the described 'regularity of observance'" is required reinforces the provision only giving "effect to usages of which the parties 'are or should be aware.'" A "regularly observed" practice of protection, of which Shell "should have been aware," was enough to constitute a usage that Nānākuli had reason to believe was incorporated into the agreement.

Nānākuli went beyond proof of a regular observance. It proved and offered to prove that price protection was probably a universal practice by suppliers to the asphaltic paving trade in 1969. It had been practiced by H.C. & D. since at least 1962, by P.C. & A. since well before 1960, and by Chevron routinely for years, with the last specific instance before the contract being March, 1969, as shown by documentary evidence. . . .

VI. Waiver Of Course Of Performance

. . . Shell protested that the jury could not have found that those two instances of price protection [in 1970 and 1971] amounted to a course of performance of its 1969 contract, relying on two Code comments. First, one instance does not constitute a course of performance. "A single occasion of conduct does not fall within the language of this section. . . ."

Although the Comment rules out one instance, it does not further delineate how many acts are needed to form a course of performance. The prior occasions here were only two, but they constituted the only occasions before 1974 that would call for such conduct. In addition, the language used by a top asphalt official of Shell in connection with the first price protection of Nānākuli indicated that Shell felt that Nānākuli was entitled to some form of price protection. . . .

Shell's second defense is that the Comment expresses a preference for an interpretation of waiver. . . . The preference for waiver only applies, however, where acts are ambiguous. . . . The jury's interpretation of those acts as a course of performance was bolstered by evidence offered by Shell that it again price protected Nānākuli on the only two occasions of post-1974 price increases, in 1977 and 1978.

VII. Express Terms As Reasonably Consistent With Usage In Course of Performance

Perhaps one of the most fundamental departures of the Code from prior contract law is found in the parol evidence rule and the definition of an agreement between two parties. Under the U.C.C., an agreement goes beyond the written words on a piece of paper. "'Agreement' means the bargain of the parties in fact as found in their language or by implication from other circumstances including course of dealing or usage of trade or course of performance as provided in [UCC § 1-205 and 2-208]." Express terms, then, do not constitute the entire agreement, which must be sought also in evidence of usages, dealings, and performance of the contract itself. The purpose of evidence of usages, which are defined in the previous section, is to help to understand the entire agreement.

(Usages are) a factor in reaching the commercial meaning of the agreement which the parties have made. The language used is to be interpreted as meaning what it may fairly be expected to mean to parties involved in the particular commercial transaction in a given locality or in a given vocation or trade. . . . Part of the agreement of the parties . . . is to be sought for in the usages of trade which furnish the background and give particular meaning to the language used, and are the framework of common understanding controlling any general rules of law which hold only when there is no such understanding.

Course of dealings is more important than usages of the trade, being specific usages between the two parties to the contract. "(C)ourse of dealing controls usage of trade." It "is a sequence of previous conduct between the parties to a particular transaction which is fairly to be regarded as establishing a common basis of understanding for interpreting their expressions and other conduct." Much of the evidence of prior dealings between Shell and Nānākuli in negotiating the 1963 contract and in carrying out similar earlier contracts was excluded by the court.

A commercial agreement, then, is broader than the written paper and its meaning is to be determined not just by the language used by them in the written contract but "by their action, read and interpreted in the light of commercial practices and other surrounding circumstances. The measure and background for interpretation are set by the commercial context, which may explain and supplement even the language of a formal or final writing." Performance, usages, and prior dealings are important enough to be admitted always, even for a final and complete agreement; only if they cannot be reasonably reconciled with the express terms of the contract are they not binding on the parties. "The express terms of an agreement and an applicable course of dealing or usage of trade shall be construed wherever reasonable as consistent with each other; but when such construction is unreasonable express terms control both course of dealing and usage of trade and course of dealing controls usage of trade."

Of these three, then, the most important evidence of the agreement of the parties is their actual performance of the contract. The operative definition of course of performance is as follows: "Where the contract for sale involves repeated occasions for performance by either party with knowledge of the nature of the performance and opportunity for objection to it by the other, any course of performance accepted or acquiesced in without objection shall be relevant to determine the meaning of the agreement." "Course of dealing . . . is restricted, literally, to a sequence of conduct between the parties previous to the agreement. However, the provisions of the Act on course of performance [Section 2-208] make it clear that a sequence of conduct after or under the agreement may have equivalent meaning." The importance of evidence of course of performance is explained: "The parties themselves know best what they have meant by their words of agreement and their action under that agreement is the best indication of what that meaning was. This section thus rounds out the set of factors which determines the meaning of the 'agreement.'" "Under this section a course of performance is always relevant to determine the meaning of the agreement."

Our study of the Code provisions and Comments, then, form the first basis of our holding that a trade usage to price protect pavers at times of price increases for work committed on nonescalating contracts could reasonably be construed as consistent with an express term of seller's posted price at delivery. Since the agreement of the parties is broader than the express terms and includes usages, which may even add terms to the agreement, and since the commercial background provided by those usages is vital to an understanding of the agreement, we follow the Code's mandate to proceed on the assumption that the parties have included those usages unless they cannot reasonably be construed as consistent with the express terms.

[Extensive analysis of case law omitted.]

"Astonishing as it will seem to most practicing attorneys, under the Code it will be possible in some cases to use custom to contradict the written agreement. . . . Therefore usage may be used to 'qualify' the agreement, which presumably means to 'cut down' express terms although not to negate them entirely."

Here, the express price term was "Shell's Posted Price at time of delivery." A total negation of that term would be that the buyer was to set the price. It is a less than complete negation of the term that an unstated exception exists at times of price increases, at which times the old price is to be charged, for a certain period or for a specified tonnage, on work already committed at the lower price on nonescalating contracts. Such a usage forms a broad and important exception to the express term, but does not swallow it entirely.

Therefore, we hold that, under these particular facts, a reasonable jury could have found that price protection was incorporated into the 1969 agreement between Nānākuli and Shell and that price protection was reasonably consistent with the express term of seller's posted price at delivery.

VIII. Good Faith In Setting Price

... The Code provides, "A price to be fixed by the seller or by the buyer means a price for him to fix in good faith." ...

Nānākuli presented evidence that Chevron, in raising its price to $76, gave at least six weeks' advance notice, in accord with the long-time usage of the asphaltic paving trade. Shell, on the other hand, gave absolutely no notice, from which the jury could have concluded that Shell's manner of carrying out the price increase of 1974 did not conform to commercially reasonable standards.

In both the timing of the announcement and its refusal to protect work already bid at the old price, Shell could be found to have breached the obligation of good faith imposed by the Code on all merchants. "Every contract or duty within this chapter imposes an obligation of good faith in its performance or enforcement," *id.* § 490:1-203, which for merchants entails the observance of commercially reasonable standards of fair dealing in the trade. The Comment to 1-203 reads:

> *This section sets forth a basic principle running throughout this Act. The principle involved is that in commercial transactions good faith is required in the performance and enforcement of all agreements or duties. Particular applications of this general principle appear in specific provisions of the Act.... It is further implemented by Section 1-205 on course of dealing and usage of trade.*

Chevron's conduct in 1974 offered enough relevant evidence of commercially reasonable standards of fair dealing in the asphalt trade in Hawaii in 1974 for the jury to find that Shell's failure to give sufficient advance notice and price protect Nānākuli after the imposition of the new price did not conform to good faith dealings in Hawaii at that time.

Because the jury could have found for Nānākuli on its price protection claim under either theory, we reverse the judgment of the District Court and reinstate the jury verdict for Nānākuli in the amount of $220,800, plus interest according to law.

REVERSED AND REMANDED WITH DIRECTIONS TO ENTER FINAL JUDGMENT.

Reflection

University of Virginia School of Law professors Charles J. Goetz and Robert E. Scott reflect extensively on Nānākuli in their seminal law review article on the interaction between express and implied contract terms. The article notes:

> *At first glance,* Nānākuli *seems to be a perfectly correct application of the rules of interpretation.... The court applied a presumption of consistency to the extrinsic evidence submitted by the buyer, holding that the express price term supplemented, rather than trumped, the price protection usage. The presumption was not overcome by the inclusion of a standard merger clause, which the court characterized as boilerplate rather than as an invoked term of art.*

The Limits of Expanded Choice: An Analysis of the Interactions between Express and Implied Contract Terms, 73 Calif. L. Rev. 261, 318 n.154 (1985). But the court's strict prioritization of extrinsic evidence over express terms is actually an oversimplification of how contracts should be interpreted:

> *Further reflection, however, reveals an underlying conceptual problem. The court in Nānākuli framed the interpretive issue as a choice between supplementary expressions and trumps. This requires a binary resolution: either the express price term trumps the context or the price protection usage fully applies.*

Professors Goetz and Scott argue that this binary does not reflect how parties actually think and behave, especially with regard to long-term contracts. Remember than Nānākuli and Shell had a longstanding close relationship.

> *In such relationships, it is equally plausible to assume that the apparent conflict between the express price term and the custom of price-protection could not have been "solved" by the parties when they crafted their agreement.*

In other words, shouldn't the Nānākuli court have recognized that parties don't really have an understanding at the time of contracting about all circumstances that will occur in the future? Aren't these long-term relational contracts more about a framework under which to work things out, and less about a set of rules courts will apply to every future circumstance?

> *This hypothesis [that the parties had no mutual assent regarding price protection] is supported by evidence that the price-protection issue first arose in 1970, seven years after the supply contract was negotiated and following major changes in Shell's management. If the formulations in Nānākuli were indeterminate rather than apparently inconsistent, then neither the outcome endorsed by the court nor the result urged by Shell would represent the optimal interpretive solution. Instead, an equitable adjustment of price would have been more consistent with the contractual instructions of the parties.*

In addition to this theoretical contribution, Goetz and Scott succinctly summarize the material facts and holdings of the case. It might be useful for law students to compare the professors' approach to this case with their own notes of key facts and holdings:

> *Nānākuli, a paving contractor, negotiated a long-term contract with Shell in which Shell agreed to supply and Nānākuli agreed to purchase all its asphalt requirements. After extensive negotiations and drafting, a written contract was signed providing that the contract price for asphalt ordered and supplied was to be determined by Shell's "posted price at the time of delivery." The written contract contained a standard merger clause. Some ten years after the original agreement was concluded, Shell increased the price on a delivery of 7,200 tons of asphalt from the $44 per ton price prevailing at the time of the order to $75 per ton, its posted price at the time of delivery. Subsequently, Nānākuli sought $220,800 in damages for breach of the contract, alleging that*

the paving trade in Hawaii followed a practice of "price protection" by extending the old price for a period of time after a new one became effective. . . .

Nānākuli claimed that Shell had protected it from price increases in two previous instances. In response, Shell argued that if the relevant market were narrowed to the supply of asphalt alone, the usage was not clearly established. Shell further claimed that the two instances of price protection were isolated waivers, not a course of performance. Finally, it said that in any event the extrinsic evidence was clearly inconsistent with the express price term in the contract and thus the price term was controlling under U.C.C. § 1-205(4).

In reinstating the jury's verdict for Nānākuli, the Ninth Circuit held that the jury could properly have found a relevant usage and course of performance, and that this extrinsic evidence was not inconsistent with the express price term in the written contract.

The above summary of the facts and holding of *Nānākuli* may therefore be a useful guide to law students on how to accurately but briefly summarize such a complex case.

Discussion

1. Is there tension between the goals of effectuating the parties' intentions and enforcing the plain meaning of written terms, or are these both means to the same ends?

2. Do you think the *Nānākuli* court correctly interpreted the contract to include price protection? Why or why not?

3. In *Nānākuli*, Shell may have gone above and beyond its contractual obligations by giving price protection to Nānākuli two times in the past. If going above and beyond in the past obligates a party to continue acting in that manner going forward, how might that impact contractual parties' willingness to do favors for each other?

Problems

Problem 13.1. IRAC Frigaliment

A party who wishes to show that a written contract should be interpreted according to the meaning it supplies usually must first show that the written term is susceptible to multiple meanings; in other words, that party must first prove the term is ambiguous. Was the term "chicken" in the *Frigaliment* case ambiguous? Would this famous historic case come out the same way under modern rules? Answer this question using the IRAC paradigm. First, frame the issue in terms of whether the word chicken is ambiguous. Second, write, cite, and explain the key rules (including a definition of what is a patent or latent ambiguity). Third, analyze the term "chicken" as it appears in the *Frigaliment* case under those rules. Finally, conclude whether the term "chicken" is ambiguous.

Chapter 14

Evaluating Intrinsic Contractual Evidence

The Canons of Construction is a collection of rules that courts will apply when determining the meaning of intrinsic evidence. In other words, the Canons of Construction are a collection of common techniques that judges often use when construing the meaning of a writing. I deliberately said that the Canons of Construction apply to writings—not just to contracts. That is because canons are also used to construe regulations, statutes, and even the Constitution! In this book, however, we focus on the Canons of Construction that specifically apply to contractual writings.

Think about each rule of construction as a tool. Just as a complete set of tools needed for a job constitutes a toolbox, a complete set of rules needed to understand a writing are grouped in a set of Canons of Construction. But just as an electrician's toolbox is likely to be different from a plumber's toolbox, different collections of rules are needed for different interpretative tasks.

Another way to think about the Canons of Construction is to compare them to the rules of grammar and style. Even a very long grammar and style manual like the Chicago Manual of Style may not contain every rule. Older grammar books, for example, will not have rules about how to cite a Twitter tweet. And some of the rules—such as whether to include the "Oxford comma" in a list—are not universally agreed upon. Still, the Chicago Manual of Style remains a very useful guide on how to write effectively!

Likewise, there is no one set of Canons of Construction that applies to all circumstances and in all courts. In fact, various courts have come up with their own specific rules. But there is broad agreement on many general principles, and some specific rules are so important as to be widely accepted and appearing universally.

For the present purpose of teaching you how to perform contractual interpretation, I have assembled an abbreviated Canons of Construction. The rules I have selected are generally accepted and nearly universally applicable, so you can feel confident applying them beyond this class. But keep in mind that it is possible to use other rules and techniques when construing the meaning of written words in contractual interpretation.

Rules

A. Ambiguity

Ambiguity is the quality of being open to more than one interpretation. For example, without more context, the word "cleave" could mean to join or to split; thus, the word "cleave" is inherently ambiguous. Parties' disagreement about a contract term may indicate that term is ambiguous. The court must determine whether a term is reasonably open to more than one meaning. If only one meaning is reasonable, the court should construe a contract with its reasonable meaning and thus conclude the dispute quickly.

Ambiguity is a double-edged sword for contract plaintiffs to wield and worry about at once. On the one hand, proving a contractual ambiguity creates issues of fact that may require a court to hear evidence and decide a case; but, on the other hand, contracts or terms may be unenforceable when they are too indefinite to show that the parties had mutual assent.

Ambiguity may be obvious from the text of a written contract itself, or ambiguity may be apparent to the judge only when the contract is viewed in light of commercial circumstances. In other words, some terms are "patently" ambiguous, while others are "latent" ambiguities. Examples of patent ambiguities include:

- In Section 1 of an Agreement, the written Agreement defines "Trial Period" as "three months." In Section 2, "Trial Period" is defined as "four months." When the term Trial Period is used in Section 3, it is ambiguous whether it means three or four months.

- A contract is for the purchase and sale of "Item 3." If Item 3 is not identified by the contract, that term is patently ambiguous. There is no way for the court to know what the parties meant by Item 3 without admitting extrinsic evidence.

A judge can discern patent ambiguities from intrinsic evidence alone. Patent ambiguities are obvious from the written terms when they cannot be made sense of without considering outside evidence. In the immortal words of Donald Rumsfeld, patent ambiguities are "known unknowns," things that you know you do not know. There is no dispute that extrinsic evidence can and should be admitted to understand patent ambiguities.

In addition to patent ambiguities, there are also "latent" ambiguities, where a term is not obviously ambiguous when read on its own, but extrinsic evidence shows the ambiguity. Latent ambiguities are therefore "unknown unknowns," which are things you thought you know but do not.

Example of latent ambiguity include:

- A breeder agrees to sell rabbits to a laboratory for "$100 per thousand." The laboratory seeks to introduce evidence that industry usage of "thousand" means 100 dozen, or 1200, rabbits. A court would not know from reading the contract alone that the word "thousand" is ambiguous, but the extrinsic evidence shows that term may have an alternative meaning.

- A seller agrees to transport cargo on "the 10 o'clock train from New York to Philadelphia." The buyer seeks to admit evidence that there were two trains departing at that time on that route: an express train and a local train. The extrinsic evidence shows that the description of the train is ambiguous.

The Restatement takes a relatively liberal approach to the admission of extrinsic evidence of usage. Comment d states:

> Language and conduct are in general given meaning by usage rather than by the law, and ambiguity and contradiction likewise depend upon usage. Hence usage relevant to interpretation is treated as part of the context of an agreement in determining whether there is ambiguity or contradiction as well as in resolving ambiguity or contradiction. There is no requirement that an ambiguity be shown before usage can be shown, and no prohibition against showing that language or conduct have a different meaning in the light of usage from the meaning they might have apart from the usage. The normal effect of a usage on a written contract is to vary its meaning from the meaning it would otherwise have.

If a term in reasonably susceptible only to one meaning, then a court should construe it according to that meaning and be done with the analysis. As the Latin maxim goes:

> Quoties in verbis nulla est ambiguitas, ibi nulla expositio contra verba expressa fienda est

Translation: when there is no ambiguity in words, then no exposition contrary to the expressed words is to be made.

When there may be an ambiguity in a contract, however, the court must then attempt to disambiguate and clarify the term. The first step in the process of disambiguation is to apply a set of rules called the semantic canons that are used to derive the meaning of contractual terms.

B. Semantic Canons

The semantic canons of construction we will apply to determine the meaning of intrinsic evidence of contractual meaning are as follows:

1. Plain Meaning Rule

Use ordinary words according to their plain or dictionary meanings.

For example: A contract prohibiting sale of "liquor" would not prohibit sales of beer.

2. Technical Meaning Rule

Use technical or specialized terms according to their technical meanings where parties are both in the same technical field.

Example one: In a sales contract between a shoe manufacturer and a shoe retailer for "300 mules," this word has technical meaning of a shoe with no backstrap, not an animal.

Example two: A contract to supply materials for a construction project includes "4 tons light iron." If the trade usage is that light iron is supplied with its supplemental steel, than the supplier is obligated to provide that steel.

3. General Terms Rule

General terms are given their general meaning (*generalia verba sunt generaliter intelligenda*) and are not arbitrarily limited.

For example: A contract for the lease of a fairground that prohibits the sale of "intoxicating beverages" would prohibit sales of beer and wine in addition to liquor.

4. Negative Implication Rule

The expression of one thing implies exclusion of others (*expressio unius est exclusio alterius*).

For example: A sales agreement defined the items for sale as "all BCI inventory, including but not limited to agricultural chemicals, fertilizers, and fertilizer materials sold by BCI to Sylvan." Despite the "including but not limited to" language, the inclusion of these specific items implies that all other items are excluded.

5. Whole Agreement Rule

Where a single transaction requires several different agreements, they should all be interpreted as one single agreement.

For example: In a venture capital financing, the Investment Agreement defines "Shares" to mean "Series A Preferred Stock." The term "Shares" in the related Stock Purchase Agreement has the same meaning.

6. Avoid Surplusage Rule

Choose an interpretation that gives force and effect to every word and every provision in an agreement.

For example: A contract says, "vessel to be loaded in turn" and "vessel to be loaded promptly." This means the vessel will be loaded promptly when it is that vessel's turn to be loaded.

7. Consistent Usage (and Meaningful Variation) Rule

Interpret the same terms in a statute the same way; a material variation in terms suggests a variation in meaning.

For example: Section 1 of a Director & Officer Insurance Agreement defines the term "insured" as "any executive officer or director." Section 6 of that agreement says, "This policy does not apply to injury to property in the care or control of the insured." Section 6 does not exclude coverage of company property in the control of employees other than executive officers or directors.

8. Negotiated Terms Rule

Separately negotiated or added terms are given greater weight than standardized terms or boilerplate language.

For example: Section 4(c) of a construction agreement prepared by a contractor contains pre-printed standard language that "contractor shall charge an agreement lump sum for any changes in the work." Section 5 of that same agreement includes a remark in the purchaser's handwriting, initialed by the contractor, that "contractor shall charge a 10% fee net of costs for changes." Section 5 prevails because it was separately negotiated.

9. Same Kind, Class, or Nature (Ejusdem Generis) Rule

General terms derive meaning from specific terms that precede them; where general words follow an enumeration of two or more things, they apply only to persons or things of the same general kind or class.

For example: A contract for sale of a farm includes transfer of "horses, cattle, sheep, pigs, goats, or any other farm animals." Despite the breadth of the general term "any other," the specific items on the list are only four-legged, hoofed mammals typically found on farms. The general term is limited to other similar animals. Thus, chickens may not be included in this sale of the farm.

10. Recognition by Association (Noscitus a Sociis) Rule

Words grouped in a list should be given related meaning.

For example: In a flood insurance agreement, covered loss includes damages from "flood, surface water, waves, tidal water or tidal wave, overflow of streams or other bodies of water, or spray from any of the foregoing, all whether driven by wind or not." The category of this list is inundation from natural sources; therefore, "flood" does not include damage from a broken water main.

11. Grammar Rule

Words are to be given the meaning that proper grammar and usage would assign them.

For example: A contract to use telephone poles for cable TV wires states: "Subject to the termination provisions of this Agreement, this Agreement shall be effective from the date it is made and shall continue in force for a period of five (5) years from the date it is made, and thereafter for successive five (5) year terms, unless and until terminated by one year prior notice in writing by either party." The second comma in the disputed phrase meant that the termination clause applied to both the initial terms and renewal terms.

12. *Legal Meaning Rule*

Presume that contracts are made for lawful purposes; therefore, if a term is susceptible to two reasonable constructions, one of which comports with the law and one which does not, construe the term in such a way that it is legal and enforceable.

For example: A mortgage company who was holding a foreclosure auction for real property made an oral promise to bid enough at that foreclosure auction to cover principal and interest of the existing loan on that property. Instead of interpreting this as an oral agreement to purchase land (which is unenforceable under the statute of frauds), the court interpreted this as a promise to start the bidding at a price which would cover the existing loan.

C. Policy Canons

When litigants dispute what a contract or term means, such that the court must determine contractual meaning, courts first determine whether the term is ambiguous. If a term is susceptible to only one reasonable meaning, the court should apply that meaning and be done with the case. But when a term is susceptible to multiple interpretations, and when the parties disagree on how that term should be read, courts must disambiguate the term — or refuse to enforce any agreement.

Courts disambiguate terms first by applying the semantic canons, which are rules regarding construction of language. If applying these rules does not produce a clear meaning, however, courts might elect one meaning or another based on so-called policy cannons. Policy cannons do not really have to do with semantic meaning per se, but rather have to do with how contracts can generally be interpreted in a way that's good for society.

The policy canons that we will discuss next involve:

- Good Faith,
- Interpretation Against the Drafter,
- Interpretation Favoring the Public, and
- Unconscionability.

Courts generally invoke policy canons only where parties dispute the meaning of a term, and its meaning cannot be resolved by logic, semantics, and credible testimony.

1. *Good Faith*

Contracts parties are in a legal relationship with each other. It is true that a contractual relationship is not quite like, for example, a spousal relationship or the relationship between lawyer and client, where two people are in a special relationship of trust and confidence. But contract parties do owe legal obligations to one another, and these obligations result from their own self-interested volitional manifestation of commitment. As a result, contract parties must treat each other reasonably well in furtherance of their mutual obligations. We call this the obligation of good faith and fair dealing.

> *Every contract imposes upon each party a duty of good faith and fair dealing in its performance and its enforcement.* R2d § 205.

Good faith is a general standard that requires case-specific analysis, because what is required or expected in one type of transaction or between one set of parties may be different from another.

> *Good faith means honesty in fact in the conduct or transaction concerned.* UCC 2-201(b)(20).

The analysis is a bit easier with merchants, who generally operate within a commercial context that has its own established standards of conduct:

> *"Good faith" in the case of a merchant means honesty in fact and the observance of reasonable commercial standards of fair dealing in the trade.* UCC § 2-103.

It is deliberately hard to pin down exactly what good faith requires, since the standard is designed to give judges freedom to consider the individual context of each transaction. But, generally, good faith requires each party to try to bring forth the fruits of the contract. For example, in *Wood v. Lucy, Lady Duff-Gordon*, 222 N.Y. 88 (1917), excerpted in Chapter 16, Lady Duff-Gordon, who was a British fashion icon and social influencer in the 1920s, agreed to put her name on clothing items that Mr. Wood selected for distribution in the American market, and then the two would share the profits. The court found that Mr. Wood had an obligation to make good faith efforts to select and distribute items.

2. Interpretation Against the Drafter

As a matter of policy, courts will also interpret a written agreement in favor of the non-drafting party. This legal concept of *contra proferentum* ("against the offeror") is based on the idea is that the drafter should feel an obligation to draft carefully; or, at least, courts should not reward drafters for drafting sloppily.

> *In choosing among the reasonable meanings of a promise or agreement or a term thereof, that meaning is generally preferred which operates against the party who supplies the words or from whom a writing otherwise proceeds.* R2d § 206.

R2d's reasoning for this rule represents legal realism par excellence:

> *Where one party chooses the terms of a contract, he is likely to provide more carefully for the protection of his own interests than for those of the other party.* R2d § 206 cmt a.

This bias against the drafter is also intended to partly correct for the typical power imbalance between the drafter and the other party. When one party drafts a contract that the other cannot even negotiate, such a take-it-or-leave-it-offer is called a contract of adhesion. In such a case of extreme power imbalance, courts should be more willing to interpret against the drafter.

On the other hand, where parties are at arm's length and take a joint role in drafting the contract, and where they are sophisticated or represented by sophisticated legal counsel, then courts should be hesitant before unduly biasing judgment toward one of two equally powerful and self-interested parties.

3. Interpretation Favoring the Public

When a contract affects the public interest, it should be interpreted with the public interest in mind. This narrowly applicable rule usually relates to public matters such as government contracts, federal patents, tax settlements, and the like.

> *In choosing among the reasonable meanings of a promise or agreement or a term thereof, a meaning that serves the public interest is generally preferred.*
> R2d § 207.

For example, courts generally disfavor private restrictions on free markets. Such restrictions can be used to generate private gains at the public expense. For example, in *Houk v. Ross*, 34 Ohio St. 2d 77 (1973), Houk purchased property from Ross subject to a deed restriction stating that only one residence could be built on the property. Houk attempted to build a duplex, which is a single residential structure designed for two different residents, on the property, and Ross sued to enjoin its construction. The court found that the term was ambiguous regarding whether a duplex was a prohibited structure, but it resolved the ambiguity in favor of the public by interpreting the less restrictive use of the land.

4. Unconscionable Contract or Term

Judges are not mere functionaries who must rubber stamp every formally valid contract. Rather, R2d specifically requires courts not to enforce "unconscionable" contracts or terms:

> *If a contract or term thereof is unconscionable at the time the contract is made a court may refuse to enforce the contract, or may enforce the remainder of the contract without the unconscionable term, or may so limit the application of any unconscionable term as to avoid any unconscionable result.* R2d § 208.

Unconscionability is term loaded with history and meaning. Courts still refer to Lord Harwicke's definition from the 1750 case *Earl of Chesterfield v. Janssen*, 28 Eng. Rep. 82 (1751):

> *Such as no man in his senses and not under delusion would make on the one hand, and as no honest and fair man would accept on the other.*

This refers to gross inequity that points so some sort of otherwise undefined unfair dealing or sharp practice. As more modern courts observe, this provision applies where an agreement falls short of being illegal or even formally unenforceable, but where, in the words of the *Campbell Soup Co v. Wentz* court, "the sum total of its provisions drives too hard a bargain for a court of conscience to assist." 172 F.2d 80, 84 (3d Cir. 1948).

For example, in *Frostifresh Corp. v. Reynoso*, 274 N.Y.S.2d 757 (1966), the Frostifresh refrigerator corporation sold a combination refrigerator-freezer to its employee, Luis Reynoso, a Spanish-speaking man who did not understand English. The contract was negotiated in Spanish by Frostifresh's Spanish-speaking sales representative. Reynoso told the representative that he could not afford the appliance, and the salesman distracted and deluded Reynoso by telling him that it would cost him nothing because Reynoso could earn commissions selling more refrigerators to his friends and neighbors. The confused Reynoso agreed, and Frostifresh charged Reynoso $900 for the appliance plus $245.88 as a credit charge, and deducted the $1,145.88 total (over $10,000 in 2022 dollars) from his paycheck.

Unsurprisingly, aside from what Frostifresh was able to deduct from his paycheck, Reynoso was unable to make any payments on the appliance. Frostifresh sued him for the balance due. The court found that Frostifresh paid $348 for the appliance. It then held that Frostifresh's $800 profit, and especially its $245.99 service charge, was inequitable under these circumstances. While a business is usually free to make whatever profits it can earn, here, this was not a fair and arm's length transaction. A large company deliberately took advantage of its employee's confusion and language difficulties. The court allowed Frostifresh to charge Reynoso its cost of $348, less amounts received, but refused to enforce "too hard a bargain and too one sided an agreement."

Such cases of unconscionability are few and far between. Courts generally enforce agreements regardless of whether there is a resulting imbalance. It is not the imbalance per se that the courts abhor; rather, a gross imbalance may evidence some sinister defect in the contracting process.

Cases

Reading Motors Liquidation Co. On June 11, 2009, General Motors, which would thus become known as "Old GM," obtained Chapter 11 bankruptcy protection in federal court. Chapter 11 of the United States Bankruptcy Code permits business entities (usually large corporations) to seek relief from creditors. When a corporation cannot pay all its debt and is thus at risk of failing completely, the law provides this way for the debtor to work out with creditors some mutually agreeable way to pay back some significant portion of the debt.

One source of corporate debt may arise from corporate torts. When a corporation harms a person, and that person successfully sues in federal court, the corporation may be required to pay damages. If the corporate harm impacts a large number of people at once, that alone could drive the corporation into a bankruptcy. In GM's case, however, many factors came together in the automotive industry crisis of 2008-2010 — including, as you will read, GM's tort liability to a certain Beverly Deutsch for an accident that occurred in June 2007 and led to her death in August 2009.

The Bankruptcy Court functions in some ways like a moderator who takes all the creditors' interests into account and approves any settlement among all the parties. In this case, the parties agreed that GM would cut expenses and raise cash, among other things, by discontinuing the Hummer and Saturn brands and by selling the Saab brand to Spyker Cars.

Substantially all of the core GM assets were auctioned off in a peculiar sale at which there was only one bidder, New GM, a corporation formed by the United States government (60.8%), the Canadian government (11.7%), the United and Canadian Auto Workers Union (17.5%) and unsecured bondholders of Old GM (10%), to "bail out" its automaker. New GM purchased Old GM according to the bankruptcy court approved Amended and Restated Master Sale and Purchase Agreement (the "MSPA"). This next case turns on the interpretation of a key provision in that MSPA.

In re Motors Liquidation Co.

447 B.R. 142 (Bankr. S.D.N.Y. 2011)

ROBERT E. GERBER, UNITED STATES BANKRUPTCY JUDGE

In this contested matter in the chapter 11 case of Motors Liquidation Company (formerly, General Motors Corp., and referred to here as "Old GM") and its affiliates, General Motors LLC ("New GM") seeks a determination from this Court that New GM did not assume the liabilities associated with a tort action in which a car accident took place before the date ("Closing Date") upon which New GM acquired the business of Old GM, but the accident victim died thereafter.

The issue turns on the construction of the documents under which New GM agreed to assume liabilities from Old GM — which provided that New GM would assume liabilities relating to "accidents or incidents" "first occurring on or after the Closing Date" — and in that connection, whether a liability of this character is or is not one of the types of liabilities that New GM thereby agreed to assume.

Upon consideration of those documents, the Court concludes that the liability in question was not assumed by New GM. However, if a proof of claim was not previously filed against Old GM with respect to the accident in question, the Court will permit one to be filed within 30 days of the entry of the order implementing this Decision, without prejudice to rights to appeal this determination.

The Court's Findings of Fact and Conclusions of Law in connection with this determination follow.

Findings of Fact

In June 2007, Beverly Deutsch was severely injured in an accident while she was driving a 2006 Cadillac sedan. She survived the car accident, but in August 2009, she died from the injuries that she previously had sustained.

In January 2010, the Estate of Beverly Deutsch, the Heirs of Beverly Deutsch, and Sanford Deutsch (collectively "Deutsch Estate") filed a Third Amended Complaint against New GM (and others) in a state court lawsuit in California (the "Deutsch Estate Action"), claiming damages arising from the accident, the injuries which Beverly sustained, and her wrongful death. The current complaint superseded the original complaint in the Deutsch Estate Action, which was filed in April 2008, before the filing of Old GM's chapter 11 case.

In July 2009, this Court entered its order (the "363 Sale Order") approving the sale of Old GM's assets, under section 363 of the Bankruptcy Code, to the entity now known as New GM. The 363 Sale Order, among other things, approved an agreement that was called an Amended and Restated Master Sale and Purchase Agreement (the "MSPA").

The MSPA detailed which liabilities would be assumed by New GM, and provided that all other liabilities would be retained by Old GM. The MSPA provided, in its § 2.3(a)(ix), that New GM would not assume any claims with respect to product liabilities (as such term was defined in the MSPA, "Product Liability Claims") of the Debtors except those that "arise directly out of death, personal injury or other injury to Persons or damage to property caused by accidents or incidents first occurring on or after the Closing Date [July 10, 2009] . . . ." Thus, those Product Liability Claims that arose from "accidents or incidents" occurring before July 10, 2009 would not be assumed by New GM, but claims arising from "accidents or incidents" occurring on or after July 10, 2009 would be.

Language in an earlier version of the MSPA differed somewhat from its final language, as approved by the Court. Before its amendment, the MSPA provided for New GM to assume liabilities except those caused by "accidents, incidents, or other distinct and discrete occurrences."

The 363 Sale Order provides that "[t]his Court retains exclusive jurisdiction to enforce and implement the terms and provisions of this Order" and the MSPA, including "to protect the Purchaser [New GM] against any of the Retained Liabilities or the assertion of any . . . claim . . . of any kind or nature whatsoever, against the Purchased Assets."

Discussion

The issue here is one of contractual construction. As used in the MSPA, when defining the liabilities that New GM would assume, what do the words "accidents or incidents," that appear before "first occurring on or after the Closing Date," mean?

It is undisputed that the accident that caused Beverly Deutsch's death took place in June 2007, more than two years prior to the closing. But her death took place after the closing. New GM argues that Beverly Deutsch's injuries arose from an "accident" and an "incident" that took place in 2007, and that her death did likewise. But the Deutsch Estate argues that while the "accident" took place in 2007, her death was a separate "incident" — and that the latter took place only in August 2009, after the closing of the sale to New GM had taken place.

Ultimately, while the Court respects the skill and fervor with which the point was argued, it cannot agree with the Deutsch Estate. Beverly Deutsch's death in 2009 was the consequence of an event that took place in 2007, which undisputedly, was an accident and which also was an incident, which is a broader word, but fundamentally of a similar type. The resulting death in 2009 was not, however, an "incident[] first occurring on or after the Closing Date," as that term was used in the MSPA.

As usual, the Court starts with textual analysis. The key provision of the MSPA, § 2.3(a)(ix), set forth the extent to which Product Liability Claims were assumed by New GM. Under that provision, New GM assumed:

> *(ix) all Liabilities to third parties for death, personal injury, or other injury to Persons or damage to property caused by motor vehicles designed for operation on public roadways or by the component parts of such motor vehicles and, in each case, manufactured, sold or delivered by Sellers (collectively, "Product Liabilities"), which arise directly out of death, personal injury or other injury to Persons or damage to property caused by accidents or incidents first occurring on or after the Closing Date and arising from such motor vehicles' operation or performance (for avoidance of doubt, Purchaser shall not assume or become liable to pay, perform or discharge, any Liability arising or contended to arise by reason of exposure to materials utilized in the assembly or fabrication of motor vehicles manufactured by Sellers and delivered prior to the Closing Date, including asbestos, silicates or fluids, regardless of when such alleged exposure occurs).*

The key words, of course, are "accidents" and "incidents," neither of which are defined anywhere else in the MSPA, and whose interpretation, accordingly, must turn on their common meaning and any understandings expressed by one side to the other in the course of contractual negotiations. Also important are the words "first occurring on or after the Closing Date," which modify the words "accidents" and "incidents," and shed light on the former words' meaning.

The word "accidents," of course, is not ambiguous. "Accidents" has sufficiently clear meaning on its own, and in any event its interpretation is not subject to debate, as both sides agree that Beverly Deutsch's death resulted from an accident that took place in 2007, at a time when, if "accidents" were the only controlling word, liability for the resulting death would not be assumed by New GM. The ambiguity, if any, is instead in the word "incidents," which is a word that by its nature is more inclusive and less precise.

But while "incidents" may be deemed to be somewhat ambiguous, neither side asked for an evidentiary hearing to put forward parol evidence as to its meaning. Though it is undisputed that "incidents" remained in the MSPA after additional words "or other distinct and discrete occurrences," were deleted, neither side was able, or chose, to explain, by evidence, why the latter words were dropped, and what, if any relevance the dropping of the additional words might have as to the meaning of the word "incidents" that remained. The words "or other distinct and discrete occurrences" could have been deleted as redundant, to narrow the universe of claims that were assumed, or for some other reason. Ultimately, the Court is unable to derive sufficient indication of the parties' intent as to the significance, if any, of deleting the extra words.

So the Court is left with the task of deriving the meaning of the remaining words "accidents or incidents" from their ordinary meaning, the words that surround them, canons of construction, and the Court's understanding when it approved the 363 Sale as to how the MSPA would deal with prepetition claims against Old GM. Ultimately these considerations, particularly in the aggregate, point in a single direction — that a death resulting from an earlier "accident[] or incident[]" was not an "incident[] first occurring" after the closing.

Starting first with ordinary meaning, definitions of "incident" from multiple sources are quite similar. They include, as relevant here, "an occurrence of an action or situation felt as a separate unit of experience"; "an occurrence of an action or situation that is a separate unit of experience"; "[a] discrete occurrence or happening"; "something that happens, especially a single event"; "a definite and separate occurrence; an event"; or, as proffered by the Deutsch Estate, "[a] separate and definite occurrence: EVENT."

In ways that vary only in immaterial respects, all of the definitions articulate the concept of a separate and identifiable event. And, and of course, from words that follow, "arising from such motor vehicles' operation or performance," the event must be understood to relate to be one that that involves a motor vehicle. Accidents, explosions or fires all fit comfortably within that description. Deaths or other consequences that result from earlier accidents, explosions or fires technically might fit as well, but such a reading is much less natural and much more strained.

Turning next to words that surround the words "accidents or incidents," these words provide an interpretive aid to the words they modify. The word "incident[]" is followed by the words "first occurring." In addition to defining the relevant time at which the incident must take place (i.e., after the closing), that clause inserts the word "first" before "occurring." That suggests, rather strongly, that it was envisioned that some types of incidents could take place over time or have separate sub-occurrences, or that one incident might relate to an earlier incident, with the earliest incident being the one that matters. Otherwise it would be sufficient to simply say "occurring," without adding the word "first." This too suggests that the consequences of an incident should not be regarded as a separate incident, or that even if they are, the incident that first occurs is the one that controls.

Canons of construction tend to cut in opposite directions, though on balance they favor New GM. The Deutsch Estate appropriately points to the canon of construction against "mere surplusage," which requires different words of a contract or statute to be construed in a fashion that gives them separate meanings, so that no word is superfluous. The Court would not go as far as to say that the words "accident" and "incident" cannot ever cover the same thing — or, putting it another way, that they always must be different. But the Court agrees with the Deutsch Estate that they cannot always mean the same thing. "Incidents" must have been put there for a reason and should be construed to add something in at least some circumstances.

But how different the two words "accidents" and "incidents" can properly be understood to be — and in particular, whether "incidents" can be deemed to separately exist when they are a foreseeable consequence, or are the resulting injury, from the accidents or incidents that cause them — is quite a different matter. A second canon of construction, "*noscitur a sociis*," provides that "words grouped in a list should be given related meaning." Colloquially, "a word is known by the company it keeps." For instance, in *Dole* [*v. United Steelworkers of America*, 494 U.S. 26 (1990)], in interpreting a phrase of the Paper Work Reduction Act, the Supreme Court invoked *noscitur a sociis* to hold that words in a list, while meaning different things, should nevertheless be read to place limits on how broadly some of those words might be construed. The *Dole* court stated:

> *That a more limited reading of the phrase "reporting and recordkeeping requirements" was intended derives some further support from the words surrounding it. The traditional canon of construction, noscitur a sociis, dictates that words grouped in a list should be given related meaning.*

Here application of the canon against surplusage makes clear, as the Deutsch Estate argues, that "incidents" must at least sometimes mean something different than "accidents" — but application of that canon does not tell us when and how. The second canon, *noscitur a sociis*, does that, and effectively trumps the doctrine of surplusage because it tells us that "accidents" and "incidents" should be given related meaning.

The Deutsch Estate argues that the Court should construe a death resulting from an earlier "accident" or "incident" to be a separate and new "incident" that took place at a later time. But ultimately, the Court concludes that it cannot do so. While it is easy to conclude that "accidents" and "incidents," as used in the MSPA, will not necessarily be the same in all cases, they must still be somewhat similar. "Incidents" cannot be construed so broadly as to cover what are simply the consequences of earlier "accidents" or other "incidents."

Applying *noscitur a sociis* in conjunction with the canon against "mere surplusage" tells us that the two words "accidents" and "incidents" must be understood as having separate meanings in at least some cases, but that these meanings should be conceptually related. At oral argument, the Court asked counsel for New GM an important question: if an "incident" would not necessarily be an "accident," what would it be? What would it cover? Counsel for New GM came back with a crisp and very logical answer; he said that "incident" would cover a situation where a car caught fire or had blown up, or some problem had arisen by means other than a collision.

Conversely, the interpretation for which the Deutsch Estate argues — that "incidents" refers to consequences of earlier accidents or incidents — is itself violative or potentially violative, of the two interpretive canons discussed above. It is violative of *noscitur a sociis*, since a death or other particular injury is by its nature distinct from the circumstance — collision, explosion, fire, or other accident or incident — that causes the resulting injury in the first place. The Deutsch Estate interpretation also tends to run counter to the doctrine against mere surplusage upon which the Deutsch Estate otherwise relies, making meaningless the words "first occurring" which follow the words "accidents or incidents," in any cases where death or other particular injury is the consequence of an explosion, fire, or other non-collision incident that causes the resulting injury.

The simple interpretation, and the one this Court ultimately provides, is that "incidents," while covering more than just "accidents," are similar; they relate to fires, explosions, or other definite events that cause injuries and result in the right to sue, as contrasted to describing the consequences of those earlier events, or that relate to the resulting damages.

Finally, this Court's earlier understanding of the purposes of New GM's willingness to assume certain liabilities of Old GM is consistent with the Court's conclusion at this time as well. When the Court approved GM's 363 Sale, this Court noted, in its opinion, that New GM had chosen to broaden its assumption of product liabilities. The MSPA was amended to provide for the assumption of liabilities not just for product liability claims for motor vehicles and parts delivered after the Closing Date (as in the original formulation), but also, for "all product liability claims arising from accidents or other discrete incidents arising from operation of GM vehicles occurring subsequent to the closing of the 363 Transaction, regardless of when the product was purchased." As reflected in the Court's decision at the time, the Court understood that New GM was undertaking to assume the liabilities for "accidents or other discrete incidents" that hadn't yet taken place.

Finally, the Deutsch Estate notes another interpretative canon, that ambiguities in a contract must be read against the drafter. If the matter were closer, the Court might consider doing so. But the language in question is not that ambiguous, and the relevant considerations, fairly decisively, all tip in the same direction. While it cannot be said that the Deutsch Estate's position is a frivolous one, the issues are not close enough to require reading the language against the drafter.

Conclusion

The Deutsch Estate's interpretation of "accident or incident" is not supportable. Thus, the Debtor's motion is granted, and the Deutsch Estate may not pursue this claim against New GM. New GM is to settle an order consistent with this opinion.

The time to appeal from this determination will run from the time of the resulting order, and not from the date of filing of this Decision.

Reflection

This bankruptcy case might have introduced some new procedural concepts or legal terms, but the core learning related directly to the Canons of Construction covered in this chapter. The case involved a contract about whose meaning two parties disagreed. One says "action or incident" means an event like a car crash or a spontaneous explosion. The other says that an incident includes the long-term consequences of an accident such as death that results years after a car crash.

To resolve such disputes, courts must first determine whether the term is ambiguous such that it is susceptible to both meanings. It then must analyze which meaning prevails using the Canons of Construction. Where both interpretations remain plausible, courts may construe the meaning to favor the non-drafting party as a last resort. The *Motors Liquidation* court follows these steps and thus illustrates how to effectively analyze and resolve a dispute regarding contractual interpretation

Discussion

1. Without the benefit of the parties' arguments, how would you go about defining what is meant by "accidents and incidents"? Does it seem more intuitive that accidents and incidents are two types of unrelated things, or that incidents are the proximate result of accidents? What evidence from common speech can you give in defense of your position?

Problems

Problem 14.1. Matching the Canons of Construction to Case Applications

Below are examples from cases that applied the Canons of Construction. Identify which canon or canons were applied in each example.

a. What canon(s) should be applied to determine whether a pharmaceutical drug is a "compound combination" in a patent license agreement?

b. What canon(s) should be applied to determine whether a sales commission was owed where an agreement for sale of real estate provided that the broker would be paid a commission "upon the signing of this agreement" by both buyer and seller, but which agreement also wrote in the last paragraph, "the commission being due and payable upon the transfer of the property"?

c. What canon(s) should be used to interpret a contract including both a printed term saying, "vessel to have turn in loading," and a handwritten term below that saying, "vessel to be loaded promptly"?

d. What canons(s) should be used determine who bears the costs of regulations where a contract between a GC and a Sub has both a specific clause shifting the cost of conforming to regulations enacted after the bid to the GC a more general clause requiring that the contractor's work to conform with all relevant regulations?

e. What canon(s) should be used to determine whether the term "insured" in an insurance policy includes company equipment operated by a company employee, where the term insured is defined as "any executive officer, director or stockholder thereof while acting within the scope of his duties"?

f. What canon(s) should be used to determine the meaning of "flood" in an insurance contract, where "flood" is defined to mean inundation from natural water sources, not damage from a broken water main, because the contract referred to loss from "flood, surface water, waves, tidal water or tidal wave, overflow of streams or other bodies of water or spray from any of the foregoing, all whether driven by wind or not"?

g. What canon(s) should be used to determine whether a lease prohibition is effective where the lease prohibits the lessee from subletting the property "for use as a pool parlor, beer parlor, or other business which would be undesirable and objectionable to the tenants in other parts of the building"? In particular, does this prohibition prevent lessee from subletting for use as a restaurant?

h. What canon(s) should be used to interpret an invoice from a contractor which contained a smaller typewritten amount and a larger handwritten number?

i. What canon(s) should be used to determine whether a franchise contract contemplated a third site where it only specifically discussed and approved two locations?

j. What canon(s) should be used to disambiguate an installment contract clause was where one of two sensible constructions would violate usury laws?

k. Is it appropriate to apply the canon of construction against the drafter to determine who has insurance coverage where the policy says it covers employees of companies "controlled by" the holding company that bought the insurance, where the insurance company primarily drafted the contract, and where the contract was negotiated between the parties for several months and involved teams of lawyers on both sides?

l. What canon(s) apply to disambiguate a guaranty agreement that contains the following phrase: "All amounts due, debts, liabilities and payment obligations described in clauses (i) and (ii), above, are referred to herein as 'Indebtedness.'" In particular, which canons helps determine whether "described in clauses (i) and (ii)" applies only to the "payment obligations," not to "amounts due, debts, liabilities"?

m. What canon(s) of constructions applies to a case where Rogers Communications of Toronto, Canada's largest cable television provider, entered into a contract with the telephone company Bell Aliant, for the use of Bell's telephone poles? The contract stated: "Subject to the termination provisions of this Agreement, this Agreement shall be effective from the date it is made and shall continue in force for a period of five (5) years from the date it is made, and thereafter for successive five (5) year terms, unless and until terminated by one year prior notice in writing by either party." During the first five-year term of the contract, Bell informed Rogers that it was terminating the contract one year early. Rogers argued that the termination provision did not apply to the initial five-year term of the contract.

Problem 14.2. **Homeowner's Insurance?**

The Hanover Commercial Umbrella Insurance Policy agreement (the "Policy") provides the following coverage and exclusions:

> *The words we, us, and our refer to the Company providing the insurance. We will pay on behalf of the Named Insured for damages because of bodily injury, property damage, personal injury, and advertising injury. This insurance does not apply to any bodily injury, property damages, personal injury, or advertising injury arising out of the actual, alleged or threatened discharge, dispersal, seepage, migration, release or escape of "pollutants." "Pollutants" means any solid, liquid, gaseous or thermal irritant or contaminant, including smoke, vapor, soot, fumes, acids, alkalis, chemicals and waste. Waste includes materials to be recycled, reconditioned or reclaimed.*

Based on your analysis of the Policy and your application of the Canons of Construction, determine:

1. Whether personal injury claims arising out of ingestion of lead from flaked paint or paint dust shall be covered under the Policy, where the Named Insured owned and operated an apartment building that it rented to Plaintiff; where an official city inspector inspected the premises and established the presence of loose, peeling, flaking, or chipped paint which contained a hazardous concentration of lead; and where Plaintiff sustained lead poisoning by ingesting lead derived from paint chips, paint flakes and dust that was contaminated with lead derived from lead based paint. *See Peace v. Northwestern Nat'l Ins. Co.*, 596 N.W.2d 429 (Wis. 1999).

2. Whether property damages claims arising out of the accumulation of bat guano between a vacation home's siding and walls shall be covered under the Policy, where the Named Insured owned a vacation home

rental business, and they discovered during an annual vacation the presence of bats and bat guano in a home, when they noticed a "penetrating and offensive odor emanating from the home," a where a contractor determined that the cause of the odor was the accumulation of bat guano between the home's siding and walls, and where the contractor determined that it was more practical financially to demolish and rebuild the home instead of attempting to spend the money to make it habitable again. *See Hirschhorn v. Auto-Owners Ins. Co.*, 809 N.W.2d 529 (Wis. 2011).

3. Whether personal injury claims arising out of the inadequate ventilation of exhaled carbon dioxide shall be covered under the Policy, where an inadequate air exchange ventilation system in an office building owned and operated by the Named Insured caused an excessive accumulation of carbon dioxide in their work area, and where the resultant poor air quality allegedly caused the plaintiffs to sustain the following injuries: headaches, sinus problems, eye irritation, extreme fatigue, upset stomach, asthma, sore throat, nausea, and pounding ears. *See Donaldson v. Urban Land Interests, Inc.*, 564 N.W.2d 728 (Wis. 1997).

Problem 14.3. What Is a "Cartoon"?

On November 28, 1998, the attorneys general of multiple states entered into a Tobacco Master Settlement Agreement ("TMSA") with major manufacturers of cigarettes, including R.J. Reynolds Tobacco Co., as part of litigation over medical expenses from tobacco-related diseases. The TMSA prohibited such cigarette manufacturers from using cartoons in advertising.

Section II(*l*) of the TMSA states as follows:

> (*l*) *"Cartoon" means any drawing or other depiction of an object, person, animal, creature or any similar caricature that satisfies any of the following criteria:*
>
>   (1) *[T]he use of comically exaggerated features;*
>
>   (2) *[T]he attribution of human characteristics to animals, plants or other objects, or the similar use of anthropomorphic technique; or*
>
>   (3) *[T]he attribution of unnatural or extrahuman abilities, such as imperviousness to pain or injury, X-ray vision, tunneling at very high speeds or transformation.*

While operating under the settlement agreement, Reynolds placed the advertisement shown here in the 40th Anniversary Edition of Rolling Stone magazine, which was published on November 15, 2007, promoting independent rock music and record labels in connection with its Camel cigarette brand and its Camel Farm campaign:

Figure 14.1. Camel cigarette ad. Is it a "cartoon"?

The Attorney General of Ohio sued Reynolds for violating the settlement agreement by promoting its cigarettes using cartoons. Reynolds claimed that the advertisement did not contain cartoons as that term is used in the settlement agreement.

Articulate the arguments that you think would support each side's interpretation of the contract. How would you rule if you were the judge?

See State ex rel. Richard Cordray v. R.J. Reynolds Tobacco Co., 2010 WL 154720, 2010 Ohio App. LEXIS 73 (2010).

Problem 14.4. Meaning of a Comma

On Jan. 1, 2000, Rappaport (Lessor) entered into a lease giving Interbroad, LLC (Lessee) the right to use the rooftop of a building to display a billboard. The lease ran until April 11, 2094. The lease gave Rappaport the following termination rights:

> *In the event that Lessor's building is damaged by fire or other casualty and Lessor elects not to restore such building, or Lessor elects to demolish the building, Lessor may terminate the Lease upon not less than 60 days notice to Lessee upon paying Lessee ten (10) times the net operating income earned by Lessee from the Advertising Structures on the Premises for the immediately preceding twelve (12) month period.*

In 2015, the building subject to the lease was purchased by BL Partners, Inc., which assumed the rights and obligations of Rappaport and so became the Lessor under the original lease. BL Partners sent Interbroad a letter stating that it had taken over the lease, had elected to demolish the building, and was terminating the lease effective

60 days from that date. The building had not been damaged by fire or any other casualty. BL Partners asked Interbroad to provide its net operating income earned by the billboard for the preceding twelve months, in order to calculate the amount owed in connection with the termination. Interbroad refused, arguing that BL Partners had no right to terminate the lease. BL Partners sought a declaratory judgment that it had the right to terminate the lease.

Articulate the arguments that you think would support each side's interpretation of the contract. How would you rule if you were the judge?

See *BL Partners Grp., L.P. v. Interbroad, LLC*, 2016 Phila. Ct. Com. Pl. LEXIS 156 (2016).

Problem 14.5. Vesting in Retirement

This problem addresses the issue of whose interpretation prevails where written agreements have internal contradictions. Before you read this problem, you may want to look up the words "vest" or "vesting" in a dictionary, as these terms may not be familiar to you. You could also consult a specialized dictionary, such as investopia .com.

First, some background: Craig Klapp worked as an insurance agent for United Insurance Group Agency, Inc. ("UIG") for seven (7) years from 1990 to 1997. Klapp is suing UIG for breach of contract, claiming that UIG promised to pay him a pension equal to 100% of commissions on renewals of policies that he originally sold. UIG claims that Klapp is not entitled to any post-retirement commission payments on renewals or otherwise.

When Klapp joined UIG, he signed two documents: an "Employment Agreement," which set forth his salary, benefits, and conditions of employment specific to him; and an "Agent's Manual," which stated the rules and policies that apply to all UIG agents and employees.

UIG's first argument is that Klapp is not entitled to any commission based on the express language of the Agent's Manual, which states:

> *Retirement is understood to be disengagement from the insurance industry.*
> *Vestment for retirement is age 65 or 10 years of service whichever is later.*

In addition, UIG wants to admit evidence that (a) an international study of retirement benefits policies of insurance companies shows that only 20% allow partial vesting, and that over ¾ of insurance company retirement plans do not fully (100%) vest until at least 10 years of continuous full-time employment.

UIG's second argument is that Klapp is not entitled to any commission because he has not relinquished his license to sell insurance; therefore Klapp has not "retired" as that term is defined in the Agent's Manual.

Klapp responds to UIG's second argument by seeking to introduce evidence that the ordinary meaning of "retired" means not currently working or immediately planning to return to work and that he is in fact not currently working nor planning to work in the insurance industry.

Klapp argues that the judge should deprioritize the definition of vesting in the Agent's Manual and instead use the definition provided in the Employment Agreement, Section 5 of which states:

5. Vested Commissions. Commissions shall be vested in the following manner:

(A) Death, disability, or retirement during term hereof. Upon the death, disability, or retirement (as those terms shall be then defined in the Agent's Manual) of Agent at any time prior to the termination of this Agreement, Agent (or Agent's designated death beneficiary who shall be designated by Agent in writing; or in the absence of such written designation, Agent's estate) shall thereafter be entitled to receive one hundred percent (100%) of such renewal commissions then payable from premiums on Agent's policies in place, in such amounts as would otherwise have been payable to Agent, until the aggregate renewals payable to Agent thereon shall equal less than Forty-One Dollars and Sixty-Seven Cents ($41.67) per month. If upon the date of death, disability, or retirement, Agent shall have aggregated eight (8) or more years of service under this Agreement, his then vesting shall be determined in accordance with the normal vesting schedule.

(B) Vesting Schedule. In the event of a termination of this Agreement for reasons of death, disability or retirement (as defined in the Agent's Manual), Agent as set forth below on the date of execution hereof shall be entitled to receive a percentage of renewal commissions then payable from premiums on Agent's policies in place, applicable to such amounts as would otherwise have been payable to Agent in accordance with the following vesting schedule:

AGENT'S YEARS OF SERVICE	% OF RENEWALS VESTED
LESS THAN 2 YEARS	0%
2 YEARS	10%
3 YEARS	30%
4 YEARS	50%
5 YEARS	70%
6 YEARS	90%
7 YEARS	100%
8 YEARS	110%
9 YEARS	120%
10 YEARS	130%
11 YEARS	140%
12 YEARS	150%

In addition, Klapp wants to admit evidence that he had a conversation with the hiring manager at UIG who provided this paperwork to him to the effect that UIG has a "policy of helping out the most valuable agents" and that UIG would "take good care" of him, as evidence that he was guaranteed full retirement benefits.

a. Characterize each piece of evidence that Klapp and UIG seek to admit as intrinsic or extrinsic and discuss what that evidence would be admitted to show or prove.

b. Does the parol evidence rule apply to any of the evidence in this case? Should any evidence be excluded from the jury pursuant to the parol evidence rule?

c. How should the court rule? Should UIG be required to pay 100% commission on renewals to Klapp?

d. How did looking up definitions for "vesting" and other financial terms affect your analysis of this case? How can you improve your ability to make legal decisions when contracts involve financial or other technical concepts?

Adapted from Klapp v. United Ins. Grp. Agency, Inc., 468 Mich. 459 (2003).

Chapter 15

The Parol Evidence Rule

Extrinsic contractual evidence — meaning, evidence aside from the written contract itself — includes (1) course of performance, (2) course of dealing, (3) trade usage, and (4) preliminary negotiations. Courts may exclude evidence of oral preliminary negotiations and even prior oral agreements pursuant to the Parol Evidence Rule that was discussed earlier. But courts generally entertain evidence of course of performance, course of dealing, and trade usage that bears upon the meaning of a disputed term in a contract.

Course of performance means how the parties acted with each other while performing the contract now under dispute.

Course of dealing means how the parties acted with each other while performing some prior or contemporaneous agreement that was reasonably like the contract now under dispute.

Trade usage refers to how parties in this trade or professor usually perform regarding similar agreements to the contract now under dispute.

Although trade usage evidence is the most removed from how the two parties subjectively think, in the sense that trade usage evidence does not usually come from the parties themselves but from impartial industry experts (who, admittedly, might be hired by the parties), it is sometimes the most compelling for the same reason that it is removed. Although trade usage does not necessarily reflect what the parties actually thought subjectively, it does tend to evidence what a reasonable commercial party should have thought. Applying this sort of constructive knowledge or reasonability makes trade usage evidence somewhat more objective, which can balance some of the subjective evidence that courts admit.

Rules

A. Excluding Parol (Oral) Evidence

When parties have written a contract, courts might prohibit them from introducing oral evidence that conflicts with or adds to the writing. This is called the Parol Evidence Rule or "PER." Note that I did not make a typo. "Parol evidence" is not to be confused with parole with an "e." Parole with an "e" was originally synonymous with a pledge or word of honor and is now used to refer to granting liberty to a prisoner. Parol without an "e", on the other hand, means an oral statement as opposed to something written. The PER is thus tantamount to the "Oral Evidence Rule," and that name precisely describes what it relates to: PER excludes oral contractual evidence that contradicts certain written contractual evidence.

The Parol Evidence Rule ("PER") connects contract law and evidence law. Contract law is a substantive doctrine: it tells you "what" elements are needed to show, for example, that a contract has been formed as a principle of law (i.e., offer, acceptance, and consideration). But contract law rarely deals with procedure. It does not necessarily tell you how that element may be shown in a physical court of law. Can you show camera footage of someone nodding to prove an offer was accepted? Is metadata such as a time stamp, or false coloring from an infrared camera, admissible as evidence of contract formation?

These questions for the most part are answered by the law of evidence, which deals with what and how evidence may be presented at trial. Civil procedure also deals with obtaining pre-trial evidence through interrogatories and depositions. The exact boundaries between procedural and substantive law are not always sharply drawn, but as a general rule, the procedural elements of contract law are dictated by other legal subjects such as evidence law and civil procedure.

PER is the exception to that general rule. It provides a rule about what kinds of evidence can be used to show that meaning of a contract.

The PER is confounding to law students because it is mired in archaic language. This chapter will provide the PER and then explain its legalese, with the forewarning that these rules require some unpacking:

> *A binding integrated agreement discharges prior agreements to the extent that it is inconsistent with them.* R2d § 213(1).

Let us break this down word by word:

"Binding" means legally enforceable. If a writing does not meet the standards of a legal contract, then the PER need not apply.

"Integrated" is the common law term for what the UCC calls "final." You can use the terms "integrated" and "final" synonymously:

> *An integrated agreement is a writing or writings constituting a final expression of one or more terms of an agreement.* R2d § 209(1).

"Agreement" was previously defined in R2d and the first module:

> *An agreement is a manifestation of mutual assent on the part of two or more persons.* R2d § 3.

"Discharges" comes from the Old French deschargier, meaning "to unload," as in unloading a wagon or cart. In fact, in Latin, "carrus" means "wagon" (and is the root of the modern words car and carriage) and "dis" means "do the opposite," such that dis-carrus means to unload or disburden. In the legal sense, discharge refers to releasing one from a legal obligation or duty. In the specific instance of the PER, this means that prior oral obligations are released and voided.

"Prior" has its simple chronological meaning. The PER does not apply to future modifications or later agreements; rather, the PER only applies to oral agreements made before the related writing was finalized.

"Inconsistent" prior oral agreements are ones that directly conflict with the written agreement at issue. For example, if the written agreement says "five dollars per ton," an oral promise to sell the first ten tons for three dollars per ton would be inconsistent.

Thus, the first element of the PER is that a final written expression supersedes any evidence of prior oral agreements that disagree in substance with the writing.

> *A binding completely integrated agreement discharges prior agreements to the extent that they are within its scope.* R2d § 213(2).

The second element of the PER adds the concept of "completely" integrated and "scope." Let us first address what is completely integrated. A completely integrated agreement is synonymous with a final and exclusive written statement of the parties' intentions with regard to a certain transaction.

> *A completely integrated agreement is an integrated agreement adopted by the parties as a complete and exclusive statement of the terms of the agreement.* R2d § 210.

In other words, a completely integrated agreement is both final and complete. This usually requires the writing itself to specify that the parties intend it to be the complete and exclusive statement of the parties' intentions with regards to the subject matter therein. Such a term is often called an integration clause or a merger clause. Here is an example of a typical integration clause:

> *This Agreement constitutes the complete, exclusive, and entire agreement between A and B regarding the Subject, all prior communications verbal or written between A and B shall be of no further effect or evidentiary value.*

Such language is usually dispositive that the parties intended the agreement to be completely integrated, but courts have found both that agreements lacking such language were completely integrated and that agreements possessing such language were not.

> *Whether an agreement is completely or partially integrated is to be determined by the court as a question preliminary to determination of a question of interpretation or to application of the parol evidence rule.* R2d § 210(3).

A classic example of an implicitly completed integrated agreement — meaning, a written contract that lacked a merger clause, but which was deemed a complete and exclusive statement of the parties' intentions about the specific transaction — is found in *Gianni v. R. Russell & Co.*, below.

Frank Gianni rented a room in R. Russell & Co's office building from where he operated a store selling tobacco, fruit, candy, and soft drinks. After some time, the parties entered into a written lease agreement, for a three-year term, which contained the following provision:

> Lessee should use the premises only for the sale of fruit, candy, soda water, etc. It is expressly understood that the tenant is not allowed to sell tobacco in any form, under penalty of instant forfeiture of this lease.

Gianni thus gave up his right to sell tobacco in exchange for Russell's continued permission to let him lease the office space.

Shortly after signing, Russell rented another space in his building to a drug store that also sold soda. Gianni protested that his contract gave him the exclusive right to sell soda in that building. He claimed Russell had promised exclusivity to him orally before signing, but the contract was silent regarding this provision.

The court needed to address the question of whether the parties intended the contract to be a complete and exclusive statement of their entire agreement — in which case Gianni's evidence of prior oral agreements regarding exclusivity should be discharged — or whether the writing was merely final and thus the agreement was susceptible to additional consistent terms.

Gianni argued that the lack of an integration clause proved that the contract was not complete and exclusive. The court disagreed, citing Wigmore on Evidence:

> In deciding upon this intent [as to whether a certain subject was intended to be embodied by the writing], the chief and most satisfactory index is found in the circumstances whether or not the particular element of the alleged extrinsic negotiation is dealt with at all in the writing. If it is mentioned, covered, or dealt with in the writing, then presumably the writing was meant to represent all of the transaction on that element; if it is not, then probably the writing was not intended to embody that element of the negotiation.

The court thus found that Gianni and Russell intended their writing to be complete and exclusive even though it lacked express intrinsic evidence of that intention.

On the other extreme are cases where a court disregards an integration clause. In *Sierra Diesel Injection Services, Inc. v. Burroughs Corp.*, below, a mechanic who ran a small business purchased a 1980s vintage computer styled as a "bookkeeping machine" from the Burroughs Corporation. Their written agreement included this integration clause:

> This Agreement constitutes the entire agreement, understanding and representations, express or implied between the Customer and Burroughs with respect to the equipment and/or related services to be furnished and this Agreement supersedes all prior communications between the parties including all oral and written proposals.

The bookkeeping machine did not perform in the manner that Burroughs's salesman promises Sierra Diesel that it would. Burroughs did not deny the salesman's promises, nor did it deny that its machine could not perform as promised. Rather, it pointed out that their agreement was complete and exclusive; therefore, it discharged any oral promises that the salesman made.

This argument may be formally true, but the court recognized the reality that a reasonable person in the buyer's position would expect a company to honor its sales-man's promises. Once again, we see that courts do not merely apply the law mechanically; rather, courts may look out for sharp dealing and refuse to read agreements in a manner contrary to ordinary expectations or logic. This is particularly true where one party asks a court to read an agreement literally, but evidence strongly shows that reasonable people would understand relevant terms differently.

The UCC is more subjectivist than R2d in that the UCC always makes admissible evidence of course of dealing, usage of trade, and course of performance to explain or supplement a written agreement. In doing this, the UCC exhibits some of the assumption (or lack of assumptions) on the part of its authors.

The UCC does not assume that the existence of a writing which appears final on some terms implies that all the terms are final. In other words, just because a final writing exists does not mean that writing is complete and exclusive.

The UCC does not assume that contractual language can be understood by looking at the law alone. Rather, judges must look at the commercial context and how terms are used in practice when interpreting contracts.

The UCC does not require a contract to be deemed ambiguous before evidence of the meaning of terms can be admitted. In other words, under the UCC, extrinsic evidence can always be introduced to show a latent ambiguity.

> *Terms with respect to which the confirmatory memoranda of the parties agree or which are otherwise set forth in a writing intended by the parties as a final expression of their agreement with respect to such terms as are included therein may not be contradicted by evidence of any prior agreement or of a contemporaneous oral agreement but may be explained or supplemented (a) by course of dealing or usage of trade (Section 1-205) or by course of performance (Section 2-208); and (b) by evidence of consistent additional terms unless the court finds the writing to have been intended also as a complete and exclusive statement of the terms of the agreement.* UCC § 2-202.

The UCC's approach to parol evidence is one of the main reasons why Williston objected to its adoption. Depending on whether you tend to be an objectivist or a subjectivist, you may find the UCC's approach to be very appealing or somewhat disconcerting. This tension is especially felt because the UCC is a statute, so, unlike common law, which can be changed over time by courts, and unlike the Restatement, which can be ignored by courts who disagree with its rationale, the UCC has the force of law and must be followed by courts in jurisdictions whose legislatures have adopted it.

B. Reflections on Parol Evidence

The Parol Evidence Rule highlights differences between the objectivist and subjectivist approach to law, especially with regard to contract interpretation. Objectivist jurists and scholars like Williston generally prefer not to admit extrinsic evidence, especially where there is a written contract that appears to be formal and final. Subjectivist jurists and scholars like Corbin would generally to prefer to hear any relevant evidence even if that evidence is offered to change the clear meaning of written terms in a contract.

The Restatement and the UCC tend to follow Corbin's subjectivist approach, but not all courts are so willing to allow extrinsic evidence of unspoken intentions to change the plain meaning of written terms.

The Restatement takes the position that a contract cannot prove itself:

> *No matter how plain a meaning may be to a layman, it may turn out to have a different and perhaps even contradictory meaning when a special usage is proven. Common experience supports this analysis: two-by-four boards are considerably smaller than two inches by four inches in dimension; psychiatrists' hours are forty-five minutes long. To hold that a contract specifying two-by-fours or a psychiatrist's hours was so unambiguous as to prevent proof of an industry-wide standard would be foolish, and none of the courts would be likely to do so despite their dicta. It is right that courts be skeptical of attempts to vary express terms through alleged usage, but the ambiguity as prerequisite approach is an oversimplified way of handling the problem.* R2d § 220, cmt. d.

Would you categorize this approach as "objective" or "subjective"? Do you think the Restatement takes the best approach to this aspect of contract interpretation?

Having reviewed these competing philosophies, rules, and cases, do you find yourself more persuaded by objective or subjective theories of contract interpretation? Spend a few minutes thinking about why you have come to your conclusions and write down your reasons for why one approach is better than the other. This will help you construct your own jurisprudential philosophy and, moreover, you will become a better advocate by learning how to articulate a rational basis for why a court should prefer an approach that favors your client.

Cases

Reading Gianni v. R. Russel & Co. Gianni demonstrates the objective approach to contract interpretation. Under the strict form of the objective approach, the express terms in the written agreement (i.e., intrinsic evidence) take absolute priority over extrinsic evidence. When the written agreement appears to be "a contract complete within itself," the presumption is even stronger: the court will not admit extrinsic evidence that is within the "scope" of the written agreement.

Gianni v. R. Russel & Co.

281 Pa. 320 (1924)

SCHAFFER, J.

The Plaintiff had been a tenant of a room in an office building in Pittsburgh wherein he conducted a store, selling tobacco, fruit, candy and soft drinks. Defendant acquired the entire property in which the storeroom was located, and its agent negotiated with plaintiff for a further leasing of the room A lease for three years was signed. It contained a provision that the lessee should "use the premises only for the sale of fruit, candy, soda water," etc., with the further stipulation that "it is expressly understood that the tenant is not allowed to sell tobacco in any form, under penalty of instant forfeiture of this lease." The document was prepared following a discussion about renting the room between the parties and after an agreement to lease had been reached. It was signed after it had been left in plaintiff's hands and admittedly had been read over to him by two persons, one of whom was his daughter.

Plaintiff sets up that in the course of his dealings with defendant's agent it was agreed that, in consideration of his promises not to sell tobacco and to pay an increased rent, and for entering into the agreement as a whole, he should have the exclusive right to sell soft drinks in the building. No such stipulation is contained in the written lease. Shortly after it was signed defendant demised the adjoining room in the building to a drug company without restricting the latter's right to sell soda water and soft drinks. Alleging that this was in violation of the contract which defendant had made with him, and that the sale of these beverages by the drug company had greatly reduced his receipts and profits, plaintiff brought this action for damages for breach of the alleged oral contract, and was permitted to recover. Defendant has appealed.

Plaintiff's evidence was to the effect that the oral agreement had been made at least two days, possibly longer, before the signing of the instrument, and that it was repeated at the time he signed; that, relying upon it, he executed the lease. Plaintiff called one witness who said he heard defendant's agent say to plaintiff at a time admittedly several days before the execution of the lease that he would have the exclusive right to sell soda water and soft drinks, to which the latter replied if that was the case he accepted the tenancy. Plaintiff produced no witness who was present when the contract was executed to corroborate his statement as to what then occurred. Defendant's agent denied that any such agreement was made, either preliminary to or at the time of the execution of the lease.

Appellee's counsel argues this is not a case in which an endeavor is being made to reform a written instrument because of something omitted as a result of fraud, accident, or mistake, but is one involving the breach of an independent oral agreement which does not belong in the writing at all and is not germane to its provisions. We are unable to reach this conclusion.

Where parties, without any fraud or mistake, have deliberately put their engagements in writing, the law declares the writing to be not only the best, but the only evidence of their agreement.

"All preliminary negotiations, conversations and verbal agreements are merged in and superseded by the subsequent written contract . . . and unless fraud, accident, or mistake be averred, the writing constitutes the agreement between the parties, and its terms cannot be added to nor subtracted from by parol evidence."

The writing must be the entire contract between the parties if parol evidence is to be excluded, and to determine whether it is or not the writing will be looked at, and if it appears to be a contract complete within itself, "couched in such terms as import a complete legal obligation without any uncertainty as to the object or extent of the engagement, it is conclusively presumed that the whole engagement of the parties, and the extent and manner of their undertaking, were reduced to writing."

When does the oral agreement come within the field embraced by the written one? This can be answered by comparing the two, and determining whether parties, situated as were the ones to the contract, would naturally and normally include the one in the other if it were made. If they relate to the same subject-matter, and are so interrelated that both would be executed at the same time and in the same contract, the scope of the subsidiary agreement must be taken to be covered by the writing. This question must be determined by the court.

In the case at bar the written contract stipulated for the very sort of thing which plaintiff claims has no place in it. It covers the use to which the storeroom was to be put by plaintiff and what he was and what he was not to sell therein. He was "to use the premises only for the sale of fruit, candy, soda water," etc., and was not "allowed to sell tobacco in any form." Plaintiff claims his agreement not to sell tobacco was part of the consideration for the exclusive right to sell soft drinks. Since his promise to refrain was included in the writing, it would be the natural thing to have included the promise of exclusive rights. Nothing can be imagined more pertinent to these provisions which were included than the one appellee avers.

In cases of this kind, where the cause of action rests entirely on an alleged oral understanding concerning a subject which is dealt with in a written contract it is presumed that the writing was intended to set forth the entire agreement as to that particular subject. "In deciding upon this intent [as to whether a certain subject was intended to be embodied by the writing], the chief and most satisfactory index . . . is found in the circumstance whether or not the particular element of the alleged extrinsic negotiation is dealt with at all in the writing. If it is mentioned, covered, or dealt with in the writing, then presumably the writing was meant to represent all of the transaction on that element, if it is not, then probably the writing was not intended to embody that element of the negotiation."

As the written lease is the complete contract of the parties, and since it embraces the field of the alleged oral contract, evidence of the latter is inadmissible under the parol evidence rule. "The [parol evidence] rule also denies validity to a subsidiary agreement within [the] scope [of the written contract] if sued on as a separate contract, although except for [that rule], the agreement fulfills all the requisites of valid contract."

There are, of course, certain exceptions to the parol evidence rule, but this case does not fall within any of them. Plaintiff expressly rejects any idea of fraud, accident, or mistake, and they are the foundation upon which any basis for admitting parol evidence to set up an entirely separate agreement within the scope of a written contract must be built. The evidence must be such as would cause a chancellor to reform the instrument, and that would be done only for these reasons and this holds true where this essentially equitable relief is being given, in our Pennsylvania fashion, through common law forms.

We have stated on several occasions recently that we propose to stand for the integrity of written contracts. We reiterate our position in this regard.

The judgment of the court below is reversed, and is here entered for defendant.

Reflection

Gianni makes the Parol Evidence Rule seem quite black and white. But you have probably already realized, the law is usually some shade of gray. After all, it is hard to craft a clear, strict rule that produces the correct result in all circumstances. Broad, vague standards give judges the discretion to provide a fair result in the instant case. But broad, vague standards create problems, too, especially in commercial law fields where people are planning business decisions. It is hard to know in advance how a random judge will rule under a broad standard. This uncertainty creates risk. Risk creates cost. Cost kills deals, since no good businessperson would engage in a deal that has a negative expected value. When dealing with a commercial law subject such as contract law, therefore, courts must maintain the delicate balance between certainty in advance (so people can plan accordingly) and fairness after the fact (so the law does not become a tool to perpetuate injustice).

You will next read how the Restatement and the UCC complicate the rule. Before moving on, pause and think about whether you understood the *Gianni* opinion. Was the rule stated clearly? Would you be able to counsel a client based on the parol evidence rule presented in *Gianni*? Record these thoughts in your mental ledger on the side that weighs for objective standard, bright-line tests, and clear rules.

Then speculate on the reason the bright-line rule in *Gianni* could result in unfair decisions. What kind of circumstances might make the rule in *Gianni* unfair? Does the bright-line objective approach articulated in *Gianni* conflict with deeper principles of contract law? One way to explore these questions is to imagine how *Gianni* itself might have come to a different conclusion if the facts were different. Why did the court mention that the written agreement in *Gianni* was reviewed by two people? If the agreement was not reviewed by anyone, would that change your opinion on whether Gianni should be bound by it? If the agreement did not prohibit Gianni from selling tobacco, would that make his argument that he was entitled to exclusive rights to sell candy stronger or weaker?

After you read the next set of rules and cases, you will see that the parol evidence rule is trying to balance objectivity and certainty on the one hand and subjective intent and fairness on the other. Which approach — objective or subjective — is the right one?

Discussion

1. What kind of intrinsic evidence would make a written agreement appear to be "a contract complete within itself"?

2. Can extrinsic evidence be used to show that a written agreement is complete within itself?

3. Can extrinsic evidence be used to show that a written agreement is not complete within itself, where the written agreement itself taken alone appears to be complete?

4. How does a court determine the "scope" of a written agreement in general? How does the *Gianni* court specifically determine that Gianni's purported consideration (the exclusive right to sell candy) is within the scope of this agreement allowing him to sell candy and forbidding him from selling tobacco?

5. What is the purpose of, or reasoning for, refusing to consider extrinsic evidence about preliminary negotiations where the intrinsic evidence appears to be the complete and exclusive statement of the parties' agreement?

Reading UAW. The next case involves a lawsuit about whether a hotel promised to staff an event only with union employees. The hotel's client, United Auto Workers-General Motors (UAW), is a labor union, so it may make sense why it wanted to vote with its dollars by hiring union staff for its event. But the legal question is whether UAW is entitled to present evidence that the parties agreed to staff the event with union workers, even though the written agreement does not mention this provision.

You should read this case for three reasons. First, this case introduces you to a new and critical concept under the parol evidence rule: a "merger clause." Also known as an integration clause, the merger clause is a written term in the agreement that effectively says (to put this in the *Gianni* court's terms) that the written agreement is a contract complete within itself. After reading this case, you should be able to identify the merger clause in an agreement — and you might be able to begin analyzing whether a potential merger clause is effective at declaring that the written agreement is a complete and exclusive statement of the parties' agreement.

Second, the majority takes a similar approach as *Gianni* and refuses to admit extrinsic evidence of preliminary negotiations where the written agreement itself seemed to be complete within itself. The *UAW* court provides some additional reasoning and support for this "objective" approach to contract interpretation. Think about why *Gianni*, which did not have a merger clause, arrived at the same result (the exclusion of extrinsic evidence of preliminary negations) that *UAW* did.

Third, the dissent in *UAW* provides your first introduction to the reasons why the objective standard can lead to unfair results. The dissent provides reasoning in support of a subjective approach that would more readily admit extrinsic evidence. Take special note of the dissent's reasoning and see whether the next case, *Sierra Diesel*, applies the same logic for its selection of the subjective approach.

Although the following cases are edited, they may still appear lengthy. That is because your humble editor felt that Professors Williston and Corbin explain competing rationales for objective and subjective approaches to the parol evidence rule better than he could, so included are many full paragraph quotations to their law treatises.

UAW-GM Human Resource Center v. KSL Recreation Corp.

228 Mich. App. 498 (1998)

MARKMAN, J.

Defendants appeal as of right a trial court order granting summary disposition to plaintiff on its claims of breach of contract, conversion, and fraud. Defendants also appeal as of right the trial court's denial of their motion for summary disposition. We reverse and remand for determination of damages pursuant to the liquidated damages formula set forth in the contract.

Facts

In December 1993, plaintiff entered into a contract with Carol Management Corporation (CMC) for the use of its property, Doral Resort and Country Club, for a convention scheduled in October 1994. The "letter of agreement" included a merger clause that stated that such agreement constituted "a merger of all proposals, negotiations and representations with reference to the subject matter and provisions." The letter of agreement did not contain any provision requiring that Doral Resort employees be union-represented. However, plaintiff contends in its appellate brief that it signed the letter of agreement in reliance on an "independent, collateral promise to provide [plaintiff] with a union-represented hotel." Plaintiff provided the affidavits of Herschel Nix, plaintiff's agent, and Barbara Roush, CMC's agent, who negotiated the contract. In his affidavit, Nix states that during the contract negotiation he and Roush discussed plaintiff's requirement that the hotel employees be union-represented and that Roush agreed to this requirement. In her affidavit, Roush states that "prior to and at the time" the contract at issue was negotiated she "was well aware" of plaintiff's requirement that the hotel employees be union-represented and that "that there is no doubt that I agreed on behalf of the Doral Resort to provide a union hotel." The letter of agreement also included a liquidated damages clause in the event plaintiff canceled the reservation "for any reason other than the following: Acts of God, Government Regulation, Disaster, Civil Disorders or other emergencies making it illegal to hold the meeting/convention."

Later in December 1993, the hotel was sold to defendants, who subsequently replaced the resort's union employees with a nonunionized work force. In June 1994, when plaintiff learned that the hotel no longer had union employees, it canceled the contract and demanded a refund of its down payment. Defendants refused to refund the down payment, retaining it as a portion of the liquidated damages allegedly owed to them pursuant to the contract.

[Facts regarding the procedural history and standard of review for summary judgment are omitted.]

Merger Clause

Defendants claim that the trial court erred in granting plaintiff's motion for summary disposition and in denying defendant's motion for summary disposition. Regarding the breach of contract count, they specifically contend that parol evidence of a separate agreement providing that the hotel would have union employees at the time of the convention was inadmissible because the letter of agreement included an express merger clause.

We begin by reiterating the basic rules regarding contract interpretation. "The primary goal in the construction or interpretation of any contract is to honor the intent of the parties."

"We must look for the intent of the parties in the words used in the instrument. This court does not have the right to make a different contract for the parties or to look to extrinsic testimony to determine their intent when the words used by them are clear and unambiguous and have a definite meaning."

In *Port Huron Ed Ass'n v Port Huron Area School Dist*, 452 Mich. 309 (1996), the Court stated:

> *The initial question whether contract language is ambiguous is a question of law. If the contract language is clear and unambiguous, its meaning is a*

question of law. Where the contract language is unclear or susceptible to multiple meanings, interpretation becomes a question of fact.

A contract is ambiguous if "its words may reasonably be understood in different ways." Courts are not to create ambiguity where none exists. "Contractual language is construed according to its plain and ordinary meaning, and technical or constrained constructions are to be avoided." If the meaning of an agreement is ambiguous or unclear, the trier of fact is to determine the intent of the parties.

The parol evidence rule may be summarized as follows: "[p]arol evidence of contract negotiations, or of prior or contemporaneous agreements that contradict or vary the written contract, is not admissible to vary the terms of a contract which is clear and unambiguous." This rule recognizes that in "[b]ack of nearly every written instrument lies a parol agreement, merged therein."

"The practical justification for the rule lies in the stability that it gives to written contracts; for otherwise either party might avoid his obligation by testifying that a contemporaneous oral agreement released him from the duties that he had simultaneously assumed in writing." 4 Williston, Contracts, § 631. In other words, the parol evidence rule addresses the fact that "disappointed parties will have a great incentive to describe circumstances in ways that escape the explicit terms of their contracts." Fried, Contract as Promise (Cambridge: Harvard University Press, 1981) at 60.

However, parol evidence of prior or contemporaneous agreements or negotiations is admissible on the threshold question whether a written contract is an integrated instrument that is a complete expression of the parties' agreement. *In re Skotzke Estate*, 216 Mich. App. 247 (1996); *NAG Enterprises, Inc v All State Industries, Inc,* 407 Mich. 407 (1979). The *NAG* Court noted four exceptions to the parol evidence rule, stating that extrinsic evidence is admissible to show (1) that the writing was a sham, not intended to create legal relations, (2) that the contract has no efficacy or effect because of fraud, illegality, or mistake, (3) that the parties did not integrate their agreement or assent to it as the final embodiment of their understanding, or (4) that the agreement was only partially integrated because essential elements were not reduced to writing. Importantly, neither *NAG* nor *Skotzke* involved a contract with an explicit integration clause.

The first issue before us is whether parol evidence is admissible with regard to the threshold question of integration even when the written agreement includes an explicit merger or integration clause. In other words, the issue is whether *NAG* applies to allow parol evidence regarding this threshold issue when a contract includes an explicit merger clause. While this issue is one of first impression, its answer turns on well-established principles of contract law. Williston on Contracts and Corbin on Contracts offer specific guidance regarding this issue. 4 Williston, Contracts, § 633, p. 1014 states in pertinent part:

Since it is only the intention of the parties to adopt a writing as a memorial which makes that writing an integration of the contract, and makes the parol evidence rule applicable, any expression of their intention in the writing in regard to the matter will be given effect. If they provide in terms that the writing shall be a complete integration of their agreement . . . the expressed intention will be effectuated.

3 Corbin, Contracts, § 578, pp. 402-411 states in pertinent part:

If a written document, mutually assented to, declares in express terms that it contains the entire agreement of the parties . . . this declaration is conclusive as long as it has itself not been set aside by a court on grounds of fraud or mistake, or on some ground that is sufficient for setting aside other contracts. . . . It is just like a general release of all antecedent claims. . . . An agreement that we do now discharge and nullify all previous agreements and warranties is effective, so long as it is not itself avoided. . . . By limiting the contract to the provisions that are in writing, the parties are definitely expressing an intention to nullify antecedent understandings or agreements. They are making the document a complete integration. Therefore, even if there had in fact been an antecedent warranty or other provision, it is discharged by the written agreement.

Thus, both Corbin and Williston indicate that an explicit integration clause is conclusive and that parol evidence is not admissible to determine whether a contract is integrated when a written contract contains such a clause. In the context of an explicit integration clause, Corbin recognizes exceptions to the barring of parol evidence only for fraud (or other grounds sufficient to set aside a contract) and for the rare situation when the written document is obviously incomplete "on its face" and, therefore, parol evidence is necessary "for the filling of gaps." The conclusion that parol evidence is not admissible to show that a written agreement is not integrated when the agreement itself includes an integration clause is consistent with the general contract principles of honoring parties' agreements as expressed in their written contracts and not creating ambiguities where none exist. This conclusion accords respect to the rules that the parties themselves have set forth to resolve controversies arising under the contract. The parties are bound by the contract because they have chosen to be so bound.

Further, and most fundamentally, if parol evidence were admissible with regard to the threshold issue whether the written agreement was integrated despite the existence of an integration clause, there would be little distinction between contracts that include an integration clause and those that do not. When the parties choose to include an integration clause, they clearly indicate that the written agreement is integrated; accordingly, there is no longer any "threshold issue" whether the agreement is integrated and, correspondingly, no need to resort to parol evidence to resolve this issue. Thus *NAG*, which allows resort to parol evidence to resolve this "threshold issue," does not control when a contract includes a valid merger clause.

3 Corbin, Contracts, § 577, p. 401 states in pertinent part:

A finding that the parties had assented to a writing as the complete integration of their then existing agreement is necessarily a finding that there is no simultaneous oral addition. On such a finding of fact, we are no longer required to decide whether proof of simultaneous oral agreement is admissible, for we have just found that there was no such oral agreement.

The conclusion that parol evidence is not admissible regarding this "threshold issue" when there is an explicit integration clause honors the parties' decision to include such a clause in their written agreement. It gives effect to their decision to establish a written agreement as the exclusive basis for determining their intentions concerning the subject matter of the contract.

This rule is especially compelling in cases such as the present one, where defendants, successor corporations, assumed performance of another corporation's obligations under a letter of agreement. Because defendants were not parties to the negotiations resulting in the letter of agreement, they would obviously be unaware of any oral representations made by CMC's agent to plaintiff's agent in the course of those negotiations. Defendants assumed CMC's obligations under the letter of agreement, which included an explicit merger clause. Defendants could not reasonably have been expected to discuss with every party to every contract with CMC whether any parol agreements existed that would place further burdens upon defendants in the context of a contract with an explicit merger clause. Under these circumstances, it would be fundamentally unfair to hold defendants to oral representations allegedly made by CMC's agent. Of the participants involved in this controversy, defendants are clearly the least blameworthy and the least able to protect themselves. Unlike plaintiff, which could have addressed its concerns by including appropriate language in the contract, and unlike CMC, which allegedly agreed to carry out obligations not included within the contract, defendants did nothing more than rely upon the express language of the instant contract, to wit, that the letter of agreement represented the full understanding between plaintiff and CMC. We believe that defendants acted reasonably in their reliance and that the contract should be interpreted in accordance with its express provisions.

[Citations to and discussion of Michigan law omitted.]

For these reasons, we hold that when the parties include an integration clause in their written contract, it is conclusive and parol evidence is not admissible to show that the agreement is not integrated except in cases of fraud that invalidate the integration clause or where an agreement is obviously incomplete "on its face" and, therefore, parol evidence is necessary for the "filling of gaps." 3 Corbin, Contracts, § 578, p. 411.

Fraud

[Discussion on invalidity of the contract for fraud or misrepresentation omitted. Misrepresentation is discussed in Module IV.]

Liquidated Damages

[Discussion on enforceability of liquidated damages provision omitted. Liquidated damages (which are enforceable) and penalties (which are unenforceable) will be discussed in Module VII.]

Finally, we will briefly respond to the dissenting opinion. The dissenting opinion indicates that no contract existed between plaintiff and defendants. Initially, we note that the parties themselves, unlike the dissent, have not suggested that no contract existed between plaintiff and defendants. In fact, the parties clearly assume that the letter of agreement is binding on them; they only disagree regarding its meaning and the effect of the alleged oral representations regarding union representation of the staff. While this Court may, of course, address essential issues not raised by the parties, we are perplexed by the dissent's reliance upon an argument that is inconsistent with the parties' positions to dispose of this matter.

[Discussion on delegation of duties omitted. Assignment and delegation will be discussed in Module VI.]

Reversed and remanded for proceedings consistent with this opinion. We do not retain jurisdiction.

HOLBROOK, J., dissenting

I respectfully dissent.

The event that precipitated this legal dispute was Carol Management's sale of the resort to defendants, without informing plaintiff during contract negotiations that the resort was for sale or that a sale was pending, and defendants' subsequent firing of the resort's union staff, less than one month after the contract with plaintiff was negotiated and signed. The contract — drafted by Carol Management — included a standardized integration or merger clause, but was silent regarding plaintiff's acknowledged requirement that the resort employ a union-represented staff. Attempts to pigeonhole these unusual facts into established black-letter rules of contract law led to harsh and unintended results. Hard cases do, indeed, make bad law.

The contract's merger clause — "a merger of all proposals, negotiations and representations with reference to the subject matter and provisions" — appears plain and unambiguous. While it is often stated that courts may not create an ambiguity in a contract where none exists, and that parol evidence is generally not admissible to vary or contradict the terms of a written contract, Professor Corbin acknowledges that strict adherence to these rules can be problematic:

> *The fact that the [parol evidence] rule has been stated in such a definite and dogmatic form as a rule of admissibility is unfortunate. It has an air of authority and certainty that has grown with much repetition. Without doubt, it has deterred counsel from making an adequate analysis and research and from offering parol testimony that was admissible for many purposes. Without doubt, also it has caused a court to refuse to hear testimony that ought to have been heard. The mystery of the written word is still such that a paper document may close the door to a showing that it was never assented to as a complete integration.*
>
> *No injustice is done by exclusion of the testimony if the written integration is in fact what the court assumes or decides that it is.*

The trouble is that the court's assumption or decision as to the complete-ness and accuracy of the integration may be quite erroneous. The writing cannot prove its own completeness and accuracy. Even though it contains an express statement to that effect, the assent of the parties thereto must still be proved. Proof of its completeness and accuracy, discharging all anteced-ent agreements, must be made in large part by the oral testimony of parties and other witnesses. The very testimony that the "parol evidence rule" is sup-posed to exclude is frequently, if not always, necessary before the court can determine that the parties have agreed upon the writing as a complete and accurate statement of terms. The evidence that the rule seems to exclude must sometimes be heard and weighed before it can be excluded by the rule. This is one reason why the working of this rule has been so inconsistent and unsatis-factory. This is why so many exceptions and limitations to the supposed rule of evidence have been recognized by various courts.

There is ample judicial authority showing that, in determining the issue of completeness of the integration in writing, evidence extrinsic to the writing itself is admissible. The oral admissions of the plaintiff that the agreement included matters not contained in the writing may be proved to show that it was not assented to as a complete integration, however complete it may look on its face. On this issue, parol testimony is certainly admissible to show the circumstances under which the agreement was made and the purposes for which the instrument was executed.

And, in § 583 of his treatise, Professor Corbin continues:

No written document can prove its own execution or that it was ever assented to as a complete integration, supplanting and discharging what preceded it. . . . There are plenty of decisions that additional terms and provisions can be proved by parol evidence, thereby showing that the written document in court is not a complete integration. This is true, even though it is clear that the additional terms form a part of one contractual transaction along with the writing. [3 Corbin on Contracts, § 583, pp. 465–467.]

Accord Stimac v Wissman, 342 Mich. 20 (1955); Restatement Contracts, 2d, § 216, comment e, p. 140 (observing that a merger "clause does not control the question of whether the writing was assented to as an integrated agreement").

The fact that plaintiff's representative read and signed the contract does not obviate the applicability of the principles outlined in Corbin, §§ 582 and 583. Indeed, Professor Corbin illustrates the principles of the section by analyzing the case of *Int'l Milling Co v Hachmeister, Inc,* 380 Pa. 407 (1955), in which the parties entered into a contract for the sale and purchase of flour. During negotiations, buyer insisted that each shipment of flour meet certain established specifications and that such a provision be included in the contract. Seller refused to put the provision in the contract, but agreed to write a confirmation letter to buyer tying in the required specifications. Buyer placed a writ-ten order, indicating that the flour must meet the required specifications. Seller sent to buyer a printed contract form, which contained none of the specifications, but did contain an express integration clause. Seller also sent a separate letter assuring delivery in accordance with the required specifications. Buyer signed the written contract form. When a subsequent shipment of flour failed to meet the specifications, buyer rejected it and canceled all other orders. The Pennsylvania Supreme Court held that extrinsic evidence of the parties' negotiations and antecedent agreements was admissible with regard to the issue whether buyer had assented to the printed contract form as a complete and accurate integration of the contract, notwithstanding its express provision to the contrary. Corbin, *supra* at 458. Professor Corbin notes that the court's decision was fully supported by § 582, and explained at p. 459:

> *It appears that in the instant case the buyer's evidence was very strong, so strong that it would be a travesty on justice to keep it from the jury. This is not because the express provision of integration was concealed from the buyer; he was familiar with the printed contract form and knew that the provision was in it and the specifications were not. The court rightly refuses to deprive him of the opportunity to prove that its statement was untrue. . . . Bear in mind, however, that throughout the chapter the author has warned against the acceptance of flimsy and implausible assertions by parties to what has turned out to be a losing contract.*

Section 582 of Corbin, allowing admission of extrinsic evidence with regard to the threshold question whether in fact the parties mutually assented to the written document as a completely integrated contract, does not contradict, but rather dovetails with, § 578, on which the lead opinion relies. Indeed, in § 578, p. 402, Professor Corbin hinges a finding of conclusiveness of an express integration clause on whether the written document was "mutually assented to." Further, in language excerpted out of the lead opinion's quotation of § 578, Professor Corbin observes:

> *The fact that a written document contains one of these express provisions does not prove that the document itself was ever assented to or ever became operative as a contract. Neither does it exclude evidence that the document was not in fact assented to and therefore never became operative . . . [P]aper and ink possess no magic power to cause statements of fact to be true when they are actually untrue. Written admissions are evidential; but <u>they are not conclusive</u>. [Id. at 405, 407 (emphasis added).]*

Thus, examination of the written document alone is insufficient to determine its completeness; extrinsic evidence that is neither flimsy nor implausible is admissible to establish whether the writing was in fact intended by the parties as a completely integrated contract.

> *The cardinal rule in the interpretation of contracts is to ascertain the intention of the parties. To this rule all others are subordinate.*

It is undisputed in this case that plaintiff's decision to hold its convention at the resort was predicated on the understanding of the representatives for both defendants' predecessor and plaintiff that the resort employed a unionized staff. Had plaintiff been made aware that the resort was for sale or that a sale was pending, I believe it is reasonable to assume that plaintiff's representative would have insisted that such a clause be incorporated into the agreement. Courts should not require that contracting parties include provisions in their agreement contemplating every conceivable, but highly improbable, manner of breach. In my opinion, the circumstances surrounding execution of the contract, as well as the material change in circumstance that occurred when the resort was sold and the union staff fired, establishes as a matter of law that plaintiff did not assent to a completely integrated agreement. Corbin's warning against the admission of "flimsy and implausible" evidence is not implicated here.

Accordingly, I would affirm the trial court's order granting summary disposition in favor of plaintiff pursuant to MCR 2.116(C)(10).

Reflection

The *UAW* case had particular facts that may have led the court to it result. The fact the parties to this lawsuit were not the original parties to the contract may have encouraged the use of Williston's objectivist approach. UAW-GW had originally contracted with CMC. KSL only learned about this contractual obligation after purchasing CMC's hotel properties. The court may have held KSL to a lower standard than CMC with regard to extrinsic evidence, since KSL had no way to know what CMC and UAW discussed in preliminary negotiations.

Discussion

1. Note that the *UAW* majority cites mainly to Professor Williston, while the *UAW* dissent cites Professor Corbin. What is the difference between these two perspectives?

2. Do you agree with the majority (who gave effect to the plain meaning merger clause) or to the dissent (who would have disregarded the merger clause based on extrinsic evidence)?

3. Does the majority or the dissent more closely follow the R2d?

4. Based on your reading of this case and the R2d rules, can you articulate a general rule on when merger clauses should be enforced and when they should be disregarded?

Reading **Sierra Diesel Injection Service, Inc. v. Burroughs Corp.** *Sierra Diesel* juxtaposes *UAW*: whereas the *UAW* court took a strict constructionist approach to the merger clause in its agreement, *Sierra Diesel* disregards a similarly clear and plain integration clause. Why would two courts arrive at such different conclusions when reviewing similar intrinsic evidence?

As you read *Sierra Diesel*, think about whether the court uses the objective approach (the "plain meaning" and "four corners" rules) or a subjective approach ("meeting of the minds") to determine whether the sales contract in this case was integrated. Consider which approach is the right one for this case and in general.

Sierra Diesel Injection Service, Inc. v. Burroughs Corp.

874 F.2d 653 (9th Cir. 1989)

STEPHENS, J.

Sierra Diesel Injection Service, Inc. (Sierra Diesel) is a family owned and operated business that services the fuel injection portions of diesel engines and sells related diesel engine parts. In September 1977, 19-year-old Caroline Cathey, the daughter-in-law of the Sierra Diesel's owner and operator James Cathey, worked as the company bookkeeper. She went to the Reno, Nevada branch office of the Burroughs Corporation (Burroughs) to purchase a posting machine to speed up Sierra Diesel's invoicing and accounting. The salespeople at Burroughs told Caroline Cathey that Sierra Diesel should buy a B-80 computer (B-80) instead of a posting machine. Caroline and James Cathey attended a demonstration of the B-80 at the Burroughs office. After the demonstration, Burroughs' sales staff sent a letter to Mr. Cathey which said that the B-80 "can put your inventory, receivables, and invoicing under complete control." The letter also informed Mr. Cathey that the information in the letter was "preliminary" and that "the order when issued shall constitute the only legally binding commitment of the parties."

In October 1977, Mr. Cathey decided to purchase the B-80. Sierra Diesel and Burroughs signed various contracts for the sale of hardware and software and for maintenance service. Mr. Cathey's highest level of formal education was a high school degree. At the time he bought the B-80 he was not knowledgeable about computers. He had a general knowledge of warranties and their limitations from the warranty service work Sierra Diesel did for diesel component parts manufacturers, but he did not understand the meaning of "merchantability." He read the contracts from Burroughs to see that they contained the correct price information and product description and he glanced at the back of the contract to see, as he put it, that "I'm not actually signing away the deed to my home or something of this nature."

The B-80 computer did not perform the invoicing and accounting functions for which it had been purchased. It experienced basic equipment breakdowns and was unable to "multi-program." Sierra Diesel personnel complained to the Burroughs service personnel. Burroughs responded to these complaints and its staff attempted to solve the problems and also attempted to repair the system during their regularly scheduled visits under the Maintenance Agreement. Eventually, the Burroughs staff recommended to Sierra Diesel that it purchase a different Burroughs computer (B-91) to remedy the problems. Sierra Diesel purchased the B-91 and took delivery in February 1981. The B-91 computer was no better able to perform the invoicing and accounting functions than the B-80. After additional unsuccessful attempts by Burroughs employees to correct the problems, Sierra Diesel employed an independent computer consultant who concluded that the Burroughs computers would never perform the functions for which they had been purchased. Sierra Diesel bought another computer from a different company. In 1984, Sierra Diesel initiated the present litigation.

[Procedural history omitted. The key point is the trial court determined that the contract was not completely integrated, despite its integration clause.]

After the trial court's ruling, Sierra Diesel and Burroughs entered into a settlement in which the court dismissed with prejudice all of Sierra Diesel's claims as to the B-91 and to most of the claims as to the B-80. The parties stipulated that Burroughs had breached its contracts with Sierra Diesel by failing to put Sierra Diesel's inventory, receivables, and invoicing under complete control and that the B-80 was not merchantable. The trial court awarded Sierra Diesel $44,000 in damages. The judgment reserved to Burroughs a right to appeal the court's integration and conspicuousness rulings. Burroughs timely appealed.

[Jurisdictional discussion omitted.]

I. Integration

The trial court found that the printed form contracts supplied by Burroughs did not represent a final integrated contract. The court considered the September 27 letter and found that the representations in the letter were part of the agreement between the parties.

Nevada has adopted the Uniform Commercial Code's parol evidence rule in NRS § 104.2202. Under the code, a trial court must make an initial determination that a writing was "intended by the parties as a final expression of their agreement." This is a question of fact and the trial court's findings are reviewed for substantial error.

In deciding whether a writing is final the most important issue is the intent of the parties. One factor is the sophistication of the parties. The trial court found that Mr. Cathey was not a sophisticated businessman, that he had little knowledge of computers or of contract terms, and that he fully expected that the representations made to him by Burroughs' representatives were part of the contract. The trial court also found that Burroughs knew of Mr. Cathey's computer needs and knew that his sole purpose for buying the computer was to get Sierra Diesel's inventory, receiving, and invoicing under control and that Mr. Cathey would not have purchased the B-80 if it were not capable of putting his inventory, receiving, and invoicing under control. The trial court's findings are supported by the record.

Burroughs argues that the presence of a merger clause should, as a matter of law, determine that the contract was integrated, and some courts have so held. However other courts and commentators have rejected this view, especially when the contract is a pre-printed form drawn by a sophisticated seller and presented to the buyer without any real negotiation. Whether several documents are integrated to form one contract is a factual question and the presence of a merger clause while often taken as a strong sign of the parties' intent is not conclusive in all cases.

The agreement between Burroughs and Sierra Diesel involved at least four different kinds of writings: the contract for the sale of the hardware, the contracts for the sale of the software, the contract to finance the transaction through what was on its face a lease, and the contract for service and maintenance. No one writing stands alone, each must be read with reference to another document. The description of the computer components does not lead to recognition of how they relate to one another without additional explanation. The hardware could not function without the software. The lease appears on its face to be inconsistent with a sale. It is not possible to understand what the basic transaction was intended to be without some coordinating explanation. It is understandable that Mr. Cathey believed that he was justified in looking beyond the four corners of anyone writing for the meaning of his agreement with Burroughs.

Additionally, the trial court found that Burroughs' efforts to repair the B-80 showed that Burroughs intended to live up to the representations made in the September 27 letter. Burroughs did not advise Sierra Diesel that the repairs were undertaken without prejudice to Burroughs' contention that there were no warranties. Burroughs' efforts are also evidence of Burroughs' knowledge of Mr. Cathey's expectations as to the scope and terms of their agreement.

[Discussion on implied warranties omitted. Implied warranties of merchantability and fitness for a particular purpose are discussed in courses focusing on the law of Sales.]

[Discussion on effect of lend-lease agreement omitted.]

Conclusion

The trial court's judgment is AFFIRMED.

Reflection

Sierra Diesel reflects Corbin's subjectivist philosophy. In this case, a clear and unequivocal formal agreement is nevertheless interpreted based on testimony of what the parties thought but did not express in writing. This is anathema to the objectivist philosophy preferred by Williston. And it reflects a general trend in the law at this time away from objectivism and toward subjectivism.

The successors of Corbin furthered the R2d's push toward subjective standards over objective formalistic rules. One of those successors was John E. Murray Jr., chancellor and a professor of law at Duquesne University, who authored the treatise Murray on Contracts. His treatise summarizes what is common about the approaches you have seen so far and functions as a brief but complete statement of the essential features of the Parol Evidence Rule:

(1) [I]f the parties intend their written expression of agreement to be merely final, the terms of that final agreement may not be contradicted by any prior or contemporaneous oral agreement. (2) Such terms in a final writing may, however, be explained or supplemented by evidence of consistent additional terms or by evidence of course of dealing, usage of trade or course of performance. (3) If the parties intended their writing to be not merely final but also a complete and exclusive statement of the terms of their agreement, evidence of consistent additional terms is excluded, but even with respect to such a complete and exclusive expression of agreement, evidence of trade usage, course of dealing, and course of performance is admissible. There is, therefore, no presumption that the writing is the complete and exclusive expression of the parties' agreement. Rather, the opposite is assumed, i.e., the writing will not be viewed as complete and exclusive unless the court finds that the parties intended it to be complete and exclusive.

As mentioned above, it is ironic that Murray was following in Corbin's subjectivist footsteps in his role in Pittsburgh while the Pennsylvania courts continued to advance the objectivist approach. The cleft between the bench and the bar show that Murray's and Corbin's efforts to reform the law have not always been well met. It is not clear whether the Restatements will continue to have so much influence over judicial decision-making if they continue to be activist in trying to change the law instead of reacting to what the law currently is.

Instead of dwelling on the *Sierra Diesel* case at this point, let's move on to critically evaluate how the R2d instructs judges to interpret contracts. As you review the Restatement's approach, consider how it accords with the reasoning articulated in *Sierra Diesel*.

Discussion

1. Compare and contrast the *UAW* and *Sierra Diesel* cases. Are they based on the same rule and reasoning, or have the courts applied different rules?

2. If the rules in *UAW* and *Sierra Diesel* are different, which rule is better and why? If the rules are the same, what are the dispositive facts that produce a different outcome in each case?

Problems

Problem 15.1. **Comparing the Common Law and the UCC**

The parol evidence rule that has been enacted in each state as Section 2-202 of the Uniform Commercial Code is nearly identical to the parol evidence rule as it previously developed in the courts as part of the common law and as it is described in R2d. There is, however, one subtle difference in the wording of the common law rule and the statutory rule.

The provisions are reproduced side by side below. In your opinion, is the difference substantive or merely semantic? In other words, is it real difference or merely a distinction without a difference?

Describe how UCC § 2-202 and R2d § 216 are different and whether those differences matter.

R2d. § 216. Consistent Additional Terms.	UCC § 2-202. Final Written Expression: Parol or Extrinsic Evidence.
(1) Evidence of a consistent additional term is admissible to supplement an integrated agreement unless the court finds that the agreement was completely integrated. (2) An agreement is not completely integrated if the writing omits a consistent additional agreed term which is (a) agreed to for separate consideration, or (b) such a term as in the circumstances might naturally be omitted from the writing.	Terms with respect to which the confirmatory memoranda of the parties agree or which are otherwise set forth in a writing intended by the parties as a final expression of their agreement with respect to such terms as are included therein may not be contradicted by evidence of any prior agreement or of a contemporaneous oral agreement but may be explained or supplemented (a) by course of dealing or usage of trade (Section 1-205) or by course of performance (Section 2-208); and (b) by evidence of consistent additional terms unless the court finds the writing to have been intended also as a complete and exclusive statement of the terms of the agreement.

Figure 15.1. R2d and UCC were drafted based on similar philosophies, but the specific language differs in material ways.

Problem 15.2. Capitol City Liquor Company

Harold S., Lester, and Eric Lee (the "Lees" or "Plaintiffs") owned 50% of Capitol City Liquor Company Inc., ("Capitol City"). Seagram (or "Defendant") is a distiller of alcoholic beverages. Capitol City is a wholesale liquor distributor located in Washington, D.C. Capitol City carries a wide variety of Seagram products, and a large portion of its sales were generated by Seagram lines, for many years.

In May 1970, then-EVP, now President, of Seagram, Jack Yogman and Harold S. Lee discussed the sale of Capitol City to Seagram, conditioned on Seagram's offer to relocate the Lees to a new distributorship of their own (100% ownership) in a different city. Yogman agreed, and the Lees trusted him based on their years of personal friendship and confidence.

About a month later, Seagram sent an officer to D.C., where the Lees negotiated and agreed to sell Capitol City. The Seagram officers prepared the paperwork (the "Merger

Agreement"), which Harold signed on behalf of the Lees. The other 50% owners of Capitol City signed for themselves as well. The promise to relocate the Lees was never reduced to writing. The Merger Agreement does not have an integration clause.

Based on these facts, answer the following questions:

a. Is the Merger Agreement final? What evidence of finality is in these facts? For each piece of evidence, classify it as intrinsic or extrinsic.

b. What is the effect of the Merger Agreement lacking an integration clause?

c. Is the promise to relocate the Lees within the scope of the Merger Agreement?

d. What do you think the parties to the oral agreement — Harold S. Lee and Jack Yogman — actually agreed?

e. If the Lees attempt to introduce evidence that Jack and Harold met and what they discussed, should a court take an objective or a subjective approach? Under that approach, how should a court rule?

f. What do you think is a fair remedy (if any) for the Lees?

See Lee v. Joseph E. Seagram & Sons, Inc., 552 F.2d 447 (2d Cir. 1977).

Problem 15.3. **Middletown Concrete Products**

Middletown Concrete Products, Inc. ("MCP") manufactures precast concrete products. Hydrotile is a corporate division of Black Clawson Co. Hydrotile makes pipe-making systems.

In 1988, David Mack, Hydrotile's regional sales manager, visited MCP and gave one of its managers a promotional brochure for one of its products, the Neptune Multipak Pipe Machine (the "Neptune"). The Neptune only works in conjunction with the other half of its pipe-making system, the Rekers Off-Bearing Unit ("Rekers").

The Neptune brochure contained a list of figures which included that the Neptune could produce round pipe at a rate of 54 pipes per hour.

After considering purchasing concrete pipe-making equipment from multiple suppliers, MCP focused on negotiations with Hydrotile. Representatives from both companies met and discussed terms including production rates. Although negotiations got heated, with MCP managers screaming, shouting, and demanding a warranty on production rates, Hydrotile never agreed orally or in writing to any particular production rate.

After about a week of negotiations, Hydrotile presented to MCP an "Acceptable Performance Letter," which contained a guaranteed round pipe production rate for the Neptune of 44 pipes per hour. The parties disagree on whether MCP orally made its payment to Hydrotile contingent on the system achieving Acceptable Performance.

After inspecting several locations where the Neptune was installed and operating, MCP agreed to purchase the machine. MCP signed two different contracts: a Neptune Sales Agreement and a Rekers Sales Agreement. Both agreements contained the following clauses:

> *There are no rights, warranties or conditions, express or implied, statutory or otherwise, other than those herein contained.*
>
> *This agreement between Buyer and Seller can be modified or rescinded only by a writing signed by both parties.*
>
> *No waiver of any provision of this agreement shall be binding unless in writing signed by an authorized representative of the party against whom the waiver is asserted and unless expressly made generally applicable shall only apply to the specific case for which the waiver is given.*

MCP's Neptune was delivered piecemeal and installed on location starting in October 1989 and began production on March 21, 1990. MCP's Neptune produces round pipe at the rate of 34 pipes per hour. MCP sued Hydrotile, claiming that Hydrotile breached its promises that the Neptune would produce 54 pipes per hour.

Based on the above facts, what evidence should the court allow MCP to admit in support of this claim?

See Middletown Concrete Products, Inc. v. Black Clawson Co., 802 F. Supp. 1135 (D. Del. 1992).

To see how concrete pipe is manufactured, visit https://youtu.be/E6jlTxhL8bg.

Problem 15.4. **Corn Delivery**

Charles Campbell is a farmer in Adams County, Pennsylvania, who entered into a written contract with Hostetter Farms, Inc., to sell 20,000 bushels of corn for $1.70 per bushel. The written agreement is signed and dated, but it lacks a merger clause.

During preliminary negotiations, the parties calculated the quantity of corn to be sold based on probable yield of Campbell's farm. Campbell claims that the parties agreed to buy and sell only what Campbell could produce. Hostetter claims that Campbell agreed to sell the specified quantity at the specified price from whatever source. However, this term was not included in their final written agreement.

The prior year, the parties the previously done business for the purchase and sale of 3,000 bushels of No. 2 wheat at $2.15 a bushel. Pursuant to an oral agreement, Campbell delivered 1,534.88 bushels of wheat, but Campbell did not deliver the remaining 1,465.12 bushels. After a little grumbling about the wheat not delivered, Hostetter paid for the wheat delivered, and the matter was concluded.

The weather was especially wet this year, and Campbell's farm did not yield as much corn as he expected. Campbell delivered 10,417.77 bushels of corn to Hostetter, who refused to pay anything given the shortage. Hostetter then purchased 20,000 bushels of corn on the open market for $2.65 a bushel.

Hostetter sued Campbell for the extra he paid to purchase the corn on the open market instead of from Campbell. In his defense, Campbell seeks to introduce evidence that (a) he only produced 12,417.77 bushels of corn, (b) he retained 2,000 bushels of corn to feed his livestock, (c) the parties discussed that Campbell was only responsible for delivering the quantity he produced, and (d) it is very common for farmers in Adams County to retain about 10% of their crop yields to feed their livestock.

Hostetter seeks to introduce evidence that the parties discussed that Campbell was responsible for obtaining the corn from another source if his farming did not yield a sufficient quantity.

a. Characterize each piece evidence that Campbell and Hostetter seek to admit as intrinsic or extrinsic and discuss what that evidence would be admitted to show or prove.

b. Does the parol evidence rule apply to any of the evidence in this case? Should any evidence be excluded from the jury pursuant to the parol evidence rule?

c. How should the court rule? Was Campbell responsible for delivering 20,000 bushels (the full amount under the contract), 12,417.77 bushels (the amount he actually produced), 10,417.77 bushels (the amount he actually delivered), or some other amount?

See Campbell v. Hostetter Farms, Inc., 251 Pa. Super. 232 (1977).

Problem 15.5. **Injury and Indemnity**

DEFINITIONS: "Drayage" means shipping goods over a short distance, as compared with long-distance shipping. "Rigging" means attaching loads to cranes or structures. G.W.'s name implies it is in the trade of moving and transporting heavy equipment. Please look up any other industrial or technical terms that are not familiar to you.

Pacific Gas & Electric Company ("PG&E"), a producer of electrical power, hired G.W. Thomas Drayage & Rigging Company ("G.W.") to remove and replace the metal cover of a steam turbine. Their written agreement, which was governed by California law, contained the following indemnity clause:

> *Contractor shall indemnify Company, its officers, agents, and employees, against all loss, damage, expense and liability resulting from injury to or death of person or injury to property, arising out of or in any way connected with the performance of this contract. Contractor shall, on Company's request, defend any suit asserting a claim covered by this indemnity. Contractor shall pay any costs that may be incurred by Company in enforcing this indemnity.*

During the work, the cover fell and damaged PG&E's turbine. PG&E sued G.W. to recover the cost to repair the turbine.

PG&E presented evidence that the term "indemnity" has a plain meaning in the law of contracts. It is defined in California Civil Code § 2772 as follows: "Indemnity is a contract by which one engages to save another from a legal consequence of the conduct of one of the parties, or of some other person."

G.W. responded by offering to admit evidence of (a) admissions of plaintiff's agents that they actually knew G.W. did not intend to indemnify PG&E, (b) evidence of defendant's conduct under similar contracts entered into with plaintiff, and (c) evidence that the trade usage of such indemnity clauses is meant to cover injury to property of third parties only and not to plaintiff's own property.

a. Characterize each piece evidence that PG&E and G.W. seek to admit as intrinsic or extrinsic and discuss what that evidence would be admitted to show or prove (i.e., would that evidence add, modify, or explain a term? Is the evidence collateral or directly related to the writing? Etc.).

b. Does the parol evidence rule apply to any of the evidence in this case? Should any evidence be excluded from the jury pursuant to the parol evidence rule?

c. How should the court rule? Should G.W. be required to indemnify PG&W and pay for the damage to its turbine?

See Pac. Gas & Elec. Co. v. G.W. Thomas Drayage & Rigging Co., 69 Cal. 2d 33 (1968).

Chapter 16

Evaluating Extrinsic Evidence

Extrinsic evidence generally refers to all the sources of contractual meaning that come from outside the verbiage of the agreement itself. When intrinsic and extrinsic evidence agree, analysis is relatively straightforward. But when there is a conflict, what rights do parties have to try and prove that the contract does not mean what it says? Here are the rules pertaining to that issue.

Rules

A. Course of Performance

Course of performance references the sequence of action parties took regarding the specific contract at issue. For example, Celeste contracts with Blue Apron Co., whereby Blue Apron ships Celeste ingredients for three meals each week for a year, in exchange for a $520 up-front payment. Under this contract, Blue Apron will perform repeatedly (fifty-two times). As Blue Apron performs, its performance time tends to evidence what Blue Apron intended this contract to mean. Meanwhile, Celeste's conduct reflects her intentions and her expectations of Blue Apron.

To understand how course of performance impacts the meaning of contracts, further imagine that Blue Apron included written recipes with instructions on how to use the ingredients in each of the first four boxes it sent to Celeste. If the fifth box contains no recipes, and Celeste complains that Blue Apron breached its promise to her regarding that fifth shipment, if Blue Apron disagrees and argues it has no obligation to send recipes, and Celeste sues, how should a court resolve this debate?

First, courts will review any written agreement between the parties. If their written contracts says that recipes shall be provided, then Celeste easily wins the case. But what if the contract is silent about recipes? If the contract is silent, courts may consider whether the parties' course of performance speaks to their contractual intention regarding the dispute. If Blue Apron provided recipes in the first four boxes, and if Celeste complained when no recipe was in the fifth box, those facts tend to show that the parties intended the shipment of ingredients to include recipes.

What if the contract said that Blue Apron is not required to include recipes with ingredients, but Blue Apron included recipes in the first four shipments anyway? This scenario is different from the immediately preceding one because now the extrinsic evidence of course of performance conflicts with the clear intrinsic evidence of the written contract itself.

Courts may or may not ignore extrinsic evidence that conflicts with unambiguous intrinsic evidence. As a technical matter, courts are supposed to exclude parol (prior oral) evidence when a completely integrated agreement is unambiguous. This rule has exceptions, of course: in the *Sierra Diesel* case from the last chapter, where a court set aside an integration clause; and in the *Nānākuli* case in Chapter 13, the appellate court found that course of performance evidence outweighed the plain meaning of a written price term.

Whether and to what extent courts consider course of performance evidence depends on various factors. The UCC summarizes its approach to consideration of course of performance evidence first by defining what is course of performance:

> A *"course of performance"* is a sequence of conduct between the parties to a particular transaction that exists if the agreement of the parties with respect to the transaction involves repeated occasions for performance by a party. . . . UCC § 1-303(a)(1).

But course of performance is not evidentiary just because one party did something repeatedly. If extrinsic evidence is to show the intention of both parties, course of performance by one party must also be understood and at least tacitly accepted by the other.

> . . . and the other party, with knowledge of the nature of the performance and opportunity for objection to it, accepts the performance or acquiesces in it without objection. UCC § 1-303(a)(2).

In sum, the hallmark of course of performance evidence is repeated behavior by one party and acquiescence by the other. This signifies that the parties tend to agree that such behavior is acceptable within the parameters of their agreement.

B. Course of Dealing

Course of dealing refers to the series of actions parties take pursuant to their various relationships and commercial dealings over time. Both R2d and UCC use virtually the same language to define course of dealing:

> A *course of dealing is a sequence of previous conduct between the parties to an agreement which is fairly to be regarded as establishing a common basis of understanding for interpreting their expressions and other conduct.* R2d § 223(1); UCC § 1-303(b).

Under both R2d and UCC, course of dealing is presumed to qualify an agreement:

> Unless otherwise agreed, a course of dealing between the parties gives meaning to or supplements or qualifies their agreement. R2d § 223(2).

R2d and UCC thus recognize that terms may become part of an agreement by tacit recognition. For this reason, both take a liberal approach to the admission of evidence showing that this tacit recognition has occurred: both would admit evidence that course of dealing informs a term regardless of whether a term is patently ambiguous:

> *There is no requirement that an agreement be ambiguous before evidence of a course of dealing can be shown, nor is it required that the course of dealing be consistent with the meaning the agreement would have apart from the course of dealing. R2d § 223 cmt. b.*

Once again, we see that the polestar of contractual interpretation is the intention of the parties. Modern courts liberally admit evidence that shows what the parties intended.

C. Usage and Trade Usage

Contracts are not made in a vacuum. Rather, they are the product of a specific need in a certain time and place. The parties who make these agreements do so with certain assumptions, whether founded or unfounded, that affect their intentions and their manifestations. Some of those assumptions are cultural, ethnic, geographic, or based on other trade or professional associations.

Evidence regarding how people use words in habitual or customary practice is called "usage":

> *Usage is habitual or customary practice. R2d § 219.*

R2d specifically recognizes that words are used differently at different times in different geographic places.

> *A particular usage may be more or less widespread. It may prevail throughout an area, and the area may be small or large — a city, a state or a larger region. A usage may prevail among all people in the area, or only in a special trade or other group. Usages change over time, and persons in close association often develop temporary usages peculiar to themselves. R2d § 219 cmt. a.*

In other words, usage is not a static concept. Parties who seek to admit evidence of usage might have to first show that usage is relevant to the parties in this transaction.

Comment b goes on to explain that dictionaries are one source of evidence of usage, but they are not the only such source. Moreover, standard English dictionaries may not accurately describe how English speakers use words in a specific geographic area or trade.

> *A word usage exists when few or many people use a word or phrase to convey a standard meaning or several standard meanings and develop a common understanding of the meaning or meanings. Dictionaries record word usages which have achieved some generality, with varying degrees of completeness and accuracy.*

R2d's definition of usage is relatively broad. This is because the polestar of contract interpretation is to ascertain the mutual intentions of the parties. Usage is a tool in the pursuit of discovering mutual intentions at the time of assent, and it should only be employed as a means when it serves the ends of shedding light on parties' actual intent.

> *An agreement is interpreted in accordance with a relevant usage if each party knew or had reason to know of the usage and neither party knew or had reason to know that the meaning attached by the other was inconsistent with the usage.* R2d § 219(1).

R2d clarifies this rule with some illustrations that are meant to demonstrate the point that neither party is bound by a meaning unless he knows or has reason to know of it. Parties are presumed to know the common usage of terms, but this presumption may be rebutted.

> *Illustration 220.1. A contracts to sell and B to buy ten bushels of oats. By very general usage 32 pounds constitutes a bushel of oats. In the absence of contrary evidence, ten bushels in the contract means 320 pounds.*

Common usage not only explains the meaning of terms like "bushel," but also may add implied terms where both parties actually knew of that usage. We will address implied terms in more details in Module IV.

> *Illustration 220.4. A and B contract for a year's employment of B by A. As both parties know, there is a usage that such a contract may be terminated by a month's notice. Unless a contrary intention is manifested, the usage is part of the contract.*

Although the Restatement focuses on the intent of the parties as the polestar of contract interpretation, it does not require a party to provide that the other party actually knew of usage. In other words, the standard for consideration of usage evidence is not actual knowledge by the parties. Rather, the Restatement would admit evidence of usage where the parties had reason to know. This is a "reasonableness" standard that may impute knowledge.

The purpose of this rule is to lower the burden of proof that usage is relevant to interpretation. It also puts the burden on parties to become aware of common usage. Some might argue that this undermines to some extent the Restatement's commitment to ascertaining the actual intentions of the parties. But parties are still free to offer evidence that they did not actually know the usage of a term.

> *An agreement is supplemented or qualified by a reasonable usage with respect to agreements of the same type if each party knows or has reason to know of the usage and neither party knows or has reason to know that the other party has an intention inconsistent with the usage.* R2d § 221.

A more specific form of usage is called usage of trade, which refers to general commercial observance.

> *A usage of trade is a usage having such regularity of observance in a place, vocation, or trade as to justify an expectation that it will be observed with*

respect to a particular agreement. It may include a system of rules regu-
larly observed even though particular rules are changed from time to time.
R2d § 222(1).

For example, in the roofing trade, five hundred shingles is nearly universally referred to as a "pack." Unless otherwise discussed, a contract between a roofer and roofing supply company for "two packs" shall mean one thousand shingles.

In another example, "Carrara Marble" refers in the homebuilding trade to a stone slab that it white-grey in color with thin, feathery veins — regardless of whether the stone originates from Carrara, Italy.

Whether and what is the usage of trade is a question of fact, meaning, a fact-finder like a trial judge or jury must hear evidence and then evaluate whether a usage is so regular in commercial practice that it should demonstrate the meaning of a disputed term in a contract.

> *The existence and scope of a usage of trade are to be determined as questions*
> *of fact. If a usage is embodied in a written trade code or similar writing the*
> *interpretation of the writing is to be determined by the court as a question of*
> *law.* R2d § 222(2).

Usage of trade only applies when both parties are involved in the trade. If the parties have no reason to know about the usage, then it might not reflect the intention of those parties, and thus it should not bear on the judicial determination of the meaning of their mutual agreement.

> *Unless otherwise agreed, a usage of trade in the vocation or trade in which*
> *the parties are engaged or a usage of trade of which they know or have rea-*
> *son to know gives meaning to or supplements or qualifies their agreement.*
> R2d § 222(3).

Nānākuli, in Chapter 13, provides a very comprehensive discussion and illustration of the admission of usage of trade evidence in a contractual dispute. In *Nānākuli*, the court found that an agreement to sell asphalt was "price protected," meaning, the seller guaranteed the buyer that the price would be equal to the price that was posted at the time the buyer agreed to use the asphalt to do paving work. The court did so even though the contract to sell the asphalt said otherwise. The reason the court interpreted the contract to mean something other than what it said is because the usage of trade was so prevalent that it actually trumped the plain meaning of the contract terms.

D. Implied Terms of Good Faith and Fair Dealing

Courts face a conundrum when parties agree they have an agreement but disagree on its material terms. You may recall from our prior study of contract formation that contracts are not actually formed when the terms are too indefinite. There is a requirement of certainty as found in R2d § 33; however, there are contracts which are certain enough to be formed but not certain enough to be enforced.

For example, *Pacific Grape Products Co. v. Commissioner of Internal Revenue*, 219 F.2d 862 (9th Cir. 1955), involved a contract for the purchase and sale of canned fruit products. The case arose when the Internal Revenue Service (the "IRS," a bureau of the U.S. Department of Treasury that enforces tax law) charged Pacific Grape with misstating its annual income. Pacific Grape used an accrual accounting system to determine its annual income. Under the accrual method, income is generated by the seller when title of goods sold passes to the buyer.

The question presented in *Pacific Grape* was whether title had passed to the buyer in a certain year, where the seller had sold goods but not shipped them to the buyer in that year. Under UCC § 2-401(2), title for goods passes from the seller to the buyer when the goods are physically delivered to the buyer, unless the parties agree otherwise. Here, the parties did not agree otherwise, so Pacific Grape argued that title did not pass in that year; therefore, income was not accrued in that year.

The IRS, however, introduced evidence that, in the canned fruit products trade in California, it is customary for title to pass from the buyer to the seller when the goods were billed, not when they were delivered. Pacific Grape billed the buyer for the goods in the year in question; therefore, income was accrued that year.

The Ninth Circuit Court of Appeals determined that the trade usage created an implied term that supplemented Pacific Grape's sales agreements. Even though the term was never actually mentioned in its sales agreements or discussed by its sales agents, Pacific Grape was presumed to understand and follow the ubiquitous trade usage.

Note that this is different from usage of trade that explains or modifies a term in a written agreement. Implied terms by definition are new terms, not modifications to or explanations of existing terms.

In these cases, courts may supply essential omitted terms. This work of the courts is especially important when the parties have already begun or completed performance under an agreement; having actually performed the contract shows they clearly intended one to exist, so the court must determine what that contract should have said such that it incorporates the intention of the parties.

> When the parties to a bargain sufficiently defined to be a contract have not agreed with respect to a term which is essential to a determination of their rights and duties, a term which is reasonable in the circumstances is supplied by the court. R2d § 204.

Usually, this rule is invoked where parties fail to foresee a situation at the time of forming the contract that poses some problem with its performance that leads to a dispute. This is particularly likely regarding long-term contracts.

For example, in *Southern Bell Tel. & Tel. Co. v. Florida East Coast R. Co.*, 399 F.2d 854 (5th Cir. 1968), Southern Bell and the Florida East Coast signed an agreement in 1917, whereby Southern Bell could run its telephone lines across East Coast Railroad's tracks. This agreement worked well until the 1960s, when East Coast demanded that Southern Bell pay more for each crossing. East Coast argued that its agreement was terminated, and Southern Bell counter-argued that the agreement did not have any express term regarding its termination, and thus, it was not terminable.

The court had to decide whether and how an agreement is terminable where it has no termination provision. The court first tried to determine the intent of the parties from their written agreement, but it was silent. The course of performance clearly showed an intent to have a long-term contract, but how long? Should courts presume an indefinite or eternal contract?

The court then incorporated a termination term based on case law. It found controlling precedent that says:

> The general rule as repeatedly stated, is that a contract for an indefinite period, which by its nature is not deemed to be perpetual, may be terminated at will on giving reasonable notice.

The court thus found that East Coast could terminate the agreement by giving reasonable notice of termination to Bell.

The *Bell* court found mandatory authorities including the weight of case law favoring the implication of reasonable termination. But what should courts do when presented with a more novel question? While the *Bell* court found a term implied by law, courts can also find a term implied in fact, where the parties obviously intended something unspoken.

Fisher v. Congregation B'Nai Yitzhok, below, illustrates the concept of terms implied in fact. Rabbi Fisher, an Orthodox Jewish rabbi, contracted with Congregation B'Nai Yitzhok, an Orthodox Jewish congregation, to officiate as cantor for six religious services for the Jewish High Holidays Season of September 1950 for $1,200.

In June 1950, when the contract was made, Orthodox Jewish law required congregations to seat men and women separately at services, and Congregation B'Nai Yitzhok complied with this practice. In July 1950, the Congregation voted to allow men and women to sit together.

When Rabbi Fisher learned that men and women would sit together at the High Holidays services he was to officiate, he protested that he would be unable to officiate as cantor because this would be a violation of his religious beliefs. It was then too late for him to obtain alternative cantorial work except for one job for which he got paid $100.

Rabbi Fisher sued for $1,100, arguing that the contract contained an implied term that the Congregation would observe Orthodox Jewish law. The Congregation argued that there was no ambiguity in their final written contract, which it claimed was a complete expression of the parties' agreement, and therefore any implied term should be excluded based on the parol evidence rule.

The court sided with Rabbi Fisher. Although the parties did not specifically discuss whether each Orthodox Jewish law from time immemorial shall be observed at the synagogue, it seems reasonable that Rabbi Fisher expected Jewish law generally to be observed. In fact, it would have been ridiculous for the parties to spell out every observance in their short-term contract. Even where contracts are more elaborate, and even when teams of lawyers write them, it may be impossible to document every eventuality and assumption. All contracts are thus susceptible to terms implied from common usage. Parties frequently fail to spell out every possible detail of every permutation. Certain terms can be implied even in the most complete of agreements.

E. Reflections on Interpretation

In this module, you learned how courts determine (interpret) the meaning of agreements.

As a preliminary matter, contractual interpretation starts with a foundation in contractual formation. We must have a valid agreement if we are to determine what that agreement means. Therefore, a preliminary step in contractual interpretation is to establish that there is a valid agreement.

In addition to an agreement, there is, of course, a disagreement that forms the basis of the legal dispute. Contract interpretation focuses on the disagreement. The first question is whether the disagreement is legitimate, or whether one party is asserting an unreasonable or overly formalistic interpretation. If a term is susceptible to only one reasonable meaning, courts should apply that meaning and resolve the case.

Harder cases involve murkier terms. Courts must disambiguify terms that are susceptible to multiple meanings. This is first done by reading the written agreement and applying to it the canons of construction. These 12 semantic rules can be applied to the written agreement, and they might resolve the agreement's meaning without the need for further evidence or inquiry.

If the semantic canons fail, courts might apply a policy canon, like construction against the drafter, as a sort of tie-breaker. Objectivist or legal-formalist courts are most likely to do this, while subjectivist or legal-realist courts are more likely to extend the inquiry further by taking extrinsic evidence into account.

Courts must take extrinsic evidence into account where the agreement regards a sale of goods because the UCC (which applies to sales of goods) is a statute that requires this inquiry. Rules regarding priority of interpretation are thus more of a standard than a rule. One form of evidence does not necessarily trump another, but some categories are certainly weighed more heavily than others.

Although blackletter law treatises like the Restatement rank extrinsic evidence into a strict order — course of performance prevails over course of dealing, and course of dealing prevails over usage of trade — things are messier in the real world. Courts generally admit evidence of trade usage because that comes from relatively impartial sources because understanding the context of the commercial arrangement helps courts arrive at the reasonable mutual understanding of the parties.

Courts also may consider evidence of implied terms: even if parties failed to discuss or write something down, it does not necessarily mean they did not have it mind. Some basic assumption upon which a contract is made might be implied by courts

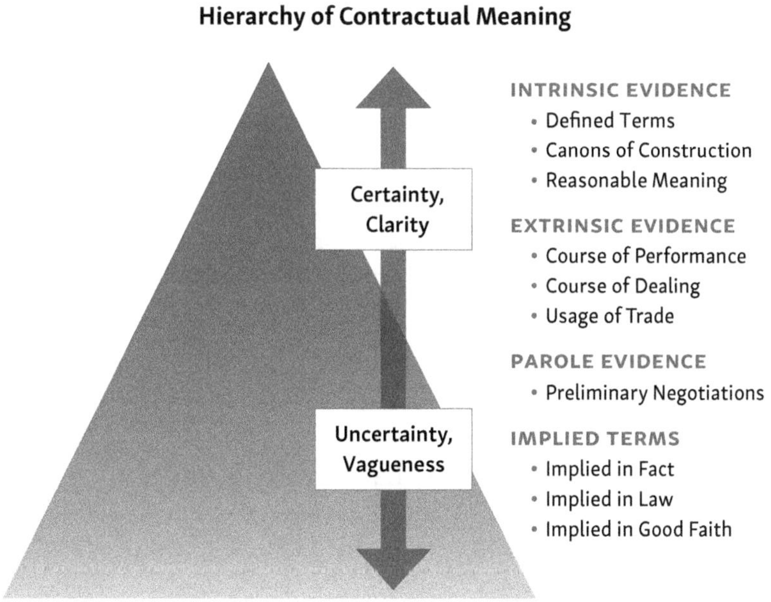

Hierarchy of Contractual Meaning

Figure 16.1. Illustration of the hierarchy of evidence used to determine contractual meaning. Credit Seth C. Oranburg.

as a matter of law or fact. For example, the weight of case law generally implies that contracts lacking a termination clause are not intended to be indefinite but rather to be terminable by either party upon reasonable notice. Other terms may be implied by the specific facts of the case. In any case, parties have an implied mutual obligation to use good faith efforts and act in fair dealing with one another in furtherance of the mutual fruits of their shared contractual endeavor.

Cases

Reading Wood v. Lucy, Lady Duff-Gordon. Before you begin to read the case of *Wood v. Lucy, Lady Duff-Gordon,* note that it can be hard to read if you do not understand the procedural posture, which is admittedly a bit confusing. In this case, the plaintiff, Otis F. Wood, has sued the defendant, Lady Duff-Gordon, on the grounds of breach of contract. Duff-Gordon defends by arguing that there is no contract at all. Her argument is that the promises were illusory, and therefore, there is no consideration. As you learned in the modules on contract formation, without consideration, there can be no contract-at-law; therefore, Duff-Gordon argues, since there is no contract, there can be no breach of contract.

Cardozo finds Duff-Gordon liable for breach of contract; therefore, he must find that some contract exists. Although he could have found there was an enforceable agreement without consideration due to promissory estoppel or some other equitable approach to contract formation, he does not make that argument. Instead, he finds that there is a contract as a matter of law, and therefore, he must find there is some consideration.

Recall that consideration is a bargained-for exchange or, as Cardozo puts it, some mutuality of agreement. To accomplish this, Cardozo must find that Duff-Gordon and Wood made mutual promises to each other. This requires Cardozo to imply a key term that creates this mutual obligation. As you read this case, pay careful attention to how Cardozo finds that the parties created a mutual obligation by virtue of a term implied in good faith.

Wood v. Lucy, Lady Duff-Gordon

222 N.Y. 88 (1917)

CARDOZO, J.

The defendant styles herself "a creator of fashions." Her favor helps a sale. Manufacturers of dresses, millinery and like articles are glad to pay for a certificate of her approval. The things which she designs, fabrics, parasols and what not, have a new value in the public mind when issued in her name.

She employed the plaintiff to help her to turn this vogue into money. He was to have the exclusive right, subject always to her approval, to place her indorsements on the designs of others. He was also to have the exclusive right to place her own designs on sale, or to license others to market them. In return, she was to have one-half of "all profits and revenues" derived from any contracts he might make. The exclusive right was to last at least one year from April 1, 1915, and thereafter from year to year unless terminated by notice of ninety days. The plaintiff says that he kept the contract on his part, and that the defendant broke it. She placed her indorsement on fabrics, dresses and millinery without his knowledge, and withheld the profits.

He sues her for the damages, and the case comes here on demurrer.

The agreement of employment is signed by both parties. It has a wealth of recitals. The defendant insists, however, that it lacks the elements of a contract. She says that the plaintiff does not bind himself to anything. It is true that he does not promise in so many words that he will use reasonable efforts to place the defendant's indorsements and market her designs.

We think, however, that such a promise is fairly to be implied. The law has outgrown its primitive stage of formalism when the precise word was the sovereign talisman, and every slip was fatal. It takes a broader view to-day. A promise may be lacking, and yet the whole writing may be "instinct with an obligation," imperfectly expressed. If that is so, there is a contract.

The implication of a promise here finds support in many circumstances. The defendant gave an exclusive privilege. She was to have no right for at least a year to place her own indorsements or market her own designs except through the agency of the plaintiff. The acceptance of the exclusive agency was an assumption of its duties. We are not to suppose that one party was to be placed at the mercy of the other.

Many other terms of the agreement point the same way. We are told at the outset by way of recital that "the said Otis F. Wood possesses a business organization adapted to the placing of such indorsements as the said Lucy, Lady Duff-Gordon has approved."

The implication is that the plaintiff's business organization will be used for the purpose for which it is adapted. But the terms of the defendant's compensation are even more significant. Her sole compensation for the grant of an exclusive agency is to be one-half of all the profits resulting from the plaintiff's efforts. Unless he gave his efforts, she could never get anything. Without an implied promise, the transaction cannot have such business "efficacy as both parties must have intended that at all events it should have."

But the contract does not stop there. The plaintiff goes on to promise that he will account monthly for all moneys received by him, and that he will take out all such patents and copyrights and trademarks as may in his judgment be necessary to protect the rights and articles affected by the agreement.

It is true, of course, as the Appellate Division has said, that if he was under no duty to try to market designs or to place certificates of indorsement, his promise to account for profits or take out copyrights would be valueless. But in determining the intention of the parties, the promise has a value. It helps to enforce the conclusion that the plaintiff had some duties. His promise to pay the defendant one-half of the profits and revenues resulting from the exclusive agency and to render accounts monthly, was a promise to use reasonable efforts to bring profits and revenues into existence. For this conclusion, the authorities are ample.

The judgment of the Appellate Division should be reversed, and the order of the Special Term affirmed, with costs in the Appellate Division and in this court.

Reflection

Cardozo's famous opinion effectively establishes the doctrine of good faith. Cardozo used this doctrine to create an enforceable obligation on the part of Lady Duff-Gorden when her promise to grant exclusivity to Wood would otherwise be unenforceable for his lack of consideration. But not every jurist would so willingly imply terms of good faith and thereby create a contract from them. For example, in *Goldstick v. ICM Realty*, 788 F.2d 456 (7th Cir. 1986), Judge Posner ignored any obligation of good faith (the term never even appears in his opinion) and instead declares a promise enforceable due to estoppel but not due to contract.

The dispute in *Goldstick* regarded a pair of out-of-luck attorneys who could not collect on a bill for a year's worth of legal services; as a cautionary tale in professional responsibility, it is worth reading in full. As to the contract points, the facts can be summarized. ICM owned some property on which back taxes were owed. ICM leased the property to John Kusmiersky, who agreed to pay the back taxes in exchange for the rights to operate the property. Kusmiersky hired the law firm of Goldstick & Smith to reduce the back taxes. The lawyers succeeded in reducing the taxes by $870,000 and billed Kusmiersky $290,000, which he refused to pay. The lawyers then entered into a settlement agreement with Kusmiersky and ICM under which ICM agreed to pay the lawyers $250,000 of out any profits ICM made if the property was sold.

ICM sold the property at a loss and refused to pay the lawyers, who sued in the Northern District of Illinois. Defendants moved for summary judgement, and the trial court granted judgment as a matter of law to ICM, on the ground that ICM did not promise to pay Goldstick & Smith unless it sold the property for a profit, and it did not sell the property for a profit, so ICM had no legal liability to Goldstick.

The Seventh Circuit reversed and remanded the case because Goldstick & Smith may have detrimentally relied on ICM. Although the appellate court could have read some duty of good faith and fair dealing into ICM's promise to Goldstick & Smith, such as an implied promise to make reasonable efforts to sell the property at a profit, the court did not even seem to entertain this idea. Rather, it employed the well-established doctrine of detrimental reliance.

The *Goldstick* case shows that Cardozo's imposition of good faith is not strictly necessary to do justice. Instead of finding a contract where the parties may not have actually promised to perform some bargained-for exchange, a judge could have found that Lady Duff-Gordon's promise to grant exclusive rights to Wood was enforceable because Wood reasonably and detrimentally relied on that promise. See R2d § 90.

The fact that Posner and Cardozo take such different approaches to this central issue in contract law indicates there is a deep tension between implying terms in good faith and respecting the express intent of the parties.

Discussion

1. In *Wood*, Cardozo seems quite willing to imply terms in this contract. He seems to be focused on achieving a fair result for the parties in the case before him; after all, that is the hallmark of his equity.

2. Equitable remedies are supposed to prevent courts and legal arrangements like contracts from becoming tools of injustice. However, allowing judicial discretion for equity creates a great deal of uncertainty. Thus, equity creates an unfairness of its own, as parties to a contract cannot easily predict how a court will re-interpret a written agreement in hindsight. In other words, judicial power to correct things in hindsight obscures parties' ability to negotiate

contracts with foresight. What is the appropriate balance? How much discretion should courts have to award equitable remedies "as justice requires"?

3. If courts are free to add, change, and modify terms, what use is the parol evidence rule? Whence is the objective theory of contract interpretation? How do lawyers help businesses plan for an uncertain legal future?

4. Is there another way to resolve *Wood* in favor of plaintiff without implying a duty of good faith as a contractual term? For example, could the doctrine of promissory estoppel (detrimental reliance) be employed to reach the same result of liability upon Lady-Duff Gordon without implying legal terms that the parties did not actually use?

Reading Fisher v. Congregation B'Nai Yitzhok. Congregation B'Nai Yitzhok is a classic case that illustrates the concept of terms implied in fact that it is actually featured as an illustration in the Restatement itself:

> *Illustration 221.2. A, an ordained rabbi, is employed by B, an orthodox Jewish congregation, to officiate as cantor at specified religious services. At the time the contract is made, it is the practice of such congregations to seat men and women separately at services, and a contrary practice would violate A's religious beliefs. At a time when it is too late for A to obtain substitute employment, B adopts a contrary practice. A refuses to officiate. The practice is part of the contract, and A is entitled to the agreed compensation.*

The illustration, however, oversimplifies the complex factual analysis the courts took on in this case. As you read this case, highlight the facts that are relevant to the court's decision and annotate each highlight you make with a comment on why that fact is relevant. This exercise will help you perform the reflections after reading *Congregation B'Nai Yitzhok* that will elevate your understanding of when courts will imply terms in fact.

> *You should also pay attention to the court's explanation for why the parol evidence rule does not apply.*

Fisher v. Congregation B'Nai Yitzhok

177 Pa. Super. 359 (1955)

HIRT, J.

Plaintiff is an ordained rabbi of the orthodox Hebrew faith. He however does not officiate except on occasion as a professional rabbi-cantor in the liturgical service of a synagogue. The defendant is an incorporated Hebrew congregation with a synagogue in Philadelphia.

Plaintiff, in response to defendant's advertisement in a Yiddish newspaper, appeared in Philadelphia for an audition before a committee representing the congregation. As a result, a written contract was entered into on June 26, 1950, under the terms of which plaintiff agreed to officiate as cantor at the synagogue of the defendant congregation "for the High Holiday Season of 1950", at six specified services during the month of September 1950. As full compensation for the above services the defendant agreed to pay plaintiff the sum of $1,200.

The purpose upon which the defendant congregation was incorporated is thus stated in its charter: "The worship of Almighty God according to the faith, discipline, forms and rites of the orthodox Jewish religion." And up to the time of the execution of the contract the defendant congregation conducted its religious services in accordance with the practices of the orthodox Hebrew faith.

On behalf of the plaintiff there is evidence that under the law of the Torah and other binding authority of the Jewish law, men and women may not sit together at services in the synagogue. In the orthodox synagogue, where the practice is observed, the women sit apart from the men in a gallery, or they are separated from the men by means of a partition [a "mechitza"] between the two groups.

The contract in this case is entirely silent as to the character of the defendant as an orthodox Hebrew congregation and the practices observed by it as to the seating at the services in the synagogue.

At a general meeting of the congregation on July 12, 1950, on the eve of moving into a new synagogue, the practice of separate seating by the defendant formerly observed was modified and for the future the first four rows of seats during religious services were set aside exclusively for the men, and the next four rows for the women, and the remainder for mixed seating of both men and women.

When plaintiff was informed of the action of the defendant congregation in deviating from the traditional practice as to separate seating, he through his attorney notified the defendant that he, a rabbi of the orthodox faith, would be unable to officiate as cantor because "this would be a violation of his beliefs." Plaintiff persisted in the stand taken that he would not under any circumstances serve as cantor for defendant as long as men and women were not seated separately. And when defendant failed to rescind its action permitting men and women to sit together during services, plaintiff refused to officiate. It then was too late for him to secure other employment as cantor during the 1950 Holiday season except for one service which paid him $100, and he brought suit for the balance of the contract price.

The action was tried before the late Judge Fenerty, without a jury, who died before deciding the issue. By agreement the case was disposed of by the late President Judge Frank Smith "on the notes of testimony taken before Judge Fenerty." At the conclusion of the trial, counsel had stipulated that the judge need not make specific findings of fact in his decision. This waiver applied to the disposition of the case by Judge Smith.

Nevertheless Judge Smith did specifically find that defendant, at the time the contract was entered into, "Was conducting its services according to the Orthodox

Hebrew Faith." Judge Smith accepted the testimony of three rabbis learned in Hebrew law, who appeared for plaintiff, to the effect: "That Orthodox Judaism required a definite and physical separation of the sexes in the synagogue." And he also considered it established by the testimony that an orthodox rabbi-cantor "could not conscientiously officiate in a 'trefah' synagogue, that is, one that violates Jewish law"; and it was specifically found that the old building which the congregation left, "had separation in accordance with Jewish orthodoxy."

The ultimate finding was for the plaintiff in the sum of $1,100 plus interest. And the court entered judgment for the plaintiff on the finding.

In this appeal it is contended that the defendant is entitled to judgment as a matter of law.

The finding for the plaintiff in this trial without a jury has the force and effect of a verdict of a jury and in support of the judgment entered by the lower court, the plaintiff is entitled to the benefit of the most favorable inferences from the evidence. Findings of fact by a trial judge, sitting without a jury, which are supported by competent substantial evidence are conclusive on appeal.

Although the contract is silent as to the nature of the defendant congregation, there is no ambiguity in the writing on that score and certainly nothing was omitted from its terms by fraud, accident or mistake. The terms of the contract therefore could not be varied under the parol evidence rule. Another principle controls the interpretation of this contract.

There is sufficient competent evidence in support of the finding that this defendant was an orthodox congregation, which observed the rule of the ancient Hebrew law as to separate seating during the services of the High Holiday Season; and also to the effect that the rule had been observed immemorially and invariably by the defendant in these services, without exception.

As bearing on plaintiff's bona fide belief that such was the fact, at the time he contracted with the defendant, plaintiff was permitted to introduce in evidence the declarations of Rabbi Ebert, the rabbi of the defendant congregation, made to him prior to signing of the contract, in which the rabbi said: "There always was a separation between men and women" and "there is going to be strict separation between men and women," referring to the seating in the new synagogue.

Rabbi Lipschitz, who was present, testified that Rabbi Ebert, in response to plaintiff's question "Will services be conducted as in the old Congregation?" replied "Sure. There is no question about that," referring to the prior practice of separate seating.

The relationship of rabbi to the congregation which he serves does not create the legal relationship of principal and agent. And Rabbi Ebert in the absence of special authority to speak for the congregation could not legally bind the defendant by his declarations to the plaintiff prior to the execution of the contract. But while the declarations of Rabbi Ebert, above referred to would have been inadmissible hearsay as proof of the truth of what was said, yet his declarations were properly admissible as bearing upon plaintiff's state of mind and his intent in entering into the contract.

In determining the right of recovery in this case the question is to be determined under the rules of our civil law, and the ancient provision of the Hebrew law relating to separate seating is read into the contract only because implicit in the writing as to the basis — according to the evidence — upon which the parties dealt.

In our law the provision became a part of the written contract under a principle analogous to the rule applicable to the construction of contracts in the light of custom or immemorial and invariable usage. It has been said that: "When a custom or usage is once established, in absence of express provision to the contrary it is considered a part of a contract and binding on the parties though not mentioned therein, the presumption being that they knew of and contracted with reference to it."

In this case there was more than a presumption. From the findings of the trial judge supported by the evidence it is clear that the parties contracted on the common understanding that the defendant was an orthodox synagogue which observed the mandate of the Jewish law as to separate seating. That intention was implicit in this contract though not referred to in the writing, and therefore must be read into it. It was on this ground that the court entered judgment for plaintiff in this case.

Judgment affirmed.

Reflection

The *Congregation B'Nai Yitzhok* appeal was decided in 1955, and the trial court below it rendered its opinion in 1950. To really understand what was happening in this case, some context about what was happening in the Jewish-American world at the time is necessary.

Congregation B'Nai Yitzhok appears to be like a snapshot of a great change in social history. In this case, we see an Orthodox rabbi cleaving to tradition while congregations in the Philadelphia suburbs modernize their practices. Perhaps the congregation's members were more inclined toward egalitarianism than its clergy. In any event, when the Congregation B'Nai Yitzhok adopted the practice of mixed seating for its High Holiday Services in September 1950, that was a major event that is best understood through the lens of its historical context.

Throughout the 19th century, American Judaism featured two prominent movements. The Orthodox movement, discussed in *Congregation B'Nai Yitzhok* above, generally held that the five books of Moses (the first five books of the Bible) contain the true and original words of God, and that the "revealed laws" therein and described by accepted oral tradition were binding and immutable. In this tradition, each year takes mankind further away from the revelation of the Torah at Mount Sinai, which the movement places at 1313 B.C.E. Under this theology, change is antithetical to core beliefs. Therefore, ancient practices including dietary laws, separation of the sexes, Hebrew language prayer, and resting on the Jewish Sabbath must be maintained.

The Reform movement, with foundations related to the German Enlightenment, generally held that theology is a continuous revelation. Many Reform Jews believe that man, not God, wrote the bible. Critical research can lead to new insights such that each generation can build upon the past to get closer and closer to a true understanding of God. Under this movement, change is necessary for the religion to remain relevant in a modern world. Therefore, changes to ancient practices are necessary so Jews can eat in restaurants, achieve equality of the sexes, pray in English, and work and drive on Saturdays.

The differences between these schools of thought are quite vast, and the rift between the members of these movements was vastly widened by an event called the "Trefa Banquet." (Recall from the *Congregation B'Nai Yitzhok* case above that "Trefa" means ritually unclean or impure under Orthodox Jewish law.) On July 11, 1883, at the Highland House Restaurant in Cincinnati, Ohio, a Reform seminary held a dinner to commemorate the graduation of its first class of rabbis. Whether by the organizers' intentions or negligence, the banquet featured many foods that are considered "trefa" under Orthodox Jewish Law. This caused great offense among the Orthodox community and may have sparked the creation of a third, middle way in Jewish theology.

Members of the Reform movement who were offended by this brash disregard for the revealed laws broke away to form a new movement that would become Conservative Judaism. The Jewish Theological Seminary was founded in 1886 to advance this middle way. Conservative Jewish theology, as expressed by JTS, seeks to combine commitment to traditional beliefs and practices with full engagement with modern society.

The pressure to modernize Judaism while cleaving to its traditions may have been amplified by the events of World War II (1939-1945) and the Holocaust, in which six million European Jews were murdered by Nazis. This event had a profound impact on the American Jewish conscience. For some, it drove them toward assimilation into American society. For others, it demanded a return to traditional practices. For all, it was a time of great upheaval and change.

World War II impacted the greater American society as well. For example, women who had joined the workforce in record numbers when men went overseas to fight were reevaluating their status and station in society, leading to renewed demands for equal rights between the sexes. Soldiers (including 550,000 Jewish men and women who served in the armed forces of the United States) returned home to a booming economy and settled in suburbs, where cars were a necessity.

Discussion

1. Given this history, do you think the court was correct in determining that separate seating was an implied term in Rabbi Fisher's contract? Was the court correct in only seeking the opinion of Orthodox rabbis? Should the court have also taken testimony from Conservative or Reform rabbis on what Jewish law requires?

2. If this case occurred today—when 35% of American Jews identify as Reform, 18% identify as conservative, and 10% identify as Orthodox—should the

court have arrived at a different result? Should a court generally be willing to hear evidence about the historical and social context of contract formation?

———————

Reading First Nat'l Bank of Lawrence v. Methodist Home for the Aged. The *Congregation B'Nai Yitzhok* case above illustrated how courts can use factual evidence, such as parties' testimonies, to determine whether terms should be implied in fact. But what if the parties are not available?

In this next case, *Methodist Home*, the plaintiff is the administrator of a decedent's estate. In other words, one of the parties to the contract is dead. Since dead people cannot give testimony—and at least one court has ruled that "evidence of deceased's wishes via Ouija board is not admissible in federal court"—courts will have to look to other sources of evidence to determine whether to imply terms.

Methodist Home concerns an agreement for lifetime tenancy in a retirement home. This lifetime membership is subject to a probationary period, during which either side could cancel the agreement. The written contract did not discuss what would happen if the tenant died during the probationary period. When such a death occurred, the estate sought to cancel the agreement and receive a refund of the lifetime tenancy fee. The court then had to determine whether such a term should be implied in this contract—and it could not call upon the decedent to determine her actual intentions at the time of contracting.

Before reading the case, consider why the parties may have omitted this term. Do you think the omission was deliberate or negligent on the part of the retirement home, who drafted the written contract? Why didn't Ms. Ellsworth insist that the contract stipulate what would happen if she died during the probationary period? Would the court actually be able to determine whether or not the parties actually discussed this term? Even if they discussed it, would the parol evidence rule bar admission of that discussion?

The court states that the written contract in question is ambiguous, but it does not explain its reasoning why. Do you think the contract is ambiguous? How does this finding of ambiguity impact the application of the parol evidence rule?

You may also note that this court helpfully outlines the rules of interpreting an ambiguous contract. It phrases these rules a bit differently than R2d—which is not surprising, given that the R2d was not yet published—but effectively goes through a similar process to the one you already learned. In fact, this court does a rather thorough job of reviewing the rules of contract interpretation in general. Highlight where the court discusses these rules and annotate your highlights with a reference to the corresponding section in R2d and any discrepancies you notice between how R2d and this court frames the rules.

Noting that the retirement home drafted the contract, do you think that the policy canon of construction against the drafter, R2d 206, plays a role in the court's analysis? Should it?

First National Bank of Lawrence v. Methodist Home for the Aged
181 Kan. 100 (1957)

PARKER, Chief Justice.

Plaintiff is a banking corporation with its place of business at Lawrence, Kansas, and the duly appointed administrator, with the will annexed, of the will of Bertha C. Ellsworth, deceased. Defendant is the Methodist Home For the Aged, a corporation, with its principal place of business at Topeka, Kansas, where it operates a home for the aged.

The events leading up to the institution of this litigation are not in controversy and should be stated at the outset in order to insure a proper understanding of the appellate issues involved.

On September 13, 1953, Bertha C. Ellsworth, who desired to be admitted to the defendant's home and was then single and more than seventy-one years of age, made a written application for admission to such home. Thereafter, having been advised her application had been approved, she was admitted to the home on May 10, 1954, and on the same date entered into the written agreement with defendant which is actually the subject of this litigation. Pertinent portions of such agreement, which we pause to note had been prepared by defendant on one of its standard forms, used for admission of members, read:

> *This Agreement, made and entered into this 10th day of May, 1954, by and between The Methodist Home for the Aged, a Corporation, of Topeka, Kansas, Party of the First Part and Bertha C. Ellsworth, of Lawrence, Kansas, Party of the Second Part, Witnesseth:*
>
> *Party of the Second Part having this day given Party of the First Part, <u>without reservation</u>, the sum of $10,779.60 to be used and disposed of in the furtherance of its benevolence and charitable work as it may deem best, Party of the First Part <u>admits Party of the Second Part into its Home as a member thereof during the period of her natural life, and agrees to furnish</u>: . . .*
>
> *Fifth: <u>It is clearly understood that Party of the Second Part has been received in accordance with the new regulations on a probation period of two months in which time she has the opportunity of finding out whether she desires to remain in the Home; and also find out whether the Home is able</u>*

to satisfy the requirements. If it should be found advisable to discontinue her stay in the Home, then her gift, with the exception of $80.00 per month shall be refunded.

The rules and regulations and bylaws of the Home as they now are and as they from time to time may be adopted and promulgated by the Board of Directors of said Party of the First Part are hereby referred to and made a part hereof and the Party of the Second Part hereby agrees to be bound by same. It is especially understood and agreed that in case of serious mental illness requiring hospital care and attention, that the First Party shall have the right to make proper arrangements for the treatment and care of the Second Party in a lawful manner in a proper State Institution, provided that if Second Party is discharged as completely cured to admit Second Party into the Home without further financial requirements. (Emphasis supplied.)

The parties concede that defendant's bylaw, article 12, was in full force and effect on the date of the execution of the agreement and therefore, according to the terms of that agreement, is a part of the contract. It reads:

Probationary membership means a short trial period while the member becomes adjusted to the life of the Home. The probationary membership shall not continue for a longer period than two consecutive months. If for any reason the trial member does not desire to remain in the Home he or she shall have the privilege of leaving. On the other hand, if the Home for any reason does not desire to continue the membership then the member shall be notified in writing and leave the Home within a week after such notice is given. Only members who do not have the money or securities to pay for their life Membership shall be granted the privilege of paying by the month. (Emphasis supplied.)

After execution of the May 10, 1954, agreement Bertha C. Ellsworth remained in the home until she died on June 10, 1954. At that time neither she nor the home had made an election as to whether she was to leave the home or remain therein after the expiration of the probationary period specified by its terms. However, it is conceded that during the interim, and on June 4, 1954, the plaintiff bank in its capacity as trustee had paid the defendant the sum of $10,799.60 by a check, which defendant had cashed, specifying that such check was "In Payment of Life Membership for Bertha C. Ellsworth in the Methodist Home for the Aged, as specified in Agreement dated May 10, 1954", and that defendant had acknowledged payment of that sum by a receipt of like import.

Upon the death of Bertha Ellsworth plaintiff was appointed by the probate court of Douglas County, Kansas, as Administrator CTA of such decedent. Thereafter it made written demand on defendant for performance under the agreement, including pertinent by-laws, and demanded that defendant refund the estate of its decedent the amount paid pursuant thereto, less any amounts due the Home under its terms, particularly the fifth clause thereof. When this demand was refused plaintiff procured authority from the probate court to institute the instant action to recover such amount as an asset of the estate of Bertha C. Ellsworth, deceased.

Following action as above indicated plaintiff commenced this lawsuit by filing a petition which, it may be stated, recites in a general way that under the more important facts, conditions and circumstances, heretofore outlined, the defendant had never attained a life membership in the home by reason of her death prior to the expiration of the probationary membership period prescribed by the contract, hence the contract should be construed as contemplating her estate was entitled to a return of the money paid by her to defendant for such a membership.

When a demurrer to this pleading, based on the ground it failed to state a cause of action, was overruled by the trial court defendant filed an answer alleging in substance that under the same facts, conditions and circumstances the contract between it and the decedent is to be construed as warranting its retention of the sum paid by such decedent for the life membership even though, prior to her death, such decedent neither indicated that she did not desire to remain in the Home nor that she desired the privilege of leaving it

It should perhaps be added that such answer contains an allegation that on May 10, 1954, decedent was permitted to enter the home without having paid her life membership; admits subsequent payment of such membership in the manner heretofore indicated; and makes decedent's application for admission to the home a part of such pleading.

With issues joined, as heretofore related, the cause came on for trial by the court.

During the trial facts, as heretofore related, were established by evidence and at the conclusion thereof the trial court, after holding that the salient question in the case was purely a question of law involving the interpretation of the contract, rendered judgment decreeing that plaintiff was entitled to recover the amount paid by Bertha C. Ellsworth to the Home, less $235 paid by the Home for her funeral expenses and less the sum of $80 provided for in the contract in the event she had elected not to remain in the Home.

Thereupon defendant perfected this appeal wherein under proper specification of errors it charges the trial court erred in overruling the demurrer to the petition; in rendering judgment for plaintiff and against defendant, wholly contrary to the law and the terms of the agreement; and in overruling its motion for a new trial.

In a preliminary way it can be said a careful examination of the record leads to the inescapable conclusion the trial court was eminently correct in holding that the all decisive question involved in this case is purely a question of law involving the interpretation of the contract entered into between the appellant and Bertha C. Ellsworth, deceased. Indeed the parties make no serious contention to the contrary.

For that reason, and others to be presently disclosed, we turn directly to appellant's claim the trial court's judgment was contrary to the terms of the agreement and to the law, mindful as we do so that where — as here — the terms of a contract are ambiguous, obscure or susceptible of more than one meaning there are certain well defined rules to which courts must adhere in construing its provisions. Four of such rules, which we believe have special application here, can be stated as follows:

1. That doubtful language in a contract is construed most strongly against the party preparing the instrument or employing the words concerning which doubt arises.

2. That where a contract is susceptible of more than one construction its terms and provisions must, if possible, be construed in such manner as to give effect to the intention of the parties at the time of its execution.

3. That in determining intention of the parties where ambiguity exists in a contract the test is not what the party preparing the instrument intended its doubtful or ambiguous words to mean but what a reasonable person, in the position of the other party to the agreement, would have understood them to mean under the existing conditions and circumstances.

4. That the intent and purpose of a contract is not to be determined by considering one isolated sentence or provision thereof but by considering and construing the instrument in its entirety.

Stated, substantially in its own language, the principal contention advanced by appellant as grounds for reversal of the judgment is that the membership agreement between it and the involved decedent was fully executed inasmuch as decedent had been admitted to the Home as a life member on May 10, 1954, and thereafter caused her life membership to be paid; hence, since nothing further needed to be done by the parties to make the portion of the agreement relating to life membership binding, provisions of the contract with respect thereto had become fully executed and title to the fee paid for such membership had vested in appellant.

If we could limit our construction of the contract to its first two paragraphs, as heretofore quoted, we might well conclude that appellant's views respecting the status of the agreement and the gift therein mentioned could be upheld. However, as has been previously demonstrated, our obligation is not to consider isolated provisions of the contract but to consider and construe such instrument in its entirety. When succeeding paragraphs of the agreement, and the incorporated by-laws, particularly portions thereof which we have heretofore italicized for purposes of emphasis, are reviewed in the light of the rule to which we have just referred, as well as others heretofore mentioned, we have little difficulty in concurring in the views expressed by the trial court in rendering its judgment that the contract had never become executed and that title to the gift paid by the decedent for a life membership had not vested in the Home.

In fact, and without repeating the emphasized portions of the agreement on which we base our conclusion, we go further and hold that, under the clear import and meaning of such emphasized provisions, Bertha C. Ellsworth, because of her untimely death during the probationary and/or trial period expressly required by their terms, never attained a life membership status in the Home. Indeed to hold otherwise would not only do violence to the language of the contract but read into it something that is not there.

One question remains in this lawsuit. Who, the Home or the decedent's estate, is entitled to the life membership fee paid by decedent to appellant? In this connection it is interesting to note that the money was paid by decedent by a check and receipted for by appellant in writing, each of which instruments contain a recital "In Payment of Life Membership for Bertha C. Ellsworth in the Methodist Home for the Aged, as specified in Agreement dated May 10, 1954." So, since it cannot be denied the contract contains no express provisions relating to where the money was to go if Bertha Ellsworth died during the probationary and/or trial period prescribed by its terms, it appears we are faced with the obligation of determining what was intended by the parties at the time of the execution of the agreement in the event of such a contingency.

Strange as it may seem, the question thus presented has been before the Courts on but few occasions. However, it has been decided under similar circumstances. An interesting discussion on the subject appears in 10 A.L.R.2d., Annotation, pp. 874, 875, § 12. It reads:

> Many entrance contracts provide for a probationary period during which the applicant for admission to the charitable home as well as the home itself can dissolve the agreement without cause. In case the applicant is refused permanent admission at the end of the trial period or withdraws during the period of his own volition, all payments made, less a fixed weekly charge for the time he stayed at the home, are refunded to him and his property rights are restored.
>
> An interesting situation arises if the applicant dies during the probationary period without having been either accepted or rejected as a permanent inmate. The legal question then is whether or not the charitable home may retain the applicant's property on the ground that the agreement had not been dissolved by either party.
>
> In a majority of cases this question has been answered in the negative and it has been held that the home may not claim or retain the applicant's property, on the ground that the death of the applicant has made it impossible to determine whether he would have become a permanent inmate at the end of the probationary period.

In connection with the foregoing quotation the author cites [sources] as supporting the conclusion reached by him in the concluding paragraph of his discussion and one case only as holding to the contrary. We may add our somewhat extended research of the books, including our own reports, discloses no other cases which can be regarded as decisive of the question presented under similar facts, conditions and circumstances.

Again reviewing the contract in the light of the heretofore stated rules, and mindful that appellant, not the decedent, prepared the involved contract, we are impelled to the view that a reasonable person, in the position of the decedent at the time of the execution of the contract, would have understood the provisions of that instrument to mean that unless and until she attained the status of a life member in the appellant's home she, or her estate would be entitled to a return of the money paid by her for that right, less amounts specified in the agreement.

Moreover we are convinced, that having prepared the contract, appellant's failure to make express provision therein for retaining the money paid by Bertha C. Ellsworth as a life membership fee, in the event of her death during the period of her probationary and/or trial membership status, precludes any construction of that agreement which would warrant its retention of such money upon the happening of that contingency.

After careful consideration of the decisions last above cited we have concluded those having the effect of holding, under similar circumstances, that the appellant cannot claim or retain Bertha Ellsworth's lifetime payment for the reason her death made it impossible for her to determine whether she was to become a permanent inmate of the Home at the end of the probation period, are more sound in principle and better reasoned that the one case holding to the contrary.

Therefore, based on the conclusions heretofore announced and on what is said and held in such decisions, we hold that the trial court did not err in rendering the judgment from which the Home has appealed.

Lest we be charged with overlooking it, we pause here to note, we regard *Old Peoples Home, etc. v. Miltner*, 149 Kan. 847, 89 P.2d 874, relied on by each of the parties in support of respective claims regarding the propriety of the judgment, as clearly distinguishable and hence of no value as a precedent controlling issues involved in the case at bar.

Contentions advanced by appellant in connection with the overruling of its demurrer to appellee's evidence and the overruling of its motion for a new trial are the same as those heretofore considered, discussed and determined. For that reason further discussion of the propriety of such rulings is neither necessary nor required.

The judgment is affirmed.

Reflection

In *Methodist Home*, the court is unable to call upon the decedent to ascertain her intentions for the obvious reason that she is dead. So, the court takes the next best approach and tries to determine what a reasonable person in the place of the decedent would have intended.

To determine the intention of a reasonable person, the court looks to case law. Fortunately for the disposition of this case, the exact matter has been litigated several times before. The court then effectively tallies up the number of analogous cases that found for the estate of the decedent versus the number of analogous cases that found for the old-age home, and it rules in favor of the decedent seemingly based on the sheer number of cases.

Fairness considerations will come to the forefront in the next section, where we consider terms implied from the duty of good faith and fair dealing.

Discussion

1. Are you comfortable with the court's approach in *Methodist Home*? Does its empirical approach approximate what a "reasonable" old-age home and its resident would intend? If the actual intention of the parties is the polestar of contract interpretation, has the court reasonably approximated that with its reasonable-person approach?

2. Consider your answer to the previous question in light of the reflections on *Congregation B'Nai Yitzhok*. If Rabbi Fisher were unavailable for testimony, could the court have determined his reasonable intentions by looking at other contracts for rabbinical services?

3. One issue with looking at precedent is that, by its very nature, it looks backwards at what has been done in the past. At times of great social, technological, industrial, or political change, does looking at precedent to determine the intentions of a reasonable person still come close enough to the actual intentions of the parties to be a valid means of determining whether to add terms to an agreement?

4. Another issue to consider is fairness. Do you think the court arrived at the correct result by refunding the decedent's money to the estate?

Problems

Problem 16.1. **Output of Toasted Bread**

Plaintiff Henry S. Levy & Sons, Inc., popularly known as Levy's, is a bakery, located first at Moore Street and Graham Avenue in Brooklyn, New York, and later on Park Avenue and 115 Thames Street, New York, NY. Levy's was famous for its cheesy bread and its rye bread, which was the subject of an offbeat advertisement campaign.

Figure 16.2. Levy's "you don't have to be Jewish" campaign was considered zany yet effective.

Defendant Crushed Toast Co. manufactures breadcrumbs. Interestingly, the term "breadcrumbs" does not refer to crumbs that may flake off bread; rather, they are a manufactured item, starting with stale or imperfectly appearing loaves and followed by removal of labels, processing through two grinders, the second of which effects a finer granulation, insertion into a drum in an oven for toasting and, finally, bagging of the finished product.

Levy's agreed to purchase "all breadcrumbs produced by Crushed Toast Co." Over the next several years, Crushed Toast Co. sold over 250 tons of breadcrumbs to Levy's.

But on May 15, 1969, the main oven at Crushed Toast Co. suddenly imploded, and the company thereafter stopped production of breadcrumbs.

Levy's brought suit, alleging that Crushed Toast Co. had a duty in good faith to repair its oven and to continue producing breadcrumbs for Levy's.

Crushed Toast Co. defended, alleging that the contract did not require defendant to manufacture breadcrumbs, but merely to sell those it did. Since none were produced after the demise of the oven, there was no duty to then deliver and, consequently from then on, no liability on its part.

Analyze both claims and discuss whether either of the parties should prevail upon a court and if so what remedies that court should award the prevailing party.

See Feld v. Levy and Sons, 37 N.Y.2d 466 (1975).

Problem 16.2. **Requirements for Corrugated Paper Boxes**

Plaintiff Fort Wayne Corrugated Paper Co. is a paper manufacturer that sells corrugated paper boxes.

Defendant Anchor Hocking Glass Corp. is a glass manufacturer that purchases and uses corrugated paper boxes to package and ship its glassware.

Defendant Anchor Glass, as buyer, entered into a written contract with Plaintiff Fort Wayne Paper, as seller, in which it was agreed that the buyer would buy not less than 90% of its entire needs of corrugated paper and solid fiber products from Fort Wayne as seller.

The buyer's needs were estimated to be 500 carloads of boxes per year.

The seller agreed to reserve production space for the manufacture of the buyer's requirements and not to make contracts for more than 50% of its production capacity. The contract was to continue for five years and thereafter until written notice of annulment was given by either party. During first two years following the making of this contract, the amount of purchases by the buyer increased from year to year.

In the third year, the contract was amended to change the proportion of its requirements which Anchor Glass agreed to buy from Fort Wayne Paper to not less than 75% of its needs. These needs were re-estimated to be approximately 800 carloads a year.

The parties did business under this arrangement satisfactorily up to the latter part of the fourth year. During the last few months of that year, there was a sudden recession of business so that the demand for glass containers fell off sharply, and from the combination of this and labor trouble at the Anchor Glass plant, there was a marked reduction in the business done there at the close of that year. It is found as a fact that the president and general manager concluded that Anchor could not hope for any substantial increase of business within a reasonably brief period of time.

In the fourth year, it was directed by resolution that operations at the plant should be suspended indefinitely. This direction was put into effect immediately. Anchor Glass promptly notified Fort Wayne Paper of its intention not to purchase any corrugated paper boxes in the fifth year of the contract.

The plaintiff, Fort Wayne Paper, brings the case upon its argument to the effect that Anchor Glass, as buyers of the plaintiff's product, were required as a matter of good faith under the contracts to continue purchasing a similar amount of corrugated paper boxes in the fifth year as it had in the first four years. Defendant Anchor Glass contends that it is under no liability, that the contract was a requirements contract, and having ceased having any requirements for plaintiff's paper boxes, they were under no obligation to take and pay for any of them.

Analyze both claims and discuss whether either of the parties should prevail upon a court, and if so, what remedies that court should award the prevailing party.

See *Fort Wayne Corrugated Paper Co. v. Anchor Hocking Glass Corp.*, 130 F.2d 471 (3d Cir. 1942).

Module VI
Performance and Breach

A contract (as a matter of law) is a set promises of performances that courts will enforce. (A contract-at-equity is a promise that courts will enforce because of some plus factor.) Promises, in turn, are manifestations to act or refrain from acting in a certain way; that is, promises are promises to perform. What, then, constitutes performance that fulfills a promissory obligation? In other words, when has a party performed its promissory obligation such that it is no longer legally liable under contract law?

Contracting parties usually are explicit about what obligations they expect one another to perform. When these obligations are unclear, ambiguous, and disputed, then courts may be called upon to interpret the meaning of these obligations. Interpretation of contractual meaning was the subject of the prior module. This module regards what happens when a party fails to receive the performance it expects.

Parties are usually wise to work out their disputes by negotiations, clarifications, cure, and assurances. Litigating in court is often the path of last resort. As French Enlightenment philosopher François-Marie Aroue, better known by his pen name Voltaire, is often quoted:

> I was never ruined but twice: once when I lost a lawsuit, and once when I won one.

Voltaire — a lawyer — thus quipped that lawsuits are prohibitively expense. Commercial lawyers are likewise wise to remember this old saw and counsel their clients to work out some accord before embroiling a business relationship with legal conflict.

R2d and UCC take a page from Voltaire's book by encouraging parties to work out their own differences. The doctrines of contractual performance that you will learn in this module are best understood in the context of such a legal framework that encourages private parties to help themselves get along.

R2d and UCC encourage parties' self-help via the application of three theoretical concepts in well established doctrine: first, parties generally intend for contractual promises to be mutual; second, mutual promises are generally intended to be conditions to each other; and third, the non-performance of a condition to a party's promise permits that party to withhold its performance. The result of these three applied concepts is that a party can lawfully threaten not to perform when its counterparty appears unwilling to perform its obligations. This threat of non-payment can itself encourage the counterparty to perform its obligation, without the parties needing to threaten to sue or to actually sue each other. Even if the counterparty is unable to perform its obligation, it might try and work things out through negotiations (e.g., I cannot do "X" that I promised to do in exchange for "Y", but, how about I do "A" in exchange for "B" instead?) instead of litigation.

Figure 17.1. François-Marie Arouet, Voltaire. Photograph by
E. Desmaisons, credit Wellcome Trust, CC-A 4.0

That said, some conflicts are unavoidable, and some relationships are irreparable. Courts are called upon to decide when parties may rightfully demand payment or refuse to perform pursuant to contractual obligations. Commercial lawyers must be able to reasonably foresee and predict how courts will respond to parties' arguments about failures in performance. In some instances, failure by one party permits the other party to withhold or cancel performance. In other instances, the aggrieved party must perform its obligations anyway. If a lawyer miscalculates and advises a client to wrongfully withhold performance, the client is now in breach, and the lawyer may be at fault.

Chapter 17

Conditions

To understand when performance is required and when it is not, lawyers and law students must first master the concept of conditions. A condition is an event that triggers a contractual obligation. A conditional promise, also known as a promise subject to a condition, is a promise to do some performance if a condition occurs. For example, Xavier says to LaVel, "I will wash and detail your car on Friday if it is not raining then in exchange for $50," and if LaVel agrees, Xavier has made a conditional promise. He must wash and detail LaVel's car only if it does not rain on Friday. If it is raining, the condition did not occur, and Xavier's obligation is not due. This stated condition is called an express condition.

Conditions may be express or implied. Most contracts are based on the implied conditions that both parties will perform their mutual obligations. The presumption of mutuality means that if one party is not ready and willing to perform, the other is not required to perform either, because each party's performance is conditional to the other's. In the prior example, if Xavier has a car detailing shop, courts might find that an implied condition to Xavier's performing is LaVel bringing his car to Xavier's shop. The parties did not discuss this, but a reasonable person would understand that car detailing would occur at the detail shop. Moreover, it's reasonable to assume that Xavier cannot detail the car if LaVel does not bring it.

Such performance of mutual obligations under a contract is generally implied to be conditional upon one another: a seller is only required to tender goods where the buyer is ready to pay for them; a general contractor is only required to pay its subcontractor when that subcontractor has finished its job; and an advertiser who promises a reward is only required to render it when a person completes the appointed task. In other words, contracts generally imply an exchange of promises, whereby one party's performance of its promise triggers the other's duty to perform.

Completely performing one's contractual obligations should obviously require the other party to perform its obligations, too. But what happens when performance is somewhat incomplete? For example, if an electrician is hired to install the electrical writing in a new-construction home, and if the electrician fails to install just one electrical outlet amid hundreds of outlets, switches, and receptacles, and if the error is discovered after the house is complete, when it is far too costly to install it, should the electrician be paid or not?

The answer to this question has legal consequences for both parties. If the electrician is entitled to payment despite the error, yet the builder refuses to pay the electrician, then the builder has breached its obligations and is liable under contract law. As a lawyer, you may ask whether one party's failure to completely perform its obligation obviates your client's obligation to pay. You must be prepared to analyze various situations and apply the rules of performance and breach to counsel clients on their actions and rights.

First, we examine express conditions, so you will understand how conditions (which are also known as contingencies) impact parties' duties to perform contract obligations. You will learn that one party's express conditions must be completely performed before the other party's obligations come due.

Second, we will discover implied conditions, which are commonly found when parties form a contract by exchanging promises to render some performance to each other. You will learn that implied conditions need only be substantially performed, and you will learn how to analyze whether one party's performance is substantial enough to require the other party to perform its contractual obligations. When one party has not substantially performed, we say that party has materially breached the contract.

Third, we will explore whether and when parties who have materially breached can cure their error and thus obtain their benefit of the bargain. The goal of contract law is not to punish people for minor transgressions. Rather, the goal of contract law is to ensure that parties receive the benefit of the bargains that they manifest an intention to perform and receive. The law gives parties an opportunity to cure material breaches, but this opportunity does not last forever. You will learn how to determine when a party has the right to cure its material breach. When that cure period has expired, we say that the party has totally breached, and is no longer entitled to receive its benefit of the bargain.

Fourth, we consider what parties must do when a counterparty refuses to perform before the time for performance is due. Imagine that the conference organizer invites a law professor to speak at a conference in New Hampshire in June, and the professor accepts. In April, the professor says he will be in Australia all of June. This could be interpreted as an anticipatory repudiation, an express statement that performance will not be forthcoming when it is due. Does the conference organizer have to wait until the conference is a flop and then sue the professor? Or may the organizers immediately declare the contract totally breached and then hire someone else to speak?

A subset of this issue involving repudiation occurs when a party shows an equivocal unwillingness or inability to perform in the future but does not make a formal act or statement declaring that it will not perform. For example, going bankrupt raises concerns about the bankrupt party's future ability to pay. If one party has reasonable insecurity about the other party's willingness and ability to perform, the insecure party may demand adequate assurances. If the assurances are insufficient or not forthcoming, then the failure to give assurances is treated like an anticipatory breach.

Fifth, and finally, there are cases where a court may not require performance because circumstances changed in an unforeseeable way that makes performance impossible or at least far more costly. This is known as impracticability, and it refers to situations where performance may be technically possible, but only at excessive cost, due to the unforeseeable and unfortunate circumstances. The final doctrine for this module is frustration of purpose, which occurs where an unforeseen event makes the value of performance virtually worthless. Parties often bear the risk that some event will impact the value of their benefit of the bargain, but excuse is granted in the exceptional cases where the unfortunate circumstances were unforeseen and the risk of them occurring was not expected to be borne by either party.

Rules

A. Conditional Obligations

A condition creates or extinguishes a contract obligation; it is an event which qualifies a contractual obligation.

> *A condition is an event, not certain to occur, which must occur, unless its non-occurrence is excused, before performance under a contract becomes due.* R2d § 224.

To understand conditions abstractly, think of a contract as a wired circuit with a power source, a switch, and a light bulb. The circuit exists whether or not the switch is on or off. This circuit is analogous to a contract that has been duly formed. But it does not function — that is, the light does not turn on — unless the switch is on. In our analogy to contracts, performance under this contract is not yet due because its conditional event did not yet occur.

A similar analogy is to a bank vault. The vault is "formed" and "completed" when it is built with a floor, four walls, a ceiling and a door. But that value is not secure until the door is closed and locked. Both an open bank vault and a closed bank vault are both vaults, but only the closed vault secures valuables.

Likewise, a contract with a condition exists, that is, the contract is formed. But the contract does not function in the sense that it does not create or "turn on" a contractual obligation until some condition occurs. In these analogies, illumination of the

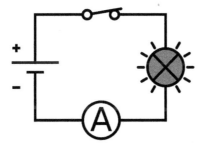

Figure 17.2. Circuit with power, amp meter, light, and switch.
Credit MikeRun. CC ASA 4 license.

bulb or security of the vault is the performance, which is dormant but ready to be activated at the flick of a switch or the lock of a door. Flicking the switch or locking the vault door is like the occurrence of a condition, which activates the conditional promise and causes a party's duty to come due.

B. Classes of Conditions

There are three forms of conditions in law, but they work in the same fundamental way. All conditions turn on or off some contractual duty. The difference between the three forms is when they operate:

Conditions precedent must occur before a duty in order to turn in on or make its performance come due.

Conditions concurrent must occur at the same time as a duty ought to be performed.

Conditions subsequent extinguish a duty by occurring at some time after the contract was formed and before it must be performed.

1. Condition Precedent: Sequential Performance

Precedent is a common word in law. Precedent typically refers to prior cases furnished as authority regarding how to decide a similar case. In commercial law, precedent refers to prior versions of a contract. The word precedent itself stems from the root precede, meaning "go before."

Similarly, a condition precedent must go before a related contractual obligation must be performed. For example, if Mason hires Wyatt to deliver a package, saying, "I will pay you twenty dollars after you deliver the package to 123 Main Street," then based on the parties' express words, Mason's promise to pay Wyatt is subject to the condition precedent that Wyatt delivers the package. Wyatt must deliver the package before Mason's obligation to pay comes due. This is an example of an express condition precedent. Express conditions must be completely performed. If Wyatt delivers the package to 122 Main Street, then Mason does not have to pay him.

Many contracts involve conditions, even where the parties do not necessarily express them as such. For example, if Jane hires Jill to mow her law, there is an implied condition precedent that Jill will mow the lawn before Jane has to pay Jill. If Jill fails to mow the lawn, Jane can sue Jill for breach of her promise to mow. But Jane has no obligations herself until Jill completes her performance. This is an example of an implied condition precedent. Later, we will explore what happens in this scenario if Jill does a mediocre but not failed job mowing the lawn, because implied conditions precedent are subject to the doctrine of substantial performance.

Terms in a contract can be promises, conditions, or both. In the first module, we learned that promises are binding manifestations to perform in some way. The failure to keep a promise can result in legal liability, because courts will enforce valid promises. Conditions, on the other hand, are not obligations in themselves but rather impact whether a related promise is obligatory. Promissory conditions are both in that promissory conditions must be performed lest they are breached, and promissory conditions also impact whether some other obligation is due.

In this case, Jill's performance is a promissory condition precedent, meaning that Jill has both made a promise to mow and given Jane a condition upon Jane's promise to pay. Jill has promised to mow the lawn and has an active contractual duty to do that; also, Jill mowing the lawn activates Jane's duty to pay. Promissory conditions precedent are commonly implied where one party performs a service that will take some time, and the other pays for the completed service.

2. Conditions Concurrent: Simultaneous Performances

Conditions concurrent always come in pairs. Both conditions concurrent shall occur at the same time. If one party is ready to perform and the other is not, the ready party is excused from performance. Such concurrent conditions are often found where parties agree to trade goods at some specific time.

For example, if Ben says to Cathy, "I will sell you my bicycle on Thursday for $45," and Cathy accepts, then the parties have agreed to perform mutual obligations at the same time. At the appointed time, Ben shall tender the bicycle, and Cathy shall pay Ben $45.

These acts of tendering the bicycle and paying $45 are conditions concurrent. They are meant to occur at the same time, and the failure of one to occur excuses the other's performance. If Cathy shows up without the money, or if she does not show up at all, then Ben does not have to tender the bicycle. His obligation to tender the bicycle did not come due (his performance "light bulb" did not turn on) because the condition to his obligation did not occur (the conditional "switch" remained off). Likewise, if Ben does not arrive with the bicycle, Cathy does not have to tender the money. The failure of one's promise excuses the performance of the other's.

Whether or not Ben and Cathy have legal liability for non-performance is a secondary matter. In addition to being conditions concurrent, Ben and Cathy's promise to tender the bicycle and pay the cash might also be promises. Later we will discuss such "promissory conditions," which doubly operate as both conditions and promises. Implied mutual promises, like an agreement to exchange goods for money on a certain date, are often intended to function as both promises and conditions at once.

3. Condition Subsequent: Excusing Performance

Conditions subsequent terminate a legal obligation if some event occurs. For example, it is typical in the sale of the house to have contingencies. The mortgage contingency typically states that, if the buyer cannot get a loan for a certain rate, then the buyer is no longer obligated to purchase the house.

Distinguishing between conditions precedent and conditions subsequent is somewhat of a philosophical exercise. One might ask, did the buyer really have an obligation to purchase the house until the mortgage contingency expired? In our light bulb analogy, conditions precedent are like starting with the light switch in the "on" position, where there is a possibility that some event will shut if off before performance is due.

As a purely technical matter, most conditions subsequent could be reengineered and formulated as conditions precedent. Instead of saying, buyer must buy the house unless you cannot obtain a mortgage, one might say, buyer must seek financing and buyer is obligated to purchase the house once buyer obtains a mortgage. "Unless" indicates a condition subsequent, while "once" indicates a condition precedent. The result is functionally the same, but there is a different emphasis on the expected outcome.

Another common example is, a man says to a barber, I will pay you for a haircut, unless I am dissatisfied with it. Semantically, this is a condition subsequent, since he has promised to pay *unless* some event occurs, in this case his dislike of the haircut, extinguishes his legal obligation.

Once again, we can restructure this as, I will pay you for a haircut if I like the finished product. The technical result is the same. We might say that the contractual "circuit" is wired the same way, only the situation stats with the switch and thus the light in different position. A condition precedent starts with the obligation in the "off" position, whereas a condition subsequent starts with the obligation in the "on" position. The technical effect is similar, if the not the same, but the rhetorical and emotional impact is different. Would you feel different if someone said, "You can practice law unless you fail the bar exam," versus, "You can only practice law if you pass the bar exam"? Some students respond that the first phrasing, which includes a condition subsequent, provides a higher expectation of receiving the result. Although, technically, both offers work the same way, the use of "if" versus "unless" tends to show the parties' intentions or expectations of that condition being met.

Conditions precedent may be express or implied where one party's performance must occur over some time, and the other party's performance is to begin or occur immediately when the first party's performance is complete. Conditions concurrent more commonly arise as implied conditions in an exchange of promises where mutual performances are to occur at the same time. Conditions subsequent are almost always found as express conditions, such as the contingences in a standard home purchase agreement, where the buyer can refuse to go forward with the purchase if he or she cannot obtain financing.

While it can sometimes be difficult to classify a particular condition as a condition precedent or a condition subsequent, usually, this classification does not make a significant impact on the legal analysis. The most critical thing to focus on is identifying what terms are conditions, what terms are promises, and what terms are both conditions and promises at once. We next look at express conditions because they are easier to spot, and then we apply these concepts to implied conditions.

C. Promissory Conditions

The tricky thing about conditions is identifying whether a term is a condition, a promise, or both. Arthur Corbin distinguished promises and conditions in his treatise on Contracts:

> *A promise in a contract creates a legal duty in the promisor and a right in the promisee; the fact or event constituting a condition creates no right or duty and is merely a limiting or modifying factor.*

Later we will exemplify this through a dispute regarding a home purchase example in *Morrison v. Bare*, where a buyer's obligation to purchase a home was conditional on the seller's repair of its furnace. In that case, the seller did not promise to repair the furnace; rather, the seller promised to sell the house, and the buyer promised to buy the house if the seller repairs the furnace. If the seller does not repair the furnace, then, the contractual "switch" is off, and the buyer does not have to perform his obligation of paying for the house. But the buyer cannot sue the seller for failing to repair the furnace. The buyer's options are limited to not purchasing the house, on the one hand, or waiving the condition and going forward with the purchase regardless.

Promises can be expressed similarly. If the buyer said, "I will buy the house if you promise to fix the furnace," there could be some debate whether the buyer intends the repair of the furnace to be a condition to the buyer's promise or an independent promise by the seller. In *Internationo-Rotterdam v. River Brand Rice Mills*, below. A rice mill agreed to sell rice to an international shipping company. The shipping contract specified as follows:

> *$8.25 F.A.S. Lake Charles and/or Houston, Texas*
>
> *Shipment to be December 1952 with two weeks call from buyer*

This merchant language requires some translation:

"F.A.S." means "freight alongside ship." This term means that the seller shall deliver the rice to the port next to the buyer's shipping vessel. The contract then provides two ports: Lake Charles, Texas, and Houston, Texas. The court interpreted this term to mean that the buyer must inform the seller as to which port to deliver the rice.

"Shipment . . . December 1952" means that the rice shall arrive at the designated port in December 1952.

"Two weeks call from buyer" means that buyer shall name the designated port at least two weeks before the delivery date. If the rice is to be delivered by the end of December 1952, then December 17, 1952, is the last date on which the buyer can specify the port.

The buyer failed to specify the port by December 17, and the seller then sold the rice to someone else. The buyer sued.

The parties did not dispute the meaning of these terms. Rather, the parties disputed whether the buyer made a promise to designate the port by December 17, 1952, or whether such designation was merely a condition to the seller's performance. The legal relevance is that, if the designation was a promise, then the buyer breached the contract, such that the seller has the right to sue the buyer for breach. If that designation was a condition, then the seller has no right to sue, since no promise to the seller was breached, although the seller also was not obligated to sell the rice to the buyer.

The court determined that the designation constituted a promissory condition. A promissory condition is both a promise and a condition.

Note there is an important distinction between a "conditional promise" and a "promissory condition." A conditional promise is a promise that only has to be performed if the relevant condition occurs. In *Morrison*, the buyer made a conditional promise to pay for the house; his promise to pay was conditioned on the repair of the furnace, and when the repair did not occur, Mr. Morrison was not obligated to buy the house.

A promissory condition, as described in *Internatio*, is both a promise and a condition. As a promise, it must be performed, lest the party who made that promise be liable for damages. As a condition, it also functions as a switch that turns on the other party's promise. To paraphrase Corbin, the non-performance of a promissory condition has a double operation: on the one hand preventing any instant duty and on the other creating a second duty to pay damages. In contrast, the non-occurrence of a pure promise only creates a duty to pay damages, while the non-occurrence of a pure condition only prevents any instant duty. A promissory condition thus performs the double function of both promises and conditions.

Courts should be reasonable in determining whether a term is intended to be a promise, a condition, or both (a promissory condition). This determination should be made in light of the purposes of promises and conditions.

> *The purpose of a promise is to create a duty in the promisor. The purpose of constituting some fact as a condition is always the postponement or discharge of an instant duty (or other specified legal relation).* Corbin on Contracts § 30.12.

A contractual promise creates a duty to perform what is promised, whereas a condition acts as switch that turns on or off that duty to perform. The function or impact of promises and conditions should also be taken into account when determining if a term is a promise or a condition.

> *The non-fulfillment of a promise is called a breach of contract and creates in the other party a secondary right to damages. It is the failure to perform a legal duty. The non-occurrence of a condition will prevent the existence of a duty in the other party; but it may not create any remedial rights and duties at all, and it will not unless someone has promised that it shall.* Corbin on Contracts § 30.12.

To recap: terms can be promises, conditions, or both. When they are both, they are called promissory conditions, and they have the double impact of creating a legal duty in another when promissory conditions are performed and creating a right to damages when they are not.

D. Express Conditions

Sometimes contracts are explicit or express about having conditions. Express conditions are ones that parties say or write into their contract, using conditional language such as "if," "on condition that," "provided that," "contingent upon," and other terms that reasonably mean parties intend promises to be conditional.

In *Morrison v. Bare*, below, a homebuyer and a seller entered into a written contract for sale of a house that contained a section titled "Special Conditions," under which it said, "Seller to repair furnace." This is an example of an express condition to a contact.

When Bare, the seller, accepted Morrison's offer, that formed a contract. But the buyer's obligation to perform under that contract was conditional on the seller's repair of the furnace, meaning, if the seller did not fix the furnace, the buyer did not have to buy the house. In other words, the buyer's obligation to purchase the house did not come due unless and until the furnace was repaired.

However, in these cases, the seller is not legally obligated to repair the furnace: note that in this simple hypothetical, the seller never promised to repair the furnace. Rather, the seller promised to sell the house, and the buyer promised to purchase the house if the seller repairs the furnace.

Express conditions are analytically simple: express conditions either occur or do not occur. In other words, express conditions are binary, like a simple light switch, which is either on or off. If the switch is off, the light is off; likewise, if the condition does not occur, the party's obligation is not due. When the switch comes on, the light turns on; likewise, when the condition occurs, the party must perform what it promised to do under the contract.

E. Implied Conditions

Most contracts contemplate an exchange of promises, whether or not the parties clearly express it. Think about it this way: if you agreed to purchase a car from a dealership, and on the appointed day, you arrived with cash in hand only to find the car had already been sold to someone else, you should not have to pay the dealer anyway. But why, as a matter of law, are you excused from performing this obligation? You made a promise to pay for the car, and that promise was binding under a contract. Recall that the Latin maxim, *pacta sunt servanda*, meaning "promises must be kept," is one of the oldest and most longstanding principles of law. We must figure out what allows deviation from this fundamental principle.

The answer to this riddle was articulated by Lord Mansfield in the 1773 case of *Kingston v. Preston*, excerpted in Chapter 18. The case arose where a silk merchant named Preston promised to sell his business to a man named Kingston, and Kingston agreed to post a bond that demonstrated his ability to pay for the business over time. Kingston never posted the bond, Preston refused to sell his business, and Kingston sued Preston. Lord Mansfield decided that Kingston was not obligated to sell his business until Preston posted the security bond because posting the bond was an implied condition to the sale:

> His Lordship then proceeded to say, that the dependance, or independence, of covenants, was to be collected from the evident sense and meaning of the parties, and, that, however transposed they might be in the deed, their precedency must depend on the order of time in which the intent of the transaction requires their performance.

Earlier, we learned that express conditions are like simple switches, which are either on or off. Now we add Lord Mansfield's concept of implied conditions. Should these conditions implied in law also function like simple on/off switches?

It turns out that the implied conditions that Lord Mansfield articulated in *Kingston v. Preston* are treated differently by courts than express conditions are. Express conditions must be strictly and completely performed, since they are terms of the contracts that represent the clearly manifested intentions of the parties. But implied conditions only need to be substantially performed. The doctrine of substantial performance was best articulated by Justice Cardozo in 1919 when he decided the famous case of *Jacob & Youngs v. Kent*, excerpted in Chapter 18.

F. Conditions of Satisfaction

Conditions are defined as events that are not certain to occur. The application of whether an objective event occurs is usually rather straightforward: whether the heat exchanger in a furnace is repaired or not (*Morrison*) or whether notification of delivery address occurred in time or not (*Internatio*) are not deep philosophical questions.

But what happens when the "event" is the satisfaction of a person? What evidence can a court review to determine whether a person is satisfied? And when the person who needs to be satisfied is also a promisor whose obligations to perform his promise will only come due if he is satisfied, does this create bad incentives?

A special issue arises when a party's contractual promise is conditional on its satisfaction with the other's performance. The special issues arising where one party's performance is conditional on its own satisfaction stem from the realistic problem that a party can lie about its subjective satisfaction with the other's performance; and, moreover, that party has strong incentives to lie where doing so can absolve it from legal liability. The law responded with special rules regarding how to deal with these so-called conditions of satisfaction.

These special rules regarding conditions of satisfaction generally do not apply when an impartial third party's satisfaction is at issue. For example, a general contractor's promise to pay a plumber for plumbing work could be conditioned on the state plumbing inspector's satisfaction of that work. So long as the inspector does not gain any personal reward for being satisfied or unsatisfied, we usually assume that inspector is impartial and will not use the condition to take advantage of one party or the other. After all, if the inspector has nothing to gain or lose regardless of whether the general contractor's duty to pay the plumber is due or not, then the law does not need to create a special situation to deal with bad behavior.

But when the contract is set up in a manner than actively encourages one party to take advantage of the other, then the law must develop new rules that reduce or eliminate the risk of this problem, so that parties to contracts do not fear that the law will facilitate their counterparties taking advantage of them.

As an initial matter, why would contracts ever have conditions of satisfaction? There are two different types of contracts in which conditions of satisfaction come up, and the law has two different rules for each.

The first situation in which conditions of satisfaction come up is in commercial agreements, such as the plumbing example above. As you will see, in commercial situations, courts generally apply a rule of "reasonable" satisfaction or "objective" satisfaction that asks whether a reasonable person in the position of the promisor would or should be satisfied with the performance. In the plumbing example, if the state inspector signs off on the plumbing work, it would probably be reasonable for the general contractor to be satisfied.

The second situation in which conditions of satisfaction come up is in agreements regarding personal or artistic matters. In such matters, there may not be a "reasonable" standard of satisfaction. As they say, one person's trash is another person's treasure; and there is no accounting for taste. When a reasonable or objective standard is not applicable as a matter of law, courts may then need to determine whether the promisor is actually satisfied in fact. This is known as "subjective" satisfaction.

Courts are very hesitant to apply a subjective standard to conditions of satisfaction. Remember that express conditions must be completely performed, otherwise the conditional promise does not have to be performed at all. This is a harsh result than can be unfair in part because of the problems with proving someone's subjective mindset.

Recall that conditions are defined as events that are not certain to occur. The application of whether an objective event occurs is usually rather straightforward: whether the heat exchanger in a furnace is repaired or not (*Morrison*) or whether notification of delivery address occurred in time or not (*Internatio*) are not deep philosophical questions.

But when the contract is set up in a manner than actively encourages one party to take advantage of the other, then the law must develop new rules that reduce or eliminate the risk of this problem, so that parties to contracts do not fear that the law will facilitate their counterparties taking advantage of them.

As an initial matter, why would contracts ever have conditions of satisfaction? There are two different types of contracts in which conditions of satisfaction come up, and the law has two different rules for each.

The first situation in which conditions of satisfaction come up is in commercial agreements, such as the plumbing example above. As you will see, in commercial situations, courts generally apply a rule of "reasonable" satisfaction or "objective" satisfaction that asks whether a reasonable person in the position of the promisor would or should be satisfied with the performance. In the plumbing example, if the state inspector signs off on the plumbing work, it would probably be reasonable for the general contractor to be satisfied.

The second situation in which conditions of satisfaction come up is in agreements regarding personal or artistic matters. In such matters, there may not be a "reasonable" standard of satisfaction. As they say, one person's trash is another person's treasure; and there is no accounting for taste. When a reasonable or objective standard is not applicable as a matter of law, courts may then need to determine whether the promisor is actually satisfied in fact. This is known as "subjective" satisfaction.

G. Non-Occurrence of a Condition

As a general matter, if a condition does not occur, then the promise subject to that condition does not need to be performed. The Restatement, however, also recognizes that sometimes this rule results in unfairness. To alleviate the unfairness of the strict performance rule, the Restatement provides that judges may excuse the non-occurrence of a condition. Such excuse of a condition is functionally equivalent to its occurrence.

Performance of a duty subject to a condition cannot become due unless the condition occurs or its non-occurrence is excused. R2d § 225(1).

Note that excuse of a condition is distinguishable from its waiver. Excuse is something that courts do as an equitable matter to ensure justice. Waiver is something parties do. The next R2d section deals with when courts should excuse the non-occurrence of a condition. Before it gets there, however, this section of R2d further explains that non-occurrence of a condition can also discharge a duty.

Unless it has been excused, the non-occurrence of a condition discharges the duty when the condition can no longer occur. R2d § 225(2).

The difference between discharging a duty and a duty not becoming due is a matter of timing and permanence. Some duty that has not become due yet can still become due in the future. Some duty that has been discharged, however, will never become due. As you will see in the next chapter on substantial performance, this concept is similar to the ideas around partial and total breach. Partial breach occurs when a party has substantially failed to meet a contractual obligation but still has time to remedy or cure that failure. Total breach occurs when one party's failure has become irredeemable, and the other party gains the right to cancel the contract.

Likewise here, there is some time when a condition has not occurred but still might occur. During this time, the promise subject to that condition is not due, but it will become due when the condition occurs. The party whose promise is subject to the condition must then remain prepared to perform. When a condition can no longer occur, however, the party no longer has to remain prepared to perform and is thus free to contract with someone else.

How long must a party who has made a conditional promise wait in this limbo state before that promisor can rest assured that performance of that conditional promise will never come due? The answer is, of course, it depends. Consider these two illustrations

> *Illustration 225.1. A contracts to sell and B to buy A's business. The contract provides that B is to pay in installments over a five-year period following the conveyance, and that A is to convey on condition that B pledge specified collateral to secure his payment. Conveyance by A does not become due until B pledges the collateral. If the agreement does not provide for the time within which the collateral is to be pledged, A's duty is discharged if it is not pledged within a reasonable time.*

> *Illustration 225.2. B gives A $10,000 to use in perfecting an invention, and A promises to repay it only out of royalties received during his lifetime from the sale of the patent rights. In spite of diligent efforts, A is unable to perfect his invention and obtain a patent, and no royalties are received. A dies after six years. B has no claim against A's estate. Receipt of royalties is a condition of A's duty to repay the money and A's duty is discharged by the non-occurrence of that condition during his lifetime.*

As these illustrations show, courts will sometimes provide a reasonable time during which a condition can still occur and thus trigger a promise to perform to come due. In other cases, the contract itself may offer a time period after which the duty to perform is forever discharged.

Finally, R2d § 225 reminds us that pure conditions are not promises, so the non-occurrence of a pure condition is not a breach. The non-occurrence of a promissory condition, however, is a breach:

> *Non-occurrence of a condition is not a breach by a party unless he is under a duty that the condition occur. R2d § 225(3).*

H. Express and Implied Conditions

In the prior section, we reviewed how an event is made a condition by agreement of the parties. In the next chapter, we will review how an event is made a condition by operation of law; in particular, we will look at the implied condition of substantial performance. This section simply states that both of these ways of creating conditions are valid in Restatement jurisdictions.

> *An event may be made a condition either by the agreement of the parties or by a term supplied by the court. R2d § 226.*

Comments and illustrations for R2d § 226 indicate that the use of language such as "on condition that," "provided that," and "if" are common ways for parties to make events conditions through their agreement. But it also states that use of such language is not necessary or even dispositive as to creating conditions. Whether a condition has been made by agreement of the parties requires an analysis of the terms and circumstances of their contracts, just like other matters of contractual interpretation do.

I. Satisfaction of the Obligor as a Condition

One special kind of condition is a condition of satisfaction, where one party's performance is dependent on its or another's satisfaction. Satisfaction is somewhat subjective in that whether a person is actually satisfied is a personal matter. This creates a problem for contract law, which prefers objective evidence. The solution, as you will see, is that conditions of satisfaction are treated objectively to the extent possible by asking not whether the party is actually satisfied but whether a reasonable person in the party's position should be satisfied.

There are two different standards of satisfaction. The first, and preferred, standard is that of reasonable or objective satisfaction. The second standard is that of honest or subjective satisfaction.

> *When it is a condition of an obligor's duty that he be satisfied with respect to the obligee's performance or with respect to something else, and it is practicable to determine whether a reasonable person in the position of the obligor would be satisfied, an interpretation is preferred under which the condition occurs if such a reasonable person in the position of the obligor would be satisfied. R2d § 228.*

No matter which standard is applied, conditions of satisfaction are subject to the requirement that parties to a contract act with good faith and fair dealing toward one another regarding their contractual obligations. This means that a party cannot claim dissatisfaction to receive a material advantage over a contract counterparty even where the standard is subjective.

Recall the case of *Ard*. In that case, the court found that Dr. Pepper's promise to license its soft drink syrup formula to Ard was conditional on Dr. Pepper's subjective satisfaction with Ard's performance. The court found that Dr. Pepper rightfully withheld its promise to pay where it was honestly dissatisfied with Ard's efforts to sanitize its bottling plant and to promote Dr. Pepper's product in the relevant territory. But if Dr. Pepper had actually wanted to dismiss Ard because another bottler was willing to do the same work at a cheaper rate, and if Dr. Pepper claimed to be dissatisfied with Ard's performance where it was actually looking only to increase its profits, then even the subjective standard of satisfaction would not protect Dr. Pepper's refusal to continue to license its product to Ard.

J. Excuse of a Condition to Avoid Forfeiture

Courts are aware that express conditions can lead to harsh and unfair results because, if such express conditions are not completely performed, then the conditional promise does not need to be performed either. Courts have equitable powers to avoid this unfair result where express conditions result in disproportionate forfeiture.

> *To the extent that the non-occurrence of a condition would cause disproportionate forfeiture, a court may excuse the non-occurrence of that condition unless its occurrence was a material part of the agreed exchange.* R2d § 229.

As stated in the comments to R2d § 229, "forfeiture" is used to refer to the denial of compensation that results when the obligee loses his right to the agreed exchange after he has relied substantially, as by preparation or performance on the expectation of that exchange. But not every forfeiture is disproportionate, as the two illustrations under this aspect of the rule attempt to make clear:

> *Illustration 229.1. A contracts to build a house for B, using pipe of Reading manufacture. In return, B agrees to pay $75,000 in progress payments, each payment to be made "on condition that no pipe other than that of Reading manufacture has been used." Without A's knowledge, a subcontractor mistakenly uses pipe of Cohoes manufacture which is identical in quality and is distinguishable only by the name of the manufacturer which is stamped on it. The mistake is not discovered until the house is completed, when replacement of the pipe will require destruction of substantial parts of the house. B refuses to pay the unpaid balance of $10,000. A court may conclude that the use of Reading rather than Cohoes pipe is so relatively unimportant to B that the forfeiture that would result from denying A the entire balance would be disproportionate, and may allow recovery by A subject to any claim for damages for A's breach of his duty to use Reading pipe.*

> *Illustration 229.2. A, an ocean carrier, carries B's goods under a contract providing that it is a condition of A's liability for damage to cargo that "written notice of claim for loss or damage must be given within 10 days after removal of goods." B's cargo is damaged during carriage and A knows of this. On removal of the goods, B notes in writing on the delivery record that the cargo is damaged, and five days later informs A over the telephone of a claim for that damage and invites A to participate in an inspection within the ten day period. A inspects the goods within the period, but B does not give written notice of its claim until 25 days after removal of the goods. Since the purpose of requiring the condition of written notice is to alert the carrier and enable it to make a prompt investigation, and since this purpose had been served by the written notice of damage and the oral notice of claim, the court may excuse the non-occurrence of the condition to the extent required to allow recovery by B.*

In the first of these two illustrations, the Restatement is summarizing the key case in the next module, which will be discussed in great detail there. In that case, Justice Cardozo transmogrified the express condition in the parties' written agreement into an implied one such that it would be subject to the lower standards of "material" achievement of an implied condition to trigger corresponding duties to come due. This will not make sense at least until you read that famous case, and it might not make sense even after that.

In the second of these two illustrations, the Restatement summarizes a more readily comprehensible case, where the purpose of the condition is accomplished but where a party wants to take advantage of its counterparty regardless.

K. Event that Terminates a Duty

Finally, the restatement acknowledges that in addition to conditions precedent (which seem to be the general subject of this section) there are also conditions subsequent, the occurrence of which terminate a duty that otherwise exists.

Recall that conditions precedent are events the occurrence of which turn on the duty to perform a contractual promise whereas a condition subsequent turns off such duties.

> *Except as stated in Subsection (2), if under the terms of the contract the occurrence of an event is to terminate an obligor's duty of immediate performance or one to pay damages for breach, that duty is discharged if the event occurs.* R2d § 230(1).

R2d does not use the term "condition subsequent" in this rule, although it does reference this term in its comments. Despite the semantics, the impact is the same.

However, the condition subsequent does not operate effectively where one party behaved badly through bad faith or unfair dealing:

> *The obligor's duty is not discharged if occurrence of the event is the result of a breach by the obligor of his duty of good faith and fair dealing,* R2d § 230(2)(a).

In other words, a party cannot be relieved of its own obligation by its own bad actions in bad faith or unfair dealing.

Courts may likewise decide not to recognize the occurrence of a condition subsequent when doing so would impose an unfair burden on one party. This is similar to the doctrine on excuse of a condition that you learned earlier.

> *The obligor's duty is not discharged if occurrence of the event could not have been prevented because of impracticability and continuance of the duty does not subject the obligor to a materially increased burden.* R2d § 230(2)(b).

In other words, conditions can either be excused or enforced to avoid injustice through unfair burdens. Parties may evidence this injustice by showing reliance on the obligation. When a party relied on an obligation, and where the other party claims that obligation is discharged because of the occurrence of a condition subsequent, courts might enforce the obligation anyway to avoid injustice.

> *The obligor's duty is not discharged if, before the event occurs, the obligor promises to perform the duty even if the event occurs and does not revoke his promise before the obligee materially changes his position in reliance on it.* R2d § 230(3).

L. Reflections on Conditions

Conditions are a fundamental part of how contracts work. Conditions are like switches that turn duties to perform contractual promises on or off. As a default, conditions are not promises, meaning the failure to perform a condition is not itself a breach. But some conditions are also promises, which means one party has an enforceable obligation to perform that promissory condition, while its nonperformance excuses the other party from performing its promise in exchange.

Conditions may be express or implied. Express conditions arise from the parties' oral and written manifestations. R2d states that courts may imply conditions even where they are not express in the written or spoken terms of the parties' agreement. Courts generally infer that promises are mutual, which is to say that the parties' promises are implied conditions concurrent to each other.

Express conditions are subject to the doctrine of strict performance. Express conditions must be completely and totally performed in order for the conditional promise to come due for performance. In our electrical analogy, an express condition is like an on/off switch, which is always in one position or the other. Such a switch must be entirely in the on position for the lamp to become illuminated; likewise, an express condition must be completely performed for the conditional promise to come due for performance.

Implied conditions are subject to the doctrine of substantial performance. Implied mutual promises and the doctrine of substantial performance are the key concepts in the next chapter.

Cases

Reading Morrison v. Bare. Our first case about conditions, *Morrison*, illustrates a clear example of a condition. In this case regarding the purchase and sale of a house, the real estate purchase agreement had a section titled "Special Conditions." In this section, the parties wrote that the seller would provide to the buyer a copy of a repair bill for the furnace.

This case is useful not only for its facts and analysis thereof, but also for its thorough description of the law of conditions. The Ohio Court of Appeals quotes and discusses treatises by Corbin, Williston, Murray, and Farnsworth and the Restatement (Second) of Contracts as those materials pertain to conditions and their impact.

As you will read in the case below, the seller tried (and failed) to argue that he was only supposed to furnish a bill, but not necessarily one that showed that a cracked heat exchanger (which is part of a furnace that heats the house) was repaired. Reflect back on the Canons of Construction and think about why the seller's position did not reflect a reasonable interpretation of the written agreement. In any event, the court dismissed this semantic gambit by the seller, so do not let that quibble distract you from the main point of this case.

The main point of reading this case is to understand what happens when a condition does not occur. To understand this point, pay careful attention to what remedies the plaintiff wanted. Note that the buyer, Mr. Morrison, is the plaintiff. The buyer is also the appellant, signifying that he must have lost at trial.

At trial, the buyer Mr. Morrison asked to court for an order of specific performance, meaning, the buyer wanted the court to require the seller to sell the house to him. Moreover, the buyer wanted the price to be the contract price minus the cost of repairing the furnace.

The court correctly refused to require the seller to sell the house at a lower cost, because that is not how conditions function. Conditions are not independent promises, where the failure to bring about such independent promises could be a breach that results in an award of money damages that equals the cost of the breach. Rather, conditions are merely switches, which turn on or off contractual promises.

Since the condition did not occur in this case, the buyer's promise to buy the house was not turned on, and the buyer could rightfully refuse to conclude the purchase. Or the buyer could waive the non-occurrence of this condition and conclude the purchase anyway pursuant to the original terms. But the buyer had no right to demand that the seller sell the house at a lower price than they originally agreed.

As you read this case, highlight the specific language that shows that the seller did not guarantee, warrant, or otherwise promise to fix the furnace. This language made clear that the condition was not a promise. You will want to compare this with the next case, *Internatio*, where the condition was a promise. Such a combination of condition and promise is called a "promissory condition." Why was the condition in *Morrison* not a promise whereas the condition in *Internatio* was?

Morrison v. Bare

2007-Ohio-6788 (Ohio Ct. App. 2007)

DICKINSON, J.

Introduction

Jack W. Morrison Jr. is in the business of buying houses, refurbishing them, and renting them to college students. Tom Campensa, a real estate agent, showed Mr. Morrison a house owned by Jonas Bare. Mr. Morrison noticed a sticker on the furnace that indicated it had a cracked heat exchanger. After checking with Mr. Bare, Mr. Campensa told Mr. Morrison that the furnace had been repaired in 2004.

Mr. Morrison executed a contract to purchase the house, but included a "special condition" in the contract that Mr. Bare would provide him a copy of the 2004 furnace repair bill within 14 days.

Mr. Bare supplied a copy of a 2004 bill for repairs, but those repairs did not include replacing the heat exchanger.

Instead of closing on the house, Mr. Morrison sued Mr. Bare for specific performance and breach of contract and sued Mr. Bare, Mr. Campensa, and Mr. Campensa's real estate agency for fraud.

The trial court granted summary judgment to all three defendants, and Mr. Morrison appealed. His sole assignment of error is that the trial court incorrectly granted the defendants summary judgment.

This court affirms the trial court's judgment because: (1) Mr. Morrison neither performed his part of the contract nor showed his "readiness and ability" to do so; (2) the requirement that Mr. Bare provide a bill showing that the heat exchanger was repaired was a condition for Mr. Morrison's performance, not a promise; and (3) Mr. Morrison did not justifiably rely upon Mr. Campensa's statement that the heat exchanger had been repaired.

Background

Mr. Morrison noticed a for-sale sign on the house at issue in this case and told Mr. Campensa he would like to look at it. Mr. Campensa walked through the house with Mr. Morrison and Mr. Morrison's father. The house was in disrepair, and the utilities were disconnected. During the walkthrough, Mr. Morrison noticed a sticker on the furnace that indicated it had a cracked heat exchanger. When he was deposed, he said the sticker had caused him concern because he knew that a cracked heat exchanger meant the furnace would have to be replaced. He further testified that he questioned Mr. Campensa about the heat exchanger and Mr. Campensa said that he would check with the seller, Mr. Bare, to see whether it had been fixed.

At some point after the walkthrough, Mr. Campensa talked to Mr. Bare about the furnace. Mr. Campensa testified that he told Mr. Bare that the furnace had a sticker on it indicating that it had a cracked heat exchanger and that Mr. Bare told him the furnace had been repaired. Mr. Bare testified that he did not recall whether Mr. Campensa had specifically mentioned the cracked heat exchanger, but that he had told Mr. Campensa the furnace had been repaired. Either way, Mr. Morrison and Mr. Campensa agree that Mr. Campensa told Mr. Morrison that the heat exchanger had been repaired.

Mr. Morrison did a second walkthrough of the house, this time with an inspector. He testified that his purpose for having the inspector look at the house with him was to try to estimate the cost of needed repairs and to "generally just look[] around the property." The utilities were still off at the time of his second walkthrough. During the second walkthrough, Mr. Morrison concluded that the kitchen floor would have to be replaced. He and his inspector also noted some problems with windows and drywall. They looked at the sticker on the furnace, but did not attempt to independently determine whether the heat exchanger had been repaired.

Following his second walkthrough, Mr. Morrison made a written offer to purchase the house for $40,000, using a form real estate purchase agreement. The form included a provision permitting Mr. Morrison to have the house inspected and, if not satisfied, to notify Mr. Bare within fourteen days of the date of the agreement. If any unsatisfactory conditions could not be resolved, Mr. Morrison could void the agreement or accept the property in its "as is" condition. The form further provided that, if Mr. Morrison did not have the home inspected or did not notify Mr. Bare of any unsatisfactory conditions, he would take the property in its "as is" condition.

Under the heading "Special Conditions," Mr. Morrison wrote: "Seller to supply buyer with copy of furnace repair bill from 2004 within 14 days." Mr. Campensa acknowledged at his deposition that the purpose of the "special condition" was to allow Mr. Morrison to satisfy himself that the heat exchanger had been repaired. At the same time he signed the written offer, Mr. Morrison also signed a property disclosure form in which he acknowledged that he was purchasing the property "as is."

Four days after he made his written offer, Mr. Morrison signed an amendment to that offer, removing his right to inspect the property. The amendment further provided that Mr. Morrison recognized that neither Mr. Bare nor Mr. Campensa was warranting the property in any manner:

> *In exercising or waiving their right to inspect, the Buyer(s) are not relying upon any representation about the property made by the Seller(s), Broker(s), Agent(s), other than those representations specified in the purchase agreement. The Buyer(s) understand that the Seller(s), Broker(s), Agent(s), and/or inspector(s) do not warrant or guarantee the condition of the property in any manner whatsoever.*

Three days later, Mr. Bare signed both the form purchase agreement and the amendment, thereby accepting Mr. Morrison's offer to purchase the house.

Prior to the date set for closing, Mr. Campensa obtained a copy of the 2004 furnace repair bill. That bill indicated that repairs totaling $234 had been made to the furnace, but that the heat exchanger had not been repaired. In fact, it included a quote to replace the furnace for $1600 and a notation that, if a new furnace was installed within 30 days, the $234 for repairs would be deducted from the cost of the new furnace.

Mr. Campensa telephoned Mr. Morrison and told him that the heat exchanger had not been repaired. At that point, Mr. Morrison told Mr. Campensa that he would close on the house only if Mr. Bare either replaced the furnace or reduced the purchase price in an amount equal to what it would cost to replace the furnace. Mr. Bare was unwilling to do either.

Mr. Campensa sent Mr. Morrison a copy of the bill, along with a proposed addendum to the purchase agreement. The proposed addendum provided that Mr. Morrison agreed to accept the property with the furnace "in its as is condition and assume all responsibility for its repair and/or replacement." Mr. Morrison refused to execute the proposed addendum.

Prior to the date set for closing, Mr. Morrison filed his complaint in this case. Mr. Bare subsequently sold the house to another purchaser, who refurbished it and rented it to college students.

This Court's Standard of Review

Mr. Morrison's sole assignment of error is that the trial court incorrectly granted the defendants summary judgment. In reviewing an order granting summary judgment, this Court applies the same test a trial court is required to apply in the first instance: whether there are any genuine issues of material fact and whether the moving party is entitled to judgment as a matter of law.

Mr. Morrison's Contract Claims

By his first cause of action, Mr. Morrison alleged that he was entitled to specific performance of his contract with Mr. Bare. In order to be entitled to specific performance of a contract, a plaintiff must either have performed his part of the contract or show his "readiness and ability" to do so. Mr. Morrison did neither. He had not paid the purchase price for the property and he had told Mr. Campensa that he was unwilling to do so unless Mr. Bare replaced the furnace or reduced the purchase price. As discussed below, the contract did not require Mr. Bare to replace the furnace or reduce the purchase price. Accordingly, Mr. Morrison is not entitled to specific performance.

Additionally, by the time the trial court granted summary judgment in this case, the property had been sold to a third party. When property has been transferred to a bona fide purchaser, specific performance is not available. Mr. Morrison has not argued that the person who purchased the property from Mr. Bare was not a bona fide purchaser. Accordingly, this is a second reason he is not entitled to specific performance.

By his second cause of action, Mr. Morrison sought damages for breach of contract. Mr. Bare has argued that the "special condition" was satisfied when he provided Mr. Morrison a copy of the 2004 bill for repairs to the furnace, even though, instead of showing that the heat exchanger had been repaired, it showed that it had not been repaired.

There can be no doubt that, in order to satisfy the "special condition" that Mr. Morrison included in his offer, the repair bill had to show that the heat exchanger had been repaired. Mr. Campensa, who was Mr. Bare's agent, acknowledged that the purpose of the "special condition" was to allow Mr. Morrison to satisfy himself that the heat exchanger had been fixed:

> Q. *All right. On line 103 it says, "Seller to supply buyer with copy of furnace repair bill from 2004 within 14 days," correct?*
>
> A. *Correct.*
>
> Q. *Why was that provision put in the contract?*
>
> A. *Because there was the potential that that was cracked in there was a cracked thing and Jack wanted to know if it was fixed or not.*
>
> Q. *Okay. Because you believed it had been repaired based on your conversation with Jonas Bare, correct?*
>
> A. *Yes.*
>
> Q. *And you had told Jack that it had been repaired, did you not?*
>
> A. *Yes.*
>
> Q. *So Jack wanted to make sure as part of this deal that that furnace had already been repaired, correct?*
>
> A. *Correct.*

Mr. Bare's argument that he satisfied the condition by supplying a bill showing that the heat exchanger had not been repaired is, at best, disingenuous. Both parties knew at the time they entered the contract that the bill Mr. Bare needed to supply to satisfy the "special condition" was a bill showing that the heat exchanger had been repaired.

That, however, does not mean that Mr. Bare breached the purchase agreement by not delivering a bill that showed the heat exchanger had been repaired and by not replacing the furnace or lowering the purchase price. To begin with, the contract does not include a promise by Mr. Bare that, if the heat exchanger was not repaired in 2004, he would replace the furnace or reduce the purchase price. Further, the "special condition" that Mr. Morrison included in the contract was just that, a condition, not a promise:

> [P]romise and condition are very clearly different in character. One who makes a promise thereby expresses an intention that some future performance will be rendered and gives assurance of its rendition to the promisee. Whether the promise is express or implied, there must be either words or conduct by the promisor by the interpretation of which the court can discover promissory intention; a condition is a fact or an event and is not an expression of

intention or an assurance. A promise in a contract creates a legal duty in the promisor and a right in the promisee; the fact or event constituting a condition creates no right or duty and is merely a limiting or modifying factor. 8 Catherine M.A. McCauliff, Corbin On Contracts, Section 30.12 (rev. ed. 1999).

Mr. Campensa told Mr. Morrison that the heat exchanger had been repaired. Mr. Morrison made his offer to purchase the house contingent upon receiving proof that it had been:

> *In contract law, "condition" is an event, other than the mere lapse of time, that is not certain to occur but must occur to <u>activate</u> an existing contractual duty, unless the condition is excused. The fact or event properly called a condition occurs during the <u>performance</u> stage of a contract, i.e., after the contract is formed and prior to its discharge.* John Edward Murray Jr., Murray on Contracts, Section 99B (4th ed. 2001) (emphasis in original)

While the failure to perform a promise is a breach of contract, the failure to satisfy a condition is not:

> *A promise is always made by the act or acts of one of the parties, such acts being words or other conduct expressing intention. A fact can be made to operate as a condition only by the agreement of both parties or by the construction of the law. The purpose of a promise is to create a duty in the promisor. The purpose of constituting some fact as a condition is always the postponement or discharge of an instant duty (or other specified legal relation). The non-fulfillment of a promise is called a breach of contract, and creates in the other party a secondary right to damages. It is the failure to perform a legal duty. The non-occurrence of a condition will prevent the existence of a duty in the other party; but it may not create any remedial rights and duties at all, and it will not unless someone has promised that it shall occur.* Corbin On Contracts, at Section 30.12.

The fact that, to satisfy the "special condition," Mr. Bare would have had to do something (supply the bill showing that the heat exchanger had been repaired) did not mean that it was a promise rather than a condition. A condition can be an act to be done by one of the parties to the contract:

> *Virtually any act or event may constitute a condition. The event may be an act to be performed or forborne by one of the parties to the contract, an act to be performed or forborne by a third party, or some fact or event over which neither party, or any other party, has any control.* Murray on Contracts, at Section 99C.

In this case, Mr. Bare had partial control over the condition. Even if he had a bill showing that the heat exchanger had been repaired in 2004, he could have chosen not to deliver it to Mr. Morrison, in which case the condition would not have been satisfied. It also, however, was partially out of his control. Since the heat exchanger had not been repaired in 2004, he was unable to satisfy the condition. The material part of the condition was that Mr. Morrison had to be satisfied that the heat exchanger had been repaired.

Section 225 of the Restatement (Second) of Contracts (1981) describes the consequences of the non-occurrence of a condition:

> (1) *Performance of a duty subject to a condition cannot become due unless the condition occurs or its non-occurrence is excused.*
>
> (2) *Unless it has been excused, the non-occurrence of a condition discharges the duty when the condition can no longer occur.*
>
> (3) *Non-occurrence of a condition is not a breach by a party unless he is under a duty that the condition occur.*

In this case, Mr. Morrison's duty to pay the purchase price did not come due because Mr. Bare could not produce a 2004 bill showing that the heat exchanger had been repaired. Once it became clear that it was impossible for Mr. Bare to produce such a bill, Mr. Morrison could have excused the condition and closed on the property. Alternatively, he could have treated his duty to close as discharged and the contract terminated:

> *[I]f a time comes when it is too late for the condition to occur, the obligor is entitled to treat its duty as discharged and the contract as terminated.* II E. Allan Farnsworth, Farnsworth On Contracts, Section 8.3 (3rd ed. 2004).

By informing Mr. Campensa that he was unwilling to close on the house unless Mr. Bare replaced the furnace or reduced the purchase price, Mr. Morrison chose to treat his duty to pay the original purchase price as discharged and the contract as terminated. His proposal to go forward under different conditions was, in effect, an offer to enter into a new contract; a new contract that Mr. Bare was free to reject, which he did.

Upon the failure of the "special condition" that he included in the real estate purchase agreement, Mr. Morrison treated the agreement as terminated, as he was entitled to do. The failure of the "special condition" was not a breach of contract.

There are no genuine issues of material fact, and Mr. Bare is entitled to judgment as a matter of law on Mr. Morrison's demand for specific performance and on his breach of contract claim. To the extent Mr. Morrison's assignment of error is addressed to the trial court's summary judgment on his contract claims, it is overruled.

Mr. Morrison's Fraud Claim

[Discussion of Morrison's fraud claim omitted.]

III.

Mr. Morrison's assignment of error is overruled. The judgment of the Summit County Common Pleas Court is affirmed.

Judgment affirmed.

Reflection

The *Morrison* case shows that conditions are not promises; that is, the failure to cause a condition to occur is not a breach of a promise. Rather, conditions are merely switches that cause another contractual promise to be due for performance or not.

Many sophisticated agreements distinguish between "buyer's conditions" and "seller's conditions." For example, in the standard form for the purchase and sale of preferred stock between a startup company and a venture capital investment firm, there are two sections named "Conditions to the Purchasers' Obligations at Closing" and "Conditions of the Company's Obligations at Closing." If any of the Conditions to the Purchasers' Obligations do not occur, then the venture capital investment firm is not required to purchase the stock. If any of the Conditions to the Company's Obligations do not occur, then the startup company is not obligated to sell. Alternatively, each side can waive the non-occurrence of its own conditions and thereby require the other party to close anyway. But neither party can sue the other for the non-occurrence of a condition.

It may be helpful to think of conditions as if they are owned by one party to the contract or the other. In the preferred stock purchase example above, the Conditions to the Purchaser's Obligations are, in a sense, held by the buyer. Like cards in a player's hand, the condition can be played or ignored by its holder. Likewise, we might frame the condition in *Morrison* (providing a bill showing that the furnace was repaired) as being owned by the buyer, Mr. Morrison. When the furnace was not repaired, Mr. Morrison held this condition like a card that he could play (thereby extinguishing his obligation to purchase the house) or ignore (allowing the transaction to go through). To be clear, this is a valuable option. As the holder of a condition that did not occur, Mr. Morrison had the option to ignore its non-occurrence and effectively give away his rights not to purchase the house. This is referred to as "waiving" the condition.

This ability to waive a condition or not gives its holder leverage or power to force a re-negotiation in some instances. Here, Mr. Morrison essentially offered to "trade" this condition with the seller in exchange for a lower purchase price. This was an offer to modify a contract that was supported by new consideration. We learn about modification of contracts obligations in Chapter 21 — Assent; for now, simply note that Mr. Morrison's offer would have resulted in a lower purchase price if Mr. Bare had accepted it. If Mr. Bare really wanted to sell his house quickly, the parties could have thereby agreed to buy and sell the house with a broken furnace for a lower price.

But that is not how Mr. Bare responded to Mr. Morrison offer. Rather, Mr. Bare rejected the offer to modify their agreement. That left Mr. Morrison with two options: waive the condition and conclude the sale on the original terms promised; or assert that his obligations to purchase the house were not due because the condition had not occurred and walk away from the deal. The key point in this case was that Mr. Morrison did not have a third option to force Mr. Bare to sell the house for less money. That is just not how conditions work as a matter of law.

Discussion

1. The court ruled that the term regarding fixing the heat exchanger was a condition and not a promise. How should the buyer have revised the contract if he intended that term to be a promise?

2. Was one party in this case trying to "pull a fast one" over the other? Do you see any evidence of bad faith or unfair dealing? If so, how does that factor into the court's resolution of this case?

Reading Internatio-Rotterdam, Inc. v. River Brand Rice Mills, Inc. In the *Morrison* case above, the court found that the "Special Condition" was just that: a condition and not a promise. But it is possible for courts to determine that a term in a contract is both a condition and a promise. Such terms are called "promissory conditions," and they perform both the function of a promise (which when breached gives rise to damages) and of a condition (the non-occurrence of which means that a conditional promise does not need to be performed).

Note there is an important distinction between a "conditional promise" and a "promissory condition." A conditional promise is a promise that only has to be performed if the relevant condition occurs. In *Morrison* above, the buyer Mr. Morrison made a conditional promise to pay for the house; his promise to pay was conditioned on the repair of the furnace, and when the repair did not occur, Mr. Morrison was not obligated to buy the house.

A promissory condition, as described in *Internatio* below, is both a promise and a condition. As a promise, it must be performed, lest the party who made that promise be liable for damages. As a condition, it also functions as a switch that turns on the other party's promise. As you read this case, make sure to highlight and annotate what is the promissory condition and how the courts finds this term has the features of both a promise and a condition.

Internatio-Rotterdam, Inc. v. River Brand Rice Mills, Inc.

259 F.2d 137 (2d Cir. 1958)

HINCKS, Circuit Judge.

Appeal from the United States District Court, Southern District of New York, Walsh, Judge, upon the dismissal of the complaint after plaintiff's case was in.

The defendant-appellee, a processor of rice, in July 1952 entered into an agreement with the plaintiff-appellant, an exporter, for the sale of 95,600 pockets of rice.

[A "pocket" is a quantity of rice. Apparently, the parties agreed upon its meaning and the court construed this term in the agreement in accordance with the parties' intentions.]

The terms of the agreement, evidenced by a purchase memorandum, indicated that the price per pocket was to be '$8.25 F.A.S. Lake Charles and/or Houston, Texas'; that shipment was to be 'December, 1952, with two weeks call from buyer'; and that payment was to be by 'irrevocable letter of credit to be opened immediately payable against' dock receipts and other specified documents.

["F.A.S." stands for "freight alongside ship," a shipment term that means the seller is responsible for delivering the goods to directly next to the ship of the buyer's choice. This is contrasted with "F.O.B." which stands for "free on board" and means that the seller is responsible for placing the goods onto the specified ship. In both cases, note that the buyer must identify the ship so that the seller can place the goods alongside or on the proper ship.]

In the fall, the appellant, which had already committed itself to supplying this rice to a Japanese buyer, was unexpectedly confronted with United States export restrictions upon its December shipments and was attempting to get an export license from the government. December is a peak month in the rice and cotton seasons in Louisiana and Texas, and the appellee became concerned about shipping instructions under the contract, since congested conditions prevailed at both the mills and the docks.

The appellee seasonably elected to deliver 50,000 pockets at Lake Charles and on December 10 it received from the appellant instructions for the Lake Charles shipments. Thereupon it promptly began shipments to Lake Charles which continued until December 23, the last car at Lake Charles being unloaded on December 31.

December 17 was the last date in December which would allow appellee the two-week period provided in the contract for delivery of the rice to the ports and ships designated. Prior thereto, the appellant had been having difficulty obtaining either a ship or a dock in this busy season in Houston. On December 17, the appellee had still received no shipping instructions for the 45,600 pockets destined for Houston. On the morning of the 18th, the appellee rescinded the contract for the Houston shipments, although continuing to make the Lake Charles deliveries.

It is clear that one of the reasons for the prompt cancellation of the contract was the rise in market price of rice from $8.25 per pocket, the contract price, to $9.75. The appellant brought this suit for refusal to deliver the Houston quota.

The trial court, in a reasoned but unreported opinion which dealt with all phases of the case, held that New York would apply Texas law. We think this ruling right, but will not discuss the point because it is conceded that no different result would follow from the choice of Louisiana law.

The area of contest is also considerably reduced by the appellant's candid concession that the appellee's duty to ship, by virtue of the two-week notice provision, did not arise until two weeks after complete shipping instructions had been given by the appellant. Thus, on brief, the appellant says:

> *we concede (as we have done from the beginning) that on a fair interpreta-*
> *tion of the contract appellant had a duty to instruct appellee by December 17,*
> *1952 as to the place to which it desired appellee to ship — at both ports, and*
> *that, being late with its instructions in this respect, appellant could not have*
> *demanded delivery (at either port) until sometime after December 31, 1952.*

This position was taken, of course, with a view to the contract provision for shipment 'December, 1952': a two-week period ending December 31 would begin to run on December 17. But although appellant concedes that the two weeks' notice to which appellee was entitled could not be shortened by the failure to give shipping instructions on or before December 17, it stoutly insists that upon receipt of shipping instructions subsequent to December 17 the appellee thereupon became obligated to deliver within two weeks thereafter. We do not agree.

It is plain that a giving of the notice by the appellant was a condition precedent to the appellee's duty to ship. Obviously, the appellee could not deliver free alongside ship, as the contract required, until the appellant identified its ship and its location. Thus the giving of shipping instructions was what Professor Corbin would classify as a 'promissory condition': the appellant promised to give the notice and the appellee's duty to ship was conditioned on the receipt of the notice.

The crucial question is whether that condition was performed. And that depends on whether the appellee's duty of shipment was conditioned on notice on or before December 17, so that the appellee would have two weeks wholly within December within which to perform, or whether, as we understand the appellant to contend, the appellant could perform the condition by giving the notice later in December, in which case the appellee would be under a duty to ship within two weeks thereafter. The answer depends upon the proper interpretation of the contract: if the contract properly interpreted made shipment in December of the essence then the failure to give the notice on or before December 17 was nonperformance by the appellant of a condition upon which the appellee's duty to ship in December depended.

In the setting of this case, we hold that the provision for December delivery went to the essence of the contract. In support of the plainly stated provision of the contract there was evidence that the appellee's mills and the facilities appurtenant thereto were working at full capacity in December when the rice market was at peak activity and that appellee had numerous other contracts in January as well as in December to fill. It is reasonable to infer that in July, when the contract was made, each party wanted the protection of the specified delivery period; the appellee so that it could schedule its production without undue congestion of its storage facilities and the appellant so that it could surely meet commitments which it in turn should make to its customers. There was also evidence that prices on the rice market were fluctuating. In view of this factor it is not reasonable to infer that when the contract was made in July for December delivery, the parties intended that the appellant should have an option exercisable subsequent to December 17 to postpone delivery until January. That in effect would have given the appellant an option to postpone its breach of the contract, if one should then be in prospect, to a time when, so far as could have been foreseen when the contract was made, the price of rice might be falling. A postponement in such circumstances would inure to the disadvantage of the appellee who was given no reciprocal option. Further indication that December delivery was of the essence is found in the letter of credit which was provided for in the contract and established by the appellant. Under this letter, the bank was authorized to pay appellee only for deliveries 'during December, 1952.' It thus appears that the appellant's interpretation of the contract, under which the appellee would be obligated, upon receipt of shipping instructions subsequent to December 17, to deliver in January, would deprive the appellee of the security for payment of the purchase price for which it had contracted.

Since, as we hold, December delivery was of the essence, notice of shipping instructions on or before December 17 was not merely a 'duty' of the appellant — as it concedes: it was a condition precedent to the performance which might be required of the appellee. The nonoccurrence of that condition entitled the appellee to rescind or to treat its contractual obligations as discharged. On December 18th the appellant unequivocally exercised its right to rescind. Having done so, its obligations as to the Houston deliveries under the contract were at an end. And of course its obligations would not revive thereafter when the appellant finally succeeded in obtaining an export permit, a ship and a dock and then gave shipping instructions; when it expressed willingness to accept deliveries in January; or when it accomplished a 'liberalization' of the outstanding letter of credit whereby payments might be made against simple forwarder's receipts instead of dock receipts.

The appellant urges that by reason of substantial part performance on its part prior to December 17th, it may not be held to have been in default for its failure sooner to give shipping instructions. The contention has no basis in the facts. As to the Houston shipments the appellant's activities prior to December 17th were not in performance of its contract: they were merely preparatory to its expectation to perform at a later time. The mere establishment of the letter of credit was not an act of performance: it was merely an arrangement made by the appellant for future performance which as to the Houston deliveries because of appellant's failure to give shipping instructions were never made. From these preparatory activities the appellee had no benefit whatever.

The appellant also maintains that the contract was single and 'indivisible' and that consequently appellee's continuing shipments to Lake Charles after December 17 constituted an election to reaffirm its total obligation under the contract. This position also, we hold untenable. Under the contract, the appellee concededly had an option to split the deliveries betwixt Lake Charles and Houston. The price had been fixed on a per pocket basis, and payment, under the letter of credit, was to be made upon the presentation of dock receipts which normally would be issued both at Lake Charles or Houston at different times. The fact that there was a world market for rice and that in December the market price substantially exceeded the contract price suggests that it would be more to the appellant's advantage to obtain the Lake Charles delivery than to obtain no delivery at all. The same considerations suggest that by continuing with the Lake Charles delivery the appellee did not deliberately intend to waive its right to cancel the Houston deliveries. Conclusions to the contrary would be so greatly against self-interest as to be completely unrealistic. The only reasonable inference from the totality of the facts is that the duties of the parties as to the Lake Charles shipment were not at all dependent on the Houston shipments. We conclude their duties as to shipments at each port were paired and reciprocal and that performance by the parties as to Lake Charles did not preclude the appellee's right of cancellation as to Houston.

Finally, we hold that the appellant's claims of estoppel and waiver have no basis in fact or in law.

Affirmed.

Reflection

The *Internatio* case states that the term in question was a "promissory condition" and cites to Corbin for support. But apparently the court found this conclusion of law so obvious that it failed to quote the supporting treatises or to really analyze the issue. Let's review what Corbin actually said in distinguishing promises and conditions:

> *A promise is always made by the act or acts of one of the parties, such acts being words or other conduct expressing intention. A fact can be made to operate as a condition only by the agreement of both parties or by the construction of the law.*

First, Corbin reminds us that contractual promises (that is, promises that courts of law will enforce) can only be formed intentionally. The law does not impose contractual obligations on unwilling parties.

Conditions, on the other hand, can be created either by the expression of intent by the parties or by constructions of law. This Chapter deals only with express conditions. Later, in Chapter 18, we will explore the doctrine of implied conditions, which are constructions of law.

Courts should be reasonable in determining whether a term is intended to be a promise, a condition, or both (a promissory condition). This determination should be made in light of the purposes of promises and conditions.

The purpose of a promise is to create a duty in the promisor. The purpose of constituting some fact as a condition is always the postponement or discharge of an instant duty (or other specified legal relation).

A contractual promise creates a duty to perform what is promised, whereas a condition acts as switch that turns on or off that duty to perform. The function or impact of promises and conditions should also be taken into account when determining if a term is a promise or a condition.

The non-fulfillment of a promise is called a breach of contract and creates in the other party a secondary right to damages. It is the failure to perform a legal duty. The non-occurrence of a condition will prevent the existence of a duty in the other party; but it may not create any remedial rights and duties at all, and it will not unless someone has promised that it shall occur.

Corbin effectively restates the rule that was necessary to decide *Morrison*: the non-occurrence of a condition (fixing the furnace) meant that the promise subject to that condition (paying for the house) did not need to be performed. But the non-occurrence of the condition is not a breach of a legal duty and does not itself give rise to damages.

Next, Corbin explains that a term can be both a promise and a condition.

> *A contract can be so made as to create a duty that the fact operative as a condition shall come into existence. . . . Such a condition might be described as a promissory condition.*

In other words, the parties might intend that a term is a promise in that the party has a duty to perform it, and that the non-occurrence of this promise extinguishes the other party's duty to perform its end of the bargain. This was a necessary reading in *Internatio*, which Corbin himself analyzes.

> Internatio-Rotterdam, Inc. v. River Brand Rice Mills, Inc. *was a suit for alleged breach of a contract to deliver goods. The promise was to deliver the goods free alongside (F.A.S.) a ship during the month of December, the ship and place to be specified by the buyer. The buyer promised to give shipping instructions at least two weeks prior to shipment. The situation was such that time was held to be of the essence. Here the notice specifying ship and place was a "promissory condition": the buyer promised to give notice at least two weeks before the end of December; and notice was also a condition to the seller's duty to make delivery.*

Let's analyze the mutual promises in this case. The seller promised to deliver rice F.A.S., which means alongside a ship to be specified by the buyer. Note that this promise cannot be accomplished unless and until the buyer specifies the ship. It is impossible to deliver goods to an unspecified location. Therefore, specifying the ship must be a condition to the seller's promise to deliver the goods.

The buyer specifying the ship is also a promise that the buyer makes to the seller. The seller cannot make the sale and get paid for the delivery until this occurs.

Internatio is a famous case that is featured in most Contracts casebooks, but this second point is made confusing because the seller did not press it claim by suing the buyer for damages caused by the buyer's failure to specify a ship for delivery. The reason why the seller did not seek damages is because it turned out that the buyer's breach benefitted the seller. The price of rice had gone up since the buyer and seller entered into their agreement, so the seller was able to sell that same rice to someone else for more money. The seller was not harmed by buyer's breach, and contract damages are meant to remedy harms.

Discussion

1. Did you notice that, when the buyer failed to provide its delivery address on time, the seller cancelled the contract immediately? Was this a reasonable response? Why did the seller not attempt to work things out?

2. The buyer breached a promissory condition. Why did the seller not sue the buyer for this breach?

3. What is happening to prices in the market for rice during the time period of this agreement? How, if at all, do those commercial realities factor in to the court's decision?

Reading Morin Building Products Co., Inc. v. Baystone Construction, Inc. As you will see in the following case, courts are very hesitant to apply a subjective standard to conditions of satisfaction. Remember that express conditions must be completely performed, otherwise the conditional promise does not have to be performed at all. This is a harsh result than can be unfair in part because of the problems with proving someone's subjective mindset. Consider how Judge Posner alleviates some of the harshness of this doctrine with his approach in *Morin Building*.

Judge Posner's opinion in the case of *Morin Building Products Co. v. Baystone Construction, Inc.*, below, illustrates how much courts disfavor the subjective standard of satisfaction. The contract in *Morin* involved putting aluminum siding on an industrial warehouse. The contract used express language that suggested that payment for this work was to be conditional on the buyer's aesthetic satisfaction with the work, and the buyer's architect claimed that "viewed in bright sunlight from an acute angle the exterior siding did not give the impression of having a uniform finish." With this claim of aesthetic dissatisfaction, the buyer refused to pay for the work.

The court disagreed. The court refused to apply such a subjective standard to a contract that was obviously for a commercial application. Judge Posner found that the seller did not intend to bind itself to the difficult and perhaps unobtainable standard of precisely matching newly milled aluminum to existing metal siding. Moreover, aesthetics are not particularly important for industrial warehouses in general. Despite the express terms and intrinsic evidence that the buyer required aesthetic perfection, the court looked at reasonableness and trade usage to find that aesthetic quality should be judged by an objective, commercially reasonable standard. The court then found the aluminum siding met this standard and decided the case in favor of the seller.

Morin shows how the process of contract interpretation and the substance of contract law go hand in hand. Courts will avoid interpreting written agreements in a manner than leads to an absurd or unfair result. Instead of relying on equitable powers, the court may simply understand the contract to mean something other than what it says. It appears that here the court read the contract to imply an objective standard of satisfaction despite its express language implying a subjective standard of satisfaction because it suspected the promisor of engaging in bad faith to avoid contractual obligations.

Morin Building Products Co., Inc. v. Baystone Construction, Inc.

717 F.2d 413 (7th Cir. 1983)

POSNER, J.

This appeal from a judgment for the plaintiff in a diversity suit requires us to interpret Indiana's common law of contracts. General Motors, which is not a party to this case, hired Baystone Construction, Inc., the defendant, to build an addition to a Chevrolet plant in Muncie, Indiana. Baystone hired Morin Building Products Company, the plaintiff, to supply and erect the aluminum walls for the addition. The contract required that the exterior siding of the walls be of "aluminum type 3003, not less than 18 B & S gauge, with a mill finish and stucco embossed surface texture to match finish and texture of existing metal siding." The contract also provided "that all work shall be done subject to the final approval of the Architect or Owner's [General Motors'] authorized agent, and his decision in matters relating to artistic effect shall be final, if within the terms of the Contract Documents"; and that "should any dispute arise as to the quality or fitness of materials or workmanship, the decision as to acceptability shall rest strictly with the Owner, based on the requirement that all work done or materials furnished shall be first class in every respect. What is usual or customary in erecting other buildings shall in no wise enter into any consideration or decision."

Morin put up the walls. But viewed in bright sunlight from an acute angle the exterior siding did not give the impression of having a uniform finish, and General Motors' representative rejected it. Baystone removed Morin's siding and hired another subcontractor to replace it. General Motors approved the replacement siding. Baystone refused to pay Morin the balance of the contract price ($23,000) and Morin brought this suit for the balance, and won.

The only issue on appeal is the correctness of a jury instruction which, after quoting the contractual provisions requiring that the owner (General Motors) be satisfied with the contractor's (Morin's) work, states: "Notwithstanding the apparent finality of the foregoing language, however, the general rule applying to satisfaction in the case of contracts for the construction of commercial buildings is that the satisfaction clause must be determined by objective criteria. Under this standard, the question is not whether the owner was satisfied in fact, but whether the owner, as a reasonable person, should have been satisfied with the materials and workmanship in question." There was much evidence that General Motors' rejection of Morin's exterior siding had been totally unreasonable. Not only was the lack of absolute uniformity in the finish of the walls a seemingly trivial defect given the strictly utilitarian purpose of the building that they enclosed, but it may have been inevitable; "mill finish sheet" is defined in the trade as "sheet having a nonuniform finish which may vary from sheet to sheet and within a sheet, and may not be entirely free from stains or oil." If the instruction was correct, so was the judgment. But if the instruction was incorrect — if the proper standard is not whether a reasonable man would have been satisfied with Morin's exterior siding but whether General Motors' authorized representative in fact was — then there must be a new trial to determine whether he really was dissatisfied, or whether he was not and the rejection therefore was in bad faith.

Some cases hold that if the contract provides that the seller's performance must be to the buyer's satisfaction, his rejection — however unreasonable — of the seller's performance is not a breach of the contract unless the rejection is in bad faith. But most cases conform to the position stated in section 228 of the Restatement (Second) of Contracts (1979): if "it is practicable to determine whether a reasonable person in the position of the obligor would be satisfied, an interpretation is preferred under which the condition [that the obligor be satisfied with the obligee's performance] occurs if such a reasonable person in the position of the obligor would be satisfied."

We do not understand the majority position to be paternalistic; and paternalism would be out of place in a case such as this, where the subcontractor is a substantial multistate enterprise. The requirement of reasonableness is read into a contract not to protect the weaker party but to approximate what the parties would have expressly provided with respect to a contingency that they did not foresee, if they had foreseen it. Therefore the requirement is not read into every contract, because it is not always a reliable guide to the parties' intentions. In particular, the presumption that the performing party would not have wanted to put himself at the mercy of the paying party's whim is overcome when the nature of the performance contracted for is such that there are no objective standards to guide the court. It cannot be assumed in such a case that the parties would have wanted a court to second-guess the buyer's rejection. So "the reasonable person standard is employed when the contract involves commercial quality, operative fitness, or mechanical utility which other knowledgeable persons can judge. . . . The standard of good faith is employed when the contract involves personal aesthetics or fancy."

We have to decide which category the contract between Baystone and Morin belongs in. The particular in which Morin's aluminum siding was found wanting was its appearance, which may seem quintessentially a matter of "personal aesthetics," or as the contract put it, "artistic effect." But it is easy to imagine situations where this would not be so. Suppose the manager of a steel plant rejected a shipment of pig iron because he did not think the pigs had a pretty shape. The reasonable-man standard would be applied even if the contract had an "acceptability shall rest strictly with the Owner" clause, for it would be fantastic to think that the iron supplier would have subjected his contract rights to the whimsy of the buyer's agent. At the other extreme would be a contract to paint a portrait, the buyer having reserved the right to reject the portrait if it did not satisfy him. Such a buyer wants a portrait that will please him rather than a jury, even a jury of connoisseurs, so the only question would be his good faith in rejecting the portrait.

This case is closer to the first example than to the second. The building for which the aluminum siding was intended was a factory — not usually intended to be a thing of beauty. That aesthetic considerations were decidedly secondary to considerations of function and cost is suggested by the fact that the contract specified mill-finish aluminum, which is unpainted. There is much debate in the record over whether it is even possible to ensure a uniform finish within and among sheets, but it is at least clear that mill finish usually is not uniform. If General Motors and Baystone had wanted a uniform finish they would in all likelihood have ordered a painted siding. Whether Morin's siding achieved a reasonable uniformity amounting to satisfactory commercial quality was susceptible of objective judgment; in the language of the Restatement, a reasonableness standard was "practicable."

But this means only that a requirement of reasonableness would be read into this contract if it contained a standard owner's satisfaction clause, which it did not; and since the ultimate touchstone of decision must be the intent of the parties to the contract we must consider the actual language they used. The contract refers explicitly to "artistic effect," a choice of words that may seem deliberately designed to put the contract in the "personal aesthetics" category whatever an outside observer might think.

But the reference appears as number 17 in a list of conditions in a general purpose form contract. And the words "artistic effect" are immediately followed by the qualifying phrase, "if within the terms of the Contract Documents," which suggests that the "artistic effect" clause is limited to contracts in which artistic effect is one of the things the buyer is aiming for; it is not clear that he was here.

The other clause on which Baystone relies, relating to the quality or fitness of workmanship and materials, may seem all-encompassing, but it is qualified by the phrase, "based on the requirement that all work done or materials furnished shall be first class in every respect" — and it is not clear that Morin's were not. This clause also was not drafted for this contract; it was incorporated by reference to another form contract (the Chevrolet Division's "Contract General Conditions"), of which it is paragraph 35. We do not disparage form contracts, without which the commercial life of the nation would grind to a halt. But we are left with more than a suspicion that the artistic-effect and quality-fitness clauses in the form contract used here were not intended to cover the aesthetics of a mill-finish aluminum factory wall.

If we are right, Morin might prevail even under the minority position, which makes good faith the only standard but presupposes that the contract conditioned acceptance of performance on the buyer's satisfaction in the particular respect in which he was dissatisfied. Maybe this contract was not intended to allow General Motors to reject the aluminum siding on the basis of artistic effect. It would not follow that the contract put Morin under no obligations whatsoever with regard to uniformity of finish. The contract expressly required it to use aluminum having "a mill finish . . . to match finish . . . of existing metal siding." The jury was asked to decide whether a reasonable man would have found that Morin had used aluminum sufficiently uniform to satisfy the matching requirement. This was the right standard if, as we believe, the parties would have adopted it had they foreseen this dispute. It is unlikely that Morin intended to bind itself to a higher and perhaps unattainable standard of achieving whatever perfection of matching that General Motors' agent insisted on, or that General Motors would have required Baystone to submit to such a standard. Because it is difficult — maybe impossible — to achieve a uniform finish with mill-finish aluminum, Morin would have been running a considerable risk of rejection if it had agreed to such a condition, and it therefore could have been expected to demand a compensating increase in the contract price. This would have required General Motors to pay a premium to obtain a freedom of action that it could not have thought terribly important, since its objective was not aesthetic. If a uniform finish was important to it, it could have gotten such a finish by specifying painted siding.

All this is conjecture; we do not know how important the aesthetics were to General Motors when the contract was signed or how difficult it really would have been to obtain the uniformity of finish it desired. The fact that General Motors accepted the replacement siding proves little, for there is evidence that the replacement siding produced the same striped effect, when viewed from an acute angle in bright sunlight, that Morin's had. When in doubt on a difficult issue of state law it is only prudent to defer to the view of the district judge, here an experienced Indiana lawyer who thought this the type of contract where the buyer cannot unreasonably withhold approval of the seller's performance.

Lest this conclusion be thought to strike at the foundations of freedom of contract, we repeat that if it appeared from the language or circumstances of the contract that the parties really intended General Motors to have the right to reject Morin's work for failure to satisfy the private aesthetic taste of General Motors' representative, the rejection would have been proper even if unreasonable. But the contract is ambiguous because of the qualifications with which the terms "artistic effect" and "decision as to acceptability" are hedged about, and the circumstances suggest that the parties probably did not intend to subject Morin's rights to aesthetic whim.

AFFIRMED.

Reflection

The contract in *Morin* involved putting aluminum siding on a warehouse. Although the contract used express language that suggested that payment for this work was to be conditional on the buyer's aesthetic satisfaction with the work, the court refused to apply such a subjective standard to a contract that was obviously for a commercial application.

Morin shows how the process of contract interpretation and the substantive contract law go hand in hand. Courts will avoid interpreting written agreements in a manner than leads to an absurd or unfair result. Instead of relying on equitable powers, the court may simply understand the contract to mean something other than what it says. It appears that here the court read the contract to imply an objective standard of satisfaction despite its express language implying a subjective standard of satisfaction because it suspected the promisor of engaging in bad faith to avoid contractual obligations.

There are, however, cases where courts will apply a subjective standard. In *Ard Dr. Pepper Bottling Co. v. Dr. Pepper Co.*, 202 F.2d 372 (5th Cir. 1953), Dr. Pepper (a manufacturer of syrup for a soft drink) granted to Ard (a bottler who used that syrup) an exclusive license in a designated territory to bottle and sell a soft drink called Dr. Pepper on specified terms for a five-year period. The contract described in detail Ard's duty to diligently market and sell Dr. Pepper in the territory and provided that Dr. Pepper could terminate the license at any time if Ard failed to "faithfully comply" with the provisions of the contract, in Dr. Pepper's "sole, exclusive and final judgment made in good faith."

Dr. Pepper sent Ard the following letter, the facts of which the court found to be accurate:

> You have failed to carry out and perform the terms, provisions and obligations imposed upon you by Dr. Pepper Bottler's License Agreement No. 329-A issued to you on July 20, 1938.
>
> Your bottled Dr. Pepper has not been up to our required standard. Your bottling machinery and equipment are inadequate and insufficient and you have failed to use modern, automatic and sanitary equipment in your Dr. Pepper bottling operations, as you have been requested to do. The building in which you operate is wholly inadequate and improperly maintained for a modern, sanitary bottling plant.
>
> You have failed to fully cover, solicit and work in a systematic and business-like manner for the promotion of Dr. Pepper the territory covered by your license agreement and all dealers therein. You have failed to at all times loyally and faithfully promote the sale of and secure thorough distribution of Dr. Pepper throughout every part of your territory and to all dealers therein, and you have failed to develop an increase in the volume of sales of Dr. Pepper satisfactory to the Dr. Pepper Company. You have failed to properly advertise Dr. Pepper in your territory.
>
> You have failed within the judgment of Dr. Pepper Company to faithfully comply with the provisions of your license agreement and the Dr. Pepper Company hereby exercises its right to terminate the aforesaid Dr. Pepper Bottler's License Agreement.

Ard defended on various grounds including that Dr. Pepper's decision was arbitrary and that the court should apply an objective standard to Ard's operations. The *Ard* court found that Dr. Pepper's termination of Ard was proper because Dr. Pepper honestly told Ard that in Dr. Pepper's judgment Ard had not performed its duty under the contract. The *Ard* court determined that Ard had no claim against Dr. Pepper since the agreement clearly provides a test of honest satisfaction.

It is not easy to distinguish between *Ard* and *Morin* as a matter of law. In both cases, the contract was fairly clear in requiring a subjective standard of satisfaction. But in *Morin*, the court refused to apply a subjective standard, whereas *Ard* did apply the subjective standard. *Ard* was not a case about artwork, nor did it involve personal taste; rather, it regarded the commercial operations of a soft drink bottling plant.

Rather than distinguishing these cases on their facts, perhaps it is more realistic to recognize them as evidencing different jurisprudential philosophies. Nominally, *Morin* seems to care deeply about extrinsic evidence like the commercial circumstances, which show a latent ambiguity in the agreement. *Ard* seems more focused on the four corners and on freedom of contract principles, stating, "The terms of the present contract in the light of its subject matter and of the circumstances of the parties leave little or no room for construction or interpretation."

The Restatement, as you will read in the next section, seems to prefer *Morin*'s approach of admitting extrinsic evidence where the written agreement is reasonably susceptible to show that the condition of satisfaction should be interpreted reasonably or objectively wherever possible.

Problems

Problem 17.1. Renewal of a Restaurant Lease

Cross Bay Chelsea (CBC) owned and operated a restaurant in Howard Beach, Queens, a neighborhood in New York, the location being rented from J.N.A. Realty Corp. pursuant to a 10-year lease agreement, the term of which ran from January 1, 1964 to December 31, 1974.

Paragraph 58 of that lease agreement granted tenant CBC an option to renew the lease of the building in Howard Beach with landlord JNA, "provided that Tenant shall notify Landlord in writing by registered or certified mail six (6) months prior to the last day of the term of the lease that tenant desires such renewal." In other words, CBC was to notify JNA of its intent to renew by June 31, 1974.

Over the course of the lease, CBC invested $40,000 in fixtures and chattels in the restaurant building. In 1974, at the end of the 10-year lease term, the restaurant business in that location was worth approximately $155,000.

CBC failed to notify JNA of its intent to renew by the end of June. JNA ignored this and continued to bill CBC for monthly rent, which CBC paid on time, until 30 days prior to end of the lease term.

On November 31, 1974, JNA informed CBC in writing that JNA was not renewing the lease and that CBC would have to vacate the premises on December 31, 1974. CBC immediately responded in writing that they wished to exercise their right to renew the lease. JNA replied that time for renewal had expired and attached a copy of the contract with Paragraph 58 highlighted. CBC protested that this was the first time they had read Paragraph 58, but JNA moved forward with eviction proceedings regardless.

The case is now before you, the judge. JNA has sued to evict CBC. CBC has countersued for breach of contract. How should you rule?

See J.N.A. Realty Corp. v. Cross Bay Chelsea, Inc., 42 N.Y.2d 392 (1977).

Problem 17.2. **Financial Satisfaction**

On August 4, 1989, Hutton and MPI executed a franchise agreement wherein MPI sold a monogramming franchise to Hutton. The franchise agreement permitted Hutton to use MPI's patented technology to sew monograms into t-shirts, hats, and bags using the Meistergram 800 XLC computerized monogramming machine that could be operated from home or at shopping mall kiosks.

There were two major costs with regard to starting up Hutton's monogram franchise small business. First, Hutton had to pay MPI for the franchise agreement. Second, Hutton had to buy or lease a Meistergram 800 XLC machine. The purchase or lease of the monogramming machine represented a critical component of the required financing because the entire operation revolved around the application of monograms to imprintable items of clothing.

Before signing, Hutton write an Appendix to the franchise agreement to which both parties agreed, which said that Hutton's purchase of the MPI franchise for $25,000 was on condition that if Hutton were "unable ... to obtain financing suitable to him" within ninety days of signing the franchise agreement, he would then be entitled to a refund of the $25,000 franchise fee.

After executing the franchise agreement and addendum, Hutton obtained a loan from Star Bank to cover the franchise fee. The loan was secured by a mortgage executed by Hutton and his wife Pamela against their residence.

The issue in this case, however, arises because Hutton was unable to obtain "suitable" financing for the monogramming machine.

To facilitate the lease or purchase of the monogramming machine, MPI issued a franchise offering circular to Hutton. The circular, which MPI was required to provide under Ohio law, estimated that the total cost of an MPI franchise varied between $32,420 and $36,720.

The fee paid by Hutton accounted for $25,000 of the $36,720 total estimated franchise cost. The circular also estimated that the monogramming machine could be leased for $520 per month for sixty months or purchased at a total cost of $21,000.

On November 20, 1989, MPI recommended to Hutton a sixty-month lease through United Leasing Corporation. The monthly lease payments totaled $751.01, with a total equipment cost of $45,060.60 over the life of the lease. The lease also required Hutton to make a ten percent down payment.

Since Hutton considered these terms to be substantially less advantageous than the terms offered in the MPI circular, he rejected the United Leasing Corporation financing offer.

Subsequently, Hutton's financing applications were rejected by Trinity Leasing and Society Bank.

After rejecting United's offer and being rejected by Trinity and Society, Hutton wrote to Larry Meyer, MPI's president, requesting a refund of the $25,000 franchise fee due to the difficulty he had experienced in securing financing. This request was denied, whereupon Hutton filed suit.

Discuss whether the term regarding MPI's return of Hutton's franchise fee is a promise, a condition, or both. If a condition, discuss whether it is a condition precedent or condition subsequent, who holds the condition, and why.

See Hutton v. Monograms Plus, Inc., 78 Ohio App. 3d 176 (1992).

Chapter 18

Performance

This chapter introduces what many scholars regard to be the heart of contract law: how courts evaluate whether a party has fulfilled its contractual obligations to its counterparty. Equally important for contract lawyers is determining whether a party can withhold its performance under a contract because the counterparty has not performed its obligations.

The situation usually plays out as some variation on the following theme: first, two parties enter into a simple bilateral agreement, where one party promises to perform services or deliver goods, and the counterparty promises to pay for those goods or services. The counterparty claims that the party's services or goods are defective somehow, and therefore the counterparty refuses to pay.

One example: a dentist promised a patient to replace a worn-out tooth with a porcelain-on-gold crown, and the patient promises to pay $1,000 for the procedure. The dentist instead uses a porcelain-only crown. Can the patient rightfully refuse to pay the dentist?

Another example: Costco Wholesalers orders 20,000 red roses from Ramakrishna Karuturi Importing Company for $1 per rose. The importing company delivers 15,000 red roses and 5,000 pink roses. Can Costco rightfully refuse to pay Ramakrishna?

A third example: Mr. Went, a wealthy individual, hires Yacov & Jung, Inc., a homebuilding company, to build an elaborate house for him according to dozens of blueprints and several pages of specifications for $1,000,000. As is custom in the homebuilding industry, Went is to pay Yacov & Jung progress payment of 1/5 of the total for each stage they complete. Went paid $800,000 upon completion of the foundation, exterior structure, electrical & plumbing, and drywall. But before making the final payment, Went discovers that Yacov & Jung installed Home Depot brand air ducts instead of Lowe's brand air ducts as required by the contract. Can Went rightfully refuse to pay Yavoc & Jung the final $200,000 payment?

To answer these questions, we must first understand why, as a matter of law, a party would have any right to refuse to fulfill its contractual promise just because its counterparty may have failed to perform its obligation. In other words, why does one party's failure to perform alleviate its counterparty's obligation to perform?

Rules

A. Discharge by Complete Performance

When one party completely performs all its obligations under a contract, that party is absolved of any further contractual liability. In this case, we say the party's duty is discharged by complete performance. The party who completely performed cannot be sued for breach.

> *Full performance of a duty under a contract discharges the duty.* R2d § 235(1).

Discharge requires complete performance, meaning, everything specified by the contract must be done correctly. If a contract requires a sugar manufacturer to deliver 100,000 tons of sugar to a buyer, and the manufacturer delivers 99,999 tons, the manufacturer has not completely performed and is liable for the breach for the remaining 1 ton of sugar. Again, any non-compliance with the agreement, no matter how slight, constitutes a breach of that agreement.

> *When performance of a duty under a contract is due any non-performance is a breach.* R2d § 235(2).

The fact of a breach, however, does not necessarily mean that the breaching party does not get paid or does not otherwise deserve the fruits of the contract. Contrarily, one party may only withhold payment from the other where a breach is material. An insubstantial breach, also known as substantial performance, occurs where a party performed enough of its obligation to merit enforcement of contractual duties owed to it, even though that party did not completely perform and therefore remains partly liable for breach.

Complete performance is usually easy to analyze. For example, if a merchant orders eleven bushels of Grade A red wheat, and a farmer delivers eleven bushels of Grade A red wheat, there is little doubt that contract was fully performed such that the merchant must pay the farmer, and the farmer is not liable for any lawsuit related to that agreement. The much more difficult question, which is addressed in the next chapter, occurs where a party did not perfectly perform but still argues it merits performance of the duties owed to it according to a contract.

B. "Kingston Covenants"

Historically, the law did not generally assume that contractual parties made mutual promises to each other. It used to be the case that every contractual promise was treated independently. Under this prior rule, a contractual promise must therefore be performed regardless of what the other party does or does not do. There was no right to withhold performance under a contract based on the other parties' failure. The aggrieved party, who did not receive what he bargained for under the contract, must pay for the goods or services anyway and then sue for any damages.

But in 1773, a famous English judge named The Right Honorable William Murray, First Earl of Mansfield (who is referred to more simply as Lord Mansfield), recognized that when parties make mutual promises to each other, these promises are often intended to be implied conditions to their obligations. He recognized this through his decision in the case of *Kingston v. Preston*, below, and thus the classification he presented is sometimes known as the "Kingston Covenants."

This casebook will clarify the modern meaning of these critical concepts. The *Kingston* case introduces what are sometimes called the "Kingston covenants." The taxonomy of promises and their interdependence that Lord Mansfield provided in this famous case remain relevant today, although the terminology varies slights. The chart below provides some of the common ways these terms are used today.

In general, contractual parties make mutual promises to each other. The assumption is that parties intend to perform and that each wants the exchange performance it expects to receive under the agreement. The parties do not want to sue each other. The right to sue is secondary. Litigation is a mechanism to ensure compliance with an agreement, and it is a costly mechanism for parties who would usually prefer to work it out themselves.

Figure 18.1. Line engraving of Lord Mansfield, 1775. Artist David Martin.
Yale Center for British Art B1979.34.5 CC0 1-0.

For this reason, one party is generally allowed to withhold its performance where its counterparty appears unable or unwilling to perform its contractual obligation. For example, if two parties have an agreement to buy and sell a certain car on Friday, and, before then, the seller calls the buyer and says the car was sold to someone else. Or it was struck by a meteor and is thus no longer available. In either case, the buyer now knows that its counterparty the seller is no longer willing and able to perform. Does that buyer have to wait until Friday and then sue the seller for breach? Or should the buyer go find another car to purchase, perhaps even another one from the same seller?

The law does not require the buyer to wait and sue because this is economically wasteful. Instead, the buyer must wait a reasonable time for the seller to cure any material failure. If the subject matter of the contract was destroyed by an errant meteor, then a reasonable time is just an instant, because there is zero chance that seller can cure this failure.

If, on the other hand, the agreement regards the construction of a house, and during the pre-closing walkthrough, the buyer discovers a leak in the roof, the buyer probably cannot instantly cancel the deal. Rather, the buyer must give the seller a reasonable time to cure this breach and thus bring about the occurrence of the condition of delivering a functional house.

KINGSTON COVENANT	MODERN TERM	DESCRIPTION	NONPERFORMANCE OF ONE GROUNDS FOR WITHHOLDING PERFORMANCE BY THE OTHER?
Mutual and Independent	Independent Promises	Neither party's performance impacts the other's duty to perform	Neither party can engage in "self help" by refusing to perform, but rather must perform and then sue for damages
Conditional and Dependent	Condition [Precedent/ Subsequent]	Occurrence of the condition triggers the duty to perform	Non-performance of the condition is usually not a breach, but the other party does not have a duty to perform until the condition is performed
Mutual Conditions	Promissory Conditions Concurrent	Each party's performance or readiness to perform triggers the other's duty to perform	If one party is not ready to perform, the other party need not perform yet but must be ready to perform for a reasonable time

Figure 18.2. Kingston Covenants Explained.

C. Exchange of Mutual Promises

R2d assumes contracts contain mutual promissory conditions. For example, Al agrees to buy Bob's car on Friday for $10,000 at the corner store parking lot. If Al fails to show up with the cash, Bob does not have to give Al the car. If Bob fails to show up with the car, Al does not have to give Bob the cash. This is because it is reasonable to assume that Al intended (implicitly) to make his promise to pay Bob conditional on Bob's transfer of the car, and because Bob probably intended (implicitly) to give Al his car only if Al pays for it. The non-occurrence of either (promissory) condition means that the promise subject to that condition need not be performed. This outcome reflects common sense and economic principles.

R2d begins its module on Performance and Non-Performance with an opening note which recognizes that parties to a contract should be encouraged to work things out first before turning to the courts. In other words, the Restatement prefers parties to engage in self-help. Self-help means that parties can enforce their own rights without the use of the courts. The courts are the last resort when self-help fails, but the mere existence of courts and the threat of a lawsuit actually encourages parties to work things out together.

> *During the course of performance, problems may arise that require a clear definition of the obligations of the parties under the contract and that may make it appropriate for them to adjust those obligations in the light of a situation not contemplated when the contract was made. When such problems arise, the parties should be encouraged to communicate with each other and seek to resolve them without outside intervention. Should their efforts fail, a court may be asked to define their obligations.*

The law does not always encourage self-help. With regard to property, for example, landlords generally cannot constructively evict tenants by changing the locks to the apartment. Likewise, criminal law discourages vigilantism. But contract law actively encourages self-help by giving contract parties the right to withhold their performance in a variety of cases. By withholding performance such as payment, the contract party can encourage its counterparty to completely or at least substantially perform its obligations.

The mechanism by which modern jurisdictions encourage self-help in cases of contract disputes is, first, to interpret mutual promises as conditions to each other. Second, the law generally allows one party to withheld performance of its conditional promise at least until the other has substantially performed. By withholding one's performance, such as payment, one can influence a counterparty to complete its performance, such as delivering conforming goods or performing services.

The Restatement generally assumes that mutual promises in a contract are usually intended to be conditioned upon each other. It makes this position clear in its opening section on this topic. Although it uses the phrase "an exchange of promises" instead of "mutual conditions" (as Mansfield did) or "promissory conditions concurrent" (as this book does), the concept is effectively the same.

> *Performances are to be exchanged under an exchange of promises if each promise is at least part of the consideration for the other and the performance of each promise is to be exchanged at least in part for the performance of the other.* R2d § 231.

The Restatement's position is that the use of exchange of promises is so widespread in our society that courts are free to assume that parties made an exchange of promises even without anything in their written agreement evidencing this intent. This assumption can be made even when the performances are not simultaneous but rather sequential, as these illustrations show:

> *Illustration 231.1. A, a shipowner, promises to carry B's cargo on his ship. B promises to pay A the stipulated freight. They exchange these promises in the expectation that there will be a subsequent exchange of those performances. A fails to carry B's cargo, and B thereupon refuses to pay the freight. A's carrying the cargo and B's paying the freight are to be exchanged under the exchange of promises. Therefore, under the rule stated in § 237, A has no claim against B.*

In the illustration above, the promises could be sequential. It is reasonable to interpret this agreement to mean that, first, A will ship the cargo, then, second, B will pay for it. Alternatively, B could pay up front, and then A could ship the goods.

There are many cases where performance cannot or usually would not occur at the same time. In fact, many services are rendered over a period of time, whereas payment occurs in an instant. R2d makes it quite clear, however, that courts can still assume that parties intended an exchange of promises even where performances do not occur at the same time, as the second illustration shows.

> *Illustration 231.2. In return for A's promise to deliver a machine, B promises to pay A $10,000 within 30 days. They exchange these promises in the expectation that there will be a subsequent exchange of those performances. A fails to deliver the machine, and B thereupon refuses to pay any part of the $10,000. A's delivery of the machine and B's payment of the $10,000 are to be exchanged under the exchange of promises. Therefore, under the rule stated in § 237, A has no claim against B.*

But this strong presumption (that parties' promises are mutual and dependent on one another) only applies where the promises are exchanged as part of a single contract. When the same parties make multiple contracts, then it becomes less reasonable to presume that the promises made in one contract are to be exchanged for promises made in an entirely separate agreement. Take a look at the two examples below.

> Example 231.A. On January 1, Walmart Stores places an order for a food-grade freezer from Subzero Inc. via a contract entitled "Food Freezer Contract," pursuant to which Subzero is to deliver a freezer and then Walmart is to pay $12,000 in equal monthly installments over a one-year period. On March 1, Walmart and Subzero enter into a second contract entitled "Pharmaceutical Freezer Contract" for a deep-freeze freezer for $10,000 to be paid within 60 days. On April 1, Walmart fails to make its installment payment for the food-grade freezer, whereupon Subzero refuses to ship the deep-freeze freezer. Walmart has a claim against Subzero for breach of the Pharmaceutical Freezer Contract because these appear to

be separate contracts. Subzero's promise to ship the deep-freeze freezer is independent from its promise to pay monthly installments for the food-grade freezer.

However, specific facts can show that promises made in separate contracts were mutual.

> *Example 231.B. Target Stores pays Dippin' Dots LLC, a manufacturer of branded novelty ice cream products, $100,000 in exchange for the exclusive rights to sell Dippin' Dots ice cream, which is dispensed through a specialized vending machine, in a 30 square mile area, pursuant to a contract entitled "Franchise Agreement." Subsequently, Target and Dippin' Dots enter into a "Vending Machine Agreement" pursuant to which Target will pay Dippin' Dots $2,000 per month for 48 months to lease and maintain a Dippin' Dots specialized vending machine. Two months after Target receives the Dippin' Dots machine, Dippin' Dots enters into another franchise agreement with a school located just ½ mile from the Target location, in violation of the exclusivity clause in the Franchise Agreement. Target may justifiably refuse to continue to pay to lease the Dippin' Dots machine because the promises in the Franchise Agreement and the Vending Machine Agreement are reasonably related to each other as part of their overall exchange of promises.*

In summary, mutual promises made pursuant to a singular contract are usually presumed to give one promise in exchange for the other. Separate contracts typically suggest independent promises, but even with separate contracts, courts may still find mutuality of obligation.

1. Presumption of an Exchange of Promises

While R2d § 231 enables courts to interpret mutual promises as dependent on one another, R2d § 232 makes it clear that this interpretation is preferred and even presumed in most contractual circumstances. In fact, the presumption for mutual dependent promises is so strong that it can only be overcome by a clear manifestation of intentions to the contrary.

> *Where the consideration given by each party to a contract consists in whole or in part of promises, all the performances to be rendered by each party taken collectively are treated as performances to be exchanged under an exchange of promises, unless a contrary intention is clearly manifested. R2d § 232.*

The reason for this presumption is to align legal rules with what contractual parties generally expect from each other:

> *When the parties have exchanged promises, there is ordinarily every reason to suppose that they contracted on the basis of such an expectation since the exchange of promises would otherwise have little purpose. R2d § 232 cmt. a.*

As a default, therefore, all promises in a contract are to be taken collectively and mutually as part of the exchange of promises, although this can be rebutted by evidence of intentions to the contrary.

2. Performance at One Time or in Installments

R2d's presumption for a mutual exchange of promises is so strong that is it not undermined simply because performance cannot occur at one time. Obligations can be mutual even where one is performed over time.

> Where performances are to be exchanged under an exchange of promises, and the whole of one party's performance can be rendered at one time, it is due at one time, unless the language or the circumstances indicate the contrary. R2d § 233(1).

The general rule is that performance shall be given at one time, but this presumption for one-time performance can be overcome by specific facts, as illustrated be these examples.

> Illustration 233.1. A contracts to sell and B to buy ten identical carloads of coal for $100,000. Delivery by A of all ten carloads is due in a single lot.

> Illustration 233.2. 1. A contracts to sell and B to buy ten identical carloads of coal for $100,000, and it is known by both A and B that only one carload of coal will be available at a time. A may deliver one carload at a time.

But when performance is done in installments, then the return performance is usually required in installments, too. In the common form of commercial agreement, where one party performs a service or delivers a good and the counterparty pays for that service or good rendered, the obligation to pay for installment performance is likewise due in installments.

> Where only a part of one party's performance is due at one time under Subsection (1), if the other party's performance can be so apportioned that there is a comparable part that can also be rendered at that time, it is due at that time, unless the language or the circumstances indicate the contrary. R2d § 233(2).

> Illustration 233.3. 1. A contracts to sell and B to buy ten identical carloads of coal for $100,000, and it is known by both A and B that only one carload of coal will be available at a time. A may deliver one carload at a time. Payment of $10,000 by B is due at the same time that A delivers each carload of coal.

Although courts can and usually do find it implied that performances are exchanged under an exchange of promises even when they cannot be rendered at one time, courts still prefer to assume that performance will be rendered simultaneously, as the next rule makes clear.

3. Order of Performances

Courts assume that promises to be exchanged under an exchange of promises are to be rendered simultaneously, although that presumption can be rebutted by specific facts to the contrary.

> Where all or part of the performances to be exchanged under an exchange of promises can be rendered simultaneously, they are to that extent due

simultaneously, unless the language or the circumstances indicate the contrary. R2d § 234(1).

The Restatement's approach prefers to find promises are to be rendered simultaneously because this promotes fairness is two ways. First, this provides greater opportunities for a party to engage in self-help by withholding their performance when its counterparty is not ready or willing to substantially perform. Second, it avoids burdening either party with the obligation to pay until its counterparty has performed.

But there are cases where simultaneous performance is not possible. R2d has an additional provision to cover situations where performance requires a period of time. Employment contracts in particular—where one party works for a time, and then the other is obligated to pay—generally reverse the presumption that mutual promises are concurrent conditions.

> *Except to the extent stated in Subsection (1), where the performance of only one party under such an exchange requires a period of time, his performance is due at an earlier time than that of the other party, unless the language or the circumstances indicate the contrary.* R2d § 234(2).

For these reasons, courts should as a default assume that performance under a contract is to be simultaneously. If one of the performances needs to occur in installments, such as the example from Illustration 233.2 in which ten carloads of coal will be delivered in ten separate installments, then the exchange of performances generally is also due in installments, as shown in Illustration 233.3 in which the $100,000 payment for all ten carloads of coal is divided up into ten payments of $10,000 each of which payments are due as each carload of coal arrives.

D. Implied Conditions

Unlike express conditions, which must be strictly and completely performed before the duty subject to that condition comes due, implied conditions must only be substantially performed in order to activate the other's duty.

This doctrine was established by the hallmark case *Jacob & Youngs v. Kent*, below, a homebuilder named Jacob & Youngs, Inc. built a mansion for a man named Kent. The builder built the expensive mansion properly except they used the wrong brand of pipe for the plumbing. Kent specified Reading brand pipe, but the builder used a mix of Reading pipe, Cohos brand pipe, and generic galvanized puddled iron pipe. Upon discovering that the mansion was not plumbed only with Reading brand pipe, Kent refused to pay Jacob & Youngs.

Justice Cardozo found that there was no difference between the various brands of galvanized puddled iron pipe, and therefore the builders had substantially performed their obligation to build the mansion. In his poetical style, Justice Cardozo opined:

> *The transgressor whose default is unintentional and trivial may hope for mercy if he will offer atonement for his wrong. . . . There will be no assumption of a purpose to visit venial faults with oppressive retribution.*

In other words, where one party substantially performs its obligation, that triggers the other party's obligation to perform its mutual obligation under the contract. The question, then, is what constitutes substantial performance? Cardozo gives little guidance as to how to apply this doctrine in other cases:

> *Where the line is to be drawn between the important and the trivial cannot be settled by a formula. In the nature of the case precise boundaries are impossible. . . . We must weigh the purpose to be served, the desire to be gratified, the excuse for deviation from the letter, the cruelty of enforced adherence. Then only can we tell whether literal fulfilment is to be implied by law as a condition.*

Fortunately for modern lawyers, case law has evolved since 1919, and the R2d provides a five-part test to determine whether a party substantially performed or materially breached.

> *In determining whether a failure to render or to offer performance is material, the following circumstances are significant: (a) the extent to which the injured party will be deprived of the benefit which he reasonably expected; (b) the extent to which the injured party can be adequately compensated for the part of that benefit of which he will be deprived; (c) the extent to which the party failing to perform or to offer to perform will suffer forfeiture; (d) the likelihood that the party failing to perform or to offer to perform will cure his failure, taking account of all the circumstances including any reasonable assurances; [and] (e) the extent to which the behavior of the party failing to perform or to offer to perform comports with standards of good faith and fair dealing.* R2d § 241.

Each of these elements will addressed in turn. But, first, we will explore the nature and consequence of breach more generally.

E. Benefit of the Bargain

There are two key principles to keep in mind whenever evaluating performance under a contract. Moreover, it is critical to keep these concepts separate and distinguishable in your mind, otherwise you will have trouble analyzing the results of contractual nonperformance

First, any failure to completely perform all the contractual obligations is a breach, no matter how minor the failure, unless that performance was excused pursuant to one of the doctrines covered in Chapter 20. As we learned in Chapter 17, any breach can lead to liability for damages. Although it is possible that a breach does not cause damages to occur (recall this occurred in the *Internatio* case), it is never possible for damages to be awarded when there has not been any breach.

Damages will be discussed extensively in later modules. To be able to read the following case, however, you need to know that nominal damages are a token amount, usually $1, awarded when a plaintiff shows there was a breach but fails to show that the breach caused harm. As mentioned above, any failure to completely perform contractual obligations is a breach, but these breaches only result in an award of money damages where the plaintiff can also show harm in addition to proving breach.

In the case of *Jacob & Youngs*, below, there was a breach: the builders promised to install well galvanized lap welded pipe manufactured by the Reading company, but instead they installed pipe manufactured by other companies. This was a breach because it was a failure to fully perform what the contract expressly required. This breach could lead to damages, and it would have if the owner would have been able to prove he was harmed by the change in pipe. But in that case, Judge Cardozo found that the pipe was of equivalent value and so, even though there was a breach, there were no damages.

But the existence of a breach does not by itself mean that the other party can withhold performance. The second key concept that you must remember when evaluating contract performance is that a party may lawfully withhold its own performance only when its counterparty materially breached the agreement. This was described as Cardozo's doctrine of substantial performance in *Jacob & Youngs*. If the breach is minor, such that performance was substantial, then the party who made a dependent promise under an exchange of promises must still perform that promise.

To put this in simpler terms, just because there was breach does not mean the nonbreaching party may engage in self-help by withholding performance. Although a nonbreaching party can sue for damages whenever there is any breach, no matter how minor, that same party cannot withhold its own performance unless the breach reaches the level of being material.

The relevant question for the remainder of this module hinges on when a breach is material such that the nonbreaching party can withhold performance, versus when performance is substantial enough such that the nonbreaching party must perform its mutual obligation (although that nonbreaching party could seek remedies from a court of law)?

In *Jacob & Youngs*, Cardozo develops a framework to employ when analyzing the builder's performance and concluded that the builder's breach was not material. Many cases cite to *Jacob & Youngs* for the proposition that a party may not withhold payment for defects in performance that are merely "venial," a term that Cardozo borrows from Christian theology that there means a sin that does not deprive the soul of divine grace.

But Cardozo's framework reflects his opened ended equitable jurisprudence. The definitions he provides are somewhat circular. Say that performance is substantial where any defects in that performance are venial is not saying much at all about how to determine the nature of the defect and the performance. This gives judges a significant degree of freedom in determining whether withholding performance is lawful.

A more recent case, *Khiterer v. Bell*, below, illustrates how a modern trial court applies Cardozo's rather loose framework. In this case, Inna Khiterer went to Dr. Mina Bell for dental treatment. Dr. Bell prescribed "gold-on-porcelain" crowns, but ended up installing all-porcelain crowns. Mrs. Khiterer was pleased with the result until an x-ray revealed that the crowns had no gold inside; then, she protested and refused to pay for the dental work. Dr. Bell sued, claiming she substantially performed.

Judge Battaglia agreed with Dr. Bell. The court found that all-porcelain crowns were medically superior and cosmetically indistinguishable. While performance was not perfect, the patient received the benefit of the bargain, and so the doctor should be paid.

The substantial performance doctrine gives judges a wide degree of freedom in deciding what justice requires for a certain case. But this freedom inherently means that it is harder for parties to predict how courts will rule. A rule like the one that the Restatement provides results in a more structured analysis. That structure gives parties more advance notice about how courts will evaluate circumstances where one party withheld performance. This makes it easier to plan actions that will not violate the law. But this also means that parties could plan their actions not to violate the specific blackletter law while violating the spirit of contract law in general, and other parties who deserve relief under the law might not receive it for technical reasons.

Whether a rule or a standard is better depends in large part on what the specific law is trying to accomplish. Recall that the Restatement's approach to this aspect of contract law is to encourage parties to engage in self-help. To accomplish this end, the Restatement needs to provide parties clarity about what is or is not lawful. A rule is a better tool than a standard when the goal is giving parties certainty or clarity in advance about how courts will decide such cases. This allows parties to accurately predict how courts will behave and to plan their actions accordingly. This may explain why the Restatement provides a more formal five-factor test in the form of a rule and not a standard, so parties can decide whether or not to withhold performance in response to their counterparties' breach.

The Restatement first deals with the black-and-white distinction between full performance and breach. Any defect in performance is a breach. This rule is sharply defined. But whether or not a defect in a contract party's performance gives rise to its counterparty's lawful right to withhold its return performance is a more complex inquiry.

R2d effectively contemplates four degrees or stages of performance, which this book characterizes as the spectrum of performance and breach: (1) complete or full performance; (2) substantial performance; (3) material breach; and (4) total breach.

F. Effect of Performance and Non-Performance

The Restatement first defines "full performance," which is where a party's obligations under a contract are completely performed. This is also called "complete performance."

Full performance of a duty under a contract discharges the duty. R2d § 235(1).

The result of full performance is therefore clear: one party's full performance absolves that party of any further contractual liability. Conversely, any lack of performance can result in liability:

> *When performance of a duty under a contract is due any non-performance is a breach.* R2d § 235(2).

This rule makes the simple, straightforward distinction between complete performance and everything else. But there is a further distinction between substantial performance, which is something less than full performance but more than enough for the other party to perform its mutual obligation, and material breach, which gives the party the right to withhold and eventually to cancel performance.

G. Evaluating Substantial Performance

To distinguish between substantial performance and material breach, R2d § 241 builds on Cardozo's framework to offer a more detailed and certain rule in the form of this five-factor test. The five-factor balancing test might be visualized as follows:

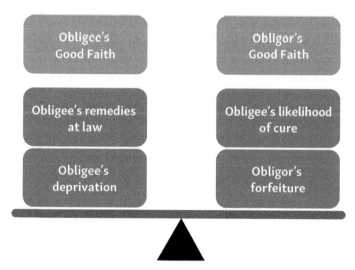

Figure 18.3. Factors in balancing test to distinguish between substantial performance and material breach.

It is very important to understand what these factors mean if one is to employ them in determining whether a party substantially performed or materially breached.

(a) The loss of benefit to the injured party, more simply known as the obligee's deprivation, attempts to quantify the money value lost as the result of the breach. This loss can be understood in light of the entire contract value. Although there is no fixed number, ratio or percentage of the contract price that makes the obligee's deprivation material, the breach is generally seen as more material where it represents a higher proportion of the contract price.

(b) Adequacy of compensation for loss refers to the degree to which the injured party can be adequately compensated by legal remedies. Courts are more likely to find that the breach was material where this leads to an award of damages that make the party whole. But when damages are uncertain or hard to calculate, then a ruling of breach is unlikely to make the plaintiff whole, since uncertain damages cannot be awarded. Thus, when the injured party's loss is clear and easy to measure, then courts will be more likely to find that breach was material.

(c) Forfeiture by the party who fails, more simply known as the obligor's forfeiture, moves to the breaching party's side of the ledger and asks how much the breaching party will lose if the breach is deemed material. When the breaching party's loss would be very large when compared to the nonbreaching party's loss, the court will be less likely to deem its breach material.

(d) Uncertainty that the obligor will cure his breach within a reasonable time justifies a court in ruling that the breach was material. If, on the other hand, a party is ready and willing to cure, the court should interpret that willingness as evidence that performance is substantial. Many facts can show a party's unwillingness or willingness to cure. For example, walking off the job site in protest is strong evidence of unwillingness to cure. Financial weakness, repeated failures to cure, and repeated defects in performance also show that cure is unlikely.

(e) An overarching factor that connects to all the other factors is whether the parties have acted in accordance with standards of good faith and fair dealing. Courts are less likely to award remedies to parties with "unclean hands," such that a party's bad actions make it less likely that a court would rule in its favor.

H. Evaluating Total Breach

Once a party has committed a material breach, its counterparty gains the right to withhold its return performance. But this withholding period is a temporary one. By their very terms, "withholding" and "suspension" of performance implies a limited time period.

This time period is known as the cure period. During the cure period, a breaching party can repair its defective performance, raising it to the level of substantial performance and thus triggering its counterparty's duty to perform in exchange.

When the cure period expires, however, the contract is forever breached. The breaching party loses the right to repair the breach, and its counterparty's duty to perform in exchange is forever discharged.

For example, if a builder of a house builds the house but fails to finish the basement, this is probably a material breach. The buyer then gains the lawful ability to withhold payment to the builder for a time while the builder can still finish the basement and receive the final payment.

How long must the home buyer wait for the builder to cure the breach? That question is answered by R2d § 242, which sets forth a test for distinguishing between material breach and total breach.

The effect of material breach is the nonbreaching party may withhold performance while the breaching party has time to cure. The effect of total breach is the cure period expires and the nonbreaching party's duty to perform is forever discharged.

> *In determining the time after which a party's uncured material failure to render or to offer performance discharges the other party's remaining duties to render performance under the rules stated in §§ 237 and 238, the following circumstances are significant: (a) those stated in § 241; (b) the extent to which it reasonably appears to the injured party that delay may prevent or hinder him in making reasonable substitute arrangements; [and] (c) the extent to which the agreement provides for performance without delay, but a material failure to perform or to offer to perform on a stated day does not of itself discharge the other party's remaining duties unless the circumstances, including the language of the agreement, indicate that performance or an offer to perform by that day is important. R2d § 242.*

The first factor in determining whether breach is total is effectively the same test for determining whether the breach is material. If the breach was so minor that performance was substantial, then there cannot be a total breach. Even if the breach was material, it still might not rise to the level of total breach. Only a breach that is very material is likely to be construed as a total breach.

The second and third factors are new, and they both directly involve time, which makes sense given that the effect of a finding of total breach is that the time for cure has expired. Finding that the breaching party still has time to cure effectively is a decision that the breach is at most material and is not total.

The second factor asks whether waiting for the breaching party to cure would further harm its injured counterparty because that delay will frustrate making substitute arrangements. As you will learn in Module VII — Remedies, injured parties have an obligation to mitigate damages. This means that injured parties have an obligation to minimize the negative impact of their counterparties' breach. This is often done by obtaining substitute performance, which is technically known as "cover."

But obtaining substitute performance may be difficult or impossible while waiting for the other party to cure. Consider the following illustrations that show how even a relatively short cure period can increase the costs of cover.

> *Illustration 242.2. A, a theater manager, contracts with B, an actress, for her performance for six months in a play that A is about to present. B becomes ill during the second month of the performance, and A immediately engages another actress to fill B's place during the remainder of the six months. B recovers at the end of ten days and offers to perform the remainder of the*

contract, but A refuses. Whether B's failure to render performance due to ill-ness immediately discharges A's remaining duties of performance, instead of merely suspending them, depends on the circumstances stated in Subsection (b) and in §241(b) and (d), and in particular on the possibility as it reason-ably appears to A when B becomes ill of the illness being only temporary and of A's obtaining an adequate temporary substitute.

Illustration 242.3. A contracts to sell and B to buy 1,000 shares of stock traded on a national securities exchange, delivery and payment to be on Feb-ruary 1. B offers to pay the price on February 1, but A unjustifiably and without explanation fails to offer to deliver the stock until February 2. B then refuses to accept the stock or pay the price. Under the circumstances stated in Subsection (b) and in §241(a) and (c), the period of time has passed after which B's remaining duties to render performance are discharged because of A's material breach and A therefore has no claim against B. B has a claim against A for breach.

The third factor regards whether the contract specified or implied that time is of the essence. Contracts often include a provision for the time or date of performance of services or delivery of goods. It may also contain a clause expressly stating that time is of the essence for the agreement. But even when the four corners of the con-tract indicate that time is of the essence, under the Restatement approach, a court should look at the contract in light of its entire commercial context before determin-ing whether a material failure to perform on the stated day gives rise to a total breach.

Illustration 242.4. A contracts to sell and B to buy land, the transfer to be on February 1. B tenders the price on February 1, but A does not tender a deed until February 2. B then refuses to accept the deed or pay the price. Under the circumstances stated in Subsections (b) and (c) and in §241(a), in the absence of special circumstances, the period of time has not passed after which B's remaining duties to render performance are discharged. Although A's breach is material, it has been cured. A has a claim against B for damages for total breach of contract, subject to a claim by B against A for damages for partial breach because of the delay.

Illustration 242.9. The facts being otherwise as stated in Illustration 4, the parties use a printed form contract that provides that "time is of the essence." Absent other circumstances indicating that performance by February 1 is of genuine importance, A has a claim against B for damages for total breach of contract.

Illustration 242.10. The facts being otherwise as stated in Illustration 4, the contract provides that A's rights are "conditional on his tendering a deed on or before February 1." A has no claim against B.

Finally, courts will consider whether one party waived its counterparty's failure to perform. A party may give its breaching counterparty time to cure even though the facts would otherwise lead a court to conclude that the cure time has expired. This acts as a waiver of the party's right to assert a total breach.

I. Evaluating Performance and Breach Under the UCC

The UCC takes a much more exacting standard with regard to breaches by the seller of goods. In what is often referred to as the Perfect Tender Rule, the buyer can reject the goods and withhold payment "if the goods or the tender of delivery fail in any respect to conform to the contract." UCC § 2-601. Even if the buyer initially accepts and does not reject the goods, the buyer can revoke acceptance if he later discovers a nonconformity that substantially impairs the value of the goods. UCC § 2-608.

This seemingly harsh standard seems to be exactly what Cardozo was hoping to avoid in *Jacob & Youngs*. The harshness of the UCC approach is softened somewhat by giving the seller additional rights to cure. UCC § 2-508. Additionally, with regard to installment contracts, buyer's rejection of one installment does not give that buyer the right to reject the entire contract unless "the non-conformity substantially impairs the value of the whole contract." UCC § 2-612.

1. Buyer's Rights on Improper Delivery

Unlike the Restatement, which employs the doctrine of substantial performance, the UCC applies the much more exacting standard known as the Perfect Tender Rule. Under this rule, if goods fail in any way to conform precisely to their description in the contract, then the buyer may reject the goods.

> *Subject to the provisions of this Article on breach in installment contracts (Section 2-612) and unless otherwise agreed under the sections on contractual limitations of remedy (Sections 2-718 and 2-719), if the goods or the tender of delivery fail in any respect to conform to the contract, the buyer may (a) reject the whole; or (b) accept the whole; or (c) accept any commercial unit or units and reject the rest. UCC § 2-601.*

2. Buyer's Revocation of Acceptance

Under the UCC, the buyer's power to reject nonconforming goods continues even after the goods are accepted, although the buyer's rights to revoke acceptance are not quite as broad as his original power to reject the goods upon delivery.

> *(1) The buyer may revoke his acceptance of a lot or commercial unit whose non-conformity substantially impairs its value to him if he has accepted it: (a) on the reasonable assumption that its non-conformity would be cured and it has not been seasonably cured; or (b) without discovery of such non-conformity if his acceptance was reasonably induced either by the difficulty of discovery before acceptance or by the seller's assurances. UCC § 2-608(1).*

The period during which a buyer may revoke is not unlimited. Rather, a buyer's revocation is only proper during a reasonable time, which is defined by when a buyer should discover any defect in the goods.

> *Revocation of acceptance must occur within a reasonable time after the buyer discovers or should have discovered the ground for it and before any substantial change in condition of the goods which is not caused by their own defects. It is not effective until the buyer notifies the seller of it.* UCC § 2-608(2).

Moreover, under the UCC, the buyer is not required to elect between revocation of acceptance or recovery of damages for breach. Both are available.

> *A buyer who so revokes has the same rights and duties with regard to the goods involved as if he had rejected them.* UCC § 2-608(3).

3. Seller's Cure

Recall that UCC employs the relatively harsh Perfect Tender Rule, which gives the buyer the ability to reject goods that fail to conform to the contract in any way, while the Restatement only allows a purchaser to refuse to pay for services that materially fail to conform to the contract. But the UCC softens this approach somewhat by giving the seller an automatic ability to cure the defect within a reasonable time (whereas under the Restatement, whether or not a party has the right to cure requires analysis under R2d § 242).

After the buyer has rejected goods, and even after the seller has taken them back and refunded the purchase price, the seller is still permitted to tender conforming goods under certain conditions. First, if the time for delivery has not yet come, the seller automatically has until the contractual time for delivery to perfect the goods.

> *Where any tender or delivery by the seller is rejected because non-conforming and the time for performance has not yet expired, the seller may seasonably notify the buyer of his intention to cure and may then within the contract time make a conforming delivery.* UCC § 2-508(1).

Even after the time for delivery has come and gone, the seller still has the ability to perfectly tender the goods when the seller had reasonable grounds to believe that the original tender would be acceptable.

> *(2) Where the buyer rejects a non-conforming tender which the seller had reasonable grounds to believe would be acceptable with or without money allowance the seller may if he seasonably notifies the buyer have a further reasonable time to substitute a conforming tender.* UCC § 2-508(2).

Once again, we see how commercial law encourages parties to engage in self-help and to work things out between themselves before litigating a contractual dispute.

For example, Jordan places an order for delivery of groceries via an application developed by Amazon.com, Inc., in which he orders a dozen items including one organic yellow banana for delivery within two hours. The local store is out of organic bananas, so two hours later, Amazon delivers a conventional yellow banana to Jordan, although with the rest of the goods he ordered. Jordan refuses to pay for the conventional banana. Even though the time for performance has expired, Amazon has a further reasonable time to provide an organic banana as a replacement.

However, if Jordan has the selected the "no substitution" options while placing his order, that would have put Amazon on reasonable notice that a substitute good would not be acceptable. If the contract has such as a "no replacement" clause, Amazon shall not have additional time to tender perfectly conforming goods.

4. Installment Contracts

Special rules apply when tender of goods occurs in installments, as opposed to a contract where tender of goods occurs all at one time. For example, A contracts to sell and B to buy ten identical carloads of coal for $100,000, with one carload to be delivered per month for ten months. This is an installment contract, according to the UCC.

It might still be interpreted to be an installment contract even if the contract includes language such as "each delivery is a separate contract" where the circumstances show that such interpretation is out of line with commercial standards. In other words, we see here again that the UCC takes a subjective approach to contract interpretation by admitting extrinsic evidence even where that conflicts with intrinsic evidence (what the contract actually says).

> An "installment contract" is one which requires or authorizes the delivery of goods in separate lots to be separately accepted, even though the contract contains a clause "each delivery is a separate contract" or its equivalent. UCC § 2-612(1).

Under an installment contract for goods, a buyer can reject any single installment pursuant to the rules stated above that apply to non-installment contracts. The question is whether a buyer can cancel the entire installment contract where one or more installments is nonconforming.

The UCC first defines installment contract broadly. Unless both parties clearly make each installment a separate contract, the UCC would have judges still interpret the contract as a unified whole.

> The buyer may reject any installment which is non-conforming if the non-conformity substantially impairs the value of that installment and cannot be cured or if the non-conformity is a defect in the required documents; but if the non-conformity does not fall within subsection (3) and the seller gives adequate assurance of its cure the buyer must accept that installment. UCC § 2-612(2).

By grouping installment contracts into a single agreement, buyers gain rights to cancel that entire agreement when a single installment is non-confirming. Delivery of a single shipment of non-conforming goods can give buyers good reason to doubt the seller's ability to perform its entire obligation. But the seller also has some ability to recognize the defect and promise to cure it. Again, commercial law wants parties to work things out and thus earn the fruits of the bargain, not to run to court as soon as issues arise.

> *Whenever non-conformity or default with respect to one or more install-ments substantially impairs the value of the whole contract there is a breach of the whole. But the aggrieved party reinstates the contract if he accepts a non-conforming installment without seasonably notifying of cancellation or if he brings an action with respect only to past installments or demands per-formance as to future installments.* UCC § 2-612(3).

As the rule above states, the buyer has the right to cancel the entire contract upon receipt of one nonconforming shipment thereunder only if that nonconforming installment substantially impairs the value of the whole contract.

J. Reflections on Substantial Performance

This module introduced three major concepts.

1. Most contract are meant to be an exchange of mutual promises, such that the performance of each promise is intended to be a condition to the performance of the other. The mutual performances under an exchange of promises are thus implied conditions concurrent to each other. This was called "mutual conditions" in *Kingston* and is also referred to as mutual and simultaneous promises.

2. Implied conditions like those found under an exchange of promises are subject to the doctrine of substantial performance. This means that, unlike express conditions, which must be completely performed before performances subject to express conditions come due, promises subject to implied conditions must be performed when the implied condition is substantially performed. Until the mutual promise is substantially performed, the counterparty may withhold its performance. This usu-ally comes up when one party refuses to pay the other because services were not completely performed.

3. A party who materially breaches (fails to substantially perform) has a reasonable amount of time known as a cure period to repair the defec-tive performance. When this cure period expires, however, the material breach decays into a state of total breach, and the nonbreaching party gains the lawful right not only to withhold or suspend performance for a time but also to cancel the contract and extinguish any future obliga-tions under it.

The UCC, however, does not apply the doctrine of substantial performance. Rather, the UCC employs the Perfect Tender Rule, which holds a buyer can reject goods that do not completely confirm to the contract in all specifications. In addition, buyers of goods subject to the UCC have some rights to revoke acceptance of goods when non-conformance with the contract substantially impairs their value to the buyer.

Cases

Reading Kingston v. Preston. In 1773, a famous English judge named The Right Honorable William Murray, First Earl of Mansfield (who is referred to more simply as Lord Mansfield), recognized that when parties make mutual promises to each other, these promises are often intended to be implied conditions to their obligations.

The original text of this famous case is reproduced below. Although the entire decision is less than a thousand words, it is hard to read due to its use of old language, British spelling, and grammatical structure that would charitably be described today as a run-on sentence. To retain the color and texture of this historic case while enhancing readability slightly, the original text has been edited only by adding paragraph breaks. Try your best to understand the fact of this case and the three kinds of covenants identified by Lord Mansfield in his analysis. After the case, this casebook will clarify the modern meaning of these critical concepts.

Kingston v. Preston

99 Eng. Rep. 437 (K.B. 1773)

MANSFIELD, J.

It was an action of debt, for non-performance of covenants contained in certain articles of agreement between the plaintiff and the defendant. The declaration stated;

That, by articles made the 24th of March, 1770, the plaintiff, for the considerations therein-after mentioned, covenanted, with the defendant, to serve him for one year and a quarter next ensuing, as a covenant-servant, in his trade of a silk-mercer, at £200 a year, and in consideration of the premises, the defendant covenanted, that at the end of the year and a quarter, he would give up his business of a mercer to the plaintiff, and a nephew of the defendant, or some other person to be nominated. By the defendant, and give up to them his stock in trade, at a fair valuation; and that, between the young traders, deeds of partnership should be executed for 14 years, and from and immediately after the execution of, the said deeds, the defendant would permit the said young traders to carry on the said business in the defendant's house.

Then the declaration stated a covenant by the plaintiff, that he would accept the business and stock in trade, at a fair valuation, with the defendant's nephew, or such other person, &c. and execute such deeds of partnership, and, further, that the plaintiff should, and would, at, and before, the sealing and delivery of the deeds, cause and procure good and sufficient security to be given to the defendant, to be approved of by the defendant, for the payment of £250 monthly, to the defendant, in lieu of a moiety of the monthly produce of the stock in trade, until the value of the stock should be reduced to £4000.

Then the plaintiff averred, that he had performed, and been ready to perform, his covenants, and assigned for breach on the part of the defendant, that he had refused to surrender and give up his business, at the end of the said year and a quarter.

The defendant pleaded, 1. That the plaintiff did not offer sufficient security; and, 2. That he did not give sufficient security for the payment of the £250, &c.

And the plaintiff demurred generally to both pleas.

On the part of the plaintiff, the case was argued by Mr. Buller, who contended, that the covenants were mutual and independent, and, therefore, a plea of the breach of one of the covenants to be performed by the plaintiff was no bar to an action for a breach by the defendant of one of which he had bound himself to perform, but that the defendant might have his remedy for the breach by the plaintiff, in a separate action.

On the other side, Mr. Grose insisted, that the covenants were dependent in their nature, and, therefore, performance must be alleged: the security to be given for the money, was manifestly the chief object of the transaction, and it would be highly unreasonable to construe the agreement, so as to oblige the defendant to give up a beneficial business, and valuable stock in trade, and trust to the plaintiff's personal security, (who might, and, indeed, was admitted to be worth nothing,) for the performance of his part.

In delivering the judgment of the Court, Lord Mansfield expressed himself to the following effect: There are three kinds of covenants:

1. Such as are called mutual and independent, where either party may recover damages from the other, for the injury he may have received by a breach of the covenants in his favor, and where it is no excuse for the defendant, to allege a breach of the covenants on the part of the plaintiff.

2. There are covenants which are conditions and dependent, in which the performance of one depends on the prior performance of another, and, therefore, till this prior condition is performed, the other party is not liable to an action on his covenant.

3. There is also a third sort of covenants, which are mutual conditions to be performed at the same time; and, in these, if one party was ready, and offered, to perform his part, and the other neglected, or refused, to perform his, he who was ready, and offered, has fulfilled his engagement, and may maintain an action for the default of the other; though it is not certain that either is obliged to do the first act.

His Lordship then proceeded to say, that the dependance, or independence of covenants, was to be collected from the evident sense and meaning of the parties, and, that, however transposed they might be in the deed, their precedency must depend on the order of time in which the intent of the transaction requires their performance. That, in the case before the Court, it would be the greatest injustice if the plaintiff should prevail: the essence of the agreement was, that the defendant should not trust to the personal security of the plaintiff, but, before he delivered up his stock and business, should have good security for the payment of the money. The giving such security, therefore, must necessarily be a condition precedent.

Judgment was accordingly given for the defendant, because the part to be performed by the plaintiff was clearly a condition precedent.

Reflection

The *Kingston* case introduces what are sometimes called the "Kingston covenants." The taxonomy of promises and their interdependence that Lord Mansfield provided in this famous case remains relevant today, although the terminology varies slightly.

Discussion

1. Prior to *Kingston*, what recourse would one party have when its counterparty breached an agreement? More specifically, what legal rights would the silk merchant in *Kingston* have if there were no such thing as dependent covenants?

2. When parties exchange promises, do they usually intend those promises to be independent or dependent? Explain your reasoning.

Reading Jacob & Youngs, Inc. v. Kent. As you will see from our next case in this chapter, *Jacob & Youngs v. Kent*, the law treats these implied conditions differently from express conditions. Recall from the prior module that express conditions precedent must be completely performed before the promise subject to that condition needs to be performed at all. This so-called doctrine of complete performance can lead to harsh and unjust results, which in the case of express conditions courts can equitably ameliorate through the excuse doctrine.

The law of implied promises developed differently. In 1921, then-Judge Benjamin Cardozo (who later became an Associate Justice of the Supreme Court of the United States) established the doctrine of substantial performance.

Jacob & Youngs, Inc. v. Kent
230 N.Y. 239 (1921)

CARDOZO, J.

The plaintiff built a country residence for the defendant at a cost of upwards of $77,000, and now sues to recover a balance of $3,483.46, remaining unpaid. The work of construction ceased in June, 1914, and the defendant then began to occupy the dwelling. There was no complaint of defective performance until March, 1915.

One of the specifications for the plumbing work provides that "all wrought iron pipe must be well galvanized, lap welded pipe of the grade known as 'standard pipe' of Reading manufacture." The defendant learned in March, 1915, that some of the pipe, instead of being made in Reading, was the product of other factories. The plaintiff was accordingly directed by the architect to do the work anew. The plumbing was then encased within the walls except in a few places where it had to be exposed. Obedience to the order meant more than the substitution of other pipe. It meant the demolition at great expense of substantial parts of the completed structure. The plaintiff left the work untouched, and asked for a certificate that the final payment was due. Refusal of the certificate was followed by this suit.

The evidence sustains a finding that the omission of the prescribed brand of pipe was neither fraudulent nor willful. It was the result of the oversight and inattention of the plaintiff's subcontractor. Reading pipe is distinguished from Cohoes pipe and other brands only by the name of the manufacturer stamped upon it at intervals of between six and seven feet. Even the defendant's architect, though he inspected the pipe upon arrival, failed to notice the discrepancy. The plaintiff tried to show that the brands installed, though made by other manufacturers, were the same in quality, in appearance, in market value and in cost as the brand stated in the contract — that they were, indeed, the same thing, though manufactured in another place. The evidence was excluded, and a verdict directed for the defendant. The Appellate Division reversed, and granted a new trial.

We think the evidence, if admitted, would have supplied some basis for the inference that the defect was insignificant in its relation to the project. The courts never say that one who makes a contract fills the measure of his duty by less than full performance. They do say, however, that an omission, both trivial and innocent, will sometimes be atoned for by allowance of the resulting damage, and will not always be the breach of a condition to be followed by a forfeiture. The distinction is akin to that between dependent and independent promises, or between promises and conditions (Anson on Contracts [Corbin's ed.], sec. 367; 2 Williston on Contracts, sec. 842). Some promises are so plainly independent that they can never by fair construction be conditions of one another. Others are so plainly dependent that they must always be conditions. Others, though dependent and thus conditions when there is departure in point of substance, will be viewed as independent and collateral when the departure is insignificant. Considerations partly of justice and partly of presumable intention are to tell us whether this or that promise shall be placed in one class or in another. The simple and the uniform will call for different remedies from the multifarious and the intricate. The margin of departure within the range of normal expectation upon a sale of common chattels will vary from the margin to be expected upon a contract for the construction of a mansion or a "skyscraper." There will be harshness sometimes and oppression in the implication of a condition when the thing upon which labor has been expended is incapable of surrender because united to the land, and equity and reason in the implication of a like condition when the subject-matter, if defective, is in shape to be returned. From the conclusion that promises may not be treated as dependent to the extent of their uttermost minutia without a sacrifice of justice, the progress is a short one to the conclusion that they may not be so treated without a perversion of intention. Intention not otherwise revealed may be presumed to hold in contemplation the reasonable and probable. If something else is in view, it must not be left to implication. There will be no assumption of a purpose to visit venial faults with oppressive retribution.

Those who think more of symmetry and logic in the development of legal rules than of practical adaptation to the attainment of a just result will be troubled by a classification where the lines of division are so wavering and blurred. Something, doubtless, may be said on the score of consistency and certainty in favor of a stricter standard. The courts have balanced such considerations against those of equity and fairness, and found the latter to be the weightier. The decisions in this state commit us to the liberal view, which is making its way, nowadays, in jurisdictions slow to welcome it (*Dakin & Co. v. Lee*, 1916, 1 K.B. 566, 579). Where the line is to be drawn between the important and the trivial cannot be settled by a formula. "In the nature of the case precise boundaries are impossible." The same omission may take on one aspect or another according to its setting. Substitution of equivalents may not have the same significance in fields of art on the one side and in those of mere utility on the other. Nowhere will change be tolerated, however, if it is so dominant or pervasive as in any real or substantial measure to frustrate the purpose of the contract. There is no general license to install whatever, in the builder's judgment, may be regarded as "just as good." The question is one of degree, to be answered, if there is doubt, by the triers of the facts, and, if the inferences are certain, by the judges of the law. We must weigh the purpose to be served, the desire to be gratified, the excuse for deviation from the letter, the cruelty of enforced adherence. Then only can we tell whether literal fulfilment is to be implied by law as a condition. This is not to say that the parties are not free by apt and certain words to effectuate a purpose that performance of every term shall be a condition of recovery. That question is not here. This is merely to say that the law will be slow to impute the purpose, in the silence of the parties, where the significance of the default is grievously out of proportion to the oppression of the forfeiture. The willful transgressor must accept the penalty of his transgression. For him there is no occasion to mitigate the rigor of implied conditions. The transgressor whose default is unintentional and trivial may hope for mercy if he will offer atonement for his wrong.

In the circumstances of this case, we think the measure of the allowance is not the cost of replacement, which would be great, but the difference in value, which would be either nominal or nothing. Some of the exposed sections might perhaps have been replaced at moderate expense. The defendant did not limit his demand to them, but treated the plumbing as a unit to be corrected from cellar to roof. In point of fact, the plaintiff never reached the stage at which evidence of the extent of the allowance became necessary. The trial court had excluded evidence that the defect was unsubstantial, and in view of that ruling there was no occasion for the plaintiff to go farther with an offer of proof. We think, however, that the offer, if it had been made, would not of necessity have been defective because directed to difference in value. It is true that in most cases the cost of replacement is the measure. The owner is entitled to the money which will permit him to complete, unless the cost of completion is grossly and unfairly out of proportion to the good to be attained. When that is true, the measure is the difference in value. Specifications call, let us say, for a foundation built of granite quarried in Vermont. On the completion of the building, the owner learns that through the blunder of a subcontractor part of the foundation has been built of granite of the same quality quarried in New Hampshire. The measure of allowance is not the cost of reconstruction. "There may be omissions of that which could not afterwards be supplied exactly as called for by the contract without taking down the building to its foundations, and at the same time the omission may not affect the value of the building for use or otherwise, except so slightly as to be hardly appreciable." The rule that gives a remedy in cases of substantial performance with compensation for defects of trivial or inappreciable importance, has been developed by the courts as an instrument of justice. The measure of the allowance must be shaped to the same end.

The order should be affirmed, and judgment absolute directed in favor of the plaintiff upon the stipulation, with costs in all courts.

McLAUGHLIN, J. (dissenting).

I dissent. The plaintiff did not perform its contract. Its failure to do so was either intentional or due to gross neglect which, under the uncontradicted facts, amounted to the same thing, nor did it make any proof of the cost of compliance, where compliance was possible.

Under its contract it obligated itself to use in the plumbing only pipe (between 2,000 and 2,500 feet) made by the Reading Manufacturing Company. The first pipe delivered was about 1,000 feet and the plaintiff's superintendent then called the attention of the foreman of the subcontractor, who was doing the plumbing, to the fact that the specifications annexed to the contract required all pipe used in the plumbing to be of the Reading Manufacturing Company. They then examined it for the purpose of ascertaining whether this delivery was of that manufacture and found it was. Thereafter, as pipe was required in the progress of the work, the foreman of the subcontractor would leave word at its shop that he wanted a specified number of feet of pipe, without in any way indicating of what manufacture. Pipe would thereafter be delivered and installed in the building, without any examination whatever. Indeed, no examination, so far as appears, was made by the plaintiff, the subcontractor, defendant's architect, or anyone else, of any of the pipe except the first delivery, until after the building had been completed. Plaintiff's architect then refused to give the certificate of completion, upon which the final payment depended, because all of the pipe used in the plumbing was not of the kind called for by the contract. After such refusal, the subcontractor removed the covering or insulation from about 900 feet of pipe which was exposed in the basement, cellar and attic, and all but 70 feet was found to have been manufactured, not by the Reading Company, but by other manufacturers, some by the Cohoes Rolling Mill Company, some by the National Steel Works, some by the South Chester Tubing Company, and some which bore no manufacturer's mark at all. The balance of the pipe had been so installed in the building that an inspection of it could not be had without demolishing, in part at least, the building itself.

I am of the opinion the trial court was right in directing a verdict for the defendant. The plaintiff agreed that all the pipe used should be of the Reading Manufacturing Company. Only about two-fifths of it, so far as appears, was of that kind. If more were used, then the burden of proving that fact was upon the plaintiff, which it could easily have done, since it knew where the pipe was obtained. The question of substantial performance of a contract of the character of the one under consideration depends in no small degree upon the good faith of the contractor. If the plaintiff had intended to, and had complied with the terms of the contract except as to minor omissions, due to inadvertence, then he might be allowed to recover the contract price, less the amount necessary to fully compensate the defendant for damages caused by such omissions. But that is not this case. It installed between 2,000 and 2,500 feet of pipe, of which only 1,000 feet at most complied with the contract. No explanation was given why pipe called for by the contract was not used, nor was any effort made to show what it would cost to remove the pipe of other manufacturers and install that of the Reading Manufacturing Company. The defendant had a right to contract for what he wanted. He had a right before making payment to get what the contract called for. It is no answer to this suggestion to say that the pipe put in was just as good as that made by the Reading Manufacturing Company, or that the difference in value between such pipe and the pipe made by the Reading Manufacturing Company would be either "nominal or nothing." Defendant contracted for pipe made by the Reading Manufacturing Company. What his reason was for requiring this kind of pipe is of no importance. He wanted that and was entitled to it. It may have been a mere whim on his part, but even so, he had a right to this kind of pipe, regardless of whether some other kind, according to the opinion of the contractor or experts, would have been "just as good, better, or done just as well." He agreed to pay only upon condition that the pipe installed were made by that company and he ought not to be compelled to pay unless that condition be performed. The rule, therefore, of substantial performance, with damages for unsubstantial omissions, has no application.

What was said by this court in *Smith v. Brady* (supra) is quite applicable here: "I suppose it will be conceded that everyone has a right to build his house, his cottage or his store after such a model and in such style as shall best accord with his notions of utility or be most agreeable to his fancy. The specifications of the contract become the law between the parties until voluntarily changed. If the owner prefers a plain and simple Doric column, and has so provided in the agreement, the contractor has no right to put in its place the more costly and elegant Corinthian. If the owner, having regard to strength and durability, has contracted for walls of specified materials to be laid in a particular manner, or for a given number of joists and beams, the builder has no right to substitute his own judgment or that of others. Having departed from the agreement, if performance has not been waived by the other party, the law will not allow him to allege that he has made as good a building as the one he engaged to erect. He can demand payment only upon and according to the terms of his contract, and if the conditions on which payment is due have not been performed, then the right to demand it does not exist. To hold a different doctrine would be simply to make another contract, and would be giving to parties an encouragement to violate their engagements, which the just policy of the law does not permit." (p. 186.)

I am of the opinion the trial court did not err in ruling on the admission of evidence or in directing a verdict for the defendant.

For the foregoing reasons I think the judgment of the Appellate Division should be reversed and the judgment of the Trial Term affirmed.

Reflection

One way to understand the dissent's criticisms of the majority opinion without throwing out Cardozo's substantial contribution to legal doctrine is to distinguish what is radical in his opinion. The criticisms boil down to a singular complaint that Cardozo transmogrified a clear express condition into an implied one. Remember that the contract was written in a manner that would reasonably lead to the conclusion that the parties intended the installation of Reading pipe to be an express condition precedent to Kent's obligation to pay Jacob & Youngs. In his effort to reach a more equitable result — and perhaps in seeking to define a new doctrine in contract law — Cardozo ignores the plain meaning of the written agreement. He is not alone in doing this: look back to cases like *Nānākuli* and *Sierra Diesel* in Module V, and you will see that judges who take a more subjective approach to contract interpretation will ignore the plain meaning when justice so requires. For an objective jurist like McLaughlin, this is error.

But once we get past Cardozo's strong application of the subjective approach to contract interpretation, such that we accept that this contract does not have an express condition to use a certain brand of pipe but at best an implied one, then the power and importance of his opinion become clear. By creating the doctrine of substantial performance of implied conditions, Cardozo finishes in 1921 what Lord Mansfield started in 1773. The law today is now better aligned with what people would expect from their contractual relationships.

The majority of jurisdictions and the Restatement have generally adopted Cardozo's approach — at least insofar as to recognize that an implied condition need only be substantially performed for the promise conditioned on that implied condition to become due. As you review the Restatement's rules on the impact of performance and non-performance, consider whether it does not go quite so far as Cardozo did.

Discussion

If you skipped the dissent in this case, stop reading here and go back to read that first. The dissent is critical to read in this case, because in it, Judge McLaughlin points out the problems with Judge Cardozo's approach.

1. McLaughlin criticizes Cardozo's new doctrine for violating principles of freedom of contract. If contracts are only enforceable at law to the extent they accord with the parties' intentions, why should a court assume that parties did not mean to make their promises depend on the complete performance of conditions precedent?

2. McLaughlin criticizes Cardozo's fact finding by questioning whether the builder's error was really so trivial and innocent. We do not really know why the builder failed to use the specified brand of pipe. We also do not know whether Reading pipe really is better than other brands — or, for that matter, whether branded pipe is better than pipe which is not branded. Courts are not experts in the quality of pipe, so how is this court justified in asserting that these pipes were identical?

3. McLaughlin criticizes Cardozo's application of equitable principles in this case as leading to unjust results in other cases. If parties' contracts will not be interpreted to mean what they say, how shall parties plan their business affairs?

Reading Khiterer v. Bell. The next case, *Khiterer*, illustrates how a modern trial court applies Cardozo's rather loose framework. Read this case twice. The first time you read it, highlight the rule that the court employed and the facts analyzed under it, and write annotations explaining how those facts impact the outcome of the rule. Then, go on to the next section, where you will learn how the Restatement created a more formal five-factor balancing test, and carefully note what are those five factors. Then, return to *Khiterer*. As you read *Khiterer* a second time, apply its facts to the balancing-test rule provided by the Restatement.

Compare your experience analyzing this case under Cardozo's loose standard against analyzing it under the Restatement's formal rule. Do you arrive at a different result? Was it easier or harder to perform this analysis with a loose standard or with a formal rule? Does one approach require more or less facts or evidence than the other? Which of these approaches do you think is more likely to help judges arrive at the right result in the majority of cases?

Khiterer v. Bell

6 Misc. 3d 1015(A), 800 N.Y.S.2d 348 (Civ. Ct. 2005)

JACK M. BATTAGLIA, J.

A patient who proves breach of a contract for professional dental services, but does not also prove personal or economic harm, may recover only nominal damages for the breach.

Inna Khiterer began treating with Dr. Mina Bell in October 2001. The treatment included root canal therapy on two teeth and the fabrication and fitting of crowns for those teeth, as well as the fabrication and fitting of a replacement crown for a third tooth. The crowns were fitted in June 2002, and, after several broken appointments, Ms. Khiterer last saw Dr. Bell in December 2002. Ms. Khiterer treated with another dentist the following summer, and, according to her testimony at trial, learned that the crowns with which she was fitted by Dr. Bell were not fabricated in accordance with their agreement. Specifically, the crowns were made totally of porcelain, rather than of porcelain on gold as they, allegedly, should have been.

Ms. Khiterer's complaint in this Small Claims Part action alleges "defective services rendered and breach of contract". Advised prior to trial that any claim in the nature of dental malpractice required expert proof, Ms. Khiterer elected to proceed on her breach of contract claim only.

"A breach of contract claim in relation to the rendition of medical or dental services by a physician or dentist will withstand a test of its legal sufficiency only when based upon an express special promise to effect a cure or accomplish some definite result." A contract cause of action might be based upon a "specific promise to deliver [a] baby without administration of blood."

The agreement alleged here, for dental services including root canal therapy and the fabrication and fitting of crowns made of porcelain on gold, had as its predominant purpose the furnishing of services, and is, therefore, governed by the general law of contracts and not by Article 2 of the Uniform Commercial Code. As will appear, however, the result would be the same in any event.

Ms. Khiterer testified that, because she had previously been fitted with crowns made of porcelain on gold (actually an 86% gold alloy, as Dr. Bell explained), she requested that the three crowns that she would receive from Dr. Bell also be made of porcelain on gold. Ms. Khiterer also offered the testimony of a friend, Sergei Leontev, who said that he was present during a conversation between Ms. Khiterer and Dr. Bell, and heard Dr. Bell assure Ms. Khiterer that she would be receiving three "golden-based crowns". Mr. Leontev also testified that he made a similar agreement with Dr. Bell that was later changed to all-porcelain crowns.

Dr. Bell testified that she had no independent recollection of any conversation with Ms. Khiterer about the composite material for the crowns. She testified further that an all-porcelain crown was therapeutically superior to a crown containing any metal, including the gold alloy, because the presence of metal created a risk of patient reaction. The cost to her, she said, of an all-porcelain crown and a porcelain-on-metal crown is the same, but the cement that binds the all-porcelain crown is more expensive.

Dr. Bell presented a copy of Ms. Khiterer's chart, showing an entry for the first visit on October 21, 2001 of "crowns metal-free". Impressions for the crowns, however, were apparently taken seven months later on May 30, 2002. Ms. Khiterer presented a summary of all treatment she received from Dr. Bell, handwritten by Dr. Bell, showing the notations for two teeth "rct/post/crown/pfm" and for one additional tooth "pfm". Dr. Bell explained that "rct" stood for "root canal therapy" and that "pfm" stood for "porcelain fused metal". She maintained that "pfm" was shorthand for any crown no matter the composition, but did not satisfactorily explain the then-redundant notation "crown/pfm".

The Court finds that the contract between Ms. Khiterer and Dr. Bell called for crowns made of porcelain on gold, but that the crowns with which Ms. Khiterer was fitted were made of all porcelain. There is no evidence that Dr. Bell intentionally substituted all porcelain for porcelain on gold. Intent is not required, of course, for a breach of contract, but, as will appear, it may affect the remedy for the breach. Dr. Bell pointed to an entry in Ms. Khiterer's chart for June 5, 2002, the date the crowns were fitted, that reads, "Patient satisfied w/esthetic [sic] cementation", as evidence that Ms. Khiterer was satisfied with the all-porcelain crowns. But the entry cannot bear that weight, particularly in light of the evidence that Ms. Khiterer could not and did not know that the crowns were all porcelain until her teeth were x-rayed by her successor dentist.

The damages recoverable in a contract action against a doctor or dentist "are restricted to payments made and to the expenditures for nurses or medicines or other damages that flow from the breach." The precise scope of this damage formula is not entirely clear. It would include the amount of the fee paid or due to the doctor or dentist, but, as the decisions make clear, would not include "pain and suffering." It would be seem, therefore, that Ms. Khiterer would be entitled to recover as damages at least the fee she paid to Dr. Bell for the fabrication and fitting of the three crowns. The opinions, however, appear to assume that there had not been substantial performance of the contract by the doctor.

Developed in the context of construction contracts, the substantial performance doctrine allows the contractor to recover or retain the contract price for the work, with a deduction for the cost of completion or correction to contract requirements. The doctrine is applicable to employment contracts, real estate brokerage agreements, and leases, and no reason suggests itself for not applying the doctrine as well to contracts for medical or dental services.

As articulated by Judge Cardozo in his seminal opinion in *Jacob & Youngs v. Kent*, 230 N.Y. 239 (1921), "The courts never say that one who makes a contract fills the measure of his duty by less than full performance. They do say, however, that an omission, both trivial and innocent, will sometimes be atoned for by allowance of the resulting damage, and will not always be the breach of a condition to be followed by a forfeiture" (*id.*, at 241). The doctrine is required by justice, so as not "to visit venial faults with oppressive retribution" (see *id.*, at 242), and "[t]he transgressor whose default is unintentional and trivial may hope for mercy if he will offer atonement for his wrong" (*id.*, at 244). But "[t]he willful transgressor must accept the penalty of his transgression." (*Id.*) "The interrupted work may have been better than called for in the plans. Even so, there can be no recovery if the contractor willfully and without excuse has substituted something else."

"[C]onveying a benefit upon a party does not ipso facto constitute substantial performance." "A contractor is not entitled to compensation from an owner even for improvements which benefit the owner unless that is a benefit for which an owner agreed to pay."

"Substitution of equivalents may not have the same significance in fields of art on the one side and in those of mere utility on the other." "Nowhere will change be tolerated, however, if it is so dominant or pervasive as in any real or substantial measure to frustrate the purpose of the contract. . . . There is no general license to install whatever, in the builder's judgment, may be regarded as 'just as good' . . . . We must weigh the purpose to be served, the desire to be gratified, the excuse for deviation from the letter, the cruelty of enforced adherence."

Where substantial performance has been rendered, the remedy is the cost of completion or correction, unless that cost "is grossly and unfairly out of proportion to the good to be attained. When that is true, the measure is the difference in value." (*Id.*, at 244; see also *Ferrari v. Barleo Homes, Inc.*, 112 A.D.2d at 137–38 [awarding "difference in value between the contract materials and the substituted materials actually utilized"].) The "difference in value rule" is applied to avoid "economic waste". (See *Bellizzi v. Huntley Estates, Inc.*, 3 N.Y.2d 112, 115 [1957]; *Lyon v. Belosky Construction Inc.*, 247 A.D.2d at 731.) But where the defect in performance is substantial, the cost of completion or correction will be awarded "notwithstanding the relatively small fee . . . charged for services rendered." (See *id.*, at 732.)

Here, as already noted, there is no evidence that Dr. Bell intentionally substituted all porcelain for porcelain on gold as the material from which Ms. Khiterer's crowns were to be fabricated. The all-porcelain crowns were clearly suitable functionally for the intended purpose; indeed, there is no evidence to contradict Dr. Bell's opinion that they were better. Nor was there evidence to contradict her testimony of economic equivalence, and Ms. Khiterer testified that the fee she was charged by Dr. Bell was significantly less than the fee she had been quoted by other dentists. There is no evidence of physical harm to Ms. Khiterer from the all-porcelain crowns; although she testified that two of the crowns have been replaced by porcelain-on-gold crowns, there was no evidence that the replacement was necessitated by the composition of the all-porcelain crowns. And Ms. Khiterer was satisfied with the all-porcelain crowns from an aesthetic perspective.

If, therefore, there is to be a determination that Dr. Bell did not substantially perform her contract with Ms. Khiterer — or, to put it differently, that her performance was substantially defective it must rest on recognition of a patient's right to control, without qualification, any material that would become part of her body. The only decision of which this Court is aware that seems relevant to the issue suggests that the contract action against a doctor or dentist does not extend that far.

In *Semel v. Culliford* (120 A.D.2d 901), the patient alleged that the doctor "fail[ed] to accomplish what he specifically undertook and agreed to do, take out all of the wire sutures" that had been implanted in the patient during previous open-heart surgery (see *id.*, at 902). The court held that, "[a]s drafted", the patient's contract cause of action could not withstand the doctor's motion for summary judgment. (See *id.*) Although the court saw "an issue of fact concerning the extent of the surgery [the doctor] actually contracted to perform, the only damage said to have been sustained is . . . pain and suffering items of injury not obtainable in a contract action." (See *id.*)

Tort cases concerning lack of consent to medical treatment address a somewhat similar issue. "Every human being of adult years and sound mind has a right to determine what shall be done with his own body; and a surgeon who performs an operation without his patient's consent, commits an assault, for which he is liable for damages." But, if the patient "fail[s] to prove any damages causally related to her lack of consent", she may recover only nominal damages. (See *Garzione v. Vassar Brothers Hospital*, 36 A.D.2d 390, 393 [1st Dept 1971], aff'd 30 N.Y.2d 857 [1972]; *Barnette v. Potenza*, 79 Misc.2d 51, 56–57 [Sup Ct, Nassau County 1974].)

And so, when a patient sued her dentist because "the wrong tooth had been extracted", but "the tooth that was extracted was badly diseased and should have been extracted", a judgment for the patient could not stand. (See *Doniger v. Berger*, 241 AD 23, 23, 26 [1st Dept 1934].) The court noted that "no injurious results to the patient were proved" and "no special contract was made." (*Id.*, at 26.) A dissenting judge disagreed on the latter issue, finding proof of a "breach of a special contract resulting in a trespass." (See *id.* [O'Malley, J, dissenting].) He would have allowed damages "predicated . . . upon the additional expense [the patient] would be required to incur for contemplated bridge work by reason of the absence of the tooth extracted." (See *id.*, at 27–28.) There was no suggestion of an award of general damages, unrelated to proof of physical or economic harm.

Whether the form of action is contract or tort, "the inquiry must always be, what is an adequate remedy to the party injured"; "the law awards to the party injured a just indemnity for the wrong which has been done him, and no more." The tort cases for lack of consent to medical treatment support a conclusion that an invasion of the interest to control one's body is not compensable beyond an award of nominal damages, in the absence of proof of other harm, presumably including, in an appropriate case, emotional harm.

The Court concludes that Dr. Bell's breach of her contract with Ms. Khiterer, fitting her with all-porcelain crowns rather than porcelain-on-gold crowns, was not substantial, so as to warrant a return of her total fee. An award based upon the cost of replacement (which, in any event, has not been established by competent evidence) would be "grossly and unfairly out of proportion to the good to be obtained." And, under the circumstances here, the "difference in value rule" yields an award of only nominal damages, to which Ms. Khiterer is entitled upon proof of breach of contract.

The Court's analysis and conclusion are supported by an analysis of Ms. Khiterer's claim, and the conclusion that would be reached, under Article 2 of the Uniform Commercial Code. The contract description of the goods, porcelain-on-gold crowns, would constitute "an express warranty that the goods shall conform to the description." (See UCC § 2-313 [1][b].) Ms. Khiterer could reject the crowns if they "fail[ed] in any respect to conform to the contract." (See UCC § 2-601.) But Ms. Khiterer's use of the crowns for approximately two years would constitute acceptance of them (see UCC § 2-606 [1][c]); and, consistent with the substantial performance doctrine in general contract law, Ms. Khiterer could revoke her acceptance of the crowns only if the "non-conformity substantially impair[ed] [their] value" (see UCC § 2-608 [1].) Without a substantial impairment of value, Ms. Khiterer's acceptance would stand, and she would be obligated to pay for the crowns "at the contract rate". (See UCC § 2-607 [1].) She would retain a claim for damages, however, measured by the "difference . . . between the value of the goods accepted and the value they would have had if they had been as warranted." (See UCC § 2-714 [2].) Applying that formula, her damages would be nominal.

Judgment is awarded to Ms. Khiterer for $10.00, plus disbursements.

Reflection

As you may have surmised from reading *Khiterer* twice — first applying Cardozo's standard for substantial performance, and second applying the Restatement's five-factor rule — there are costs and benefits to both rules and standards.

A standard like the one Cardozo provides for determining substantial performance gives judges a wide degree of freedom in deciding what justice requires for a certain case. But this freedom inherently means that it is harder for parties to predict how courts will rule. A rule like the one that the Restatement provides results in a more structured analysis. That structure gives parties more advance notice about how courts will evaluate circumstances where one party withheld performance. This makes it easier to plan actions that will not violate the law. But this also means that parties could plan their actions not to violate the specific blackletter law while violating the spirit of contract law in general, and other parties who deserve relief under the law might not receive it for technical reasons.

Whether a rule or a standard is better depends in large part on what this specific law is trying to accomplish. Recall that the Restatement's approach to this aspect of contract law is to encourage parties to engage in self-help. To accomplish this end, the Restatement needs to provide parties clarity about what is or is not lawful. A rule is a better tool than a standard when the goal is giving parties certainty or clarity in advance about how courts will decide such cases. This allows parties to accurately predict how courts will behave and to plan their actions accordingly. This may explain why the Restatement provides a more formal five-factor test in the form of a rule and not a standard, so parties can determine with greater certainty whether or not to withhold performance in response to their counterparties' breach.

Discussion

1. When you apply the R2d test to the facts in *Khiterer*, do you arrive at the same or a different legal result?

2. Are you suspicious of either Khiterer's or Bell's motives in this case? Does either party appear to be acting in bad faith? Or was this just an innocent and good faith mistake?

Problems

Problem 18.1. Direct Timber Shipment

In the 19th century, a ship captain and a timber producer entered into a contract for the shipment of timber from Riga, the capital of Latvia, to Portsmouth, United Kingdom. The contract specified that the ship would "sail with the first favorable wind direct to Portsmouth."

The contract also has a "Choice of Law" clause that specifies: "The validity of this agreement, its construction, interpretation, and enforcement, and the rights of the parties hereto shall be determined under, and construed in accordance with, the laws of the State of Delaware." Assume for purposes of this problem that Delaware follows the Restatement and has adopted the UCC.

Instead of sailing directly to Portsmouth, the ship stopped along the way in Copenhagen, Denmark, where it was detained for several weeks. Upon arriving at Portsmouth, the producer's agent accepted delivery of the timber, but the producer refused to pay the ship captain, citing both the delay and the detour.

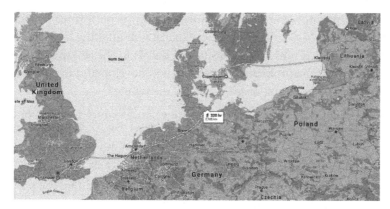

Figure 18.4. Map showing the relative locations of Riga, Copenhagen, and Portsmouth.

How would you characterize the promises and/or conditions in this agreement? Based on that characterization, analyze whether or not the timber producer's duty to pay the ship captain has come due.

See Bornmann v. Tooke, 170 Eng. Rep. 991 (1807).

Problem 18.2. Sewer System

This case involves a sewer system that was not fully completed. In June 2004, appellant Roberts Contracting Company, Inc. (Roberts) agreed to build and complete a sewer system for appellee Valentine-Wooten Road Public Facility Board (VWR) by April 12, 2005. The contract provided that VWR would pay $2,088,166 for Roberts to build the sewer system, which was to be accepted by the City of Jacksonville, and that, if Roberts did not complete the work on time, it would pay $400 per day until completion. Roberts received an extension from VWR until October 20, 2005 but did not finish the job by then.

Although VWR agreed to obtain all necessary easements, it did not resolve disputes with two landowners, Pickens and Harris, until very late in the project. Those issues, along with wet weather and a contract dispute between the project engineer, Bond Consulting Engineers, Inc., and Pulaski County delayed construction. The parties disagree about whether VWR's failure to fulfill its obligations hindered Roberts's ability to perform.

By fall 2005, Roberts had installed and tested the sewer lines, and had installed five pump stations and the force-main pipes and related equipment. But the pump station on the Pickens property still lacked power, and Mr. Harris had damaged a force main on his property that Roberts had, at VWR's direction, placed outside the easement. The Pickens easement was finally settled in January 2006, but the Harris dispute was not resolved until May 2006. Further, Bond Consulting Engineers stopped its on-site supervision of the job in December 2005 after a dispute with Pulaski County over payment.

More than a year past the original completion date, with at least one extension granted, Roberts walked off the job, and VWR refused to pay all of Roberts's last bill. The sewer system was not operational. A video inspection performed by Jacksonville Waste Water Utility in November 2006, more than a year after the lines had been successfully tested, revealed numerous defects and debris in the sewer system. Roberts took the position that the problems in the lines had developed during the year-long interval between its completion of the lines and the taping.

On May 16, 2006, VWR refused to pay Roberts the entire amount of a bill on the ground that it had not completed all of the work. The pay estimate indicated that retainage (from work already performed and partially paid) at that time was $104,408.30, and that Roberts had earned an additional $57,532.50, which had not yet been paid. Roberts refused to perform further and asserted that the purportedly incomplete work was not within the scope of the contract. It also claimed that its ability to perform had been hampered by VWR's failure to perform its obligations.

Roberts sued VWR for breach of contract, alleging that it had substantially performed, and seeking $162,502.80. VWR filed a counterclaim for damages caused by Roberts's failure to complete and repair the system.

Evaluate the competing claims based on whether the parties substantially performed pursuant to the rule articulated in the Restatement. Specifically, evaluate whether any failure to completely, substantially, or materially perform has any impact on the other party's duty to perform its obligations. Make sure to characterize any contractual obligations as mutual or independent promises, conditions, or promissory conditions.

See Roberts Contracting Co. v. Valentine-Wooten Rd. Pub. Facility Bd., 2009 Ark. App. 437.

Problem 18.3. Newspaper Stock

As of July 8, 1961, Paul, Spindler was the owner of a majority of the shares of S & S Newspapers, a corporation which, since April 1, 1959, had owned and operated a newspaper in Santa Clara known as the Santa Clara Journal. In addition, Spindler, as president of S & S Newspapers, served as publisher, editor, and general manager of the Journal.

On July 8, 1961, Spindler entered into a written agreement with Sheldon Sackett whereby the latter agreed to purchase 6,316 shares of stock in S & S Newspapers, this number representing the total number of shares outstanding. The contract provided for a total purchase price of $85,000 payable as follows:

- $6,000 on or before July 10,
- $20,000 on or before July 14, and
- $59,000 on or before August 15.

In addition, the agreement obligated Sackett to pay interest at the rate of 6 percent on any unpaid balance. And finally, the contract provided for delivery of the full amount of stock to Sackett free of encumbrances when he made his final payment under the contract.

Sackett paid the initial $6,000 installment on time and made an additional $19,800 payment on July 21. On August 10, Sackett gave Spindler a check for the $59,200 balance due under the contract; however, due to the fact that the account on which this check was drawn contained insufficient funds to cover the check, the check was never paid.

Meanwhile, however, Spindler had acquired the stock owned by the minority shareholders of S & S Newspapers, had endorsed the stock certificates, and had given all but 454 shares to Sackett's attorneys to hold in escrow until Sackett had paid Spindler the $59,200 balance due under the contract. However, on September 1, after the $59,200 check had not cleared, Spindler reclaimed the stock certificates held by Sackett's attorney.

Thereafter, on September 12, Spindler received a telegram from Sackett to the effect that the latter "had secured payments our transaction and was ready, willing and eager to transfer them" and that Sackett's new attorney would contact Spindler's attorney. In response to this telegram Spindler, by return telegram, gave Sackett the name of Spindler's attorney. Subsequently, Sackett's attorney contacted Spindler's attorney and arranged a meeting to discuss Sackett's performance of the contract.

At this meeting, which was held on September 19 at the office of Sackett's attorney, in response to Sackett's representation that he would be able to pay Spindler the balance due under the contract by September 22, Spindler served Sackett with a notice to the effect that unless the latter paid the $59,200 balance due under the contract plus interest by that date, Spindler would not consider completing the sale and would assess damages for Sackett's breach of the agreement.

Also discussed at this meeting was the newspaper's urgent need for working capital. Pursuant to this discussion Sackett on the same date paid Spindler $3,944.26 as an advance for working capital.

However, Sackett failed to make any further payments or to communicate with Spindler by September 22, and on that date, the latter, by letter addressed to Sackett, again extended the time for Sackett's performance until September 29. Again, Sackett failed to tender the amount owing under the contract or to contact Spindler by that date.

The next communication between the parties occurred on October 4 in the form of a telegram by which Sackett advised Spindler that Sackett's assets were now free as a result of the fact that his wife's petition to impress a receivership on his assets had been dismissed by the trial court in which divorce proceedings between Sackett and his wife were pending; that he was "ready, eager and willing to proceed to . . . consummate all details of our previously settled sale and purchase"; and that the decision of the trial court dismissing his wife's petition for receivership "will clear way shortly for full financing any unpaid balance." Accordingly, Sackett, in this telegram, urged Spindler to have his attorney contact Sackett's attorney "regarding any unfinished details."

In response to this telegram, Spindler's attorney, on October 5, wrote a letter to Sackett's attorney stating that as a result of Sackett's delay in performing the contract and his unwillingness to consummate the agreement, "there will be no sale and purchase of the stock."

Following this letter, Sackett's attorney, on October 6, telephoned Spindler's attorney and offered to pay the balance due under the contract over a period of time through a "liquidating trust." This proposal was rejected by Spindler's attorney, who, however, informed Sackett's attorney at that time that Spindler was still willing to consummate the sale of the stock provided Sackett would pay the balance in cash or its equivalent. No tender or offer of cash or its equivalent was made, and Sackett thereafter failed to communicate with Spindler until shortly before the commencement of suit.

During the period scheduled for Sackett's performance of the contract, Spindler found it increasingly difficult to operate the paper at a profit, particularly due to the lack of adequate working capital. In an attempt to remedy this situation, Spindler obtained a loan of approximately $4,000 by mortgaging various items of personal property owned by him. In addition, in November, Spindler sold half of his stock in S & S Newspapers for $10,000. Thereafter, in December, in an effort to minimize the cost of operating the newspaper, Spindler converted the paper from a daily to a weekly. Finally, in July 1962, Spindler repurchased for $10,000 the stock which he had sold the previous November and sold the full 6,316 shares for $22,000, which sale netted Spindler $20,680 after payment of brokerage commission.

Sackett (the buyer) then commenced this action against Spindler (the seller), claiming that Spindler has breached his promise to sell the stock to Sackett.

a. Did Sackett completely perform, such that Spindler had to perform his obligations under the contract?

b. Did Sackett substantially perform or materially breach, such that Spindler could withhold his performance but not cancel the contract?

c. Did Sackett have time to cure, or did he totally breach his promise to Spindler, such that Spindler was legally able to cancel the contract?

See Sackett v. Spindler, 248 Cal. App. 2d 220 (1967).

Chapter 19

Anticipatory Repudiation

Repudiation occurs when a party to a contract indicates its intention not to perform its obligations under that contract. This disavowal of an obligation in advance has the same effect as failing to perform when the time for performance is due. This seemingly simple concept raises some unexpectedly complex issues. First and foremost, what constitutes a repudiation? Does a repudiation require words, or can it arise from actions?

Rules

A. What Counts as a Repudiation?

R2d takes what some scholars have called the "modern view" on repudiation. Unlike more traditional jurisdictions like Pennsylvania, which require an "absolute and unequivocal" repudiation, R2d requires only that the party's language "be sufficiently positive to be reasonably interpreted to mean that the party will not or cannot perform."

While "sufficiently positive" is less than "absolute and unequivocal," the statement by the purportedly repudiating party cannot be a "mere expression of doubt as to his willingness or ability to perform."

What R2d gains in flexibility it loses in certainty. It can be difficult under the modern view to determine when a statement or act is a repudiation. Perhaps this opacity is deliberate, such that judges are free to consider all the facts and circumstances when determining when a statement or act is a repudiation.

Fortunately, the effects of a repudiation, once found, are clear. A repudiation under R2d acts like a total breach, immediate extinguishing the non-repudiating party's mutual obligations and giving rise to damages under the contract.

R2d classifies a statement or act as a repudiation when such statement or act declares the actor's intention not to perform except on conditions which go beyond the contract.

> *A repudiation is a statement by the obligor to the obligee indicating that the obligor will commit a breach that would of itself give the obligee a claim for damages for total breach under § 243. R2d § 250(a).*

While many repudiations take the form of verbal or written manifestations, they can also take the form of actions which are reasonably interpreted to demonstrate an intent not to perform:

> *A reproduction is a voluntary affirmative act which renders the obligor unable or apparently unable to perform without such a breach.* R2d § 250(b).

Illustrations of Repudiation. Comments to the Restatement suggest that the words of repudiation must be spoken to someone who has some rights under the contract, although it is not clear whether such words when spoken to someone who is not a beneficiary of the contractual promise could still constitute an act of repudiation.

> *Illustration 250.1. On April 1, A contracts to sell and B to buy land, delivery of the deed and payment of the price to be on July 30. On May 1, A tells B that he will not perform. A's statement is a repudiation.*

> *Illustration 250.3. On April 1, A contracts to sell and B to buy land, delivery of the deed and payment of the price to be on July 30. On May 1, A tells B, "I am not sure that I can perform, and I do not intend to do so unless I am legally bound to." A's statement is not a repudiation.*

> *Illustration 250.4. On April 1, A contracts to sell and B to buy land, delivery of the deed and payment of the price to be on July 30. On May 1, A tells C, a third person having no right under the contract, and not B, that he will not perform. C informs B of this conversation, although not requested by A to do so. A's statement is not a repudiation.*

The distinction between Illustration 250.1 and Illustration 250.4 seem to imply that a statement to a third party cannot be a repudiation. But this is only half of the story. While it is true that, according to R2d, statements to a third party cannot be a repudiation by words, such statements can still be a repudiation by action.

A voluntary and affirmative action can constitute a repudiation where such action makes it actually or apparently impossible for the purportedly repudiating party to perform its obligations under the contract, as demonstrated by the following illustrations.

> *Illustration 250.5. On April 1, A contracts to sell and B to buy land, delivery of the deed and payment of the price to be on July 30. On May 1, A says nothing to B on May 1, but on that date he contracts to sell the land to C. A's making of the contract with C is a repudiation.*

> *Illustration 250.6. On April 1, A contracts to sell and B to buy land, delivery of the deed and payment of the price to be on July 30. On May 1, A says nothing to B on May 1, but on that date he mortgages the land*

> *to C as security for a $40,000 loan which is not payable until one year later. A's mortgaging the land is a repudiation.*
>
> Additionally, words to a third party that would otherwise constitute a repudiation or equivocal actions that do not quite rise to the level of repudiation by one party can still give its counterparty reasonable grounds to demand assurances of performance. To better understand how a party's actions can give rise to a counterparty's right to demand assurances, and how the failure to provide those assures can thereby constitute a repudiation, consider the next case and then the Restatement rules following it.

B. Effect of Repudiation

Assuming that we can identify what is and is not a repudiation, when we identify a repudiation, what is the effect of such a repudiation? Should this be tantamount to a breach, even if the time for the repudiating party's performance has not yet come due? If repudiation has the effect of breach, should it be treated like a material breach, where the counterparty withholds performance for a reasonable time, or should it be treated like a total breach, where the counterparty can cancel the contract and forever extinguish its obligations thereunder?

The second issue (what is the effect of a repudiation) turns out to be simpler than the first. The effect of a repudiation is now well defined under common law. The Restatement clearly states that repudiation acts like a total breach, giving rise to a claim for damages and discharging the other party's duties to perform any promises that were conditioned on the repudiating party's performance. The UCC takes a slightly different approach, treating repudiation more like a material breach. But under both common and statutory contract law, repudiation has the immediate effect of a breach, even when the time for performance has not yet come due.

The effect of a repudiation as an immediate breach was resolved in in the famous case of *Hochster v. De La Tour*, 2 E & B 678, QB, 118 ER 922 (1853). Edgar Frederick De La Tour hired Albert Hochster to be his personal courier on a three-month tour around Europe, pursuant to a contract executed on April 12, 1852. The tour was to begin on June 1, 1852. On May 11, 1852, De La Tour wrote to Hochster that he had changed his mind and no longer required his services. De La Tour refused to pay Hochster.

Hochster then sought out another client and entered into an engagement with Lord Ashburton on equally good terms to serve as his courier

The question presented in this case was whether in law it is possible to break a contract before the day for its performance comes? In other words, should the law recognize an anticipatory repudiation?

The consequence of recognizing such an anticipatory repudiation means that the repudiating party has totally breached, even where the time for performance is not yet due, and therefore its nonrepudiating counterparty is immediately free to mitigate damages by seeking other employment. If anticipatory repudiation is not recognized, however, then the nonrepudiating counterparty must wait for the repudiating party until the time for performance is due, even if this results in piling up damages.

The effect of a repudiation is therefore rather simple and well established, but perhaps students are confused by the different ways that courts refer to this doctrine. While the Restatement and many courts and scholars simply use the term "repudiation," the UCC and many other courts and scholars use the term "anticipatory repudiation." Still others use the term "anticipatory breach." These all amount to the same thing.

In truth, it is redundant to append the term "anticipatory" before "repudiation" because repudiation already indicates an unwillingness not to perform in the future. The only valuable distinction one could make between these two terms is that repudiation is the term used by the Restatement, whereas anticipatory repudiation is the term used by the UCC. One can imply which law governs the case by using the correct term.

Some make a further distinction between express repudiation (repudiation made by using clear, unequivocal words and actions) and implied repudiation (repudiation shown by acts indicating an unwillingness to perform as promised). These distinctions are not particularly helpful as there is no difference in the effect of so-called express and implied repudiation.

Yet another unhelpful addition to this legal lexicon is total repudiation (an unconditional refusal by a party to perform the acts required by a contract). It does not matter whether or not a repudiation is unconditional. Repudiation either occurred or did not occur.

The most challenging part of the doctrine of repudiation is determining whether or not a repudiation has occurred. The consequences for such a repudiation are quite clear, but the test for whether or not some words or action constitutes a repudiation is of necessity murkier. Like Justice Stewart's (in)famous test for what is an "obscenity" ("I know it when I see it."), sometimes the law needs to provide some room for a reasonable interpretation of something as complex as human behavior under commercial arrangements.

C. Retraction of Express Repudiation

Even where a party has expressly and unequivocally repudiated, that repudiating party has limited rights to retract that repudiation, thereby reinstating the contract. Repudiation is a wrongful act, itself giving rise to damages for breach, and courts will not reward a wrongful act, nor will they penalize a blameless party to benefit a blameworthy one. But there are situations where it is more efficient (better for society) for the parties to resume their course of performance, despite a repudiation. Thus courts do allow the "nullification" of repudiation where the non-repudiating party has not yet materially changed its position in reliance on the repudiation.

For example, imagine that you have decided to purchase your dream car from a Porsche dealership. You have specified a racing yellow Porsche Boxster 718 with the chrono package and several other special features such that the car needs to be custom ordered from Germany. You place the special order at your local Porsche dealership, with the understanding that it will arrive in four to six weeks, and you put a 10% down payment of $6,500 toward the $65,000 purchase price. After three weeks, however, the dealership calls you and regretfully informs you that there is a worldwide chip shortage that has prevented Porsche from building any new cars. There is no end to the shortage in sight, and the company plans to stop making the model you specified, so the dealership will not be able to deliver the car to you and offers to refund your deposit.

This is clearly a repudiation—it is an unequivocal refusal to perform—but you might not immediately take action based on this. Perhaps you spend some time mournfully starting at your poster of your dream car and then get on with your day and your week. Two days later, to your surprise, the Porsche dealership calls you back and joyfully announces that one final shipment of microchips apparently made it to the car manufacturer, who has updated the system to show your car is now in production and will arrive in your location in about three weeks, so they will not be refunding your deposit but instead delivering the car to you. This is the dealership's attempt to retract its repudiation. Do you have to accept this return to the status quo?

According to both R2d § 264 and UCC § 2-611, yes, this appears to be a valid nullification or retraction of a repudiation. The legal standard is whether the non-repudiating party has materially changed its position in reliance on the revocation. Since you have not changed your position in any way since the revocation, the dealership has the right to reinstate the contract.

> *When either party repudiates the contract with respect to a performance not yet due the loss of which will substantially impair the value of the contract to the other, the aggrieved party may (a) for a commercially reasonable time await performance by the repudiating party; or (b) resort to any remedy for breach (Section 2-703 or Section 2-711), even though he has notified the repudiating party that he would await the latter's performance and has urged retraction; and (c) in either case suspend his own performance or proceed in accordance with the provisions of this Article on the seller's right to identify goods to the contract notwithstanding breach or to salvage unfinished goods (Section 2-704).* UCC § 2-610.

But what if you had acted differently? What if, instead of simply regretting that you would not receive your dream car, you went ahead and put a down payment on another car—say, a red Chevrolet Corvette—that you were now obligated to purchase? This would constitute precisely the kind of material change in position that would make the Porsche dealership's attempted nullification or retraction (both synonymous with revocation) of its repudiation ineffective.

The same is true for contracts for services as it is for contracts for sales of goods like the car example above. For example, Jane hires Peter to be the photographer at her daughter's wedding. Eleven days before the wedding, Peter calls Jane and tells her that he feels unwell and, according to CDC guidelines, will need to self-quarantine for fourteen days to prevent the spread of COVID-19 at the wedding; therefore, Peter informs Jane, he will not be able to photograph the wedding. This constitutes a repudiation. Jane frantically calls the other wedding photographers in her area until she reaches Phil, who agrees to photograph the wedding and requires a non-refundable down payment, which Jane pays. Subsequently, Peter calls Jane and tells her that he took a PCR test for COVID-19 that came up negative, and that he is feeling better, so that he is now able to photograph the wedding after all. Jane does not have to accept Peter's attempt to nullify or retract his repudiation. Jane has already materially relied on Peter's repudiation by changing her position — she paid a non-refundable down payment to Phil — therefore, Peter's attempted nullification of his repudiation is ineffective. If Jane had not yet hired another wedding photograph or otherwise changed the wedding plans, however, then Peter would be able to nullify his repudiation and reinstate the mutual duties to perform under the contract.

Note that the repudiation is still a breach, regardless of whether it is nullified, retracted, and revoked. Jane may have been injured by this repudiation even if she did not make a material change in reliance thereon. For example, if Jane employed a wedding planner who was paid by the hour, the wedding planner may have charged Jane for two hours of making phone calls to find an alternate photographer, even if those calls did not result in hiring anyone to replace Peter. In that case, Peter would be liable for damages to Jane for the harm his repudiation caused, even if that repudiation was later revoked. Jane would have the legal right to withhold this amount of payment from Peter's bill, even as she would be required to go forward with employing him for his services and otherwise paying him the contract amount.

Under both R2d and UCC, repudiation can be retracted until the nonrepudiating party has detrimentally relied on the repudiation.

> Until the repudiating party's next performance is due he can retract his repudiation unless the aggrieved party has since the repudiation cancelled or materially changed his position or otherwise indicated that he considers the repudiation final. UCC § 2-611(1).

> Retraction may be by any method which clearly indicates to the aggrieved party that the repudiating party intends to perform, but must include any assurance justifiably demanded under the provisions of this Article (Section 2-609). UCC § 2-611(2).

> Retraction reinstates the repudiating party's rights under the contract with due excuse and allowance to the aggrieved party for any delay occasioned by the repudiation. UCC § 2-611(3).

Furthermore, a party who repudiates and then successfully nullifies that repudiation may begin to cause the other party to have reasonable insecurity about future performance. In this example, Jane might reasonably worry that Peter is overexposing himself to the risk of disease such that he may still get sick and be unable to photograph her daughter's wedding. Jane might then reasonably ask Peter to assure her that he is taking precautions to prevent getting sick such that he will be available to photograph her event. If Peter does not provide adequate assurances of his future performance, Jane may be allowed to terminate the contract under the theory that Peter's failure to provide adequate assurances itself constitutes a repudiation, as discussed in the next section.

D. Failure to Assure as Implied Repudiation

Although some words or actions by a contract party may not rise to the level of being a repudiation in themselves, they may still cause a reasonable counterparty to become insecure about the party's ability and willingness to perform. We describe a state as "reasonable insecurity." For example, where a buyer has failed to pay on time, the seller might have the right to inquire why the delay and how it will be resolved.

In general, when the state of reasonable insecurity arises, then the insecure party has the right to demand adequate assurances from its counterparty.

> *Where reasonable grounds arise to believe that the obligor will commit a breach by non-performance that would of itself give the obligee a claim for damages for total breach under § 243, the obligee may demand adequate assurance of due performance and may, if reasonable, suspend any performance for which he has not already received the agreed exchange until he receives such assurance.* R2d § 251(1).

If its counterparty fails to reasonably reassure the insecure party that performance will be forthcoming, then the insecure party can treat that failure to provide assurances as a repudiation.

> *The obligee may treat as a repudiation the obligor's failure to provide within a reasonable time such assurance of due performance as is adequate in the circumstances of the particular case.* R2d § 251(2).

In other words, failure to give assurances may be treated as a repudiation (which in turn functions as a total breach under the Restatement approach) when the assurances demanded were reasonable in light of the insecurity.

For example, Professor Hamburger, a United States resident, enters into a contract on January 1, 2020, with the Paris-Sorbonne University, which is located in France, to teach a week-long in-person course starting May 1, 2020. On April 1, 2020, the French government issues a travel ban, forbidding any United States residents from entering France for at least 60 days. Although this event does not constitute a repudiation because it is not a statement by the obligor (Hamburger) to the obligee (Sorbonne), it does give Sorbonne reasonable grounds to believe that the obligor will not perform under the agreement to teach in person. Sorbonne thus gains the right to demand assurances from Hamburger, who will almost certainly be unable to provide such assurances that he will appear in person at Sorbonne next month given that the national government has forbidden such travel for the next 60 days. When Hamburger fails to provide assurances, that may be treated as a repudiation, which functions as a total breach.

A party does not have an unlimited right to demand assurances whenever it wants from its counterparty. Rather, the right to demand assurances comes from the implied duty of good faith and fair dealing. The UCC has extended this duty of good faith to specifically "impose [] an obligation on each party that the other's expectation of receiving due performance will not be impaired." UCC § 2-609. Therefore, when one party makes the other reasonably insecure that due performance will be received, the insecure party gains the right to demand assurance of performance. R2d has incorporated the UCC's approach, so these two legal regimes are harmonized in this respect.

> *A contract for sale imposes an obligation on each party that the other's expectation of receiving due performance will not be impaired. When reasonable grounds for insecurity arise with respect to the performance of either party the other may in writing demand adequate assurance of due performance and until he receives such assurance may if commercially reasonable suspend any performance for which he has not already received the agreed return.* UCC § 2-609(1).

> *Between merchants the reasonableness of grounds for insecurity and the adequacy of any assurance offered shall be determined according to commercial standards.* UCC § 2-609(2).

> *Acceptance of any improper delivery or payment does not prejudice the aggrieved party's right to demand adequate assurance of future performance.* UCC § 2-609(3).

> *After receipt of a justified demand failure to provide within a reasonable time not exceeding thirty days such assurance of due performance as is adequate under the circumstances of the particular case is a repudiation of the contract.* UCC § 2-609(4).

Whether under the common law or the UCC, the first analytical step is to resolve whether reasonable grounds have arisen for the obligee to believe that the obligor will not perform. This must be determined in light of the circumstances of the particular case. The question is not whether the obligee actually has insecurity but rather whether a reasonable person in the obligee's position would be insecure. This requires courts to understand the circumstances of the obligee's position.

For example, Pucciano Lavorotti, a world-famous opera singer, contracts with Lang-Lang Pa, one of the world's top pianists, to play his musical accompaniment for an opera show at the Sydney Opera House in Australia on June 5. On June 1, Lavorotti receives an advertisement to purchase tickets to a live concert featuring Pa on June 4 at the Grand Théâtre de Casablanca in Morocco, which is about 11,200 miles from Sydney. Lavorotti writes to Pa, expressing his insecurity that Pa will perform at Sydney based on the immense distance between that venue and the venue he plays at the day before the opera show. Is his insecurity reasonable?

The answer depends on facts and circumstances. For example, Lavorotti might offer evidence that commercial air travel from Casablanca to Sydney takes at least 25 hours, plus delays, and therefore it is impossible for Pa to play in Casablanca one day and appear in Sydney the next. This evidence tends to show that Lavorotti's concerns are reasonable.

Pa might submit evidence that he is well known to travel by a private supersonic jet that can easily reach any major city on the globe within about 12 hours. That would tend to show that Lavorotti's concerns are less reasonable (although perhaps not totally unfounded). Both parties might respond by submitting witness testimony about industry practices, delays in private travel, Pa's reputation for timeliness, etc.

The second element to resolve is whether the demand is reasonable. Under common law, the demand does not have to be in writing, although the UCC does have such a writing requirement. But the demand in both cases must comport with the duty of good faith and fair dealing: "Harassment by means of frequent unjustified demands may amount to a violation of the duty of good faith and fair dealing." R2d § 251 cmt. d.

In the example above regarding the contract between Lavorotti and Pa, imagine that Lavorotti asks Pa to send his travel itinerary showing that he will arrive in Sydney in time for the opera show there. Under these circumstances, that seems to be a reasonable request.

What if Lavorotti demanded to see not only Pa's travel schedule to Sydney but also requested a copy of all his concert booking and travel arrangements for two weeks prior to the opera show? Although Lavorotti's insecurity is reasonable, his demand seems disproportionate to the insecurity, and therefore, his demand is probably unreasonable.

Asking for a performer's travel schedule in this manner may or may not be reasonable depending on the circumstances. What if Pa's concert in Morocco occurred five days before the opera show in Sydney, instead of the events being just one day apart? That would make Lavorotti's insecurity less reasonable and also make his demand for assurances less reasonable.

Consider a more extreme example, where Lavorotti and Pa enter into their contract on January 1 for a performance on June 5, more than six months away. If Lavorotti demands on January 2 to see Pa's flight schedule for June 5, and threatens to cancel the contract if such schedule is not provided within 24 hours, that is more likely to be considered harassing behavior that does not comport with good faith and fair dealing.

The third element to resolve is whether the demand was reasonably met. Once again, this does not ask whether the obligee himself is assured, but whether a reasonable person in the obligee's position should be assured by the obligor's words or actions. And once again, this requires an analysis of all the facts and circumstances.

The Restatement offers a series of illustrations of how this rule operates. Read these illustrations carefully, noting which facts change from one illustration to the next, and how those changes impact the legal outcome.

> *Illustration 251.1. A contracts to let B use his concert hall on the evening of May 7 for a performance by B's string quartet, in return for B's promise to perform and to pay a percentage of the receipts. The contract provides that B is not discharged even if he is unable to transport his quartet to A's hall. On May 6, because of an unexpected airline strike, A reasonably believes that B's quartet will be unable to come the 3,000 miles necessary to perform in his hall as scheduled. Without demanding adequate assurance of due performance under the rule stated in this Section, A then contracts with C to let C hold a meeting in the hall on the evening of May 7. A's contract with C is a repudiation of his contract with B (§ 250), which gives rise to a claim by B against A for damages for total breach (§ 253). If, however, B is in fact unable to bring his quartet to A's hall on May 7, B's claim against A is discharged (§ 254).*

> *Illustration 251.2. The facts being otherwise as stated in Illustration 251.1, B succeeds in chartering a plane and flies the 3,000 miles with his quartet in his private plane. He arrives in time to perform, but is unable to do so because C is using the hall. B has a claim against A for damages for total breach (§ 243).*

> *Illustration 251.6. The facts being otherwise as stated in Illustration 251.1, before contracting with C, A telephones B on May 6 and asks B to assure him that he will be there on May 7. B says only "We will do our best to get there." B succeeds in chartering a plane and flies the 3,000 miles with his quartet. He arrives in time to perform, but is unable to do so because C is using the hall. In the absence of countervailing circumstances, a court should conclude that, as a result of B's apparent inability to perform, A had reasonable grounds to believe that B would commit a breach by non-performance that would of itself have given a claim for damages for total breach, that because of the shortness of time a demand by telephone conformed to the duty of good faith and fair dealing (§ 205), that B failed upon such a demand to give adequate assurance of due performance, and therefore that A properly treated B's failure as a repudiation. A then has a claim against B for damages for total breach.*

> *Illustration 251.7. The facts being otherwise as stated in Illustration 251.1, before contracting with C, A telephones B on May 6 and asks B to assure him that he will be there on May 7. B explains over the telephone that he has been able to charter a plane and expects to come as planned. B then flies the 3,000 miles with his quartet. He arrives in time to perform, but is unable to do so because C is using the hall. The assurance given by B was adequate in*

view of what it was reasonable to require, and therefore A could not treat B's failure to do more as a repudiation. B then has a claim against A for damages for total breach.

Illustration 251.8. The facts being otherwise as stated in Illustration 251.1, before contracting with C, A telephones B on May 6 and asks B to assure him that he will be there on May 7. B replies that he hopes to be able to charter a plane and that he will telephone A to let him know. A tells B that he must know by noon on May 7 in order to make alternative arrangements with C. B succeeds in chartering a plane and flies the 3,000 miles with his quartet. After he has arrived on the afternoon of May 7, he telephones A to assure him that he will perform. A court may conclude that, as a result of B's apparent inability to perform, A had reasonable grounds to believe that B would commit a breach by non-performance that would of itself have given a claim for damages for total breach, that the assurances given by B were not within a reasonable time, and therefore that A properly treated B's delay in giving them as a repudiation. A then has a claim against B for damages for total breach.

A key takeaway from these illustrations that may not be patently obvious at first is that if an obligee unreasonably demands assurances, the obligee might inadvertently become the breaching party. By threatening to cancel the contract where there are no grounds for doing so, the obligee has repudiated and therefore breached! For this reason, a party should be careful to analyze whether insecurity is reasonable and what assurances are proportional to that insecurity before demanding assurances and threatening to cancel a contract.

E. Reflections on Repudiation

This chapter explained how parties can effectively breach a contract in advance by repudiating their performance under it. The Restatement defines repudiation narrowly such that it must be a statement or action by the obligor to the obligee that indicates that the obligor will not fulfill its obligation under the contract. Some states such as Pennsylvania define this even more narrowly by requiring the statement to be an unequivocal disavowal of the contractual obligation.

There is, however, a back door of sorts to the repudiation result. If an obligee becomes reasonably unsure about its obligor's future performance — regardless of whether that insecurity is due to the obligor's own words or actions — then that obligee can lawfully demand reasonable assurances. The failure to provide such assurances counts as a repudiation.

The UCC and the common law according to the Restatement are fairly well aligned with regards to the doctrine of what constitutes a repudiation. One important distinction between the UCC and R2d, however, regards the effect of repudiation. R2d treats repudiation as a total breach, giving the nonrepudiating party the immediate ability to cancel the contract and find substitute performance. The UCC treats repudiation as a material breach, giving the nonrepudiating party the right to withhold performance and to sue for damages for any harm from this breach, but the nonrepudiating party must wait and cannot cancel the contract for a reasonable time unless that delay would substantially impair the value of the contract or would significantly hinder the ability to make substitute arrangements.

Cases

Reading McCloskey & Co. v. Minweld Steel Co. The most challenging part of the doctrine of repudiation is determining whether or not a repudiation has occurred. The consequences for such a repudiation are quite clear, but the test for whether or not some words or actions constitute a repudiation is of necessity murkier. Like Justice Stewart's (in)famous test for what is "obscenity" ("I know it when I see it."), sometimes the law needs to provide some room for a reasonable interpretation of something as complex as human behavior under commercial arrangements.

As you read the next case, pay careful attention to the words and actions of both parties. Highlight what they said and did that could possibly be construed as a repudiation and annotate those highlights with your opinion on whether those words and actions should be considered a repudiation. Hopefully, you too, will know it when you see it.

McCloskey & Co. v. Minweld Steel Co.
220 F.2d 101 (3d Cir. 1955)

McLAUGHLIN, Circuit Judge.

Plaintiff-appellant, a general contractor, sued on three contracts alleging an anticipatory breach as to each. At the close of the plaintiff's case the district judge granted the defense motions for judgment on the ground that plaintiff had not made out a cause of action.

By the contracts involved the principal defendant, a fabricator and erector of steel, agreed to furnish and erect all of the structural steel required on two buildings to be built on the grounds of the Hollidaysburg State Hospital, Hollidaysburg, Pa. and to furnish all of the long span steel joists required in the construction of one of the two buildings. Two of the contracts were dated May 1, 1950 and the third May 26, 1950. By Article V of each of the contracts:

Should the Sub-Contractor (the defendant herein) . . . at any time refuse or neglect to supply a sufficiency . . . of materials of the proper quality, . . . in and about the performance of the work required to be done pursuant to the provisions of this agreement, or fail, in the performance of any of the agreements herein contained, the Contractor shall be at liberty, without prejudice to any other right or remedy, on two days' written notice to the Sub-Contractor, either to provide any such . . . materials and to deduct the cost thereof from any payments then or thereafter due the Sub-Contractor, or to terminate the employment of the Sub-Contractor for the said work and to enter upon the premises.

There was no stated date in the contracts for performance by the defendant sub-contractor. Article VI provided for completion by the subcontractor of its contract work "by and at the time or times hereafter stated to-wit:"

Samples, Shop Drawings and Schedules are to be submitted in the quantities and manner required by the Specifications, for the approval of the Architects, immediately upon receipt by the Sub-Contractor of the contract drawings, or as may be directed by the Contractor. All expense involved in the submission and approval of these Samples, Shop Drawings and Schedules shall be borne by the Sub-Contractor.

All labor, materials and equipment required under this contract are to be furnished at such times as may be directed by the Contractor, and in such a manner so as to at no time delay the final completion of the building.

It being mutually understood and agreed that prompt delivery and installation of all materials required to be furnished under this contract is to be the essence of this Agreement.

Appellee Minweld Steel Co., Inc., the subcontractor, received contract drawings and specifications for both buildings in May, 1950. On June 8, 1950, plaintiff McCloskey & Co. wrote appellee asking when it might "expect delivery of the structural steel" for the buildings and "also the time estimated to complete erection." Minweld replied on June 13, 1950, submitting a schedule estimate of expecting to begin delivery of the steel by September 1, and to complete erection approximately November 15. On July 20, 1950 plaintiff wrote Minweld threatening to terminate the contracts unless the latter gave unqualified assurances that it had effected definite arrangements for the procurement, fabrication and delivery within thirty days of the required materials. On July 24, 1950 Minweld wrote McCloskey & Co. explaining its difficulty in obtaining the necessary steel. It asked McCloskey's assistance in procuring it and stated that, "We are as anxious as you are that there be no delay in the final completion of the buildings or in the performance of our contract."

Plaintiff-appellant claims that by this last letter, read against the relevant facts, defendant gave notice of its positive intention not to perform its contracts and thereby violated same. Some reference has already been made to the background of the July 24th letter. It concerned Minweld's trouble in securing the steel essential for performance of its contract. Minweld had tried unsuccessfully to purchase this from Bethlehem Steel, US Steel and Carnegie-Illinois. It is true as appellant urges that Minweld knew and was concerned about the tightening up of the steel market. And as is evident from the letter it, being a fabricator and not a producer, realized that without the help of the general contractor on this hospital project particularly by it enlisting the assistance of the General State Authority, Minweld was in a bad way for the needed steel. However, the letter conveys no idea of contract repudiation by Minweld. That company admittedly was in a desperate situation. Perhaps if it had moved earlier to seek the steel its effort might have been successful. But that is mere speculation for there is no showing that the mentioned producers had they been solicited sooner would have been willing to provide the material.

Minweld from its written statement did, we think, realistically face the problem confronting it. As a result it asked its general contractor for the aid which the latter, by the nature of the construction, should have been willing to give. Despite the circumstances there is no indication in the letter that Minweld had definitely abandoned all hope of otherwise receiving the steel and so finishing its undertaking. One of the mentioned producers might have relented. Some other supplier might have turned up. It was McCloskey & Co. who eliminated whatever chance there was. That concern instead of aiding Minweld by urging its plea for the hospital construction materials to the State Authority which represented the Commonwealth of Pennsylvania took the position that the subcontractor had repudiated its agreement and then moved quickly to have the work completed. Shortly thereafter, and without the slightest trouble as far as appears, McCloskey & Co. procured the steel from Bethlehem and brought in new subcontractors to do the work contemplated by the agreement with Minweld.

Under the applicable law Minweld's letter was not a breach of the agreement. The suit is in the federal court by reason of diversity of citizenship of the parties. Though there is no express statement to that effect the contracts between the parties would seem to have been executed in Pennsylvania with the law of that state applicable. In *McClelland v. New Amsterdam Casualty Co.*, 1936, 322 Pa. 429, 433, 185 A. 198, 200, the Pennsylvania Supreme Court held in a case where the subcontractor had asked for assistance in obtaining credit, "In order to give rise to a renunciation amounting to a breach of contract, there must be an absolute and unequivocal refusal to perform or a distinct and positive statement of an inability to do so." Minweld's conduct is plainly not that of a contract breaker under that test.

Restatement of Contracts, Comment (i) to Sec. 318 (1932) speaks clearly on the point saying:

> *Though where affirmative action is promised mere failure to act, at the time when action has been promised, is a breach, failure to take preparatory action before the time when any performance is promised is not an anticipatory breach, even though such failure makes it impossible that performance shall take place, and though the promisor at the time of the failure intends not to perform his promise.*

Appellant contends that its letter of July 20, requiring assurances of arrangements which would enable appellee to complete delivery in thirty days, constituted a fixing of a date under Article VI of the contracts. The short answer to this is that the thirty day date, if fixed, was never repudiated. Appellee merely stated that it was unable to give assurances as to the preparatory arrangements. There is nothing in the contracts which authorized appellant to demand or receive such assurances.

The district court acted properly in dismissing the actions as a matter of law on the ground that plaintiff had not made out a prima facie case.

The order of the district court of July 14, 1954 denying the plaintiff's motions for findings of facts, to vacate the judgments and for new trials will be affirmed.

Reflection

In reading the *McCloskey* case, did you wonder why the McCloskey corporation was so concerned about Minweld's ability to obtain the steel needed for its building? To pressure one's counterparty so early and so often into the relationship belies some deeper tensions. What was happening in the world around this time?

The dispute arose in the Summer of 1950, which coincides precisely with the beginning of the Korean War on June 25, 1950. America troops were deployed to the region in July of that same year to defend the "38th Parallel," the geographic boundary between the Democratic People's Republic of Korea to its north and the Republic of Korea to its south. Despite having similar names, these governments could not be more different. The Democratic People's Republic of what is now referred to as North Korea was a Communist regime, while what we now call South Korea was a pro-Western Democracy. The Korean War was thus seen by America as a war against Communism itself. America was prepared to put its full force into this war effort, which ended in July 1953, but not before some five million soldiers and civilians lost their lives.

Wars require a lot of steel. During World War II, which had ended just five years earlier, there were frequent shortages of steel and other metals. One could not purchase a new tube of toothpaste or a tub of shaving cream without first turning in the old container. Ration books issued by the Office of Price Administration gave American families a limited number of coupons needed to purchase necessities like car tires, and a national speed limit of 35 miles per hour was instituted to conserve gasoline. Such recent memories of severe war-time rationing during World War II might justify anxiety about such rationing happening again for the Korean War.

Meanwhile, taxes were raised to pay for the war effort, while wages did not keep apace. Labor unions, especially steel unions, were upset about the declining purchase power of working-class Americans. The steel unions were in an especially strong position to demand higher wages, as their products were vital to the war effort and to the economy at large. Steel worker strikes were threatened several times. President Harry S. Truman responded by threating to nationalize the steel industry, just as President Woodrow Wilson nationalized the railroad industry to prevent workers from striking during the First World War. A 1948 amendment to the Selective Service Act allowed the President to seize industry factors that failed to fulfill government orders, so threats on all sides were very real and likely to result in severe disruptions and shortages.

Although the steel workers did not strike during the times relevant to this case, they did plan to go on strike starting on April 9, 1952. President Truman made good on his threats, responding by nationalizing the entire American steel industry on that very day. In a case better suited for another casebook, the Supreme Court of the United States determined that the president lacked the authorize to seize the steel mills, ending this brief period of industrial nationalization.

Pennsylvania, the jurisdiction in which *McCloskey* originated, produced much of the nation's steel in the 1950s. It is thus a fitting site for this famous case.

By an odd turn of fate, Pennsylvania was not only the jurisdiction that gave rise to the famous *McCloskey* case was decided, but the Pennsylvania Supreme Court also seemingly rejected this approach in a later decision, *2401 Pennsylvania Avenue Corp. v. Federation of Jewish Agencies of Greater Philadelphia*, 507 Pa. 166 (1985). In that case, Chief Justice Nix, writing for the majority, concluded that a determination of repudiation required a finding that the purported repudiating party make an "absolute and unequivocal refusal to perform or a definite and positive statement of an inability to fulfill its obligations under the contract." In doing so, Pennsylvania staked out a minority position of requiring a much higher standard than R2d, which requires only an apparent inability to perform.

Justice Larsen dissented, arguing that the majority's position does not comply with how modern business transactions actually operate. The dissent then cited the following portions from the treatise on contracts written by Dr. John Murray, who taught contract law in Pittsburgh, Pennsylvania:

> *The modern view as to what constitutes a repudiation may be stated as follows: A positive statement by the obligor to the obligee which is reasonably interpreted by the obligee to mean that the obligor will not or cannot perform his contractual duty constitutes a repudiation.*
>
> *Statements of doubt by the obligor as to his ability or willingness to perform are insufficient though such statements may suggest reasonable grounds for insecurity and ultimately constitute a repudiation. Moreover, language which, alone, would not be sufficient to constitute a repudiation, may constitute a repudiation when accompanied by some nonperformance by the obligor. A positive manifestation that the obligor cannot or will not perform need not be expressed in language. It may be inferred from conduct which is wholly inconsistent with an intention to perform. Any voluntary affirmative act which actually or apparently precludes the obligor from performing amounts to a repudiation.*

It would seem that Pennsylvania is thus a jurisdiction at war with itself, at least with regard to the doctrine of repudiation. Even at the time of *McCloskey*, the courts in Pennsylvania might have been moving towards a higher standard for what counts as repudiation. As you consider the Restatement's approach below, think about whether the case would have been decided differently if it occurred in another place or time.

Discussion

1. When you read Minweld's letter, does it seem like an unequivocal refusal to perform? Why or why not?

2. Why did McCloskey treat Minweld's letter as a repudiation? Was this a good faith interpretation of the letter, or did McCloskey have ulterior motives?

Reading Hornell Brewing Co., Inc. v. Spry. The case of *Hornell Brewing* requires a court to determine whether and when one party had a reasonable insecurity about the other's performance. Students looking for sharp lines and easy answers will be disappointed. It turns out that matters such as reasonableness occur on a continuum. Insecurity develops over time as trust erodes. There may be some points where insecurity is obviously unreasonable and others where insecurity is obviously present, but most circumstances requiring legal advice fall somewhere in between. Lawyers must operate in this gray area between the lines, giving advice regarding fuzzy concepts and ambiguous facts.

The predicament of judging from vague predicates or fuzzy standards is known in philosophy as the sorties paradox. Sorties is derived from the Greek word for "heap" (σωρός), as in a heap of sand. The paradox goes something like this: if you take a heap of sand and remove one grain, is it still a heap? If so, how many grains must one remove to turn the heap of sand into a mere pile? There is, of course, no absolute number of grains of sand that constitute a heap. Likewise, there is no absolute amount of insecurity that makes it inherently reasonable to demand assurances, nor is there so specific quantity of assurance that resolve such insecurity. Although the rule that a party who is reasonably insecure can demand adequate assurances is straightforward enough, it can be difficult to determine exactly when insecurity is reasonable to feel, what assurances are reasonable to demand, and whether an insecure party has been reasonable reassured. The next case will help you better understand how courts will analyze the reasonableness of parties in such a case.

Hornell Brewing Co., Inc. v. Spry

174 Misc. 2d 451 (N.Y. Sup. Ct. 1997)

LOUISE GRUNER GANS, Justice.

Plaintiff Hornell Brewing Co., Inc. ("Hornell"), a supplier and marketer of alcoholic and non-alcoholic beverages, including the popular iced tea drink "Arizona," commenced this action for a declaratory judgment that any rights of defendants Stephen A. Spry and Arizona Tea Products Ltd. to distribute Hornell's beverages in Canada have been duly terminated, that defendants have no further rights with respect to these products, including no right to market and distribute them, and that any such rights previously transferred to defendants have reverted to Hornell.

In late 1992, Spry approached Don Vultaggio, Hornell's Chairman of the Board, about becoming a distributor of Hornell's Arizona beverages. Vultaggio had heard about Spry as an extremely wealthy and successful beer distributor who had recently sold his business. In January 1993, Spry presented Vultaggio with an ambitious plan for distributing Arizona beverages in Canada. Based on the plan and on Spry's reputation, but without further investigation, Hornell in early 1993 granted Spry the exclusive right to purchase Arizona products for distribution in Canada, and Spry formed a Canadian corporation, Arizona Iced Tea Ltd., for that express purpose.

Initially, the arrangement was purely oral. In response to Spry's request for a letter he needed to secure financing, Hornell provided a letter in July 1993 confirming their exclusive distributorship arrangement, but without spelling out the details of the arrangement. Although Hornell usually had detailed written distributorship agreements and the parties discussed and exchanged drafts of such an agreement, none was ever executed. In the meantime, Spry, with Hornell's approval, proceeded to set himself up as Hornell's distributor in Canada. During 1993 and until May 1994, the Hornell line of beverages, including the Arizona beverages, was sold to defendants on 10-day credit terms. In May 1994, after an increasingly problematic course of business dealings, Hornell de facto terminated its relationship with defendants and permanently ceased selling its products to them.

The problem dominating the parties' relationship between July 1993 and early May 1994 was defendants' failure to remit timely payment for shipments of beverages received from plaintiff. Between November and December 1993, and February 1994, defendants' unpaid invoices grew from $20,000 to over $100,000, and their $31,000 check to Hornell was returned for insufficient funds. Moreover, defendants' 1993 sales in Canada were far below Spry's initial projections.

In March and April 1994, a series of meetings, telephone calls, and letter communications took place between plaintiff and defendants regarding Spry's constant arrearages and the need for him to obtain a line and/or letter of credit that would place their business relationship on a more secure footing. These contacts included a March 27, 1994 letter to Spry from Vanguard Financial Group, Inc. confirming "the approval of a $1,500,000 revolving credit facility" to Arizona Tea Products Ltd., which never materialized into an actual line of credit; Spry sent Hornell a copy of this letter in late March or early April 1994.

All these exchanges demonstrate that during this period plaintiff had two distinct goals: to collect the monies owed by Spry, and to stabilize their future business relationship based on proven, reliable credit assurances. These exchanges also establish that during March and April, 1994, Spry repeatedly broke his promises to pay by a specified deadline, causing Hornell to question whether Vanguard's $1.5 million revolving line of credit was genuine.

On April 15, 1994, during a meeting with Vultaggio, Spry arranged for Vultaggio to speak on the telephone with Richard Worthy of Metro Factors, Inc. The testimony as to the content of that brief telephone conversation is conflicting. Although Worthy testified that he identified himself and the name of his company, Metro Factors, Inc., Vultaggio testified that he believed Worthy was from an "unusual lending institution" or bank which was going to provide Spry with a line of credit, and that nothing was expressly said to make him aware that Worthy represented a factoring company. Worthy also testified that Vultaggio told him that once Spry cleared up the arrears, Hornell would provide Spry with a "$300,000 line of credit, so long as payments were made on a net 14 day basis." According to Vultaggio, he told Worthy that once he was paid in full, he was willing to resume shipments to Spry "so long as Steve fulfills his requirements with us."

Hornell's April 18, 1994 letter to Spry confirmed certain details of the April 15 conversations, including that payment of the arrears would be made by April 19, 1994. However, Hornell received no payment on that date. Instead, on April 25, Hornell received from Spry a proposed letter for Hornell to address to a company named "Metro" at a post office box in Dallas, Texas. Worthy originally sent Spry a draft of this letter with "Metro Factors, Inc." named as the addressee, but in the copy Vultaggio received the words "Factors, Inc." were apparently obliterated. Hornell copied the draft letter on its own letterhead and sent it to Metro over Vultaggio's signature. In relevant part, the letter stated as follows:

> *Gentlemen:*
>
> *Please be advised that Arizona Tea Products, Ltd. (ATP), of which Steve Spry is president, is presently indebted to us in the total amount of $79,316.24 as of the beginning of business Monday, April 25, 1994. We sell to them on "Net 14 days" terms. Such total amount is due according to the following schedule: . . .*
>
> *Upon receipt of $79,316.24. (which shall be applied to the oldest balances first) by 5:00 P.M. (EST) Tuesday, May 2, 1994 by wire transfer(s) to the account described below, we shall recommence selling product to ATP on the following terms:*
>
> 1) *All invoices from us are due and payable by the 14th day following the release of the related product.*
>
> 2) *We shall allow the outstanding balance owed to us by ATP to go up to $300,000 so long as ATP remains "current" in its payment obligations to us. Wiring instructions are as follows: . . .*

Hornell received no payment on May 2, 1994. It did receive a wire transfer from Metro of the full amount on May 9, 1994. Upon immediate confirmation of that payment, Spry ordered 30 trailer loads of "product" from Hornell, at a total purchase price of $390,000 to $450,000. In the interim between April 25, 1994 and May 9, 1994, Hornell learned from several sources, including its regional sales manager

Baumkel, that Spry's warehouse was empty, that he had no managerial, sales or office staff, that he had no trucks, and that in effect his operation was a sham.

On May 10, 1994, Hornell wrote to Spry, acknowledging receipt of payment and confirming that they would extend up to $300,000 of credit to him, net 14 days cash "based on your prior representation that you have secured a $1,500,000. US line of credit." The letter also stated,

> *Your current balance with us reflects a 0 [zero] balance due. As you know, however, we experienced considerable difficulty and time wasted over a five week time period as we tried to collect some $130,000 which was 90–120 days past due.*
>
> *Accordingly, before we release any more product, we are asking you to provide us with a letter confirming the existence of your line of credit as well as a personal guarantee that is backed up with a personal financial statement that can be verified. Another option would be for you to provide us with an irrevocable letter of credit in the amount of $300,000.*

Spry did not respond to this letter. Spry never even sent Hornell a copy of his agreement with Metro Factors, Inc., which Spry had signed on March 24, 1994 and which was fully executed on March 30, 1994. On May 26, 1994, Vultaggio met with Spry to discuss termination of their business relationship. Vultaggio presented Spry with a letter of agreement as to the termination, which Spry took with him but did not sign. After some months of futile negotiations by counsel this action by Hornell ensued.

At the outset, the court determines that an enforceable contract existed between plaintiff and defendants based on the uncontroverted facts of their conduct. Under Article 2 of the Uniform Commercial Code, parties can form a contract through their conduct rather than merely through the exchange of communications constituting an offer and acceptance.

Section 2-204(1) states: "A contract for sale of goods may be made in any manner sufficient to show agreement, including conduct by both parties which recognizes the existence of such a contract." Sections 2-206(1) and 2-207(3) expressly allow for the formation of a contract partly or wholly on the basis of such conduct. 1 White & Summers, Uniform Commercial Code, ibid.

Here, the conduct of plaintiff and defendants which recognized the existence of a contract is sufficient to establish a contract for sale under Uniform Commercial Code sections 2-204(1) and 2-207(3). Both parties' undisputed actions over a period of many months clearly manifested mutual recognition that a binding obligation was undertaken. Following plaintiff's agreement to grant defendant an exclusive distributorship for Canada, defendant Spry took certain steps to enable him to commence his distribution operation in Canada. These steps included hiring counsel in Canada to form Arizona Tea Products, Ltd., the vehicle through which defendant acted in Canada, obtaining regulatory approval for the labelling of Arizona Iced Tea in conformity with Canadian law, and obtaining importation approvals necessary to import Arizona Iced Tea into Canada. Defendants subsequently placed orders for the purchase of plaintiff's products, plaintiff shipped its products to defendants during 1993 and early 1994, and defendants remitted payments, albeit not timely nor in full. Under the Uniform Commercial Code, these uncontroverted business dealings constitute "conduct . . . sufficient to establish a contract for sale," even in the absence of a specific writing by the parties.

Notwithstanding the parties' conflicting contentions concerning the duration and termination of defendants' distributorship, plaintiff has demonstrated a basis for lawfully terminating its contract with defendants in accordance with section 2-609 of the Uniform Commercial Code. Section 2-609(1) authorizes one party upon "reasonable grounds for insecurity" to "demand adequate assurance of due performance and until he receives such assurance . . . if commercially reasonable suspend any performance for which he has not already received the agreed return." The Official Comment to section 2-609 explains:

> This section rests on the recognition of the fact that the essential purpose of a contract between commercial men is actual performance and they do not bargain merely for a promise, or for a promise plus the right to win a lawsuit and that a continuing sense of reliance and security that the promised performance will be forthcoming when due, is an important feature of the bargain. If either the willingness or the ability of a party to perform declines materially between the time of contracting and the time for performance, the other party is threatened with the loss of a substantial part of what he has bargained for. A seller needs protection not merely against having to deliver on credit to a shaky buyer, but also against having to procure and manufacture the goods, perhaps turning down other customers. Once he has been given reason to believe that the buyer's performance has become uncertain, it is an undue hardship to force him to continue his own performance.

Whether a seller, as the plaintiff in this case, has reasonable grounds for insecurity is an issue of fact that depends upon various factors, including the buyer's exact words or actions, the course of dealing or performance between the parties, and the nature of the sales contract and the industry.

Subdivision (2) defines both "reasonableness" and "adequacy" by commercial rather than legal standards, and the Official Comment notes the application of the good faith standard.

Once the seller correctly determines that it has reasonable grounds for insecurity, it must properly request assurances from the buyer. Although the Code requires that the request be made in writing, UCC § 2-609(1), courts have not strictly adhered to this formality as long as an unequivocal demand is made. After demanding assurance, the seller must determine the proper "adequate assurance." What constitutes "adequate" assurance of due performance is subject to the same test of commercial reasonableness and factual conditions.

Applying these principles to the case at bar, the overwhelming weight of the evidence establishes that at the latest by the beginning of 1994, plaintiff had reasonable grounds to be insecure about defendants' ability to perform in the future. Defendants were substantially in arrears almost from the outset of their relationship with plaintiff, had no financing in place, bounced checks, and had failed to sell even a small fraction of the product defendant Spry originally projected.

Reasonable grounds for insecurity can arise from the sole fact that a buyer has fallen behind in his account with the seller, even where the items involved have to do with separate and legally distinct contracts, because this "impairs the seller's expectation of due performance."

Here, defendants do not dispute their poor payment history, plaintiff's right to demand adequate assurances from them and that plaintiff made such demands. Rather, defendants claim that they satisfied those demands by the April 15, 1994 telephone conversation between Vultaggio and Richard Worthy of Metro Factors, Inc., followed by Vultaggio's April 18, 1994 letter to Metro, and Metro's payment of $79,316.24 to Hornell, and that thereafter plaintiff had no right to demand further assurance.

The court disagrees with both plaintiff and defendants in their insistence that only one demand for adequate assurance was made in this case to which there was and could be only a single response. Even accepting defendants' argument that payment by Metro was the sole condition Vultaggio required when he spoke and wrote to Metro, and that such condition was met by Metro's actual payment, the court is persuaded that on May 9, 1994, Hornell had further reasonable grounds for insecurity and a new basis for seeking further adequate assurances.

Defendants cite the UCC for the proposition that "[i]f a party demands and receives specific assurances, then absent a further change of circumstances, the assurances demanded and received are adequate, and the party who has demanded the assurances is bound to proceed." Repeated demands for adequate assurances are within the contemplation of section 2-609.

Here, there was a further change of circumstances. Vultaggio's reported conversation with Worthy on April 15 and his April 25 letter to Metro both anticipate that once payment of defendants' arrears was made, Hornell would release up to $300,000 worth of product on the further condition that defendants met the 14 day payment terms. The arrangement, by its terms, clearly contemplated an opportunity for Hornell to test out defendants' ability to make payment within 14-day periods.

By placing a single order worth $390,000 to $450,000 immediately after receipt of Metro's payment, Spry not only demanded a shipment of product which exceeded the proposed limit, but placed Hornell in a position where it would have no opportunity learn whether Spry would meet the 14-day payment terms, before Spry again became indebted to Hornell for a very large sum of money.

At this point, neither Spry nor Worthy had fully informed Hornell what assurance of payment Metro would be able to provide. Leaving aside the question whether the factoring arrangement with Metro constituted adequate assurance, Hornell never received any documentation to substantiate Spry's purported agreement with Metro. Although Spry's agreement with Metro was fully executed by the end of March, Spry never gave Hornell a copy of it, not even in response to Hornell's May 10, 1994 demand. The March 27, 1994 letter from Vanguard coincided with the date Spry signed the Metro agreement, but contained only a vague reference to a $1.5 million "revolving credit facility," without mentioning Metro Factors, Inc. Moreover, based on the Vanguard letter, Hornell had expected that payment would be forthcoming, but Spry once again offered only excuses and empty promises.

These circumstances, coupled with information received in early May (on which it reasonably relied) that Spry had misled Hornell about the scope of his operation, created new and more acute grounds for Hornell's insecurity and entitled Hornell to seek further adequate assurance from defendants in the form of a documented line of credit or other guarantee.

Defendants' failure to respond constituted a repudiation of the distributorship agreement, which entitled plaintiff to suspend performance and terminate the agreement.

Even if Hornell had seen Spry's agreement with Metro, in the circumstances of this case, the agreement did not provide the adequate assurance to which plaintiff was entitled in relation to defendants' $390,000–$450,000 order. Spry admitted that much of the order was to be retained as inventory for the summer, for which there would be no receivables to factor within 14 days. Although the question of whether every aspect of Hornell's May 10 demand for credit documentation was reasonable is a close one, given the entire history of the relationship between the parties, the court determines that the demand was commercially reasonable. This case is unlike *Pittsburgh-Des Moines Steel Co. v. Brookhaven Manor Water Co.*, 532 F.2d 572 (7th Cir.1976), cited by defendants, in that plaintiff's demand for credit assurances does not modify or contradict the terms of an elaborated written contract.

The court notes in conclusion that its evaluation of the evidence in this case was significantly influenced by Mr. Spry's regrettable lack of credibility. The court agrees with plaintiff, that to an extent far greater than was known to Hornell in May 1994, Mr. Spry was not truthful, failed to pay countless other creditors almost as a matter of course, and otherwise engaged in improper and deceptive business practices.

For the foregoing reasons, it is hereby

ORDERED and ADJUDGED that plaintiff Hornell Brewing Co., Inc. have a declaratory judgment that defendants Stephen A. Spry and Arizona Tea Products,

Ltd. were duly terminated and have no continuing rights with respect to plaintiff Hornell Brewing Co.'s beverage products in Canada or elsewhere.

Reflection

Although Spry's entire pattern of behavior constitutes grounds for reasonable insecurity, it is difficult to pin down exactly which action tipped the scales and created Hornell's right to demand assurances. It may also be hard to fix exactly when Hornell gained the right to cancel its contract with Spry. Remember that the parties — and their attorneys — usually do not have knowledge of all the facts and circumstances at the time they must decide how to act. Parties act with incomplete information about the circumstances and uncertainty with regard to how a court would interpret those circumstances and thereby assign rights and responsibilities. Parties who cancel a contract or threaten to cancel it if they do not receive certain assurances of performance are taking the risk that a court might find that action wrongful.

Discussion

1. When exactly did Spry give Hornell grounds to demand assurances? Which specific action by Spry engendered this right in Hornell?

2. If you were attorney for Hornell Brewing, when exactly would you advise your client that Spry has repudiated? Which specific act made it reasonable for Hornell to cancel the contract?

3. What are the risks to Hornell of cancelling or threatening to cancel its contract with Spry before Spry technically repudiated?

Problems

Problem 19.1. The Rumored Bankruptcy

RingGold Pharmacy purchases its house-branded over-the-counter inventory from MiracleDrug Distributors. MiracleDrug has an exclusive arrangement with RingGold. Under the contract, RingGold is not permitted to purchase house-branded products from any other distributor.

Earlier this week, Erin Ringgold, the owner of the pharmacy, heard a rumor from another reliable pharmacist that MiracleDrug was near bankruptcy. If true, Ring-Gold would have to quickly find another distributor willing to package and sell products that the pharmacy would sell under the RingGold name.

What should Erin do? Should RingGold cancel the contract with MiracleDrug based upon this rumor?

Problem 19.2. **Circuit Boards**

EI (a Pennsylvania corporation) manufactures electronic components for military and civilian aircraft. On March 1, 2015, EI was awarded a contract to supply components for a military aircraft. The contract included detailed specifications and a strict deadline of August 31, 2015, for delivery of the components. On March 15, 2015, EI subcontracted with Circuits, Inc. (Circuits"), to manufacture and supply certain circuit boards that EI needed to make the components for the military contract. EI had never worked with Circuits. The subcontract required Circuits to meet the strict specifications of the military contract, pass sample testing during manufacture, and deliver the required circuit boards by July 31, 2015.

In early April, Al (EI's president) learned the Circuits was having financial difficulties, had several judgments entered against it, and was running late on making deliveries under its existing contracts with other customers. Also, the first circuit board that EI received from testing from Circuits failed the test. Al immediately wrote to the president of Circuits and asked for an updated financial statement from Circuits and written verification that it would be able to deliver circuit boards complying with the contract specifications on time. He also asked that Circuits provide another circuit board for testing. In early May, having received no response to his earlier demand, Al repeated his request in writing to Circuits' president. As of today, Al has received no response from Circuits.

Concerned about Circuits' ability to perform, Al has found another supplier for the circuit boards, Boards, Inc. ("Boards"), which has the required circuit boards in its inventory. A purchase of the circuit boards from Boards will cost EI $20,000 more (inclusive of shipping costs) than the contract price with Circuits. Respond to the following questions with a thorough legal analysis:

a. Was EI within its rights to demand assurances from Circuits that it would be able to fulfill its obligations under the subcontract, and what is the effect of Circuits' failure to respond?

b. Can EI buy the circuit boards it needs from Boards, and, if so, is there any basis for EI to recover the $20,000 excess cost from Circuits?

Chapter 20

Excuse

The general rule of contract law is that any failure to completely perform a contractual obligation is a breach. As R2d puts it, "contract liability is strict liability":

> *The obligor is therefore liable in damages for breach of contract even if he is without fault and even if circumstances have made the contract more burdensome or less desirable than he had anticipated.* R2d Chap. 11 Introductory Note.

But you have already seen that this doctrine has many exceptions. The duty to perform might not have come due because a condition did not occur. The contractual promise may be unenforceable because it lacks consideration. A party may have lacked capacity to form a binding promise. Or the statute of frauds might prevent its enforcement.

But all those other reasons are based on the terms of the agreement and the parties' intentions when forming it. The excuse doctrines we learn about in this chapter are different because they deal with unforeseen events. By definition, parties cannot have had intentions about unforeseen events, since they definitively did not consider such events at the time of contracting. The question for this chapter is, what happens when an unforeseen event fundamentally changes the basis for a contract?

This is really about allocation of risk. When an unforeseen event happens, one party effectively gets stuck with the bill for it. The question is, who bears the risk for such events?

Since the excuse doctrines only apply to unforeseen events, we must define foreseeability in order to determine whether the doctrines even apply. Foreseeability is usually studied more deeply in tort law (where its relation to proximate cause is often a dispositive factor in determining negligence) than in contract law. Contract law prefers to focus on effectuating the intent of the parties to the contract. Where the parties have not sufficiently expressed their intent, courts might say there is no contract. But parties cannot account for every possible eventuality, nor are they obligated to negotiate everything that may happen ahead of time in order for promises to be sufficiently definite as to be enforceable.

Rules

A. Impracticability

Taylor and *Krell* were landmark cases for their time because each broadened the scope of performances that would be excused. But those doctrines have since been broadened further still in the modern era. In particular, the doctrine formerly known as "impossibility" has broadened into "impracticability."

> *Where, after a contract is made, a party's performance is made impracticable without his fault by the occurrence of an event the non-occurrence of which was a basic assumption on which the contract was made, his duty to render that performance is discharged, unless the language or the circumstances indicate the contrary.* R2d § 261.

But just because the excuse doctrine was broadened from impossibility to impracticability does not mean it is limitless. The Supreme Court case of *Transatlantic Financing Coro. v. United States*, below, highlight the limits of the impracticability doctrine. In this case, the United States government hired American Transatlantic Co. to ship a full cargo of wheat from Galveston, Texas to Bandar Shapur, Iran. The typical route for this trip goes through the Suez Canal, which is an artificial waterway offering a significant shortcut to the Middle East instead of going around the Horn of Africa. Soon after the parties formed the agreement, the Government of Egypt took control of the Suez Canal and blockaded it. Transatlantic Financing argued that the blockade constituted an unforeseeable superseding event that made its performance of the contract impracticable.

The Supreme Court disagreed. It found that completing the shipment was made practicable by changing course and going around the Cape of Good Hope. This deviation made the journey about 15% longer and more expensive for the shipper, but this did not constitute an "impracticability." Rather, the risk of delays and expenses en route fall squarely on the shipper and not the buyer in such cases, unless the contract expressly provides otherwise. Moreover, a 15% increase in price is not enough to make performance impracticable—such impracticability is more commonly found where cost of performance increases by an order of magnitude such as an eight to twelve times increase in cost.

A key to understanding the modern doctrine of excuse is to recognize that a party's performance is excused "by the occurrence of an event the non-occurrence of which was a basic assumption on which the contract was made." In the case of *Transatlantic*, war was brewing in the Middle East when the contract was formed. Egypt's blockade of the Suez was foreseeable and, moreover, the shipping company generally assumes the risk of any additional cost of transit.

In the absence of a supervening event, the doctrine of excuse does not come into play. If at the time of contracting, the parties foresaw or should have foreseen the occurrence of an event, and the contract explicitly or implicitly assigned the risk of that occurrence to one of the parties, then that party's performance is not excused upon the happening of that event.

There are, however, three special circumstances where courts usually do recognize that performance is impracticable. They are: one, where a party necessary for performance dies or becomes incapacitated; two, when something necessary for performance is destroyed or fails to come into existence; and, three, when a governmental order prevents performance of a contractual obligation.

1. Death or Incapacity of Necessary Person

Perhaps the most obvious example of "impossibility" is if a person who is contractually obligated to perform personal services for another person dies, then that person is not considered to have breached the contract. In reality, it is difficult to hold a dead person specifically liable for failing to perform some obligation. In practice, that person's performance is excused. The person's estate may have to make restitution of any amounts that the other party had paid in advance, but the person's estate could not be sued for breach of contract, unless the estate or some other corporate entity or trust also had responsibility for the contract.

> *If the existence of a particular person is necessary for the performance of a duty, his death or such incapacity as makes performance impracticable is an event the non-occurrence of which was a basic assumption on which the contract was made. R2d § 262.*

Since the death or incapacity of a person makes that person's performance impossible, it necessarily also makes that performance impracticable, as impracticability is a lower standard than impossibility.

2. Destruction of Necessary Thing

The lack of existence of an essential thing necessary for performance is the second case of legal impossibility. If, for example, a person promises to sell a car that is destroyed in a freak wildfire, the seller should be excused from liability.

> *If the existence of a specific thing is necessary for the performance of a duty, its failure to come into existence, destruction, or such deterioration as makes performance impracticable is an event the non-occurrence of which was a basic assumption on which the contract was made. R2d § 263.*

In another, if a couple reserved space at a hotel to hold a wedding reception but the hotel was destroyed by a tornado before the wedding took place, the hotel's performance would be excused due to impossibility. The hotel would have to return the couple's deposit, but it would not be liable for breach of contract.

The rationale is that the parties both expected the thing to exist at the time of performance. If neither took the risk of its unforeseeable non-existence, then neither should be liable for contractual damages.

3. Prevention by Law

The third case of legal impossibility is where performance is not "impracticable" but for a law or regulation which makes it illegal. Contracts to perform illegal obligations are unenforceable at law; thus, contractual obligations made illegal by law are excused.

> If the performance of a duty is made impracticable by having to comply with a domestic or foreign governmental regulation or order, that regulation or order is an event the non-occurrence of which was a basic assumption on which the contract was made. R2d § 264.

Whether a governmental regulation or order makes performance "impractical" or "frustrates" the purpose of performance is discussed in the case below, *New Beginnings*.

B. Frustration of Purpose

As discussed above, buyers as well as sellers may avail themselves of excuse defenses. Buyers' defenses are generally characterized as frustration of purpose, whereas sellers' defenses are generally characterized as impracticability. But the rules permitting excuse in both cases are very similar:

> Where, after a contract is made, a party's principal purpose is substantially frustrated without his fault by the occurrence of an event the non-occurrence of which was a basic assumption on which the contract was made, his remaining duties to render performance are discharged, unless the language or the circumstances indicate the contrary. R2d § 265.

Discharge by supervening frustration is typically a buyer's remedy, not a seller's remedy, as it is typically the buyer who values the contractual promise, such that when that value is lost, it is the buyer who may be excused from paying for the performance.

C. UCC Excuses

Article 2 of the UCC excuses a party's performance in two circumstances. First, under Section 2-613, the seller's performance may be excused if there has been "casualty to identified goods." Second, under Section 2-615, the seller's performance may be excused if an event preventing performance has occurred that the parties assumed would not occur, such as a natural disaster or the adoption of a government regulation.

1. Casualty to Identified Goods

Under UCC § 2-613, if the contract requires for its performance goods identified when the contract is made, and if those goods are destroyed before the risk of loss has shifted to the buyer, then under Section 2-613, the seller's performance is excused.

> *Where the contract requires for its performance goods identified when the contract is made, and the goods suffer casualty without fault of either party before the risk of loss passes to the buyer, or in a proper case under a "no arrival, no sale" term (Section 2-324) then (a) if the loss is total the contract is avoided; and (b) if the loss is partial or the goods have so deteriorated as no longer to conform to the contract the buyer may nevertheless demand inspection and at his option either treat the contract as avoided or accept the goods with due allowance from the contract price for the deterioration or the deficiency in quantity but without further right against the seller. UCC § 2-613.*

If the loss is partial, the buyer may demand inspection and at its option either treat the contract as avoided or accept the goods with due allowance.

2. Excuse by Failure of Presupposed Conditions

The UCC includes a gap filler provision regarding excuse of performance. If the parties have not adopted a force majeure clause, then under Section 2-615, a party's performance is excused if performance is rendered "impracticable" by "the occurrence of a contingency the non-occurrence of which was a basic assumption of the contract" or by "compliance in good faith with any applicable foreign or domestic governmental regulation or order."

> *Except so far as a seller may have assumed a greater obligation and subject to the preceding section on substituted performance:*
>
> (a) *Delay in delivery or non-delivery in whole or in part by a seller who complies with paragraphs (b) and (c) is not a breach of his duty under a contract for sale if performance as agreed has been made impracticable by the occurrence of a contingency the non-occurrence of which was a basic assumption on which the contract was made or by compliance in good faith with any applicable foreign or domestic governmental regulation or order whether or not it later proves to be invalid.*
>
> (b) *Where the causes mentioned in paragraph (a) affect only a part of the seller's capacity to perform, he must allocate production and deliveries among his customers but may at his option include regular customers not then under contract as well as his own requirements for further manufacture. He may so allocate in any manner which is fair and reasonable.*
>
> (c) *The seller must notify the buyer seasonably that there will be delay or non-delivery and, when allocation is required under paragraph (b), of the estimated quota thus made available for the buyer. UCC § 2-615.*

608   20 • EXCUSE

Note that increased cost alone does <u>not</u> excuse performance. Every contract is entered into in order to protect against changes in the market price. The buyer normally assumes the risk that the price will drop and that it could have obtained the goods at a lower price if it had not entered into the contract. The seller assumes the risk that the market price will rise and that it could have obtained a better price for the goods had it not entered into the contract. The whole point of entering into a contract is to minimize the risk of loss against fluctuations in the market. Accordingly, changes in market price alone do not justify excusing a party's performance and cancelling the contract. According to UCC commentary:

> *Increased cost alone does not excuse performance unless the rise in cost is due to some unforeseen contingency which alters the essential nature of the performance.*
>
> *Neither is a rise or a collapse in the market in itself a justification, for that is exactly the type of business risk which business contracts made at fixed prices are intended to cover. But a severe shortage of raw materials or of supplies due to a contingency such as war, embargo, local crop failure, unforeseen shutdown of major sources of supply or the like, which either causes a marked increase in cost or altogether prevents the seller from securing supplies necessary to his performance, is within the contemplation of this section.*

As indicated by the reporter's comment to the UCC above, what matters is the cause of the change in the ability of the party to perform. Was there some unforeseen event that impaired the ability of the party to perform — an event that the parties had assumed would not occur?

D. Reflections on Excuse

Normally, if a party fails to perform any duty under a contract, that constitutes a breach of contract. However, if a party's performance is excused, then its failure to perform its duty is not a breach of contract. Instead, the legal consequence of excuse of performance is as if the contract had been cancelled. Each party must make restitution to the other of any partial performance, but neither party is liable to the other for any expectancy or consequential damages.

A key to understanding the modern doctrine of excuse is to recognize that a party's performance is excused "by the occurrence of an event the non-occurrence of which was a basic assumption on which the contract was made."

In the absence of a supervening event, the doctrine of excuse does not come into play. If at the time of contracting, the parties foresaw or should have foreseen the occurrence of an event, and the contract explicitly or implicitly assigned the risk of that occurrence to one of the parties, then that party's performance is not excused upon the happening of that event.

Cases

Reading Taylor v. Caldwell. Historically, courts held parties to contracts regardless of circumstances. By the mid-19th century, however, courts recognized that parties should not be forced to carry out obligations that were made impossible by some intervening event. In the famous case of *Taylor v. Caldwell*, below, the plaintiffs agreed to rent Surrey Music Hall and Gardens from defendant. Before the appointed date, the hall burned down due to a fire that was neither party's fault. The court held that the defendant was excused from renting the hall because it could not have foreseen its burning down. Likewise, the plaintiff was not responsible for this risk. Accordingly, the court excused both parties' performance under the agreement.

In the *Taylor* case the owner was excused, but buyers can be excused as well. In *Krell v. Henry*, further below, an English case, a man rented an apartment at a significantly above market rate simply because it afforded an excellent view of the King's coronation. The King, however, got appendicitis, and the coronation was postponed. A court found that the buyer was excused from renting the room because his purpose in renting it was completely frustrated by the postponement.

The next two cases featured in this chapter are perhaps two of the most important cases under English law for understanding modern American contract law. Although the American common law system was substantially inherited from the English system, the systems have been drifting apart from even before the American Revolution began in 1775, yet they have also dovetailed from time to time since then.

Taylor v. Caldwell
122 E.R. 309 (1863)

The declaration alleged that by an agreement, bearing date the 27th May, 1861, the defendants [Caldwell & Bishop] agreed to let, and the plaintiffs [Taylor & Lewis] agreed to take, on the terms therein stated, The Surrey Gardens and Music Hall, Newington, Surrey, for the following days, that is to say, Monday the 17th June, 1861, Monday the 15th July, 1861, Monday the 5th August, 1861, and Monday the 19th August, 1861, for the purpose of giving a series of four grand concerts and day and night fêtes, at the Gardens and Hall on those days respectively, at the rent or sum of £1001 for each of those days.

On the trial, before Blackburn J., at the London Sittings after Michaelmas Term, 1861, it appeared that the action was brought on the following agreement:

Royal Surrey Gardens, 27th May, 1861. Agreement between Messrs. Caldwell & Bishop, of the one part, and Messrs. Taylor & Lewis of the other part, whereby the said Caldwell & Bishop agree to let, and the said Taylor & Lewis agree to take, on the terms hereinafter stated, The Surrey Gardens and Music Hall, Newington, Surrey, for the following days: [Monday the 17th June, 1861, Monday the 15th July, 1861, Monday the 5th August, 1861, and Monday the 19th August, 1861] for the purpose of giving a series of four grand concerts and day and night fêtes at the said Gardens and Hall on those days respectively at the rent or sum of £1001 for each of the said days.

The said Caldwell & Bishop agree to find and provide at their own sole expense, on each of the aforesaid days, for the amusement of the public and persons then in the said Gardens and Hall, an efficient and organised military and quadrille band, the united bands to consist of from thirty-five to forty members; al fresco entertainments of various descriptions; coloured minstrels, fireworks and full illuminations; a ballet or divertissement, if permitted; a wizard and Grecian statues; tight rope performances; rifle galleries; air gun shooting; Chinese and Parisian games; boats on the lake, and (weather permitting) aquatic sports, and all and every other entertainment as given nightly during the months and times above mentioned . . .

And the said Taylor & Lewis agree to pay the aforesaid respective sum of £1001. in the evening of the said respective days by a crossed cheque, and also to find and provide, at their own sole cost, all the necessary artistes for the said concerts, including Mr. Sims Reeves, God's will permitting.

[The contract was signed by signed by J. Caldwell and C. Bishop and witnessed by S. Denis.]

On the 11th June the Music Hall was destroyed by an accidental fire, so that it became impossible to give the concerts.

The judgment of the Court was now delivered by BLACKBURN J.

[Blackburn's recitation of the facts omitted as they are virtually identical to the statement of facts given by the court reporter above.]

The effect of the whole is to shew that the existence of the Music Hall in the Surrey Gardens in a state fit for a concert was essential for the fulfilment of the contract, such entertainments as the parties contemplated in their agreement could not be given without it.

After the making of the agreement, and before the first day on which a concert was to be given, the Hall was destroyed by fire. This destruction, we must take it on the evidence, was without the fault of either party, and was so complete that in consequence the concerts could not be given as intended. And the question we have to decide is whether, under these circumstances, the loss which the plaintiffs have sustained is to fall upon the defendants. The parties when framing their agreement evidently had not present to their minds the possibility of such a disaster, and have

Figure 20.1. The Adelphi Theatre Calendar revised, reconstructed and amplified.
Credit Alfred L. Nelson, Gilbert B. Cross, Joseph Donohue. CC-A 3.0 License.

made no express stipulation with reference to it, so that the answer to the question must depend upon the general rules of law applicable to such a contract.

[Lengthy discussion of precedent in English and Roman law omitted. This discussion is to the effect that where promises are independent, the contractor must perform or pay damages for not performing. But when there is some express stipulation that the destruction of a person or thing shall excuse performance, or when such excuse is a condition implied by law, then the destruction of said person or thing shall excuse the performance conditioned on its existence.]

[Here,] excuse is by law implied, because from the nature of the contract it is apparent that the parties contracted on the basis of the continued existence of the particular person or chattel. In the present case, looking at the whole contract, we find that the parties contracted on the basis of the continued existence of the Music Hall at the time when the concerts were to be given; that being essential to their performance.

We think, therefore, that the Music Hall having ceased to exist, without fault of either party, both parties are excused, the plaintiffs from taking the gardens and paying the money, the defendants from performing their promise to give the use of the

Hall and Gardens and other things. Consequently the rule must be absolute to enter the verdict for the defendants [Caldwell & Bishop, such that they do not have to pay for the use of Surrey Music Hall].

Rule absolute.

Reflection

While it may seem obvious after reading *Taylor* that neither party should be obligated to perform under a contract where its subject matter was destroyed, the court does not address why the owners of Surrey Music Hall did not bear responsibility for ensuring it remained. Why did the owners of the hall not bear the risk of its loss? The owners are in the better position to prevent fires or to maintain insurance that covers the risk of this loss.

Discussion

1. Consider how the doctrine of mistake would apply to this case. A party is only entitled to void a contract on the basis of mistake where that party does not bear the risk of that mistake. Should a party be able to use the excuse defense where its performance became impossible due to its own fault? What would be the economic impact of such a rule?

2. How could a court determine whether a party's impossibility in performance is due to its own fault? Tort law uses the idea of "proximate causation" to determine fault for negligence. Does contract law also imply some idea of proximate causation for impossibility? Should it? If so, how?

Krell v. Henry

2 K.B. 740 (1903)

Vaughan Williams, L.J.

The real question in this case is the extent of the application in English law of the principle of the Roman law which has been adopted and acted on in many English decisions, and notably in the case of *Taylor v. Caldwell*. That case at least makes it clear that where, from the nature of the contract, it appears that the parties must from the beginning have known that it could not be fulfilled unless, when the time for the fulfilment of the contract arrived, some particular specified thing continued to exist, so that when entering into the contract they must have contemplated such continued existence as the foundation of what was to be done; there, in the absence of any express or implied warranty that the thing shall exist, the contract is not to be considered a positive contract, but as subject to an implied condition that the parties shall be excused in case, before breach, performance becomes impossible from the perishing of the thing without default of the contractor.

Thus far it is clear that the principle of the Roman law has been introduced into the English law. The doubt in the present case arises as to how far this principle extends. The Roman law dealt with obligationes de certo corpore.

Whatever may have been the limits of the Roman law, the case of *Nickoll v. Ashton* makes it plain that the English law applies the principle not only to cases where the performance of the contract becomes impossible by the cessation of existence of the thing which is the subject-matter of the contract, but also to cases where the event which renders the contract incapable of performance is the cessation or non-existence of an express condition or state of things, going to the root of the contract, and essential to its performance.

Now what are the facts of the present case? The contract is contained in two letters of June 20 which passed between the defendant and the plaintiff's agent, Mr. Cecil Bisgood. These letters do not mention the coronation [of King Edward VII and Alexandria that was scheduled for June 26, 1902], but speak merely of the taking of Mr. Krell's chambers, or, rather, of the use of them, in the daytime of June 26 and 27, for the sum of £751, £251 then paid, balance £501 to be paid on the 24th.

But the affidavits, which by agreement between the parties are to be taken as stating the facts of the case, shew that the plaintiff exhibited on his premises, third floor, 56A, Pall Mall, an announcement to the effect that windows to view the Royal coronation procession were to be let, and that the defendant was induced by that announcement to apply to the housekeeper on the premises, who said that the owner was willing to let the suite of rooms for the purpose of seeing the Royal procession for both days, but not nights, of June 26 and 27.

In my judgment the use of the rooms was let and taken for the purpose of seeing the Royal procession.

It was not a demise of the rooms, or even an agreement to let and take the rooms. It is a licence to use rooms for a particular purpose and none other. And in my judgment the taking place of those processions on the days proclaimed along the proclaimed route, which passed 56A, Pall Mall, was regarded by both contracting parties as the foundation of the contract; and I think that it cannot reasonably be supposed to have been in the contemplation of the contracting parties, when the contract was made, that the coronation would not be held on the proclaimed days, or the processions not take place on those days along the proclaimed route; and I think that the words imposing on the defendant the obligation to accept and pay for the use of the rooms for the named days, although general and unconditional, were not used with reference to the possibility of the particular contingency which afterwards occurred.

It was suggested in the course of the argument that if the occurrence, on the proclaimed days, of the coronation and the procession in this case were the foundation of the contract, and if the general words are thereby limited or qualified, so that in the event of the nonoccurrence of the coronation and procession along the proclaimed route they would discharge both parties from further performance of the contract.

Figure 20.2. Procession passing along a busy London thoroughfare during the Coronation of Edward VII (1841–1910) on August 9, 1902. The view from the apartment on Pall Mall would have been similar to this. Public domain work.

[Counsel argued that the following hypothetical is analogous to the instant case:] if a cabman was engaged to take someone to Epsom on Derby Day at a suitable enhanced price for such a journey, say £10, both parties to the contract would be discharged in the contingency of the race at Epsom for some reason becoming impossible. [This was counsel's effort to make a slippery slope argument; that is, if the court excuses the renter's payment in this case, it must also excuse many other payments, and this cannot be the correct result because too many contractual promises would thus be excused.]

[Judge Williams distinguished the counsel's hypothetical thus:] but I do not think this follows, for I do not think that in the cab case the happening of the race would be the foundation of the contract. No doubt the purpose of the engager would be to go to see the Derby, and the price would be proportionately high; but the cab had no special qualifications for the purpose which led to the selection of the cab for this particular occasion. Any other cab would have done as well.

Moreover, I think that, under the cab contract, the hirer, even if the race went off, could have said, "Drive me to Epsom; I will pay you the agreed sum; you have nothing to do with the purpose for which I hired the cab," and that if the cabman refused he would have been guilty of a breach of contract, there being nothing to qualify his promise to drive the hirer to Epsom on a particular day.

Whereas in the case of the coronation, there is not merely the purpose of the hirer to see the coronation procession, but it is the coronation procession and the relative position of the rooms which is the basis of the contract as much for the lessor as the hirer; and I think that if the King, before the coronation day and after the contract, had died, the hirer could not have insisted on having the rooms on the days named.

It could not in the cab case be reasonably said that seeing the Derby race was the foundation of the contract, as it was of the licence in this case. Whereas in the present case, where the rooms were offered and taken, by reason of their peculiar suitability from the position of the rooms for a view of the coronation procession, surely the view of the coronation procession was the foundation of the contract, which is a very different thing from the purpose of the man who engaged the cab — namely, to see the race — being held to be the foundation of the contract.

[The judge, having distinguished the Epsom cab analogy from the instant case, goes on to discuss general rules that can apply in all such cases.]

Each case must be judged by its own circumstances. In each case one must ask oneself:

1. first, what, having regard to all the circumstances, was the foundation of the contract?

2. Secondly, was the performance of the contract prevented?

3. Thirdly, was the event which prevented the performance of the contract of such a character that it cannot reasonably be said to have been in the contemplation of the parties at the date of the contract?

If all these questions are answered in the affirmative (as I think they should be in this case), I think both parties are discharged from further performance of the contract.

I think that the coronation procession was the foundation of this contract, and that the non-happening of it prevented the performance of the contract; and, secondly, I think that the non-happening of the procession, to use the words of Sir James Hannen in *Baily v. De Crespigny*, was an event

> *of such a character that it cannot reasonably be supposed to have been in the contemplation of the contracting parties when the contract was made, and that they are not to be held bound by general words which, though large enough to include, were not used with reference to the possibility of the particular contingency which afterwards happened.*

The test seems to be whether the event which causes the impossibility was or might have been anticipated and guarded against. It seems difficult to say, in a case where both parties anticipate the happening of an event, which anticipation is the foundation of the contract, that either party must be taken to have anticipated, and ought to have guarded against, the event which prevented the performance of the contract.

[Extensive discussion of English case law omitted.]

It is not essential to the application of the principle of *Taylor v. Caldwell* that the direct subject of the contract should perish or fail to be in existence at the date of

Figure 20.3. Le Derby de 1821 à Epsom, an 1821 painting by Théodore Géricault
in the Louvre Museum, showing The Derby (the main horse race or 'course de chevaux')
of that year. Public domain work distributed by DIRECTMEDIA Publishing GmbH.

performance of the contract. It is sufficient if a state of things or condition expressed
in the contract and essential to its performance perishes or fails to be in existence at
that time.

In the present case the condition which fails and prevents the achievement of that
which was, in the contemplation of both parties, the foundation of the contract, is
not expressly mentioned either as a condition of the contract or the purpose of it;
but I think for the reasons which I have given that the principle of *Taylor v. Caldwell*
ought to be applied. This disposes of the plaintiff's claim for £501 unpaid balance of
the price agreed to be paid for the use of the rooms. . . . I think this appeal ought to
be dismissed.

Reflection

Krell offers a more sophisticated analysis than *Taylor*, which is unsurprising given
that *Krell* benefited from the precedent of *Taylor* and other precedent analysis. But
the *Krell* court does not seem to explicitly discuss why the tenant or, alternatively, the
landlord bears any risk or responsibility for the cancellation of an event. Instead, the
court seems to excuse the tenant because the landlord is in a better position to afford
the loss of the rental. (The landlord can re-let the premises, presumably for a similar
rate, when the coronation is reconvened.) This appears to be based on the reliance
interest, which you will learn about in the chapter on money damages. But it does

not account for the expectation interest, which, as you will learn, is the typical measure of damages. This deviation from the norm signifies that the court was considering equitable basis for excuse.

Discussion

1. Why is "foreseeability" the basis for the frustration of purpose excuse? Should a court consider instead, or also, which party bears the risk of frustration of purpose? How would this consideration change the outcome in this case?

2. How would the rule apply to similar matters, such as renting an expensive hotel room in order attend the Super Bowl, where the event is cancelled due to outbreak of a virulent disease?

3. How does the *Krell* rule impact incentives on parties to be careful, or careless, when transacting about goods, services, or real or intellectual property that is to be used for a particular purpose? Specifically, does this rule encourage parties to disclose their purposes, or does it encourage them to keep information private?

Reading Transatlantic Financing Corp. v. United States. The cases above are featured in the introduction because they established the foundation for the excuse doctrines we have today. Both *Taylor* and *Krell* were landmark cases for their time because each broadened the scope of performances that would be excused. But those doctrines have since been broadened further still in the modern era. In particular, the doctrine formerly known as "impossibility" has broadened into "impracticability." The correlated doctrine of frustration of purpose has likewise broadened, as you will see.

Today, courts may excuse performance even where it is not strictly impossible but only highly impracticable such that it has become unfair to hold both parties to the bargain.

Since the excuse doctrines only apply to unforeseen events, we must define foreseeability in order to determine whether the doctrines even apply. Foreseeability is usually studied more deeply in tort law (where its relation to proximate cause is often a dispositive factor in determining negligence) than in contract law. Contract law prefers to focus on effectuating the intent of the parties to the contract. Where the parties have not sufficiently expressed their intent, courts might say there is no contract. But parties cannot account for every possible eventuality, nor are they obligated to negotiate everything that may happen ahead of time in order for promises to be sufficiently definite as to be enforceable.

Transatlantic Financing Corp. v. United States

363 F.2d 312 (D.C. Cir. 1966)

J. SKELLY WRIGHT, Circuit Judge:

This appeal involves a voyage charter between Transatlantic Financing Corporation, operator of the SS CHRISTOS, and the United States covering carriage of a full cargo of wheat from a United States Gulf port to a safe port in Iran. The District Court dismissed a libel filed by Transatlantic against the United States for costs attributable to the ship's diversion from the normal sea route caused by the closing of the Suez Canal. We affirm.

On July 26, 1956, the Government of Egypt nationalized the Suez Canal Company and took over operation of the Canal. On October 2, 1956, during the international crisis which resulted from the seizure, the voyage charter in suit was executed between representatives of Transatlantic and the United States. The charter indicated the termini of the voyage but not the route. On October 27, 1956, the SS CHRISTOS sailed from Galveston for Bandar Shapur, Iran, on a course which would have taken her through Gibraltar and the Suez Canal. On October 29, 1956, Israel invaded Egypt. On October 31, 1956, Great Britain and France invaded the Suez Canal Zone. On November 2, 1956, the Egyptian Government obstructed the Suez Canal with sunken vessels and closed it to traffic.

On or about November 7, 1956, Beckmann, representing Transatlantic, contacted Potosky, an employee of the United States Department of Agriculture, who appellant concedes was unauthorized to bind the Government, requesting instructions concerning disposition of the cargo and seeking an agreement for payment of additional compensation for a voyage around the Cape of Good Hope. Potosky advised Beckmann that Transatlantic was expected to perform the charter according to its terms, that he did not believe Transatlantic was entitled to additional compensation for a voyage around the Cape, but that Transatlantic was free to file such a claim. Following this discussion, the CHRISTOS changed course for the Cape of Good Hope and eventually arrived in Bandar Shapur on December 30, 1956.

Transatlantic's claim is based on the following train of argument. The charter was a contract for a voyage from a Gulf port to Iran. Admiralty principles and practices, especially stemming from the doctrine of deviation, require us to imply into the contract the term that the voyage was to be performed by the "usual and customary" route. The usual and customary route from Texas to Iran was, at the time of contract, via Suez, so the contract was for a voyage from Texas to Iran via Suez. When Suez was closed this contract became impossible to perform. Consequently, appellant's argument continues, when Transatlantic delivered the cargo by going around the Cape of Good Hope, in compliance with the Government's demand under claim of right, it conferred a benefit upon the United States for which it should be paid in quantum meruit.

The doctrine of impossibility of performance has gradually been freed from the earlier fictional and unrealistic strictures of such tests as the "implied term" and the parties' "contemplation." It is now recognized that "A thing is impossible in legal contemplation when it is not practicable; and a thing is impracticable when it can only be done at an excessive and unreasonable cost." The doctrine ultimately represents the ever-shifting line, drawn by courts hopefully responsive to commercial practices and mores, at which the community's interest in having contracts enforced according to their terms is outweighed by the commercial senselessness of requiring performance. When the issue is raised, the court is asked to construct a condition of performance based on the changed circumstances, a process which involves at least three reasonably definable steps. First, a contingency-something unexpected- must have occurred. Second, the risk of the unexpected occurrence must not have been allocated either by agreement or by custom. Finally, occurrence of the contingency must have rendered performance commercially impracticable. Unless the court finds these three requirements satisfied, the plea of impossibility must fail.

The first requirement was met here. It seems reasonable, where no route is mentioned in a contract, to assume the parties expected performance by the usual and customary route at the time of contract. Since the usual and customary route from Texas to Iran at the time of contract was through Suez, closure of the Canal made impossible the expected method of performance. But this unexpected development raises rather than resolves the impossibility issue, which turns additionally on whether the risk of the contingency's occurrence had been allocated and, if not, whether performance by alternative routes was rendered impracticable.

Proof that the risk of a contingency's occurrence has been allocated may be expressed in or implied from the agreement. Such proof may also be found in the surrounding circumstances, including custom and usages of the trade. The contract in this case does not expressly condition performance upon availability of the Suez route. Nor does it specify "via Suez" or, on the other hand, "via Suez or Cape of Good Hope." Nor are there provisions in the contract from which we may properly imply that the continued availability of Suez was a condition of performance. Nor is there anything in custom or trade usage, or in the surrounding circumstances generally, which would support our constructing a condition of performance. The numerous cases requiring performance around the Cape when Suez was closed, indicate that the Cape route is generally regarded as an alternative means of performance. So the implied expectation that the route would be via Suez is hardly adequate proof of an allocation to the promisee of the risk of closure. In some cases, even an express expectation may not amount to a condition of performance. The doctrine of deviation supports our assumption that parties normally expect performance by the usual and customary route, but it adds nothing beyond this that is probative of an allocation of the risk.

If anything, the circumstances surrounding this contract indicate that the risk of the Canal's closure may be deemed to have been allocated to Transatlantic. We know or may safely assume that the parties were aware, as were most commercial men with interests affected by the Suez situation, see *The Eugenia, supra,* that the Canal might become a dangerous area. No doubt the tension affected freight rates, and it is arguable that the risk of closure became part of the dickered terms. We do not deem the risk of closure so allocated, however. Foreseeability or even recognition of a risk does not necessarily prove its allocation. Parties to a contract are not always able to provide for all the possibilities of which they are aware, sometimes because they cannot agree, often simply because they are too busy. Moreover, that some abnormal risk was contemplated is probative but does not necessarily establish an allocation of the risk of the contingency which actually occurs. In this case, for example, nationalization by Egypt of the Canal Corporation and formation of the Suez Users Group did not necessarily indicate that the Canal would be blocked even if a confrontation resulted. The surrounding circumstances do indicate, however, a willingness by Transatlantic to assume abnormal risks, and this fact should legitimately cause us to judge the impracticability of performance by an alternative route in stricter terms than we would were the contingency unforeseen.

We turn then to the question whether occurrence of the contingency rendered performance commercially impracticable under the circumstances of this case. The goods shipped were not subject to harm from the longer, less temperate Southern route. The vessel and crew were fit to proceed around the Cape. Transatlantic was no less able than the United States to purchase insurance to cover the contingency's occurrence. If anything, it is more reasonable to expect owner-operators of vessels to insure against the hazards of war. They are in the best position to calculate the cost of performance by alternative routes (and therefore to estimate the amount of insurance required), and are undoubtedly sensitive to international troubles which uniquely affect the demand for and cost of their services. The only factor operating here in appellant's favor is the added expense, allegedly $43,972.00 above and beyond the contract price of $305,842.92, of extending a 10,000 mile voyage by approximately 3,000 miles. While it may be an overstatement to say that increased cost and difficulty of performance never constitute impracticability, to justify relief there must be more of a variation between expected cost and the cost of performing by an available alternative than is present in this case, where the promisor can legitimately be presumed to have accepted some degree of abnormal risk, and where impracticability is urged on the basis of added expense alone.

We conclude, therefore, as have most other courts considering related issues arising out of the Suez closure, that performance of this contract was not rendered legally impossible. Even if we agreed with appellant, its theory of relief seems untenable. When performance of a contract is deemed impossible it is a nullity. In the case of a charter party involving carriage of goods, the carrier may return to an appropriate port and unload its cargo, subject of course to required steps to minimize damages. If the performance rendered has value, recovery in quantum meruit for the entire performance is proper. But here Transatlantic has collected its contract price, and now seeks quantum meruit relief for the additional expense of the trip around the Cape. If the contract is a nullity, Transatlantic's theory of relief should have been quantum meruit for the entire trip, rather than only for the extra expense. Transatlantic attempts to take its profit on the contract, and then force the Government to absorb the cost of the additional voyage. When impracticability without fault occurs, the law seeks an equitable solution, and quantum meruit is one of its potent devices to achieve this end. There is no interest in casting the entire burden of commercial disaster on one party in order to preserve the other's profit. Apparently the contract price in this case was advantageous enough to deter appellant from taking a stance on damages consistent with its theory of liability. In any event, there is no basis for relief.

Affirmed.

Reflection

Transatlantic not only shows how the impossibility excuse broadened into the impracticability defense. It also shows the limits of the broader excuse doctrine. Impracticability does not require impossibility of performance, but it does require performance to be so onerous that it would be unconscionable for a court to require it. You will learn in the chapter on remedies that courts usually award to an aggrieved party money damages calculated pursuant to the expectation interest when one party breaches a contract. This measure of damages is useful because it ensures parties to a contract get what they expected (or its monetary value). As you will learn in subsequent chapters, this measure of damages encourages the efficient result of performance when it is socially beneficial and payment when it is not.

But excusing performance has a different result. Excusing performance makes it as if the contract was not formed. This leaves parties in a difficult position, and, moreover, it puts courts in the challenging position of trying to assess what damages should be owed when the expectation interest must be disregarded.

Discussion

1. If the court had excused the contract in *Transatlantic*, assuming that the United Stated had not yet paid anything for shipment, how much should the United States pay Transatlantic? Answer this based on your intuition and allow yourself to change your view after you learn the rules regarding money damages.

2. If the cost of delivering the wheat to Iran becomes more expensive than the value of the wheat itself, due to geopolitical issues involving shipping that were beyond the control of either party, should Transatlantic be required to deliver the wheat anyway? What does justice require? What judgment is most economically efficient? Is there a difference between equitable results and efficient results in cases regarding commercial matters?

_____

> *Reading Adbar, L.C. v. New Beginnings C-Star.* Frustration of purposes operates in much the same way that impracticability does, but it is phrased in such a way that this tends to be a buyer's excuse, whereas impracticability tends to be a seller's excuse. As you read the next case, *Adbar v. New Beginnings*, think about whether the buyer's purpose in renting a building was totally or substantially frustrated, and also think about who should bear the risk that the event which caused the purported frustration would occur.

Adbar, L.C. v. New Beginnings C-Star

103 S.W.3d 799 (Mo. Ct. App. 2003)

GLENN A. NORTON, Judge.

Adbar, L.C. appeals the judgment in favor of New Beginnings C Star on Adbar's claim for breach of lease. We reverse in part and affirm in part.

I. Background

New Beginnings provides rehabilitation services for alcohol and drug abuse to both adults and adolescents. In the fall of 1999, New Beginnings was searching for a new location and entered into negotiations with Adbar for lease of a building in the City of St. Louis. New Beginnings received a preliminary indication from the City's zoning administrator that its use of the property constituted a permitted use under the zoning regulations. New Beginnings and Adbar subsequently entered into a three-year lease. The total rent due for the three-year term was $273,000.

After the lease was executed, the City denied New Beginnings' application for an occupancy permit on the grounds that the operation constituted a nuisance use under the zoning regulations. At trial, Alderman Freeman Bosley, Sr. testified that due to his opposition to New Beginnings moving into his Ward, he had called the zoning administrator and asked him to reverse his preliminary indication that New Beginnings' operation constituted a permitted use.

New Beginnings appealed the denial of the occupancy permit to the board of adjustment. Alderman Bosley and other neighborhood residents testified in opposition to New Beginnings at the board's hearing. The board affirmed the denial of the permit. New Beginnings then sought a writ, which was granted by the circuit court, and New Beginnings was issued an occupancy permit. Alderman Bosley contacted the judge who issued the writ and asked him to reverse his decision. The judge declined. A few weeks later, at the City counselor's request, the City revoked New Beginnings' occupancy permit. New Beginnings filed a motion for contempt with the circuit court. The motion was granted, and the City re-issued the occupancy permit.

After the permit was reissued, New Beginnings began preparing to move in, including having some construction done on the building. At this same time, Alderman Bosley contacted then State Representative Paula Carter, chairwoman of the appropriations committee responsible for New Beginnings' state funding. Alderman Bosley asked Representative Carter to "pull the funding" for New Beginnings. Alderman Bosley did not get a commitment from Representative Carter, but told her that "if you don't get their funding, you are going to have trouble running" for re-election.

New Beginnings alleges that it was then contacted by Michael Couty, director of the Missouri Division of Alcohol and Drug Abuse, who threatened to rescind all state contracts with New Beginnings if it moved into the new location. New Beginnings convened a meeting of its board of directors to conduct a conference call with Director Couty. New Beginnings alleges that during that conference call Director Couty repeated his threat to rescind funding if it moved into the new location. At the end of the meeting, New Beginnings' board decided not to occupy the building they had leased from Adbar. At trial Director Couty denied making any such threats to New Beginnings.

Adbar filed a petition for breach of the lease. New Beginnings asserted a defense of legal impossibility. On the first day of the trial, New Beginnings was granted leave to amend its answer to add the defense of commercial frustration. Following a bench trial, the trial court ruled that New Beginnings was excused from its performance under the lease because of commercial frustration. This appeal follows.

II. Discussion

On review of this court-tried case, we will sustain the judgment of the trial court unless there is no substantial evidence to support it, it is against the weight of the evidence, it erroneously declares the law, or it erroneously applies the law. We accept the evidence and inferences favorable to the prevailing party and disregard all contrary evidence. We will defer to the factual findings of the trial judge, who is in a superior position to assess credibility; however, we independently evaluate the court's conclusions of law.

A. Commercial Frustration

In its first point on appeal, Adbar asserts that the trial court erroneously applied the law when it excused New Beginnings' performance under the lease due to the doctrine of commercial frustration. We agree.

[Under common law,] the doctrine of commercial frustration grew out of demands of the commercial world to excuse performance under contracts in cases of extreme hardship. Under the doctrine of commercial frustration, if the occurrence of an event, not foreseen by the parties and not caused by or under the control of either party, destroys or nearly destroys the value of the performance or the object or purpose of the contract, then the parties are excused from further performance.

If, on the other hand, the event was reasonably foreseeable, then the parties should have provided for its occurrence in the contract. The absence of a provision in the contract providing for such an occurrence indicates an assumption of the risk by the promisor. In determining foreseeability, courts consider the terms of the contract and the circumstances surrounding the formation of the contract. The doctrine of commercial frustration should be limited in its application so as to preserve the certainty of contracts.

[Here, in this case,] New Beginnings alleged that the troubles it faced obtaining its occupancy permit, along with the actions of Alderman Bosley and Director Couty, combined to rise to commercially frustrate the lease agreement with Adbar. Ultimately, New Beginnings' funding was never rescinded. In this case the intervening event was merely the possibility that the funding may be rescinded. For an organization that receives funding from the State, the possibility that their funding may be reduced or even completely rescinded is foreseeable.

Furthermore, while the zeal with which Alderman Bosley attempted to keep New Beginnings out of his ward may have been surprising to the parties, it is certainly foreseeable that a drug and alcohol abuse treatment facility might encounter neighborhood resistance when attempting to move into a new location. At trial, the CEO of New Beginnings admitted that both the elimination of New Beginnings' funding and opposition from neighborhood groups were foreseeable.

[Citations to analogous cases omitted.]

The possibility that New Beginnings' funding may be threatened was foreseeable. Yet, New Beginnings did not provide for that possibility in the lease. Therefore, New Beginnings assumed the risk that their funding may be threatened and that it might frustrate the purpose of the lease.

In addition to this event being foreseeable, neither the value of the performance nor the purpose of the lease was destroyed. The purpose of the lease was to allow New Beginnings to operate a rehabilitation center at the location of the property. New Beginnings' funding was never rescinded or even restricted. Alderman Bosley's continued interference with New Beginnings efforts to provide rehabilitation treatment to addicts of drugs and alcohol certainly made, and would have continued to make, business difficult for New Beginnings. However, neither the value of the performance nor the object or purpose of the lease was destroyed or nearly destroyed.

Therefore, the doctrine of commercial frustration does not excuse New Beginnings performance under the lease. Point I is granted.

III. Conclusion

The judgment that New Beginnings is excused from the lease under the defense of commercial frustration is reversed and the cause is remanded for a new trial in accordance with this opinion. The judgment in all other respects is affirmed.

Reflection

The *New Beginnings* case is an example of a foreseeable event that occurred. Since the event was foreseeable, it cannot be grounds for excuse due to frustration of purpose.

Why was it foreseeable in this case that an addiction treatment facility would meet resistance to its operation by local government officials? There is a concept called NIMBY, which stands for "not in my backyard." The idea is that, although a development will be a net positive for society as a whole, it is seen negatively by those who are most immediately impacted by it. The residents who oppose the development are called Nimbys, and their viewpoints is called Nimbyism.

Wikipedia lists a variety of projects that are likely to be opposed by local residents:

- housing development
- bicycle and pedestrian infrastructure
- skyscrapers
- homeless shelters
- oil wells
- chemical plants
- industrial parks
- military bases
- sewage treatment systems
- fracking
- wind turbines
- desalination plants
- landfill sites
- incinerators
- power plants

- quarries
- prisons
- pubs and bars
- adult entertainment clubs
- concert venues
- firearms dealers
- mobile phone masts
- electricity pylons
- abortion clinics
- children's homes
- nursing homes
- youth hostels
- sports stadiums
- shopping malls
- retail parks
- railways

- highway expansions
- airports
- seaports
- nuclear waste repositories
- storage for weapons of mass destruction
- cannabis dispensaries and recreational cannabis shops
- methadone clinics
- accommodation of persons applying for asylum, refugees, and displaced persons

Perhaps you can see some similarities among the items on this list. When a promotor proposes a development that typically engenders a NIMBY reaction, it is reasonably foreseeable that the promoter might not gain local government support for that development project.

Since local government support is often required for development projects such as the addiction treatment clinic in *New Beginnings* to operate, courts generally will not find that the promotor's performance (e.g., paying rent) is excused where operating permits are not forthcoming from the local authorities.

Discussion

1. When an entrepreneur embarks on a business project such as developing an adult entertainment club or a methadone clinic, should that entrepreneur bear the risk that local governments oppose the project? Should the person transacting with the entrepreneur bear this risk?

2. In general, which contractual party should bear the economic risk that government will prevent some activity?

Problems

Problem 20.1. Super Bowl LV

On January 1, 2020, Alex, who lives in Minnesota, decides she wants to get away from the cold winters and go to Florida to attend Super Bowl LV in Tampa, Florida. On that day, she enters into the following transactions:

- Alex agrees to buy from Will two tickets to Super Bowl LV, which is scheduled to be held at the Raymond James Stadium in Tampa Bay, Florida, on Sunday, February 7, 2021, for $1,000 each.

- Alex purchases two round-trip airplane tickets from Delta Airlines for travel on Friday from Minneapolis-Saint Paul International Airport to Tampa International Airport for $125 each.

- Alex agrees to rent from Colin his one-bedroom apartment in Tampa the four nights from Friday, February 5 to Tuesday, February 9. Colin's apartment is located in the Cove Apartments on the Bay at 4003 S. West Shore Blvd., Tampa, FL, for $500 per night ($2,000 total).

In March of that year, the novel coronavirus known as COVID-19 began infecting people worldwide. Governments responded by shutting down businesses and limiting in-person gatherings throughout that Spring and Summer. Some airlines cancelled flights and refunded passengers for travel in early April and May, and confusion continued through the year.

On December 15, 2020, Alex decided to cancel her trip and asked Will, Colin, and Delta Airlines for a refund. They all refused, noting the following facts:

- Delta Airlines stated that, unless the Florida, Minnesota, or federal government(s) order another shutdown, it will be flying the MSP-TPA route, so her travel is possible. Alex has purchased a standard-fair ticket, which has a $200 change fee.

- Colin made plans to stay at his mother's house in West Palm Beach, Florida, in order to make his apartment available to Alex. He also did not rent it to others during the Super Bowl period because Alex had reserved it. He also hired a professional cleaning company to sanitize the vacant apartment before her arrival, for which service he put down a $100 non-refundable deposit.

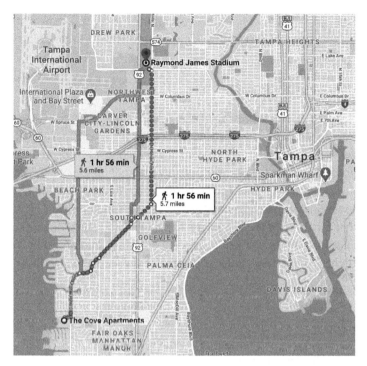

Figure 20.4. Map showing the relative locations of the rented apartment and the football stadium.

- Will cannot get his money back for or resell the Super Bowl LV tickets because as of that date, the NFL Commissioner Roger Goodell still has not announced whether in person attendance will be permitted at that game. The Tampa Bay Times quoted Commissioner Goodell saying, "We will be working with public officials and the health officials to define [the capacity for the game] as we get closer to the game." Will added that he will refund Alex if the NFL refunds him for his ticket.

In addition to these facts, note that these are real locations and events, so you can use the internet to learn more about them. Do some "Google research" and consider things like comparable price, location, and other details that are significant to your determination of this case. You should also look at news articles to determine when cancelling live attendance at the Super Bowl due to COVID-19 was reasonably foreseeable.

Based on these facts and your research, discuss:

a. Whether Alex has the immediate right to cancel her promises to pay Colin and/or Will, and/or whether she is legally entitled to receive a refund from Delta Airlines.

b. Whether Alex would have the right to cancel or receive a refund if it turns out that she will not be permitted by the NFL to attend the game live and in person.

c. Whether Alex's request for a cancellation or a refund constitutes either a repudiation or provides grounds for any of Colin, Will, or Delta Airlines to demand assurances.

Problem 20.2. **Lot Number 1285**

Naomi purchased 3 tons of nitrogen fertilizer for her farm from Grozit, a local feed and fertilizer distributor in Carlisle, Pennsylvania. Ever careful, before Naomi signed the purchase agreement, she visited the warehouse, inspected the fertilizer, and had 3 tons of it set aside for her and designated "Lot Number 1285." The purchase agreement dated March 1 specified that Grozit would deliver "Lot Number 1285" to Naomi on May 1. Unfortunately, a small fire destroyed Lot Number 1285 on April 15. Grozit has other fertilizer of the same type that is available, but the market price has risen and Grozit insists that the prior agreement is now void and that Naomi must sign a new purchase agreement at a higher price if she wants the fertilizer.

Is Grozit within its rights? Analyze whether Grozit's performance is excused.

Problem 20.3. **Excessive Rain**

Bob is a potato broker. Bob entered into a contract with McDonald's to provide 80 tons of potatoes to be delivered by November 1. There was excessive rain in the Midwest that ruined the potato crop, thus raising the price of potatoes nationwide by 25%, making the contract with McDonald's relatively unprofitable for Bob. Bob claims that this unforeseen event should excuse his performance under the contract. McDonald's demands that he either deliver the potatoes or be liable for breach of contract.

All of Bob's contracts for obtaining potatoes were with farmers in the Midwest, none of whom have any potatoes for sale. McDonald's was aware of Bob's regional affiliations with farmers, and contracted with potato brokers in many different regions around the country specifically to protect against localized and regional crop failures.

Analyze who wins the breach of contract dispute.

Chapter 21

Assent

This module regarding performance and breach of contractual obligations began by describing when one party's performance of its contractual promise is due: performance is due when conditions to it have occurred. Such conditions include express conditions, including conditions precedent, such as where one party says to another "I will pay you twenty dollars to mow my lawn on Friday on condition that it does not rain before then."

Conditions also include implied conditions. Implied conditions concurrent are especially common where parties have made an exchange of promises. Courts assume that promises given in exchange for one another are mutually conditional; that is, one person need not perform unless the other is ready and willing to perform. For example, if a salesman agrees to sell a woman a certain car next Wednesday, the woman does not have to pay the salesman if he does not show up with the car, and the salesman does not have to deliver the car to the woman if she is not able to pay for it. This may seem obvious, but the law of contracts only began recognizing this mutuality of obligation around the time of the American Revolution, although it is a well established principle today.

Once conditions occur, performance is due. A party who completely performs thus discharges any further obligation. But a party who does not fully perform has thereby breached. As you will learn in the next module, breach creates liability for damages. But one party's breach does not necessarily give the other party the right not to perform its mutual obligations. The doctrine of substantial performance holds that when one party substantially performs, then the other party must perform, too. If the other party fails to perform, that constitutes a breach by the other party.

Refusing to perform in advance is called repudiation or anticipatory repudiation. It can occur when one party wrongly believes the other has not substantially performed. Repudiation can also occur due to changed circumstances or market conditions. In general, parties who do not perform cannot blame circumstantial changes and will remain liable for their breach. But in rare instances, courts might excuse non-performance because of some unforeseen and unforeseeable change in circumstances that makes performance impracticable or renders its purpose frustrated. These excuses are the exception to the general rule expressed in the Latin maxim *pacta sunt servanda*, which means that promises must be kept.

The other exception to the maxim *pacta sunt servanda* occurs where parties relieve each other of their obligations. Just as parties can make agreements, parties can agree to end or change them. While some texts divide these concepts into two doctrines — contract modification on the one hand and discharge by assent on the other — this casebook combines them, because conceptually, modification is simply a milder form of discharge. Both modification and discharge require assent from the other party, and in both instances, such assent must be given freely as the result of fair and equitable circumstances. The difference between them is a matter of degree: discharge modifies an obligation completely.

But the law is wary of one party who claims the other let it "off the hook," so to speak. Why would one party rationally release another from a valuable obligation? A party who wants to take advantage of the other could coerce its release from some obligation or demand additional payment for some service. For this reason, the courts developed the cautionary pre-existing duty rule to guard against unreasonable modification and discharge by so-called assent.

The original pre-existing duty rule held that parties could not agree to modify or discharge an existing obligation without paying some new consideration. More recently, courts have relaxed the rule. Nowadays, parties can modify their agreement to the extent such modification is fair and reasonable. Instead of prohibiting modification, courts usually require parties to perform under the new agreement in order to be discharged from the old obligation. This process is called accord and satisfaction, where the accord is the new agreement, and its performance is the satisfaction.

Parties can also modify who is liable under a contract through various legal processes such as substitution and novation.

Rules

A. The Traditional Pre-Existing Duty Rule

Once parties are in a contractual relationship, they often take action in reliance on their counterparty's promises to perform. This creates an opportunity for mischief, as one party could take advantage of the other party's reliance by extorting more value from the bargain.

For example, imagine that you live in Pennsylvania and want to sell your car for $10,000. You post an ad online (which is not an offer but an invitation for offers), and you receive an offer from a prospective buyer in California. California is 3,000 miles away, and you estimate it will cost you $500 in gas and tolls to drive there, plus two nights in a hotel for $300, plus a one-way plane ticket for $200, for a total of $1,000. But this buyer has offered you a price of $12,000, so you decide it's worth the hassle to earn an extra $1,000 in profit, so you accept. You drive the car to California, and when you arrive, the buyer says he will only pay you $10,000. Now what should you do? It will cost you $1,000 to drive the car home, where you can only get $10,000 for the car, plus you'll have to re-list it and go through the entire sales process again. You are better off taking the $10,000 instead of driving the car home, so you agree to "modify" the contract.

Does something about this situation seem unfair to you? Well, it should! The buyer took advantage of your reliance on his promise in order to extract more value from the transaction. The question is, how should contract law handle situations like this?

Historically, courts dealt with coercive contract modification by applying the pre-existing duty rule. According to this rule, doing or promising what a party is already legally bound to do insufficient consideration for a new promise. The rule has been applied to a variety of factual contexts, including

- the promise of a debtor to pay less than the full amount due,
- the promise of an owner to pay a contractor more for completion of construction,
- a promise of an employer to pay more to an employee for his work, and
- a promise of a buyer to pay more to a seller for goods.

Perhaps the most famous case involving the pre-existing duty rule is *Alaska Packers' Association v. Domenico*, below. In this case, Domenico and his business associates hired a group of sailors who formed the Alaska Packers Association to fish for salmon off of Pyramid Harbor, Alaska in Spring, 1900. Upon transporting the sailors from San Francisco to California, the sailors organized and demanded double pay for the same work they had already bargained to do. Domenico was left with no alternative but agree to pay them, since otherwise he would earn nothing that fishing season.

When the parties arrived back in San Francisco, Domenico paid them their original wage but refused to pay double. The sailors sued.

The Ninth Circuit Court of Appeals ruled in favor of Domenico. Its ruling was based on the presumption that contract modification must be supported by sufficient consideration. Promising to perform a pre-existing duty cannot be consideration, because such a promise does not involve relinquishing or taking on a legal duty. The promising party already has the duty to perform, so it is really promising nothing at all. Nothing is, of course, insufficient to be consideration, which, by definition, is something given in exchange for a promise.

B. Modern Relaxation of the Pre-Existing Duty Rule

The *Alaska Packers* case makes a compelling argument for a strict application of the pre-existing duty rule — which states that contracts cannot be modified without new consideration — but more recent case law shows why this rule creates problems of its own. Problems with the pre-existing duty rule led courts to relax it in some cases and abandon it in others.

To understand why modern courts generally do not strictly apply the pre-existing duty rule, it makes sense to first review why the rule — which, again, states that a contract cannot be modified without new consideration — was established in the first place.

The obvious reason for the pre-existing duty rule is to prevent a party from taking advantage of a counterparty who has put himself in a helpless position, at the other's

Figure 21.1. Over a Barrel. Unknown artist. Public domain work.

mercy, by relying on promises made in a legal contract. To put it another way, the law should not allow one party to take advantage of another who is "over a barrel" due to the contractual agreement itself.

But there are serious problems with the pre-existing duty rule itself. The rule effectively prohibits contract modifications from enforcement even where the parties were cooperating voluntarily and in their mutual long-term best interests. It also allows one party to take advantage of the other by proving just a modicum of consideration — a "peppercorn," in Farnsworth's terms, is enough to make the modification enforceable.

The pre-existing duty rule is thus both over-inclusive and under-inclusive at the same time. It is over-inclusive in that it fails to distinguish between situations in which the party desiring modification is in fact playing a hold-up game and one in which such party is motivated by the discovery of circumstances or the occurrence of unexpected events that makes his performance far more burdensome than originally expected; as a result, it is a serious impediment to good faith contract modifications. At the same time, it is under-inclusive, because even if bad faith or overreaching underlies the party's desire to modify, if it is coupled with even the most modest form of consideration, then the modification will be upheld.

For these reasons, the UCC does not require consideration as a predicate for the enforceability of modifications of contracts involving goods; rather, "an agreement modifying a contract within this Article needs no consideration to be binding." UCC § 2-209. This provision acknowledges that, under the common law, without consideration, no contract modifications would be recognized, whether coerced or made voluntarily by the parties.

Common-law courts have also moved away from a strict application of the pre-existing duty rule. Courts have formulated various legal fictions to circumvent the rule, including:

- Pretending that parties mutually rescinded the agreement prior to execution of the new agreement.

- Holding that the responding party had, through gift, waiver, or release, relieved the other party of his obligations under the earlier contract.
- Finding additional consideration to support the new promise.

Some courts simply ignored the pre-existing duty rule or acknowledged it before relegating it to the dustbin of history. *Angel v. Murray*, below, is perhaps the most famous example of a court disavowing the pre-existing duty rule. This case is cited by R2d § 89, which likewise adopts the new rule that contractual modifications are binding even without new consideration so long as they are "fair and equitable."

> *A promise modifying a duty under a contract not fully performed on either side is binding if the modification is fair and equitable in view of circumstances not anticipated by the parties when the contract was made.* R2d § 89(1).

The erosion of the pre-existing duty rule reflects a larger move away from the requirement of consideration more generally. Most courts, however, are more willing to dispense with the need for consideration where parties in an arm's length relationship engage in what appears to be mutually agreed upon bargains and modification of those bargains.

C. Substitution, Novation, Accord, and Satisfaction

Substitution is where a new agreement replaces a prior one. As soon as the substitution is effective, the prior obligation is immediately and permanently discharged. Once a substitution is effective, parties can only sue for breach of the new agreement, not the prior one.

R2d distinguishes between substituted performance and substituted contract. The difference between the two regards when the proposal to modify occurs, but they are analytically very similar.

Substituted performance occurs where one party offers a performance different from what was promised. For example, Frankfurt promises to sell a Model F131 tractor to Hoegaarden on Wednesday. At the appointed time, Hoegaarden appears with cash in hand at Frankfurt's dealership, but Frankfurt has not yet received his shipment of those tractors. Frankfurt instead offers to sell Hoegaarden a Model F130 for the same price. If Hoegarden accepts the Model F130, that is a valid substitute performance.

> *If an obligee accepts in satisfaction of the obligor's duty a performance offered by the obligor that differs from what is due, the duty is discharged.* R2d § 278(1).

Upon accepting the substituted performance, the performing party's duty is discharged, just as if it had performed the original promise.

A substituted contract occurs when, ahead of the time for performance, one party offers a new contract that is inconsistent with the old one, and the other party accepts it with the intention not to enforce the old bargain:

A substituted contract is a contract that is itself accepted by the obligee in satisfaction of the obligor's existing duty. R2d § 279(1).

Returning to our tractor sale example, if Frankfurt called Hoegaarden two days before the Wednesday on which they agreed to consummate the sale and then offered to sell a F130 tractor instead of the F131 model, that would be an offer for a substituted contract.

If Hoegaarden agreed to the substituted contract, but then Frankfurt fails to deliver a Model F130 tractor on Wednesday, Hoegaarden can sue Frankfurt for breach of his promise to deliver the F130, but Hoegaarden cannot sue Frankfurt for breach of his promise to deliver the F131, because that old obligation to deliver the Model F131 was discharged by the agreement to deliver the Model F130 instead.

The substituted contract discharges the original duty and breach of the substituted contract by the obligor does not give the obligee a right to enforce the original duty. R2d § 279(2).

A novation is a special kind of substituted contract where a new party replaces a prior one.

A novation is a substituted contract that includes as a party one who was neither the obligor nor the obligee of the original duty. R2d § 280.

Just like a substituted contract, which immediately discharges the old one, as soon as the new party effectuates the new agreement, the prior party is immediately and permanently released from its prior obligations. Once a novation is effective, the new parties can only sue for breach of the new agreement, not the prior one.

A party does not always intend to release another from its old obligation. In fact, courts assume that, in most cases, parties intend to hold each other to their old obligations until new promises are performed. This is a situation called accord and satisfaction.

Accord is where a new agreement, an "accord," suspends a prior one, but does not terminate it.

An accord is a contract under which an obligee promises to accept a stated performance in satisfaction of the obligor's existing duty. Performance of the accord discharges the original duty. R2d § 281(1).

If the accord is not performed, or "satisfied," the injured party has a choice: it may either sue for breach of the accord, or it may sue for breach of the prior agreement.

Until performance of the accord, the original duty is suspended unless there is such a breach of the accord by the obligor as discharges the new duty of the obligee to accept the performance in satisfaction. If there is such a breach, the obligee may enforce either the original duty or any duty under the accord. R2d 281(2).

The accord thus suspends, but does not cancel, the old agreement until one of two things happens. Either the accord is performed or satisfied, in which case the obligor's obligations are discharged, or the accord is breached, in which case the obligor is liable for either the non-performance of the old promise or of the accord, but not both, at the obligee's election:

> Breach of the accord by the obligee does not discharge the original duty, but the obligor may maintain a suit for specific performance of the accord, in addition to any claim for damages for partial breach. R2d § 281(3).

Bar examiners seem especially keen to trick law students with some of the technicalities regarding discharge by assent. Let's review some of the common problems, so you are not caught unaware.

The first issue is distinguishing between a substitution and an accord, and this is the counterintuitive bit: the law presumes parties to be making accords, not substitutions, even where the parties do not plainly express their intention to merely suspend, and not supersede, a prior agreement. *Birdsall v. Saucier*, below, relates a relatively common situation where a creditor provides its debtor with some alternative way to repay the debt. Such situations are generally regarded as accords, not substitutions, but the reasoning in this case will help you to understand why a court would find one or the other.

The second issue is distinguishing between a novation, on the one hand, and an assignment or a delegation on the other. Again, courts generally presume that parties intended an accord and satisfaction, not a substituted contract, unless they clearly manifest intentions to the contrary.

D. Recission and Release

Perhaps the most extreme example of a contract modification is where the obligations are discharged completely. An agreement discharging another's obligation is called an agreement of recission.

> An agreement of rescission is an agreement under which each party agrees to discharge all of the other party's remaining duties of performance under an existing contract. R2d § 283(1).

An agreement of rescission is, first and foremost, an agreement. That means it must be brought about by mutual assent. Moreover, the R2d's comments go on to clarify that such agreement of recession requires consideration. The special thing about such consideration, however, is that consideration is provided by each party's discharge of the other's obligations. For this reason, rescission must be mutual for it to be effective.

> An agreement of rescission discharges all remaining duties of performance of both parties. It is a question of interpretation whether the parties also agree to make restitution with respect to performance that has been rendered. R2d § 283(2).

For rescission to constitute consideration, both parties must still have some remaining contractual obligations, the discharge of which constitutes the consideration for the rescission. In other words, rescission only applies to executory contracts, that is, contracts which have not yet been fully performed on either side. Such a rescission may be in writing or oral.

A release, on the other hand, refers to the unilateral discharge of one party's obligations by the other. According to R2d, such a release must be in writing:

> A release is a writing providing that a duty owed to the maker of the release is discharged immediately or on the occurrence of a condition. R2d § 284(1).

Traditionally, release was made under seal, which is a type of formal contract that does not require consideration. In modern courts, release is effective when proved by a writing and supported by consideration. Alternatively, release may be effective without consideration pursuant to statute or because the released party reasonably relied on the release.

E. Assignment and Delegation

Parties to contracts have rights and responsibilities. Within limits, contractual rights can be assigned to others, while responsibilities can also be delegated to third parties.

As assignment occurs where one party transfers its rights to receive contractual benefits to another:

> An assignment of a right is a manifestation of the assignor's intention to transfer it by virtue of which the assignor's right to performance by the obligor is extinguished in whole or in part and the assignee acquires a right to such performance. R2d § 317(1).

The default rule is that contractual rights are freely assignable, although parties can limit each other from assigning rights through their contract itself:

> A contractual right can be assigned unless (a) the substitution of a right of the assignee for the right of the assignor would materially change the duty of the obligor, or materially increase the burden or risk imposed on him by his contract, or materially impair his chance of obtaining return performance, or materially reduce its value to him, or (b) the assignment is forbidden by statute or is otherwise inoperative on grounds of public policy, or (c) assignment is validly precluded by contract. R2d § 317(2).

Once a contractual right is duly assigned, the assignor (who originally had the right) can no longer enforce it. Only the assignee (who receives the right) can enforce breach of any assigned promise.

Contractual duties are also generally delegable:

> An obligor can properly delegate the performance of his duty to another unless the delegation is contrary to public policy or the terms of his promise. R2d § 318(1).

Contracts are not delegable, however, where a promise requires performance by a particular person. For example, if you hire Beyonce to perform at your birthday party, she cannot simply delegate that performance to her understudy.

Unless otherwise agreed, a promise requires performance by a particular person only to the extent that the obligee has a substantial interest in having that person perform or control the acts promised. R2d § 318(2).

Unlike as an assignor who can no longer enforce an assigned right, a delegor (who delegates the performance of his duty to another) remains liable to the obligee. For a delegator's liability to end, the obligator would need to formally release the delegator through the release process described in R2d § 284. Alternatively, if the parties enter into a novation, which is a special sort of substitute contract that replaces the obligor with a third party, then the original obligee is released from liability.

Unless the obligee agrees otherwise, neither delegation of performance nor a contract to assume the duty made with the obligor by the person delegated discharges any duty or liability of the delegating obligor. R2d § 318(3).

Even if the delegator is not released from liability, however, the delegee may be liable to the delegor. Whether the delegee is liable depends on various factors including whether the delegee is the delegor's agent, whether the delegee received consideration for assuming the delegated responsibility, and whether the delegee's promise to assume the responsibility was gratuitous. Unless the delegee and the obligee have a direct contractual relationship, however, they are not in privity, and therefore, the obligee has no contractual recourse against the delegee directly. Instead, the obligee must sue the delegor who can in turn attempt to collect indemnity from the delegee.

F. Conclusion: Modification and Discharge by Assent

Parties can agree to absolve each other of contractual liability through contractual modification, substitution, accord and satisfaction, recission, release, assignment, and delegation. They key is remembering the differences between them so you can identify each and then apply the correct rules.

A novation is readily distinguishable from a substitution or an accord because a novation will always involve some new third party who was not involved in the prior agreement. This new third party steps into the shoes of one of the prior parties, effectively taking its place. Since a substitution or accord always involves a new agreement between the same parties, and not any new parties, it is usually not confusing whether a discharge is a novation, on the one hand, or an accord or satisfaction, on the other.

But a novation can look deceptively similar to other legal concepts, namely, assignment and delegation.

Assignment is the transfer of a right, or contractual benefit, to a third party.

Novation is the transfer of both rights and duties to a third party. R2d § 280.

Delegation is the transfer of a duty, or contractual obligation, to a third party. R2d § 318.

It may see odd, at first, that a third party would be willing to take on an obligation in this way. But a third party does not usually take on such an obligation gratuitously, and, if it does, that gratuitous promise is not binding for want of consideration, unless some substitute such as promissory restitution applies.

Delegation is not so freely available as assignment, especially where the contract is for a personal service. If Beyonce promises to perform at a concert, for example, she cannot simply delegate that obligation to another singer.

The definitions and rules regarding contract modification and discharge by assent may seem clear enough, but beneath the verbiage lurk some rather thorny and seemingly unsolved problems.

First, the line between modification and substitution is blurry, and this presents a doctrinal problem. R2d states that a contract modification does not require consideration so long as the modification is fair and equitable, while a substituted contract does require consideration. But it does not resolve is the difference between a modification and a substitution. Nor does case law illuminate any bright line between these concepts.

It seems that the distinction between modification and substitution is a matter of degree, not of kind. R2d § 279 cmt. a states, "If the parties intend the new contract to replace all of the provisions of the earlier contract, the contract is a substituted contract." Whereas, if the contract only intends to replace some of the provisions, it is merely a modification. This seems like a bright-line distinction — "some" versus "all" of the provisions — but R2d seemingly contradicts this conclusion, stating, "A common type of substituted contract is one that contains a term that is inconsistent with a term of an earlier contract between the parties." In this sentence, R2d says "a" term, not "all" terms.

Perhaps the Restatement authors are as ambivalent about the pre-existing duty rule as the courts seem to be. This is not a well-settled doctrine, and it may never be, as there will always be trade offs between protecting parties from unfair advantage and allowing parties to freely modify their agreements.

Another problem with the Restatement's approach to these doctrines is the vague distinction between "substituted performance" (R2d § 278) and "substituted contract" (R2d § 279). Why does the Restatement go out of its ways to distinguish these provisions? What is the difference? While the difference between an immediate performance and a promise to perform in the future is clear, why the distinction matters is less obvious.

It seems the distinction is merely semantic. R2d § 278 (substituted performance) stipulates that such a substituted performance can be made either by the original obligor or a third party, whereas R2d § 279 (substituted contract) stipulates that such a substituted contract can only be made by the original obligor, because a substituted contract with a new obligor is instead called a novation (R2d § 280).

However, the legal effect of all three are the same. Regardless of whether the discharge is technically a substituted performance, a substituted contract, or a novation, the effect is to immediately destroy the old obligation upon creation of the new. Perhaps this is why some courts refer to all three simply as a "novation."

The key thing is not to get caught up in these semantics. It's best to leave these mind games for law review articles. To effectively practice in contract law, its is not necessary to distinguish between substituted performance, substituted promise, and novation; rather, it is necessary to distinguish between all three, on the one hand, and an accord, on the other. An accord does not immediately destroy the old obligation, but merely suspends it until the promised accord has either been performed, in which case the remaining duties are discharged, or breached, in which case the obligee can select to sue either for breach of the new accord or for breach of the old obligation.

As with all matters of contract law, let the intentions of the parties guide your analysis. In general, assume that parties intend an accord, not a substation, when they radically change the terms of the agreement between them. In general, obligors do not reduce their rights for no reason, but rather because doing so in some way makes the obligor better off. When a new third party take the place of one of the original parties, however, then you should presume that is a novation.

The following chart is designed to help you remember the key details and distinctions between the various terms and provisions involved in contract modification and discharge by assent.

R2d §	Concept	Impact	Consideration Required?	Effective Immediately?	Involves Only Original Parties?
§ 89	Contract Modification	Changes some terms	No	Immediately	Original parties
§ 278	Substituted Performance	Discharges a promise in exchange for immediate alternative performance	Yes	Immediately	Original parties
§ 279	Substituted Contract	Discharges a promise in exchange for an alternative promise	Yes	Immediately	Original parties
§ 280	Novation	Substitutes one or more parties	Yes	Immediately	Third party required
§ 281	Accord & Satisfaction	Suspends a prior obligation pending performance ("satisfaction") of a new obligation (the "accord")	Yes	Upon satisfaction	Third party OK but not required

§ 317	Assignment	Transfers contractual rights and benefits to a new obligee	Yes	Immediately	Third party (new obligee) required
§ 318	Delegation	Creates a new obligor	Yes	Immediately	Third party (new obligor) required

Cases

Reading Alaska Packers Association v. Domenico. Perhaps the most famous case involving the pre-existing duty rule is the following one, *Alaska Packers*, in which some sailors refuse to work unless they got paid more than they originally bargained for. As you read this case, think about what the pre-existing duty rule is and whether it makes sense.

Spoiler alert! The *Alaska Packers* case makes a compelling argument for a strict application of the pre-existing duty rule — which states that contracts cannot be modified without new consideration — but more recent case law shows why this rule creates problems of its own. The cases that follow will sharpen your understanding of why the pre-existing duty rule has more recently fallen out of favor. But, for now, enjoy this classic case.

Alaska Packers Association v. Domenico
117 F. 99 (9th Cir. 1902)

The libel in this case was based upon a contract alleged to have been entered into between the libelants and the appellant corporation on the 22d day of May, 1900, at Pyramid Harbor, Alaska, by which it is claimed the appellant promised to pay each of the libelants, among other things, the sum of $100 for services rendered and to be rendered. In its answer the respondent denied the execution, on its part, of the contract sued upon, averred that it was without consideration, and for a third defense alleged that the work performed by the libelants for it was performed under other and different contracts than that sued on, and that, prior to the filing of the libel, each of the libelants was paid by the respondent the full amount due him thereunder, in consideration of which each of them executed a full release of all his claims and demands against the respondent.

The evidence shows without conflict that on March 26, 1900, at the city and county of San Francisco, the libelants entered into a written contract with the appellants, whereby they agreed to go from San Francisco to Pyramid Harbor, Alaska, and return, on board such vessel as might be designated by the appellant, and to work for the appellant during the fishing season of 1900, at Pyramid Harbor, as sailors and fishermen, agreeing to do "regular ship's duty, both up and down, discharging and loading; and to do any

Figure 21.2. Cannery at Pyramid Harbor, 1899. Public domain work.

other work whatsoever when requested to do so by the captain or agent of the Alaska Packers' Association." By the terms of this agreement, the appellant was to pay each of the libelants $50 for the season, and two cents for each red salmon in the catching of which he took part.

On the 15th day of April, 1900, 21 of the libelants signed shipping articles by which they shipped as seamen on the Two Brothers, a vessel chartered by the appellant for the voyage between San Francisco and Pyramid Harbor, and also bound themselves to perform the same work for the appellant provided for by the previous contract of March 26th; the appellant agreeing to pay them therefor the sum of $60 for the season, and two cents each for each red salmon in the catching of which they should respectively take part.

Under these contracts, the libelants sailed on board the Two Brothers for Pyramid Harbor, where the appellants had about $150,000 invested in a salmon cannery. The libelants arrived there early in April of the year mentioned, and began to unload the vessel and fit up the cannery.

A few days thereafter, to wit, May 19th, they stopped work in a body, and demanded of the company's superintendent there in charge $100 for services in operating the vessel to and from Pyramid Harbor, instead of the sums stipulated for in and by the contracts; stating that unless they were paid this additional wage they would stop work entirely, and return to San Francisco.

The evidence showed, and the court below found, that it was impossible for the appellant to get other men to take the places of the libelants, the place being remote, the season short and just opening; so that, after endeavoring for several days without success to induce the libelants to proceed with their work in accordance with their contracts, the company's superintendent, on the 22d day of May, so far yielded to their demands as to instruct his clerk to copy the contracts executed in San Francisco, including the words "Alaska Packer's Association" the end, substituting, for the $50 and $60 payments, respectively, of those contracts, the sum of $100, which document, so prepared, was signed by the libelants before a shipping commissioner whom they had requested to be brought from Northeast Point; the superintendent, however, testifying that he at the time told the libelants that he was without authority to enter into any such contract, or to in any way alter the contracts made between them and the company in San Francisco.

Upon the return of the libelants to San Francisco at the close of the fishing season, they demanded pay in accordance with the terms of the alleged contract of May 22d, when the company denied its validity, and refused to pay other than as provided for by the contracts of March 26th and April 5th, respectively. Some of the libelants, at least, consulted counsel, and, after receiving his advice, those of them who had signed the shipping articles before the shipping commissioner at San Francisco went before that officer, and received the amount due them thereunder, executing in consideration thereof a release in full, and the others paid at the office of the company, also receipting in full for their demands.

. . .

The real questions in the case as brought here are questions of law, and, in the view that we take of the case, it will be necessary to consider but one of those. Assuming that the appellant's superintendent at Pyramid Harbor was authorized to make the alleged contract of May 22d, and that he executed it on behalf of the appellant, was it supported by a sufficient consideration?

From the foregoing statement of the case, it will have been seen that the libelants agreed in writing, for certain stated compensation, to render their services to the appellant in remote waters where the season for conducting fishing operations is extremely short, and in which enterprise the appellant had a large amount of money invested; and, after having entered upon the discharge of their contract, and at a time when it was impossible for the appellant to secure other men in their places, the libelants, without any valid cause, absolutely refused to continue the services they were under contract to perform unless the appellant would consent to pay them more money.

Consent to such a demand, under such circumstances, if given, was, in our opinion, without consideration, for the reason that it was based solely upon the libelants' agreement to render the exact services, and none other, that they were already under contract to render.

The case shows that they willfully and arbitrarily broke that obligation. As a matter of course, they were liable to the appellant in damages, and it is quite probable, as suggested by the court below in its opinion, that they may have been unable to respond in damages. But we are unable to agree with the conclusions there drawn, from these facts, in these words:

> Under such circumstances, it would be strange, indeed, if the law would not
> permit the defendant to waive the damages caused by the libelants' breach,
> and enter into the contract sued upon, — a contract mutually beneficial to all
> the parties thereto, in that it gave to the libelants reasonable compensation

for their labor, and enabled the defendant to employ to advantage the large capital it had invested in its canning and fishing plant.

Certainly, it cannot be justly held, upon the record in this case, that there was any voluntary waiver on the part of the appellant of the breach of the original contract. The company itself knew nothing of such breach until the expedition returned to San Francisco, and the testimony is uncontradicted that its superintendent at Pyramid Harbor, who, it is claimed, made on its behalf the contract sued on, distinctly informed the libelants that he had no power to alter the original or to make a new contract, and it would, of course, follow that, if he had no power to change the original, he would have no authority to waive any rights thereunder. The circumstances of the present case bring it, we think, directly within the sound and just observations of the supreme court of Minnesota in the case of *King v. Railway Co.*, 61 Minn. 482, 63 N.W. 1105:

> *No astute reasoning can change the plain fact that the party who refuses to perform, and thereby coerces a promise from the other party to the contract to pay him an increased compensation for doing that which he is legally bound to do, takes an unjustifiable advantage of the necessities of the other party. Surely it would be a travesty on justice to hold that the party so making the promise for extra pay was estopped from asserting that the promise was without consideration. A party cannot lay the foundation of an estoppel by his own wrong, where the promise is simply a repetition of a subsisting legal promise. There can be no consideration for the promise of the other party, and there is no warrant for inferring that the parties have voluntarily rescinded or modified their contract. The promise cannot be legally enforced, although the other party has completed his contract in reliance upon it.*

In *Lingenfelder v. Brewing Co.*, 103 Mo. 578, 15 S.W. 844, the court, in holding void a contract by which the owner of a building agreed to pay its architect an additional sum because of his refusal to otherwise proceed with the contract, said:

> *It is urged upon us by respondents that this was a new contract. New in what? Jungenfeld was bound by his contract to design and supervise this building. Under the new promise, he was not to do anything more or anything different.*
>
> *What benefit was to accrue to Wainwright? He was to receive the same service from Jungenfeld under the new, that Jungenfeld was bound to tender under the original, contract.*
>
> *What loss, trouble, or inconvenience could result to Jungenfeld that he had not already assumed? No amount of metaphysical reasoning can change the plain fact that Jungenfeld took advantage of Wainwright's necessities, and extorted the promise of five per cent on the refrigerator plant as the condition of his complying with his contract already entered into.*
>
> *Nor had he even the flimsy pretext that Wainwright had violated any of the conditions of the contract on his part. Jungenfeld himself put it upon the*

simple proposition that 'if he, as an architect, put up the brewery, and another company put up the refrigerating machinery, it would be a detriment to the Empire Refrigerating Company,' of which Jungenfeld was president.

To permit plaintiff to recover under such circumstances would be to offer a premium upon bad faith, and invite men to violate their most sacred contracts that they may profit by their own wrong.

That a promise to pay a man for doing that which he is already under contract to do is without consideration is conceded by respondents.

The rule has been so long imbedded in the common law and decisions of the highest courts of the various states that nothing but the most cogent reasons ought to shake it. [Citing a long list of authorities.]

. . .

What we hold is that, when a party merely does what he has already obligated himself to do, he cannot demand an additional compensation therefor; and although, by taking advantage of the necessities of his adversary, he obtains a promise for more, the law will regard it as nudum pactum, and will not lend its process to aid in the wrong.

. . .

It results from the views above expressed that the judgment must be reversed, and the cause remanded, with directions to the court below to enter judgment for the respondent, with costs. It is so ordered.

Reflection

The obvious reason for the pre-existing duty rule is to prevent a party from taking advantage of a counterparty who has put himself in a helpless position, at the other's mercy, by relying on promises made in a legal contract. To put it another way, the law should not allow one party to take advantage of another who is "over a barrel" due to the contractual agreement itself.

But there are serious problems with the pre-existing duty rule itself. The rule effectively prohibits contract modifications from enforcement even where the parties were cooperating voluntarily and in their mutual long-term best interests. It also allows one party to take advantage of the other by proving just a modicum of consideration — a "peppercorn," in Farnsworth's terms, is enough to make the modification enforceable.

Discussion

1. Do you think that the sailors took unfair advantage of circumstances in this case? If so, why was this case not decided as a matter of breach of the implied duty of good faith and fair dealing?

2. What does the pre-existing duty rule add to the duty of good faith and fair dealing?

Reading Angel v. Murray. In the case of *Angel v. Murray*, a waste disposal company contracted with the City of Newport, Rhode Island, for waste disposal services. Pursuant to the five-year agreement, the waste disposal company was entitled to receive a set amount of money in return for removing all the waste materials generated within the city limits. However, the city grew surprisingly and substantially during the contract term. The waste disposal company petitioned the city council for a pay increase to compensate for the additional waste, and the council agreed.

A citizen of Newport named Alfred L. Angel brought a civil action against the city Director of Finance, John E. Murry, Jr., alleging that the city official wrongfully overpaid the waste disposal company. The citizen's argument was based on the pre-existing duty rule: the agreement to increase the disposal company's pay was invalid because it was unsupported by new consideration; therefore, the city wrongfully paid the additional amount.

The Supreme Court of Rhode Island disagreed. It found that the contract modification was fair and reasonable under the circumstances of a dramatic and unforeseen population increase that resulted in much greater expense and less profit for the waste disposal company. The council was not coerced or subject to any undue influence; unlike in *Alaska Packers*, where Domenico had no commercial alternative but to agree to pay the sailors more then they originally agreed to work for, the city could have hired some other waste disposal company. In this case, there was no coercion or duress.

Moreover, the *Angel* court expressly disavowed the pre-existing duty rule:

> *Although the preexisting duty rule has served a useful purpose insofar as it deters parties from using coercion and duress to obtain additional compensation, it has been widely criticized as a general rule of law.*

The *Angel* court goes on to cite the 1963 edition of Corbin's treatise on Contracts, upon which the R2d was substantially based.

> *There has been a growing doubt as to the soundness of this doctrine as a matter of social policy. In certain classes of cases, this doubt has influenced courts to refuse to apply the rule, or to ignore it, in their actual decisions. Like other legal rules, this rule is in process of growth and change, the process being more active here than in most instances. The result of this is that a court should no longer accept this rule as fully established. It should never use it as the major premise of a decision, at least without giving careful thought to the circumstances of the particular case, to the moral deserts of the parties, and to the social feelings and interests that are involved. It is certain that the rule, stated in general and all-inclusive terms, is no longer so well-settled that a court must apply it though the heavens fall.*

The UCC, which was principally authored by Corbin's protégé, Llewellyn, completely dispenses with the requirement of consideration for an agreement to modify a contract for the sale of goods.

An agreement modifying a contract within this Article needs no consideration to be binding. UCC § 2-209(1).

R2d contemplates this statutory section, again showing its tendency toward the relaxation of the pre-existing duty rule:

A promise modifying a duty under a contract not fully performed on either side is binding to the extent provided by statute. R2d § 89(2).

Harmony between R2d and UCC continues, with both including an additional exception to the pre-existing duty rule where one party reasonably relied on the modification:

A promise modifying a duty under a contract not fully performed on either side is binding to the extent that justice requires enforcement in view of material change of position in reliance on the promise. R2d § 89(3).

The UCC's language is different, but its impact is similar:

A party who has made a waiver affecting an executory portion of the contract may retract the waiver by reasonable notification received by the other party that strict performance will be required of any term waived, unless the retraction would be unjust in view of a material change of position in reliance on the waiver. UCC § 2-209(5).

We thus see that both the common law and the UCC are moving away from a hardline pre-existing duty rule and towards a more flexible standard that allows for greater degrees of freedom regarding mutual assent for contract modification.

Angel v. Murray

113 R.I. 482 (1974)

This is a civil action brought by Alfred L. Angel and others against John E. Murray, Jr., Director of Finance of the City of Newport, the city of Newport, and James L. Maher, alleging that Maher had illegally been paid the sum of $20,000 by the Director of Finance and praying that the defendant Maher be ordered to repay the city such sum. The case was heard by a justice of the Superior Court, sitting without a jury, who entered a judgment ordering Maher to repay the sum of $20,000 to the city of Newport. Maher is now before this court prosecuting an appeal.

The record discloses that Maher has provided the city of Newport with a refuse-collection service under a series of five-year contracts beginning in 1946. On March 12, 1964, Maher and the city entered into another such contract for a period

Figure 21.3. Tourist's map of Newport, Rhode Island.

of five years commencing on July 1, 1964 and terminating on June 30, 1969. The contract provided, among other things, that Maher would receive $137,000 per year in return for collecting and removing all combustible and noncombustible waste materials generated within the city.

In June of 1967 Maher requested an additional $10,000 per year from the city council because there had been a substantial increase in the cost of collection due to an unexpected and unanticipated increase of 400 new dwelling units. Maher's testimony, which is uncontradicted, indicates the 1964 contract had been predicated on the fact that since 1946 there had been an average increase of 20 to 25 new dwelling units per year. After a public meeting of the city council where Maher explained in detail the reasons for his request and was questioned by members of the city council, the city council agreed to pay him an additional $10,000 for the year ending on June 30, 1968. Maher made a similar request again in June of 1968 for the same reasons, and the city council again agreed to pay an additional $10,000 for the year ending on June 30, 1969.

The trial justice found that each such $10,000 payment was made in violation of law. His decision, as we understand it, is premised on two independent grounds. First, he found that the additional payments were unlawful because they had not been recommended in writing to the city council by the city manager. Second, he found that Maher was not entitled to extra compensation because the original contract already required him to collect all refuse generated within the city and, therefore, included the 400 additional units. The trial justice further found that these 400 additional units were within the contemplation of the parties when they entered into the contract. It appears that he based this portion of the decision upon the rule that Maher had a preexisting duty to collect the refuse generated by the 400 additional units, and thus there was no consideration for the two additional payments.

I.

[Part I discusses the first basis for the trial court's decision, that the payment increase was unlawful because not requested in writing, but this is not relevant to the contract issue. The appellate court ruled that a written request was not required as a matter of law. Although a statute literally stated that such increases must be in writing, "this court will not undertake to read an enactment literally if to do so would result in attributing to the Legislature an intention that is contradictory of or inconsistent with the evident purposes of the act."]

II.

Having found that the city council had the power to modify the 1964 contract without the written recommendation of the city manager, we are still confronted with the question of whether the additional payments were illegal because they were not supported by consideration.

A

[Omitted]

B

It is generally held that a modification of a contract is itself a contract, which is unenforceable unless supported by consideration. . . . In *Rose v. Daniels*, 8 R.I. 381 (1866), this court held that an agreement by a debtor with a creditor to discharge a debt for a sum of money less than the amount due is unenforceable because it was not supported by consideration.

Rose is a perfect example of the preexisting duty rule. Under this rule an agreement modifying a contract is not supported by consideration if one of the parties to the agreement does or promises to do something that he is legally obligated to do or refrains or promises to refrain from doing something he is not legally privileged to do. In *Rose* there was no consideration for the new agreement because the debtor was already legally obligated to repay the full amount of the debt.

Although the preexisting duty rule is followed by most jurisdictions, a small minority of jurisdictions, Massachusetts, for example, find that there is consideration for a promise to perform what one is already legally obligated to do because the new promise is given in place of an action for damages to secure performance. *See Swartz v. Lieberman*, 323 Mass. 109 (1948) . . . . *Swartz* is premised on the theory that a promisor's forbearance of the power to breach his original agreement and be sued in an action for damages is consideration for a subsequent agreement by the promisee to pay extra compensation. This rule, however, has been widely criticized as an anomaly.

The primary purpose of the preexisting duty rule is to prevent what has been referred to as the "hold-up game." [Citing Corbin.] A classic example of the "hold-up game" is found in *Alaska Packers' Ass'n v. Domenico*, 117 F. 99 (9th Cir. 1902). There 21 seamen entered into a written contract with Domenico to sail from San Francisco to Pyramid Harbor, Alaska. They were to work as sailors and fishermen out of

Pyramid Harbor during the fishing season of 1900. The contract specified that each man would be paid $50 plus two cents for each red salmon he caught. Subsequent to their arrival at Pyramid Harbor, the men stopped work and demanded an additional $50. They threatened to return to San Francisco if Domenico did not agree to their demand. Since it was impossible for Domenico to find other men, he agreed to pay the men an additional $50. After they returned to San Francisco, Domenico refused to pay the men an additional $50. The court found that the subsequent agreement to pay the men an additional $50 was not supported by consideration because the men had a preexisting duty to work on the ship under the original contract, and thus the subsequent agreement was unenforceable.

Another example of the "hold-up game" is found in the area of construction contracts. Frequently, a contractor will refuse to complete work under an unprofitable contract unless he is awarded additional compensation. The courts have generally held that a subsequent agreement to award additional compensation is unenforceable if the contractor is only performing work which would have been required of him under the original contract. See, e.g., *Lingenfelder v. Wainwright Brewery Co.,* 103 Mo. 578 (1891), which is a leading case in this area.

These examples clearly illustrate that the courts will not enforce an agreement that has been procured by coercion or duress and will hold the parties to their original contract regardless of whether it is profitable or unprofitable. However, the courts have been reluctant to apply the preexisting duty rule when a party to a contract encounters unanticipated difficulties and the other party, not influenced by coercion or duress, voluntarily agrees to pay additional compensation for work already required to be performed under the contract. For example, the courts have found that the original contract was rescinded, *Linz v. Schuck,* 106 Md. 220, 67 A. 286 (1907); abandoned, *Connelly v. Devoe,* 37 Conn. 570 (1871), or waived, *Michaud v. McGregor,* 61 Minn. 198, 63 N.W. 479 (1895).

Although the preexisting duty rule has served a useful purpose insofar as it deters parties from using coercion and duress to obtain additional compensation, it has been widely criticized as a general rule of law. With regard to the preexisting duty rule, one legal scholar [Corbin] has stated:

> *There has been a growing doubt as to the soundness of this doctrine as a matter of social policy. . . . In certain classes of cases, this doubt has influenced courts to refuse to apply the rule, or to ignore it, in their actual decisions. Like other legal rules, this rule is in process of growth and change, the process being more active here than in most instances. The result of this is that a court should no longer accept this rule as fully established. It should never use it as the major premise of a decision, at least without giving careful thought to the circumstances of the particular case, to the moral deserts of the parties, and to the social feelings and interests that are involved. It is certain that the rule, stated in general and all-inclusive terms, is no longer so well-settled that a court must apply it though the heavens fall.*

The modern trend appears to recognize the necessity that courts should enforce agreements modifying contracts when unexpected or unanticipated difficulties arise during the course of the performance of a contract, even though there is no consideration for the modification, as long as the parties agree voluntarily.

Under the Uniform Commercial Code, s 2-209(1) . . . "(a)n agreement modifying a contract (for the sale of goods) needs no consideration to be binding." Although at first blush this section appears to validate modifications obtained by coercion and duress, the comments to this section indicate that a modification under this section must meet the test of good faith imposed by the Code, and a modification obtained by extortion without a legitimate commercial reason is unenforceable.

The modern trend away from a rigid application of the preexisting duty rule is reflected by s 89D(a) of the American Law Institute's Restatement Second of the Law of Contracts, which provides "A promise modifying a duty under a contract not fully performed on either side is binding (a) if the modification is fair and equitable in view of circumstances not anticipated by the parties when the contract was made."

We believe that s 89D(a) is the proper rule of law and find it applicable to the facts of this case. It not only prohibits modifications obtained by coercion, duress, or extortion but also fulfills society's expectation that agreements entered into voluntarily will be enforced by the courts. See generally Horwitz, *The Historical Foundations of Modern Contract Law*, 87 Harv.L.Rev. 917 (1974). Section 89D(a), of course, does not compel a modification of an unprofitable or unfair contract; it only enforces a modification if the parties voluntarily agree and if (1) the promise modifying the original contract was made before the contract was fully performed on either side, (2) the underlying circumstances which prompted the modification were unanticipated by the parties, and (3) the modification is fair and equitable.

The evidence, which is uncontradicted, reveals that in June of 1968 Maher requested the city council to pay him an additional $10,000 for the year beginning on July 1, 1968, and ending on June 30, 1969. This request was made at a public meeting of the city council, where Maher explained in detail his reasons for making the request. Thereafter, the city council voted to authorize the Mayor to sign an amendment to the 1964 contract which provided that Maher would receive an additional $10,000 per year for the duration of the contract. Under such circumstances we have no doubt that the city voluntarily agreed to modify the 1964 contract.

Having determined the voluntariness of this agreement, we turn our attention to the three criteria delineated above. First, the modification was made in June of 1968 at a time when the five-year contract which was made in 1964 had not been fully performed by either party. Second, although the 1964 contract provided that Maher collect all refuse generated within the city, it appears this contract was premised on Maher's past experience that the number of refuse-generating units would increase at a rate of 20 to 25 per year. Furthermore, the evidence is uncontradicted that the 1967-1968 increase of 400 units "went beyond any previous expectation." Clearly the circumstances which prompted the city council to modify the 1964 contract were unanticipated. Third, although the evidence does not indicate what proportion of the total this increase comprised, the evidence does indicate that it was a "substantial" increase. In light of this, we cannot say that the council's agreement to pay Maher the $10,000 increase was not fair and equitable in the circumstances.

The judgment appealed from is reversed, and the cause is remanded to the Superior Court for entry of judgment for the defendants.

Reflection

Angel presents a somewhat unusual procedural posture. Note who the parties are in the case: a citizen is suing the director of finance of a governmental entity and a waste management service. The government entity and a waste management service were the parties to the contract. Thus, the parties to the case are not the same as the parties to the contract. In fact, both parties to the contract appear on the same side of the 'v'.

The court does not explicitly address whether this unusual posture impacted its disposition, but it stands to reason that it does. The simple fact that both parties to the contract are in accord with its enforceability tends to show that the alteration to that agreement was not only mutual but reasonable.

Discussion

1. Some scholars say that *Angel* abrogated the pre-existing duty rule. Others say that *Angel* merely followed precedent that had already abrogated it. As you read the court's opinion in *Angel*, did you find that the court was changing the law, or does the court merely recognize that the law about the pre-existing duty rule has already changed?

2. There are similar discussions about whether R2d (which was drafted around the time that *Angel* was decided) modified the pre-existing duty rule in an activist attempt to change judicial outcomes, or whether R2d was simply restating the law as it had changed. Notably, R2d § 89 ("Modification of an Executory Contract") is new. The first Restatement of Contract does not have a parallel provision. Read the comments to R2d § 89 and discuss whether R2d is merely restating the law as it has changed since *Alaska Packers*, or whether R2d is pushing the law towards a new direction.

Reading Birdsall v. Saucier. Remember that contract parties are often not lawyers. They may not even become aware of the legal consequences of some of their actions until their agreement turns into a dispute in court. Then, lawyers and judges have to figure out how the parties' intentions map onto legal concepts.

One concept that parties rarely consider in advance of agreeing to modify a contract is whether they intend to make a substituted contract or an accord and satisfaction. It is the lawyer's job to recognize that the law presumes parties to be making accords, not substitutions, even where the parties do not plainly express their intention to merely suspend, and not supersede, a prior agreement.

The next case, *Birdsall*, relates a relatively common situation where a creditor provides its debtor with some alternative way to repay the debt. Such situations are generally regarded as accords, not substitutions, but the reasoning in this case will help you to understand why courts would find one or the other. Admittedly, the *Birdsall* case is a bit long, but it relates the pertinent details of the famous *Pinnel's Case*, and I find this modern court's discussion of those facts much more readable than the original case from 1602.

The second issue is distinguishing between a novation, on the one hand, and an assignment or a delegation on the other. This issue will be discussed after the *Birdsall* case.

Birdsall v. Saucier

1992 WL 37731 (Conn. Super. Ct. Feb. 24, 1992)

One of the peculiarities of the common law is that a creditor may accept anything in satisfaction of a liquidated debt except a lesser sum of money. Almost four centuries ago, Sir Edward Coke opined that a creditor might take "a horse, hawk, or robe" if he chose and that would be accord and satisfaction. *Pinnel's Case*, 77 Eng.Rep. 237 (C.P. 1602). The only thing that he may not take is ninety cents on the dollar. The present case involves a modern debtor who did not have a horse, hawk, or robe but did settle a debt with the assignment of a promissory note of a third party. The court holds that this assignment, which was satisfactory to the creditor at the time (much to her present chagrin), was sufficient consideration to satisfy the debt.

Virginia Birdsall is a real estate broker who does business under the names of Birdsall Agency and Birdsall Realty in Middlebury. Roy Birdsall ("Birdsall") is a real estate broker in her employ. Fernando Saucier ("Saucier") is a real estate entrepreneur who at the time of the events in question was the president and sole shareholder of B & S Realty of Bristol, Inc. ("B & S"). The only substantial asset of B & S, a now-dissolved corporation, was a large office and restaurant building in Bristol. The Birdsalls are the plaintiffs in this action; Saucier and B & S are the defendants. Their dispute was tried to the court on October 17-18, 1991. From the evidence submitted at the hearing, the court finds the following facts.

In the spring of 1985, Saucier wanted to sell the building owned by B & S. He had previously met Birdsall in connection with the sale of some Bristol apartments and, on May 1, 1985, entered into an open listing agreement with the Birdsall Agency to sell the building owned by B & S. This agreement is a written contract signed by Birdsall and Saucier (signing for B & S). The agreement states that "In consideration of your efforts to sell said property, I/we agree that if you are able to procure a customer ready, willing and able to buy said property at a sale price of $1,275,000 or at a price or terms acceptable to me/us, I/we will pay you a commission of ten % of the gross sale price." The open listing was to remain in effect for 180 days.

Armed with this agreement, Birdsall went to work. Eventually he found two buyers for the building, Mark Silverstein and Aryeh Shander. On August 6, 1985, Silverstein and Shander signed an agreement with B & S, agreeing to purchase the building for $1,150,000. The closing was to take place within thirty days. B & S was to pay the Birdsall Agency "whatever commission is due to the broker."

The closing occurred on August 15, 1985. At some point between August 6 and August 15, Saucier met with Birdsall. Although extensive documentation has been submitted on most aspects of the case, the details of this meeting have been lost in the vague memories of the participants. Birdsall testified that Saucier asked him to take some of his commission (which at 10% of the purchase price would have been $115,000) in "paper" and some in cash. According to Birdsall it was understood that about half of the commission would be in "paper," but the terms were not otherwise discussed. Saucier testified in somewhat greater detail. A few days before the closing he realized that very little cash would be left after closing costs. He approached Birdsall and told him that if the closing were to go through, arrangements would have to be made. Birdsall said (according to Saucier) "I don't need money. I'd rather take payments." He said that he would take a third mortgage on the property in question. He (Birdsall) further said that he felt very comfortable and confident taking payment from the doctors. (Silverstein and Shander were physicians.) Saucier agreed with Birdsall's testimony that the exact terms of payment were not discussed. Saucier's testimony was amply corroborated by the events about to be described. The court finds it credible.

Birdsall and Saucier were both present at the closing. The building, of course, was purchased by Silverstein and Shander for $1,150,000. As part of this purchase price, they assumed a mortgage to one Nathan Mafale in the amount of $560,000. A second mortgage was given to Saucier in the amount of $295,000. (For reasons never explained to the court, the proceeds of the sale were paid to Saucier personally rather than to B & S.) The Birdsall Agency received a check in the amount of $29,500, which it subsequently endorsed and deposited. The balance of Birdsall's compensation was what the parties termed "paper." The documents constituting this compensation must be described in some detail.

Silverstein and Shander gave a third mortgage to Saucier in the amount of $73,000. This was accompanied by a mortgage note in the same amount. The note provided for quarterly payments of interest for five years commencing on January 1, 1986. The interest specified was ten percent per annum, and the quarterly interest payments were consequently $1,825. At the end of this period, on August 1, 1991, the unpaid principal balance was to be paid in full. The note expressly provides that its obligations "shall be without personal recourse against any individual, partnership or corporate maker and the mortgagee's sole recourse in the event of a default shall be against the mortgaged property." At the closing, Saucier assigned his entire interest in this note to Birdsall.

At or shortly after the closing (Saucier testified that it was within a week) Birdsall gave B & S a written receipt. The receipt acknowledges the payment of $29,500 as a commission for the sale to Silverstein and Shander and the assignment of the $73,000 note. It concludes with the words "Commission paid in full." It is signed by Birdsall.

Birdsall thus received a cash payment of $29,500 and a $73,000 note. The sum of these two amounts is $102,500. This is not the sum that was originally to have been Birdsall's fee. That original sum was to have been $115,000 (ten percent of the $1,150,000 purchase price).

In other words, Birdsall, on the face of it, received $12,500 less than he was due.

On the stand, however, Birdsall expressly disavowed any claim to the $12,500 difference. He certainly registered no complaint at the time. As just recounted, he gave B & S a receipt stating that his commission had been "paid in full." There is no evidence whatsoever of any contemporaneous dissatisfaction with this arrangement. The court finds that Birdsall—and, by inference, his employer, Virginia Birdsall (who did not testify)—was satisfied with what he received.

Perhaps the reason for this lies in simple mathematics. Had the note from Silverstein and Shander been fully paid, Birdsall would have received $22,500 in interest payments plus $73,000 in principal (admittedly after a delay of five and a half years). These payments when added to the $29,500 check that Birdsall received at the closing, would have equaled $125,000, or $10,000 more than he was originally entitled to receive. Of course, Birdsall was also aware from his previous meeting with Saucier that, if he had not been willing to take part of his compensation in "paper," the closing would not have gone through and his practical ability to collect the fee he was legally owed might well have been seriously impaired. It is a fair inference from these facts that there was a meeting of the minds between Birdsall and Saucier that the $29,500 in cash and the assignment of the $73,000 note were to constitute full satisfaction of any claim for commission against Saucier that Birdsall might have.

In any event, the building was sold, and Birdsall had his check and his "paper." Birdsall proceeded to contentedly collect his interest payments from Silverstein and Shander for three years. Then, Birdsall's bargain melted into the air. The last interest payment paid was that of January 1, 1989 (apparently paid sometime in December 1988). On April 1, 1989, Birdsall's mailbox was as bare as Mother Hubbard's cupboard. So, for that matter, was Saucier's. (Saucier was owed a substantially greater amount on his second mortgage.) Demands to Silverstein and Shander from all quarters proved fruitless. Nothing was paid thereafter.

At some point after the default, Saucier asked Birdsall to find a new buyer for the building. Birdsall was eager to do this since a sale of the building might result in the payment of his $73,000 note. Nothing, however, was put in writing between

Saucier and Birdsall, and as far as the record indicates, the owners of the building, Silverstein and Shander, were wholly unaware of this arrangement at the time. Birdsall eventually found an interested purchaser, one Anthony Rugens. On October 25, 1989, Rugens signed a written offer to purchase the building for $25,000 plus the assumption of all indebtedness (including the indebtedness to Birdsall). Silverstein and Shander, however, never signed the offer. On October 27, 1989, Saucier's attorney signed a complaint commencing a foreclosure action against them. *Saucier v. Silverstein*, No. CV-89-0437356S (Hartford-New Britain J.D.).

The Birdsalls allege in their complaint that Saucier told Birdsall that he did not wish to have the building sold during or after the foreclosure action and that if Birdsall stopped his effort to sell the property, Saucier would pay him the $73,000. No credible evidence has been advanced to support this claim. On the contrary, Saucier testified that he planned the foreclosure action independently, and that Rugens independently decided not to pursue his bid until the foreclosure was over so that Birdsall would be out of the picture. Rugens did not testify. The court finds Saucier's testimony on this matter credible.

Because of his interest in the premises, Birdsall was named as a co-defendant in the foreclosure action. On June 18, 1990, a judgment of strict foreclosure was entered. Because the value of the property was by now greatly diminished, Birdsall's note and mortgage were rendered worthless. His mortgage was not redeemed. On March 22, 1991, the Birdsalls commenced the present action.

The complaint is in three counts. The first count seeks recovery of $73,000 as the allegedly unpaid balance of the plaintiffs' commission for their services under the open listing agreement of May 1, 1985. The second count alleges that Saucier is liable for the unpaid debts of B & S (which dissolved shortly after the 1985 closing) and that one of these debts is the $73,000 owed to the plaintiffs. The third count alleges that Saucier breached his agreement to pay Birdsall $73,000 if Birdsall dropped his efforts to sell the building at the time of the foreclosure. As already noted, the factual basis of the third count has simply not been established, and that count will not be further discussed. Because the first two counts involve the same underlying debt, they can be conveniently discussed together. As an affirmative defense to the first two counts, the defendants have pleaded accord and satisfaction. The court finds that defense to be established.

"An accord is a contract between creditor and debtor for the settlement of a claim by some performance other than that which is due. Satisfaction takes place when the accord is executed." An accord, however, is an agreement, and an agreement will not be considered binding by the courts unless it is supported by consideration.

At an early date in English history it was held that a creditor could not take five pounds in satisfaction of a fifteen pound debt because he received no consideration for the other ten pounds. *Cumber v. Wane*, 93 Eng.Rep. 613 (1718); *Pinnel's Case*, *supra*. From the day this rule was announced, however, it has been recognized that dictates of fairness and considerations of business require that the rule be subject to certain exceptions. One well known exception is that an accord may be made "when there is a good faith dispute about the existence of a debt or about the amount that is owed." That exception is not applicable here. There are, however, other well-established exceptions that are highly relevant to the instant case.

It was, in the first place, recognized in *Pinnel's Case* itself that, while a lesser sum cannot be satisfaction for a greater sum, "the gift of a horse, hawk, or robe . . . in satisfaction is good." 77 Eng.Rep. at 237. From that day to this, it has not been doubted that,

> *A liquidated money demand may, with the consent of the parties, be discharged by the delivery of property in payment thereof or by delivery of part money and part property; if the latter is received by the creditor in full discharge of the indebtedness, there is a good accord and satisfaction. The relative value of the property is immaterial as affecting the validity of the accord and satisfaction.*

1 Am.Jur.2d Accord and Satisfaction Sect. 40 (1962).

This exception has long been acknowledged in Connecticut. In *Warren v. Skinner*, 20 Conn. 559 (1850), which recognized both the ancient English rule and its traditional exceptions, it was stated that an agreement in satisfaction of a debt will be recognized when it "rests on a new and adequate consideration; as where the debtor pays a part of the debt . . . in a collateral article, agreed to be received in full payment." The Connecticut Supreme Court subsequently found this exception applicable in *Rose v. Hall*, 26 Conn. 392 (1857) (holding a combination of bills of exchange and cloth to be adequate consideration), and *Bull v. Bull*, 43 Conn. 455 (1876) (holding a debt to be satisfied by the payment of some pictures).

Of course, not every debtor has a stock of cloth or pictures handy to pay off his debts. Commercially sensible arrangements are acceptable as well. In particular, it is well established that "[t]he acceptance, by a creditor, of the note of a third person, in satisfaction of an existing debt, is an extinguishment of such original indebtedness, and constitutes a good accord and satisfaction thereof, whether the note be for the full amount of the debt, or for a lesser sum."

This latter exception has been recognized in Connecticut for over a hundred years. In *Argall v. Cook*, 43 Conn. 160, 166 (1875), it was held that a note endorsed by a third person may be taken in accord and satisfaction of a debt even when the note is for a lesser amount. The Supreme Court [of Connecticut] explained that, "The additional security which [the creditor] received by the indorsement was a sufficient legal consideration for the discharge." *Id.*

Birdsall argues that the assignment here cannot extinguish the underlying debt unless it amounts to a novation. This is not, however, the case.

"'Novation' is a term usually used to refer to instances in which a new party is introduced into a new contract." A novation "creates a new contractual duty." 15 Samuel Willison, A Treatise on the Law of Contracts Sect. 1865 at 590 (3d ed. 1972).

A substitution of a new creditor brought about by an assignment "is seldom referred to as a novation." 6 Arthur Corbin, Corbin on Contracts Sect. 1297 at 216 (1962). "Thus," as Corbin explains, "if we suppose that A owes B $100, B can assign his right to C, without A's assent." *Id.* That is exactly what happened here.

The real question here is a factual one: did the parties — i.e. Birdsall and Saucier — agree that the settlement agreement itself constituted satisfaction of the original cause of action or did they instead agree that the performance of the agreement was to be the satisfaction. This depends entirely "upon the intention of the parties." While there is "a strong presumption that the plaintiff would not, claiming a substantially undisputed amount to be due her, accept a mere promise to pay a much smaller sum in discharge of the larger amount," *id.*, that presumption is not applicable here, and to the extent that it is applicable, it is overcome by the facts.

Here, Birdsall did not "accept a mere promise to pay a much smaller sum in discharge of the larger amount." As explained above, the note that he accepted, had it been fully paid, would have given him a larger sum at the end. In any event, there is no credible evidence that either party intended that the original debt of Saucier to Birdsall was to continue after the assignment of the note. There is, in contrast, credible evidence that both parties intended that the original debt was to be extinguished by the assignment. Were the facts otherwise, Birdsall — an experienced real estate broker — would not have given Saucier a written receipt stating "commission paid in full." It bears repeating that Birdsall was willing to do this because he wanted to save the deal and knew that a bird in the hand was worth two in the bush.

Birdsall was satisfied with the monetary payment of $29,500 and the note assigned to him by Saucier. He took money from Silverstein and Shander for three years without complaint. The debt that B & S owed to Birdsall was extinguished, and both parties intended it to be so. By any measure, the assignment of the note constituted a new and valid consideration. When Birdsall signed his receipt "commission paid in full," there was accord and satisfaction. Because of this he cannot now recover against the defendants no matter how bad his bargain has turned out to be.

Judgment shall enter for the defendants.

Aff'd, 29 Conn. App. 921 (1992).

Reflection

As substituted contract immediately replaces an old obligation with a new one. An accord and satisfaction, on the other hand, does not immediately destroy the old obligation, but merely suspends it until the promised accord has either been performed, in which case the remaining duties are discharged, or breached, in which case the obligee can select to sue either for breach of the new accord or for breach of the old obligation.

When determining whether parties have agreed to a substituted contract or to an accord and satisfaction, as with all matters of contract law, let the intentions of the parties guide your analysis. In general, assume that parties intend an accord, not a substitution, when they radically change the terms of the agreement between them. In general, obligors do not reduce their rights for no reason, but because doing so in some way makes the obligor better off.

Discussion

1. The law of contracts purports to codify reasonable parties' intention when bargaining. The law of sales, in particular, is said to have developed from custom amid merchants' guilds. In this way, contracts rules such as the presumption that parties generally intend to make an accord and satisfaction instead of a substituted contract function as default rules. But does this rule reflect ordinary intentions?

2. Consider whether you had any notion of "accord and satisfaction" before taking this course. If you were Saucier, without knowledge of the R2d's default presumption, would you have presumed that you were entitled to payment on the old note until you received payment of the new one? Or would you have intended to give up your rights to the old note in exchange for rights to the new one?

Problems

Problem 21.1. **Fair and Reasonable Modification**

Angel dismisses the pre-existing duty rule and replaces it with the ability to modify a contract on fair and equitable terms. Do you think this case moves the law in the right or wrong direction? Discuss and explain your position.

Problem 21.2. **Accord and Satisfaction**

Birdsall explained its reasoning why parties generally intend an accord and satisfaction, and not a substituted contract, when one party agrees to take less than it was owed under the original contract. Do you agree with this presumption, or is it misplaced? In answering this question, make sure to explain the difference in form and function between a substituted contract, on the one hand, and accord and satisfaction, on the other. Then discuss what merits a presumption that the parties intend to engage in one of these two forms.

Module VII
Remedies

Remedy comes from the Anglo-French term meaning the cure for a disease. By the mid-15th century, the Anglican use of the term came to mean legal redress. The term appears to come from the root *re-*, meaning "back to the original place," and -med, meaning "take appropriate measure." (The root *med* also relates to the concepts judge, estimate, and measure out.)

A remedy is thus a sort of legal solution that takes appropriate measures to put parties in their original place. If you imagine the scales of justice, the remedy is the weight required to restore balance that has been disrupted by some wrong. This etymologically conveys the gist of remedies, although you will soon learn that not all modern remedies are backwards looking in this way. Contractual remedies are rather framed as protecting specific interests known as the expectation interest, the reliance interest, and the restitution interest:

> *Judicial remedies under the rules stated in this Restatement serve to protect one or more of the following interests of a promisee:*
>
> *(a) his "expectation interest," which is his interest in having the benefit of his bargain by being put in as good a position as he would have been in had the contract been performed,*
>
> *(b) his "reliance interest," which is his interest in being reimbursed for loss caused by reliance on the contract by being put in as good a position as he would have been in had the contract not been made, or*
>
> *(c) his "restitution interest," which is his interest in having restored to him any benefit that he has conferred on the other party.*

Modern contractual remedies come in two main forms: money damages, which is some amount of cash that courts require one party to pay the other, and specific performance and injunctions, which are where a court compels a party to do or not to do something other than pay money. In both cases, the goal of contractual remedies is not usually to put the aggrieved party back in the place it was before the contract, but rather to put the aggrieved party in the position it would have been in but for the breach.

Contractual remedies being forward-looking, the most common contractual remedy is expectation damages. Expectation damages is most simply stated as the sum of money paid by a breaching party to an aggrieved party that puts the party in the position it reasonably expected to be in had the contract been performed. For example, a seller who fails to deliver goods may be responsible for the profits the buyer would have earned reselling them.

Sometimes this predictive calculation is difficult or impossible, however, in which case, courts will award reliance damages, which cleave more closely to the etymology of the term remedies and seek to put the aggrieved party in the position it would have been in if the contract had never been formed. Courts may also order restitution, which is the return of a liable party's ill-gotten gains under a contractual relationship. For example, a court may require a seller to return the purchase price upon failing to deliver goods.

In rarer cases, courts will order specific performance, where a party must do what it promised to do and not merely pay money. Courts will generally not order specific performance where money damages can adequately compensate an injured party. One notable exception is for sales of land. Land is considered unique under the law, and so sellers may be required to transfer land instead of paying buyers its value.

Finally, courts may order an injunction, which stems from the Latin *injunctio*, meaning, a command. It is related to the term *iungere*, meaning "fasten to a yoke." An injunction, therefore, is a command that binds, halts, or harnesses. Under contract law, an injunction is where a court prohibits a party from doing some act that is prohibited by contract. For example, some employment contracts have non-compete covenants, whereby the employee promises not to work for an employer's competitors for a specified time. Although many have argued that such non-competes should be unenforceable as a matter of public policy favoring entrepreneurial liberty, courts in many states enforce these covenants through negative injunctions.

> *The judicial remedies available for the protection of the interests stated in § 344 include a judgment or order*
>
> > *(a) awarding a sum of money due under the contract or as damages,*
> >
> > *(b) requiring specific performance of a contract or enjoining its non-performance,*
> >
> > *(c) requiring restoration of a specific thing to prevent unjust enrichment,*
> >
> > *(d) awarding a sum of money to prevent unjust enrichment,*
> >
> > *(e) declaring the rights of the parties, and*
> >
> > *(f) enforcing an arbitration award. R2d § 345.*

Chapter 22

Expectation Damages

Legal remedies are the means by which courts enforce rights. When a party wins a court case, that winning party is entitled to a remedy. Remedies is the subject of an entire law school course on its own, but here we will focus on contract remedies. In other words, this casebook will next discuss how courts of law enforce contractual rights.

There are two main forms of remedies at contract law, and one is much more common than the other. We will first discuss the common remedy of money damages, which is when a court requires the losing party to pay the winning party. In Chapter 24, we will discuss equitable remedies, including specific performance, where a court will force the losing party to perform some action other than simply paying the winning party.

The initial distinction among the various types of remedies, therefore, is the nature of the relief that the aggrieved party is seeking. A person asserting a claim for breach of contract may seek money damages or may seek a court order directing the breaching party to engage in certain conduct, either to specifically perform the contract or to be enjoined from acting in a manner inconsistent with their obligations under the contract.

In general, money damages are referred to as "remedies at law," and specific performance and injunctions are considered to be "remedies at equity."

The legal tradition in the United States favors money damages over equitable remedies, because money awards promote finality and involve less judicial supervision.

The injured party has a right to damages for any breach by a party against whom the contract is enforceable unless the claim for damages has been suspended or discharged. R2d § 346(1).

Whenever a promise or a contract is breached, the promisee is entitled to a remedy. But the remedy will vary. The favored remedy for contract breaches are expectation damages.

Rules

A. Direct Expectation Damages

The purpose of awarding expectation damages is to place the injured party in as good a position as it would have been in had the other party fully performed the contract. For this reason, direct expectancy damages are measured by reference to the terms of the contract. The two most common measurements of direct expectation damages are the cost of obtaining a substitute performance for what the breaching party failed to do under the contract, or the difference in value between what the breaching party promised to do under the contract and what the breaching party actually did. R2d sets out what amounts to a formula for figuring out expectation damages:

> *Subject to the limitations stated in §§ 350-53, the injured party has a right to damages based on his expectation interest as measured by (a) the loss in the value to him of the other party's performance caused by its failure or deficiency, plus (b) any other loss, including incidental or consequential loss, caused by the breach, less (c) any cost or other loss that he has avoided by not having to perform. R2d § 347.*

This primary measure of expectation damages is also known as the loss in value method of calculating damages. Loss in value is the preferred method of calculating damages when courts can fairly determine what that loss is. When that loss is hard to determine or calculate, however, courts have three alternative formulas for expectation damages. The first pertains specifically to the loss of use of property that has a rental or interest value:

> *If a breach delays the use of property and the loss in value to the injured party is not proved with reasonable certainty, he may recover damages based on the rental value of the property or on interest on the value of the property. R2d § 348(1).*

Second, and generally regarding construction projects, expectation damages can alternatively be calculated by diminution in market value where there is a market that can be used to determine such value. For example, if a carpenter builds one lopsided house in a neighborhood where similar well-built houses recently sold for $100,000, and if the lopsided house sells for $80,000, then the direct expectation damage is the difference, or $20.000.

> *If a breach results in defective or unfinished construction and the loss in value to the injured party is not proved with sufficient certainty, he may recover damages based on the diminution in the market price of the property caused by the breach. R2d § 378(2)(a).*

If there is not such a ready market, then courts may determine the direct expectation by the cost of completing performance. For example, if it costs $30,000 to make a lopsided house straight, that is the measure of loss in value damages.

> *If a breach results in defective or unfinished construction and the loss in value to the injured party is not proved with sufficient certainty, he may recover damages based the reasonable cost of completing performance or of remedying the defects if that cost is not clearly disproportionate to the probable loss in value to him. R2d § 348(2)(b).*

Courts should select the measure of expectation damages that best fulfill the purpose of the expectation remedy generally. Expectancy remedies are intended to put the aggrieved party in as good a position as if the breaching party had fully performed the contract. What distinguishes expectancy remedies from other categories of damages is that expectancy remedies are always determined by the terms of the contract. The law requires the breaching party either to perform their duty under the contract or to pay damages that will be the dollar value equivalent of any duty that the breaching party failed to perform.

There are four measures of expectation damages: (1) loss in value; (2) delayed use of property; (3) diminution in market price; and (4) cost of completing performance.

Illustration of Expectation Damages. One clear way of measuring the difference between what a party received and what it bargained for is determining the cost to complete full performance. We can thus draw a simplistic equation:

Expectation Damages = Value Expected – Value Received

The courts do not always order a breaching party to fully perform their obligation under a contract, but in some situations it is appropriate. The most common situation where the courts will order full performance is where the aggrieved party has fully performed a service or delivered goods that were accepted by the buyer and the customer or buyer did not pay for that service or those goods. Under those circumstances, the courts will order the customer to pay any unpaid portion of the contract price.

In other situations, the courts are more reluctant to order full performance in accordance with the terms of the contract. For example, if the customer or buyer repudiates the contract before the seller or service provider has performed, the courts are unlikely to allow the seller or service provider to perform and to order the customer or buyer to pay the entire contract price; instead, the customer or buyer will be liable for one of the following lesser amounts of expectancy damages such as lost profits or the extra cost of substitute performance.

If the seller or service provider is the breaching party, the normal remedy for the aggrieved customer or buyer is not a judicial order of "strict performance" (which is an "equitable remedy") but rather an award of expectancy and consequential damages. There are circumstances, however, where the courts will order a breaching seller or service provider to strictly perform the contract: for example, in contracts for the sale of land and contracts for the sale of goods where the buyer is unable to "cover," that is, where the buyer needs the goods and cannot obtain the same or similar goods from another source.

B. Indirect Expectation Damages

Direct expectation damages are measured by (1) loss in value; (2) delayed use of property; (3) diminution in market price; or (4) cost of completing performance. But this does not account for all the aggrieved party's costs of breach. The aggrieved party may also incur expenses in avoiding further damages. These costs incurred in avoiding further damages from another's breach are called incidental damages or damages incurred in mitigating breach.

The purpose of awarding incidental damages is to reimburse the injured party for any costs incurred in mitigating its damages after the other party breached the contract. When a breach occurs, the injured party may not simply allow itself to be harmed if the harm could be reasonably prevented. Instead, the injured party may have to pay money, whether it is for covering a hole in the roof left by a defaulting contractor or storing a boat that the breaching buyer failed to take delivery of or paying a headhunter's fee to find another job after being wrongfully terminated. The measure of incidental damages is the out-of-pocket expense incurred by the injured party after and as a result of the breach.

Incidental damages are expenses incurred by the aggrieved party in stopping performance or otherwise in mitigating damages after and as a result of the other party's breach. Consequential damages are harms reasonably foreseeable and caused by the breach.

1. Incidental Damages

Incidental damages are costs incurred by the injured party while reasonably trying to mitigate the breach. For example, if a farmer delivers the wrong kind of tomatoes to a supermarket, the supermarket might put that product in a cooler at the expense of its own sales floor and electrical bill to keep them from spoiling. Spending money in this way is economically efficient, since society is better off with edible tomatoes than with rotten ones. To encourage this behavior, courts established two rules. First, parties can recover incidental damages spent as a direct result of mitigating the breach.

Second, an aggrieved party has an obligation to mitigate and not pile up damages:

> *Except as stated in Subsection (2), damages are not recoverable for loss that the injured party could have avoided without undue risk, burden or humiliation.* R2d § 350(1).

As you can see, the R2d frames the rules in the negative by denying recovery of damages that could have been avoided. This removes the incentive for one party to pile up damages by, for example, not reporting a non-conforming produce delivery until it has already rotted.

> *The injured party is not precluded from recovery by the rule stated in Subsection (1) to the extent that he has made reasonable but unsuccessful efforts to avoid loss.* R2d § 350(2).

Although an argument could be made that incidental and consequential damages have more in common with "reliance damages," traditionally, both incidental and consequential damages have been classified as "indirect expectancy damages." As a form of expectancy damages, only aggrieved parties are entitled to recover incidental damages.

2. Attorney's Fees

Under the common law of contracts and the Uniform Commercial Code, each party is normally responsible for its own attorney fees that are incurred in resolving disputes with the other party. In the United States, each party is expected to pay its own attorney fees for negotiation, arbitration or litigation of disputes. Attorney fees for asserting a claim or defense are awarded only under certain civil rights statutes or consumer protection statutes, or under the Rules of Civil Procedure if the other party pursues a frivolous claim or defense in court or abuses the process of discovery.

However, if an attorney conducts activities not related to dispute resolution, but rather other actions made necessary by the breach of the other party, then the attorney's fees are recoverable as incidental damages.

3. Consequential Damages

Consequential damages are losses that do not flow directly and immediately from an injurious act but that result indirectly from the act. Consequential damages are also termed indirect damages. Professors Spies and McCoid explained:

> No discussion of consequential damages can be profitable unless we first define what we mean by this elusive concept. Admittedly, the concept is ambiguous and equivocal. Nevertheless, it is a usual and useful rubric to denote varied types of losses, for some of which the courts consistently allow recovery, for others of which there is never recovery, and for still others of which the courts allow or deny recovery depending upon the degree of remoteness, the pertinent constitution and the philosophy of the judges deciding the issue. . . . Consequential damages typically embrace such indirect and uncompensated losses as good will, business profits, removal expenses, and losses resulting from obstruction to light, air, view and access. E.G. Spies & J.C. McCoid, *Recovery of Consequential Damages in Eminent Domain*. 48 Va. L. Rev. 437 (1962).

Consequential damages for breach of contract are commonly awarded for the following types of harms caused by the breaching party:

- Personal injury;
- Injury to property; and
- Economic harm such as lost profits.

Consequential damages in the form of lost profits were the subject of *Hadley v. Baxendale*, from the ye olde court in England in 1854, which declared that delays from shipment are foreseeable. Mr. Hadley and Mr. Anor owned a mill as partners in the city of Gloucester. One day, the central crankshaft of a critical steam engine at the mill broke. Hadley arranged for W. Joyce & Co. to make a new one, which was to be transported by Baxendale.

Baxendale failed to deliver the crankshaft on time, and Hadley sued for the cost of his mill being offline for longer than expected. Baron Sir Edward Hall Alderson, sitting as judge in the Court of Exchequer, considered whether Hadley should be allowed to recover these lost profits from Baxendale. First, Judge Alderson sets forth the rule regarding such consequential damages:

> *Where two parties have made a contract which one of them has broken, the damages which the other party ought to receive in respect of such breach of contract should be such as may fairly and reasonably be considered either arising naturally, i.e., according to the usual course of things, from such breach of contract itself, or such as may reasonably be supposed to have been in the contemplation of both parties, at the time they made the contract, as the probable result of the breach of it.*

The question, therefore, focuses on whether Baxendale reasonably supposed that his delay would cost the mill lost profits. The court heard convincing testimony that most mills had at least one spare crankshaft, such that the delay of a replacement crankshaft should not cause the mill to remain shut down. Baxendale, for his part, had no special reason to know that Hadley lacked this spare part. Since a shipper in ordinary circumstances would not expect his delay to cause such lost profits, and since there was nothing in this case which took its facts out of the ordinary, Baxendale was not liable for Hadley's lost profits.

The modern legal standard for limitations on consequential is found in R2d § 351.

> *Damages are not recoverable for loss that the party in breach did not have reason to foresee as a probable result of the breach when the contract was made.* R2d § 351(1).

R2d adopts as a general rule that consequential damages are recoverable if the loss was "foreseeable" at the time that the parties entered into the contract.

> *Loss may be foreseeable as a probable result of a breach because it follows from the breach (a) in the ordinary course of events, or (b) as a result of special circumstances, beyond the ordinary course of events, that the party in breach had reason to know.* R2d § 351(2).

The Uniform Commercial Code adopts as a general rule that consequential damages in the form of injury to person and property are recoverable if the breach was the "proximate cause" of the loss.

Both the Restatement and the Uniform Commercial Code adopt a higher standard in cases where the loss was due to "special" circumstances or requirements.

In certain cases, it is not enough for the plaintiff to prove that its loss was "foreseeable" or that the loss was "proximately caused" by the breach. In those cases — primarily cases involving "special" circumstances or requirements resulting in economic loss such as lost profits — the plaintiff must prove that the seller or service provider had "reason to know" of the "special" circumstances or requirements. In general, courts have wide power to limit consequential damages where they are too attenuated or speculative.

Figure 22.1. Windmill by Piet Mondrian. Public domain work.

A court may limit damages for foreseeable loss by excluding recovery for loss of profits, by allowing recovery only for loss incurred in reliance, or otherwise if it concludes that in the circumstances justice so requires in order to avoid disproportionate compensation. R2d § 351(3).

Returning to the case of *Hadley*, where the shipper did not know that the mill would be offline while the shipment was delayed, the shipper could not reasonably foresee and did not actually know about the loss. Therefore, court did not award this loss in the calculation of damages from the breach of delay.

Let's return to the case in *Hadley v. Baxendale*, a British case decided by the Court of Exchequer in 1854. In that case a mill had to shut down because a carrier was slow in delivering a mill shaft to be repaired, and the owners of the mill sought to recover their lost profits from the carrier. However, the court ruled in favor of the carrier because the mill owners had not informed the carrier that this would be the consequence of any delay. (For example, the carrier might have assumed that the mill had a spare shaft). The rule that emerges from that case is that a breaching party is not liable for lost profits unless the "special circumstances" giving rise to the loss were "fairly and reasonably contemplated" by the parties at the time that the contract was entered into.

C. Punitive Damages

Contract law is not designed to punish breaking promises but rather to rationally encourage keeping promises. The default measure of damages, expectation damages, seeks to ensure that contractual parties get their financial benefit of the bargain regardless of whether the other party performs.

In fact, there is a concept called efficient breach where the most socially productive solution is for one party to breach and pay damages. For example, imagine that Pixie grows carrot and enters into a contract to sell her entire fall crop for $1 per ton to Campbell's Soup. Before harvest time, a scientist discovery that Pixie's carrots contain an enzyme that can be used to treat ocular cancer. The scientist is willing to pay Pixie $100 per ton for her carrots, which he hopes to use to make medicine that will cure thousands and make millions of dollars in the process.

In this situation, both Pixie and society are better off if her carrots become medicine and not soup, so from their perspective, she should breach her agreement with Campbell's and sell to the scientist. But what about Campbell's — how can that party be made whole? Let's say that similar carrots, which are equal substitutes in the soup-making process, cost $2 ton. Pixie should sell her carrots to the scientist for $100 per ton and pay Campbell's $1 per ton. Then Campbell's can go out and get carrots for the net cost of $1 per ton that it bargained for.

In the eyes of contract law, Pixie has done nothing ethically wrong under this situation. Whether her own morals dictate otherwise is another matter. For this reason, contract law generally does not punish breaching parties but only makes them make the aggrieved party whole:

> *Punitive damages are not recoverable for a breach of contract unless the conduct constituting the breach is also a tort for which punitive damages are recoverable. R2d § 355.*

There are exceptions to this rule where contractual breaches are also torts or crimes. But even in those cases, the additional punitive damages come from those other violations, not from contract law itself.

D. Liquidated Damages and Penalties

Liquidated damages are an amount contractually stipulated as a reasonable estimation of actual damages to be recovered by one party if the other party breaches. If the parties to a contract have properly agreed on liquidated damages, the sum fixed is the measure of damages for a breach, whether it exceeds or falls short of the actual damages. Liquidated damages are also termed stipulated damages or estimated damages.

> *Where the terms of a contract specify a sum payable for non-performance, it is a question of construction whether this sum is to be treated as a penalty or as liquidated damages. The difference in effect is this: The amount recoverable*

in case of a penalty is not the sum named, but the damage actually incurred. The amount recoverable as liquidated damages is the sum named as such. In construing these terms a judge will not accept the phraseology of the parties; they may call the sum specified "liquidated damages," but if the judge finds it to be a penalty, he will treat it as such.

As ATIYAH'S INTRODUCTION TO THE LAW OF CONTRACTS says:

The distinction between a penalty and genuine liquidated damages, as they are called, is not always easy to apply, but the Courts have made the task simpler by laying down certain guiding principles. In the first place, if the sum payable is so large as to be far in excess of the probable damage on breach, it is almost certainly a penalty. Secondly, if the same sum is expressed to be payable on any one of a number of different breaches of varying importance, it is again probably a penalty, because it is extremely unlikely that the same damage would be caused by these varying breaches. Thirdly, where a sum is expressed to be payable on a certain date, and a further sum in the event of default being made, this latter sum is prima facie a penalty, because mere delay in payment is unlikely to cause damage. Finally, it is to be noted that the mere use of the words "liquidated damages" is not decisive, for it is the task of the Court and not of the parties to decide the true nature of the sum payable. William R. Anson, Principles of the Law of Contract 470 (Arthur L. Corbin ed., 3d Am. ed. 1919).

Liquidated damages must therefore be "reasonable." Liquidated damages that are unreasonably large constitute a "penalty" rather than compensation and are unenforceable; and liquidated damages that are unreasonably small may be unconscionable and unenforceable.

Damages for breach by either party may be liquidated in the agreement but only at an amount that is reasonable in the light of the anticipated or actual loss caused by the breach and the difficulties of proof of loss. A term fixing unreasonably large liquidated damages is unenforceable on grounds of public policy as a penalty. R2d § 356(1).

Bonds are specific financial instruments whose contractual functions are subject to special rules. Generally, a corporation, municipality, or government issues a bond to raise money. The terms of the bond are that the bearer pays a certain amount for the bond in exchange for the right to earn a fixed amount of intertest over a specified period of time before being permitted to reclaim the initial amount invested.

Bonds are complex instruments that may involve conditions such as that the issue must maintain a certain debt to income ratio. If these conditions or "covenants" are breached, the holder may be entitled to a certain amount of money. Just as liquidated damages in other contracts are limited so they do not constitute penalties, similar terms in bonds must also not function as penalties.

A term in a bond providing for an amount of money as a penalty for non-occurrence of the condition of the bond is unenforceable on grounds of public policy to the extent that the amount exceeds the loss caused by such non-occurrence. R2d § 356(2).

E. Reflections on Expectation Damages

Any breach creates liability for damages, but which measure of damages should courts use? Expectation damages are the preferred method of calculating damages. Expectation damages are intended to award to the aggrieved party the benefit that it bargained for and reasonably expected.

Expectation damages can include incidental damages, which are expenses incurred by the aggrieved party in stopping performance or otherwise in mitigating damages after and as a result of the other party's breach, including attorney's fees in some cases.

Expectation damages can also include consequential damages, which are injuries or losses proximately and foreseeably caused by the breach such as personal injury, damage to property, or economic loss like lost profits or lost customers.

Aggrieved parties have a duty to mitigate damages. If an aggrieved party fails to take reasonable action to mitigate damages, then expectation damages may be reduced or eliminated.

As an alternative to expectation damages, a party may instead be awarded reliance damages, especially when expectation damages are difficult to calculate with reasonable certainty. Reliance damages are expenses that are incurred in preparation for or in performance of a contract.

At the fringe of contract law is restitution damages, which stand in stark contrast to expectation damages. Expectation damages are intended to put the aggrieved party in the position it would have been in if the contract were completely performed, whereas restitution damages seek to put the aggrieved party in the position in was in before the contract was formed.

Restitution is the subject of its own treatises, but as applied to contract law, recovery in restitution for contractual breach is measured by the value of the benefit that was conferred upon the other party, not the contract price. Restitution is available in quasi-contract and even in cases where a contract at law does not exist.

Cases

Reading Peevyhouse v. Garland Coal & Mining Co. The following famous case, *Peevyhouse*, explains why courts will not require breaching parties to pay the cost of completing performance, but rather the loss in value (normal expectation damages) of the breach.

Peevyhouse v. Garland Coal & Mining Co.

1962 OK 267 (1962)

W.R. WALLACE, JR., Judge.

In the trial court, plaintiffs Willie and Lucille Peevyhouse sued the defendant, Garland Coal and Mining Company, for damages for breach of contract. Judgment was for plaintiffs in an amount considerably less than was sued for. Plaintiffs appeal and defendant cross-appeals.

In the briefs on appeal, the parties present their argument and contentions under several propositions; however, they all stem from the basic question of whether the trial court properly instructed the jury on the measure of damages.

Briefly stated, the facts are as follows: plaintiffs owned a farm containing coal deposits, and in November, 1954, leased the premises to defendant for a period of five years for coal mining purposes. A "stripmining" operation was contemplated in which the coal would be taken from pits on the surface of the ground, instead of from underground mine shafts. In addition to the usual covenants found in a coal mining lease, defendant specifically agreed to perform certain restorative and remedial work at the end of the lease period. It is unnecessary to set out the details of the work to be done, other than to say that it would involve the moving of many thousands of cubic yards of dirt, at a cost estimated by expert witnesses at about $29,000.00. However, plaintiffs sued for only $25,000.00.

. . . .

Plaintiffs contend that the true measure of damages in this case is what it will cost plaintiffs to obtain performance of the work that was not done because of defendant's default. Defendant argues that the measure of damages is the cost of performance "limited, however, to the total difference in the market value before and after the work was performed".

. . . .

We therefore hold that where, in a coal mining lease, lessee agrees to perform certain remedial work on the premises concerned at the end of the lease period, and thereafter the contract is fully performed by both parties except that the remedial work is not done, the measure of damages in an action by lessor against lessee for damages for breach of contract is ordinarily the reasonable cost of performance of the work; however, where the contract provision breached was merely incidental to the main purpose in view, and where the economic benefit which would result to lessor by full performance of the work is grossly disproportionate to the cost of performance, the damages which lessor may recover are limited to the diminution in value resulting to the premises because of the non-performance.

. . . .

Under the most liberal view of the evidence herein, the diminution in value resulting to the premises because of non-performance of the remedial work was $300.00.

After a careful search of the record, we have found no evidence of a higher figure, and plaintiffs do not argue in their briefs that a greater diminution in value was sustained. It thus appears that the judgment was clearly excessive, and that the amount for which judgment should have been rendered is definitely and satisfactorily shown by the record.

IRWIN, J (dissenting).

By the specific provisions in the coal mining lease under consideration, the defendant agreed as follows:

> *7b Lessee agrees to make fills in the pits dug on said premises on the property line in such manner that fences can be placed thereon and access had to opposite sides of the pits.*

> *7c Lessee agrees to smooth off the top of the spoil banks on the above premises.*

> *7d Lessee agrees to leave the creek crossing the above premises in such a condition that it will not interfere with the crossings to be made in pits as set out in 7b.*

> *7f Lessee further agrees to leave no shale or dirt on the high wall of said pits.*

. . . .

Defendant admits that it failed to perform its obligations that it agreed and contracted to perform under the lease contract and there is nothing in the record which indicates that defendant could not perform its obligations. Therefore, in my opinion defendant's breach of the contract was wilful and not in good faith.

. . . .

Defendant has received its benefits under the contract and now urges, in substance, that plaintiffs' measure of damages for its failure to perform should be the economic value of performance to the plaintiffs and not the cost of performance.

. . . .

In the instant action defendant has made no attempt to even substantially perform. The contract in question is not immoral, is not tainted with fraud, and was not entered into through mistake or accident and is not contrary to public policy. It is clear and unambiguous and the parties understood the terms thereof, and the approximate cost of fulfilling the obligations could have been approximately ascertained. There are no conditions existing now which could not have been reasonably anticipated when the contract was negotiated and executed. The defendant could have performed the contract if it desired. It has accepted and reaped the benefits of its contract and now urges that plaintiffs' benefits under the contract be denied. If plaintiffs' benefits are denied, such benefits would inure to the direct benefit of the defendant.

Therefore, in my opinion, the plaintiffs were entitled to specific performance of the contract and since defendant has failed to perform, the proper measure of damages should be the cost of performance. Any other measure of damage would be holding for naught the express provisions of the contract; would be taking from the plaintiffs the benefits of the contract and placing those benefits in defendant which has failed to perform its obligations; would be granting benefits to defendant without a resulting obligation; and would be completely rescinding the solemn obligation of the contract for the benefit of the defendant to the detriment of the plaintiffs by making an entirely new contract for the parties.

Reflection

The court in *Peevyhouse* effectively said that that the defendant breached its contract and in doing so made plaintiff's land uglier. That appears to be true. The image below shows how mining terraforms flat land into hills. Note that the process also stopped a small river from flowing through the land.

Figure 22.2. "Garland Coal sure left a lot of hills behind." Credit Tim Root, "Case of the Day — Monday, June 15, 2020," Tree and Neighbor Blog.

The question was weather defendant had to pay for restoration of the land to its prior state — which as you can image would be a considerable expense — or merely for the diminution to its value. The latter, diminution to value, was selected because it more closely approximated the financial deal the parties struck or would have struck.

Given that some damage was foreseeable, the extent of the damage was beyond what Garland bargained for. The court therefore awarded him the difference between what he got (some cash and totally destroyed land) for what he bargained for (some cash and moderately damaged land) according to what was the reasonably foreseeable outcome of this agreement.

The court's business about "reasonable cost" and "unreasonable economic waste" is a poetic way of identifying this as a commercial agreement, whereas courts might instead use the concept of a "reasonable person" where dealing with noncommercial agreements. But this distinction also makes cases somewhat easier to resolve because we have a sharper view of the commercially reasonable person than we do in noncommercial contexts: we generally presume that commercial parties are economically rational, that is, they want to make money. Parties to commercial agreements allocate risk and reward in the manner that they deem most likely to generate the most profit for themselves. Here, the court effectively found that a commercially reasonable bargain could have been struck in exchange for the total destruction of Peevyhouse's land, but no commercially reasonable strip miner would have bargained for the cost of totally restoring land to perfect condition after it had mined the resources out of it. It then enforces the terms of the commercially reasonable bargain, thus putting commercial reality in line with contractual obligations.

Discussion

1. Peevyhouse was paid for use of his land by a strip mining company. Was some damage to the land foreseeable?

2. How do you square the commercial reality of strip mining with the plain meaning of the written term to restore the land?

3. If the court made Garland Coal pay the Peevyhouses the estimated cost to restore the land to its original condition, would the Peevyhouses spend the money on doing that? Does your answer to this question impact whether courts should award this remedy? If so, why?

Reading Hadley v. Baxendale. One of the most famous and most durable cases in the law of contracts is *Hadley v. Baxendale*, a British case decided by the Court of Exchequer in 1854. In that case a mill had to shut down because a carrier was slow in delivering a mill shaft to be repaired, and the owners of the mill sought to recover their lost profits from the carrier. However, the court ruled in favor of the carrier because the mill owners had not informed the carrier that this would be the consequence of any delay. (For example, the carrier might have assumed that the mill had a spare shaft). The rule that emerges from that case is that a breaching party is not liable for lost profits unless the "special circumstances" giving rise to the loss were "fairly and reasonably contemplated" by the parties at the time that the contract was entered into.

The contract was for shipment of a crankshaft for a windmill. The language of this case is a bit archaic, so I have provided summaries and guide points for you in [square brackets] in the text below. I have also added paragraph breaks, since the court did not seem to possess an "enter" key and often went on for dozens of lines at a time. Otherwise, I have been mainly faithful to the original so you can hear the color and texture of the court's famous language.

See R2d § 351 for the modern statement of the rule on the reasonable foreseeability limitations of awards of expectation damages.

Hadley v. Baxendale

56 Eng. Rep. 145, 9 Exch. 341 (1854)

[Summary: Hadley ran a windmill that broke its crankshaft. Baxendale promises to deliver a crankshaft to a manufacturer within 2 days, but it took ten extra days. Hadley's mill was out of commission during that time because of Baxendale's delay in delivery of the crankshaft to the manufacturer, so Hadley sued Baxendale for the delay as measured by lost profits. The trial court awarded lost profit damages to Hadley, and Baxendale appealed.]

At the trial before Crompton, J., at the last Gloucester Assizes, it appeared that the plaintiffs carried on an extensive business as millers at Gloucester; and that, on the 11th of May, their mill was stopped by a breakage of the crank shaft by which the mill was worked.

The steam-engine was manufactured by Messrs. Joyce & Co., the engineers, at Greenwich, and it became necessary to send the shaft as a pattern for a new one to Greenwich.

The fracture was discovered on the 12th, and on the 13th the plaintiffs sent one of their servants to the office of the defendants, who are the well-known carriers trading under the name of Pickford & Co., for the purpose of having the shaft carried to Greenwich.

The plaintiffs' servant told the clerk that the mill was stopped, and that the shaft must be sent immediately; and in answer to the inquiry when the shaft would be taken, the answer was, that if it was sent up by twelve o'clock that day, it would be delivered at Greenwich on the following day.

On the following day the shaft was taken by the defendants, before noon, for the purpose of being conveyed to Greenwich, and the sum of 2l. 4s. was paid for its carriage for the whole distance; at the same time the defendants' clerk was told that a special entry, if required, should be made to hasten its delivery.

The delivery of the shaft at Greenwich was delayed by some neglect; and the consequence was, that the plaintiffs did not receive the new shaft for several days after they would otherwise have done, and the working of their mill was thereby delayed, and they thereby lost the profits they would otherwise have received.

[Hadley won: the trial court awarded him lost profits for Baxendale's negligent delay.]

On the part of the defendants, it was objected that these damages were too remote, and that the defendants were not liable with respect to them. The learned Judge left the case generally to the jury, who found a verdict with 25l. damages beyond the amount paid into Court.

[Baxendale appealed, arguing that he did not know Hadley would suffer this loss; therefore, he should not be liable for paying it.]

Whateley, in last Michaelmas Term, obtained a rule nisi for a new trial, on the ground of misdirection.

The judgment of the [Appellate] Court was now delivered by

ALDERSON, B. We think that there ought to be a new trial in this case; but, in so doing, we deem it to be expedient and necessary to state explicitly the rule which the Judge, at the next trial, ought, in our opinion, to direct the jury to be governed by when they estimate the damages.

Now we think the proper rule is such as the present is this: — Where two parties have made a contract which one of them has broken, the damages which the other party ought to receive in respect of such breach of contract should be such as may fairly and reasonably be considered either:

> arising naturally, i.e., according to the usual course of things, from such breach of contract itself, or

> such as may reasonably be supposed to have been in the contemplation of both parties, at the time they made the contract, as the probable result of the breach of it.

If the special circumstances under which the contract was:

> actually made where communicated by the plaintiffs to the defendants, and

> thus known to both parties,

Then the damages resulting from the breach of such a contract, which they would reasonably contemplate, would be the amount of injury which would ordinarily follow from a breach of contract under these special circumstances so known and communicated.

But, on the other hand, if these special circumstances were wholly unknown to the party breaking the contract, he, at the most, could only be supposed to have had in his contemplation the amount of injury which would arise generally, and in the great multitude of cases not affected by any special circumstances, from such a breach of contract.

Such loss would neither have flowed naturally from the breach of this contract in the great multitude of such cases occurring under ordinary circumstances, nor were the special circumstances, which, perhaps, would have made it a reasonable and natural consequence of such breach of contract, communicated to or known by the defendants.

The Judge ought, therefore, to have told the jury, that, upon the facts then before them, they ought not to take the loss of profits into consideration at all in estimating the damages.

There must therefore be a new trial in this case. Rule absolute.

[Remanded to trial court to determine whether Hadley's damages were reasonably foreseeable to Baxendale under the new rule stated above.]

Reflection

Whether *Hadley* is the best of cases or the worst of cases, it surely is the most popular of cases, and among the most cited.

Hadley, a miller, contracted with Baxendale, a carrier, to have a broken shaft sent to the manufacturer for repairs. Due to some neglect, the shaft was not sent on time, and Hadley lost profits due to the delay; so, he sued, and he won.

On appeal, the court granted a new trial, and the jury was to be instructed not to consider lost profits because the circumstances did not show that the mill would lose profits if the shaft was not delivered on time. What carrier should have known this? Maybe Hadley had another shaft he could use; maybe another machine had broken and the mill couldn't run anyway; or maybe zombies arrived to save the day. Not to quibble, but it would be a very bad day to have two essential machines break down; and as to the backup shaft, was Hadley compulsive?

Of course, had Hadley told Baxendale that his was a unique case and that he had a pressing need for the shaft, things might have turned out differently. Alas, he only said that the "article to be carried was the broken shaft of a mill and that the plaintiffs were millers of the mill." Hold on there! In the first paragraph we are told that Hadley told Baxendale, "the mill was stopped, that the shaft must be delivered immediately, and that a special entry, if necessary, must be made to hasten its delivery." Now my short-term memory is not what it used to be, but come on, five short paragraphs? Maybe the clerk who transcribed the opinion was in his cups — gin was very popular at the time — but let us simply assume that, for whatever reason, the statement of these facts is incorrect, and move on.

Baxendale made a promise, he did not keep it, and that breach injured Hadley. Why should he, rather than Hadley, take the loss? The jury thought he should, but the court tells us that this would be the "greatest injustice." In tort law, you take the plaintiff as you find her — none of this "before you throw that apple let me tell you I have a very rare heart condition" nonsense. Why give the promisor a break? Between the two, it is more likely that the promisor would envision consequents of breach, as he is focusing on whether he can keep his word; the promisee is focusing on the price. It seems, however, that the greatest injustice does not turn on fault or who can better envision the harm, but rather on the harm that would flow if the jury did not buy into the notion of a cheap contract. But that is another article, and justice is beyond my scope.

"[I]f the jury [is] left without any definite rule to guide [it], it will . . . manifestly lead to the greatest injustice."

Put aside the notion that jurors might have a better idea of justice than do judges and focus instead on the notion "we cannot trust jurors." A core notion in the law is that is we cannot trust anyone to do the right thing. Jurors are roped in by the instructions (which they must follow), by parties via their carefully drafted contracts (which they often ignore), by judges, and, alas, by *Hadley*.

Discussion

1. *Hadley* distinguishes between "incidental" and consequential damages, as does the R2d. But is this diction necessary? Not all courts distinguish between different kinds of indirect damages in this way. As an alternative to distinguishing between incidental damages, which directly arise from direct damages, and consequential damages, which indirectly arise and only count as damages where they are reasonably foreseeable, could a court simplify this analysis with a rule that says all indirect damages count to the extent they are reasonably foreseeable? Or do the separate concepts of incidental and consequential damages do some additional work beyond making reasonably unforeseeable losses unrecoverable?

Problems

Problem 22.1. Dynamo Products

Dynamo Products entered into a contract to sell Republic Manufacturing a large-scale lithium wall battery for Republic's new factory for a price of $130,000. The battery was delivered to Republic; Republic inspected the battery fully and accepted it. Under the contract, Republic was to pay Dynamo for the battery 30 days after delivery; however Republic failed to make payment.

Assuming that Republic thereby breached, what damages should a court order Republic to pay to Dynamo?

Problem 22.2. Francis the Plumber

Francis, a plumber, had a contract with the Bistro Hotel to replace the old cast iron pipes in the hotel with copper pipes. The agreed upon contract price was $20,000. Before Francis started work, Bistro repudiated the contract. Bistro had paid nothing in advance. Francis had expected to pay workers and suppliers $15,000 and expected to earn a profit of $5,000 from the contract.

Assuming that Bistro's repudiation is a total breach, what damages should a court order Bistro to pay to Francis?

Problem 22.3. Gateway Packaging

Gateway Packaging of Scranton, Pennsylvania signed a contract with Xanadu Freight Lines to take fourteen thousand unfolded cardboard boxes to Pennington's Online Sales Company in Youngstown, Ohio, shipping date of June 18. Gateway informed Xanadu that "time was of the essence" and that the shipment must occur on that date or Pennington's would refuse the shipment. Gateway was to pay $1,000 to Xanadu to carry the freight to Youngstown.

On June 17, Xanadu informed Gateway that it had entered into too many shipping contracts and that it would not be able to take the boxes to Youngstown. Gateway then contacted another company, Cassiopeia Trucking, and had to pay them $1,600 to take the boxes to Youngstown the next day.

What damages should a court order Xanadu pay to Gateway?

Problem 22.4. Yugo Motors — Diminution in Value

Blake ordered a luxury automobile loaded with accessories from Yugo Motors for a contract price of $66,000. When the car arrived, Blake discovered that it lacked four of the features that Blake had ordered. Yugo refused to take back the car and order a new one.

What damages should be awarded to Blake?

Problem 22.5. The Oysters

Haverfield Aquatic Farms raises various shellfish including oysters. Angstrom Food Distributors buys food from producers and sells it to restaurants and food processors. Angstrom placed an order with Haverfield for 400 pounds of oysters to be delivered on August 1; the agreed-upon price was $6 per pound. Angstrom then entered into contracts with six restaurants and a food processor to resell the oysters at $10 per pound. During July, the market price for oysters was rising, and when the market price reached $7 per pound, Haverfield sent Angstrom an email stating that it was repudiating the contract; Haverfield resold the oysters to another distributor for $7 per pound.

What is Angstrom's remedy if it is able to cover by purchasing oysters from another source for $6.50 per pound, and it also spent an extra $100 arranging for the substitute purchase?

What is Angstrom's remedy if it is unable to cover?

What is Angstrom's remedy if it could have covered by purchasing oysters from another source but chose not to?

Chapter 23

Alternative Money Damages

Expectation damages are the preferred measure of damages because they put the party in the place it would have been in had the contract been performed. This calculation makes difficult for one contractual party to cheat the other, since it will have to pay for the value of the contract whether it completes that contract or not. However, as we saw earlier, expectation damages may be hard to calculate in some case and inappropriate for others. This chapter reviews the alternative measures of money damages that courts will resort to when expectation damages are not appropriate.

Rules

A. Reliance Damages

Reliance damages are expenses that are incurred in preparation for or in performance of a contract.

Reliance damages are an alternative to expectation damages. Reliance damages are typically awarded when a party is unable to prove expectancy damages; e.g., when expectancy damages are speculative or uncertain. Reliance damages may not be awarded in addition to direct expectancy damages.

Recall that expectation damages include both direct and indirect loss, and that indirect loss includes consequential and incidental damages. How are reliance damages different from incidental damages?

The purpose of awarding reliance damages is to grant some relief to an injured party in situations where expectancy or consequential damages are not available. For example, after a breach of contract, the injured party may be unable to prove the extent of expectancy or consequential damages to a degree of reasonable certainty, so instead the courts may grant the injured party reliance damages as some measure of justice.

> *As an alternative to the measure of damages stated in § 347, the injured party has a right to damages based on his reliance interest, including expenditures made in preparation for performance or in performance, less any loss that the party in breach can prove with reasonable certainty the injured party would have suffered had the contract been performed. R2d § 349.*

For example, in cases involving promissory estoppel, the courts often find that it is not appropriate to fully enforce the promise of the promisor and that granting the promisee its reliance damages is all that justice requires. In breach of contract cases, reliance damages consist of expenses incurred in performing or preparing to perform a contract. In promissory estoppel cases, reliance damages consist of expenses incurred in reasonable reliance upon the promise of the other party. In contrast to incidental damages, reliance damages are expenses incurred before the other party breached. It may be more appropriate to restore a party to its pre-reliant state than to create and enforce a contract where none existed as a matter of law.

B. Punitive Damages

Normally, the purpose of the law of contract is not punitive but merely economic; to enforce promises that have a tendency to increase value and to encourage commercial practices that prevent economic waste. However, punitive damages are awarded for breach of contract where the breaching party engaged in "outrageous conduct" characterized by "evil motive" or "reckless indifference to the rights of others." This is the same standard that is used in awarding punitive damages in tort cases. The purpose of awarding punitive damages for breach of contract is also the same as it is in the law of tort: to punish and deter outrageous conduct.

The amount of punitive damages is measured by taking into account the nature of the defendant's conduct, the extent of harm suffered by the injured party, and the wealth of the defendant. Punitive damages must be large enough to discourage outrageous conduct but not so large as to destroy the defendant.

Punitive damages are damages in excess of expectation, reliance, or restitution. As their name implies, they are designed to punish a contract party.

In general, punitive damages are disfavored for breach of contract because the purpose of the law of contracts is economic in nature, not moral. The law of contracts is designed to encourage voluntary, bargained-for exchanges supported by valid consideration, not to enforce promise-keeping. Contract law even permits the "efficient breach." Remedies for breach of contract are normally compensatory in nature, not punitive.

However, when a party's conduct is not only a breach of contract but is also a tort for which punitive damages might be awarded, then the courts will allow the trier of fact to consider awarding punitive damages for breach of contract. Punitive damages may be awarded for conduct that is outrageous or when the breaching party had an evil motive or acted with reckless indifference to the rights of others.

If a punitive damages award is so large that it appears to be the product of passion and prejudice, it will be overturned. As a matter of constitutional law, an award of punitive damages must also be in some measure proportionate to the amount of compensatory damages.

C. Nominal Damages

The purpose of awarding nominal damages (usually in the amount of $1 or $10) is to acknowledge that the breaching party committed a breach and that the aggrieved party, though uninjured, is the victor of the lawsuit.

> *If the breach caused no loss or if the amount of the loss is not proved under the rules stated in this Chapter, a small sum fixed without regard to the amount of loss will be awarded as nominal damages.* R2d § 346.

Nominal damages may be legally significant for a number of reasons: assigning court costs, awarding attorney fees, or in complex litigation involving multiple parties, a "nominal" victory against one party may insulate a party from liability to other parties. In any event, they are symbolic of one party's victory.

D. Liquidated Damages and Penalties

Liquidated damages are amounts of damages for breach of contract that the parties have agreed to in their contract. The purpose of awarding liquidated damages is to honor the parties' freedom of contract and to respect their estimate of the damages that would flow from a breach. However, liquidated damages that are unreasonably large may be struck down as a penalty, and liquidated damages that are unreasonably small may be struck down as unconscionable.

The parties to a contract may agree in advance to establish the damages for breach contractually by means of a "liquidated damages clause." Damages which are established in advance by the parties in a contract are known as "liquidated" damages.

Courts will only enforce liquidated damages that are "reasonable." The "reasonableness" of the amount of liquidated damages depends upon the interaction of two factors: (1) whether the amount of liquidated damages reflects the anticipated or actual harm caused by the breach, and (2) the difficulties that the aggrieved party would have in proving loss.

A liquidated damages clause is valid so long as it is reasonable in light of either anticipated or actual harm caused to the aggrieved party.

The easier it would be to prove that a loss had occurred and the easier it would be to prove the amount of the loss, the less discretion the parties would have in setting the amount of liquidated damages in advance. In other words, the reasonableness of liquidated damages is inversely proportional to the ability to prove expectation damage to a reasonable certainty.

Liquidated damages that are unreasonably large constitute a "penalty" rather than compensation and are unenforceable; and liquidated damages that are unreasonably small may be unconscionable and unenforceable.

E. Reflections on Alternative Money Damages

Expectation damages, the most common form of damages awarded for breach of contract, seek to put an aggrieved party in the position it would have been in had the contract been performed.

When expectation damages are inappropriate, courts may award reliance damages. Reliance damages are expenses that are incurred in preparation for or in performance of a contract before the other party breached and even before the contract was made.

Punitive damages are unavailable for a mere contractual breach. Punitive damages are generally available only where a breach is also a tort or crime.

Nominal damages are a token amount awarded to show who won a lawsuit where there was not other damages to speak of.

Liquidated damages are an agreed set of damages parties agree to pay in the event of breach. Courts generally enforce liquidated damages except in cases where the breaching party claims they constitute an inappropriate penalty.

Chapter 24

Equitable Remedies

Despite the Latin maxim *pacta sunt servanda*, promises must be kept, who should require this? Courts have limited enforcement powers. Should a court order some action, generally a member of the executive branch such as a sheriff must ensure that order is carried out. This is a more onerous and invasive process than merely requiring someone to pay money or even garnishing a bank account. For this reason, these equitable remedies are somewhat exceptional and rarely granted.

Rules

A. Specific Performance

"Specific performance" is a court order directing one party to a contract to perform its obligations under that contract. The result is the rendering, as nearly as practicable, of a promised performance through a judgment or decree. It is a court-ordered remedy that requires precise fulfillment of a legal or contractual obligation.

> *Subject to the rules stated in §§ 359-69, specific performance of a contract duty will be granted in the discretion of the court against a party who has committed or is threatening to commit a breach of the duty.* R2d § 357(1).

Specific performance is only granted when monetary damages are inappropriate or inadequate, as when the sale of real estate or a rare article is involved. It is an equitable remedy that lies within the court's discretion to award whenever the common-law remedy is insufficient, either because damages would be inadequate or because the damages could not possibly be established. Specific performance is also termed "specific relief" and "performance in specie."

B. Prohibitory Injunction

An "injunction"—also known as a "negative injunction" or "prohibitory injunction"—is a court-ordered prohibition that prevents an action. In this way, an injunction is the opposite of specific performance, which is where a court requires a party to complete performance under a contract.

> *Subject to the rules stated in §§ 359-69, an injunction against breach of a contract duty will be granted in the discretion of the court against a party who has committed or is threatening to commit a breach of the duty if (a) the*

duty is one of forbearance, or (b) the duty is one to act and specific perfor-
mance would be denied only for reasons that are inapplicable to an injunc-
tion. R2d § 357(2).

In general, a court will not grant injunctive relief unless four conditions are satisfied:

- Likelihood of serious and irreparable harm. Without the injunction, the party seeking the injunction will likely suffer serious and irreparable harm.
- Availability of an adequate remedy at law. The party seeking the injunction cannot be adequately compensated by means of an award of money damages.
- Balancing the equities between the parties. The benefit of the injunction to the party seeking the injunction outweighs the harm to the party against whom the injunction is sought.
- Public interest. Granting the injunction will not unduly harm the public interest.

There are three common types of contractual provisions that a party might seek to enforce by means of a prohibitory injunction: (1) non-compete agreements, (2) non-solicitation agreements, and (3) non-disclosure agreements.

1. Non-Compete Agreements

A non-competition agreement is an agreement to not accept employment with a competitor or to set up a competing business. In certain businesses and professions, it is common for employees to be required to sign a "non-compete."

The law of most states disfavors "non-competes" and will enforce them only to protect a legitimate business purpose, not simply to eliminate competition. Furthermore, courts routinely strike down or limit non-compete agreements if they extend for too long a period of time, have too broad a geographic scope, or if they are in conflict with the public interest.

As with all contractual provisions, the employee must receive consideration for signing the non-compete. If an employer attempts to impose a non-compete on an existing employee as a condition of future employment, the employer would be wise to offer some material inducement.

Moreover, if an employer fires an employee without cause, the courts are less likely to enforce the non-compete agreement.

2. Non-Solicitation Agreements

Non-solicitation agreements are a more targeted form of non-compete agreement and are more likely to be enforced than a general non-compete. Solicitation of existing customers or fellow employees during the period of employment is a serious breach of the duty of loyalty that an employee owes to an employer. A non-solicitation agreement represents an attempt to extend that duty once the employment has terminated. As with non-competes, however, a court may find that a non-solicitation agreement is unreasonably broad in its duration or geographic scope.

3. Non-Disclosure Agreements

The parties to a contract may enter into a non-disclosure agreement prohibiting the disclosure or use of trade secrets or customer lists.

However, non-disclosure of trade secrets may be enforced even in the absence of an express non-disclosure agreement. The Uniform Trade Secrets Act has been adopted in nearly all the states. The UTSA prohibits the "misappropriation" of trade secrets, that is, the disclosure or use of trade secrets which were obtained by "improper means." Under this statute, the courts are authorized to enjoin a former employee from disclosing information that the former employee knew was to be kept confidential.

4. Enforceability of Negative Covenants

Specific (equitable) enforceability of these "negative covenants" varies from state to state. Pursuant to the Uniform Trade Secrets Act, prohibitory injunctions enforcing non-disclosure of trade secrets may be issued even in the absence of an express non-disclosure agreement. Non-compete and non-solicitation agreements may be limited or invalidated if they are too broad in duration or geographic scope or if they are in conflict with the public interest. Courts are more likely to enforce restrictive covenants against a party that has sold a business than they are against a former employee.

C. Restitution

The purpose of awarding restitution damages is to prevent unjust enrichment. This is the only type of monetary damages for breach of contract that is recoverable by both the breaching party as well as the injured party. When a breach occurs, the party who breached may be unjustly enriched unless the law grants a remedy to the injured party, but it is also possible that the party who did not breach may be unjustly enriched unless the law grants the breaching party a remedy.

> A party is entitled to restitution under the rules stated in this Restatement only to the extent that he has conferred a benefit on the other party by way of part performance or reliance. R2d § 370.

The measure of restitution damages is the value of the benefit that one party conferred upon the other party. For example, if a contractor abandoned work for the construction of a garage when the work was partially completed, the owner is entitled to the return of any partial payment that was made to the contractor, and the contractor is presumptively entitled to restitution for the value of the work that was performed. A breaching party who acted in bad faith may be denied any recovery for restitution.

> If a sum of money is awarded to protect a party's restitution interest, it may as justice requires be measured by either (a) the reasonable value to the other party of what he received in terms of what it would have cost him to obtain it

from a person in the claimant's position, or (b) the extent to which the other party's property has been increased in value or his other interests advanced. R2d § 371.

The purpose of restitutionary remedies is to restore a party to the position it was in before the contract was formed. The restorative purpose of restitution contrasts with expectancy damages, whose purpose is to place a party in the position it would have been in if the other party had fully performed.

The purpose of restitution and reliance, however, are very similar. Both remedies seek to put the party in the position her, she, or it would have been if the contract was never formed. So how do they differ?

Restitution is a body of law that is based on unjust enrichment: when one party retains a benefit conferred by another not as a gift, but instead under circumstances where compensation is reasonably expected. Restitutionary remedies at contract law, thereby, are based not on the plaintiff's loss, but rather on the defendant's gain. The benefit that one party received from the other party in the performance of a contract may include goods, land, or securities; services; or money. Restitution therefore consists of returning the value of those items, services or money to the other party.

Reliance damages, on the other hand, focus on costs incurred by the plaintiff. This is distinguishable from restitution damages, which focus on benefits received by the defendant.

Recovery for restitution is measured by the value of the benefit that was conferred upon the other party, not the contract price, which distinguishes restitution from expectation damages.

However, restitution under contract law may be limited by the contract price. If the parties entered into a valid contract, many courts would be reluctant to grant a party more in restitution than what it would have earned under the contract that it bargained for. Many courts would find that the contract price should represent a ceiling on the amount of restitution that a party is entitled to recover.

Restitution is a unique remedy in that, in many cases, both parties are entitled to restitution. Both parties may be required to "disgorge" the benefits received under the bargain. This may in effect return the parties to the status quo that existed before the contract was formed, which would be the same effect as reliance damages, but this need not necessarily be the case.

D. Reflections on Equitable Remedies

Specific performance is a court order directing one party to a contract to perform its obligation under the contract. Specific performance is an equitable remedy; accordingly, issuance of an order of specific performance is subject to the sound discretion of the issuing court; a party is not entitled to an order of specific performance if an award of money damages would be an adequate remedy; and the party seeking an order of specific performance must not be in breach of the contract or guilty of bad faith.

The inverse of specific performance is a prohibitory injunction, a court order which prohibits a contract party from taking action that would be a violation of a contract. Prohibitory injunctions are subject to the four requirements that are generally applied to injunctions:

1. Likelihood of serious and irreparable harm.
2. Availability of an adequate remedy at law.
3. Balancing the equities between the parties.
4. Public interest.

There are three common types of contractual provisions that a party might seek to enforce by means of a prohibitory injunction:

1. Non-compete agreement.
2. Non-solicitation agreement.
3. Non-disclosure agreement.

Traditionally specific performance was awarded only in cases involving the sale of land, pieces of art, or unique items such as heirlooms. Today, however, the trend is for the courts to award specific performance "in other proper circumstances," for example, to protect a party's continued supply of raw materials. The UCC also grants buyers rights to "replevin" or recovery of goods in certain circumstances.

Cases

Reading Bauer v. Sawyer. Courts generally prefer to award money damages to resolve contract disputes. But, sometimes, money is not a sufficient remedy to an aggrieved contract party. For one thing, it can be hard to value certain broken promises, even when the courts recognize that such promises have significant value. As another matter, parties sometimes make promises that contemplate specific performance and not money damages for breach.

The following case is one where a party agreed to join a medical partnership and promised not to compete with it even if he departed. Such promises, known as non-compete agreements, are rather contentious. On the one hand, they obviously restrain trade — the doctor who promises not to compete cannot practice his trade during the time and in the place contemplated by the non-compete — and restraints of trade are disfavored in law. On the other hand, if you look at the situation *ex ante*, that is, before the parties agreed to work together in the first play, you may find that the parties would never have agreed to work together if one party did not have assurances that the other party would not take advantage of that work by opening a competing shop just down the block.

As you read this case, think about balancing these two concerns: first, the concern that restraints of trade are either unconscionable or bad for public policy and social welfare; and second, the concern that parties will not cooperate in the first place if they cannot prevent competition that arises from their prior collaboration. A business does not want to generate its own competition, after all.

Bauer v. Sawyer
8 Ill. 2d 351 (1956)

SCHAEFER, J.

All of the parties to this action are doctors. Prior to March 31, 1954, they were associated together in a medical partnership known as the Kankakee Clinic. On that date Dr. P.W. Sawyer, the principal defendant, withdrew from the partnership and in May of 1954 he opened offices for the practice of medicine and surgery in the city of Kankakee. Five of the eleven remaining partners instituted this action, alleging that the partnership agreement prohibited a retiring partner from practicing medicine in the city of Kankakee and seeking an injunction to restrain Dr. Sawyer from violating the agreement. The other six remaining partners were joined as defendants. They admitted the allegations of the complaint, but sought no relief against Dr. Sawyer. Dr. Sawyer also admitted the allegations of the complaint, but defended on the ground that the partnership agreement contemplated that a withdrawing partner had the alternative right to perform the agreement or to pay liquidated damages. The case was submitted upon the pleadings and a stipulation of facts. The circuit court entered a decree dismissing the complaint. The Appellate Court reversed, and we granted leave to appeal.

The partnership agreement provides that the interest of an individual partner may be terminated by retirement based on physical incapacity, by voluntary withdrawal, or by expulsion for unprofessional conduct or for failure to carry out the provisions of the agreement. In each instance the remaining partners are to purchase the interest of the outgoing partner at a stated percentage of its value as shown on the partnership books: 100 per cent in case of retirement for incapacity, 80 per cent in case of voluntary withdrawal, and 75 per cent in case of expulsion. By the agreement each partner covenants that after the termination of his interest he will not engage in the practice of medicine, surgery or radiology within a radius of 25 miles of Kankakee for a period of five years. The agreement also provides that if the former partner violates this covenant, he shall forfeit any unpaid portion of the purchase price of his interest. In the case of a partner withdrawing voluntarily, one half the purchase price is payable 30 days after withdrawal and the other half is to be evidenced by notes payable in one year which are to be delivered to an escrow agent, who is directed to cancel the notes upon certification by the remaining partners that the former partner has resumed practice. At the time of his withdrawal from the firm Dr. Sawyer was paid 40 per cent of the value of his partnership interest, and a note for the remaining 40 per cent was turned over to an escrow agent in accordance with the agreement.

Although Dr. Sawyer admits that he resumed practice in Kankakee in violation of the contract, he contends that the contract ought not to be specifically enforced against him, (1) because it is an unreasonable restraint of trade and contrary to public policy, and (2) because it contains a provision for liquidated damages which bars specific enforcement.

The principles governing cases of this kind were stated in *Ryan v. Hamilton*, in which a contract by a physician not to engage in practice in a specified community was enforced by injunction: "That contracts in general restraint of trade are generally held to be illegal is beyond controversy. But the rule admits of well defined exceptions, and among the exceptions are contracts of the kind and character presented in this case. Contracts of this class, where the limitation as to territory is reasonable and there exists a legal consideration for the restraint, are valid and enforceable in equity, and in such cases relief by injunction is customary and proper."

In determining whether a restraint is reasonable it is necessary to consider whether enforcement will be injurious to the public or cause undue hardship to the promisor, and whether the restraint imposed is greater than is necessary to protect the promisee.

In this case the interest of the public is in having adequate medical protection, and it is of course true, as suggested by Dr. Sawyer, that if the injunction is granted the number of doctors available in the Kankakee community will be reduced. A stipulation entered into by the parties, however, shows that there are now 70 doctors serving the area. We are unable to say that the reduction of this number by one will cause such injury to the public as to justify us in refusing to enforce this contract. In any case, there is no reason why Dr. Sawyer cannot serve the public interest equally well by practicing in another community. No special hardship to Dr. Sawyer appears which would justify the denial of relief in this case. He may resume practice in Kankakee after five years and in the meantime he may practice elsewhere. The territorial limitation to the city of Kankakee and the surrounding area is not, we think, unreasonable in the light of modern methods of transportation and communication.

Agreements unlimited in time have heretofore been enforced, although other authorities hold that the restraint must be limited in time as well as space. We need not here consider whether a time limitation is essential, because in any event the present five-year period does not appear unreasonable.

It thus appears that the agreement is not contrary to public policy by the tests that have heretofore been employed. Dr. Sawyer contends, however, that the prior cases decided by this and other courts are distinguishable because they involved either the sale of an established practice or the taking of a newcomer into an established practice, as employee or partner. Pointing out that in this case there was no express sale of the practice of any of the partners, and each of the partners was a practicing physician when the agreement was entered into, he argues that "If there is no established practice sold and no newcomer as a potential usurper, there is no need for the restraint being enforced by injunction."

With this contention we do not agree. No case is cited which holds that the members of a partnership may not by their agreement reasonably protect themselves against the competition of an outgoing partner. Indeed such agreements are classic illustrations of reasonable restraints of trade. "A legitimate method of enhancing the good will of continuing partners in professional, as well as commercial, partnerships is to secure forbearance from competition by a retired partner. He may agree not to compete, within reasonable limits as to time and space, and such an undertaking will be enforced by injunction. . . . The contract of a partner not to compete with the partnership either directly or indirectly is not opposed to public policy; but such an agreement must be ancillary to the relation or contract of partnership or to a contract by which a partner disposes of his interest."

Our own decision in *Storer v. Brock* enforced an agreement, entered into between two doctors upon the dissolution of their partnership, which restricted the future practice of the retiring partner. The distinction attempted to be drawn is without merit.

The most significant of the two remaining contentions of the defendant relates to the effect of the forfeiture clause. Under the partnership agreement the purchase price to be paid to an outgoing partner is payable in equal annual installments. In the event of a retirement for incapacity, there is one installment; if there is voluntary withdrawal, as in this case, there are two installments, and in the case of an ouster there are three installments. The first installment is payable thirty days after the withdrawal and notes are issued for the other installments. Interest is payable on the outstanding balance, and the partners have the privilege of prepayment. The notes are to be deposited with an escrow agent, who is directed to deliver them to the outgoing partner on the due date, unless the remaining partners have certified that the outgoing partner has breached the conditions of the agreement limiting his subsequent practice of medicine. If the remaining partners make such a certification, the agreement provides that the "escrow agent shall turn over and deliver the remaining unpaid notes to the makers thereof for cancellation, it being the intention of the parties hereto that the retiring or withdrawing Partner who has breached the [said] provisions . . . shall thereby forfeit a portion of the value of his Partnership interest."

Dr. Sawyer claims that the contract gave him the option to resume practice by giving up the unpaid portion of the value of his partnership interest, in this case $7451, which he characterizes as liquidated damages. Of course an agreement may be so formulated as to give an option to perform the contract or pay the stipulated damages. That was the case in *Davis v. Eisenstein*, where the agreement provided that "Upon payment thereof [of the stipulated liquidated damages] this contract is to become null and void." That agreement was held to give an option to each party to perform the contract or to pay the stipulated damages. There is no similar language in the present contract. On the contrary, the entire agreement indicates the intention of the parties that the covenant restricting the future activities of a former partner was intended to be enforced.

Upon the assumption that the provision contemplates liquidated damages, it is also argued that the existence of the liquidated damage clause bars the issuance of an injunction, and in support of the argument, *Bartholomae & Roesing Brewing and Malting Co. v. Modzelewski* is relied upon. That case was decided upon many grounds. Its statements to the effect that a provision for liquidated damages operates as a bar to an injunction have been sharply criticized. In accordance with our earlier and later decisions and with the weight of authority elsewhere, we hold that even if the provision in question is construed as one for liquidated damages the right to an injunction is not barred. To the extent that the *Modzelewski* case may be thought to hold otherwise, it is overruled.

While this case was under advisement in the Appellate Court, the continuing partners, including the plaintiffs, certified to the escrow agent that the condition as to subsequent practice had been breached by Dr. Sawyer. Under the agreement the escrow agent was required to return the notes to the makers for cancellation. Dr. Sawyer contends that liquidated damages have been collected, and that it would therefore be inequitable to enforce performance of the agreement by injunction. Plaintiffs argue that their certification was made with the thought that the clause was a penalty, and that the certification so stated. They say that the penalty cannot be enforced in its face amount and that they are still liable to Dr. Sawyer for $7451, the amount of the notes, less such actual damages as may have been sustained by the partnership.

> An agreement, made in advance of breach, fixing the damages therefor, is not enforceable as a contract and does not affect the damages recoverable for the breach, unless (a) the amount so fixed is a reasonable forecast of just compensation for the harm that is caused by the breach, and (b) the harm that is caused by the breach is one that is incapable or very difficult of accurate estimation.

In the present case it is not disputed that damages are difficult to ascertain. Indeed, plaintiffs' complaint so alleges. The more difficult question is whether the parties intended to forecast and fix the probable damages which would result from a breach. We think that they did not, and that they intended the clause as an additional sanction, by way of penalty, to enforce performance of the covenant not to re-engage in practice. In determining intent the language used by the parties is significant. Here, the parties speak not in the language of damages, but in terms of forfeiture. Although it is not controlling, the use of the word "forfeit" tends to exclude the idea of liquidated damages.

So, too, the method of payment suggests that the purpose of the parties was to secure performance rather than to settle damages. The money is withheld, in this instance for a year, in the case of an excluded partner for two years. If settlement of damages alone had been intended, it would have been sufficient to have provided for initial payment of the value of the partnership interest, and for subsequent recovery of the stipulated amount of damages in the event of breach.

There are other indications that the purpose of the clause was not to fix the amount of damages. Although the covenant not to re-engage in practice runs for five years, the clause in question covers only one year in the case of a withdrawing partner and only two years in the case of an expelled partner. No satisfactory reason explains why the provision, if it is for liquidated damages, does not cover the entire period of the restraint. Nor, assuming that the clause is a liquidated damage provision, is there any satisfactory explanation of what is to happen if a breach occurs after the escrow agent has delivered the notes to the outgoing partner. It can hardly be assumed that no damages at all were intended. The suggestion of defendant that the plaintiffs would then be entitled to an injunction, or to actual damages, as assessed by a court or jury, has no support in the language of the clause.

Nor does the clause fulfill the requirement that the amount of damages fixed be a reasonable forecast of just compensation for the harm caused by the breach. The defendant suggests that a percentage of the value of the partnership interest is probably as good a measure of damages as any test which could be devised by a court or jury. Assuming that, no reason appears for the discrimination between withdrawing and expelled partners. If a breach occurs during the first year, an expelled partner loses 50 per cent of the value of his interest in the partnership, while a withdrawing partner loses only 40 per cent. If a breach occurs during the second year an expelled partner would lose 25 per cent, while a withdrawing partner would presumably be liable for actual damages, whether they were greater or less than 25 per cent of the value of his interest. These differences seem to us impossible to explain on the assumption that the clause was intended as a forecast of just compensation for the harm caused by a breach. The reason for this discrimination does not appear to be that there would be greater damage in the case of a breach by an expelled partner, but rather than there was thought to be greater likelihood of a breach. Accordingly, more stringent sanctions to secure performance were inserted.

Defendant Sawyer argues that the failure to provide damages for a breach occurring in the second and following years, in the case of a withdrawing partner, may be explained on the ground that a physician's goodwill would be largely lost if he remained out of practice for a year, and damages in that situation would be negligible. But even if we assume that a withdrawing physician's goodwill is as perishable as defendant suggests, we are unable to understand why an expelled physician's goodwill would last longer.

We conclude that the provision is a penalty and that the partners therefore remain liable to Dr. Sawyer in the amount of the outstanding unpaid balance. Plaintiffs' conduct was not, we think, inequitable or inconsistent with their theory of recovery and does not bar injunctive relief. The issuance of an injunction need not await the assessment of interim damages and the determination of a net balance.

Dr. Sawyer's final contention is that the Appellate Court lacked jurisdiction to reverse the trial court, because the trial court was composed of three judges and therefore lacked jurisdiction to enter a valid final judgment. The record shows that because of the importance of the questions presented by this case the three judges of the Twelfth Judicial Circuit decided to hear the case *en banc*. We are of the opinion that if there was error in the organization of the court, it was waived by the defendant's failure to raise the objection in the trial court.

The judgment of the Appellate Court, reversing the decree of the trial court and remanding the cause with directions to issue the injunction, is affirmed, with further directions to proceed in accordance with the views expressed herein.

Judgment affirmed.

Reflection

Equitable remedies are exceptional, especially where one party wants to restrain the free trade of another. You may recall from the Declaration of Independent that America was founded on desires for "Life, Liberty and the pursuit of Happiness." This is generally interpreted to include the right to ply a trade and to make something of oneself through work.

But rights are not unlimited, and, in some cases, parties can contractually bind themselves not to enjoy these rights in certain circumstances. For example, while the Second Amendment provides a right to bear arms, an employer may ask an employee not to bring a firearm to work as a condition of employment. Whether or not courts would enforce such an employee's promise not to bear arms in that workplace depends on many factors, including state law. In fact, such an issue gave rise to the case of *Hansen v. Am. Online, Inc.*, 96 P.3d 950 (Utah 2004), where the Supreme Court of Utah determined that a freely entered into contract between an employee and an employer not to bring weapons into the workplace is enforceable. That case was decided under color of specific Utah law, and so it does not necessarily inform the common law of contracts generally, but it highlights the problems involved in enforcing a contract where on person promises to give up fundamental rights.

You might observe from this brief discussion how such contractual restraints on constitutional liberties are problematic and contentious. The level of contentiousness rises exponentially when a court not only awards money damages for failure to keep such a promise not to exercise one's rights, but also where that court physically stops such person from doing so. An equitable remedy such as an injunction requires the court to physically command a person to do or not to do a certain action, and courts are especially reluctant to issue such a command where the action involves essential freedoms such as the right to gainfully work.

Discussion

1. If the *Bauer* case did not involve doctors in a medical practice but instead involved a similar agreement between two eighteen-year-olds who agreed to

operate a lemonade stand together, would the court have reached a different result? Is the nature of the work significant in determining whether an agreement not to ply that trade within a certain time and space is valid?

2. Why did the doctors agree to the non-compete in the first place? What business purpose did this provision solve?

3. Was there any evidence of bad faith in the *Bauer* case? In general, equitable remedies are special — what about this case was special such that it rose to the level of meriting an equitable remedy?

Problems

Problem 24.1. **The Ink Factory**

Pigment Producers, Inc., produces ink for printers. However, sources of raw materials for several pigments are drying up. For example, the chemicals MX and diketene that are used in the production of yellow pigment are in very short supply because of a crackdown on air pollution in China and a factory explosion in China. Pigment Producers has a long-term requirements contract with Okinawa Chemical, a Japanese company, for both MX and diketene. The choice-of-law clause of this contract provides that the CISG does not apply and that any disputes arising under this contract are to be governed by the law of Pennsylvania, which has adopted the Uniform Commercial Code.

If Okinawa Chemical backs out of the contract because it can obtain a higher price by selling Pigment Producer's quota to other ink producers, is Pigment Producers entitled to specific performance, or will Pigment Producers be limited to a recovery of money damages?

Problem 24.2. **Pesky Provisions**

Orkin Exterminating Co., a national pest control company, hired Tony A. Martin to work as a pest exterminator at their office in Miami, Florida, which provided pest control services throughout Miami-Dade County. At the time of employment, the parties entered into a written contract which contained a covenant not to compete. The covenant restricted Martin from engaging in the pest control business anywhere in Miami-Dade County for two years following his termination of employment.

Martin voluntarily terminated his employment and began working in Miami-Dade County with one of Orkin's competitors. Orkin sued, asking for an injunction prohibiting Martin from working as an exterminator in Miami-Dade County.

Miami-Dade County has a total land area of 2,431 square miles and a total population of 2,700,000 people.

Should the court enforce Martin's non-complete agreement by issuing a injunction again his working in Miami-Dade County as an exterminator for two years?

Chapter 25

UCC Damages

The UCC approach to damages is to give the buyer and seller significant flexibility in terms of how each wants to deal with a breach. This accords with the UCC's general disposition to encouraging self-help in matters regarding commercial (dis) agreements.

Although the coverage of the UCC provisions in this chapter may seem extensive or even overwhelming compared to the R2d approach, the UCC actually offers a more straightforward system of default rules that apply to breach. To understand UCC damages, one should think separately about breaches by the buyer, on the one hand, and breaches by the seller, on the other.

Rules

A. Buyer's Breaches

Under the UCC, the buyer typically breaches by accepting goods yet failing to pay the seller for them. When the buyer breaches by accepting and failing to pay for goods, it does not matter whether the goods are conforming or non-conforming. Although the buyer initially has the right to reject non-conforming goods pursuant to the perfect tender rule, that right is not consequential when the buyer has accepted non-conforming goods. In any case, when the seller tenders the goods, and the buyer accepts those goods, then the seller is entitled to the contract price.

A more complicated situation arises where the buyer does not accept the goods but instead repudiates the contract or rejects the goods.

In some cases, the buyer thus acts rightfully; for example, if the goods are non-conforming, the buyer has the right to reject them, such that rejecting non-conforming goods and returning them to the seller is not a breach by the buyer. Likewise, there are circumstances that make a buyer's repudiation appropriate. For purposes of discussing a buyer's breach, we will set aside cases where the buyer rightfully repudiated or rejected the goods.

If the buyer's rejection or repudiation is wrongful, however, then that repudiation or rejection is a breach. The seller's remedies for such a breach, however, depend on which of three things the seller does in response:

First, if the seller is makes good faith efforts to resell the goods, then the seller is entitled to the contract price. Whether the buyer must pay that price to the seller in damages, however, depends on whether the seller resold the goods. If the seller was able to resell the goods, that is called "cover," and the court should require the buyer to pay damages to the seller in the amount of the contract price less the amount the seller received by covering and reselling the goods. If the seller sold the goods to someone else for full value, then the difference between the contract price and the cover price is zero, and there are no money damages. If the cover price is less than the original contract price, the buyer must pay the difference so that the seller ends up as well off as it expected to be had the buyer fully performed its obligation.

A seller who resells repudiated or rejected goods may also be entitled to collect from the buyer incidental damages incurred as the cost of reselling the goods.

Second, if the seller does not make efforts to resell the goods, the law effectively assumes that the seller keeps the goods at their market price. A seller who does not attempt to resell rejected good is thus entitled to the contract price less the market price.

Third, if the seller sells resells rejected goods to someone who would have purchased more goods anyway, this is a special case of a lost volume sale. The seller did not really mitigate its damages in this case. Note that the seller expected to sell two batches of goods, thus profiting twice, but due to a buyer's breach, the seller only sold one batch and thus earned only one profit. In this case, the lost profits from the lost volume of sales is the correct measure of damages. Lost profits are generally calculated as the contract price minus seller's cost of acquiring or producing the goods.

But a seller is not required to complete delivery of goods to a buyer who is not intending to pay for them. In fact, sellers are entitled to stop delivery of goods to buyers who repudiate obligations to pay for them:

> Where the buyer wrongfully rejects or revokes acceptance of goods or fails to make a payment due on or before delivery or repudiates with respect to a part or the whole, then with respect to any goods directly affected and, if the breach is of the whole contract (Section 2-612), then also with respect to the whole undelivered balance, the aggrieved seller may
>
> (a) withhold delivery of such goods;
>
> (b) stop delivery by any bailee as hereafter provided (Section 2-705);
>
> (c) proceed under the next section respecting goods still unidentified to the contract;
>
> (d) resell and recover damages as hereafter provided (Section 2-706);
>
> (e) recover damages for non-acceptance (Section 2-708) or in a proper case the price (Section 2-709);
>
> (f) cancel. UCC § 2-703.

The seller can even treat a buyer's insolvency as a repudiation such that a seller can withhold delivery from a bankrupt buyer.

Where the seller discovers the buyer to be insolvent he may refuse delivery except for cash including payment for all goods theretofore delivered under the contract, and stop delivery under this Article. UCC § 2-207(1).

B. Seller's Breaches

Although, as a technical matter, the perfect tender rule states that the buyer can reject any non-conforming goods, the UCC is actually designed for parties to work out such disputes and arrive at a mutual agreement. The UCC's policy is to encourage self-help and private resolution of contractual disputes. To accomplish this purpose, the UCC dispels some of the buyer's remedies upon the proper retender of seller's delivery. This encourages the seller to correct any non-conformance in the shipment of goods.

(1) *Where the seller fails to make delivery or repudiates or the buyer rightfully rejects or justifiably revokes acceptance then with respect to any goods involved, and with respect to the whole if the breach goes to the whole contract (Section 2-612), the buyer may cancel and whether or not he has done so may in addition to recovering so much of the price as has been paid*

(a) *"cover" and have damages under the next section as to all the goods affected whether or not they have been identified to the contract; or*

(b) *recover damages for non-delivery as provided in this Article (Section 2-713).*

(2) *Where the seller fails to deliver or repudiates the buyer may also*

(a) *if the goods have been identified recover them as provided in this Article (Section 2-502); or*

(b) *in a proper case obtain specific performance or replevy the goods as provided in this Article (Section 2-716).*

(3) *On rightful rejection or justifiable revocation of acceptance a buyer has a security interest in goods in his possession or control for any payments made on their price and any expenses reasonably incurred in their inspection, receipt, transportation, care and custody and may hold such goods and resell them in like manner as an aggrieved seller (Section 2-706).* UCC § 2-711.

Once again, we can understand buyer's remedies based on, first, how the seller breached and, second, how the buyer responded to that breach. There are two main ways in which a seller might breach: first, a seller may entirely fail to deliver goods. This failure to deliver may result from a repudiation that occurs before the time for performance is due. Or it may simply occur when it is time for the goods to arrive and they do not show up at the buyer's address.

If the seller failed to deliver goods, and if those goods are "unique," a court might award specific performance under which the seller is required to produce and deliver those goods. If the goods were shipped to someone else, the buyer may have a right to replevin, which means recovery of the goods.

If the goods are not unique, then the buyer can make reasonable efforts to cover by obtaining similar goods from someone else. If the buyer is able to cover, then the buyer is entitled to the cover price minus the contract price. If the buyer makes good faith efforts but is unable to cover, then the buyer is entitled to the market price minus the contract price. In both cases, the buyer may also be entitled to incidental and consequential damages as measured by costs incurred covering the breach.

Second, a seller may deliver non-conforming goods. Pursuant to the perfect tender rule, buyers have the right to reject non-conforming goods; but remember, buyers also have the right to accept them.

If a buyer accepts non-conforming goods, that buyer should then pay the contract price less any damages for non-conformity.

If the buyer rejects non-conforming goods, the buyer has similar remedies to a buyer who did not receive goods at all. The buyer who receives non-conforming goods may cover and then recover the difference between the cover price and the contract price. If the buyer fails to cover, the buyer is entitled to the difference between the market price and the contract price.

C. Incidental and Consequential UCC Damages

The Uniform Commercial Code adopts as a general rule that consequential damages in the form of injury to person and property are recoverable if the breach was the "proximate cause" of the loss. This is true for both buyers and sellers, although the seller's rule is simpler:

> *Incidental damages to an aggrieved seller include any commercially reasonable charges, expenses or commissions incurred in stopping delivery, in the transportation, care and custody of goods after the buyer's breach, in connection with return or resale of the goods or otherwise resulting from the breach.* UCC § 2-710.

In short, sellers can recover costs of "cover" (finding a substitute buyer) and mitigating breach (taking care of the goods). This encourages seller to cover and mitigate damages by providing recovery for costs thus incurred.

The Buyer's remedy works much the same way, but it is more complicated, because buyers may also incur consequential damages from not receiving the goods. A buyer who does not receive conforming goods is unable to resell the goods to others or to use those goods in productions of its own goods or services. When a buyer's business is harmed in this way, the buyer has limited remedies for these consequential damages:

(1) *Incidental damages resulting from the seller's breach include expenses reasonably incurred in inspection, receipt, transportation and care and custody of goods rightfully rejected, any commercially reasonable charges, expenses or commissions in connection with effecting cover and any other reasonable expense incident to the delay or other breach.*

(2) *Consequential damages resulting from the seller's breach include*

    (a) *any loss resulting from general or particular requirements and needs of which the seller at the time of contracting had reason to know and which could not reasonably be prevented by cover or otherwise; and*

    (b) *injury to person or property proximately resulting from any breach of warranty. UCC 2-715.*

The primary purpose of this code section is to encourage buyers to cover and mitigate damages from a seller's breach. The UCC effectuates this by providing reimbursement for buyers' reasonable expenses in obtaining replacement goods and in handling the rightfully rejected (or revoked) goods.

In doing this, the UCC modifies the common law's approach to consequential damages. Recall from *Hadley v. Baxendale* and the R2d that, under the common law, the seller is liable for all consequential damages of which he had "reason to know." In the *Hadley* case, the shipper had no reason to know that the mill would be inoperative while the crankshaft shipment was delayed. But if the shipper knew that the miller had but one essential crankshaft, then the shipper would have had to pay for lost profits while the mill was down as consequential damages.

UCC § 2-715(2) modifies the common law rule by disallowing recovery for consequential damages unless the buyer could not reasonably have prevented the loss by cover or otherwise. This further encourages buyers to cover and mitigate damages.

A seller is thus liable for consequential damages when that seller had reason to know of the buyer's general or particular requirements at the time of contracting, and where the buyer took reasonable efforts to prevent negative consequences stemming from the seller's breach and related to those requirements.

This rule does not require the seller to actually know about those requirements; it is an objective standard based on what a reasonable seller should know. If a seller wishes to limit this risk of consequential damages, the seller must affirmatively limit this remedy through contractual agreement.

Cases

Reading North American Foreign Trading Corp. v. Direct Mail Specialist.
Once a court determines that a party breached an agreement, it usually must assess damages. Plaintiffs generally seek maximal damages, but such an award

is not always in the interests of justice. The following case regards an aggrieved seller who seeks direct damages in the form of lost profits plus incidental damages in the form of storage fees and interest costs. It is these incidental damages which here are more questionable.

Before delving into the case, consider the bigger picture of why incidental damages are awarded to sellers. The purpose of incidental damage awards are to encourage sellers to make the best use of goods that buyers refuse to take. Sellers are incentivized to retrieve, store, and resell these goods because they can, in theory, collect damages for reasonable costs so incurred. If these incentives work, then breaches are less likely to result in wasted and ruined goods. Not wasting valuable goods is generally positive for social welfare, but the rule can also be abused by sellers who spend unreasonable time or costs with regard to repudiated, rejected, or revoked goods. The next case discusses how courts should apply the rule in a manner that strikes the appropriate balance.

North American Foreign Trading Corp. v. Direct Mail Specialist
697 F. Supp. 163 (S.D.N.Y. 1988)

KRAM, JUDGE

In this breach of contract action, plaintiffs are suing to recover on a contract through which they were to provide certain goods to defendant. Defendant and the additional counterclaim defendant have counterclaimed for breach of contract and fraud. Presently before the Court is plaintiffs' motion *in limine* for a determination of the proper method of calculating the appropriate amount of statutory pre-judgment interest in this action. The dispute over this legal issue has stymied the parties' attempts at a negotiated settlement.

Background

Based on an affirmation submitted by plaintiffs, the following appear to be the facts relevant to the present motion. In May, 1983, the parties met to discuss the sale of a blackjack game to defendant DMS, Inc. ("DMS"). Through an exchange of correspondence, the parties agreed that plaintiff North American Foreign Trading Corporation ("NAFTC") would supply defendant with a total 164,968 units in minimum monthly installments of 15,000 units at a cost of $12 per unit. Defendant provided plaintiffs with a deposit of $100,000 to be applied only to the last shipment.

NAFTC made monthly shipments of 15,000 units to defendant from May, 1983 through August, 1983. DMS paid the contract price of $ 12 per unit for each of these shipments. In September, 1983, DMS requested NAFTC to delay the monthly shipments until February or March, 1984 to allow DMS to consume its current inventories. By letter dated September 15, 1983, Gordon Nelms, defendant's representative, stated the reasons for requesting the delay, noted that plaintiffs had refused to delay shipments and then proceeded to cancel the outstanding purchase order for that month. Nelms concluded the letter by stating that "no further shipments will be accepted by this organization."

Plaintiffs commenced this action shortly thereafter. Plaintiffs state that they attempted to sell the remaining 104,968 units, but only managed to sell small quantities during the period from September, 1983 through mid-1986. In mid-1986, plaintiffs began selling the product in bulk to a single purchaser at a price of $11 per unit. All of the units were eventually sold. Plaintiffs still have possession of defendant's $100,000 deposit.

Discussion

On the assumption that plaintiffs would prevail on all issues, plaintiffs argue that it would be entitled to recover: (1) the contract price of the goods less the amount realized by NAFTC upon resale of the goods, (2) storage and insurance costs and (3) interest at the statutory rate of nine percent (9%) on the full contract price and the storage and insurance costs for the period September, 1983 through the time of resale in mid-1986 and interest on the contract price less the amount received upon resale for the period of mid-1986 through the time of judgment. Defendant counters that plaintiffs would only be entitled to interest on the net amount of damages, i.e., the contract price plus storage and insurance costs less the amount received upon resale.

Since jurisdiction in this action is premised on diversity of citizenship, the Court will apply New York law. Section 5001(a) of the Civil Practice Law and Rules ("CPLR") of New York states that "Interest shall be recovered upon a sum awarded because of a breach of performance of a contract." (McKinney's 1963). Section 5001(b) states that

> Interest shall be computed from the earliest ascertainable date the cause of action existed, except that interest upon damages incurred thereafter shall be computed from the date incurred. Where such damages were incurred at various times, interest shall be computed upon each item from the date it was incurred or upon all of the damages from a single reasonable intermediate date.

Defendant argues that the statute speaks for itself and restricts any computation of interest to the net amount of damages, or the "sum awarded" for breach of performance. Plaintiffs, choosing not to discuss the nuances of this limiting language, stresses that the purpose behind this section and the damage sections of the Uniform Commercial Code as applied in New York is to put a party in the same position it would have enjoyed but for the breach. The Court finds merit in each parties' argument.

Each side calls the Court's attention to a few cases, none of which directly reaches the question presently before the Court. In *Intermeat, Inc. v. American Poultry, Inc.,* the Court awarded the seller interest on the full contract price for the period from the date of breach until the buyer remitted further monies to seller, and thereafter, on the difference between the contract price and the monies remitted. Although the Court awarded interest consistent with plaintiffs' position in this case, one important difference must be noted. In *Intermeat*, the seller had shipped the goods to the buyer who then repudiated the contract but retained possession of the goods.

Similarly, in *Bulk Oil (U.S.A.), Inc. v. Sun Oil Trading Co.,* the buyer accepted delivery of the goods and thereafter repudiated the contract. In this case, on the other hand, the seller retained possession of the goods before and after the alleged repudiation. Thus, any argument made that interest should be awarded on the full contract price makes greater sense in the cases cited by plaintiffs in light of the fact that the seller had already delivered the goods to the buyer.

Defendant's cases are also distinguishable, though for different reasons. Defendant cites *Pro-Specialties, Inc. v. Thomas Funding Corp.,* for the proposition that interest should be awarded only on the net amount recovered. In that case, the seller sought damages from a third-party guarantor. The buyer defaulted in August, 1982 and the guarantor made only one payment of $5000 in October, 1982. The District Court awarded damages to the seller in the amount of the outstanding invoices less the $5000 received from the guarantor, and then awarded interest on this net amount of damages from the date of breach in August, 1982.

Although the Court awarded interest in a manner consistent with defendant's position in this case, the Court believes that the cases are factually distinguishable. In *Pro-Specialties*, the delay between the time of breach and the time the seller received the $5000 was only two to three months, and the $5000 received was only a fraction of the amount due. The seller thus received interest on the bulk of the contract price from the date of breach, and the lost time-value of the $5000 for the three months was relatively minuscule. In this case, on the other hand, plaintiffs claim that they had to wait some three years before receiving any significant amount of money due on the contract. Defendant's theory of the appropriate interest recovery would deny plaintiffs any substantial recovery for the funds not received during those three years.

Under the provisions of New York's Uniform Commercial Code seller's damages can be calculated in a few ways, depending on the circumstances. See N.Y. U.C.C. §§ 2-703 et seq. The seller may resell the goods and recover the difference between the contract price and the resale price, plus incidental damages, assuming the resale was accomplished in a commercially reasonable time. *Id.* § 2-706.

An aggrieved party must mitigate damages by resale if feasible. If the aggrieved seller fails to resell in a commercially reasonable time, then damages can be calculated as the difference between the unpaid contract price and the market price of the goods at the time and place of tender, plus incidental damages. N.Y. U.C.C. § 2-708(1). If that amount is inadequate to put the seller in as good a position as performance would have done, then damages may be calculated by awarding the seller the lost profit, including reasonable overhead and incidental damages. *Id.* § 2-708(2). The seller may also sue for the price of the goods, plus incidental damages, either for goods accepted by the seller or for "goods identified to the contract if the seller is unable after reasonable effort to resell them at a reasonable price or the circumstances reasonably indicate that such effort will be unavailing." *Id.* § 2-709.

The damages provisions are designed to put the seller in the same position he would have enjoyed had the buyer not breached the contract. N.Y. U.C.C. § 1-106 (U.C.C. provisions should be construed liberally so that the aggrieved party may be put in the position he would have enjoyed had the other party fully performed). Defendant's proposed method of interest calculation would not put plaintiffs in the same position they would have enjoyed had defendant performed — if resale during the three-year period between the time of breach and mid-1986, when the goods were in fact resold, was not reasonably feasible at a reasonable price. If resale was not reasonably feasible, then plaintiffs suffered losses during the three-year period for the lost time value of the money they would have received had defendant fully performed.

In *Bulk Oil*, the Second Circuit recognized that an aggrieved seller could recover as incidental damages interest payments made to a bank that would not have been made had the buyer performed. Similarly, in *Intermeat*, the Court awarded as incidental damages finance charges the seller incurred as a result of the buyer's breach. The Second Circuit intimated that the time value of money is recoverable in noting that "the rate used in computing statutory interest is an assumption about the value of the use of money." The Court thus decides that plaintiffs would be entitled to recover interest at the statutory rate on the contract price (less the $100,000 deposit) from the date of breach until the time at which the seller could reasonably have resold the goods with reasonable effort for a reasonable price. Plaintiffs are entitled to such interest only if the delay was reasonable under the circumstances. If the delay were unreasonable, plaintiff would be entitled to interest on damages based on the difference between the contract price and the market price at the time of breach or some reasonable time thereafter, see N.Y. U.C.C. § 2-708(1), or on the lost profit, see N.Y. U.C.C. § 2-708(2). Whether the three-year delay before the goods were resold was reasonable is a question that remains to be resolved at trial.

SO ORDERED.

Reflections

The prior case demonstrated how courts will evaluate sellers' remedies under the UCC. Recall that sellers are not entitled to consequential damages, but incidental damages may be available to sellers who expect costs in dealing appropriately with repudiated, rejected, or revoked goods. *N. Am. Foreign Trading* thus provides an effective review of the rules regarding UCC damages for sellers.

This case also brings up a new concept that is worth highlighting: time value of money. The simple version of this idea is that, in ordinary economic conditions, a dollar today is worth more than a dollar tomorrow. For one thing, you can spend a dollar that you have presently, but you cannot spend a dollar you do not yet have, and this alone tends to make having the dollar sooner more valuable. Also, the future is inherently uncertain, and there is some risk that dollars promised in the future never arrive, whereas the one in your wallet, you already possess. Time value of money is related to the interest rate, which is the amount one pays to borrow money. The fact that people pay interest to borrow money shows that having money now is worth more than having that money later, and that value is measurable by the interest paid for the privilege of having that money sooner.

Another way to think of time value of money is as a discount rate; that is, money in the future is (generally) worth less than money today; and the longer in the future one expects to receive money, the greater the diminution in its value. For this reason, we say that future dollars are "discounted" in relation to present value. For example, if we can determine that receiving a dollar in a week is worth ninety cents today — meaning, you would be equivocal whether you got a dollar in a week or ninety cents today — we can say that that future dollar is subject to a 10% discount.

It is beyond the scope of this course to refine economic understanding of such concepts to an operational level, but, for present purpose, it is critical to note that courts must take economic reality into account when measuring damages. Lawyers and law professors (who have a reputation for being averse to mathematics in general) tend to overlook such economic complexities as time value of money. The *N. Am. Foreign Trading* court itself laments this point in a footnote not included here. The Court criticizes a 1984 law review article titled *An Economic Analysis of the Lost-Volume Retail Seller*, 49 ALBANY L. REV. 889 (1985), observing that "This Comment, though quite complete in most respects, does not discuss the time value of money as an element of economic damages, reflecting a lack of discussion of this topic generally in this area."

Fortunately, the law and economics movement has made great progress in the past 40 years. Courts, academics, and even practicing attorneys have greater knowledge of economic principles, and these principles are applied to render more appropriate decisions. Students who plan to practice commercial law should likewise consider how to expand their knowledge of and comfort with using economic concepts and analysis to make legal arguments.

Discussion

1. The *N. Am. Foreign Trading* court remands the question of whether the three-year period before reselling the goods at issue was reasonable. What factors should the trial court consider when determining what constitutes a reasonable time to resell goods?

2. What is the logical connection between the economic concept of time value of money and the legal concept of awarding incidental damages for interest?

Reading Ramirez v. Autosport. Ramirez is a relatively modern classic. The case is popular in part because the Supreme Court of New Jersey takes the time and effort to extensively discuss and describe the meaning and purpose of UCC remedies. In addition, its subject matter — the purchase and sale of an RV — is not especially technical. The court also does an excellent job analyzing the readily comprehensible facts of this case under the UCC rules. Students thus derive two benefits from reading *Ramirez*. First, *Ramirez* reviews the UCC remedies and explains them by integrating case law and commentary from a variety of leading authorities, thus helping students understand what this complex area of law involves and requires. Second, *Ramirez* analyzes an understandable (albeit unfortunate) situation under these rules, thus helping students see how UCC remedies analysis should be conducted. As you read this case, take this opportunity to refine your knowledge and understanding of the UCC remedies rules and to learn by example of how to analyze facts and make and balance arguments under these rules.

Ramirez v. Autosport

88 N.J. 277 (1982)

POLLACK, J

This case raises several issues under the Uniform Commercial Code ("the Code" and "UCC") concerning whether a buyer may reject a tender of goods with minor defects and whether a seller may cure the defects. We consider also the remedies available to the buyer, including cancellation of the contract. The main issue is whether plaintiffs, Mr. and Mrs. Ramirez, could reject the tender by defendant, Autosport, of a camper van with minor defects and cancel the contract for the purchase of the van.

The trial court ruled that Mr. and Mrs. Ramirez rightfully rejected the van and awarded them the fair market value of their trade-in van. The Appellate Division affirmed in a brief *per curiam* decision which, like the trial court opinion, was unreported. We affirm the judgment of the Appellate Division.

I

Following a mobile home show at the Meadowlands Sports Complex, Mr. and Mrs. Ramirez visited Autosport's showroom in Somerville. On July 20, 1978 the Ramirezes and Donald Graff, a salesman for Autosport, agreed on the sale of a new camper and the trade-in of the van owned by Mr. and Mrs. Ramirez. Autosport and the Ramirezes signed a simple contract reflecting a $14,100 purchase price for the new van with a $4,700 trade-in allowance for the Ramirez van, which Mr. and Mrs. Ramirez left with Autosport. After further allowance for taxes, title and documentary fees, the net price was $9,902. Because Autosport needed two weeks to prepare the new van, the contract provided for delivery on or about August 3, 1978.

On that date, Mr. and Mrs. Ramirez returned with their checks to Autosport to pick up the new van. Graff was not there so Mr. White, another salesman, met them. Inspection disclosed several defects in the van. The paint was scratched, both the electric and sewer hookups were missing, and the hubcaps were not installed. White advised the Ramirezes not to accept the camper because it was not ready.

Mr. and Mrs. Ramirez wanted the van for a summer vacation and called Graff several times. Each time Graff told them it was not ready for delivery. Finally, Graff called to notify them that the camper was ready. On August 14 Mr. and Mrs. Ramirez went to Autosport to accept delivery, but workers were still touching up the outside paint. Also, the camper windows were open, and the dining area cushions were soaking wet. Mr. and Mrs. Ramirez could not use the camper in that condition, but Mr. Leis, Autosport's manager, suggested that they take the van and that Autosport would replace the cushions later. Mrs. Ramirez counteroffered to accept the van if they could withhold $2,000, but Leis agreed to no more than $250, which she refused. Leis then agreed to replace the cushions and to call them when the van was ready.

On August 15, 1978 Autosport transferred title to the van to Mr. and Mrs. Ramirez, a fact unknown to them until the summer of 1979. Between August 15 and September 1, 1978 Mrs. Ramirez called Graff several times urging him to complete the preparation of the van, but Graff constantly advised her that the van was not ready. He finally informed her that they could pick it up on September 1.

When Mr. and Mrs. Ramirez went to the showroom on September 1, Graff asked them to wait. And wait they did — for one and a half hours. No one from Autosport came forward to talk with them, and the Ramirezes left in disgust.

On October 5, 1978 Mr. and Mrs. Ramirez went to Autosport with an attorney friend. Although the parties disagreed on what occurred, the general topic was whether they should proceed with the deal or Autosport should return to the Ramirezes their trade-in van. Mrs. Ramirez claimed they rejected the new van and requested the return of their trade-in. Mr. Lustig, the owner of Autosport, thought, however, that the deal could be salvaged if the parties could agree on the dollar amount of a credit for the Ramirezes. Mr. and Mrs. Ramirez never took possession of the new van and repeated their request for the return of their trade-in. Later in October, however, Autosport sold the trade-in to an innocent third party for $4,995. Autosport claimed that the Ramirez' van had a book value of $3,200 and claimed further that it spent $1,159.62 to repair their van. By subtracting the total of those two figures, $4,159.62, from the $4,995.00 sale price, Autosport claimed a $600-700 profit on the sale.

On November 20, 1978 the Ramirezes sued Autosport seeking, among other things, rescission of the contract. Autosport counterclaimed for breach of contract.

II

Our initial inquiry is whether a consumer may reject defective goods that do not conform to the contract of sale. The basic issue is whether under the UCC, adopted in New Jersey as N.J.S.A. 12A:1-101 et seq., a seller has the duty to deliver goods that conform precisely to the contract. We conclude that the seller is under such a duty to make a "perfect tender" and that a buyer has the right to reject goods that do not conform to the contract. That conclusion, however, does not resolve the entire dispute between buyer and seller. A more complete answer requires a brief statement of the history of the mutual obligations of buyers and sellers of commercial goods.

In the nineteenth century, sellers were required to deliver goods that complied exactly with the sales agreement. That rule, known as the "perfect tender" rule, remained part of the law of sales well into the twentieth century. By the 1920's the doctrine was so entrenched in the law that Judge Learned Hand declared "[t]here is no room in commercial contracts for the doctrine of substantial performance."

The harshness of the rule led courts to seek to ameliorate its effect and to bring the law of sales in closer harmony with the law of contracts, which allows rescission only for material breaches. Nevertheless, a variation of the perfect tender rule appeared in the Uniform Sales Act.

The chief objection to the continuation of the perfect tender rule was that buyers in a declining market would reject goods for minor nonconformities and force the loss on surprised sellers.

To the extent that a buyer can reject goods for any nonconformity, the UCC retains the perfect tender rule. Section 2-106 states that goods conform to a contract "when they are in accordance with the obligations under the contract". Section 2-601 authorizes a buyer to reject goods if they "or the tender of delivery fail in any respect to conform to the contract". The Code, however, mitigates the harshness of the perfect tender rule and balances the interests of buyer and seller. See R2d § 241 cmt. b. The Code achieves that result through its provisions for revocation of acceptance and cure.

Initially, the rights of the parties vary depending on whether the rejection occurs before or after acceptance of the goods. Before acceptance, the buyer may reject goods for any nonconformity. Because of the seller's right to cure, however, the buyer's rejection does not necessarily discharge the contract. Within the time set for performance in the contract, the seller's right to cure is unconditional. Some authorities recommend granting a breaching party a right to cure in all contracts, not merely those for the sale of goods. See R2d ch. 10, especially §§ 237 and 241. Underlying the right to cure in both kinds of contracts is the recognition that parties should be encouraged to communicate with each other and to resolve their own problems.

The rights of the parties also vary if rejection occurs after the time set for performance. After expiration of that time, the seller has a further reasonable time to cure if he believed reasonably that the goods would be acceptable with or without a money allowance. The determination of what constitutes a further reasonable time depends on the surrounding circumstances, which include the change of position by and the amount of inconvenience to the buyer. Those circumstances also include the length of time needed by the seller to correct the nonconformity and his ability to salvage the goods by resale to others. Thus, the Code balances the buyer's right to reject non-conforming goods with a "second chance" for the seller to conform the goods to the contract under certain limited circumstances.

After acceptance, the Code strikes a different balance: the buyer may revoke acceptance only if the nonconformity substantially impairs the value of the goods to him. This provision protects the seller from revocation for trivial defects. It also prevents the buyer from taking undue advantage of the seller by allowing goods to depreciate and then returning them because of asserted minor defects. Because this case involves rejection of goods, we need not decide whether a seller has a right to cure substantial defects that justify revocation of acceptance.

Other courts agree that the buyer has a right of rejection for any nonconformity, but that the seller has a countervailing right to cure within a reasonable time.

We conclude that the perfect tender rule is preserved to the extent of permitting a buyer to reject goods for any defects. Because of the seller's right to cure, rejection does not terminate the contract.

A further problem, however, is identifying the remedy available to a buyer who rejects goods with insubstantial defects that the seller fails to cure within a reasonable time. The Code provides expressly that when "the buyer rightfully rejects, then with respect to the goods involved, the buyer may cancel."

"Cancellation" occurs when either party puts an end to the contract for breach by the other. Nonetheless, some confusion exists whether the equitable remedy of rescission survives under the Code.

The Code eschews the word "rescission" and substitutes the terms "cancellation", "revocation of acceptance", and "rightful rejection". Although neither "rejection" nor "revocation of acceptance" is defined in the Code, rejection includes both the buyer's refusal to accept or keep delivered goods and his notification to the seller that he will not keep them. Revocation of acceptance is like rejection, but occurs after the buyer has accepted the goods. Nonetheless, revocation of acceptance is intended to provide the same relief as rescission of a contract of sale of goods.

In brief, revocation is tantamount to rescission. Similarly, subject to the seller's right to cure, a buyer who rightfully rejects goods, like one who revokes his acceptance, may cancel the contract. We need not resolve the extent to which rescission for reasons other than rejection or revocation of acceptance, e.g. fraud and mistake, survives as a remedy outside the Code. Accordingly, we recognize that explicit Code remedies replace rescission, and disapprove suggestions the UCC expressly recognizes rescission as a remedy.

Although the complaint requested rescission of the contract, plaintiffs actually sought not only the end of their contractual obligations, but also restoration to their pre-contractual position. That request incorporated the equitable doctrine of restitution, the purpose of which is to restore plaintiff to as good a position as he occupied before the contract. In UCC parlance, plaintiffs' request was for the cancellation of the contract and recovery of the price paid.

General contract law permits rescission only for material breaches, and the Code restates "materiality" in terms of "substantial impairment". The Code permits a buyer who rightfully rejects goods to cancel a contract of sale. Because a buyer may reject goods with insubstantial defects, he also may cancel the contract if those defects remain uncured. Otherwise, a seller's failure to cure minor defects would compel a buyer to accept imperfect goods and collect for any loss caused by the nonconformity.

Although the Code permits cancellation by rejection for minor defects, it permits revocation of acceptance only for substantial impairments. That distinction is consistent with other Code provisions that depend on whether the buyer has accepted the goods. Acceptance creates liability in the buyer for the price, and precludes rejection. Also, once a buyer accepts goods, he has the burden to prove any defect. By contrast, where goods are rejected for not conforming to the contract, the burden is on the seller to prove that the nonconformity was corrected.

Underlying the Code provisions is the recognition of the revolutionary change in business practices in this century. The purchase of goods is no longer a simple transaction in which a buyer purchases individually-made goods from a seller in a face-to-face transaction. Our economy depends on a complex system for the manufacture, distribution, and sale of goods, a system in which manufacturers and consumers rarely meet. Faceless manufacturers mass-produce goods for unknown consumers who purchase those goods from merchants exercising little or no control over the quality of their production. In an age of assembly lines, we are accustomed to cars with scratches, television sets without knobs and other products with all kinds of defects. Buyers no longer expect a "perfect tender". If a merchant sells defective goods, the reasonable expectation of the parties is that the buyer will return those goods and that the seller will repair or replace them.

Recognizing this commercial reality, the Code permits a seller to cure imperfect tenders. Should the seller fail to cure the defects, whether substantial or not, the balance shifts again in favor of the buyer, who has the right to cancel or seek damages. In general, economic considerations would induce sellers to cure minor defects. Assuming the seller does not cure, however, the buyer should be permitted to exercise his remedies under the Code. The Code remedies for consumers are to be liberally construed, and the buyer should have the option of cancelling if the seller does not provide conforming goods.

To summarize, the UCC preserves the perfect tender rule to the extent of permitting a buyer to reject goods for any nonconformity. Nonetheless, that rejection does not automatically terminate the contract. A seller may still effect a cure and preclude unfair rejection and cancellation by the buyer.

III

The trial court found that Mr. and Mrs. Ramirez had rejected the van within a reasonable time. The court found that on August 3, 1978, Autosport's salesman advised the Ramirezes not to accept the van and that on August 14, they rejected delivery and Autosport agreed to replace the cushions. Those findings are supported by substantial credible evidence, and we sustain them. Although the trial court did not find whether Autosport cured the defects within a reasonable time, we find that Autosport did not effect a cure. Clearly the van was not ready for delivery during August, 1978 when Mr. and Mrs. Ramirez rejected it, and Autosport had the burden of proving that it had corrected the defects. Although the Ramirezes gave Autosport ample time to correct the defects, Autosport did not demonstrate that the van conformed to the contract on September 1. In fact, on that date, when Mr. and Mrs. Ramirez returned at Autosport's invitation, all they received was discourtesy.

On the assumption that substantial impairment is necessary only when a purchaser seeks to revoke acceptance, the trial court correctly refrained from deciding whether the defects substantially impaired the van. The court properly concluded that plaintiffs were entitled to "rescind" — i.e., to "cancel" — the contract.

Because Autosport had sold the trade-in to an innocent third party, the trial court determined that the Ramirezes were entitled not to the return of the trade-in, but to its fair market value, which the court set at the contract price of $4,700. A buyer who rightfully rejects goods and cancels the contract may, among other possible remedies, recover so much of the purchase price as has been paid.

The Code, however, does not define "pay" and does not require payment to be made in cash.

A common method of partial payment for vans, cars, boats and other items of personal property is by a "trade-in". When concerned with used vans and the like, the trade-in market is an acceptable, and perhaps the most appropriate, market in which to measure damages. It is the market in which the parties dealt; by their voluntary act they have established the value of the traded-in article. In other circumstances, a measure of damages other than the trade-in value might be appropriate.

The ultimate issue is determining the fair market value of the trade-in. This Court has defined fair market value as "the price at which the property would change hands between a willing buyer and a willing seller when the former is not under any compulsion to buy and the latter is not under any compulsion to sell, both parties having reasonable knowledge of relevant facts." Although the value of the trade-in van as set forth in the sales contract was not the only possible standard, it is an appropriate measure of fair market value.

For the preceding reasons, we affirm the judgment of the Appellate Division.

Reflection

Part II of *Ramirez* effectively functions as a mini-treatise on UCC buyers' remedies. I selected this case instead of a selection from Williston's or Corbin's treatises because I find this case more readable and efficient than the relevant sections from those luminaries' treatises. Still, perhaps it is useful to reiterate some key points.

First, the UCC nominally has a perfect tender rule, but this does not give buyers the right to reject goods willy-nilly. Rather, buyers have a good faith obligation which extends to their rejection rights. Sellers, meanwhile, have some rights to cure, and buyers have some obligation to give them time to cure. Remember, the goal of contract law is not to meet venial faults with harsh oppression, but, rather, to ensure that parties receive the mutual benefits of their commercial agreements. The UCC in particular encourages behavior that is socially efficient by encouraging parties to work things out before litigating their issues.

Discussion

1. Is substantial performance or perfect tender the more appropriate standard? Why should this standard be different in contracts for services versus contracts for goods?

2. Does the UCC really require perfect tender in the first instance? Or must the rule be read more softly such that there is room for sellers' errors without their loss of right to payment?

Problems

Problem 25.1. Retiring Road Commissioner

Until March, 1972, Everett D. Dehahn was road commissioner for the Town of Wayne, Maine. In his work for the town, he used, for the most part, his own heavy equipment and was compensated for his services at an hourly rate. Failing reelection at the annual town meeting in 1972, the plaintiff sought to interest Richard A. Innes in purchasing his business, including incidental goodwill, for the price of $60,000.00.

Dehahn and Innes reached an agreement of purchase and sale at the end of April. By oral contract, Dehahn agreed to sell and Innes agreed to buy for the price of $35,000.00 the plaintiff's 52 acre gravel pit, a back hoe, a bulldozer, a loader, a dump truck with plow, another truck with plow and a home-made low bed trailer. But the parties did not agree to buy and sell the business as such.

Dehahn orally agreed to deliver the equipment in a "ready-to-go condition." In compliance with this part of the agreement, Dehahn sent his employee Riggs to do the jobs which needed to be done, such as the removal of the plows from the trucks, plus such other maintenance work as was necessary. Riggs moved Dehahn's equipment to a field that Innes owned that was across from the driveway to his home. He left keys to the equipment in the machines.

Innes used the bulldozer on one job, when he determined that the bulldozer was not in good condition. Innes then inspected the rest of the equipment and complained that none of it was in "ready-to-go condition." After Innes made numerous complaints to Dehahn about Dehahn's failure to put the equipment in a "ready-to-go condition," Innes informed Dehahn that he was cancelling the agreement. Innes never made any payments pursuant to the contract.

Dehahn sued Innes to recover the contract price of $35,000.00. Innes presented the statute of frauds as an affirmative defense, but this failed, because the UCC provides an exception to the statute of frauds, where the party to be charged actually admits the contract exists. The court then proceeded to determine at trial that Innes breached his promise to pay pursuant to the agreement because, as a finding of fact, the trial court determined that the equipment sold was in substantially ready-to-go condition under commercially reasonable standards.

The court must now determine what remedy should be awarded to Dehahn. For that purpose, the court found the following facts:

- Dehahn recovered the equipment
- Dehahn resold the equipment to someone else for $26,200.00
- Dehahn spend $200.00 locating the new buyer

If you were the clerk for the judge in this case, how would you calculate damages? Make sure to explain whether resale price is a valid measure of damages, and cite to UCC provisions discussing this.

See Dehahn v. Innes, 356 A.2d 711 (Me. 1976).

Problem 25.2. **Rash Delivery**

Rash Ranco Corporation ("Rash Ranco") is an Illinois corporation with its principal place of business in Chicago, Illinois. Rash Ranco sells wholesale and retail goods to customers in foreign countries. BLB is a New York corporation with its principal place of business in Fairview, New Jersey. BLB is also engaged in the sale of goods.

On January 25, 1990, Rash Ranco entered into an agreement with BLB to purchase 1,100 motors at $8 each, for a total of $8,800. BLB faxed Rash Ranco an invoice for the goods, and Rash Ranco sent BLB a deposit check for the sum of $4,000.

On or around February 7, 1990, Rash Ranco contacted a customer in Egypt and began arrangements for sale of the motors. Around that same date, Rash Ranco advised BLB that it was negotiating with an Egyptian customer for resale of the motors. On March 6, 1990, BLB notified Rash Ranco that it sold the motors to another party and, therefore, BLB would not sell the motors to Rash Ranco.

Rash Ranco sued BLB, seeking $ 111,800 in damages. Specifically, the company requests $19,800 in lost profits plus $92,000 in cover expenses.

Is Rash Ranco entitled to these damages?

See *Rash Ranco Corp. v. B.L.B. Inc.*, 762 F. Supp 1339 (N.D. Ill. 1990).

Problem 25.3. Cumene Repudiation

Koppers Company makes industrial wood preserving and fire preventing chemical formulations, such as the chemicals used to pressure treat wood for construction uses. An input to Koppers's products is cumene, a colorless oily hydrocarbon. Cumene, in turn, is manufactured through a process called Friedel-Crafts alkylation that combines benzene with propylene. (Side note: 20% of the world's benzene supply is used to make cumene.)

Koppers contracted to buy 1,000 tons of cumene from Nobs Chemical, Inc., a distributor of industrial chemicals, for $540,000, including delivery to Koppers's facility. Nobs then located and contracted with Brazilian Chemical, a manufacturer who agreed to produce the cumene for $400 a ton and to deliver the cumene to Koppers and/or Nobs for $45 a ton, provided that Nobs purchased 4,000 tons of cumene. Nobs agreed and placed its order for 4,000 tons of cumene for $1,780,000.00, with the intention of selling 1,000 tons of cumene to Koppers and then storing the additional 3,000 tons until it could find a buyer for that additional cumene.

After Koppers placed the order for its input materials but before Nobs was obligated to deliver the cumene to Koppers, Koppers repudiated the contract by stating in writing that it no longer needed the cumene and no longer intended to pay for it. Nobs contacted Brazilian Chemical, who offered to reduce the order from 4,000 tons to 3,000 tons, provided that Nobs pay $70 a ton for shipment. Nobs accepted this modification. Then Nobs sued Koppers for breach.

The court determined that Koppers breached, and now it must calculate damages. Nobs expected to profit $95,000 on its sale of cumene to Koppers. Are lost profits the proper way for the court to calculate direct expectation damages? Should the court count the additional $75,000 that Nobs will pay in delivery costs as either incidental or consequential damages due to Kopper's breach? What is the total amount of damages that the court should award Nobs?

See *Nobs Chem., U.S.A., Inc. v. Koppers Co.*, 616 F.2d 212, 216 (5th Cir. 1980).

Problem 25.4. Graphics Cards I

Cooper Technologies entered into a contract with Carolina Circuits to sell Carolina 2,500 high-performance graphics cards for a total cost of $30,000. When the cards were delivered Carolina inspected them, found that they were non-conforming, returned them to Cooper, and canceled their order. Carolina did not give Cooper an opportunity to cure the defect in the cards.

Was Carolina rightful or wrongful in its rejection of Cooper's goods?

Problem 25.5. Graphics Cards II

Cooper Technologies entered into a contract with Carolina Circuits to sell Carolina 2,500 high-performance graphics cards for a total cost of $30,000. When the cards were delivered, Carolina inspected them, but Carolina failed to discover a latent defect in the cards. Carolina paid Cooper for the cards.

Six months later, the latent defect surfaced. Carolina promptly notified Cooper of the defect and gave Cooper an opportunity to cure it. Cooper was unable to cure the defect.

Analyze and describe Carolina's remedies under the UCC.

Index